Essentials of Criminal Justice

Siegel | Worrall

CENGAGE
Learning·

Australia • Brazil • Japan • Korea • Mexico • Singapore • Spain • United Kingdom • United States

CENGAGE
Learning·

Essentials of Criminal Justice

Essentials of Criminal Justice, 8th Edition
Siegel | Worrall

© 2013 Cengage Learning. All rights reserved.

Senior Project Development Manager:
Linda deStefano

Market Development Manager:
Heather Kramer

Senior Production/Manufacturing Manager:
Donna M. Brown

Production Editorial Manager:
Kim Fry

Sr. Rights Acquisition Account Manager:
Todd Osborne

For product information and technology assistance, contact us at
Cengage Learning Customer & Sales Support, 1-800-354-9706

For permission to use material from this text or product,
submit all requests online at **cengage.com/permissions**
Further permissions questions can be emailed to
permissionrequest@cengage.com

This book contains select works from existing Cengage Learning resources and was produced by Cengage Learning Custom Solutions for collegiate use. As such, those adopting and/or contributing to this work are responsible for editorial content accuracy, continuity and completeness.

Compilation © 2013 Cengage Learning
ISBN-13: 978-1-285-89050-0

ISBN-10: 1-285-89050-7

Cengage Learning
5191 Natorp Boulevard
Mason, Ohio 45040
USA
Cengage Learning is a leading provider of customized learning solutions with office locations around the globe, including Singapore, the United Kingdom, Australia, Mexico, Brazil, and Japan. Locate your local office at:
international.cengage.com/region.

Cengage Learning products are represented in Canada by Nelson Education, Ltd.
For your lifelong learning solutions, visit **www.cengage.com/custom.**
Visit our corporate website at **www.cengage.com.**

Printed in the United States of America

ABOUT THE AUTHORS

Larry Siegel

Larry J. Siegel was born in the Bronx in 1947. While living on Jerome Avenue and attending City College of New York in the 1960s, he was swept up in the social and political currents of the time. He became intrigued with the influence contemporary culture had on individual behavior: Did people shape society or did society shape people? He applied his interest in social forces and human behavior to the study of crime and justice. After graduating CCNY, he attended the newly opened program in criminal justice at the State University of New York at Albany, earning both his M.A. and Ph.D. degrees there. After completing his graduate work, Dr. Siegel began his teaching career at Northeastern University, where he was a faculty member for nine years. After leaving Northeastern, he held teaching positions at the University of Nebraska–Omaha and Saint Anselm College in New Hampshire. He is currently a professor at the University of Massachusetts–Lowell. Dr. Siegel has written extensively in the area of crime and justice, including books on juvenile law, delinquency, criminology, criminal justice, and criminal procedure. He is a court certified expert on police conduct and has testified in numerous legal cases. The father of four and grandfather of three, Larry Siegel and his wife, Terry, now reside in Bedford, New Hampshire, with their two dogs, Watson and Cody.

John Worrall

John L. Worrall is Professor of Criminology and Program Head at the University of Texas at Dallas. A Seattle native, he received a B.A., double majoring in psychology and law and justice, from Central Washington University in 1994. Both his M.A. (criminal justice) and Ph.D. (political science) were received from Washington State University, where he graduated in 1999. From 1999–2006, he was a member of the criminal justice faculty at California State University, San Bernardino. He joined UTD in Fall 2006. Dr. Worrall has published articles and book chapters on a wide range of topics ranging from legal issues in policing to crime measurement. He is the author of *Crime Control in America: What Works?* (2nd ed., Allyn and Bacon, 2008) and *Criminal Procedure: From First Contact to Appeal* (4th ed., Prentice Hall, 2013); coauthor of *Police Administration* (3rd ed., Cengage, 2013), *Policing Today* (Prentice Hall, 2010), and *Criminal Evidence: An Introduction* (Oxford University Press, 2005); and co-editor of *The Changing Role of the American Prosecutor* (SUNY, 2009). He is also editor of the journal *Police Quarterly*.

BRIEF CONTENTS

CONTENTS

3 Criminal Law: Substance and Procedure   52

PART 2   THE POLICE AND LAW ENFORCEMENT   72

4 Police in Society: History and Organization   74

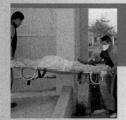

5 The Police: Role and Function 93

6 Issues in Policing: Professional, Social, and Legal 116

PART 3 COURTS AND ADJUDICATION 142

7 Courts, Prosecution, and the Defense 144

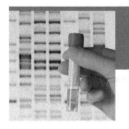

8 Pretrial and Trial Procedures 169

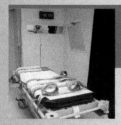

PART 4 CORRECTIONS AND ALTERNATIVE SANCTIONS 226

11 Corrections: History, Institutions, and Populations 254

12 Prison Life: Living in and Leaving Prison 276

CAREER PROFILES

PART 1 Investigator
Daisy Mongeau, Investigator,
New Hampshire Public Defender's Office
Concord, New Hampshire

PART 1 Probation Officer
Samantha O'Hara, Probation Officer,
U.S. District Court
Southern District of Iowa
Des Moines, Iowa

PART 1 Lawyer
Ralph C. Martin II, Attorney, Managing
Partner at Bingham McCutchen LLP
and Leader of the Bingham
McCutchen Diversity Task Force
Boston, Massachusetts

PART 2 Patrol Training Officer
Stephen Bishopp, Sergeant, Patrol
Division Training Coordinator
Dallas, Texas

PART 2 State Trooper
John Sullivan, Massachusetts State
Trooper
Revere, Massachusetts

PART 3 Court Reporter
Carlos Martinez, Court Reporter
Sonoma County Superior Courts,
California

PART 3 Judge
Ruben Andres Martino, Presiding Justice,
Harlem Community Justice Center
Harlem, New York

PART 4 Probation Officer
Ann Beranis, Probation Officer
Supervisor, DuPage County Probation
and Court Services
Wheaton, Illinois

PART 4 Correctional Officer
Gina Curcio, Correctional Officer,
Essex County House of Corrections,
Middleton, Massachusetts

PART 5 Juvenile Probation Officer
Kevin Kellems, Intensive Juvenile
Probation Officer
Calhoun County, Michigan

PART 5 Homeland Security
Special Agent
Mark O., Special Agent, Department of
Homeland Security, Immigration and
Customs Office of Investigations

There are certain incidents that we remember all our lives—where we were, what we were doing when they occurred. For some of us, it was events such as the Kennedy and King assassinations, the day the *Challenger* blew up, the day John Lennon was shot. For the students using this text, May 1, 2011, the day Osama bin Laden, the world's most wanted man, was located and killed, will forever be a milestone. While Bin Laden was not a "traditional" criminal and his death was at the hands of a Navy SEAL team, in the aftermath of 9/11 the control of terrorism is now a significant justice system issue. Federal, state, and local law enforcement agencies have been ferreting out terrorists, courts have conducted terrorist trials, and prisons now incarcerate convicted terrorists.

The control of terrorism illustrates how the challenges faced by the justice system are constantly changing. In the 1980s, the crack epidemic occupied the center of attention. In the 1990s, gang violence seemed out of control, and during the past decade, there has been an ongoing concern about terrorist activities. Yet terrorists comprise only a very small percentage of the critical cases now being brought to justice each year. The criminal justice system routinely processes millions of cases involving fraud, theft, violence, drug trafficking, and other crimes. How does this vast enterprise, which costs billions of dollars and involves millions of people, operate? What are its most recent trends and policies? How effective are its efforts to control crime? What efforts are being made to improve its efficiency? We have written the eighth edition of *Essentials of Criminal Justice* in an attempt to help answer these questions in a clear and concise manner.

Goals and Objectives

Because the study of criminal justice is a dynamic, ever-changing field of scientific inquiry, and because the concepts and processes of justice are constantly evolving, we have updated *Essentials of Criminal Justice* to reflect the most critical legal cases, research studies, and policy initiatives that have taken place in the past few years. *Essentials* lays a foundation for the study of criminal justice by analyzing and describing the agencies of justice and the procedures they use to identify and treat criminal offenders. It covers what most experts believe are the crucial issues in criminal justice and analyzes their impact on the justice system. This edition focuses on critical policy issues in the criminal justice system, including efforts to control and contain terrorism, cyber crime, and transnational gangs, as well as serial killers, car thieves, and burglars.

Our primary goals in writing this eighth edition remain the same as they have been for the previous seven editions:

- Provide students with a thorough knowledge of the criminal justice system
- Be as readable and interesting as possible
- Be objective and unbiased
- Describe current methods of social control and analyze their strengths and weaknesses

Every attempt has been made to make the presentation of material interesting, balanced, and objective. No single political or theoretical position dominates the text; we try to be as objective as possible. Accordingly, we have included the many diverse views that are represented within criminal justice and that characterize its interdisciplinary nature.

Organization of the Text

Our major goal when creating the eighth edition of *Essentials of Criminal Justice* was to simplify the presentation and write as clearly and concisely as possible. Therefore, we have streamlined the text while maintaining the essential features of past editions. We have made every effort to ensure that the book is informative, comprehensive, interesting, well organized, and impartial, yet stimulating and thought-provoking.

Part One gives the student a basic introduction to crime, law, and justice. The first chapter covers the agencies of justice, outlines the formal justice process, and introduces the concept of the informal justice system, which involves discretion, deal making, and plea bargains. Chapter 1 examines the major perspectives on justice and shows how they shape justice policy. Chapter 2 discusses the nature and extent of crime and victimization: How is crime measured? Where and when does it occur? Who commits crime? Who are its victims? What social factors influence the crime rate? Chapter 3 provides a discussion of the criminal law and its relationship to criminal justice. It covers the legal definition of crime, the types of defenses available to those charged with having committed a crime, as well as issues in constitutional procedural law.

Part Two offers an overview of law enforcement. Three chapters cover the history and development of police departments, the functions of police in modern society, issues in policing, and the police and the rule of law. Special emphasis is placed on community policing and crime prevention, technology and policing, law enforcement and terrorism, and changes in police procedures.

Part Three is devoted to the court process, from pretrial indictment to the sentencing of criminal offenders. In this section, individual chapters focus on the organization of the court system and the roles of its major participants (judge, prosecutor, and defense attorney), pretrial procedures, the criminal trial, and sentencing. The topics explored include bail, court reorganization, sentencing, and capital punishment.

Part Four focuses on the correctional system, including probation and the intermediate sanctions of house arrest, intensive supervision, and electronic monitoring. Although the traditional correctional system of jails, prisons, community-based corrections, and parole is discussed at length, there is also a new focus on restorative justice programs. Such issues as the crisis of overcrowding in prisons and jails, house arrest, correctional workers, super-maximum-security prisons, and parole effectiveness are discussed.

Part Five explores current issues in justice. One chapter deals with the problem of juveniles who break the law. What should be done with them and how should they be treated? There is information on the development of juvenile justice, on waiving youth to the adult court, and on the death penalty for children. Chapter 14, which appears for the first time in this edition, focuses on a number of critical issues currently facing the justice system: business crime, green crime, cyber crime, and transnational organized crime. It illustrates the dynamic nature of the justice process and the fact that the problems it faces are constantly evolving.

Key Changes to the Eighth Edition

We have made a number of revisions to the eighth edition. The Reality Check feature that first appeared in the seventh edition has been ravamped for balance—to ensure an even mix of myth and reality. Chapter summaries were shortened and organized by their corresponding learning objectives. Each chapter was shortened considerably, without loss of critical information, to make the discussions leaner than ever before. Marginal learning objectives were added. Chapter and part openers were also updated and revised. Following is a summary of the chapter-specific revisions:

Chapter 1, Crime and Criminal Justice, now opens with the story of the Tucson massacre and mass murderer Jared Lee Loughner, who opened fire in a supermarket parking lot in Tucson, Arizona, in an attempt to kill Congresswoman Gabrielle Giffords. The data on the criminal justice process has been updated. A new Contemporary Issues in Criminal Justice: Evidence-Based Justice feature looks at the provocative question, *Does Monitoring Sex Offenders Really Work?*

Chapter 2, The Nature of Crime and Victimization, begins with a vignette on the sensational Casey Anthony case, which captivated the nation and resulted in the acquittal of a young mother accused of murdering her own child. Crime data has been updated to include the most recent trends. A Contemporary Issues in Criminal Justice box seeks to answer the question, Is the United States Crime Prone? We have also updated the sections on victimization.

Chapter 3, Criminal Law: Substance and Procedure, begins with a vignette on cyber laws designed to control new types of crimes called vishing and smishing, Internet identity theft schemes. There are new and updated sections that discuss controlling technology with laws designed to control criminal acts involving theft of access numbers and software piracy, identity theft, and similar cyber crimes. Another new section on legalizing marijuana tells how 16 states have legalized the use of marijuana for medical purposes and some, including California, allow dispensaries to fill prescriptions. There is an analysis of the 2008 case *Baze and Bowling v. Rees*, in which the Supreme Court upheld the use of lethal injections in capital punishment, and the 2011 Defense Authorization Bill, which contains provisions preventing the transfer of Guantánamo prisoners to the mainland or to other foreign countries. The 2009 case of *Herring v. United States* involves interpretation of the exclusionary rule.

Chapter 4, Police in Society: History and Organization, features a new opening vignette on the importance of budget cuts in contemporary law enforcement. It highlights many of the financial problems America's police agencies have endured in recent years. The section on technology and law enforcement was updated. Sections on police organizational characteristics were updated with the most recent data.

Chapter 5, The Police: Role and Function, begins with a brief examination of U.S.–Mexico border violence and possible spillover effects. A new Contemporary Issues in Criminal Justice box features an evidence-based look at the deterrent effects of preventive patrol. Uninformed observers often conclude that preventive patrol is essential for crime control. A number of scientific studies have told a different story, however.

Chapter 6, Issues in Policing: Professional, Social, and Legal, opens with a summary of the Supreme Court's decision in *Arizona v. Gant*, a recent case involving police searches. Critics of the Court's decision in *Gant* claim it hampers law enforcement effectiveness. We leave it to the reader to draw his or her own conclusion. A new police corruption exhibit is included. The section "Police and the Rule of Law" was updated and given a new *Miranda* exhibit. The chapter also contains a new section on non-deadly force.

Chapter 7, Courts, Prosecution, and the Defense, opens with a new vignette featuring the case of George Hayward, a Baltimore man convicted of sexual abuse of a minor. Learning objectives were revised. A new Contemporary Issues in Criminal Justice box features no-drop prosecution. Prosecutors often have difficulty charging domestic abusers because victims sometimes fail to cooperate. No-drop policies make it so prosecutors can press charges regardless of the victim's wishes.

Chapter 8, Pretrial and Trial Procedures, begins with a vignette featuring a recent Supreme Court case dealing with DNA testing in the criminal trial context. In *District Attorney's Office v. Osborne*, the Supreme Court concluded that there is no constitutional right for convicted persons to access the state's evidence and perform additional DNA testing. The chapter was also reduced in length, as it was one of the seventh edition's longer chapters. Learning objectives were revised and reorganized to reflect the improvements.

Chapter 9, Punishment and Sentencing, begins with a new chapter-opening vignette featuring the case of William Johnson, a man who was on Florida's death row for over three decades. The latest sentencing data are presented throughout the chapter. The section on arguments for and against the death penalty was revised and streamlined. Added to it was a comparison of capital punishment in countries around the globe.

Chapter 10, Community Sentences: Probation, Intermediate Sanctions, and Restorative Justice, has been tightened and shortened. It begins with the story of celebrities who are on or who have been on probation, including Lindsay Lohan, Lawrence Taylor, Mel Gibson, Lil Wayne, and Eminem. A new Contemporary Issues in Criminal Justice: Evidence-Based Justice box entitled "Treating Probationers with Cognitive Behavioral Therapy" covers cognitive behavioral therapy (CBT), a correctional treatment approach that focuses on patterns of thinking and beliefs, attitudes, and values and whether this approach can be successful with probationers. The data on the number of people on probation and the success of probation have been updated.

Chapter 11, Corrections: History, Institutions, and Populations, begins with the story of Keaira Brown, who was just 13 years old when she was charged with a murder that was a result of a carjacking that went wrong. In addition, the data on correctional populations and costs have been updated. There is also an analysis of recent trends, showing that the nation's prison population may be "maxing out" because the long-term effects of the crime rate drop may finally be taking effect.

Chapter 12, Prison Life: Living in and Leaving Prison, opens with a new vignette telling the story of Kevin James, a man who grew up in South Central Los Angeles, became a member of the 76th Street Crips gang, was convicted of robbery and given a 10-year sentence, and became a recruit in a terror gang. He was later convicted of plotting terror attacks. The chapter includes recent data on sexual assaults in prison. We cover a 2011 report by the Pew Foundation on a study they sponsored measuring parole success. We also look at what strategies work best for released inmates and the effect of close parole supervision on inmate re-entry success. A new Contemporary Issues in Criminal Justice box adopts an evidence-based focus and looks at Arizona's Getting Ready Program, which is designed to reduce post-release recidivism.

Chapter 13, Juvenile Justice in the Twenty-First Century, opens with a controversial case involving the murder of James Alenson, a young boy whose 16-year-old killer had never met him prior to the killing. Learning objectives have been revamped completely and the chapter has been reorganized. Recent court cases and the latest research have been added.

Chapter 14, Crime and Justice in the New Millennium, has been totally revised and rewritten to include new topics such as corporate fraud, green crime, and transnational crime along with cyber crime. It begins with the story of WikiLeaks, an international organization that published classified and secret U.S. government documents. We also discuss the challenges to the justice system presented by multibillion dollar corporate enterprise crimes and the collapse of the subprime mortgage system. Next, we examine laws making it a crime to pollute or damage the environment. Finally, we updated the sections on cyber crime and included new material on cyber war, acts aimed at undermining the social, economic, and political system of an enemy nation by destroying its electronic infrastructure and disrupting its economy. There is also a new Contemporary Issues in Criminal Justice box that focuses on global sex trafficking.

Chapter Features

The eighth edition of *Essentials of Criminal Justice* contains the following boxed features in various places throughout the text.

Careers in Criminal Justice

We believe that helping students focus on possible careers is an important element in a criminal justice course. Therefore we now have part openers featuring possible career paths and interviews with professionals who have gone down those paths.

We also use boxed features within chapters that contain detailed information on salaries, educational requirements, and future prospects, and we have a "Word to the Wise" section in these features, discussing the potential pitfalls of that career area, as well as what might disqualify a person from the career or job highlighted.

Criminal Justice and Technology

These boxes review some of the more recent technological and scientific advances that can aid the justice system. For example, in Chapter 4, a Criminal Justice and Technology feature on so-called fusion centers describes law enforcement efforts to exchange information and intelligence, streamline their operations, and prevent crime—all with the extensive use of technology. Fusion centers are law enforcement's digital "nerve center."

Learning Objectives

Each chapter begins with a list of key learning objectives. These objectives are then revisited in the summary at the end of the chapter, where they are directly tied to the material covered in the text.

Contemporary Issues in Criminal Justice

The Contemporary Issues in Criminal Justice boxes, found in most chapters, help students to think critically about current criminal justice issues and policies. Several of the boxes were revised for the eighth edition to take on an evidence-based focus. For example, the Chapter 5 box examines the research as to whether preventive police patrol is beneficial from a crime control standpoint.

RealityCheck

One of the goals of this book is to expose some of the myths that persist about crime, criminals, and the criminal justice system. Given the popularity of television series such as *CSI* and *Law & Order*, which purport to strip away the veneer of the justice system and expose the truth, it has become essential to help students separate rhetoric from reality in the criminal justice system: Is the crime rate really out of control? Are unemployed people more likely than others to commit crime? Do detectives solve the most serious crimes? Does incarceration really work? Does the death penalty deter people from committing murder? Making it clear what is true and what is merely legend is one of the greatest challenges for instructors teaching the first course in criminal justice. The RealityCheck feature in *Essentials of Criminal Justice* meets that challenge head on. Its purpose is to separate myth from reality and thereby inform students of the incorrect notions, perceptions, and biases they bring to class as a result of what they see on television or read in fiction and on the Internet.

Ancillaries

To access additional course materials, including CourseMate, please visit www .cengagebrain.com. At the CengageBrain.com home page, search for the ISBN of your title (from the back cover of your book) using the search box at the top of the page. This will take you to the product page where these resources can be found.

An extensive package of supplemental aids accompanies this edition. Many separate items have been developed to enhance the course and to assist instructors and students. Available to qualified adopters. Please consult your local sales representative for details.

For the Instructor. Instructor's Resource Manual with Test Bank. The manual, written by Laura Hahn of Towson University, includes learning objectives, key terms, a detailed chapter outline, a chapter summary, discussion topics, student activities, and a Test Bank. Each chapter's Test Bank contains questions in multiple-choice, true-false, fill-in-the-blank, and essay formats, with a full answer key. The Test Bank is coded to the learning objectives that appear in the main text, and it includes the page numbers in the main text where the answers can be found. Finally, each question in the Test Bank has been carefully reviewed by experienced criminal justice instructors for quality, accuracy, and content coverage. Our Instructor Approved seal, which appears on the front cover, is our assurance that you are working with an assessment and grading resource of the highest caliber.

Online PowerPoint Lectures. These handy Microsoft PowerPoint slides developed by Kelly Gould of Sacramento City College, which outline the chapters of the main text in a classroom-ready presentation, will help you in making your lectures engaging and in reaching your visually oriented students. The presentations are available for download on the password-protected website and can also be obtained by e-mailing your local Cengage Learning representative.

PowerLecture with ExamView. This one-stop digital library and presentation tool includes preassembled Microsoft® PowerPoint® lecture slides linked to the learning objectives for each chapter. Also included are an electronic copy of the Instructor's Resource Manual with Test Bank, the Online Lesson Plans, ExamView computerized testing, and more. Based on the learning objectives outlined at the beginning of each chapter, the enhanced PowerLecture lets you bring together text-specific lecture outlines and art from this text, along with new video clips, animations, and learning modules from the Web or your own materials—culminating in a powerful, personalized, media-enhanced presentation. PowerLecture also integrates ExamView®—a computerized test bank available for PC and Macintosh computers—software for customizing tests of up to 250 items that can be delivered in print or online. With ExamView you can create, deliver, and customize tests and study guides in minutes. You can easily edit and import your own questions and graphics, change test layouts, and reorganize questions. And, using ExamView's complete word-processing capabilities, you can enter an unlimited number of new questions or edit existing questions.

Online Lesson Plans. Revised to reflect content in the new edition, the Lesson Plans bring accessible, masterful suggestions to every lesson. Developed by Kelly Gould of Sacramento City College, this supplement includes a sample syllabus, learning objectives, lecture notes, discussion topics, in-class activities, a detailed lecture outline, assignments, media tools, and "What if…" scenarios. Current events and real-life examples in the form of articles, websites, and video links are incorporated into the class discussion topics, activities, and assignments. The lecture outlines are correlated with PowerPoint® slides for ease of classroom use. Lesson Plans are included on the PowerLecture™ resource and available for download from the password-protected instructor book companion website.

WebTutor™ on Blackboard® and WebCT®. Jump-start your course with customizable, rich, text-specific content within your Course Management System. Whether you want to web-enable your class or put an entire course online, WebTutor delivers. WebTutor offers a wide array of resources, including media assets, test bank, practice quizzes linked to chapter learning objectives, and additional study aids. Visit www.cengage.com/webtutor to learn more.

Criminal Justice Media Library on WebTutor. Cengage Learning's Criminal Justice Media Library includes nearly 300 media assets on the topics you cover in your courses. Available to stream from any web-enabled computer, the Criminal Justice Media Library's assets include such valuable resources as Career Profile Videos featuring interviews with criminal justice professionals from a range of roles and locations, simulations that allow students to step into various roles and practice their decision-making skills, video clips on current topics from ABC® and other sources, animations that illustrate key concepts, interactive learning modules that help students check their knowledge of important topics, and RealityCheck exercises that compare expectations and preconceived notions against the real-life thoughts and experiences of criminal justice professionals. Video assets include assessment questions that can be delivered straight to the gradebook. The Criminal Justice Media Library can be uploaded and customized within many popular Learning Management Systems. Please contact your Cengage Learning representative for ordering and pricing information.

The Wadsworth Criminal Justice Video Library. So many exciting new videos—so many great ways to enrich your lectures and spark discussion of the material in this text. Your Cengage Learning representative will be happy to provide details on our video policy by adoption size. The library includes these selections and many others.

ABC® Videos. ABC videos feature short, high-interest clips from current news events as well as historic raw footage going back 40 years. Perfect for discussion starters or to enrich your lectures and spark interest in the material in the text, these brief videos provide students with a new lens through which to view the past and present, one that will greatly enhance their knowledge and understanding of significant events and open up to them new dimensions in learning. Clips are drawn from such programs as *World News Tonight, Good Morning America, This Week, PrimeTime Live, 20/20,* and *Nightline,* as well as numerous ABC News specials and material from the Associated Press Television News and British Movietone News collections.

- *Cengage Learning's "Introduction Criminal Justice Video Series"* features videos supplied by the BBC Motion Gallery. These short, high-interest clips from CBS and BBC news programs—everything from nightly news broadcasts and specials to *CBS News Special Reports, CBS Sunday Morning, 60 Minutes,* and more—are perfect classroom discussion starters. Designed to enrich your lectures and spark interest in the material in the text, these brief videos provide students with a new lens through which to view the past and present, one that will greatly enhance their knowledge and understanding of significant events and open up to them new dimensions in learning. Clips are drawn from BBC Motion Gallery.

For the Student

CourseMate. Cengage Learning's Criminal Justice CourseMate brings course concepts to life with interactive learning, study, and exam preparation tools that support the printed textbook. CourseMate includes an integrated e-book, quizzes mapped to chapter learning objectives, flashcards, videos, and EngagementTracker, a first-of-its-kind tool that monitors student engagement in the course. The accompanying instructor website offers access to password-protected resources such as an electronic version of the instructor's manual and PowerPoint® slides.

Study Guide. An extensive student guide has been developed by Todd Scott of Schoolcraft College for this edition, featuring a variety of pedagogical aids to help students with diverse learning styles. Students will find learning objectives, chapter outlines and summaries, definitions of major terms, and self-tests with answers. Test questions are correlated to learning objectives; the objective with which each question correlates is cited in the answer key.

Careers in Criminal Justice Website. *Available bundled with this text at no additional charge.* Featuring plenty of self-exploration and profiling activities, the interactive Careers in Criminal Justice Website helps students investigate and focus on the criminal justice career choices that are right for them. Includes interest assessment, video testimonials from career professionals, résumé and interview tips, peripheral skills such as courtroom demeanor and preparation for testimony, effective communication skills, ethics and professionalism, and more.

CLeBook. CLeBook allows students to access Cengage Learning textbooks in an easy-to-use online format. Highlight, take notes, bookmark, search your text, and (in some titles) link directly into multimedia: CLeBook combines the best aspects of paper books and e-books in one package.

Current Perspectives: Readings from Infotrac® College Edition. These readers, designed to give students a closer look at special topics in criminal justice, include free access to InfoTrac College Edition. The timely articles are selected by experts in each topic from within InfoTrac College Edition. They are available free when bundled with the text and include the following titles:

- Introduction to Criminal Justice
- Community Corrections
- Cyber Crime
- Victimology
- Juvenile Justice
- Racial Profiling
- White-Collar Crime
- Terrorism and Homeland Security
- Public Policy and Criminal Justice
- Technology and Criminal Justice
- Ethics in Criminal Justice
- Forensics and Criminal Investigation
- Corrections
- Law and Courts
- Policy in Criminal Justice

Acknowledgments

Many people helped make this book possible. The following reviewers of this edition offered a number of suggestions that we addressed to the best of our ability:

Jennifer M. Allen, North Georgia College and State University

James Blair, South Texas College

George J. Ellefson, Bismarck State College

Peter Galante, Farmingdale State College

LiYing Li, Metropolitan State College of Denver

Ellen Marshall, Delaware Technical and Community College

John M. Reinholz, Bryant and Stratton College

Hamin D. Shabazz, Stevenson University

Gary A. Sokolow, College of the Redwoods

Ivy Yarckow-Brown, Missouri State University

Thanks to our terrific editor, Carolyn Henderson Meier, who does it all for us all the time. (She is our unnamed co-author.) Plenty of credit for getting this book out must also go to the marvelous Shelley Murphy, developmental editor extraordinaire, to whom we can never give enough praise no matter how hard we try. Special thanks to our outstanding production manager, Christy Frame; to our wonderful and professional production editor, Aaron Downey; to the precise and knowledgeable copyeditor, Lunaea Weatherstone, who did a thorough and professional job; and to the ever-creative photo researcher, Kim Adams Fox, who brought the book to life with colorful imagery. And of course, we are totally in debt to our incredible marketing manager, the astonishing Michelle Williams. This skilled team's efforts have resulted in an exceptional new edition.

LARRY SIEGEL
Bedford, New Hampshire

JOHN WORRALL
Dallas, Texas

ESSENTIALS OF
CRIMINAL
JUSTICE

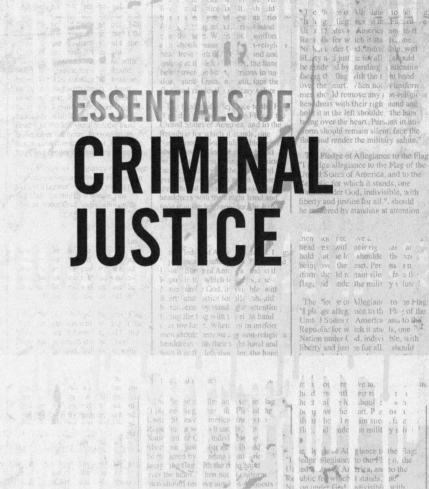

THE NATURE OF CRIME, LAW, AND CRIMINAL JUSTICE

Interested in a career in criminal justice? Some opportunities are centered around the investigation of crime, the apprehension of criminals, and their prosecution in a court of law. Take for instance Daisy Mongeau, an investigator with the New Hampshire Public Defender's Office in Concord. Her job involves interviewing witnesses, writing reports, obtaining medical/court records, subpoenaing witnesses, taking pictures, interacting with clients, helping attorneys in trial preparation, and testifying at hearings. She finds that a lot of her friends just can't understand why she works so hard to defend people who are guilty, even those who have confessed to the crime. They don't seem to understand that everyone is entitled to a criminal defense even if they actually committed the crime! After Mongeau earned her bachelor's degree in Sociology and Justice Studies from the University of New Hampshire, she chose her career in criminal justice because she likes fighting for the underdog who would have no chance in the legal system without representation. "The job is challenging," she claims. Mongeau has to locate witnesses who may not have a phone or permanent address and track them down through neighbors, friends, acquaintances, or anyone else who might know their location. What is her greatest reward? "Getting the prosecutor to drop the case, *nolle prosequi*, because of what a witness told me during an investigation." She finds that clients are thrilled that someone actually believed them and helped them win the case. These are people not used to being given a helping hand.

The modern criminal justice system has evolved since ancient times. Some elements, such as courts and punishment, have been with us for thousands of years. Others, like police and corrections, are newer concepts, some developing in the United States in the nineteenth century. For example, probation is a relatively new concept, begun in 1841; today, probation officers supervise 4 million clients. One of them, Samantha J. O'Hara, is a U.S. probation officer for the U.S. District Court in the Southern District of Iowa, headquartered in Des Moines. O'Hara thoroughly enjoys her job.

I like learning of people's stories and how they became involved in their offenses. The contact with a variety of people, including offenders, their families, assistant U.S. attorneys, defense counsel, case agents,

and the federal judges makes for an extremely diverse mix. It is personally rewarding to me to see that the final product is helpful to the U.S. district court judges, later the Federal Bureau of Prisons, and eventually to my colleagues in the U.S. probation officer supervision units across the country.

Some students will go on and gain professional degrees. Many want to become attorneys and work within the court system. Ralph C. Martin II was a student in the criminal justice program at Northeastern University before receiving his law degree at Northeastern School of Law. His career is rather unique. Martin served as the district attorney of Suffolk County, Massachusetts, and, in that capacity, was the chief elected law enforcement official for Boston, Chelsea, Revere, and Winthrop from 1992 to 2002. He was appointed in 1992 and won election to the office in 1994 by a margin of almost 20 percent. He ran unopposed in 1998 and became the first African-American and Republican district attorney in Suffolk County's history. Now a partner at the Bingham McCutchen law firm in Boston, Martin put his more than 20 years experience as a trial lawyer and prosecutor to good use in his practice, which covers the areas of corporate governance and investigations, white collar defense, and general civil litigation. While not everyone can be as successful as Ralph Martin, many criminal justice students will go on to law school when they graduate. Here they will gain an extensive knowledge of the law and the legal system in order to defend the rights of their clients and protect their best interests. Cases may be settled in court or more commonly through a negotiated settlement that helps both sides avoid a lengthy trial. They also act as legal advisors and engage in such activities as drawing up and/or interpreting a legal document or contract, and advising clients of changes in existing laws. Some work for the federal, state, or local government; others take advantage of increasing opportunities for employment within businesses.

Part 1 of this text covers the basic issues and concepts of crime, law, and justice. Chapter 1 covers the justice process and the organizations that are entrusted with conducting its operations: the police, courts, and corrections; it provides an overview of the justice system and sets out its most important agencies, processes and concepts. Chapter 2 looks at the nature and extent of crime, and tries to answer the question, why do people commit crime? Chapter 3 covers the criminal law, analyzing both its substantive and procedural components.

> *"I like learning of people's stories and how they became involved in their offenses. The contact with a variety of people, including offenders, their families, assistant U.S. attorneys, defense counsel, case agents, and the federal judges makes for an extremely diverse mix."*
>
> Samantha J. O'Hara

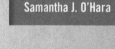

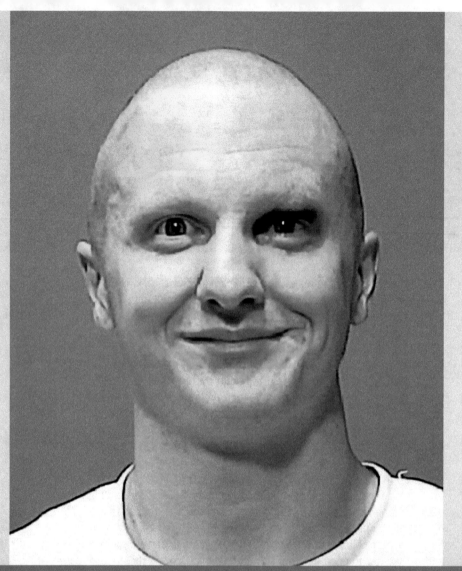

1 Crime and Criminal Justice

Learning Objectives

LO1 Discuss the formation of the criminal justice system in America

LO2 Be able to define the concept of a criminal justice system

LO3 Be familiar with the basic component agencies of criminal justice

LO4 Comprehend the size and scope of the contemporary justice system

LO5 Trace the formal criminal justice process

LO6 Know what is meant by the term *criminal justice assembly line*

LO7 Characterize the informal criminal justice system

LO8 Describe the "wedding cake" model of justice

LO9 Be familiar with the various perspectives on justice

LO10 Understand the ethical issues involved in criminal justice

Who of us can ever forget the events of January 8, 2011, the day a disturbed young man named Jared Lee Loughner opened fire in a supermarket parking lot in Tucson, Arizona, in an attempt to kill Congresswoman Gabrielle Giffords? Before the shooting stopped, 19 people were hit, 6 of them fatally, including Gabe Zimmerman, an aide to Giffords; John Roll, a federal judge; and Christina-Taylor Green, a 9-year-old girl interested in politics, who had been brought to the meeting by neighbor Susan Hileman. How could this tragedy have occurred? Investigations quickly found that Loughner was a deeply disturbed person. His friends told authorities that he had undergone a radical change in personality. Mounting evidence of his abnormal behavior came to light, including the fact that after numerous run-ins with campus security and bizarre outbursts in class, Loughner had been suspended from Pima Community College in October 2010. School officials had sent a letter to Loughner's parents stating that if he wished to return to the school, he would have to "obtain a mental health clearance indicating, in the opinion of a mental health professional, his presence at the college does not present a danger to himself or others." Rather than get help, Loughner decided to drop out. ∎

How can we truly understand why a young man raised in a middle-class environment, who had friends, a Facebook page, and attended college, suddenly became a cold-blooded killer? Was his violent rampage the product of a diseased mind or, as some critics charged, the end-product of an era of poisonous political rhetoric?

Loughner's attempt to kill Gabrielle Giffords also focused attention on a number of other important social and legal issues. How is it possible for a disturbed individual such as Loughner to obtain a semi-automatic weapon and buy ammo at the local Walmart? The Tucson massacre is just one of a spate of shootings involving disturbed people using high-powered weapons. On Monday, April 16, 2007, 23-year-old Seung-Hui Cho methodically took the lives of 32 people—27 students and 5 professors—at Virginia Tech before taking his own life.[1] On February 14, 2008, Steven Kazmierczak entered Cole Hall at Northern Illinois University armed with a shotgun and three handguns, killed five people, and wounded 16 others before taking his own life. Considering these and similar incidents, many people believe that handguns should be more tightly controlled.

The Tucson shootings also focused attention on the nation's mental health system and its ability to help people avoid violent crime. Should Loughner's potential for violence have been diagnosed sooner and steps taken to treat or at least confine him taken before tragedy occurred?

The Tucson incident also raises questions about punishment and correction. Can a person as disturbed as Loughner be considered "legally sane" and sentenced to death? Did his own words and writings describing his intent and planning show that he is rational and therefore a candidate for the death penalty? Should a person's psychological problems exempt him from harsh criminal sanctions?

The Tucson massacre is but one of the millions of cases that enter the **criminal justice system** each year. Defined as the system of law enforcement, adjudication, and correction that is directly involved in the apprehension, prosecution, and control of those charged with criminal offenses, this loosely organized collection of agencies is responsible for, among other matters, protecting the public, maintaining order, enforcing the law, identifying transgressors, bringing the guilty to justice, and treating criminal behavior. The public depends on this vast system not only to protect them from evil doers and to bring justice to their lives but also to maintain order and protect the fabric of society.

This textbook serves as an introduction to the study of criminal justice. This area of research and scholarship includes describing, analyzing, and explaining the behavior of those agencies authorized by law and statute to dispense justice—police departments, courts, and correctional agencies—and helping these institutions to identify effective and efficient methods of crime control.

Myth vs. Reality

As we engage in this study of crime and justice, a unifying theme is exposing, analyzing, and setting straight some of the myths and legends that have grown up about the justice system. Many people form opinions about criminal justice from the media, which often leads to false impressions and unrealized expectations. In the movies and on TV, it takes police about an hour to catch even the most wily criminal. Shootouts and car chases are routine, and every criminal defendant receives a lengthy trial in front of an attentive jury. Journalists help perpetuate these myths: the media routinely feature stories exposing brutal cops and violent prisons. How true are these images of justice? How can we separate myth from reality? Throughout this textbook, we will confront such myths and legends and try to sort out the facts from the fiction.

This chapter introduces some basic issues, beginning with a discussion of the history of crime in America and the development of criminal justice. The major organizations of the criminal justice system are then introduced as an overview of how the **criminal justice process** functions. Because there is no single view of the underlying goals that help shape criminal justice, the varying perspectives on what criminal justice really is, or should be, are set out in some detail.

Developing the Criminal Justice System

During the nineteenth century, America experienced a surge in violent behavior. You have all seen movie Westerns featuring the likes of badmen such as Jesse James, Billy the Kid, and Butch Cassidy and the Sundance Kid. These outlaws were not merely media legends, they actually robbed trains, rustled cattle, and engaged in Western land wars. On the East Coast, large and deadly urban gangs such as the North End Gang, Dead Rabbits, Plug Uglies, and Hudson Dusters set up operations in cities such as New York and Boston. Responding to public outcry over rising crime rates in the United States and abroad, the first criminal justice agencies began to appear. The emergence of criminal gangs and groups in the nineteenth century and a general sense of lawlessness spurred development of formal agencies of criminal justice. In 1829, the first police agency, the London Metropolitan Police, was developed to keep the peace and identify criminal suspects. In the United States, the first police agencies were created in Boston (1838), New York (1844), and Philadelphia (1854). The penitentiary, or prison, was created to provide nonphysical correctional treatment for convicted offenders; these were considered "liberal" innovations that replaced corporal or capital punishment.

During the first century of their existence, these fledgling agencies of justice rarely worked together in a systematic fashion. It was not until 1919—when the Chicago Crime Commission, a professional association funded by private contributions, was created—that the work of the criminal justice system began to be recognized.[2] This organization acted as a citizens' advocate group and kept track of the activities of local justice agencies. The commission still carries out its work today.

In 1931, President Herbert Hoover appointed the National Commission of Law Observance and Enforcement, which is commonly known today as the Wickersham Commission. This national study group made a detailed analysis of the U.S. justice system and helped usher in the era of treatment and rehabilitation. The final report found that thousands of rules and regulations governed the system and made it difficult for justice personnel to keep track of the system's legal and administrative complexity.[3]

The Modern Era of Justice

The modern era of criminal justice can be traced to a series of research projects begun in the 1950s under the sponsorship of the American Bar Foundation.[4] Originally designed to provide in-depth analysis of the organization, administration, and operation of criminal justice agencies, the ABF project discovered that the justice system contained many procedures that had been hidden from the public view. The research focus then shifted to an examination of these previously obscure processes and their interrelationship—investigation, arrest, prosecution, and plea negotiations. It became apparent that justice professionals used a great deal of personal choice in decision making, and showing how this discretion was used became a prime focus of the research effort. For the first time, the term *criminal justice system* began to be used, reflecting a view that justice agencies could be connected in an intricate yet often unobserved network of decision-making processes.

Federal Involvement in Criminal Justice

In 1967, the President's Commission on Law Enforcement and Administration of Justice (the Crime Commission), which had been appointed by President Lyndon Johnson, published its final report, entitled *The Challenge of Crime in a Free Society*.[5] This group of practitioners, educators, and attorneys was given the responsibility of creating a comprehensive view of the criminal justice process and recommending reforms. In 1968, Congress passed the Safe Streets and Crime Control Act, providing for the expenditure of federal funds for state and local crime control efforts and launching a massive campaign to restructure the justice system.[6] It funded the National Institute of Law Enforcement and Criminal Justice (NILECJ), which encouraged research and development in criminal justice. Renamed the National Institute of Justice (NIJ) in 1979, it has continued its mission as a major source of funding for the implementation and evaluation of innovative experimental and demonstration projects in the criminal justice system.[7]

The Safe Streets Act provided funding for the **Law Enforcement Assistance Administration (LEAA)**, which granted hundreds of millions of dollars in aid to local and state justice agencies. Throughout its 14-year history, the LEAA provided the majority of federal funds to states for criminal justice activities. On April 15, 1982, the program came to an end when Congress terminated its funding. However, the federal government continues to fund innovation in the criminal justice system through the National Institute of Justice and the Bureau of Justice Assistance (BJA).

The Contemporary Criminal Justice System

The criminal justice system is society's instrument of **social control**. Some behaviors are considered so dangerous that they must either be strictly controlled or prohibited outright, and some people are so destructive that they must be monitored or even confined. It is the task of the agencies of justice to prevent or deter outlawed behavior by apprehending, adjudicating, and sanctioning lawbreakers. Society maintains other forms of informal social control, such as parental and school discipline, but these are designed to deal with moral, not legal, misbehavior. Only the

RealityCheck

MYTH OR REALITY? Police departments are an American creation, the first having been formed in New York City after the Civil War.

MYTH. *The first formal police department was created in London, England in 1829, headquartered in Scotland Yard.*
Police agencies in the United States developed in the latter half of the nineteenth century. What social conditions present at that time encouraged the creation of formal police agencies?

LO1 Discuss the formation of the criminal justice system in America

Law Enforcement Assistance Administration (LEAA)
Funded by the federal government's Safe Streets Act, this agency provided technical assistance and hundreds of millions of dollars in aid to local and state justice agencies between 1969 and 1982.

social control
The control of an individual's behavior by social and institutional forces in society.

criminal justice system maintains the power to control crime and punish those who violate the law.

Contemporary criminal justice agencies are political entities whose structure and function are lodged within the legislative, judicial, and executive branches of the government. They typically can be divided into three main components (Figure 1.1): law enforcement agencies, which investigate crimes and apprehend suspects; court agencies, in which charges are brought, indictments submitted, trials conducted, and sentences formulated; and correctional agencies, which are charged with monitoring, treating, and rehabilitating convicted offenders.

Because of its varied and complex mission, the contemporary criminal justice system in the United States is monumental in size. The cost of law enforcement, court agencies, and correctional agencies has increased significantly during the past 25 years. Per capita expenditure for criminal justice functions is now more than $720 each year for every American! One reason the justice system is so expensive to run is because it employs more than 2.4 million people in thousands of independent law enforcement, court-related, and correctional agencies. The nation now has almost 18,000 law enforcement agencies, including more than 12,000 local agencies, 3,000 county sheriffs' offices, and 49 state police departments (every state has one except Hawaii). In addition, there are 2,000 other specialized law enforcement agencies ranging from transit police in large cities to county constables. These police and law enforcement agencies now employ more than 1 million people, including more than 700,000 sworn police personnel (those with general arrest powers) and the rest civilian employees. Of these, about 600,000 are in local agencies, 330,000 work in county sheriffs' offices, and the rest (90,000) work for

RealityCheck

MYTH OR REALITY? At its core, the justice system is designed to protect the public from those people who cannot abide by or obey the law.

REALITY. *The justice system dispenses formal social control, and is made up of a group of government agencies empowered to control and punish people who violate the criminal law.*

What behaviors that are currently illegal would you decriminalize and make legal? Conversely, what behaviors that are now legal do you believe should be criminalized?

Police	Courts	Corrections
Police departments are those public agencies created to maintain order, enforce the criminal law, provide emergency services, keep traffic on streets and highways moving freely, and develop a sense of community safety. Police officers work actively with the community to prevent criminal behavior; they help divert members of special needs populations, such as juveniles, alcoholics, and drug addicts, from the criminal justice system; they participate in specialized units such as a drug prevention task force or antirape unit; they cooperate with public prosecutors to initiate investigations into organized crime and drug trafficking; they resolve neighborhood and family conflicts; and they provide emergency services, such as preserving civil order during strikes and political demonstrations.	The criminal courthouse is the scene of the trial process. Here the criminal responsibility of defendants accused of violating the law is determined. Ideally, the court is expected to convict and sentence those found guilty of crimes, while ensuring that the innocent are freed without any consequence or burden. The court system is formally required to seek the truth, to obtain justice for the individual brought before its tribunals, and to maintain the integrity of the government's rule of law. The main actors in the court process are the judge, whose responsibilities include overseeing the legality of the trial process, and the prosecutor and the defense attorney, who are the opponents in what is known as the adversary system. These two parties oppose each other in a hotly disputed contest —the criminal trial—in accordance with rules of law and procedure.	In the broadest sense, correctional agencies include community supervision or probation, various types of incarceration (including jails, houses of correction, and state prisons), and parole programs for both juvenile and adult offenders. These programs range from the lowest security, such as probation in the community with minimum supervision, to the highest security, such as 24-hour lockdown in an ultra-maximum security prison. Corrections ordinarily represent the postadjudicatory care given to offenders when a sentence is imposed by the court and the offender is placed in the hands of the correctional agency.

Figure 1.1 Components of the Criminal Justice System

state police.[8] There are nearly 17,000 courts; more than 8,000 prosecutorial agencies employ around 80,000 people; and about 1,200 correctional institutions (such as jails, prisons, and detention centers) employ around half a million people. There are also thousands of community corrections agencies, including more than 3,500 probation and parole departments.

The system is massive because it must process, treat, and care for millions of people. Although the crime rate has declined substantially in the past decade, more than 14 million people are still being arrested each year, including more than 2 million for serious felony offenses.[9] In addition, the juvenile courts handle about 1.5 million juveniles. Today, state and federal courts convict a combined total of over 1 million adults on felony charges.[10] It is not surprising, considering these numbers, that today more than 7 million people are under some form of correctional supervision, including 2 million men and women in the nation's jails and prisons and an additional 5 million adult men and women being supervised in the community while on probation or parole. More people are being convicted today than ever before and, if sent to prison or jail, are serving more of their sentence behind bars.[11] The cost of corrections is now almost $70 billion per year, a cost of about $30,000 per inmate, reinforcing the old saying, "It costs a lot more to put a person in the state pen, than to send a student to Penn State."

L03 Be familiar with the basic component agencies of criminal justice

L04 Comprehend the size and scope of the contemporary justice system

The Formal Criminal Justice Process

Another way of understanding criminal justice is to view it as a process that takes an offender through a series of decision points beginning with arrest and concluding with reentry into society. During this process, key decision makers resolve whether to maintain the offender in the system or discharge the suspect without further action. This decision making is often a matter of individual discretion, based on a variety of factors and perceptions. Legal factors, including the seriousness of the charges, available evidence, and the suspect's prior record, are usually considered legitimate influences on decision making. Troubling is the fact that such extralegal factors as the suspect's race, gender, class, and age may also influence decision outcomes. Some critics believe that a suspect's race, class, and gender largely determine the direction a case will take, whereas supporters argue that the system is relatively fair and unbiased.[12]

In reality, few cases actually are processed through the entire formal justice system. Most are handled informally and with dispatch. The system of justice has been roundly criticized for its "backroom deals" and bargain justice. Although informality and deal making are in fact the rule, the concept of the formal justice process is important because it implies that every criminal defendant charged with a serious crime is entitled to a full range of rights under law. The fact that most criminal suspects are actually treated informally may be less important than the fact that all criminal defendants are entitled to a full range of legal rights and constitutional protections.

A comprehensive view of the formal criminal process would normally include the following:

1. *Initial contact.* In most instances, an offender's initial contact with the criminal justice system takes place as a result of a police action:

   - Patrol officers observe a person acting suspiciously, conclude the suspect is under the influence of drugs, and take her into custody.
   - Police officers are contacted by a victim who reports a robbery; they respond by going to the scene of the crime and apprehending a suspect.
   - An informer tells police about some ongoing criminal activity in order to receive favorable treatment.
   - Responding to a request by the mayor or other political figure, the local department may initiate an investigation into an ongoing criminal enterprise such as gambling, prostitution, or drug trafficking.
   - A person walks into the police station and confesses to committing a crime—for example, killing his wife after an altercation.

in-presence requirement
The condition that in order to make an arrest in a misdemeanor, the arresting officer must have personally witnessed the crime being committed.

nolle prosequi
The term used when a prosecutor decides to drop a case after a complaint has been formally made. Reasons for a *nolle prosequi* include evidence insufficiency, reluctance of witnesses to testify, police error, and office policy.

grand jury
A type of jury responsible for investigating alleged crimes, examining evidence, and issuing indictments.

true bill of indictment
A written statement charging a defendant with the commission of a crime, drawn up by a prosecuting attorney and considered by a grand jury. If the grand jury finds sufficient evidence to support the indictment, it will issue a true bill of indictment.

information
Charging document filed by the prosecution that forms the basis of the preliminary hearing.

probable cause hearing
Term used in some jurisdictions for a preliminary hearing to show cause to bring a case to trial.

2. *Investigation.* The purpose of the criminal investigation is to gather sufficient evidence to identify a suspect and support a legal arrest. An investigation can take only a few minutes, as in the case where a police officer sees a crime in progress and can apprehend the suspect quickly. Or it can take many years and involve hundreds of law enforcement agents. Dennis Rader, the notorious BTK ("Bind, Torture, Kill") serial killer, began his murderous streak in 1974 and was finally apprehended in 2005 after an investigation that lasted more than 20 years.[13]

3. *Arrest.* An arrest is considered legal when all of the following conditions exist: (1) the police officer believes there is sufficient evidence, referred to as *probable cause*, that a crime is being or has been committed and the suspect is the person who committed it; (2) the officer deprives the individual of freedom; and (3) the suspect believes that he is now in the custody of the police and has lost his liberty. The police officer is not required to use the word "arrest" or any similar term to initiate an arrest, nor does the officer have to bring the suspect to the police station. To make an arrest in a misdemeanor, the officer must have witnessed the crime personally, a provision known as the **in-presence requirement**. Some jurisdictions have passed laws allowing misdemeanor arrests based on victim complaints in cases involving child or domestic abuse. Arrests can also be made when a magistrate, presented with sufficient evidence by police and prosecutors, issues a warrant authorizing the arrest of the suspect.

4. *Custody.* After an arrest and while the suspect is being detained, the police may wish to search for evidence, conduct an interrogation, or even encourage a confession. Witnesses may be brought to view the suspect in a lineup or in a one-on-one confrontation. Because these procedures are so crucial and can have a great impact at trial, the U.S. Supreme Court has granted suspects in police custody protection from the unconstitutional abuse of police power, such as illegal searches and intimidating interrogations.

5. *Charging.* If the arresting officers or their superiors believe that sufficient evidence exists to charge a person with a crime, the case will be turned over to the prosecutor's office. The prosecutor's decision to charge the suspect with a specific criminal act involves many factors, including evidence sufficiency, crime seriousness, case pressure, and political issues, as well as personal factors such as a prosecutor's own specific interests and biases. After conducting a preliminary investigation of its legal merits, prosecutors may decide to take no further action in a case; this is referred to as a **nolle prosequi**.

6. *Preliminary hearing/grand jury.* The U.S. Constitution mandates that before a trial can take place, the government must first prove probable cause that the accused committed the crime for which he is being charged. In about half the states and in the federal system, this determination is made by a **grand jury** in a closed hearing. If the prosecution can present sufficient evidence, the grand jury will issue a **true bill of indictment**, which specifies the exact charges on which the accused must stand trial. In the remaining states, the prosecution will file a charging document (usually called an **information**) before a lower trial court, which then conducts an open hearing on the merits of the case. During this procedure, which is sometimes referred to as a **probable cause hearing**, the defendant and the defendant's attorney may appear and dispute the prosecutor's charges. The suspect will be called to stand trial if the presiding magistrate or judge accepts the prosecutor's evidence as factual and sufficient.

7. *Arraignment.* Before the trial begins, the defendant will be arraigned, or brought before the court that will hear the case. At this time, formal charges are read, the defendant is informed of his constitutional rights (for example, the right to be

The grand jury determines whether sufficient evidence exists to bring a criminal suspect to trial. Here, IMF leader Dominique Strauss-Kahn (seated) appears at a court hearing in New York on May 19, 2011, at which a grand jury found enough evidence for an indictment on charges that he sexually abused a hotel maid. Later, the maid's statements were questioned, placing the prosecution under a cloud. Strauss-Kahn was released on bail and the prosecution placed in jeopardy. The Strauss-Kahn case, which made national headlines because he was a frontrunner to become president of France, illustrates how cases can be dropped due to witness and evidence problems before they ever get to trial.

AP Photo/NBC, Pool

represented by legal counsel), an initial plea (not guilty or guilty) is entered, a trial date set, and bail issues are considered.

8. *Bail/detention.* Bail is a money bond levied to ensure the return of a criminal defendant for trial, allowing the defendant to remain in the community prior to trial. Defendants who do not show up for trial forfeit their bail. Those people who cannot afford to put up bail or who cannot borrow sufficient funds for it will remain in state custody prior to trial. In most instances, this means an extended stay in a county jail or house of correction. If they are stable members of the community and have committed nonviolent crimes, defendants may be released on their own recognizance (promise to the court), without bail.

9. *Plea bargaining.* After an arraignment, or even before, the defense and prosecution will discuss a possible guilty plea in exchange for the prosecution's reducing or dropping some of the charges or agreeing to a request for a more lenient sentence. It is generally accepted that almost 90 percent of all cases end in a plea bargain, rather than a criminal trial.

10. *Trial/adjudication.* If an agreement cannot be reached or if the prosecution does not wish to arrange a negotiated settlement of the case, a criminal trial will be held before a judge (bench trial) or jury, who will decide whether the prosecution's evidence against the defendant is sufficient beyond a reasonable doubt to prove guilt. If a jury cannot reach a decision—that is, if it is deadlocked—the case is left unresolved, leaving the prosecution to decide whether it should be retried at a later date.

11. *Sentencing/disposition.* If after a criminal trial the accused has been found guilty as charged, he will be returned to court for sentencing. Possible sentencing dispositions include a fine, probation, some form of community-based corrections, a period of incarceration in a penal institution, or, in rare instances, the death penalty.

12. *Appeal/postconviction remedies.* After conviction, the defense can ask the trial judge to set aside the jury's verdict because the jury has made a mistake of law—for example, by misinterpreting the judge's instructions or convicting on a charge that was not supported by the evidence. Failing that, an appeal may be filed if after conviction the defendant believes that his constitutional rights were violated by errors in the trial process. Appellate courts review such issues as whether evidence was used properly, the judge conducted the trial in an approved fashion, jury selection was properly done, and the attorneys in the case acted appropriately. If the court rules that the appeal has merit, it can hold that the defendant be given a new trial or, in some instances, order his outright release.

13. *Correctional treatment.* After sentencing, the offender is placed within the jurisdiction of state or federal correctional authorities. The offender may serve a probationary term, be placed in a community correctional facility, serve a term in a county jail, or be housed in a prison. During this stage of the criminal justice process, the offender may be asked to participate in rehabilitation programs designed to help him make a successful readjustment to society.

14. *Release.* Upon completion of the sentence and period of correction, the offender will be free to return to society. Most inmates do not serve the full term of their sentence but are freed through an early-release mechanism, such as parole or pardon or by earning time off for good behavior. Offenders sentenced to community supervision simply finish their term and resume their lives in the community.

15. *Postrelease.* After termination of their correctional treatment, offenders may be asked to spend some time in a community correctional center, which acts as a bridge between a secure treatment facility and absolute freedom. Offenders may find that their conviction has cost them some personal privileges, such as the right to hold certain kinds of employment. These privileges may be restored by court order once the offenders have proved their trustworthiness and willingness to adjust to society's rules.

L05 Trace the formal criminal justice process

The Criminal Justice Assembly Line

To justice expert Herbert Packer, the image that this process evokes is an assembly line conveyor belt down which moves an endless stream of cases, never stopping.[14] According to this view, each of the 15 stages is actually a *decision point* through which cases flow. At the investigatory stage, police must decide whether to pursue the case or terminate involvement because there is insufficient evidence to identify a suspect, the case is considered trivial, the victim decides not to press charges, and so on. At the bail stage, a decision must be made whether to set bail so high that the defendant remains in custody, to set a reasonable bail, or to release the defendant on his or her own recognizance without requiring any bail at all. Each of these decisions can have a critical effect on the defendant, the justice system, and society. If an error is made, an innocent person may suffer or a dangerous individual may be released to continue to prey upon society.

Figure 1.2 illustrates the approximate number of offenders removed from the criminal justice system at each stage of the process. As the figure shows, most people who commit crime escape detection, and of those who do not, relatively few are bound over for trial, convicted, and eventually sentenced to prison. About 30 percent of people arrested on felony charges are eventually convicted in criminal court; however, nearly a third of those convicted on felony charges are sentenced to probation and released back into the community without doing time in prison.[15] For every 1,000 crimes, about 20 people are sent to prison.

In actual practice, many suspects are released before trial because of a procedural error, evidence problems, or other reasons that result in a case dismissal by the prosecutor, or *nolle prosequi*. Although most cases that go to trial end in a conviction, others are dismissed by the presiding judge because of a witness

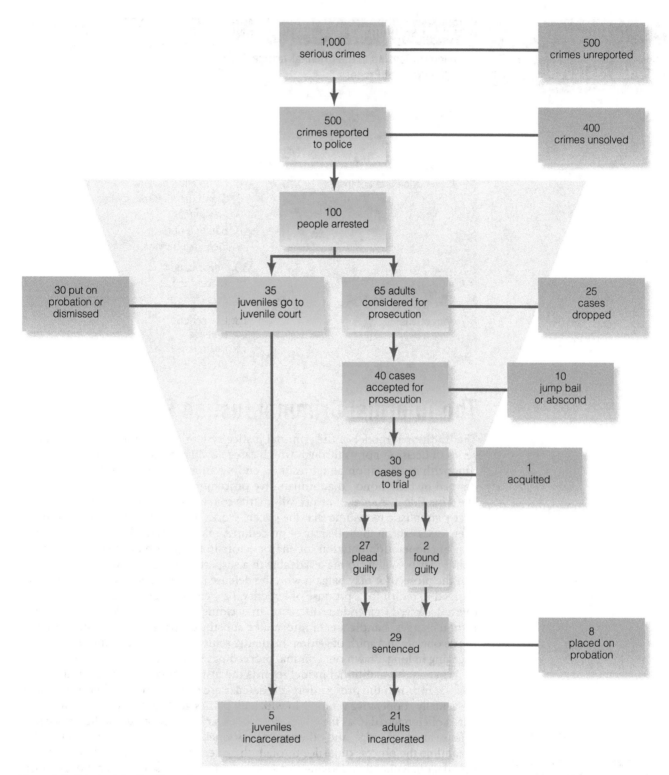

Figure 1.2 Criminal Justice Funnel

Sources: Thomas Cohen and Tracey Kyckelhahn, *Felony Defendants in Large Urban Counties, 2006* (Washington, DC: Bureau of Justice Statistics, 2010); Matthew Durose and Patrick Langan, *Felony Sentences in State Courts, 2004* (Washington, DC: Bureau of Justice Statistics, 2007).

or a complainant's failure to appear or procedural irregularities. Thus the justice process can be viewed as a funnel that holds many cases at its mouth and relatively few at its end. Concept Summary 1.1 shows the interrelationship of the component agencies of the criminal justice system and the criminal justice process.

L06 Know what is meant by the term *criminal justice assembly line*

Concept Summary 1.1

The Interrelationship of the Criminal Justice System and the Criminal Process

The System: Agencies of Crime Control	The Process
1. Police	1. Contact
	2. Investigation
	3. Arrest
	4. Custody
2. Prosecution and defense	5. Complaint/charging
	6. Grand jury/preliminary hearing
	7. Arraignment
	8. Bail/detention
	9. Plea negotiations
3. Court	10. Adjudication
	11. Disposition
	12. Appeal/postconviction remedies
4. Corrections	13. Correction
	14. Release
	15. Postrelease

The Informal Criminal Justice Process

The traditional model of the criminal justice system depicts the legal process as a series of decision points through which cases flow. Each stage of the system, beginning with investigation and arrest and ending after a sentence has been served, is defined by time-honored administrative procedures and controlled by the rule of law. This "ideal" model of justice still merits concern and attention, but it would be overly simplistic to assume that the system works this way for every case. Although a few cases exhibit the full array of procedures, many are settled in an informal pattern of cooperation between the major actors in the justice process. For example, police may be willing to make a deal with a suspect in order to gain his cooperation, and the prosecutor may bargain with the defense attorney to gain a plea of guilty as charged in return for a promise of leniency. Law enforcement agents and court officers are allowed tremendous discretion in deciding whether to make an arrest, bring formal charges, handle a case informally, substitute charges, and so on. Crowded courts operate in a spirit of getting the matter settled quickly and cleanly, rather than engaging in long, drawn-out criminal proceedings with an uncertain outcome.

Whereas the traditional model regards the justice process as an adversarial proceeding in which the prosecution and defense are combatants, most criminal cases are actually cooperative ventures in which all parties get together to work out a deal; this is often referred to as the **courtroom work group**.[16] Made up of the prosecutor, defense attorney, judge, and other court personnel, the courtroom work group helps streamline the process of justice through the extensive use of deal making and plea negotiation. Rather than looking to provide a spirited defense or prosecution, cooperation rather than conflict between prosecutor and defense attorney appears to be the norm. It is only in a few widely publicized criminal cases involving rape or murder that the adversarial process is called into play. Consequently, upward of 80 percent of all felony cases and over 90 percent of misdemeanors are settled without trial.

The "Wedding Cake" Model of Justice

Samuel Walker, a justice historian and scholar, has come up with a rather unique way of describing this informal justice process: he compares it to a four-layer cake, as depicted in Figure 1.3.[17]

courtroom work group
The phrase used to indicate that all parties in the adversary process work together cooperatively to settle cases with the least amount of effort and conflict.

Level I The first layer of Walker's model is made up of celebrated cases involving the wealthy and famous, such as O. J. Simpson and Lindsay Lohan, or the not-so-powerful who victimize a famous person—such as Jared Lee Loughner, who shot Congresswoman Gabrielle Giffords. Other cases fall into the first layer because they are widely reported in the media and become the subject of widespread media interest. For example, there was an avalanche of media interest in the kidnapping of Elizabeth Smart from her Salt Lake City home on June 5, 2002, and her rescue nine months later. Media attention rebounded in 2010 when her abductors, Brian David Mitchell and Wanda Barzee, were tried and convicted of the crime.[18]

Cases in the first layer of the criminal justice wedding cake usually receive the full array of criminal justice procedures, including competent defense attorneys, expert witnesses, jury trials, and elaborate appeals. Because of the media focus on Level I cases and the Hollywood treatment of them, the public is given the impression that most criminals are sober, intelligent people who receive the full range of procedural rights afforded by the justice system and that most victims are members of the upper classes, a patently false impression.

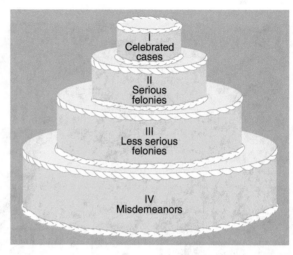

Figure 1.3 The Criminal Justice "Wedding Cake"

Source: Based on Samuel Walker, *Sense and Nonsense About Crime* (Belmont, CA: Wadsworth, 2001). There are a number of new editions that may also be of interest, including *Sense and Nonsense About Crime, Drugs, and Communities 2010.*

Level II The second layer contains serious felonies—rapes, robberies, and burglaries. Police, prosecutors, and judges all agree that these cases are worthy of the full attention of the justice system. The factors placing them in the Level II category include:

- They are committed by experienced, repeat offenders.
- The amount of money stolen in a burglary or larceny is significant.
- Violent acts are committed by a stranger who uses a weapon.
- Robberies involve large amounts of money taken by a weapon-wielding criminal.

Offenders in Level II cases quite often receive a full jury trial and, if convicted, can look forward to a prison sentence.

Level III Although they can also be felonies, crimes that fall in the third layer of the wedding cake either are less serious offenses, committed by young or first-time offenders, or involve people who knew each other or were otherwise related, such as a domestic abuse case or a drunken brawl involving people in a "love triangle." Level III crimes may be dealt with by an outright dismissal, a plea bargain, reduction in charges, or (most commonly) a probationary sentence.

Level IV The fourth layer of the cake is made up of the millions of misdemeanors—disorderly conduct, shoplifting, public drunkenness, and minor assault—that are handled by the lower criminal courts in assembly-line fashion. Few defendants insist on exercising their constitutional rights, because the delay would cost them valuable time and money, and punishment is typically a fine or probation.[19]

The wedding cake model of informal justice is an intriguing alternative to the traditional criminal justice flowchart. Criminal justice officials handle individual cases quite differently, yet there is a high degree of consistency with which particular types or classes of cases are handled in every legal jurisdiction. For example, police and prosecutors in Los Angeles and Boston will handle the murder of a prominent citizen in a similar fashion. They will also deal with the death of an unemployed street person killed in a brawl in a similar manner. The wedding cake model is useful because it helps us realize that public opinion about criminal justice is often formed on the basis of what happened in an atypical case.

RealityCheck

MYTH OR REALITY? There is equal justice under the law, and everyone can expect to get their day in court.

MYTH. *In practice, few cases find their way to court, and most are settled informally with a plea bargain.*

Do you have an alternative to the plea bargaining system? What would happen if all criminal cases were settled with a formal trial rather than a plea agreement?

LO8 Describe the "wedding cake" model of justice

■ Some defendants and cases fall in the top tier of the criminal justice wedding cake because they make national headlines and are widely covered by the media. Here, Brian David Mitchell is escorted into the Frank E. Moss Federal Courthouse on November 1, 2010, in Salt Lake City for his trial related to the kidnapping of Elizabeth Smart in 2002. On May 25, 2011, Mitchell was sentenced to life in prison.

Perspectives on Justice

Even though it has been more than 40 years since the field of criminal justice began to be the subject of both serious academic study and attempts at unified policy formation, significant debate continues over the actual meaning of *criminal justice* and how the problem of crime control should be approached. After decades of effort in research and policy analysis, it is clear that criminal justice is far from a unified field. Practitioners, academics, and commentators alike have expressed irreconcilable differences concerning its goals, purpose, and direction. Considering the complexity of criminal justice, it is not surprising that no single perspective or philosophy dominates the field. What are the dominant views of the criminal justice system today? What is the role of the justice system, and how should it approach its tasks? The different perspectives on criminal justice are discussed next.

Crime Control Perspective

crime control perspective
A model of criminal justice that emphasizes the control of dangerous offenders and the protection of society. Its advocates call for harsh punishments as a deterrent to crime and support availability of the death penalty.

People who hold the **crime control perspective** believe that the proper role of the justice system is to prevent crime through the judicious use of criminal sanctions. Because the public is outraged by violent crimes, it demands an efficient justice system that hands out tough sanctions to those who choose to violate the law.[20] If the justice system were allowed to operate in an effective manner, unhampered by legal controls, potential criminals would be deterred from violating the law. Those who did commit a crime would be apprehended, tried, and punished so that they would never dare commit a crime again. Crime rates trend upward, the argument goes, when criminals do not sufficiently fear apprehension and punishment. If the efficiency of the system could be increased and the criminal law could be toughened, crime rates would eventually decline. Effective law enforcement, strict mandatory punishment, incarceration of dangerous criminals, and the judicious use of capital punishment are the keys to reducing crime rates. Crime control may be expensive, but reducing the pain inflicted by criminal activity is well worth the price. If punishment were swift, certain, and severe, few would be tempted to break the law.

Crime control advocates do not want legal technicalities to help the guilty go free and tie the hands of justice. They lobby for the abolition of legal restrictions on a police officer's ability to search for evidence and interrogate suspects. They want law enforcement officers to be able to profile people at an airport in order to identify terrorists, even if it means singling out individuals because of their gender, race, or ethnic origin. They are angry at judges who let obviously guilty people go free because a law enforcement officer made an unintentional procedural error.

In sum, the key positions of the crime control perspective are these:

- The purpose of the justice system is to deter crime through the application of punishment.
- The more efficient the system, the greater its effectiveness.
- The justice system is not equipped to treat people but, rather, to investigate crimes, apprehend suspects, and punish the guilty.

Rehabilitation Perspective

Whereas the crime control perspective views the justice system in terms of protecting the public and controlling criminal elements, advocates of the **rehabilitation perspective** view crime as an expression of frustration and anger created by social inequality. They see the justice system as a means of caring for and treating people who have been the victims of this inequity. According to this view, crime can be controlled by giving people the means to improve their lifestyle and helping them overcome any personal and or psychological problems caused by their life circumstances.

The rehabilitation concept assumes that people are at the mercy of social, economic, and interpersonal conditions and interactions. Criminals themselves are the victims of racism, poverty, strain, blocked opportunities, alienation, family disruption, and other social problems. Violent killers such as Jared Loughner and Seung-Hui Cho seem mentally and emotionally unstable. Others live in socially disorganized neighborhoods that are incapable of providing proper education, health care, or civil services. Society must help them in order to compensate for their social problems. Punishment cannot deter these people, but proper treatment may prevent their crimes.

Rehabilitation advocates believe that government programs can help reduce crime on both a societal (macro) and individual (micro) level. On the macro or societal level, rehabilitation efforts are aimed at preventing crimes before they occur. If legitimate opportunities increase, crime rates decline.[21] This goal may be achieved at the neighborhood level by increasing economic opportunities through job training, family counseling, educational services, and crisis intervention. On a micro or individual level, rehabilitation efforts are aimed at known offenders who have already violated the law. The best way to reduce crime and recidivism (repeat offending) rates is to help offenders, through intensive one-on-one counseling, adopt prosocial changes in attitudes and improved cognitive thinking patterns.[22] Although the public may want to "get tough" on crime, many are willing to make exceptions—for example, by advocating leniency for younger offenders.[23]

The key provisions of the rehabilitation model are these:

- In the long run, it is better to treat than punish.
- Criminals are society's victims.
- Helping others is part of the American culture.
- Convicted criminals can be successfully treated within the confines of the justice system.

rehabilitation perspective
The view that the primary purpose of criminal justice is helping to care for people who cannot manage themselves. Crime is an expression of frustration and anger created by social inequality and can be controlled by giving people the means to improve their lifestyle through conventional endeavors.

Due Process Perspective

due process perspective
Due process is a basic constitutional principle based on the concept of an individual's expectations of civil rights and justice and the complementary concept of limitation on governmental power; it is a safeguard against arbitrary and unfair state procedures in judicial or administrative proceedings. Embodied in the due process concept are the basic rights of a defendant in criminal proceedings and the requirements for a fair trial.

According to the **due process perspective**, the justice system should be dedicated to providing fair and equitable treatment to those accused of crime.[24] This means providing impartial hearings, competent legal counsel, evenhanded treatment, and reasonable sanctions to ensure that no one suffers from racial, religious, or ethnic discrimination and that their basic constitutional rights are respected.

Those who advocate the due process orientation are quick to point out that the justice system remains an adversarial process that pits the forces of an all-powerful state against those of a solitary individual accused of a crime. If concern for justice and fairness did not exist, the defendant who lacked resources could easily be overwhelmed; miscarriages of justice are all too common. Numerous criminal convictions have been overturned because newly developed DNA evidence later showed that the accused could not have committed the crimes; many of the falsely convicted spend years in prison before their release.[25] Evidence also shows that many innocent people have been executed for crimes they did not commit.[26] Because such mistakes can happen, even the most apparently guilty offender deserves all the protection the justice system can offer.

The key positions advocated by due process supporters include the following:

- Every person deserves her or his full array of constitutional rights and privileges.
- Preserving the democratic ideals of American society takes precedence over the need to punish the guilty.
- Because of potential errors, decisions made within the justice system must be carefully scrutinized.
- Steps must be taken to treat all defendants fairly regardless of their sex, socioeconomic status, race, religion, or ethnicity.

Nonintervention Perspective

nonintervention perspective
A view of criminal justice that emphasizes the least intrusive treatment possible. Among its central policies are decarceration, diversion, and decriminalization. In other words, less is better.

Supporters of the **nonintervention perspective** believe that justice agencies should limit their involvement with criminal defendants. They believe that regardless of whether intervention is designed to punish people or to treat them,

Due process advocates fear that without careful protections innocent people will be prosecuted, convicted, and face harsh punishments. Here, on May 12, 2011, in Dallas, Texas, Natalie Roetzel, left, chief staff attorney with the Innocence Project of Texas hugs Johnny Pinchback, who spent 27 years in prison for aggravated sexual assault before DNA evidence proved him innocent. Pinchback, the 22nd person to be exonerated through DNA testing in Dallas County since 2001, was found to have been wrongly convicted of raping two teenage girls in 1984.

AP Photo/Tony Gutierrez

Does Monitoring Sex Offenders Really Work?

Noninterventionists worry that contemporary technology will reduce the privacy of American citizens, especially those convicted of crime who now have a permanent and public record. Take for instance the effort to monitor former sex offenders by requiring them to be placed on Web-based sex offender registration lists. Does this violate the privacy of offenders who have served their time? After all, there are no arsonist, drug dealer, or even murderer lists, even though those offenders may present an equally significant danger to society. Even if it is intrusive, sex offender registration may be justified if it significantly reduces the incidence and rate of offending.

Sex offender registration laws are now used in all 50 states. They appeal to politicians who may be swayed by media crusades against child molesters (such as "To Catch a Predator" on *Dateline NBC*), and appease the public's desire to "do something" about child predators. But do they actually work? Does registration deter offenders from committing further sex offenses and reduce the incidence of predatory acts against children?

To answer this question, criminologists Kristen Zgoba and Karen Bachar conducted an in-depth study of the effectiveness of the New Jersey registration law, commonly called Megan's Law (after Megan Kanka, a young girl killed by a sex offender living in her community). They found that, although the system was maintained at great cost to the state, it did not produce effective results. Sex offense rates were in steep decline in New Jersey before the system was installed, and

the rate of decline actually slowed down after the law took effect. The study showed that the greatest rate of decline in sex offending occurred *prior* to the passage and implementation of Megan's Law. Zgoba and Bachar also found that the passage and implementation of Megan's Law did not reduce the number of rearrests for sex offenses, nor did it have any demonstrable effect on the time between when sex offenders were released from prison and the time they were rearrested for any new offense, such as a drug offense, theft, or another sex offense.

Zgoba and Bachar's results can be used to rethink legal changes such as sex offender registration. Rather than deterring crime, such laws may merely cause sex offenders to be more cautious, while giving parents a false sense of security. For example, sex offenders may target victims in other states or in communities where they do not live and parents are less cautious.

CRITICAL THINKING

Is it fair to monitor sex offenders and have sex offender registration lists made open to the public? After all we do not have lists of embezzlers or rapists who have served time and now live in the community. Nor do we let neighbors know when a burglar has moved next door. Should sex offenders who have served their time be singled out while other former felons escape this form of public stigma?

---

the ultimate effect of any involvement is harmful and will have long-term negative consequences. Once involved with the justice system, criminal defendants develop a permanent record that follows them for the rest of their lives. They may be watched and kept under surveillance. Bearing an official label disrupts their personal and family life and harms their own self-image; they may view themselves as bad, evil, outcasts, troublemakers, or crazy. Official labels then may promote rather than reduce the continuity in antisocial activities.[27] When people are given less stigmatized forms of punishment, such as probation, they are less likely to become repeat offenders.[28] As the Contemporary Issues in Criminal Justice feature shows, efforts to keep criminals under constant surveillance does not always work as intended.

Fearing the harmful effects of stigma and labels, noninterventionists have tried to place limitations on the government's ability to control people's lives. They have called for the **decriminalization** (reduction of penalties) and outright **legalization** of nonserious victimless crimes, such as the possession of small amounts of marijuana. Noninterventionists have sponsored the removal of nonviolent offenders from the nation's correctional system, a policy referred to as **deinstitutionalization**. They support the placement of first offenders who commit minor crimes in informal, community-based treatment programs, a process referred to as **pretrial diversion**.

Noninterventionists fear that efforts to help or treat offenders may actually stigmatize them beyond the scope of their actual offense; this is referred to as **widening the net of justice**. Their efforts have resulted in rulings stating that these laws can be damaging to the reputation and the future of offenders who have not been given an opportunity to defend themselves from the charge that they are

decriminalization
Reducing the penalty for a criminal act but not actually legalizing it.

legalization
The removal of all criminal penalties from a previously outlawed act.

deinstitutionalization
The policy of removing as many offenders as possible from secure confinement and treating them in the community.

pretrial diversion
A program that provides nonpunitive, community-based alternatives to more intrusive forms of punishment such as jail or prison.

widening the net of justice
The view that programs designed to divert offenders from the justice system actually enmesh them further in the process by substituting more intrusive treatment programs for less intrusive punishment-oriented outcomes.

chronic criminal sex offenders.[29] As a group, noninterventionist initiatives have been implemented to help people avoid the stigma associated with contact with the criminal justice system.

The key elements of the nonintervention perspective include the following:

- The justice process stigmatizes offenders.
- Stigma locks people into a criminal way of life.
- Less is better. Decriminalize, divert, and deinstitutionalize whenever possible.

Equal Justice Perspective

equal justice perspective
The view that all people should be treated equally before the law. Equality may best be achieved through individual discretion in the justice process.

According to those who take the **equal justice perspective**, the greatest challenge facing the American criminal justice system is its ability to dispense fair and equal justice to those who come before the law. It is unfair for police to issue a summons to one person for a traffic violation while letting a second offender off with a warning, or to have two people commit the same crime but receive different sentences or punishments. Unequal and inconsistent treatment produces disrespect for the system, suspiciousness, and frustration; it also increases the likelihood of recidivism. Therefore, law violators should be evaluated on the basis of their current behavior, not on what they have done in the past (they have already paid for that behavior) or on what they may do in the future (because future behavior cannot be accurately predicted). The treatment of criminal offenders must be based solely on their present behavior: punishment must be equitably administered and based on "just desserts."

The equal justice perspective has had considerable influence in molding the nation's sentencing policy. There has been an ongoing effort to reduce discretion and to guarantee that every offender convicted of a particular crime receives equal punishment. There have been a number of initiatives designed to achieve this result, including mandatory sentences requiring that all people convicted of a crime receive the same prison sentence. **Truth-in-sentencing laws** now require offenders to serve a substantial portion of their prison sentence behind bars, limiting their eligibility for early release on parole.[30]

truth-in-sentencing laws
A sentencing scheme requiring that offenders serve at least 85 percent of their original sentence before being eligible for parole or other forms of early release.

The key elements of the equal justice perspective are these:

- People should receive equal treatment for equal crimes.
- Decision making in the justice system must be standardized and structured by rules and regulations.
- Whenever possible, individual discretion must be reduced and controlled.
- Inconsistent treatment produces disrespect for the system.

Restorative Justice Perspective

restorative justice perspective
A view of criminal justice that advocates peaceful solutions and mediation rather than coercive punishments.

According to the concept of restorative justice, the criminal justice system should promote a peaceful and just society; the justice system should aim for peacemaking, not punishment.[31] Advocates of the **restorative justice perspective** view the efforts of the state to punish and control as encouraging crime rather than discouraging it. The violent, punishing acts of the state are not dissimilar to the violent acts of individuals.[32] Therefore, mutual aid rather than coercive punishment is the key to a harmonious society. Without the capacity to restore damaged social relations, society's response to crime has been almost exclusively punitive.

According to restorative justice, resolution of the conflict between criminal and victim should take place in the community in which it originated, not in some far-off prison. Under these conditions, the victim has a chance to tell his story, and the offender can directly communicate his need for social reintegration and treatment. The goal is to enable the offender to appreciate the damage he has caused, to make amends, and to be reintegrated into society.

Restorative justice programs are now being devised to reflect these principles. Police officers, as elements of community policing programs, are beginning to use mediation techniques to settle disputes, rather than resorting to formal arrest.[33] Mediation and conflict resolution programs are common features in many communities and are being used in efforts to resolve harmful human interactions ranging from domestic violence to hate crimes.[34] Financial and community service restitution programs as an alternative to imprisonment have been in operation for more than two decades.

The most important elements of the restorative justice model are the following:

- Offenders should be reintegrated into society.
- Coercive punishments are self-defeating.
- The justice system must become more humane.

Perspectives in Perspective

Advocates of each view have attempted to promote their vision of what justice is all about and how it should be enforced. During the past decade, the crime control and equal justice models have dominated. Laws have been toughened and the rights of the accused curtailed, the prison population has grown, and the death penalty has been employed against convicted murderers. Because the crime rate has been dropping, these policies seem to be effective; they may be questioned if crime rates once again begin to rise. At the same time, efforts to rehabilitate offenders, to provide them with elements of due process, and to give them the least intrusive treatment have not been abandoned. Police, courts, and correctional agencies supply a wide range of treatment and rehabilitation programs to offenders in all stages of the criminal justice system. Whenever possible, those accused of crime are treated informally in nonrestrictive, community-based programs, and the effects of stigma are guarded against. Although the legal rights of offenders are being closely scrutinized by the courts, the basic constitutional rights of the accused remain inviolate. Guardians of the process have made sure that defendants are allowed the maximum protection possible under the law. For example, criminal defendants have been awarded the right to competent legal counsel at trial; merely having a lawyer to defend them is not considered sufficient legal protection.

In sum, understanding the justice system today requires analyzing a variety of occupational roles, institutional processes, legal rules, and administrative doctrines. Each predominant view of criminal justice provides a vantage point for understanding and interpreting these rather complex issues. No single view is *the* right or correct one. Each individual must choose the perspective that best fits his or her own ideas and judgment—or propose a different view that combines elements of all the perspectives or expresses the individual's own view in a new and unique way.

LO9 Be familiar with the various perspectives on justice

Ethics in Criminal Justice

The general public and criminal justice professionals are also concerned with the application of ethics in the criminal justice system.[35] Both would like every police officer on the street, every district attorney in court, and every correctional administrator in prison to be able to discern what is right, proper, and moral, to be committed to ethical standards, and to apply equal and fair justice. These demands are difficult because justice system personnel are often forced to work in an environment where moral ambiguity is the norm. For example, should a police officer be forced to arrest, a prosecutor charge, and a correctional official punish a woman who for many years was the victim of domestic abuse and who in desperation retaliated against her abusive spouse? Who is the victim here and who is the aggressor? And what about the parent who attacks the man who has sexually abused her young child? Should she be prosecuted as a felon? But what happens if the parent mistakenly attacks and injures the wrong person? Can a clear line be drawn between righteous retribution and vigilante justice? As students of justice, we are concerned with identifying the behavioral standards that should govern each of the elements of justice. If these can be identified, is it possible to find ways to apply these standards to police, court, and correctional agencies around the nation?

Ethics in criminal justice is an especially important topic today because of the power granted to those who control the justice system. We rely on the justice system to exert power over people's lives and to be society's instrument of social control, so we grant the system and its agents the authority to deny people their personal liberty on a routine basis. A police officer's ability to arrest and use force, a judge's power to sentence, and a correctional administrator's ability to punish an inmate give them considerable personal power that must be governed by ethical considerations. Without ethical decision making, it is possible that individual civil rights will suffer and that personal liberties guaranteed by the U.S. Constitution will be trampled upon. The need for an ethical criminal justice system is further enhanced by cyber-age advances in record keeping and data recording. Agents of the criminal justice system now have immediate access to our most personal information, ranging from arrest records to medical history. Issues of privacy and confidentiality—which can have enormous economic, social, and political consequences—are now more critical than ever.

Ethical issues transcend all elements of the justice system. Yet each branch has specific issues that shape its ethical standards, as we will see in the following sections.

Ethics and Law Enforcement

Ethical behavior is particularly important in law enforcement because, quite simply, police officers have the authority to deprive people of their liberty. And, in carrying out their daily activities, they also have the right to use physical and even deadly force.

Depriving people of liberty and using force are not the only police behaviors that require ethical consideration. Police officers exercise considerable discretion when they choose whom to investigate, how far the investigation should go, and how much effort is required—for example, undercover work, listening devices, or surveillance. In carrying out their duties, police officers must be responsive to the public's demand for protection, while at the same time remaining sensitive to the rights and liberties of those they must deter and/or control. In this capacity, they serve as the interface between the power of the state and the citizens it governs. This duality creates many ethical dilemmas. Consider the following:

- Should law enforcement agents target groups whom they suspect are heavily involved in crime and violence, or does this lead to racial/ethnic profiling? Is it unethical for a security agent to pay closer attention to a young Arab male getting on an airline flight than she pays to a well-groomed American soldier from upstate New York? After all, there have been no terrorist activities among army personnel, and the 9/11 terrorists were of Arab descent. But don't forget that clean-cut Tim McVeigh, who grew up in rural Pendleton, New York, and spent more than three years in the army, went on to become the Oklahoma City bomber. How can police officers balance their need to protect public security with the ethical requirement that they safeguard citizens' legal rights?
- What limits should be placed on the use of technology? Should law enforcement agencies be allowed to use tracking devices to monitor movements, take facial scans, listen in on cell phones, or hack into computers in order to keep watch on potential criminals and terrorists? Does the end justify the means? The Criminal Justice and Technology feature addresses this issue.

Using Biometrics to Fight Terrorism: US-VISIT

Is it possible to identify people by computer-based recognition of their facial characteristics or their fingerprints? Sounds like science fiction, or is it? Biometrics, the science of using digital technology to identify individuals, has been installed in airports, land border points (border crossings), and seaports. The Department of Homeland Security's US-VISIT program uses biometric scans to determine the identity of all travelers from foreign countries who attempt to enter the United States.

HOW IT WORKS

Nearly all foreign citizens, regardless of country of origin, who travel into the United States must comply with US-VISIT requirements. The process of registering for travel into the United States sometimes starts far from U.S. soil. Individuals who wish to travel to the United States must first visit the U.S. consular office in their country and apply for a visa. When they apply for the visa, they will have their biometrics collected in two separate ways. First, photographs will be taken of every applicant, and those photographs will be entered into the US-VISIT database, along with digital finger scans. The digital finger scans will be taken of both index fingers of the applicant. This information will be loaded into a database and then checked to see whether the individual matches any criminal or suspected terrorist already in the system. In 2009, DHS announced that it had completed an upgrade from two-fingerprint to ten-fingerprint scanners at major U.S. ports of entry, increasing scanning accuracy. Once an applicant passes the database check, he or she can be issued a visa to travel to the United States. Upon arrival at a U.S. point of entry, the traveler will be required to undergo a scan to determine whether he or she is the same person who applied for the visa.

Entry procedures were started in 115 airports at the beginning of 2004. US-VISIT entry procedures are now in place in 116 airports, 15 seaports, and the secondary inspection areas of 154 land points of entry. Homeland Security believes that implementing these new security procedures will result in fewer criminals or terrorists entering the country and will also reduce the incidence of identity theft and fraud that may occur upon entry into or exit from the country. However, there are critics who say that the process violates ethical standards and makes too much personal information about travelers and U.S. citizens available to U.S. Customs and Immigration. Despite privacy concerns, the Department of Homeland Security is committed to using the US-VISIT program, in conjunction with other government programs, to increase the security of the United States, and Congress has increased funding for the program to more than $370 million per year.

CRITICAL THINKING

1. *Are you afraid that futuristic security methods such as biometric technology will lead to the loss of personal privacy and the erosion of civil liberties?*
2. *Would you want your personal medical information to be posted on a computer network where it could potentially be accessed by future employers and others?*

- Should police officers tell the truth even if it means that a guilty person goes free? For example, a police officer stops a car for a traffic violation and searches it illegally. He finds a weapon used in a particularly heinous shooting in which three children were killed. Would it be ethical for the officer to lie on the witness stand and say the gun was resting on the car seat in plain sight (thereby rendering its seizure legal and proper)? Or should he tell the truth and risk having the charges dismissed, leaving the offender free to kill again?
- Should police officers be loyal to their peers even when they know a colleague has violated the law? For example, a new officer soon becomes aware that his partner is taking gratuities from local gangsters in return for looking the other way and allowing their prostitution and bookmaking operations to flourish. Should the rookie file a complaint and turn in his partner? Will she be labeled a "rat" and lose the respect of her fellow officers? After all, gambling and prostitution are not violent crimes and don't really hurt anyone. Or do they?

What help is available to law enforcement officers in making ethical decisions? Various national organizations have produced model codes of conduct that can serve as behavioral guides. One well-known document created by the International Association of Chiefs of Police says, in part,

As a law enforcement officer my fundamental duty is to serve mankind; to safeguard lives and property; to protect the innocent against deception, the weak against oppression or intimidation, and the peaceful against violence or disorder; and to respect the constitutional rights of all men to liberty, equality, and justice. . . .[36]

Ethics and the Courts

Ethical concerns do not stop with an arrest. As an officer of the court and the "people's attorney," the prosecutor must seek justice for all parties in a criminal matter and should not merely be targeting a conviction. To be fair, prosecutors must share evidence with the defense, must not use scare tactics or intimidation, and must represent the public interest. It would be inexcusable and illegal for prosecutors to suppress critical evidence, a practice that might mean the guilty walked free and the innocent were convicted.

Prosecutorial ethics become tested when the dual role of prosecutors cause them to experience role conflict. On the one hand, a prosecutor represents the people and has an obligation to present evidence, uphold the law, and obtain convictions as vigorously as possible. In the adversary system, it is the prosecutor who takes the side of victims and on whom they rely for justice.

But as a fair and impartial officer of the court, the prosecutor must oversee the investigation of crime and make sure that all aspects of the investigation meet constitutional standards. If during the investigation it appears that the police have violated the constitutional rights of suspects—for example, by extracting an illegal confession or conducting an illegal search—then the prosecutor has an ethical obligation to take whatever action is necessary and appropriate to remedy legal or technical errors, even if it means rejecting a case in which the defendant's rights have been violated. Moreover, the canon of legal ethics in most states forbids the prosecutor from pursuing charges when there is no probable cause and mandates that all evidence that might mitigate guilt or reduce the punishment be turned over to the defense.

Defense Attorney As an officer of the court, along with the judge, prosecutors, and other trial participants, the defense attorney seeks to uncover the basic facts and elements of the criminal act. In this dual capacity of being both a defensive advocate and an officer of the court, the attorney is often confronted with conflicting obligations to his client and profession. Suppose a client confides that she is planning to commit a crime. What are the defense attorney's ethical responsibilities in this case? Obviously, the attorney would have to counsel the client to obey the law; if the attorney assisted the client in engaging in illegal behavior, the attorney would be subject to charges of unprofessional conduct and even criminal liability.

What about the situation where an attorney knows that his or her client is guilty because the client admitted as much during pretrial conferences? Should the defense lawyer still try for an acquittal? What is said privately before trial, even at a plea discussion, is never admissible during trial. An attorney would be accused of incompetence if she or he did not try to raise reasonable doubt in every case. The attorney's job is not to decide whether the client committed the offense but to provide a vigorous defense and ensure that the client is not convicted unless the prosecution can prove its case beyond a reasonable doubt. And it is impossible to make the prosecution meet its burden without aggressively challenging the evidence, even if the defender believes the client committed the crime. However, if a client attempted to take the stand and lie about his involvement in the crime, then the attorney would be required to tell the judge.[37]

RealityCheck

MYTH OR REALITY? Defense attorneys do not represent clients they know to be guilty.

MYTH. *A defense attorney must provide her client with a rigorous defense even if she knows that the client did the act in question. It is possible that a client is not guilty legally even if he actually did the act for which he is charged—for example, if he acted in self defense or were legally insane. Therefore, even someone who admits committing a crime requires a rigorous defense.*

Ethics and Corrections

Ethical issues do not disappear once a defendant has been convicted. The ethical issues in punishment are too vast to discuss here, but they include the following:

- Is it fair and ethical to execute a criminal? Can capital punishment ever be considered a moral choice?
- Should people be given different punishments for the same criminal law violation? Is it fair and just when some convicted murderers and rapists receive probation for their crimes while others are sentenced to prison for the same offense?

- Is it fair to grant leniency to criminals who agree to testify against their co-conspirators and therefore allow them to benefit from their perfidy, while others, who are not given the opportunity to "squeal," are forced to bear the full brunt of the law?
- Should some criminal inmates be granted early release because they can persuade the parole board that they have been rehabilitated, while others, who are not as glib, convincing, or well spoken, are forced to serve their entire sentence behind bars?
- Should technology be used to monitor offenders in the community? Would it be ethical to track a probationer's movements with a GPS unit attached to an ankle bracelet she is required to wear at all times? Should her Internet use and computer downloads be monitored?

Ethics are also challenged by the discretion afforded to correctional workers and administrators. Discretion is involved when a correctional officer decides whether to report an inmate for disorderly conduct, which might jeopardize his or her parole. And although the Supreme Court has issued many rulings related to prisoners' rights, no justices are at the scene of the prison to make sure that their mandates are carried out reliably and consistently.

Correctional officers have significant coercive power over offenders. They are under a legal and professional obligation not to use unnecessary force or take advantage of inmate powerlessness. Examples of abuse would be an officer who beats an inmate, or a staff member who coerces sex from an inmate. The possibility that these abuses of power will be perpetrated exists because of the powerlessness of the offender relative to the correctional professional. A recent national survey uncovered evidence that this breach of ethics is significant: An estimated 8,210 allegations of sexual violence were reported by correctional inmates. About 42 percent of the reported allegations of sexual violence involved staff-on-inmate sexual misconduct, and 11 percent involved staff sexual harassment of inmates. In other words, staff members were accused of more cases of sexual violence and harassment in correctional facilities than were other inmates![38]

Ethical considerations transcend all elements of the justice system. Making ethical decisions is an increasingly important task in a society that is becoming more diverse, pluralistic, and complex every day.

Ethical Challenge

Some experts believe that the justice system could operate more effectively if drugs were legalized and their trade controlled so that they could not fall into the hands of adolescents. This would be similar to the way we now regulate the sale of alcohol and cigarettes.

Write an essay addressing this issue. Remember to consider such topics as the consequences of regulating the sale of drugs. If juveniles, criminals, and members of other at-risk groups were forbidden to buy drugs, who would be the customers? Noncriminal, nonabusing, middle-aged adults? And would not those adolescents prohibited from legally buying drugs create an underground market almost as vast as the one for illegal alcohol?

Summary

LO1 Discuss the formation of the criminal justice system in America There was little in the way of a formal criminal justice system until the nineteenth century when the first police agencies were created. The term *criminal justice system* became prominent around 1967, when the President's Commission on Law Enforcement and the Administration of Justice began a nationwide study of the nation's crime problem.

LO2 Be able to define the concept of a criminal justice system The term *criminal justice* refers to both the agencies that dispense justice and the process in which justice is carried out. It is assumed that these agencies work in concert to protect society and dispense fair and equal justice.

LO3 Be familiar with the basic component agencies of criminal justice On an ideal level, the criminal justice system functions as a cooperative effort among the primary agencies—police, courts, and corrections. However, all too often these agencies act independently from one another.

LO4 Comprehend the size and scope of the contemporary justice system The contemporary criminal justice system in the United States is monumental in size. It now costs federal, state, and local governments more than $200 billion per year for civil and criminal justice. The system is massive because it must process, treat, and care for millions of people. As a result, the system now employs more than 2 million people.

L05 Trace the formal criminal justice process The criminal justice process consists of the actual steps the offender takes from the initial investigation through trial, sentencing, and appeal. The justice process contains 15 stages, each of which is a decision point through which cases flow. Each of these decisions can have a critical effect on the defendant, the justice system, and society.

L06 Know what is meant by the term *criminal justice assembly line* Some experts believe that the justice system processes cases in a routine, ritualized manner resembling an assembly line. Because justice is often dispensed in a hasty fashion, an innocent person may suffer a false accusation while a dangerous individual may be released to continue to prey upon society. The system acts as a "funnel": most people who commit crime escape detection, and of those who do not, relatively few are bound over for trial, convicted, and eventually sentenced to prison.

L07 Characterize the informal criminal justice system A great deal of the criminal justice process is informal, involving deal making and plea bargaining. Rather than engage in the adversarial process, prosecution and defense work together to settle cases efficiently. Bargains and informal negotiations are more common than formal trials.

L08 Describe the "wedding cake" model of justice There are significant differences in the way each case is treated. Criminal acts that are very serious or notorious may receive the full complement of criminal justice processes, from arrest to trial. However, less serious cases are often settled when a bargain is reached between the prosecution and the defense.

L09 Be familiar with the various perspectives on justice The role of criminal justice system can be interpreted in many ways. People who study the field or work in its agencies bring their own ideas and feelings to bear when they try to decide on the right course of action to take or recommend. Thus there are a number of different perspectives on criminal justice today ranging from the most conservative (crime control) to the most liberal (restorative justice).

L010 Understand the ethical issues involved in criminal justice It is sometimes difficult to determine what is fair and just and to balance it with the need to protect the public. There are ethical issues facing police, court, and correctional agencies ranging from ethnic and racial profiling to the use of the death penalty.

Review Questions

1. Can a single standard of ethics be applied to all criminal justice agencies? Or is the world too complex to legislate morality and ethics?

2. Describe the differences between the formal and informal justice systems. Is it fair to treat some offenders informally?

3. What are the layers of the criminal justice "wedding cake"? Give an example of a crime for each layer.

4. What are the basic elements of each model or perspective on justice? Which best represents your own point of view?

5. How would each perspective on criminal justice consider the use of the death penalty as a punishment for first-degree murder?

6. What amendments to the Constitution are most important for the administration of justice?

© AP Photo/Joe Burbank, Pool

2 The Nature of Crime and Victimization

Learning Objectives

LO1 Be able to discuss how crime is defined

LO2 Be familiar with the methods used to measure crime

LO3 Discuss the strengths and weaknesses of crime measures

LO4 Recognize the trends in the crime rate

LO5 Comment on the factors that influence crime rates

LO6 Be familiar with international crime trends and how the United States compares to other nations

LO7 Know the various crime patterns

LO8 Understand the concept of the criminal career

LO9 Be able to discuss the characteristics of crime victims

LO10 Distinguish among the various views of crime causation

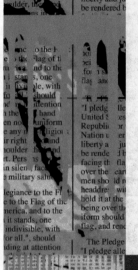

MYTH OR REALITY?

- The content of the criminal law represents the moral values of the general public.
- Most people report their criminal victimizations to police.
- Crime and violence rates are out of control and getting worse every day.
- The police assign more patrol cars to areas where minority populations are disproportionately high.
- A poor economy and high unemployment cause crime rates to increase.
- Crime victims are people who are in the wrong place at the wrong time.
- The elderly are the age group most vulnerable to predatory criminals.
- Most crimes are committed by strangers.
- Mothers who smoke and drink during pregnancy increase the likelihood their children will be prone to antisocial behavior.
- Kids who watch a lot of violence on TV are more likely to get involved in violent behavior themselves.

In 2011, in a case that captured immense media attention, Casey Anthony, a young Florida mother, was tried for the murder of her daughter Caylee Marie, whose disappearance and death had captivated America for three years.[1] Though Caylee had gone missing on June 16, 2008, shortly before her third birthday, Casey Anthony failed to report the child's absence to police for 31 days. She told people that Caylee was being taken care of by a nanny and had been taken on trips and outings. Casey's mother finally notified police, and Casey admitted that the child had been missing for more than a month. After a frantic search, Caylee's remains were found on December 11, 2008, in a wooded lot not far from the Anthony home. After Casey spent more than two years in jail awaiting trial, her defense team claimed that the baby had accidentally drowned and that Casey and her father, in a panic, covered up the accident. Why had Casey gone along with the scheme? The defense claimed she had been sexually abused by her father and had been forced to lie about it her whole life. In contrast, the prosecution argued that Casey had murdered her daughter in cold blood, sedating her with chloroform, suffocating her with duct tape, and dumping her body in a wooded area. Why did she commit this horrible crime? According to the prosecution, she killed her daughter so she could be free to live a life of partying and clubbing. Casey had gotten a tattoo that read "bella vita"— beautiful life—after Caylee had disappeared, a signal that she wanted to begin a new and carefree life. Despite the prosecution's best efforts, on July 5, 2011, Casey Anthony was found not guilty of first-degree murder, aggravated manslaughter of a child, and aggravated child abuse. She was found guilty of four misdemeanor counts of providing false information to a law enforcement officer and released soon after having been credited for time served. What swayed the day was the lack of physical evidence. The body was too decomposed to tell the cause or time of death, nor could evidence be found in the home or in Casey's car, allegedly used to transport the body. The jury could not condemn a young woman to death without clear and convincing evidence that she had murdered her child. ■

The Anthony case illustrates how violent crime has become an ever-present part of American society. Americans are fascinated by highly publicized murder cases, even when the defendant is found not guilty, as Casey Anthony was. They are bombarded daily with stories of child abductions, gang killings, and drug busts. They are also stunned by highly publicized mass killings, such as the well-publicized incidents of mass murder that occurred in Tucson, Arizona, and Oslo, Norway, in 2011. People hearing about these violent incidents demand that their legal representatives "do something about crime." How accurate is this vision? Is the crime rate truly skyrocketing or has intense media coverage given the public a false impression about crime

in America? When people read headlines about a violent crime spree, they begin to fear crime and take steps to protect themselves, perhaps avoiding public places and staying at home in the evening.[2] When asked if they fear walking in their neighborhood at night, more than one-third of all American citizens say yes.[3] About one-quarter say they bought a gun for self-protection, and more than 10 percent claim they carry guns for defense.[4]

The public's impression about violent crime may also help shape criminal justice policy. Responding to public fear, lobbying groups may demand that state legislators pass legislation not only making it more difficult to buy firearms but also imposing mandatory prison terms on anyone caught with an illegally obtained handgun.

Are Americans justified in their fear of crime? Should they barricade themselves behind armed guards? Are crime rates actually rising or falling? Where do most crimes occur and who commits them? To answer these and similar questions, elaborate methods of crime data collection have been devised. These sources of crime data are essential to get an accurate reading on the nature and extent of crime as well as the nature of crime trends and patterns. Without this data it would be impossible to create effective crime control policies and assess their effectiveness.

This chapter reviews some basic questions about crime addressed by criminal justice professionals: How is crime defined? How is crime measured? How much crime is there, and what are its trends and patterns? Why do people commit crime? How many people become victims of crime, and under what circumstances does victimization take place?

How Is Crime Defined?

The justice system revolves around crime and its control. Although for most of us the concept of "crime" seems rather simple—a violation of criminal law—the question remains: Why are some acts considered a violation of the law and others, seemingly more serious, legal and noncriminal? There are three views of how and why some behaviors become illegal and are considered crimes whereas others remain noncriminal.

Consensus View

According to what is known as the **consensus view of crime**, crimes are behaviors that are essentially harmful to a majority of citizens living in society and therefore have been controlled or prohibited by the existing criminal law. Using this definition, criminal law is a set of rules, codified by state authorities, that express the norms, goals, and values of the *vast majority of society*. The definition implies that criminal law, and the behaviors it defines as crimes, represent the *consensus* of public opinion and that there is general agreement about which behaviors society needs to control and which should be beyond state regulation.

The consensus view rests on the assumption that criminal law has a social control function—restraining those who might otherwise engage in antisocial behavior. Criminal law works to control behaviors that are inherently destructive and dangerous in order to maintain the existing social fabric and ensure the peaceful functioning of society.

consensus view of crime
The majority of citizens in a society share common ideals and work toward a common good. Crimes are acts that are outlawed because they conflict with the rules of the majority and are harmful to society.

Conflict View

According to the **conflict view of crime**, the content of criminal law, and consequently the definition of crime, are shaped and controlled by the ongoing class struggle between the rich and poor, the haves and have-nots. According to this view, criminal law is created and enforced by the ruling class as a mechanism for controlling dissatisfied, have-not members of society. The law is the instrument that enables the wealthy to maintain their position of power and control the behavior of those who oppose their ideas and values or who might rebel against the unequal distribution of wealth.[5]

conflict view of crime
The law is controlled by the rich and powerful who shape its content to ensure their continued economic domination of society. The criminal justice system is an instrument of social and economic repression.

interactionist view of crime
Criminal law reflects the values of people who use their social and political power to shape the legal system.

moral entrepreneurs
People who wage moral crusades to control criminal law so that it reflects their own personal values.

Interactionist View

According to the **interactionist view of crime**, the criminal law is structured to reflect the preferences and opinions of people who hold social power and use their influence to shape the legal process.[6] These so-called **moral entrepreneurs** wage campaigns (moral crusades) to control behaviors they view as immoral and wrong (such as abortion) or, conversely, to legalize behaviors they consider harmless social eccentricities (such as smoking marijuana). In essence, they dedicate themselves to molding the law to reflect their own world views. According to the interactionist view, then, many crimes are not inherently evil or immoral acts but are illegal because they are in conflict with social norms. So, for example, it is perfectly legal to purchase liquor, even though 18 million Americans have alcohol problems and more people die from the effects of alcoholism every year than any other cause.[7]

crime
A violation of societal rules of behavior as interpreted and expressed by a criminal legal code created by people holding social and political power. Individuals who violate these rules are subject to sanctions by state authority, social stigma, and loss of status.

Defining Crime Although these views of crime differ, they generally agree on four points: (1) Criminal law defines crime; (2) the definition of crime is constantly changing and evolving; (3) social forces mold the definition of crimes; and (4) criminal law has a social control function. Therefore, as used here, the term **crime** is defined as follows:

> Crime is a violation of social rules of conduct, interpreted and expressed by a written criminal code, created by people holding social and political power. Its content may be influenced by prevailing public sentiments, historically developed moral beliefs, and the need to protect public safety. Individuals who violate these rules may be subject to sanctions administered by state authority, which include social stigma and loss of status, freedom, and, on occasion, their lives.

On October 21, 2010, in Los Angeles, celebrities Danny Glover, Melissa Etheridge, Hal Sparks, and marijuana legalization advocate Sarah Lovering take part in a news conference in support of California's Proposition 19 to regulate, control, and tax marijuana. If they succeed, behavior that has been a crime will now be legal. Interactionists believe that no act is inherently evil; crimes are created by those in power. What is considered a crime today may be legal tomorrow as public attitudes and perceptions shift and change.

AP Photo Chris Pizzello

How Is Crime Measured?

In addition to understanding how an act becomes a crime, it is important for criminal justice scholars to measure the nature, extent, and trends in the crime rate. They use a variety of techniques to study crime and its consequences. Three principal types of crime data have been developed—official data, victim data, and self-report data—each having particular strengths and weaknesses. The following sections review these methods in some detail and what they tell us about the crime problem in the United States and abroad.

LO1 Be able to discuss how crime is defined

Official Crime Data: The Uniform Crime Reports (UCR)

The FBI's **Uniform Crime Reports (UCR)** is the best known and most widely cited source of criminal records.[8] Data from the UCR are published in an annual volume called *Crime in the United States* and serves as the nation's **official crime statistics**.

How is the UCR compiled? The FBI receives reports from over 17,000 police departments serving a majority of the U.S. population. Its main unit of analysis involves **Part I crimes**: criminal homicide (including murder and nonnegligent manslaughter, and manslaughter by negligence), forcible rape, robbery, aggravated assault, burglary, larceny/theft, motor vehicle theft, and arson.

Local police departments enter into their database all reported incidents involving these crimes and send the information to the FBI. The Bureau tallies the local police reports and then compiles the numbers of known offenses by city, county, standard metropolitan statistical area, and geographical divisions of the United States. Besides these statistics, the UCR also provides a number of other pieces of crime data. Most important, it calculates the number and characteristics (age, race, and gender) of individuals who have been arrested for these and all other crimes—**Part II crimes**—such as prostitution and drug trafficking.

The UCR uses three methods to express crime data. First, the number of crimes reported to the police and arrests made are expressed as raw figures. For example, an estimated 15,241 persons were murdered nationwide in 2009. Second, crime rates per 100,000 people are computed. That is, when the UCR indicates that the murder rate was 5.0 in 2009, it means about 5 people in every 100,000 were murdered between January 1 and December 31 of 2009. This is the equation used:

$$\frac{\text{Number of Reported Crimes}}{\text{Total U.S. Population}} \times 100{,}000 = \text{Rate per } 100{,}000$$

Third, the FBI computes changes in rate of crime over time. The 15,241 murders in 2009 were a 7.3 percent decrease from 2008, a 9.0 percent decrease from 2005, and a 2.2 percent decrease from the number of murders committed in 2000.[9]

How Accurate Is the UCR? The UCR's accuracy has long been suspect. Many serious crimes are not reported to police and therefore are not counted by the UCR. The reasons for not reporting vary:

- Victims consider the crime trivial or unimportant and choose not to call the police.
- Some victims fail to report because they do not trust the police or have little confidence in their ability to solve crime.
- People without property insurance believe it is useless to report theft.
- Victims fear reprisals from an offender's friends or family.
- Victims have "dirty hands" and are involved in illegal activities themselves. They do not want to get involved with the police.

Because of these and other factors, less than half of all criminal incidents are reported to the police.

The way police departments record and report criminal activity also affects the validity of UCR statistics. Some departments may define crimes loosely—reporting a trespass as a burglary or an assault on a woman as

Uniform Crime Reports (UCR)
The FBI's yearly publication of where, when, and how much serious crime occurred in the prior year.

official crime statistics
Compiled by the FBI in its Uniform Crime Reports, these are a tally of serious crimes reported to police agencies each year.

Part I crimes
The eight crimes for which, because of their seriousness and frequency, the FBI reports their incidence in its annual Uniform Crime Reports. The Part I crimes are murder, rape, assault, robbery, burglary, arson, larceny, and motor vehicle theft.

Part II crimes
All other crimes except the eight Part I crimes. The FBI records all arrests made for Part II crimes, including race, gender, and age information.

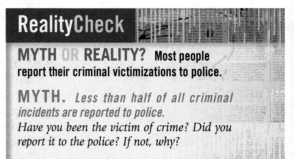

RealityCheck

MYTH OR REALITY? Most people report their criminal victimizations to police.

MYTH. *Less than half of all criminal incidents are reported to police.*
Have you been the victim of crime? Did you report it to the police? If not, why?

an attempted rape—whereas others pay strict attention to FBI guidelines. Some make systematic errors in UCR reporting—for example, counting an arrest only after a formal booking procedure, even though the UCR requires arrests to be counted when the suspect is released without a formal charge. These reporting practices may help explain interjurisdictional differences in crime.

Some critics take issue with the way the FBI records data and counts crimes. According to the "Hierarchy Rule," in a multiple-offense incident, only the most serious crime is counted. So if an armed bank robber commits a robbery, assaults a patron as he flees, steals a car to get away, and damages property during a police chase, only the robbery is reported because it is the most serious offense.

Although these issues are troubling, the UCR continues to be one of the most widely used sources of criminal statistics. Because the UCR is collected in a careful and systematic way, it is considered a highly reliable indicator of crime patterns and trends. That is, even if reporting problems compromise computing the exact number of crimes committed in a single year, measurement of year-to-year change should be accurate because measurement problems are stable over time. In other words, half of all burglaries will be reported both in 2010 and 2011, making an accurate count impossible. However, if the number of burglaries increases between the two years, we can conclude that more burglaries were committed in 2011 than in 2010 since half of all the crimes *were reported in both years*.

The National Crime Victimization Survey (NCVS)

Because many victims choose not to call police, crime experts have devised surveys to ask victims about their criminal experiences in order to tally both reported and unreported criminal incidents. The most prominent of these data sources is the **National Crime Victimization Survey (NCVS)**. This federally sponsored survey uses a large, carefully drawn sample of citizens who are queried about their experiences with criminal activity during the past year.[10]

National Crime Victimization Survey (NCVS)
The ongoing victimization study conducted jointly by the Justice Department and the U.S. Census Bureau that surveys victims about their experiences with law violation.

How is the NCVS conducted? A nationally representative sample of approximately 40,000 households (about 75,000 people) is selected. People are interviewed twice a year, so that approximately 150,000 interviews of persons age 12 or older are conducted annually. Households stay in the sample for three years.[11] Those contacted are asked to report on the frequency, characteristics, and consequences of criminal victimization for such crimes as rape, sexual assault, robbery, assault, theft, household burglary, and motor vehicle theft.

Because of the care with which the samples are drawn and the high completion rate, NCVS data is considered a relatively unbiased, valid estimate of all victimizations for the target crimes included in the survey. Yet, like the UCR, the NCVS may suffer from methodological problems. As a result, its findings must be interpreted with caution. Some of the potential problems include:

- Victims may overreport as a consequence of their misinterpretation of events; for example, a lost wallet may be reported as stolen, or an open door may be viewed as a burglary attempt.
- Victims may underreport because they are embarrassed about reporting crime to interviewers, fear getting in trouble, or simply forget an incident.
- There may be an inability to record the personal criminal activity of those interviewed, such as drug use or gambling; murder is not included for obvious reasons.
- Sampling errors may produce a group of respondents that does not represent the nation as a whole.
- A faulty question format may invalidate responses; some groups, such as adolescents, may be particularly susceptible to error because of question format.
- For some crimes, such as rape, the number of people reporting victimization is quite small so that even a slight year-to-year change can produce significant results. For example, between 2008 and 2009, victims reported 39 percent fewer rapes. While this decline is remarkable, it was based on a drop of 20 cases (from 56 in 2008 to 36 in 2009).

Self-Report Surveys

Self-report surveys, the third source of crime data, ask subjects to describe their past and current criminal activities, including whether they have ever been involved in substance abuse, theft, and/or violence; how often they engage in these activities; what specific kinds of drugs they took; and whether they acted alone or in groups. It is assumed that respondents will be willing to describe their illegal activities accurately because self-report surveys are typically administered in groups, anonymously and unsigned. The idea is to measure crimes that would neither be reported to the police nor show up in victim surveys, such as using cocaine. The ability of self-reports to get at these "dark figures of crime" makes it possible to track the incidence of criminal acts that are not reflected in official statistics.

Most self-report studies are administered among middle school and high school youth. Because school attendance is universal in the United States, a school-based self-report survey represents a cross section of the community. However, self-reports are not restricted to youth crime. They are also used to examine the offense histories of prison inmates, drug users, and other segments of the population.

While most self-report studies are conducted with limited samples, the Monitoring the Future (MTF) study, conducted by the Institute of Survey Research at the University of Michigan, uses a national high school sample of around 50,000 that has been collected annually for more than three decades.[12]

Although they are widely used, how valid are self-reports? Is it reasonable to expect people to candidly admit illegal acts? They have nothing to gain, and the ones who would be taking the greatest risk are the ones with official records, who may be engaging in the most criminality. Some people may exaggerate their criminal acts, forget some of them, or be confused about what is being asked. Response rate is also critical. Even if 90 percent of a school population voluntarily participates in a self-report survey, researchers can never be sure whether the few who refuse to participate or are absent that day account for a significant portion of the school's population of persistent, high-rate offenders.[13] It is also unlikely that the most serious chronic offenders in the teenage population are the most willing to cooperate with university-based criminologists administering self-report tests.[14] Although these drawbacks are troubling, crime experts have used a variety of techniques to verify the accuracy of self-report data.[15] While questions remain, as with the UCR, the errors in self-report data remain consistent over time. Consequently, self-report surveys such as the MTF are quite capable of showing trends and patterns in crime and substance abuse over time. While critics may question their validity, self-reports are reliable and consistent.

Compatibility of Crime Data Sources

Are the various sources of crime data compatible? Each has strengths and weaknesses. The FBI survey is carefully tallied and contains data on the number of murders and people arrested—information that the other data sources lack. However, this survey omits the many crimes that victims choose not to report to police, and it is subject to the reporting caprices of individual police departments.

The NCVS contains unreported crime and important information on the personal characteristics of victims, but the data consist of estimates made from relatively limited samples of the total U.S. population, so that even narrow fluctuations in the rates of some crimes can have a major impact on findings. It also relies on personal recollections that may be inaccurate. Furthermore, the NCVS does not include data on important crime patterns, including murder and drug abuse.

Self-report surveys can provide information on the personal characteristics of offenders that is not available from any other source, such as their attitudes, values, beliefs, and psychological profiles. Yet, at their core, self-reports rely on the honesty of criminal offenders and drug abusers, a population not generally known for accuracy and integrity.

Despite these differences, the data sources seem more compatible than was first believed. Although their tallies of crimes are certainly not in sync, the crime patterns and trends they record are often similar.[16] All three sources generally agree about the

self-report survey
A research approach that requires subjects to reveal their own participation in delinquent or criminal acts.

LO2 Be familiar with the methods used to measure crime

LO3 Discuss the strengths and weaknesses of crime measures

personal characteristics of serious criminals (such as age and gender) and about where and when crime occurs (such as urban areas, nighttime, and summer months).

Crime Trends

Crime is not new to this century.[17] Studies have indicated that a gradual increase in the crime rate, especially in violent crime, occurred from 1830 to 1860. Following the Civil War, this rate increased significantly for about 15 years. Then, from 1880 up to the time of the First World War, with the possible exception of the years immediately preceding and following the war, the number of reported crimes decreased. After a period of readjustment, the crime rate steadily declined until the Depression (about 1930), when another crime wave was recorded. As measured by the UCR, crime rates increased gradually following the 1930s until the 1960s, when the growth rate became much greater. The homicide rate, which had actually declined from the 1930s to the 1960s, also began a sharp increase that continued through the 1970s.

By 1991, police recorded about 14.5 million crimes. Since then, the number of crimes has been in decline; in 2009, about 10.5 million crimes were reported to the police, a drop of 4 million recorded crimes from the peak despite an increasing national population; preliminary data indicate crime continued to decline in 2010. Despite a severe economic downturn, property crime dropped 3 percent and violent crime more than 5 percent between 2009 and 2010, indicating a disjunction between crime rates and the state of the economy.

During the same period, the number of victimizations reported to the NCVS also showed a significant downturn. For example, in 2009, the NCVS recorded about 4 million violent crimes (rapes or sexual assaults, robberies, aggravated assaults, and simple assaults), almost 16 million property crimes (burglaries, motor vehicle thefts, and household thefts), and 133,000 personal thefts (picked pockets and snatched purses).[18] This number has dropped by half since 1991, when 43 million crimes were reported, including more than 10 million violent crimes. The victimization rate for violence was more than 50 incidents per 1,000 population, while today it is less than 20; in 1991, victims reported more than 300 incidents of property crime per 1,000 population, while today it is less than 150.[19] Figure 2.1 shows the violent crime rate trends since 1993. As you can see, both violent crimes reported to police and violent victimizations reported to the NCVS have been in decline for almost two decades.

Trends in Self-Reporting

Self-report studies indicate that the use of drugs and alcohol increased markedly in the 1970s, leveled off in the 1980s, increased until the mid-1990s, and has been in decline ever since. Although a self-reported crime wave has not occurred, neither has there been any visible reduction in self-reported criminality. According to MTF national data, drug use has declined since 1980 when more than 50 percent of high school students reported using drugs during the past year; substance abuse had stabilized during the past decade. In 2010, about 38 percent of 12th graders reported using drugs during the past year, compared to about 41 percent in the year 2000.[20]

Among the key recent MTF findings:

- Marijuana use has been rising among teens for the past few years, a sharp contrast to the considerable decline of the preceding decade.

- Ecstasy use—which fell out of favor in the early 2000s as concerns about its dangers grew—appears to be making a comeback, following a considerable recent decline in the belief that its use is dangerous.

Four measures of serious violent crime

Offenses in millions

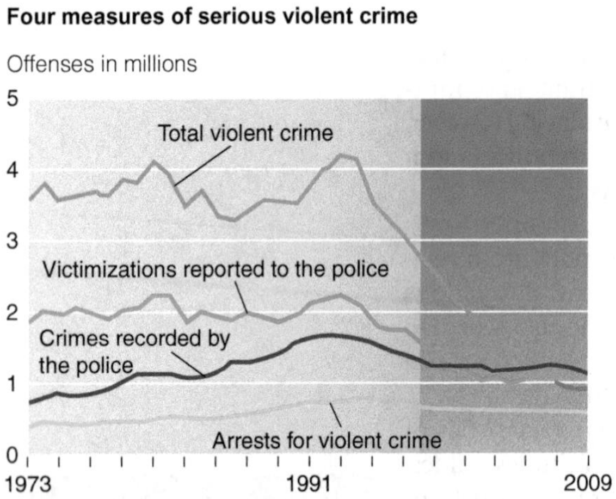

Figure 2.1 Four Measures of Serious Violent Crime

Source: Bureau of Justice Statistics, "Key Facts at Glance," http://bjs.ojp.usdoj.gov/content/glance/cv2.cfm (accessed May 22, 2011).

- Alcohol use—and, specifically, occasions of heavy drinking—continued its long-term decline among teens, reaching historically low levels.

The factors that help explain the upward and downward movement in crime rates, such as the one we have experienced for the past two decades, are discussed in Exhibit 2.1.

L04 Recognize the trends in the crime rate

L05 Comment on the factors that influence crime rates

Exhibit 2.1

Factors that Influence Crime Trends

Crime experts have identified a variety of social, economic, personal, and demographic factors that influence crime rate trends. Although crime experts are still uncertain about how these factors impact these trends, directional change seems to be associated with changes in crime rates.

Age Structure As a general rule, the crime rate follows the proportion of teens in the population: more kids, more crime! Crime rates skyrocketed in the 1960s when the baby boomers became teens and the 13 to 19 population grew rapidly. Crime rate drops since 1993 can be explained in part by an aging society: the elderly commit relatively few crimes.

Immigration Immigration has a suppressor effect on crime. Research shows that immigrants are less crime prone than the general population, so that as the number of immigrants increases per capita crime rates decline. During the past two decades, cities with the largest increases in immigration have experienced the largest decreases in crime rates, especially homicides and robberies.

Unemployment The general public believes that crime rates increase as the economy turns down and unemployment rises. However, there is little correlation between these indicators of economic prosperity and crime rates. Unemployed people do not suddenly join gangs or commit armed robberies. Criminals are usually unemployed or underemployed and therefore not affected by short-term economic conditions.

Abortion There is evidence that the recent drop in the crime rate is linked to the availability of legalized abortion. In 1973, *Roe v. Wade* legalized abortion nationwide, and the drop in crime rate began approximately 18 years later, in 1991. Crime rates began to decline when the first groups of potential offenders affected by the abortion decision began reaching the peak age of criminal activity. It is possible that the link between crime rates and abortion is the result of two mechanisms: (1) selective abortion on the part of women most at risk to have children who would engage in criminal activity, and (2) improved child rearing or environmental circumstances caused by better maternal, familial, or fetal care because women are having fewer children.

Gun Availability The availability of firearms may influence the crime rate: as the number of guns in the population increases, so do violent crime rates. Handguns are especially dangerous if they fall into the hands of teens. Surveys of high school students indicate that between 6 and 10 percent carry guns at least some of the time. Guns also cause escalation in the seriousness of crime. As the number of gun-toting students increases, so too does the seriousness of violent crime as a schoolyard fight turns into murder.

Gangs Another factor that affects crime rates is the explosive growth in teenage gangs. Surveys indicate that there are about 800,000 gang members in the United States. Data collected by the National Youth Gang Center show that gang members are responsible for a large proportion of all violent offenses committed during the adolescent years. Boys who are members of gangs are far more likely to possess guns than non-gang members; criminal activity increases when kids join gangs. Gangs involved in the urban drug trade recruit juveniles because they work cheaply, are immune from heavy criminal penalties, and are daring and willing to take risks. Arming themselves for protection, these drug-dealing children present a menace to their community, which persuades non–gang-affiliated neighborhood adolescents to arm themselves for protection. The result is an arms race that produces an increasing spiral of violence. As gangs become more organized, so too does their level of violence and drug dealing. Without gang influence, the crime rate might be much lower.

Drug Use Some experts tie increases in the violent crime rate between 1985 and 1993 to the crack epidemic, which swept the nation's largest cities, and to drug-trafficking gangs that fought over drug turf. These well-armed gangs did not hesitate to use violence to control territory, intimidate rivals, and increase market share. As the crack epidemic subsided, so too did the violence

(Continued)

Exhibit 2.1 *Continued*

rates in New York City and other metropolitan areas where crack use was rampant. A sudden increase in drug use, on the other hand, may be a harbinger of future increases in the crime rate, especially if guns are easily obtained and fall into the hands of gang members.

Media Some experts argue that violent media can influence the direction of crime rates. As the availability of media with a violent theme skyrocketed with the introduction of home video players, DVDs, cable TV, computer and video games, and so on, so too did teen violence rates. Efforts to curb violence on TV may help account for a declining crime rate.

Medical Technology Some crime experts believe that the presence and quality of health care can have a significant impact on murder rates. Murder rates might be up to five times higher than they are today without medical breakthroughs in treating victims of violence developed over the past 40 years. The big breakthrough occurred in the 1970s when technology developed to treat injured soldiers in Vietnam was applied to trauma care in the nation's hospitals. Since then, fluctuations in the murder rate can be linked to the level and availability of emergency medical services.

Justice Policy Some law enforcement experts have suggested that a reduction in crime rates may be attributed to adding large numbers of police officers and using them in aggressive police practices that target "quality of life" crimes such as panhandling, graffiti, petty drug dealing, and loitering. By showing that even the smallest infractions will be dealt with seriously, aggressive police departments may be able to discourage potential criminals from committing more serious crimes. Cities employing aggressive, focused police work may be able to lower homicide rates in the area.

It is also possible that tough laws imposing lengthy prison terms on drug dealers and repeat offenders can affect crime rates. The fear of punishment may inhibit some would-be criminals and place a significant number of potentially high-rate offenders behind bars, lowering crime rates. As the nation's prison population expanded, the crime rate has fallen.

However, justice policy can sometimes backfire and actually lift crime rates. Take for instance the long-term effect of incarceration. The imprisonment boom has resulted in more than 2 million people behind bars. While this policy may take some dangerous offenders off the street, eventually most get out. About 600,000 inmates are now being released each year, and many return to their communities without marketable skills or resources. The number of releasees will rise for the foreseeable future as more and more sentences bestowed during the high crime rate 1990s are completed. The recidivism rate of paroled inmates is quite high, averaging about 40 percent for those released from federal penitentiaries and 67 percent for those released from state custody. Inmates reentering society may have a significant effect on local crime rates.

Sources: Tim Wadsworth, "Is Immigration Responsible for the Crime Drop? An Assessment of the Influence of Immigration on Changes in Violent Crime Between 1990 and 2000," *Social Science Quarterly* 91 (2010): 531–553; Amy Anderson and Lorine Hughes, "Exposure to Situations Conducive to Delinquent Behavior: The Effects of Time Use, Income, and Transportation," *Journal of Research in Crime and Delinquency* 46 (2009): 5–34; National Gang Intelligence Center, *National Gang Threat Assessment, 2009*, www.justice.gov/ndic/pubs32/32146/gangs .htm (accessed May 22, 2011); Ramiro Martinez, Jr., and Matthew Amie Nielsen, "Local Context and Determinants of Drug Violence in Miami and San Diego: Does Ethnicity and Immigration Matter?" *International Migration Review* 38 (2004): 131–157; National Youth Gang Center, "What Proportion of Serious and Violent Crime Is Attributable to Gang Members?" www.nationalgangcenter.gov/About/FAQ#q13 (accessed May 22, 2011); Steven Levitt, "Understanding Why Crime Fell in the 1990s: Four Factors that Explain the Decline and Six that Do Not," *Journal of Economic Perspectives* 18 (2004): 163–190; Brad Bushman and Craig Anderson, "Media Violence and the American Public," *American Psychologist* 56 (2001): 477–489; John J. Donohue and Steven D. Levitt, "The Impact of Legalized Abortion on Crime," *Quarterly Journal of Economics* 116 (2001): 379–420.

What the Future Holds

It is risky to speculate about the future of crime trends because current conditions can change rapidly. It's possible that crime rates may rise in the future if the unemployment rate remains high for a prolonged period of time and the current generation of teens lose hope of ever gaining legitimate employment. Without the hope or possibility of a legitimate job, gang membership may increase and those involved in gangs may remain active for a longer period time. However, even if teens commit more crime in the future, their contribution may be offset by the aging of the population, which will produce a large number of senior citizens and elderly, a group with a relatively low crime rate.[21] The immigrant population is also increasing, another factor that may reduce crime rates.

Such prognostications are reassuring, but there is, of course, no telling what changes are in store that may influence crime rates. Technological developments such as e-commerce on the Internet have created new classes of crime that are not recorded by any of the traditional methods of crime measurement. It's possible that some crimes such as fraud, larceny, prostitution, obscenity, vandalism, stalking, and harassment have increased during the past decade but remain undetected because Internet crimes fall under the radar of official crime data. For example, the number of people arrested for prostitution has declined 17 percent during the past decade. It's possible that (a) there are simply fewer prostitutes, (b) police are less likely to arrest prostitutes than they were a decade ago, or (c) prostitution is booming, but because it's being conducted via the Internet, prostitutes are more likely now to avoid detection. Nonetheless, the rate of violent crimes has also decreased significantly, an indication that the crime drop is real and not merely a product of shifts into unrecorded crime.

How does the United States stack up against other nations around the world? Is the crime drop in America unique or a global phenomenon? And, as some people believe, is the United States the most crime-ridden nation in the world?

LO6 Be familiar with international crime trends and how the United States compares to other nations

Crime Patterns

By studying crime data, experts can determine whether there are stable patterns in the crime rate, which may help us to better understand where crime occurs, who commits crime, and why they violate the law. What are these enduring and stable patterns?

Ecological Patterns

There are distinct ecological patterns in the crime rate:

- Rural and suburban areas have much lower crime rates than large metropolitan centers, suggesting that urban problems—overcrowding, poverty, social inequality, narcotics use, and racial conflict—are related to crime rates.
- Crime rates are highest in the summer months, probably because people spend so much time outdoors and are less likely to secure their homes, and because schools are closed and young people have greater opportunity for criminal activity.
- Crime rates are also related to the region of the country. The West and South usually have significantly higher rates than the Midwest and New England.

Though crime rates have been declining, high-profile cases sometimes give the public the impression that crime is getting out of control. These photos show, from left, Melissa Barthelemy, of New York's Erie County; Maureen Brainard-Barnes, of Norwich, Connecticut; Megan Waterman, of Scarborough, Maine; and Amber Lynn Costello, of North Babylon, New York, all slain by a suspected serial killer who may have killed up to 10 people and dumped them on a desolate stretch of a New York barrier island. These women were believed to be prostitutes who advertised online.

AP Photo/Suffolk County Police Department

Is the United States Crime Prone?

It was a long-held belief that the United States was fatally crime prone compared to our friends and neighbors in other nations. People blamed American culture, love of guns, and frontier mentality for skyrocketing American crime rates. Now we know that crime has declined significantly in the U.S. for almost two decades. What has been happening in the rest of the world?

To find out, the International Crime Victims Survey (ICVS) is now being conducted in 60 countries and managed by the Ministry of Justice of the Netherlands, the Home Office of the United Kingdom, and the United Nations Interregional Crime and Justice Research Institute. The ICVS has become a reliable source of cross-cultural crime and victimization trends.

What do these data sources tell us about crime in other cultures? According to the most recent ICVS, about 16 percent of the people surveyed around the world were the victim of a common crime (e.g., burglary, robbery, theft, assault) in the course of a year. The countries with the highest scores are Ireland, England and Wales, New Zealand, and Iceland. Lowest overall victimization rates are found in Spain, Japan, Hungary, and Portugal. The cities in developed countries with the lowest victimization rates are Hong Kong, Lisbon, Budapest, Athens, and Madrid; highest victimization rates are found in London and Tallinn, Estonia.

Similar to the United States, there has been a distinct downward trend in the level of crime and victimization during the past decade. The drops are most pronounced in property crimes such as vehicle-related crimes (bicycle theft, thefts from cars, and joyriding) and burglary. In most countries, crime rates are back at the level of the late 1980s. One reason is that people around the world are taking precautions to prevent crime. Improved security may well have been one of the main forces behind the universal drop in crimes such as joyriding and household burglary.

While crime rates seem to be dropping all over, does that mean the United States still leads the world in this dubious category of social problems? Actually, many nations, especially those experiencing social or economic upheaval, have crime rates much higher than the United States. For example, Colombia experiences more than 60 homicides per 100,000 people, and South Africa has 50, compared to fewer than 6 in the United States. During the 1990s, there were more homicides in Brazil than in the United States, Canada, Italy, Japan, Australia, Portugal, Britain, Austria, and Germany combined. Why are murder rates so high in Brazil? Law enforcement officials link the upsurge in violence to drug trafficking, gang feuds, vigilantism, and disputes over trivial matters, in which young, unmarried, uneducated males are involved.

Murder is not the only crime pattern in which the rest of the world has caught up to the United States. Countries with more reported robberies than the United States include England and Wales, Portugal, and Spain. The United States also has lower burglary rates than Australia, Denmark, Finland, England and Wales, and Canada.

CRITICAL THINKING

As recent events have shown, young people in all nations who experience economic and income inequalities are highly disaffected and angry at their place in the social order. In some nations, such as Egypt and Libya, this has led to revolutionary movements, while in others there has been an increase in violent crime. Can anything be done to help alleviate these social problems?

Violence is not unique to the United States. On July 22, 2011, in an act of violence that shocked the world, Anders Behring Breivik, a right-wing extremist, set off a car bomb that destroyed a government building in Oslo, Norway, killing eight people and wounding many others. Breivik then proceeded to a youth camp organized by the liberal Norwegian Labour Party on the island of Utøya, where he mercilessly gunned down 69 people, mostly young teens. When police finally arrived, the 32-year-old Breivik quickly surrendered. He later claimed that his actions were spurred by an effort to prevent Muslim immigration and preserve the Norwegian culture. His murder spree was the largest mass shooting by one person to date.

AP Photo/via Scanpix

Gender Patterns

UCR arrest data consistently show that males have a much higher crime rate than females. The UCR arrest statistics indicate that the overall male–female arrest ratio is about 3 male offenders to 1 female offender; for serious violent crimes, the ratio is closer to 4 males to 1 female. Male–female arrest ratios have been much higher in the past; thirty years ago, the violent crime ratio was 8:1 in favor of males.

How can gender differences in the crime rates be explained? A number of views have been put forward:

- Males are stronger and better able to commit violent crime.
- Hormonal differences make males more aggressive.
- Girls are socialized to be less aggressive than boys and consequently develop moral values that strongly discourage antisocial behavior.[22]
- Girls have better verbal skills and use them to resolve conflict.
- Males are granted greater personal freedom and therefore have more opportunities to commit crime. Girls are subject to greater parental control.

When female arrest rates rose more rapidly than male arrests between 1970 and 1995, some experts began to proclaim the emergence of a "new female criminal" whose antisocial behaviors were similar to those of their male counterparts.[23] The thinking was that as gender role differences at home, school, and the workplace narrowed, female participation in traditionally male-oriented forms of criminality such as violent crime and juvenile gang membership would increase.[24]

Racial Patterns

Official crime data indicate that members of minority groups are involved in a disproportionate share of criminal activity. According to UCR reports, African Americans make up almost 14 percent of the general population, yet they account for about 39 percent of Part I violent crime arrests and about 30 percent of the property

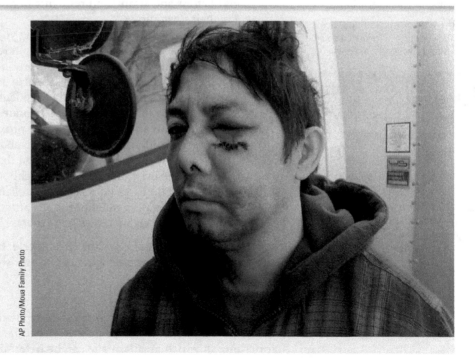

Koua Moua, 39, is shown after he was arrested by Milwaukee police and allegedly beaten. Supporters believe that police targeted Moua because of his racial makeup. Some experts believe that racial differences in the crime rate are more a function of police behavior than actual between-group differences in offending.

AP Photo/Moua Family Photo

crime arrests. How can these racial differences in the crime rate be explained? There are a number of competing views on this issue:

racial threat hypothesis
The view that the percentage of minorities in the population shapes the level of police activity.

- *Systemic racism.* Police are more likely to arrest racial minorities because of discriminatory patterns such as racial profiling. According to what is known as the **racial threat hypothesis**, as the percentage of minorities in the population increases, so too does the amount of social control that police direct at minority group members.[25] Police are more likely to aggressively patrol minority neighborhoods; suspect, search, and arrest minority group members; and make arrests for minor infractions, helping to raise the minority crime rate.[26] The result is a stepped-up effort to control and punish minority citizens, which segregates minorities from the economic mainstream and reinforces their physical and social isolation.[27]
- *Institutional racism.* Racism infects educational, government, and corporate institutions, creating differential opportunity and powerlessness in the minority community. The high rate of crime committed by African Americans is an expression of their anger and frustration at an unfair social order.[28]
- *Structural racism.* African American families are forced to live in some of the nation's poorest communities that cannot provide economic opportunities. The resulting lack of opportunity creates a sense of hopelessness that serves as an incentive to commit crime.

According to most experts, if and when interracial economic, social, and educational differences converge, so too will crime rates.

RealityCheck

MYTH OR REALITY? The police assign more patrol cars to areas where minority populations are disproportionately high.

REALITY. *According to the racial threat hypothesis, the more minorities in the population, the greater the assignment of police patrols.*
Should police departments be required to assign cars and officers evenly across their jurisdiction in order to avoid the reality or perception of racial bias?

Social Class Patterns

Though short-term economic trends do not seem to influence crime rates, there is no question that the official data indicate that crime rates are highest in deprived, inner-city areas. As the level of poverty and social disorganization in an area increases, so too do neighborhood crime rates.

Why are lower-class neighborhoods more likely than affluent communities to be afflicted by crime?

relative deprivation
The view that extreme social and economic differences among people living in the same community exacerbate criminal activity.

broken windows hypothesis
The view that deteriorated communities attract criminal activity.

- Communities that lack economic and social opportunities also produce high levels of stress and strain, and residents may then turn to criminal behavior to relieve their frustration.[29]
- Family life is disrupted, and law-violating youth groups and gangs thrive in a climate where adult supervision has been undermined.[30]
    - Socially disorganized neighborhoods lack the ability to exert social control over their residents. Lack of informal social control significantly increases the likelihood that residents will engage in criminality.
    - Crime rates are high in deteriorated areas where the disadvantaged and the affluent live in close proximity. In these neighborhoods, social differences are magnified, and less affluent residents experience a feeling of **relative deprivation** that results in a higher crime rate.[31]
- People living in lower-class neighborhoods experience poverty, dilapidated housing, poor schools, broken families, drugs, and street gangs. Deteriorating neighborhoods attract law violators (this is known as the **broken windows hypothesis**).

Whatever the reason, the crime data tell us that rates of violent and property crime are higher in impoverished areas.

RealityCheck

MYTH OR REALITY? A poor economy and high unemployment cause crime rates to increase.

MYTH. *Under some circumstances, crime rates decline during an economic downturn.*
Does it seem possible that one of your relatives or family members would suddenly become a criminal or rob a bank just because they got laid off from their job during a recession?

Age Patterns

Official statistics tell us that young people are arrested at a rate disproportionate to their numbers in the population; victim surveys generate similar findings for crimes in which assailant age can be determined. As a general rule, the peak age for property crime is believed to be 16 and for violence 18. In contrast, the elderly are particularly resistant to the temptations of crime; elderly males age 65 and over are arrested predominantly for alcohol-related matters (public drunkenness and drunk driving) and elderly females for larceny (shoplifting). The elderly crime rate has remained stable for the past 20 years.

When violence rates surged in the 1980s, the increase was due almost entirely to young people; the adult violence rate remained stable. How can the age–crime relationship be explained?

- Young people are part of a youth culture that favors risk taking, short-run hedonism, and other behaviors that may involve them in law violation. The high-risk lifestyle of most youths ends as they mature and become involved in forming a family and a career.[32]
- Adolescents are psychologically immature and are therefore unlikely to appreciate the wrongfulness or destructive consequences of their antisocial acts.
- Youths have limited financial resources and may resort to theft and drug dealing for income.
- Young people have the energy, strength, and physical skill needed to commit crime, and all of these erode with age.[33]
- Adolescents are aware that the juvenile justice system is not as punitive as the adult court system and are therefore more likely to risk committing criminal acts.

L07 Know the various crime patterns

Career Patterns: The Chronic Offender

Chronic offenders commit crime at a very early age, maintain a high rate of criminal violations throughout their lifetime, and are immune to both the ravages of age and the punishments of the justice system. They are responsible for a significant portion of all serious criminal behavior. The **chronic offender** is one who has serious and persistent brushes with the law, who is building a career in crime, and whose behavior may be excessively violent and destructive.

chronic offender
A delinquent offender who is arrested five or more times before he or she is 18 and who stands a good chance of becoming an adult criminal; these offenders are responsible for more than half of all serious crimes.

The concept of the chronic offender is most closely associated with the research efforts of Marvin Wolfgang and his associates at the University of Pennsylvania. In 1972, Wolfgang, Robert Figlio, and Thorsten Sellin published a landmark study entitled *Delinquency in a Birth Cohort.*[34] The researchers used official records to follow the criminal careers of a cohort of 9,945 boys born in Philadelphia in 1945 until they reached age 18 in 1963. Here is what they found:

- About two-thirds of the cohort (6,470) never had contact with police authorities.
- About one-third (3,475) had at least one contact with the police during their minority.
- Of the repeat offenders, a relatively small subgroup (627 boys) were arrested five times or more. These were the chronic offenders, who made up 6 percent of the total (600 out of 10,000).
- The chronic offenders were responsible for 5,305 arrests, or 51.9 percent of the total arrests. They committed 71 percent of the homicides, 73 percent of the rapes, 82 percent of the robberies, and 69 percent of the aggravated assaults.
- Arrest and punishment did little to deter chronic offenders. In fact, punishment was inversely related to chronicity—the stricter the sanctions they received, the more likely they were to engage in repeated criminal behavior.

Since the Philadelphia survey was carried out, a number of other independent studies, including one of a larger Philadelphia cohort of children born in 1958, have confirmed the existence of a repeat offender.[35] Here are some of the key findings about chronic offenders:

- Chronic offender research indicates that young persistent offenders grow up to become adult repeat offenders. This phenomenon is referred to as persistence or continuity of crime.

- Chronic delinquents who commit the most serious violent acts as youngsters have the greatest chance of later becoming adult offenders.[36]
- Youthful offenders who persist are more likely to abuse alcohol, to get into trouble while in military service, to become economically dependent, to have lower aspirations, to get divorced or separated, and to have a weak employment record.

The chronic offender concept has had a great impact on the criminal justice system. If a small group of offenders commits almost all of the serious crime, then it stands to reason that their incarceration might have an appreciable influence on the crime rate. This thought pattern has been responsible for the "get-tough" laws designed to put habitual offenders behind bars for long periods of time. As a consequence of these get-tough sentences, the prison population has trended upward even as crime rates have fallen.

LO8 Understand the concept of the criminal career

Victim Patterns

In addition to information on the nature and extent of crime, the various sources of crime data, especially the NCVS, can also tell us something about crime victims. How many crime victims are there in the United States, and what are the trends and patterns in victimization?

Today, about 21 million criminal victimizations occur each year.[37] While this total is significant, it represents a significant 20-year-long decline from a 1998 peak of more than 40 million reported victimizations. Between 1998 and 2009, violence rates dropped more than 40 percent and property victimizations dropped more than 30 percent. The NCVS data provides a snapshot of the social and demographic characteristics of crime victims.

Gender Gender affects one's risk of victimization. Men are much more likely than women to be victims of robbery and aggravated assault; they are also more likely to experience theft, but the differences are less pronounced. Although females are far more likely to be victims of sexual assault, thousands of men are sexually assaulted each year.

When men are the victims of violent crime, the perpetrator is usually described as a stranger. Women are much more likely to be attacked by a relative than men are; about two-thirds of all attacks against women are committed by a husband or boyfriend, family member, or acquaintance. In two-thirds of sexual assaults as well, the victim knows the attacker.

RealityCheck

MYTH OR REALITY? Crime victims are people in the wrong place at the wrong time.

MYTH. *Victimization is not random. People who live risky lives—drinking, partying, hanging out with a bad crowd—are most likely to become a crime victim.*

Comment on how a risky lifestyle influences the chances of becoming a victim. How can a college student avoid victimization risks?

Age Young people face a much greater victimization risk than older persons do. Victim risk diminishes rapidly after age 25. The elderly, who are thought of as being the helpless targets of predatory criminals, are actually much safer than their grandchildren. People over age 65, who make up 14 percent of the population, account for 1 percent of violent victimizations; teens aged 12 to 19, who also make up 14 percent of the population, typically account for more than 30 percent of crime victims.

What factors explain the age–victimization association?

- Adolescents often stay out late at night, go to public places, and hang out in places where crime is most likely to occur.
- Teens spend a great deal of time in the presence of their adolescent peers, the group most likely to commit crime.

Income The poorest Americans might be expected to be the most likely victims of crime, since they live in areas that are crime-prone: inner-city, urban neighborhoods. The NCVS does in fact show that the least affluent (annual incomes of less than $7,500) are by far the most likely to be victims of violent crimes, and this association occurs across all gender, racial, and age groups.

Marital Status Unmarried or never married people are victimized more often than married people or widows and widowers. These relationships are probably influenced by age, gender, and lifestyle:

- Unmarried people tend to be younger, and young people have the highest victim risk.
- Widows, who are more likely to be older women, suffer much lower victimization rates because they interact with older people, are more likely to stay home at night, and avoid public places.

Race African Americans are victimized by violent crime at a higher rate than other groups. NCVS data show that African Americans have strikingly higher rates of violent personal crime victimizations than whites. Although these two groups are more similar in their risk of theft victimization, African Americans are still more likely to be victimized than whites.

Crimes committed against African Americans tend to be more serious than those committed against whites. African Americans experience higher rates of aggravated assault, whereas whites are more often the victims of simple assault. African Americans are about three times as likely to become robbery victims as whites. Young African American males are also at great risk for homicide victimization. They face a murder risk 4 or 5 times greater than that of young African American females, 5 to 8 times higher than that of young white males, and about 20 times higher than that of young white females.[38]

Why do these discrepancies exist? One clear reason is that young black males tend to live in the largest U.S. cities, in areas beset by alcohol and drug abuse, poverty, racial discrimination, and violence. Because they are forced to live in the most dangerous areas, their lifestyle places them in the highest at-risk population group.

Ecological Factors There are distinct ecological patterns in the victim rate:

- Most victimizations occur in large urban areas; rural and suburban victim rates are far lower.
- Most incidents occur during the evening hours (6:00 PM to 6:00 AM). More serious crimes take place after 6:00 PM, less serious crimes before 6:00 PM.
- The most likely site for a victimization—especially a violent crime such as rape, robbery, or aggravated assault—is an open, public area such as a street, park, or field.
- One of the most dangerous public places is a public school building. Each year about 10 percent of all U.S. youths aged 12 to 19 (approximately 2 million) are crime victims while on school grounds.
- An overwhelming number of criminal incidents involve a solo victim.
- Most victims report that their assailant was not armed (except for the crime of robbery, where about half the offenders carry weapons). The use of guns and the use of knives are about equal, and there does not seem to be a pattern of a particular weapon being used for a particular crime.

Victim–Offender Relationships The NCVS can tell us something about the characteristics of people who commit crime. This information is available only on criminals who actually came in contact with the victim through such crimes as rape, assault, or robbery.

- About 50 percent of all violent crimes are committed by strangers. The other half of violent crimes are committed by people who were known to the victim, including family members, spouses, parents, children, and siblings.
- Women seem much more likely than men to be victimized by acquaintances; a majority of female assault victims know their assailants.

Most people who commit murder were acquainted with their victims. Here aspiring hard-core rapper Richard "Sam" McCroskey is led into the Prince Edward County Courthouse in Farmville, Virginia, on June 22, 2010. McCroskey faced capital murder charges in the deaths of his girlfriend, 16-year-old Emma Niederbrock; her parents, Presbyterian minister Mark Niederbrock and Longwood University professor Debra Kelley; and Emma's 18-year-old friend Melanie Wells of Inwood, West Virginia. He was later sentenced to life in prison.

AP Photo/Steve Helber

LO9 Be able to discuss the characteristics of crime victims

- A majority of victims report that the crime was committed by a single offender over the age of 20.
- About 25 percent of victims indicate that their assailant was a young person 12 to 20 years of age. This may reflect the criminal activities of youth gangs and groups in the United States.
- Whites are the offenders in a majority of single-offender rapes and assaults; there is no racial pattern in single-offender robberies. However, multiple-offender robberies are more likely to be committed by African Americans.

Repeat Victimization Research shows that individuals who have had prior victimization experiences have a significantly higher chance of repeat victimization than people who have not been victims.[39] Households that have experienced victimization are the ones most likely to experience it again.[40] Some combination of personal and social factors may possibly encourage victimization risk. Repeat victimizations are most likely to occur in areas with high crime rates.[41]

Most revictimizations happen soon after a previous crime, suggesting that repeat victims share some personal characteristics that make them a magnet for predators.[42] Not fighting back, not reporting crime to police, and repurchasing stolen goods may encourage repeat victimization.

Causes of Crime and Victimization

Although the various sources of crime statistics can tell us about the nature of crime patterns and trends, knowing why an individual commits crime in the first place is also important. Such knowledge is critical if programs are to be devised to deter or prevent crime. If, for example, people commit crime because they are poor and desperate, the key to crime prevention might be a job program and government economic aid. If, however, the root cause of crime is a poor family life marked by conflict and abuse, then providing jobs will not help lower the crime rate; family counseling and parenting skills courses are likely to be more effective.

Some criminologists view crime as a social phenomenon and study the social and economic factors that influence human behavior. Others view crime as an individual-level phenomenon and attempt to identify the cognitive and psychological processes that result in antisocial behavior. Regardless of their point of view, criminologists study crime data in order to identify the factors and motivations that predict crime and to assess the most effective responses to crime by various methods of law enforcement. Because there is still a great deal of uncertainty about the "real" cause of crime and the most effective methods of crime prevention, some of the more popular explanations are discussed in the following sections.

Choice Theory

According to what is known as **rational choice theory**, crime is a matter of rational decision making and personal choice. Crime is attractive because it holds the promise of great rewards without corresponding effort. It's a lot easier to steal a car than to earn the money for its purchase. The gains from robbing a bank take a lot less effort than earning the sum through a minimum wage job.

According to this view, motivated people, after thoughtful consideration, will commit crime if they believe that it will provide immediate benefits without the threat of long-term risks.[43] Before concluding a drug sale, experienced traffickers will mentally balance the chances of making a large profit against the consequences of being apprehended and punished for drug dealing. They know that most drug deals are not detected and that the potential for enormous, untaxed profits is great. They evaluate their lifestyle and determine how much cash they need to maintain their standard of living, which is usually extravagant. They may have borrowed to finance the drug deal, and their creditors are not usually reasonable if loans cannot be repaid promptly. They also realize that they could be the target of a "sting" operation by undercover agents and, if caught, would get a long mandatory sentence in a forbidding federal penitentiary. They may be aware that law enforcement agents are now using sophisticated technology such as hidden cameras and facial recognition technology to monitor their whereabouts and spy on their drug deals.[44]

If they conclude that the potential for profits is great enough, their need for cash urgent, and the chances of apprehension minimal, they will carry out the deal. If, however, they believe that the transaction will bring them only a small profit and a large risk of apprehension and punishment, they may forgo the deal as too risky. The more often they are arrested, the less likely they are to engage in a risky deal.[45]

When deciding to commit crime, potential offenders balance their perceptions of getting caught and punished against the perceived benefits of crime. Benefits include not only monetary gains but also psychic rewards such as excitement and increased social status among their peers.[46] Experience may play a hand in the decision-making process. Veteran criminals may not fear some future punishment because they know firsthand that apprehension risk is actually quite low.[47] Some may be deterred in the short run but soon return to their criminal ways.[48] Others, convinced that the pains of punishment outweigh the benefits of crime, may become more wary and willing to desist from a criminal career.[49]

Biosocial Theory

If criminals choose crime, why do they do so? After all, millions of people live in poverty, yet most choose to live law-abiding, conventional lives. So what causes a relatively few people to select a criminal way of life? According to **biosocial theory**, elements of the environment (e.g., family life, community factors) interact with biological factors (e.g., diet, neurological makeup) to control and influence behavior. People choose crime because of a preexisting physical condition, present at birth or soon after, that makes them predisposed to being crime prone.

Biosocial theories can be divided into three broad areas of focus: biochemical factors, neurological problems, and genetic abnormalities.

Biochemical Factors Some criminologists believe that biochemical abnormality may lead to antisocial behaviors. Such biochemical factors as vitamin and mineral deficiencies, hormone imbalance, and environmental contaminants (such as the presence of lead and other metals) have been linked to antisocial behavior.[50] The

rational choice theory
People will engage in delinquent and criminal behavior after weighing the consequences and benefits of their actions. Delinquent behavior is a rational choice made by a motivated offender who perceives the chances of gain as outweighing any perceived punishment or loss.

biosocial theory
Human behavior is a function of the interaction of biochemical, neurological, and genetic factors with environmental stimuli.

influence of damaging chemical and biological contaminants may begin before birth: maternal alcohol abuse and/or smoking during gestation have long been linked to prenatal damage and subsequent antisocial behavior in adolescence.[51] Adolescents exposed to harmful chemicals and poor diet may be prone to antisocial behavior choices.[52]

Neurological Factors There is now evidence that decision making may in fact be regulated and controlled by the brain.[53] Some people may engage in antisocial behaviors because some neurological impairment reduces impulse control and self-control, which then leads people to make damaging behavioral choices.

Brain dysfunction is sometimes manifested as attention deficit/hyperactivity disorder (ADHD), which has been linked to antisocial behavior. About 3 percent of all U.S. children, primarily boys, are believed to suffer from this disorder. Some psychologists believe that the syndrome is essentially a chemical problem, specifically an impairment in the chemical system that supports rapid and efficient communication in the brain's management system.[54] The condition may result in poor school performance, bullying, stubbornness, and a lack of response to discipline.[55]

Genetic Factors Violent behavior is possibly inherited and a function of a person's genetic makeup. One approach to testing this theory has been to evaluate the behavior of adopted children. If an adopted child's behavior patterns ran parallel to those of his or her biological parents, it would be strong evidence to support a genetic basis for crime. Studies conducted in Europe have indicated that the criminality of the biological father is in fact a strong predictor of a child's antisocial behavior.[56] The probability that a youth will engage in crime is significantly enhanced when both biological and adoptive parents exhibit criminal tendencies.

Psychological Theory

Considering incidents such as the Tucson and Virginia Tech massacres, it comes as no surprise that some experts believe criminality is caused by psychological factors. There are actually a number of views on the psychological basis of crime.

psychodynamic view
Criminals are driven by unconscious thought patterns, developed in early childhood, that control behaviors over the life course.

Psychodynamic Theory According to the **psychodynamic view**, some people encounter problems during their early development that cause an imbalance in their personality. The most deeply disturbed are referred to as psychotics, who cannot restrain their impulsive behavior. One type of psychosis is schizophrenia, a condition marked by incoherent thought processes, a lack of insight, hallucinations, and feelings of persecution. Schizophrenics may suffer delusions and feel persecuted, worthless, and alienated.[57] Other offenders may suffer from a wide variety of mood and behavior disorders that render them histrionic, depressed, antisocial, or narcissistic.[58] They may suffer from conduct disorders, which include long histories of antisocial behavior, or mood disorders characterized by disturbance in expressed emotions. Among the latter is **bipolar disorder**, in which moods alternate between periods of wild elation and deep depression.[59] Some offenders are driven by an unconscious desire to be punished for prior sins, either real or imaginary. As a result, they may violate the law or even harm their parents to gain attention.

bipolar disorder
A psychological condition marked by mood swings between periods of wild elation and deep depression.

According to this view, crime is a manifestation of feelings of oppression and of the individual's inability to develop the proper psychological defenses and rationales to keep these feelings under control. Criminality may allow these troubled people to survive by producing positive psychic results: it helps them to feel free and independent, and confers an opportunity for excitement and the chance to use their skills and imagination. It also provides them with the promise of positive gain, as well as allowing them to blame others (such as the police) for their predicament. Finally, it gives them a chance to rationalize their sense of failure ("If I hadn't gotten into trouble, I could have been a success").[60]

■ Psychological theories assume some problem relating to mental well-being influences criminal behaviors. Therefore programs that improve mental well-being should help offenders reduce or avoid engaging in illegal behavior. Here, inmates Donnell Johnson, James Washington, and Patrick Baker participate in a wellness self-management class at Fishkill Correctional Facility in Beacon, New York. A prison may not seem like the most obvious place for self-actualization, with its imposing brick walls and barbed-wire fences. But a program at Fishkill Correctional Facility is trying to help mentally ill inmates learn more about their conditions. The hope is that the program will help inmates cope better in prison and after release, potentially reducing discipline problems and recidivism.

AP Photo/Mike Groll

This view has great appeal, but research results are conflicting. Some studies find a link between mental disturbance and crime; others indicate that the mentally ill are not any more crime prone than the mentally sound. The mentally ill who are violent or criminal typically manifest other problems such as drug abuse and alcoholism, conditions that have been linked to criminality.[61]

Behavioral/Social Learning Theory Another psychological view is that criminal behavior is learned through interactions with others. One assumption is that people act aggressively because as children they experienced violence firsthand, either observing it at home or being a target of violent parents. Children model their behavior after the violent acts of adults. Observed and experienced violence may have an interactive effect: kids who live in high-crime neighborhoods and witness violence in the community and at home, who are the direct victims of domestic and community-based violence, are the ones most likely to commit crime.[62]

One area of particular interest to **social learning** theorists is whether the media can influence violence. Studies have shown that youths exposed to antisocial behavior in the media are likely to copy that violent behavior. Some studies have found that violence on television can lead to aggressive behavior. Yet millions of kids who watch violent media are not violent themselves, so the true association is still unknown.[63]

social learning theory
Behavior patterns are modeled and learned in interactions with others.

Cognitive Theory Law violators may lack the ability to perform cognitive functions in a normal and orderly fashion.[64] Because they have inadequate cognitive processing, criminals perceive the world as stacked against them; they believe they have little control over the negative events in their life.[65] Some may be sensation seekers who are constantly looking for novel experiences, whereas others lack deliberation and rarely think through problems. Some may give up easily, whereas others act without thinking when they get upset.[66]

This distorted view of the world shapes their thinking and colors their judgments. Crime is viewed as an appropriate means to satisfy their

RealityCheck

MYTH OR REALITY? Kids who watch a lot of violence on TV are more likely to get involved in violent behavior themselves.

MYTH. *Millions of kids watch violent TV shows and remain nonviolent.*
The link between violent media and violent behavior is still being debated. In the meantime, should young children be prevented from watching media violence?

immediate personal needs, which take precedence over more distant social needs and such abstract moral concepts as "obey the law" and "respect the rights of others."[67]

Personality Theory It is also possible that people who possess a disturbed personality structure are prone to criminal behavior. For example, people who possess an **antisocial personality** (which used to be referred to as **sociopathic** or **psychopathic personality**) are believed to be dangerous, aggressive individuals who act in a callous manner. They neither learn from their mistakes nor are deterred by punishment.[68] From an early age, they have had home lives filled with frustration, bitterness, and quarreling.[69] They exhibit low levels of guilt and anxiety and persistently violate the rights of others. Although they may exhibit charm and be highly intelligent, these qualities mask a disturbed personality that makes them incapable of forming enduring relationships.[70]

The concept of the antisocial personality is important for understanding the cause of crime because it has been estimated that somewhere between 10 and 30 percent of all prison inmates can be classified as psychopaths or sociopaths or as having similar character disorders.[71]

Social Structure Theory

Another view is that the basis of crime can be found in the relationship a person has to social structures and institutions. According to **social structure theory**, the United States is a stratified society, where there are a few thousand "super rich" making more than $5 million per year, and 40 million Americans who live beneath the poverty line, calculated at about $22,000 per year for a family of four.[72]

Those living in poverty face dead-end jobs, unemployment, and social failure. Because of their meager economic resources, lower-class citizens are often forced to live in poor areas marked by substandard housing, inadequate health care, renters rather than homeowners, poor educational opportunities, underemployment, and despair. These indicators of neighborhood disorder are highly predictive of crime rates.[73]

The problems of lower-class culture are particularly acute for racial and ethnic minorities, who have an income level significantly below that of whites and an unemployment rate almost twice as high. In the inner cities, more than half of all black men do not finish high school. In addition, they face the burden of racism and racial stereotyping. Research shows that whites are averse to living in or visiting black neighborhoods because they consider them crime-ridden, even if these neighborhoods actually have relatively low crime rates.[74]

The crushing burden of urban poverty results in the development of a **culture of poverty** marked by apathy, cynicism, helplessness, and distrust.[75] The culture is passed from one generation to another such that its members become part of a permanent underclass, "the truly disadvantaged."[76] In these areas people live in constant fear and suffer social and physical incivilities—rowdy youths, trash and litter, graffiti, abandoned storefronts, burned-out buildings, littered lots, strangers, drunks, vagabonds, loiterers, prostitutes, noise, congestion, angry words, dirt, and stench.[77] Forced to endure substandard housing and schools in deteriorated inner-city, socially disorganized neighborhoods, and cut off from conventional society, the urban poor face a constant assault on their self-image and sense of worth. Criminal acts and drug dealing provide a means of survival in an otherwise bleak existence. Those living in impoverished neighborhoods are continuously exposed to the opportunity to buy drugs and engage in antisocial acts.[78]

A socially disorganized area is one in which institutions of social control, such as the family, commercial establishments, and schools, have broken down and can no longer carry out their expected or stated functions.[79] Living in deteriorated, crime-ridden neighborhoods exerts a powerful influence that is strong enough to neutralize any positive effects of a supportive family and close social ties.[80]

Strain Theory Social and economic goals are common to people in all economic strata, but ability to obtain these goals is class dependent. Most people in the United States

---

antisocial (sociopathic, psychopathic) personality Individuals who are always in trouble and do not learn from either experience or punishment. They are loners who engage in frequent callous and hedonistic behaviors, are emotionally immature, and lack responsibility, judgment, and empathy.

social structure theory A person's position in the social structure controls his or her behavior. Those in the lowest socioeconomic tier are more likely to succumb to crime-promoting elements in their environment, whereas those in the highest tier enjoy social and economic advantages that insulate them from crime-producing forces.

culture of poverty The crushing lifestyle of slum areas produces a culture of poverty, passed from one generation to the next, marked by apathy, cynicism, feelings of helplessness, and mistrust of social institutions, such as schools, government agencies, and the police.

Structural theory links crime to the disorganization and limited social control found in inner city poverty areas. In this February 13, 2011, picture, Sean Brown, foreground left, of the Young Urban Leaders, uses a microphone to speak in Camden, New Jersey, at a rally remembering Anjanea Williams, who died after she was hit by a stray bullet outside a nearby deli. Anjanea's mother, Latonya Williams (in the blue coat) joined the rally. The city has among the nation's highest unemployment, school dropout, and homeless rates. The latest census data finds 53.6 percent of the city's residents in poverty, the highest in the nation. Camden is now the nation's second-most dangerous city. The UCR reports that Camden suffers more than 2,300 violent crimes per 100,000 residents—more than five times the national average.

AP Photo/Mel Evans

desire wealth, material possessions, power, prestige, and other comforts.[81] Members of the lower class are unable to achieve these symbols of success through conventional means. Consequently, they feel anger, frustration, and resentment. Lower-class citizens either can accept their condition, and live out their days as socially responsible, if unrewarded, citizens, or can choose an alternative means of achieving success, such as theft, violence, or drug trafficking. Although there are other sources of strain, such as negative life experiences or losing a loved one, the strain imposed by limited opportunities may help explain why lower-class areas have such high crime rates.[82]

Cultural Deviance Theory Combining elements of both strain and social disorganization, cultural deviance theory holds that because of strain and social isolation, a unique lower-class culture has developed in disorganized, poverty-ridden neighborhoods. The independent **subcultures** maintain a unique set of values and beliefs that are in conflict with conventional social norms. Criminal behavior is an expression of conformity to lower-class subcultural values, which stress toughness, independence, and standing up to authority. These subcultural values are handed down from one generation to the next in a process called **cultural transmission**. Neighborhood youths who hold these values and incorporate them into their own personal code of behavior are much more likely to join gangs and violate the law than those who reject the deviant subculture.

subculture
A substratum of society that maintains a unique set of values and beliefs.

cultural transmission
The passing of cultural values from one generation to the next.

Social Process Theory

Still another view is that people commit crime as a result of the experiences they have while they are being socialized by the various organizations, institutions, and processes of society. People are most strongly impelled toward criminal behavior by poor family relationships, destructive peer-group relations, educational failure, and labeling by agents of the justice system. Although lower-class citizens bear the added burdens of poverty and strain, even middle-class or upper-class citizens may turn to crime if their socialization is poor or destructive.

The social process approach has several independent branches. The first branch, social learning theory, suggests that people learn the techniques and attitudes of

social process theory
An individual's behavior is shaped by interactions with key social institutions—family, school, peer group, and the like.

crime from close and intimate relationships with criminal peers; crime is a learned behavior. The second branch, social control theory, maintains that everyone has the potential to become a criminal but that most people are controlled by their bond to society. Crime occurs when the forces that bind people to society are weakened or broken. The third branch, social reaction (labeling) theory, says people become criminals when significant members of society label them as such and they accept those labels as a personal identity.

Put another way, social learning theory assumes people are born good and learn to be bad; social control theory assumes people are born bad and must be controlled in order to be good; social reaction theory assumes that whether good or bad, people are controlled by the reactions of others.

Social Conflict Theory

social conflict theory
Human behavior is shaped by interpersonal conflict, and those who maintain social power use it to further their own interests.

Social conflict theory views the economic and political forces operating in society as the fundamental causes of criminality. The criminal law and criminal justice systems are viewed as vehicles for controlling the poor members of society. The criminal justice system is believed to help the powerful and rich impose their particular morality and standards of good behavior on the entire society, while it protects their property and physical safety from the have-nots, even though the cost may be the legal rights of the lower class. Those in power control the content and direction of the law and legal system.

Crimes are defined in a way that meets the needs of the ruling classes. The theft of property worth $5 by a poor person can be punished much more severely than the misappropriation of millions by a large corporation. Those in the middle class are drawn into this pattern of control because they are led to believe that they too have a stake in maintaining the status quo and should support the views of the upper-class owners of production.[83]

L10 Distinguish among the various views of crime causation

Developmental Theory

developmental theory
Social interactions that are developed over the life course shape behavior. Some interactions (such as involvement with deviant peers) encourage law violations, whereas others (such as marriage and military service) may help people desist from crime.

According to **developmental theory**, even as toddlers, people begin relationships and behaviors that will determine their adult life course.[84] These transitions are expected to take place in a prescribed order—beginning with completing school, entering the workforce, getting married, and having children. Some individuals, however, are incapable of maturing in a reasonable and timely fashion because of family, environmental, or personal problems. In some cases, transitions can occur too early—for example, when adolescents engage in precocious sex. In other cases, transitions may occur too late, as when a student fails to graduate on time because of bad grades. Sometimes disruption of one trajectory can harm another. For example, teenage childbirth is likely to disrupt educational and career development. And kids who are schoolyard bullies may later engage in aggressive behavior and crime.[85] Because developmental theories focus on the associations between life events and deviant behaviors, they are sometimes referred to as life-course theories.

Disruptions in life's major transitions can be destructive and ultimately can promote criminality. Those who are already at risk because of socioeconomic problems or family dysfunction are the most susceptible to these awkward transitions. The cumulative impact of these disruptions sustains criminality from childhood into adulthood.

Because a transition from one stage of life to another can be a bumpy ride, the propensity to commit crimes is neither stable nor constant; it is a developmental process. A positive life experience may help some criminals desist from crime for a while, whereas a negative one may cause them to resume their activities. Criminal careers are said to be developmental because people are influenced by the behavior of those around them and in turn influence others' behavior. A youth's antisocial behavior may turn his more conventional friends against him; their rejection solidifies and escalates his antisocial behavior.

Ethical Challenge

A criminologist proposes a research project to test the association between IQ and crime. She wants to look at the associations among race, intelligence, and delinquent behavior. To carry out the project, she wants to conduct IQ tests with K–12 students in the local school district, use a self-report instrument, and gather arrest data from local police. She guarantees that all data will be confidential. Take the role of school board member who must approve of the project. Would you grant her permission to conduct the research? Explain your answer in detail. What possible harm could be done by her project and to whom?

Summary

L01 **Be able to discuss how crime is defined** There are three independent views on how behaviors become crimes. The consensus view holds that criminal behavior is defined by laws that reflect the values and morals of a majority of citizens. The conflict view states that criminal behavior is defined in such a way that economically powerful groups can retain their control over society. The interactionist view portrays criminal behavior as a relativistic, constantly changing concept that reflects society's current moral values.

L02 **Be familiar with the methods used to measure crime** We get our information on crime from a number of sources, including surveys, records, interviews, and observations. One of the most important of these sources is the Uniform Crime Reports (UCR) compiled by the FBI. This national survey compiles criminal acts reported to local police. The acts are called Part I crimes (murder, rape, burglary, robbery, assault, larceny/theft, and motor vehicle theft). All other crimes are referred to as Part II crimes; the FBI reports arrests for Part II crimes. The National Crime Victimization Survey (NCVS) asks people about their experiences with crime. A third form of information is self-report surveys, which ask offenders themselves to tell about their criminal behaviors.

L03 **Discuss the strengths and weaknesses of crime measures** The validity of the UCR has been suspect because many people fail to report crime to police because of fear, apathy, or lack of respect for law enforcement. Many crime victims also do not report criminal incidents to the police because they believe that nothing can be done or that they should not get involved. Self-reports depend on the accuracy of respondents, many of whom are drug users. While imperfect, the crime patterns found in all three data sources may be more similar than some critics believe.

L04 **Recognize the trends in the crime rate** Crime peaked in the 1930s and declined afterward. In the 1960s, crime rates began a rapid increase for almost 30 years. Crime rates have been in a downward trend the past two decades. Even violent crimes have dropped significantly.

L05 **Comment on the factors that influence crime rates** Changes in the crime rate have been attributed to social factors, including the age structure of society. Crime rate increases have been tied to substance abuse levels. While unemployment does not influence crime rates in the short term, long periods of economic decline may promote crime. Crime trends have been linked to abortion. Criminal justice policy may also have an influence on crime rates.

L06 **Be familiar with international crime trends and how the United States compares to other nations** Crime rates have traditionally been higher in the United States than abroad. In recent years, crime rates have been climbing overseas while declining in the United States. Crime rates may be spiraling upward in nations undergoing rapid changes in their social and economic makeup.

L07 **Know the various crime patterns** Crime occurs more often in large cities during the summer and at night. Some geographic areas (the South and West) have higher crime rates than others (the Midwest and New England). Arrest data indicate that males, minorities, the poor, and the young have relatively high arrest rates. Victims of crime tend to be poor, young, male, and members of minority groups.

L08 **Understand the concept of the criminal career** One of the most important findings in the crime statistics is the existence of the chronic offender. The data show that repeat, career criminals are responsible for a significant amount of all law violations. Cohort data find that career criminals begin offending early in life and, instead of aging out of crime, continue to commit crimes in adulthood.

L09 **Be able to discuss the characteristics of crime victims** About 20 million U.S. citizens are victims of crime each year. Data show that, as with crime, victimization has stable patterns and trends. Violent crime victims tend to be young, poor, single males living in large cities. Females are more likely than males to be victimized by someone they know. Adolescents maintain a high risk of being physically and sexually victimized.

L10 **Distinguish among the various views of crime causation** Diverse schools of criminological theory approach the understanding of the cause of crime and its consequences. Some theories focus on the individual, whereas others view social factors as the most important element in producing crime. Developmental theories integrate variables at the social, individual, and societal levels.

Review Questions

1. Why are crime rates higher in the summer than during other seasons?

2. What factors account for crime rate trends?

3. What factors that are present in poverty-stricken urban areas produce high crime rates?

4. It seems logical that biological and psychological factors might explain why some people commit crime. But if crime is based on individual traits, how would we explain the fact that crime rates are higher in the West and South than the Midwest and East?

5. Considering the patterns that victimization takes, what steps should you take to avoid becoming a crime victim?

3

Criminal Law: Substance and Procedure

Learning Objectives

L01 Know the similarities and differences between criminal law and civil law

L02 Understand the concept of substantive criminal law and its history

L03 Discuss the sources of the criminal law

L04 Be familiar with the elements of a crime

L05 Define the term *strict liability*

L06 Be able to discuss excuses and justification defenses for crime

L07 Be familiar with the most recent developments in criminal law reform

L08 Describe the role of the Bill of Rights in shaping criminal procedure

L09 List the elements of due process of law

L010 Know about the role the Supreme Court plays in interpreting the Constitution and shaping procedural law

One day you receive a text message or an automated phone call on your cell phone saying there's a problem with your bank account or your ATM number. The message gives you a phone number to call or a website to log into and you are then directed to identify yourself so that your account can be "fixed." You might be asked to provide personal identifiable information—like a bank account number, ATM PIN number, Social Security or credit card number—to fix the problem. The website looks legit and contains a logo that looks exactly like Bank of America, TD Bank, or any other large national bank. Sounds good, but you have just become the victim of a crime called "smishing" or "vishing." The person monitoring the website is not a bank employee but a criminal intent on collecting your personal information in order to help themselves to your money via your cell phone. Armed with your personal information, vishers can steal from your bank accounts, charge purchases on your charge cards, create a phony ATM card to drain your account, and so on. If you happen to log onto the phony website with a smart phone rather than your laptop, vishers can begin downloading malicious software that gives them access to anything and anyone in your phone's contact list. With the growth of mobile banking and the ability to conduct financial transactions online, smishing and vishing attacks may become even more attractive and lucrative for cyber criminals. ■

Vishing and smishing schemes were hardly what the founding fathers had in mind in the eighteenth century when they created the U.S. Constitution or when the first written criminal codes were formulated. It comes as no surprise that to keep up with the changes in society the law must be flexible and designed to quickly react to technological innovations such as the Internet, smart phones, online banking, and the like. Sometimes, these contemporary criminal acts fall under laws controlling traditional crimes such as larceny and fraud. For example, vishing and smishing are considered violations of Chapter 63 of the United States Criminal Code, which controls mail fraud.[1] In other instances, new laws must be devised specifically to control criminal innovations. For example, when millions of people were besieged by spam messages, some attempting to get them to give out personal information, Congress passed the CAN-SPAM act of 2003 (full name, Controlling the Assault of Non-Solicited Pornography and Marketing Act of 2003) to reduce and regulate the use of Internet spam.[2]

Creating new laws to control cyberspace is just one element of contemporary criminal law. Today, the rule of law governs almost all phases of human enterprise, including crimes, family life, property transfer, and the regulation of interpersonal conflict. It can generally be divided into four broad categories:

- *Substantive criminal law.* The branch of the law that defines crimes and their punishment. It involves such issues as the mental and physical elements of crime,

substantive criminal law
A body of specific rules that declare what conduct is criminal and prescribe the punishment to be imposed for such conduct.

criminal procedure
The rules and laws that define the operation of criminal proceedings. Procedural law describes the methods that must be followed in obtaining warrants, investigating offenses, effecting lawful arrests, conducting trials, introducing evidence, sentencing convicted offenders, and reviewing cases by appellate courts.

civil law
All law that is not criminal, including the law of torts (personal wrongs) and contract, property, maritime, and commercial law.

tort
A personal injury or wrong for which an action for damages may be brought.

public law
The branch of law that deals with the state or government and its relationships with individuals or other governments.

crime categories, and criminal defenses. Exhibit 3.1 sets out the main goals of **substantive criminal law**.

- *Procedural law.* Those laws that set out the basic rules of practice in the government, including the criminal justice system. Some elements of the law of **criminal procedure** are the rules of evidence, the law of arrest, the law of search and seizure, questions of appeal, jury selection, and the right to counsel.
- *Civil law.* The set of rules governing relations between private parties, including both individuals and organizations (such as business enterprises and/or corporations). **Civil law** is used to resolve, control, and shape such personal interactions as contracts, wills and trusts, property ownership, and commerce. The element of civil law most relevant to criminal justice is **torts**, or the law of personal injuries.
- *Public or administrative law.* The branch of law that deals with the government and its relationships with individuals or other governments is known as **public law**. It governs the administration and regulation of city, county, state, and federal government agencies.

Exhibit 3.1

The Goals of Substantive Criminal Law

Enforce social control Substantive criminal law is the main instrument of control at the disposal of an existing government. It is used by those who hold political power to eliminate behaviors they believe pose a threat to society or challenge the government's authority.

Distribute retribution By punishing people who infringe on the rights, property, and freedom of others, the law shifts the burden of revenge from the individual to the state. Although the thought of state-sponsored retribution may be offensive to some, it is greatly preferable to a system in which injured parties or their friends and relatives would seek to redress their injuries through personal vengeance or revenge.

Express public opinion and morality Criminal law reflects public opinions and moral values. It reflects both traditional and contemporary moral values, and it may undergo change according to existing social conditions and attitudes. The criminal law is used to codify changing social values and to educate the public about what is expected of them.

Deter criminal behavior Criminal law is designed, through its application of punishment, to control, restrain, and deter illegal acts before they actually occur. During the Middle Ages, public executions drove this point home; today, long prison sentences and an occasional execution are designed to achieve the same result.

Punish wrongdoing If the deterrent power of criminal law fails to prevent crime, the law gives the state the right to sanction or punish offenders. Those who violate criminal law are subject to physical coercion and punishment.

Maintain social order All legal systems are designed to support and maintain the boundaries of the social system they serve. The free enterprise system is supported and sustained by criminal laws that protect property transfer and control market operations.

Restoration Victims deserve restitution or compensation for their pain and loss. The criminal law can be used to restore to the victims what they have lost. Because we believe in equity and justice, it is only fair that the guilty help repair the harm they have caused others by their crimes. Punishments such as fines, forfeiture, and restitution are connected to this legal goal.

LO1 Know the similarities and differences between criminal law and civil law

There is of course overlap between these branches of the law. In some instances, a person who has been the victim of a criminal act may also sue the perpetrator for damages in a civil tort; some crime victims may forgo criminal action and choose to file a tort claim alone. It is also possible to seek civil damages from a perpetrator even if he or she is found not guilty of crime, because the evidentiary standard in a tort action (by a preponderance of the evidence) is less than is needed for a criminal conviction (beyond a reasonable doubt). In one famous case, the families of Nicole Brown and Ron Goldman successfully sued O. J. Simpson for damages, even though he was found not guilty of murder.

People having conflicts with the government may find redress through the administrative law. The government has the option to pursue a legal matter through the criminal process, file a tort action, or both. White-collar crimes, including mail, wire, tax-related, or computer fraud and money-laundering violations, often involve both criminal and civil penalties, giving the government the choice of pursuing one type of action or both.

Historical Development of the Criminal Law

The roots of contemporary criminal codes can be traced to such early legal charters as the Babylonian Code of Hammurabi (2000 BCE), which rested on the concept of proportionality, **lex talionis** (an eye for an eye), that is still the basis of law today Some of its provisions include:

- If a man puts out the eye of an equal, his eye shall be put out.
- If a man knocks the teeth out of another man, his own teeth will be knocked out.
- If the slave of a freed man strikes the body of a freed man, his ear shall be cut off.[3]

lex talionis
Latin for "law as retaliation." From Hammurabi's ancient legal code, the belief that the purpose of the law is to provide retaliation for an offended party and that the punishment should fit the crime.

The Mosaic Code of the Israelites (1200 BCE), better known today as the Ten Commandments, contains prohibitions against theft, violence, and perjury that still hold sway in the modern criminal law.

The early formal legal codes were lost during the Dark Ages (500–1000 AD). In their place, a legal system featuring monetary compensation, called *wergild* (*wer* means "worth" and refers to what the person, and therefore the crime, was worth), was developed for criminal violations. Guilt was determined by two methods: "compurgation," which involved having the accused person swear an oath of innocence while being backed up by a group of 12 to 25 oath-helpers, who would attest to his or her character and claims of innocence, and "ordeal," which was based on the principle that divine forces would not allow an innocent person to be harmed.

Determining guilt by ordeal involved such measures as having the accused place his or her hand in boiling water or hold a hot iron. If the wound healed, the person was found innocent; if the wound did not heal, the accused was deemed guilty. Another ordeal, trial by combat, allowed the accused to challenge his accuser to a duel, with the outcome determining the legitimacy of the accusation.

Common Law and the Principle of *Stare Decisis*

Soon after William, Duke of Normandy, conquered England in 1066—a feat that transformed him into William the Conqueror—he sent his royal administrators to travel throughout the land, holding court in each county of his new domain. When court was in session, the royal administrator, or judge, summoned a number of citizens who would, on their oath, tell of the crimes and serious breaches of the peace that had occurred since the judge's last visit. The royal judge then decided what to do in each case, using local custom and rules of conduct as his guide in a system known as *stare decisis* (Latin for "to stand by decided cases").

stare decisis
Latin for "to stand by decided cases." The legal principle by which the decision or holding in an earlier case becomes the standard by which subsequent similar cases are judged.

LO2 Understand the concept of substantive criminal law and its history

The present English system of law came into existence during the reign of Henry II (1154–1189), when royal judges began to publish their decisions in local cases. This allowed judicial precedents to be established and a national law to accumulate. Other judges began to use these written decisions as a basis for their decision making, and eventually a fixed body of legal rules and principles emerged. If the new rules were successfully applied in a number of different cases, they would become precedents, which would then be commonly applied in all similar cases. This unified system evolved into a **common law** of the country that incorporated local custom and practice into a national code. Crimes that were *mala in se*, inherently evil and depraved (such as murder, burglary, and arson), and were the cornerstone of the common law, were joined by new *mala prohibitum* crimes such as embezzlement, which reflected existing social and economic conditions.

Before the American Revolution, the colonies, then under British rule, were subject to the common law. After the colonies acquired their independence, state legislatures standardized common-law crimes such as murder, burglary, arson, and rape by codifying them (putting them into statutory form in criminal codes). As in England, whenever common law proved inadequate to deal with changing social and moral issues, the states and Congress supplemented it with legislative statutes, creating new elements in the various state and federal legal codes. Similarly, statutes prohibiting such offenses as identity theft and the pirating of videotapes have recently been passed to control human behavior unknown at the time the common law was formulated.

Sources of the Criminal Law

The contemporary American legal system is codified by state and federal legislatures. Each jurisdiction precisely defines crime in its legal code and sets out the appropriate punishments. However, like its English common-law roots, American criminal law is not static and is constantly evolving. A state statute based on common law may define first-degree murder as the "unlawful killing, with malice and premeditation, of one human being by another." Over time, state court decisions might help explain the meaning of the term "malice" or clarify whether "human being" refers only to someone "born and alive" or whether it can also refer to an unborn fetus. More than half the states have expanded their legal codes to include feticide law, which makes the killing of an unborn fetus murder.

The content of the law may also be influenced by judicial decision making. A criminal offense is no longer enforceable when an appellate judge rules that the statute is vague, deals with an act no longer of interest to the public, or is an unfair exercise of state control over an individual. Conversely, a judicial ruling may expand the scope of an existing criminal law, thereby allowing control over behaviors heretofore beyond its reach.

RealityCheck

MYTH OR REALITY? Because it is designed to control such acts as murder, theft, and rape, the criminal law rarely if ever changes.

REALITY. *The criminal law changes all the time.*

Can you think of acts that have been criminalized during your lifetime? What about those that have been decriminalized or legalized?

Constitutional Limits

Regardless of its source, all criminal law in the United States must conform to the rules and dictates of the Constitution.[4] Any criminal law that conflicts with the various provisions and articles of the Constitution will eventually be challenged in the appellate courts and stricken from the legal code by judicial order (or modified to adhere to constitutional principles). The Constitution has been interpreted to forbid any criminal law that violates a person's right to be treated fairly and equally; this principle is referred to as substantive due process. This means that before a new law can be created, the state must show a compelling need to protect public safety or morals.[5]

Criminal laws have been interpreted as violating constitutional principles if they are too vague or broad for their intent to be clear. A law

■ The Constitution forbids bills of attainder—legislative acts finding a person guilty of treason or a felony without a trial. By forbidding attainder, the founding fathers did not want to repeat the ills of the English system that was used to persecute people considered to be disloyal to the government. This woodcut shows the execution of Thomas Wentworth, Earl of Strafford (1593–1641), an English politician, impeached by Commons led by John Pym and convicted on a bill of attainder.

The Execution of the Earl of Strafford (1593–1641) on Tower Hill, 12th May 1641 (engraving) by German School (17th century) Ashmolean Museum, University of Oxford, UK/The Bridgeman Art Library

forbidding adults to engage in "immoral behavior" could not be enforced, because it does not use clear and precise language or give adequate notice as to which conduct is forbidden.[6] The Constitution also prohibits laws that make a person's status a crime. Being a heroin addict is not a crime, although laws can forbid the sale, possession, and manufacture of heroin. Finally, the Constitution limits laws that are overly cruel and/or capricious.[7]

The Constitution also forbids bills of attainder, which are legislative acts that inflict punishment without a judicial trial. This device, used by the English kings to punish rebels and seize their property, was particularly troublesome to American colonials when it was used to seize the property of people considered disloyal to the crown; hence, attainder is forbidden in the Constitution. Nor does the Constitution permit the government to pass ex post facto laws, which are defined as follows:

- A law that makes an action that was done before the passing of the law, and that was innocent when done, criminal and punishes such action
- A law that makes a crime more serious after the fact than it was when first committed
- A law that inflicts a greater punishment than was available when the crime was committed
- A law that makes it easier to convict the offender than it was at the time the crime was committed[8]

Crimes and Classifications

All states and the federal government have developed their own body of criminal law that defines and grades offenses, sets levels of punishment,

RealityCheck

MYTH OR REALITY? A murderer cannot be executed unless the state had a death penalty statute in place before his or her trial began.

REALITY. *The Constitution prohibits imposing a more severe punishment than that which was in place when the crime was first committed. It does not matter when the criminal was caught or when they were brought to trial.*

A person who commits a murder cannot be executed in a non–death penalty state even if the state legalizes the death penalty before the culprit is identified, caught, and tried. Do you agree with this principle?

and classifies crimes into categories. Crimes are generally grouped into three categories:

- Felonies, the most serious crimes punishable by imprisonment, such as criminal homicide, robbery, and rape, as well as such crimes against property as burglary and larceny.
- Misdemeanors, less serious crimes punishable by a jail term, including petit (or petty) larceny, assault and battery, and the unlawful possession of marijuana.
- Violations (also called infractions), which are violations of city or town ordinances such as traffic violations or public intoxication, punishable by a fine. Some states consider violations civil matters, whereas others classify them as crimes.

Distinguishing between a **felony** and a **misdemeanor** is sometimes difficult. Simply put, a felony is a serious offense, and a misdemeanor is a less serious one.

The felony/misdemeanor classification has a direct effect on the way an offender is treated within the justice system. Police may arrest a felon if there is an arrest warrant issued by a court and/or probable cause that he or she committed a crime. In contrast, misdemeanants may be taken into custody only with an arrest warrant or if the police officer observed the infraction personally; this is known as the in-presence requirement. There are, however, some instances when police can make a misdemeanor arrest without observing its occurrence. For example, a number of jurisdictions have passed domestic violence prevention acts, which allow arrests based merely on the accusation of the injured party. These laws have been created in an effort to protect the target of the abuse from further attacks.[9]

If convicted, a person charged with a felony may be barred from certain fields of employment or some professions, such as law and medicine. A felony offender's status as an alien in the United States might also be affected, or the offender might be denied the right to hold public office, vote, or serve on a jury.[10] These and other civil liabilities exist only when a person is convicted of a felony offense, not of a misdemeanor.

felony
A more serious offense that carries a penalty of incarceration in a state prison, usually for one year or more. Persons convicted of felony offenses lose such rights as the right to vote, hold elective office, or maintain certain licenses.

misdemeanor
A minor crime usually punished by less than one year's imprisonment in a local institution, such as a county jail.

L03 Discuss the sources of the criminal law

The Legal Definition of a Crime

Almost all common-law crime contains both mental and physical elements. For example, in order to commit the crime of armed burglary, offenders must do the following things:

- Willfully enter a dwelling
- Be armed or arm themselves after entering the house, or commit an actual assault on a person who is lawfully in the house
- Knowingly and intentionally commit the crime

For the prosecutor to prove a crime occurred, and that the defendant committed it, the prosecutor must show (a) that the accused engaged in the guilty act (*actus reus*, or guilty act) and (b) that the act was intentional and purposeful (*mens rea*, or guilty mind). Under common law, both the *actus reus* and the *mens rea* must be present for the act to be considered a crime. Thoughts of committing an act do not alone constitute a crime; there must also be an illegal act. Let us now look more closely at these issues.

Actus Reus

The *actus reus* is a *voluntary and deliberate* illegal act, such as taking someone's money, burning a building, or shooting someone; an accident or involuntary act would not be considered criminal. However, even an unintentional act can be considered a crime if it is the result of negligence and/or disregard for the rights of others.

actus reus
An illegal act. The *actus reus* can be an affirmative act, such as taking money or shooting someone, or a failure to act, such as failing to take proper precautions while driving a car.

mens rea
Guilty mind. The mental element of a crime or the intent to commit a criminal act.

A person cannot be held criminally liable for assault if while walking down the street he has a seizure and as a result his arm strikes another person in the face; his act was not voluntary and therefore not criminal. However, if this same person knew beforehand that he might have a seizure and unreasonably put himself in a position where he was likely to harm others—for instance, by driving a car—he could be criminally liable for his behavior because his actions were negligent and disregarded the rights of others.

In addition, there are occasions when the failure or omission to act can be considered a crime:

- *Failure to perform a legally required duty that is based on relationship or status.* These relationships include parent and child and husband and wife. If a husband finds his wife unconscious because she took an overdose of sleeping pills, he is obligated to save her life by seeking medical aid. If he fails to do so and she dies, he can be held responsible for her death. Parents are required to look after the welfare of their children; failure to provide adequate care can be a criminal offense.
- *Imposition by statute.* Some states have passed laws that require a person who observes an automobile accident to stop and help the other parties involved.
- *Contractual relationship.* These relationships include lifeguard and swimmer, doctor and patient, and babysitter or au pair and child. Because lifeguards have been hired to ensure the safety of swimmers, they have a legal duty to come to the aid of drowning persons. If a lifeguard knows a swimmer is in danger and does nothing about it, and the swimmer drowns, the lifeguard can be held legally responsible for the swimmer's death.

In these cases, the duty to act is a legal and not a moral duty. The obligation arises from the relationship between the parties or from explicit legal requirements. In contrast, a private citizen who sees a person drowning is under no legal obligation to save that person. Although we may find it morally reprehensible, the private citizen could walk away and let the swimmer drown without facing legal sanctions.

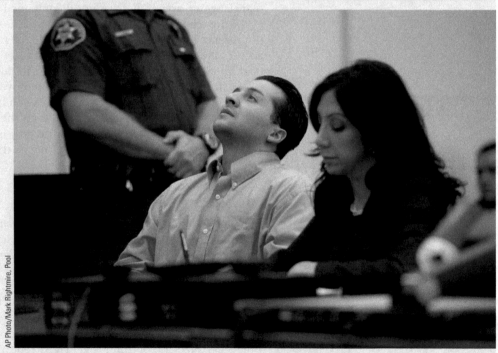

If a driver's act of drunk driving results in the death of another person, the driver will be charged with some form of homicide even though he did not intend to kill his or her victim. His negligent disregard for the safety of others constitutes intent. Here, Andrew Gallo reacts as he is sentenced to 51 years in prison, in Santa Ana, California, on December 22, 2010. At right is his attorney, Jacqueline Goodman. Gallo was convicted of three counts of second-degree murder and single counts of drunken driving, hit-and-run driving, and driving under the influence of alcohol and causing great bodily injury. Killed in the crash were Los Angeles Angels pitcher Nick Adenhart, 20-year-old Courtney Stewart, and 25-year-old Henry Pearson. A fourth passenger, Jon Wilhite, was severely injured.

AP Photo/Mark Rightmire, Pool

Mens Rea

For an act to constitute a crime, it must be done with deliberate purpose or criminal intent. A person who enters a store with a gun with the intention of stealing money indicates by his actions the intent to commit a robbery. Criminal intent is implied if the results of a person's action, though originally unintended, are certain to occur. When Mohammed Atta and his terrorist band crashed an aircraft into the World Trade Center on September 11, 2001, they did not intend to kill any particular person in the building. Yet the law would hold that Atta, and any others conspiring with him, would be substantially certain that people in the building would be killed in the blast and that they therefore had the criminal intent to commit the crime of murder.

In some situations, intent is derived from recklessness or negligence. A drunk driver may not have intended to kill her specific victim, yet her negligent and reckless behavior—driving while drunk—creates a condition that a reasonable person can assume may lead to injury.

The Relationship between *Mens Rea* and *Actus Reus*

For an act to constitute a crime, the law requires a connection be made between the *mens rea* and the *actus reus*, thereby showing that the offender's conduct was the proximate cause of the criminal act. If a man chases a woman into the street intending to assault her, and the victim is struck by a car and killed, the accused cannot claim at trial that the death was an accident caused by the inopportune passing of the motor vehicle. The law holds that the victim would never have run into the street had she not been pursued by the defendant, and that, therefore, (a) the defendant's reckless disregard for the victim's safety makes him responsible for her death, and (b) his action was the proximate cause of her death.

Criminal Harm Thought alone is not a crime. For a person to be considered to have committed a crime, some act is required to prove the actor's willingness to cause harm. It is the nature of the harm that ultimately determines what crime the person committed. If someone trips another with the intent of making the person fall down and be embarrassed in public, he has committed the crime of battery. If by some chance the victim dies from the fall, the harm caused elevates the crime to manslaughter, even if that was not the intended result.

In the crime of robbery, the *actus reus* is taking the property from the person or presence of another. In order to satisfy the harm requirement, the robber must acquire the victim's possessions, referred to as "asportation." The legal definition of robbery is satisfied when even for a brief moment possession of the property is transferred to the robber. If a robber removes a victim's wallet from his pocket and immediately tosses it over a fence when he spies a police officer approaching, the robbery is complete because even the slightest change in possession of the property is sufficient to cause harm. Nor is the value of the property important: actual value is unimportant as long as the property had some value to the victim.

L04 Be familiar with the elements of a crime

strict liability crime
Illegal act whose elements do not contain the need for intent, or *mens rea*; usually, an act that endangers the public welfare, such as illegal dumping of toxic wastes.

L05 Define the term *strict liability*

Strict Liability

There are certain statutory offenses in which *mens rea* is not essential. These offenses fall in a category known as public safety or **strict liability crimes**. A person can be held responsible for such a violation independent of the existence of intent to commit the offense. Strict liability criminal statutes generally include narcotics control laws, traffic laws, health and safety regulations, sanitation laws, and other regulatory statutes. A motorist could not defend herself against a speeding ticket by claiming that she was unaware of how fast she was going and did not intend to speed, nor could a bartender claim that a juvenile to whom he sold liquor looked quite a bit older. No state of mind is generally required where a strict liability statute is violated.[11]

Criminal Defenses

In 1884, two British sailors, desperate after being shipwrecked for days, made the decision to kill and eat a suffering cabin boy who was on their lifeboat. Four days later, they were rescued by a passing ship and returned to England. English authorities, wanting to end the practice of shipwreck cannibalism, tried the two men and convicted them of murder. Clemency was considered, and a reluctant Queen Victoria commuted the death sentences to six months.[12] Were the seamen justified in killing a shipmate to save their lives? If they had not done so, it is likely they all would have died. Did they act out of necessity or malice? Can there ever be a good reason to take a life? Can we ever justify killing another? Before you answer, remember that we can kill in self-defense, to prevent lethal crimes, or in times of war (more on necessity defenses later).

When people defend themselves against criminal charges, they must refute one or more of the elements of the crime of which they have been accused. Defendants may deny the *actus reus* by arguing that they were falsely accused and the real culprit has yet to be identified. Defendants may also claim that although they did engage in the criminal act they are accused of, they lacked the *mens rea*, or mental intent, needed to be found guilty of the crime. If a person whose mental state is impaired commits a criminal act, it is possible for the person to excuse his criminal actions by claiming he lacked the capacity to form sufficient intent to be held criminally responsible. **Insanity**, intoxication, and ignorance are also among the types of excuse defenses.[13]

Another type of defense is justification. Here, the individual admits committing the criminal act but maintains that the act was justified and that, given the circumstances, anyone would have acted in a similar manner; because her act was justified, she should not be held criminally liable. Among the justification defenses are necessity, duress, **self-defense**, and **entrapment**. We will now examine some of these defenses and justifications in greater detail.

Excuse Defenses

Excuses refer to situations in which the criminal defendants admit to performing the physical act of crime but claim they are not responsible for it because they lacked free will. It is not their fault, they claim, because they had no control over their actions; therefore, they should be "excused" from criminal responsibility.

Ignorance or Mistake People sometimes defend themselves by claiming either that their actions were a mistake or that they were unaware (ignorant) of the fact that their behavior was a crime. For example, they did not realize they had stepped onto private property and were guilty of trespassing.

As a general rule, ignorance of the law is no excuse. According to the great legal scholar William Blackstone, "Ignorance of the law, which everyone is bound to know, excuses no man."[14] Consequently, a defendant cannot present a legitimate defense by saying he was unaware of a criminal law, had misinterpreted the law, or believed the law to be unconstitutional.

In some instances, mistake of fact, such as taking someone else's coat that is similar to your own, may be a valid defense; an honest mistake may remove the defendant's criminal responsibility. Mistake can also be used as a defense when the government failed to make enactment of a new law public or when the offender relies on an official statement of the law that is later deemed incorrect.

Insanity Insanity is a defense to criminal prosecution in which the defendant's state of mind negates his or her criminal responsibility. A successful insanity defense results in a verdict of "not guilty by reason of insanity."[15]

Insanity is a legal category. As used in U.S. courts, it does not necessarily mean that everyone who suffers from a form of mental illness can be excused

insanity
A legal defense that maintains a defendant was incapable of forming criminal intent because he or she suffers from a defect of reason or mental illness.

self-defense
A legal defense in which defendants claim that their behavior was legally justified by the necessity to protect their own life and property, or that of another victim, from potential harm.

entrapment
A criminal defense that maintains the police originated the criminal idea or initiated the criminal action.

For a defendant who commited a criminal act to be considered insane, a jury must believe that mental instability made it impossible for him or her to have had the intent to commit crime. Even some bizarre cases do not qualify as insanity. Take, for instance, Sheila LaBarre, who on June 20, 2008, was found guilty of murder in Rockingham County Superior Court in New Hampshire. LaBarre, who claimed she was an angel sent from God to punish pedophiles, was convicted of murdering two boyfriends after a jury rejected her insanity plea.

RealityCheck

MYTH OR REALITY? People who are mentally ill cannot be found guilty of a crime.

MYTH. *Mentally ill people can be convicted of a crime unless they are legally insane. You can suffer mental illness but be aware of your behavior and in control; therefore you would be legally responsible for your acts.*

Do you agree? Or should mental illness excuse guilt? Is it possible to be suffering from severe mental illness yet have the intent to commit crime? Can we really say someone like Jeffrey Dahmer, the cannibal who raped, killed, and ate 17 men and boys, was not insane? Yet, he was found guilty of his crimes and given 15 life sentences; he was later killed in prison.

from legal responsibility. Many people who are depressed, suffer mood disorders, or have a psychopathic personality can be found legally sane. Instead, insanity means that the defendant's state of mind at the time the crime was committed made it impossible for that person to have the necessary *mens rea* to satisfy the legal definition of a crime. A person can be undergoing treatment for a psychological disorder but still be judged legally sane if it can be proved that at the time he committed the crime, he had the capacity to understand the wrongfulness of his actions.

If a defendant uses the insanity plea, it is usually left to psychiatric testimony to prove that the person understood the wrongfulness of her actions and was therefore legally sane, or conversely, was mentally incapable of forming intent. The jury then must weigh the evidence in light of the test for sanity currently used in the jurisdiction. Such tests vary throughout the United States; the commonly used tests are listed in Exhibit 3.2.

Intoxication As a general rule, intoxication, which may include drunkenness or being under the influence of drugs, is not considered a defense. However, a defendant who becomes involuntarily intoxicated under duress or by mistake may be excused for crimes committed. Involuntary intoxication may also reduce the degree of the crime; a judgment may be decreased from first- to second-degree murder because the defendant uses intoxication to prove the lack of the critical element of *mens rea*.

Age The law holds that a child is not criminally responsible for actions committed at an age that precludes full realization of the gravity of certain types of behavior. Under common law, there is generally a conclusive presumption of incapacity for a child under age 7, a reliable presumption for a child between the ages of 7 and 14, and no presumption for a child over the age of 14. This generally means that a child under age 7 who commits a crime will not be held criminally responsible for these actions and that a child between ages 7 and 14 may be held responsible. These common-law rules have been changed by statute in most jurisdictions. Today, the maximum age of criminal responsibility for children ranges from age 14 to 17 or 18, and the minimum age may be set by statute at age 7 or under age 14.[16]

Various Insanity Defense Standards

The M'Naghten rule The M'Naghten rule, first formulated in England in 1843, defines a person as insane if, at the time she committed the act she stands accused of, she was laboring under such a defect of reason, arising from a disease of the mind, that she could not tell or know the nature and quality of the act or, if she did know it, that she did not know what she was doing was wrong. In other words, she could not "tell right from wrong." The M'Naghten rule is used in the majority of the states.

The irresistible impulse The irresistible impulse test was formulated in Ohio in 1834. It is used quite often in conjunction with M'Naghten and defines a person as insane if she should or did know that her actions were illegal but, because of a mental impairment, could not control her behavior. Her act was a result of an uncontrollable or irresistible impulse. A person who commits a crime during a "fit of passion" would be considered insane under this test. The most famous use of this defense occurred in 1994, when Lorena Bobbitt successfully defended herself against charges that she cut off the penis of her husband, John, after suffering abuse at his hands.

The Durham rule The Durham rule, or "product test," was set forth by the U.S. Court of Appeals for the District of Columbia Circuit in 1954 and states that "an accused is not criminally responsible if her unlawful act was the product of mental disease or defect." It was used for some time in the state of New Hampshire.

The Insanity Defense Reform Act The Insanity Defense Reform Act, Title 18, U.S. Code, Section 17, was enacted by Congress in 1984 and states that a person accused of a crime can be judged not guilty by reason of insanity if "the defendant, as a result of a severe mental disease or defect, was unable to appreciate the nature and quality or the wrongfulness of her acts."

The substantial capacity test The substantial capacity test was defined by the American Law Institute in its Model Penal Code. This argues that insanity should be defined as a lack of substantial capacity to control one's behavior. Substantial capacity is defined as "the mental capacity needed to understand the wrongfulness of [an] act, or to conform . . . behavior to the . . . law." This rule combines elements of the M'Naghten rule with the concept of irresistible impulse.

Justification Defenses

Justifications arise in situations in which the defendants don't deny they committed a crime but claim that anyone in their situation would have acted in a similar fashion. Justification defenses deny *mens rea*: "I did a bad act, but I did it for all the right reasons."

Consent A person may not be convicted of a crime if the victim consented to the act in question. In other words, a rape does not occur if the victim consents to sexual relations; a larceny cannot occur if the owner voluntarily consents to the taking of property. Consent is an essential element of these crimes, and it is a valid defense where it can be proved or shown that consent existed at the time the act was committed. In some crimes, such as statutory rape, however, consent is not an element of the crime and is considered irrelevant because the state presumes that young people are not capable of providing consent.

Self-Defense Defendants may justify their actions by saying they acted in self-defense. To establish the necessary elements to constitute self-defense, the defendant must have acted under a reasonable belief that he was in danger of death or great harm and had no means of escape from the assailant.

As a general legal rule, a person defending himself may use only such force as is reasonably necessary to prevent personal harm. A person who is assaulted by another with no weapon is ordinarily not justified in hitting the assailant with a baseball bat; a person verbally threatened is not justified in striking the other party. Persons can be found guilty of murder in the first degree if, after being attacked during a brawl, they shot and killed an unarmed person in self-defense. Despite the fact that it was the victim who initiated the fray and pummeled his opponent first, the imbalance in weaponry (gun versus fist) would mitigate a finding of self-defense.[17]

To exercise the self-defense privilege, the danger to the defendant must be immediate; it is not justifiable to kill someone who threatened you with death a year ago. In addition, most jurisdictions require that the defendants prove that they sought alternative means of avoiding the danger, such as escape, retreat, or assistance from others, before they defended themselves with force.

In some instances, women (or men) may kill their mates after years of abuse; this is known as battered-wife syndrome (or, in cases involving child abuse, battered-child syndrome). Although a history of battering can be used to mitigate the seriousness of the crime, a finding of not guilty most often requires the presence of imminent danger and the inability of the accused to escape from the assailant.

Stand Your Ground Most self-defense statutes require a duty to retreat before reacting to a threat with physical violence. An exception is one's own home. According to the "castle exception" ("every man's home is his castle"), a person is not obligated to retreat within his or her residence before fighting back. Some states, most notably Florida, now have "stand your ground" laws, which allow people to use force in a wide variety of circumstances and eliminate or curtail the need to retreat, even if they are not in their own home but in a public place.

Florida's law, enacted on October 1, 2005, allows the use of deadly force when a person reasonably believes it necessary to prevent the commission of a "forcible felony," including carjacking, robbery, and assault.[18] The new law allows average citizens to use deadly force when they reasonably believe that their homes or vehicles have been illegally invaded. The Florida law authorizes the use of defensive force by anyone "who is not engaged in an unlawful activity and who is attacked in any other place where he or she has a right to be." Furthermore, under the law, such a person has no duty to retreat and can stand his or her ground and meet force with force. The statute also grants civil and criminal immunity to anyone found to have had such a reasonable belief.[19]

Entrapment Defendants can claim their criminal activity was justified because law enforcement agents used traps, decoys, and deception to induce criminal action; this is referred to as entrapment. It is generally legitimate for law enforcement officers to set traps for criminals by getting information about crimes from informers, undercover agents, and codefendants. Police officers are allowed to use ordinary opportunities for defendants to commit crime and to create these opportunities that involve a defendant in a crime. For example, they can pose as prostitutes or drug dealers, hang out in an area known for drug dealing and prostitution, and make an arrest if they are solicited for crime. However, entrapment occurs when the police instigate the crime, implant criminal ideas, and coerce individuals into bringing about crime.

In *Sherman v. United States*, the Supreme Court found that the function of law enforcement is to prevent crime and apprehend criminals, not to implant a criminal design originating with officials of the government in the mind of an innocent person.[20]

RealityCheck

MYTH OR REALITY? It is illegal for a policewoman to dress like a prostitute, hang out on a street corner, and arrest someone who solicits her for sex; that is called entrapment.

MYTH. *It is perfectly legal to arrest a suspect who approaches a provocatively dressed police officer and solicits her for sex.*

What would happen if the provocatively dressed police officer made the first move?

Duress To prove duress, defendants must show they have been forced into committing a crime in order to prevent death or serious harm to self or others. For example, a bank employee might be excused from taking bank funds if she can prove that her family was being threatened and that consequently she was acting under duress. But there is widespread general agreement that duress is no defense for an intentional killing.

Necessity Sometimes criminal defendants, like the two sailors who killed and ate the cabin boy, argue that they acted out of "necessity." To be successful, a defense of necessity must show that considering the circumstances and conditions at the time the crime occurred, the defendant (or any reasonable person) could not have behaved in any other way. For example, a husband steals a car to take his pregnant wife to the hospital for an emergency delivery, or a hunter shoots an animal of an endangered species that was about to attack his child. The defense has been found inapplicable in cases where defendants sought to shut down nuclear power plants or abortion clinics or to destroy missile components under the belief that the action was necessary to save lives or prevent a nuclear war.

LO6 Be able to discuss excuses and justification defenses for crime

Reforming the Criminal Law

In recent years, many states and the federal government have been examining their substantive criminal law. In some instances, what was formerly legal is now a crime, and in other instances, what was previously considered illegal has been legalized or decriminalized (in other words, the penalties have been reduced). An example of the former can be found in changes to the law of rape. In seven states, including California, it is now considered rape when the following sequence of events occurs: (1) The woman consents to sex, (2) the sex act begins, (3) she changes her mind during the act and tells her partner to stop, and (4) he refuses and continues. Before the legal change, such a circumstance was not considered rape.[21]

There are also many instances in which the law has been changed so that what was considered illegal is now legal and noncriminal. Until recently, sexual relations between consenting same-sex adults was punished as a serious felony under sodomy statutes. In an important 2003 case, *Lawrence v. Texas*, the Supreme Court declared that laws banning sodomy are unconstitutional if they restrict adults' private sexual behavior and impose on their personal dignity. As a result of this decision, laws banning same-sex relations between consenting adults in the United States are now unconstitutional and therefore non-enforceable.[22]

Creating New Crimes

In some instances, new laws have been created to conform to emerging social issues and to deal with threats to people and the environment. Some of the new crimes and legal categories created in this era of law reform are discussed below.

Physician-Assisted Suicide Doctors helping people to end their life became the subject of a national debate when Dr. Jack Kevorkian began practicing what he called **obitiatry**, helping people take their lives.[23] In an attempt to stop Kevorkian, Michigan passed a statutory ban on assisted suicide, reflecting what lawmakers believed to be prevailing public opinion; Kevorkian was convicted and imprisoned.[24] He was released on June 1, 2007, on parole due to good behavior and died of natural causes on June 3, 2011, at age 83. Forty-four states now disallow assisted suicide either by statute or common law, including Michigan.[25]

obitiatry
Helping people take their own lives.

Stalking More than 25 states have enacted **stalking** statutes, which prohibit and punish acts described typically as "the willful, malicious, and repeated following and harassing of another person."[26] Stalking laws were originally formulated to protect women terrorized by former husbands and boyfriends, although celebrities often are plagued by stalkers as well. In celebrity cases, these laws often apply to stalkers who are strangers or casual acquaintances of their victims.

stalking
The willful, malicious, and repeated following and harassing of another person.

Community Notification Laws These laws require the registration of people convicted of sex-related crimes; they were enacted in response to concern about sexual predators moving into neighborhoods. One of the best-known such statutes, New Jersey's "Megan's Law," was named after 7-year-old Megan Kanka of Hamilton Township, New Jersey, who was killed in 1994. Charged with the crime was a convicted sex offender who (unknown to the Kankas) lived across the street. On May 17, 1996, President Clinton signed Megan's Law, which contained two components:

- *Sex offender registration.* Requires the states to register individuals convicted of sex crimes against children.
- *Community notification.* Compels the states to make private and personal information on registered sex offenders available to the public.

Controlling Technology The opening vignette discussed two new Internet crimes, vishing and smishing. These cyber crimes are not unique, and their effect on the criminal law has been profound. Such technologies as automatic teller machines and cellular phones have already spawned a new generation of criminal acts involving theft of access numbers and software piracy. Identity theft has become a national problem, and as a result, there has been an ongoing effort by state legislatures to change their criminal codes to penalize sending out bulk email messages designed to trick consumers into revealing bank account passwords, Social Security numbers, and other personal information, as a felony offense.[27]

Protecting the Environment In response to the concerns of environmentalists, the federal government has passed numerous acts designed to protect the nation's well-being. The Environmental Protection Agency has successfully prosecuted significant violations of these and other new laws, including data fraud cases (e.g., private laboratories submitting false environmental data to state and federal environmental agencies); indiscriminate hazardous waste dumping that resulted in serious injuries and death; industrywide ocean dumping by cruise ships; oil spills that caused significant damage to waterways, wetlands, and beaches; and illegal handling of hazardous substances such as pesticides and asbestos that exposed children, the poor, and other especially vulnerable groups to potentially serious illness.[28]

Legalizing Marijuana About 16 states have legalized the use of marijuana for medical purposes and some, including California, allow dispensaries to fill prescriptions.[29] New Jersey Senate Bill 119, signed into law on January 18, 2010,

Environmental laws are designed to protect the public from green-criminals who may dump toxic chemicals in the water supply rather than pay to have them effectively treated. A number of laws protect the water supply in the United States. For example, the Clean Water Act of 1972 prohibits the dumping of toxic chemicals and medical waste. The Safe Drinking Water Act of 1974 set maximum allowable contaminant levels for drinking water and calls for the regular monitoring of groundwater. And the Ocean Dumping Ban prohibited the marine disposal of sewage and industrial waste after 1991.

AP Photo/Damian Dovarganes

protects "patients who use marijuana to alleviate suffering from debilitating medical conditions, as well as their physicians, primary caregivers, and those who are authorized to produce marijuana for medical purposes" from "arrest, prosecution, property forfeiture, and criminal and other penalties."[30]

While providing medical marijuana has strong public support, the federal government still criminalizes any use of marijuana, and federal agents can arrest users even if they have prescriptions from doctors in states where medical marijuana is legal (though federal guidelines "suggest" to local prosecutors that they concentrate their efforts on abusers and not patients in need). In *Gonzales v. Raich*, the Supreme Court ruled that the federal government can prosecute medical marijuana patients, even in states with compassionate use laws.[31]

Fighting Terrorism Soon after the September 11 terrorist attacks, the U.S. government enacted several laws focused on preventing further acts of violence against the United States and creating greater flexibility in the fight to control terrorist activity. Most important, Congress passed the **USA Patriot Act (USAPA)** on October 26, 2001. The bill is over 342 pages long, creates new laws, and makes changes to over 15 different existing statutes. Its aim is to give sweeping new powers to domestic law enforcement and international intelligence agencies in an effort to fight terrorism, to expand the definition of terrorist activities, and to alter sanctions for violent terrorism. USAPA expands all four traditional tools of surveillance—wiretaps, search warrants, pen/trap orders (installing devices that record phone calls), and subpoenas. The Foreign Intelligence Surveillance Act (FISA), which governs domestic operations by intelligence agencies, is also expanded. USAPA gives the FBI greater power to check and monitor phone, Internet, and computer records without first having to demonstrate that they were being used by a suspect or the target of a court order. The act also expands the definition of "terrorism" and enables the government to monitor more closely those people suspected of "harboring" and giving "material support" to terrorists (Sections 803, 805). It increases the authority of the U.S. attorney general to detain and deport noncitizens with little or no judicial review. The attorney general may certify that he has "reasonable grounds to believe" that a noncitizen endangers national security and is therefore eligible for deportation. The attorney general and secretary of state are also given the authority to designate domestic groups as terrorist organizations and to deport any noncitizen who is a member of such an organization.

USA Patriot Act (USAPA)
A law designed to grant new powers to domestic law enforcement and international intelligence agencies in an effort to fight terrorism.

L07 Be familiar with the most recent developments in criminal law reform

Constitutional Criminal Procedure

Whereas substantive criminal law primarily defines crimes, the law of criminal procedure consists of the rules and procedures that govern the pretrial processing of criminal suspects and the conduct of criminal trials. The main source of the procedural law is the body of the Constitution and the first ten amendments added to the Constitution on December 15, 1791, which are collectively known as the **Bill of Rights**. The purpose of these amendments is to prevent the government from usurping the personal freedoms of citizens. The U.S. Supreme Court's interpretation of these amendments has served as the basis for the creation of legal rights of the accused. Of primary concern are the Fourth, Fifth, Sixth, and Eighth Amendments, which limit and control the manner in which the federal government operates the justice system. In addition, the due process clause of the Fourteenth Amendment has been interpreted to apply these limits on governmental action to the state and local levels:

- The Fourth Amendment bars illegal "searches and seizures," a right especially important for the criminal justice system because it means that police officers

RealityCheck

MYTH OR REALITY? Under the Fourth Amendment, in order to search a person, the police must first obtain a search warrant.

MYTH. *Police can search without a warrant in emergency circumstances or if the courts have granted them permission to do so. This loophole has spurred many legal cases defining when and where police can conduct warrantless searches.*

Should a guilty person be allowed to go free simply because police officers made a mistake when they conducted a search? For example, if they opened the trunk of a car and found a dead body in the vehicle, should the driver go free if the search was later ruled illegal? Is there some other possible remedy?

Bill of Rights
The first ten amendments to the U.S. Constitution.

exclusionary rule
Evidence seized in violation of the
Fourth Amendment cannot be used
in a court of law.

cannot indiscriminately use their authority to investigate a possible crime or arrest a suspect. Searching an individual without legal justification represents a serious violation of the Fourth Amendment right to personal privacy. However, the police can search without a warrant in exigent circumstances, such as a search for weapons after a person has been legally arrested. Under the **exclusionary rule**, evidence seized in violation of the Fourth Amendment cannot be used in a court of law; it is as though it never existed.

- The Fifth Amendment limits the admissibility of confessions that have been obtained unfairly. In the 1966 landmark case *Miranda v. Arizona*, the Supreme Court held that a person accused of a crime has the right to refuse to answer questions when placed in police custody.[32] The Fifth Amendment also guarantees defendants the right to a grand jury hearing and to protection from being tried twice for the same crime (double jeopardy). Its due process clause guarantees defendants the right to fundamental fairness and the expectation of fair trials, fair hearings, and similar procedural safeguards.

- The Sixth Amendment guarantees the defendant the right to a speedy and public trial by an impartial jury, the right to be informed of the nature of the charges, and the right to confront any prosecution witnesses. It also contains the right of a defendant to be represented by an attorney—a privilege that has been extended to numerous stages of the criminal justice process, including pretrial custody, identification and lineup procedures, preliminary hearing, submission of a guilty plea, trial, sentencing, and postconviction appeal.

- According to the Eighth Amendment, "Excessive bail shall not be required, nor excessive fines imposed, nor cruel and unusual punishments inflicted." Bail is a money bond put up by the accused to attain freedom between arrest and trial. Bail is meant to ensure a trial appearance, because the bail money is forfeited if the defendant misses the trial date. The Eighth Amendment does not guarantee a constitutional right to bail but, rather, prohibits the use of excessive bail, which is typically defined as an amount far greater than that imposed on similar defendants who are accused of committing similar crimes. The Eighth Amendment also forbids the use of cruel and unusual punishment. This prohibition protects both the accused and convicted offenders from actions regarded as unacceptable by a civilized society, including corporal punishment and torture. Capital punishment, however, is legal unless it is employed in a random, haphazard fashion or if especially cruel means of execution are used.[33] One method used to avoid "cruelty" is lethal injection. In the 2008 case *Baze and Bowling v. Rees*, the Court upheld the use of this method unless there is a "substantial risk of serious harm" that the drugs will not work effectively.[34]

- The Fourteenth Amendment is the vehicle used by the courts to apply the protection of the Bill of Rights to the states. It affirms that no state shall "deprive any person of life, liberty, or property, without due process of law." In essence, the same general constitutional restrictions applicable to the federal government can be imposed on the states.

L08 **Describe the role of the Bill of Rights in shaping criminal procedure**

RealityCheck

MYTH OR REALITY? All U.S. citizens accused of a crime have the right to be released on bail before trial.

MYTH. *Criminal defendants do not have a right to bail, only a right to reasonable bail if pretrial release is granted. Dangerous offenders and those who are a flight risk can be denied bail. Do you agree? Should a person accused of murder ever be given bail? What about rapists? What message does that send to crime victims who have to testify against their attackers who are free in the community?*

Due Process of Law

The concept of due process, found in both the Fifth and Fourteenth Amendments, has been used to evaluate the constitutionality of legal statutes and to set standards and guidelines for fair procedures in the criminal justice system. As you may recall from Chapter 1, some criminal justice experts believe that the concept of due process is the lens through which the criminal justice system must be examined. Without the application of due process, civil rights and constitutional protections are meaningless. In seeking to define the term, most legal experts believe that it refers to the essential elements of fairness under law.[35] This definition basically refers to the legal system's need for rules and regulations that protect individual rights.

■ Under the concept of due process, Courts are asked to decide the fundamental rights of American citizens. In *Mapp v. Ohio*, 367 U.S. 643 (1961), the United States Supreme Court decided that evidence obtained from the home of Dolree Mapp (shown on left) without a warrant was in violation of the Fourth Amendment, and could not be used in criminal prosecutions in state courts, as well as federal courts. While *Mapp* increased suspect rights, the Court narrowed them in *Herring v. United States*, 555 U.S. 135 (2009), when it decided that a search is legal if a police officer makes an arrest and search based on an outstanding warrant in another jurisdiction, only to later find out that the warrant has already been withdrawn. Because the mistake was inadvertent, the evidence was allowed at trial and Herring (shown on right) was convicted and sent to prison.

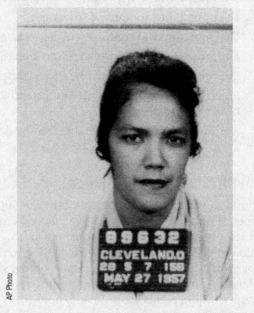

Due process can actually be divided into two distinct categories, substantive and procedural. Substantive due process refers to the citizen's right to be protected from criminal laws that may be biased, discriminatory, and otherwise unfair. These laws may be vague or may apply unfairly to one group and not others. Civil libertarians are troubled by some of the actions taken by the various law enforcement agencies to combat terrorism, maintaining that the harshest measures are eroding civil rights. For example, there are provisions in the Patriot Act that permit the government to share information from grand jury proceedings and from criminal wiretaps with intelligence agencies. There is concern that the Patriot Act authority is not limited to true terrorism but that investigations cover a much broader range of activity involving reasonable political dissent. Even though many critics have called for its repeal, it was reauthorized in 2006 with a slew of provisions ensuring that the Act did not violate civil rights by limiting its surveillance and wiretap authorizations.

There has also been significant controversy over the long-term detention of suspected terrorists without trial at the Guantánamo camp in Cuba. Although this complex issue is far from resolved, in *Boumediene v. Bush* the Supreme Court held that the Guantánamo prisoners had a right to *habeas corpus* protection under the United States Constitution.[36] *Boumediene*, along with similar cases, indicates that terror suspects are not denied the protection of the U.S. Constitution and that their indefinite detention without trial is not legally permissible. On January 7, 2011, President Obama signed the 2011 Defense Authorization Bill, which contains provisions preventing the transfer of Guantánamo prisoners to the mainland or to other foreign countries, a measure that continues the use of this overseas detention facility.

Procedural due process seeks to ensure that no person will be deprived of life, liberty, or property without proper and legal criminal process. Basically, procedural due process is intended to guarantee that fundamental fairness exists in each individual case. Specific due process procedures include the following:

1. Freedom from illegal searches and interrogations
2. Prompt notice of charges and a formal hearing

L09 List the elements of due process of law

3. The right to counsel or some other representation
4. The opportunity to respond to charges
5. The opportunity to confront and cross-examine witnesses and accusers
6. The privilege to be free from self-incrimination
7. The opportunity to present one's own witnesses
8. A decision made on the basis of substantial evidence and facts produced at the hearing
9. A written statement of the reasons for the decision
10. An appellate review procedure

LO10 Know about the role the Supreme Court plays in interpreting the Constitution and shaping procedural law

Interpreting the Constitution

Within the context of due process, how the Supreme Court decides a specific case depends on the facts of the case, the federal and state constitutional and statutory provisions, previous court decisions, and judicial philosophy.[37] The judicial interpretation of the Constitution is not fixed but reflects what society deems fair and just at a particular time and place. The degree of loss suffered by the individual (victim or offender), balanced against the state's interests, also determines how many constitutional requirements are ordinarily applied. When the Supreme Court justices are conservative, as they are now, they are less likely to create new rights and privileges and more likely to restrict civil liberties. Take the 2009 case of *Herring v. U.S.*, which involved interpretation of the exclusionary rule.[38] Bennie Dean Herring had been searched after the police were informed that there was an outstanding warrant against him on a felony charge. The search turned up methamphetamine and a pistol. Soon after, it was discovered that the warrant had actually been withdrawn five months earlier and had been left in the computer system by mistake. Should the evidence be discarded because the police made an error? Or should it be allowed because they acted in good faith based on existing evidence that later proved inaccurate? The majority decision ruled that "When police mistakes leading to an unlawful search are the result of isolated negligence attenuated from the search, rather than systemic error or reckless disregard of constitutional requirements, the exclusionary rule does not apply." The Court ruled that the errors in the *Herring* case did not amount to deliberate police misconduct that should trigger the exclusionary rule.

Ethical Challenge

In 1997, Louise Woodward, a teenage British nanny, was accused of first-degree murder; she was alleged to have shaken to death Matthew Eappen, the infant she was babysitting. Prosecutors claimed that Woodward was so frustrated by the crying child that she first shook him and then slammed the infant against a hard surface to silence him. Woodward's defense claimed that she did not cause Eappen's death and that a prior incident must have caused the baby's skull fracture.

After the jury found Woodward guilty of second-degree murder, Hiller B. Zobel, the trial judge, reduced Woodward's sentence to manslaughter because he concluded that the intent to do bodily harm or act with malice was not present. Involuntary manslaughter is a killing with no intention to cause serious bodily harm, such as acting without proper caution. Woodward was soon released.

Write an essay commenting on the judge's behavior: Is it fair for a trial judge to overturn a jury verdict and impose his will on the people? Does that allow a single person to control the content of the law? What are some harmful outcomes that might occur if this became a common practice? What are some of the benefits?

Summary

LO1 **Know the similarities and differences between criminal law and civil law** The law today can generally be divided into four broad categories. Substantive criminal law defines crimes and their punishment. Procedural criminal law sets out the basic rules of practice in the criminal justice system. Civil law governs relations between private parties, including both individuals and organizations (such as business enterprises and/or corporations). Administrative or public law controls the behavior of government agencies.

L02 **Understand the concept of substantive criminal law and its history** The roots of the criminal codes used in the United States can be traced to such early legal charters as the Babylonian Code of Hammurabi (2000 BCE) and the Mosaic Code of the Israelites (1200 BCE). In the Middle Ages, societies developed legal systems featuring monetary compensation, called *wergild*. After the Norman Conquest, royal judges would decide what to do in each case, using local custom and rules of conduct as a guide in a system known as *stare decisis* (Latin for "to stand by decided cases"). Eventually this system evolved into a common law of the country that incorporated local custom and practice into a national code.

L03 **Discuss the sources of the criminal law** The contemporary American legal system was codified by state and federal legislatures. The content of the law may also be influenced by judicial decision making. Regardless of its source, all criminal law in the United States must conform to the rules and dictates of the Constitution.

L04 **Be familiar with the elements of a crime** Almost all common-law crime contains both mental and physical elements. The *actus reus* is a voluntary and deliberate illegal act, such as taking someone's money, burning a building, or shooting someone. For an act to constitute a crime, it must be done with deliberate purpose or criminal intent, or *mens rea*.

L05 **Define the term *strict liability*** Thought alone is not a crime. For a person to be considered to have committed a crime, some act is required to prove her or his willingness to cause harm. Certain statutory offenses exist in which *mens rea* is not essential. These offenses fall in a category known as public safety or strict liability crimes.

L06 **Be able to discuss excuses and justification defenses for crime** When people defend themselves against criminal charges, they must refute one or more of the elements of the crime of which they have been accused.

Defendants may deny the *actus reus* by arguing that they were falsely accused and the real culprit has yet to be identified. Defendants may also claim that even though they did engage in the criminal act they are accused of, they should be excused because they lacked *mens rea*.

L07 **Be familiar with the most recent developments in criminal law reform** The criminal law is constantly changing and being updated. New crimes have been created to control stalking, environmental damage, cyber crime, and terrorism. Others have been decriminalized or legalized, such as sodomy. In some cases, such as distributing medical marijuana, states may legalize acts that are still banned by federal law.

L08 **Describe the role of the Bill of Rights in shaping criminal procedure** The main source of the procedural law is the body of the Constitution and the first ten amendments—the Bill of Rights—added to the Constitution on December 15, 1791. Of primary concern are the Fourth, Fifth, Sixth, and Eighth Amendments, which limit and control the manner in which the federal government operates the justice system.

L09 **List the elements of due process of law** The concept of due process is found in both the Fifth and Fourteenth Amendments. Due process has been used to evaluate the constitutionality of legal statutes and to set standards and guidelines for fair procedures in the criminal justice system.

L010 **Know about the role the Supreme Court plays in interpreting the Constitution and shaping procedural law** The law of criminal procedure consists of the rules and procedures that govern the pretrial processing of criminal suspects and the conduct of criminal trials. It is the job of the Supreme Court to interpret the Constitution and set limits on governmental behavior—for example, limiting the ability of the police in their searching, questioning, and punishing those suspected of crime.

Review Questions

1. What are the specific aims and purposes of the criminal law? To what extent does the criminal law control behavior?

2. What kinds of activities should be labeled criminal in contemporary society? Why?

3. What is a criminal act? What is a criminal state of mind? When are individuals liable for their actions?

4. Discuss the various kinds of crime classifications. To what extent or degree are they distinguishable?

5. Numerous states are revising their penal codes. Which major categories of substantive crimes do you think should be revised?

6. Entrapment is a defense when the defendant was lured, beguiled, or enticed into committing the crime by police. Is it ever ethical for law enforcement agents to encourage people to commit crime?

7. What legal principles can be used to justify self-defense? Given that the law seeks to prevent crime, not promote it, are such principles sound?

8. What are the minimum standards of criminal procedure required in the criminal justice system?

THE POLICE AND LAW ENFORCEMENT

There are a number of career options in law enforcement, the most common being that of a municipal police officer. Duties include:

- Enforcing the laws of the jurisdiction
- Patrolling, investigating crime, testifying in court, and writing reports
- Specialized tasks if assigned to a particular unit, such as SWAT (Special Weapons and Tactics)

Advantages of police work include job security, good salary, the potential for excitement and action, and helping the public and preserving public safety. The downside can include:

- Stress from encounters with hostile people and unpleasant situations
- Shifts that fall on weekends and holidays
- Overtime work (this is also a benefit to some because of the added pay)

Steve Bishopp, a sergeant with the Dallas Police Department, knows firsthand some of the frustrations that can result from a career in law enforcement. Besides the usual frustrations, he feels another challenge is dealing with family and friends who are not cops.

People don't understand how we can describe a gruesome and violent crime scene and joke about it, but that is sometimes how we deal with the difficult situations we face. I also don't care much to be introduced everywhere I go as "Steve Bishopp, the cop." It bothers me when the conversation turns to, "Hey, why do you cops always..."

At the same time, Steve loves his job. He feels that its most rewarding aspect is the opportunity to put truly bad people in jail.

I've come across some truly violent, vicious people that should never be out in society. I have worked many bloody and violent murders and sexual assaults, and putting those people in jail (particularly after assisting

the prosecution in getting a conviction) gives me a huge sense of accomplishment and pride.

Numerous law enforcement careers are available beyond the local level. One such position is that of a state trooper. State troopers perform many of the same functions as local law enforcement officials, but depending on the states in which they work, they may focus primarily on traffic enforcement or exercise general police powers throughout the whole state.

Massachusetts State Trooper John Sullivan thinks the greatest challenges on his job are keeping a positive attitude and avoiding the temptation to become cynical. Law enforcement officials are often called upon to make difficult decisions, and some of these decisions come to the attention of the press. John feels that, unfortunately, many times reporters portray the police in a critical light. This sometimes makes it hard for him and his colleagues to maintain a favorable attitude toward the public.

While it is true that a law enforcement career can be difficult, it also carries with it the potential for great personal fulfillment. John especially prizes his capability to turn what could otherwise become a negative encounter with the public into a positive one. Not every interaction with the police has to result in a citation, arrest, or other formal sanction. Part of the job, he says, is community caretaking.

"I've come across some truly violent, vicious people that should never be out in society . . . and putting those people in jail (particularly after assisting the prosecution in getting a conviction) gives me a huge sense of accomplishment and pride."
Steve Bishopp

Part 2 of this text covers policing. Chapter 4 looks at the history and organization of law enforcement organizations at all levels of government. Chapter 5 discusses the role and function of policing, including patrol, investigations, and community policing. Chapter 6 tackles a number of contemporary issues in policing, among them police culture, discretion, stress fatigue, and use of force. Chapter 6 also provides an introduction to the legal environment within which the police must operate.

Morganne Portyka, 11, holds a sign she made on behalf of her father, Delaware State Police Officer Andrew Portyka, during a rally held by state employees outside of Legislative Hall in Dover. State workers were protesting the governor's proposal to cut their pay in order to help balance the budget.

AP Photo/*The News Journal*, Bob Herbert

4

Police in Society: History and Organization

Learning Objectives

LO1 Describe how law enforcement developed in feudal England

LO2 Summarize characteristics of the first law enforcement agencies

LO3 Discuss the development of law enforcement in the United States

LO4 Analyze the problems of early police agencies

LO5 Discuss how reformers attempted to create professional police agencies

LO6 Describe the major changes in law enforcement between 1970 and today

LO7 Be familiar with the major federal law enforcement agencies

LO8 Summarize the differences among state, county, and local law enforcement

LO9 Explain the role of technology in police work

Cities all across the country are being forced to cope with budget cuts. Services are being curtailed, employees are being furloughed, and capital improvements are being delayed—if not canceled altogether. Throughout history, police department spending has rarely landed on the chopping block, but in light of the difficult economic conditions America is facing, no public agency is immune. No one likes to cut spending for crime prevention, but in some locales it has become necessary. ■

Police departments nationwide are adopting a range of creative—and controversial—strategies to respond to mandates that they limit spending. Some of them, such as in Temecula, California, have placed limits on overtime, putting caps on the amount of extra work officers can put in.[1] Other cities, including Philadelphia, have left hundreds of positions unfilled.[2] Still others are offering senior officers early retirement. In one extreme case, the city of Toledo, Ohio, made cost-saving alterations to police and fire contracts without union input.[3] Citing falling tax revenues, officials said that economic conditions amounted to an "exigent circumstance" that gave them no choice.

Spending limits and budget cuts seem to prevail more than growth and expansion. Interestingly, the New York City Police Department is now around the same size it was 20 years ago.[4] This trend raises interesting questions for public safety. Do cuts in hiring affect crime? Do other restrictions limit police effectiveness? Will we see an increase in crime because of criminal justice spending cuts? Only time will tell.

The police are the gatekeepers of the criminal justice process. They initiate contact with violators of the law and decide whether to arrest them formally and start their journey through the criminal justice system, to settle the issue in an informal way (such as by issuing a warning), or to take no action at all. The strategic position of law enforcement officers, their visibility and contact with the public, and their use of weapons and arrest power kept them in the forefront of public thought for most of the twentieth century.

This and the following two chapters evaluate the history, role, organizational issues, and procedures of police agents and agencies and discuss the legal rules that control police behavior.

The History of Police

The origin of U.S. police agencies, like the origins of criminal law, can be traced to early English society.[5] Before the Norman Conquest in 1066 BCE, no regular English police force existed. Every person living in the villages scattered throughout the countryside was responsible for aiding neighbors and protecting the settlement from thieves and marauders. This was known as the "pledge system." People were grouped in collectives of 10 families, called **tithings**, and were entrusted with policing their own minor problems. When trouble occurred, the citizen was expected to make a **hue and cry**. Ten tithings were grouped into what was called a **hundred**, whose affairs were supervised by a **constable** appointed by the local nobleman. The constable, who might be considered the first real police officer, dealt with more serious breaches of the law.[6]

Shires, which resembled the counties of today, were controlled by the **shire reeve**, who was appointed by the Crown or by a local landowner to supervise the territory and ensure that order was kept. The shire reeve, a forerunner of today's **sheriff**, soon began to pursue and apprehend law violators as part of his duties.

tithing
In medieval England, a group of 10 families who collectively dealt with minor disturbances and breaches of the peace.

LO1 **Describe how law enforcement developed in feudal England**

hue and cry
In medieval England, a call for assistance. The policy of self-help that prevailed in villages demanded that everyone respond if a citizen raised a hue and cry to get their aid.

hundred
In medieval England, a group of 100 families responsible for maintaining order and trying minor offenses.

constable
In medieval England, an appointed official who administered and supervised the legal affairs of a small community.

shire reeve
In medieval England, the senior law enforcement figure in a county; the forerunner of today's sheriff.

sheriff
The chief law enforcement officer in a county.

LO2 **Summarize characteristics of the first law enforcement agencies**

watch system
During the Middle Ages in England, men were organized in church parishes to guard at night against disturbances and breaches of the peace under the direction of the local constable.

justice of the peace
Established in 1326 England, the office was created to help the shire reeve in controlling the county; it later took on judicial functions.

In the thirteenth century, the **watch system** was created to help protect property in England's larger cities and towns. Watchmen patrolled at night and helped protect the community against robberies, fires, and disturbances. They reported to the area constable, who became the primary metropolitan law enforcement agent. In larger cities, such as London, the watchmen were organized within church parishes and were usually members of the parish they protected.

In 1326, the office of **justice of the peace** was created to assist the shire reeve in controlling the county. Eventually, these justices took on judicial functions in addition to their primary role as peacekeepers. The local constable became the operational assistant to the justice of the peace, supervising the night watchmen, investigating offenses, serving summonses, executing warrants, and securing prisoners. This system helped establish the relationship between police and the judiciary, which has continued for more than 670 years.

Private Police and Thief Takers

As the eighteenth century began, rising crime rates encouraged a new form of private, monied police, who profited both legally and criminally from the lack of formal police departments. These private police agents, referred to as "thief takers," were universally corrupt, taking profits not only from catching and informing on criminals but also from receiving stolen property, theft, intimidation, perjury, and blackmail. They often relieved their prisoners of money and stolen goods and made even more income by accepting hush money, giving perjured evidence, swearing false oaths, and operating extortion rackets. Petty debtors were especially easy targets for those who combined thief taking with the keeping of alehouses and taverns. While prisoners were incarcerated, their health and safety were entirely at the whim of the thief takers, who were free to charge virtually whatever they wanted for board and other necessities. Court bailiffs who also acted as thief takers were the most passionately detested legal profiteers. They seized debtors and held them in small lockups, where they forced their victims to pay exorbitant prices for food and lodging.

The thief takers' use of violence was notorious. They went armed and were prepared to maim or kill in order to gain their objectives. Before he was hanged in 1725, Jack Wild, the most notorious thief taker, "had two fractures in his skull and his bald head was covered with silver plates. He had seventeen wounds in various parts of his body from swords, daggers, and gunshots, [and] . . . his throat had been cut in the course of his duties."[7]

Henry Fielding (famed author of *Tom Jones*), along with Saunders Welch and his brother John Fielding, sought to clean up the thief-taking system. Appointed a city magistrate in 1748, Henry Fielding operated his own group of monied police out of Bow Street in London, directing and deploying them throughout the city and its environs, deciding which cases to investigate and what streets to protect. His agents were carefully instructed on their legitimate powers and duties. Fielding's Bow Street Runners were a marked improvement over the earlier monied police, because they actually had an administrative structure that improved record keeping and investigative procedures.

Creating Public Police

In 1829, Sir Robert Peel, England's home secretary, guided through Parliament an "Act for Improving the Police in and near the Metropolis." The Metropolitan Police Act established the first organized police force in London. Composed of over 1,000 men, the London police force was structured along military lines; its members were known from then on as "bobbies," after its creator. They wore a distinctive uniform and were led by two magistrates, who were later given the title of commissioner. However, the ultimate responsibility for the police fell to the home secretary and consequently to the Parliament.

The early bobbies suffered from many of the same ills as their forebears. Many were corrupt, they were unsuccessful at stopping crime, and they were influenced by the wealthy. Owners of houses of ill repute, who in the past had guaranteed their undisturbed operations by bribing watchmen, now turned their attention to the bobbies. Metropolitan police administrators fought constantly to terminate cowardly, corrupt, and alcoholic officers, dismissing in the beginning about one-third of the bobbies each year.

Law Enforcement in Colonial America

Law enforcement in colonial America paralleled the British model. In the colonies, the county sheriff became the most important law enforcement agent. In addition to keeping the peace and fighting crime, sheriffs collected taxes, supervised elections, and handled a great deal of other legal business.

The colonial sheriff did not patrol or seek out crime. Instead, he reacted to citizens' complaints and investigated crimes that had occurred. His salary, related to his effectiveness, was paid on a fee system. Sheriffs received a fixed amount for every arrest made. Unfortunately, their tax-collecting chores were more lucrative than fighting crime, so law enforcement was not one of their primary concerns. In the cities, law enforcement was the province of the town marshal, who was aided, often unwillingly, by a variety of constables, night watchmen, police justices, and city council members. However, local governments had little power of administration, and enforcement of the criminal law was largely an individual or community responsibility. In rural areas in the South, slave patrols charged with recapturing escaped slaves were an early—if loathsome—form of law enforcement.[8] When these patrols apprehended runaway slaves, they administered "justice" on the spot, often with violence. In the western territories, individual initiative was encouraged by the practice of offering rewards for the capture of felons. If trouble arose, the town vigilance committee might form a posse to chase offenders. These **vigilantes** were called on to eradicate such social problems as theft of livestock through force or intimidation; the San Francisco Vigilance Committee actively pursued criminals in the mid-nineteenth century.

Early Police Agencies

The modern police department was born out of urban mob violence that wracked the nation's cities in the nineteenth century. Boston created the first formal U.S. police department in 1838. New York formed its police department in 1844, Philadelphia in 1854. The new police departments replaced the night-watch system and relegated constables and sheriffs to serving court orders and running jails.

At first, the urban police departments inherited the functions of the institutions they replaced. For example, Boston police were charged with maintaining public health until 1853, and in New York the police were responsible for street sweeping until 1881. Politics dominated the departments and determined the recruitment of new officers and the promotion of supervisors. An individual with the right connections could be hired despite a lack of qualifications. Early police agencies were corrupt, brutal, and inefficient.[9] At first, police were expected to live in the area they patrolled, but as the nineteenth century drew to a close, officers left the most dangerous areas and commuted to work, thereby separating themselves from the people they were being asked to supervise and control.[10]

In the late nineteenth century, police work was highly desirable because it paid more than most other blue-collar jobs. By 1880, the average factory worker earned $450 a year, whereas a metropolitan police officer made $900 annually. For immigrant groups, having enough political clout to be appointed to the police department was an important step up the social ladder.[11] However, job security was uncertain because it depended on the local political machine staying in power.

Police work itself was primitive. There were few of even the simplest technological innovations common today, such as centralized record keeping. Most officers patrolled on foot, without backup or the ability to call for help. Officers

vigilantes
Groups of citizens who tracked down wanted criminals in the Old West.

LO3 Discuss the development of law enforcement in the United States

■ John X. Beidler, pictured here, was leader of the Montana Vigilantes, a secretive band formed to fight crime in Montana in the 1860s. He later became a stagecoach guard and a deputy U.S. marshal. Vigilante groups like Beidler's were precursors to organized police forces in colonial America.

© Print Collector/HIP/The Image Works

were commonly taunted by local toughs and responded with force and brutality. The long-standing conflict between police and the public was born in the difficulty that untrained, unprofessional officers had in patrolling the streets of nineteenth-century U.S. cities and in breaking up and controlling labor disputes. Police were not crime fighters as we know them today. Their main role was maintaining order, and their power was almost unchecked. The average officer had little training, no education in the law, and a minimum of supervision, yet the police became virtual judges of law and fact with the ability to exercise unlimited discretion.[12]

Police during the nineteenth century were regarded as incompetent and corrupt and were disliked by the people they served. The police role was only minimally directed at law enforcement. Its primary function was serving as the enforcement arm of the reigning political power, protecting private property, and keeping control of the ever-rising numbers of foreign immigrants.

Police agencies evolved slowly through the second half of the nineteenth century. Uniforms were introduced in 1853 in New York. The first technological breakthroughs in police operations came in the area of communications. The linking of precincts to central headquarters by telegraph began in the 1850s. In 1867, the first telegraph police boxes were installed; an officer could turn a key in a box, and his location and number would automatically register at headquarters. Additional technological advances were made in transportation. The Detroit Police Department outfitted some of its patrol officers with bicycles in 1897. By 1913, the motorcycle was being used by departments in the eastern part of the nation. The first police car was used in Akron, Ohio, in 1910, and the police wagon became popular in Cincinnati in 1912.[13] Nonpolice functions, such as care of the streets, had begun to be abandoned by police departments after the Civil War.

RealityCheck

MYTH OR REALITY? During the nineteenth century, the police were regarded as competent and professional.

MYTH. *Policing in the 1800s was anything but professional. Competence often was lacking as well. It would not be until the 1900s that police departments began making major strides toward professionalism.*

Is policing a profession today? What are the hallmarks of a profession?

The control of police departments by local politicians impeded effective law enforcement and fostered an atmosphere of graft and corruption. In the nineteenth century, big-city police were still not respected by the public, were largely unsuccessful in their role as crime stoppers, and were involved in no progressive activities.

L04 Analyze the problems of early police agencies

Policing in the Twentieth Century

The modern era of policing can be traced from the turn of the nineteenth century to the present. What are the major events that occurred during this period?

The Emergence of Professionalism

In an effort to reduce police corruption, civic leaders in a number of jurisdictions created police administrative boards to reduce local officials' control over the police. These tribunals were responsible for appointing police administrators and controlling police affairs. In many instances, these measures failed because the private citizens appointed to the review boards lacked expertise in the intricacies of police work. Another reform movement was the takeover of some metropolitan police agencies by state legislators. Although police budgets were financed through local taxes, control of police was usurped by rural politicians in the state capitals. New York City temporarily lost authority over its police force in 1857. It was not until the first decades of the twentieth century that cities regained control of their police forces.

The Boston police strike of 1919 heightened interest in police reform. The strike came about basically because police officers were dissatisfied with their status in society. Other professions were unionizing and increasing their standard of living, but police salaries lagged behind. The Boston police officers' organization, the Boston Social Club, voted to become a union affiliated with the American Federation of Labor. The officers went out on strike on September 9, 1919. Rioting and looting broke out, resulting in Governor Calvin Coolidge's mobilization of the state militia to take over the city. Public support turned against the police, and the strike was broken. Eventually, all the striking officers were fired and replaced by new recruits. The Boston police strike ended police unionism for decades and solidified power in the hands of reactionary, autocratic police administrators. In the aftermath of the strike, various local, state, and federal crime commissions began to investigate the extent of crime and the ability of the justice system to deal with it effectively; they then made recommendations to improve police effectiveness.[14] With the onset of the Depression, however, justice reform became a less important issue than economic revival, and for many years little changed in the nature of policing.

At about the same time, a number of nationally recognized leaders called for measures to help improve and professionalize the police. In 1893, the International Association of Chiefs of Police (IACP), a professional society, was formed. The IACP called for creating a civil service police force and for removing political influence and control. The most famous police reformer of the time was August Vollmer. While serving as police chief of Berkeley, California, Vollmer instituted university training for young officers and helped develop the School of Criminology at the University of California at Berkeley. Vollmer's disciples included O. W. Wilson, who pioneered the use of advanced training for officers and was instrumental in applying modern management and administrative techniques to policing. During this period, police professionalism was equated with an incorruptible, tough, highly trained, rule-oriented department organized along militaristic lines. The most respected department was that of Los Angeles, which emphasized the police as incorruptible crime fighters who would not question the authority of the central command.

L05 Discuss how reformers attempted to create professional police agencies

Great precaution is taken to guard police headquarters in Pemberton Square during the Boston police strike of 1919. Here the cavalrymen of the state guard ride horses previously used by the mounted policemen who went on strike. The Boston police strike ended police unionism for decades and solidified power in the hands of reactionary, autocratic police administrators. In the aftermath of the strike, various local, state, and federal crime commissions began to investigate the extent of crime and the ability of the justice system to deal with it and made recommendations to improve police effectiveness.

© AP Images/Boston Public Library

The 1960s and Beyond

Turmoil and crisis were the hallmarks of policing during the 1960s. Throughout this decade, the Supreme Court handed down a number of decisions designed to control police operations and procedures. Police officers were now required to follow strict legal guidelines when questioning suspects, conducting searches, and wiretapping, among other duties. As the civil rights of suspects were significantly expanded, police complained that they were being "handcuffed by the courts."

Also during this time, civil unrest produced a growing tension between police and the public. African Americans, who were battling for recognition and enforcement of their rights and freedoms in the civil rights movement, found themselves confronting police lines. When riots broke out in New York, Detroit, Los Angeles, and other cities between 1964 and 1968, the spark that ignited conflict often involved the police. When students across the nation began marching in anti–Vietnam War demonstrations, local police departments were called on to keep order. Police forces were ill equipped and poorly trained to deal with these social problems; it is not surprising that the 1960s were marked by a number of bloody confrontations between the police and the public.

Confounding these problems was a rapidly growing crime rate. The number of violent and property crimes increased dramatically. Drug addiction and abuse grew to be national concerns, common among all social classes. Urban police departments could not control the crime rate, and police officers resented the demands placed on them by dissatisfied citizens.

The 1970s witnessed many structural changes in police agencies themselves. The end of the Vietnam War significantly reduced tensions between students and police. The relationship between police and minorities was still rocky, however. Local fears and distrust, combined with conservative federal policies, encouraged police departments to control what was perceived as an emerging minority group "threat."[15]

Increased federal government support for criminal justice greatly influenced police operations. During the decade, the Law Enforcement Assistance Administration (LEAA) devoted a significant portion of its funds to police agencies. Although a number of police departments used this money to purchase little-used hardware, such as antiriot gear, most of it went to supporting innovative research on police work and advanced training of police officers. Perhaps most significant, the

LEAA's Law Enforcement Education Program helped thousands of officers further their college education. Hundreds of criminal justice programs were developed on college campuses around the country, providing a pool of highly educated police recruits. LEAA funds were also used to transfer technology originally developed in other fields into law enforcement. Technological innovations involving computers transformed the way police kept records, investigated crimes, and communicated with one another. State training academies improved the way police learned to deal with such issues as job stress, community conflict, and interpersonal relations. More women and minorities were recruited into police work. Affirmative action programs helped to slowly alter the ethnic, racial, and gender composition of U.S. policing.

As the 1980s began, the police role seemed to be changing significantly. A number of experts acknowledged that the police were not simply crime fighters and called for police to develop a greater awareness of community issues, which resulted in the emergence of the community policing concept.[16]

Police unions, which began to grow again in the late 1960s, continued to have a great impact on departmental administration in the 1980s. Unions fought for and won increased salaries and benefits for their members. In many instances, union efforts eroded the power of the police chief to make unquestioned policy and personnel decisions. During the decade, chiefs of police commonly consulted with union leaders before making significant decisions about departmental operations.

Although police operations improved markedly during this time, police departments were also beset by problems that impeded their effectiveness. State and local budgets were cut back during the Reagan administration, and federal support for innovative police programs was severely curtailed with the demise of the LEAA.

Police–community relations continued to be a major problem. Riots and incidents of urban conflict occurred in some of the nation's largest cities.[17] They triggered persistent concern about what the police role should be, especially in inner-city neighborhoods.

The 1990s began on a sour note and ended with an air of optimism. The incident that helped change the face of American policing occurred on March 3, 1991, when Rodney King and his friend Bryant Allen were driving in Los Angeles, California. They refused to stop when signaled by a police car behind them but instead increased their speed; King, the driver, was apparently drunk or on drugs. When police finally stopped the car, they delivered 56 baton blows and 6 kicks to King in a period of two minutes, producing 11 skull fractures, brain damage, and kidney damage. They did not realize that their actions were being videotaped by an observer, who later gave the tape to the media. The officers involved were eventually tried and acquitted in a suburban court by an all-white jury, a decision that set off six days of rioting.[18]

The King case prompted an era of reform. Several police experts decreed that the nation's police forces should be evaluated not on their crime-fighting ability but on their courteousness, deportment, and helpfulness. Interest was renewed in reviving an earlier style of police work featuring foot patrols and increased citizen contact. Police departments began to embrace new forms of policing that stressed cooperation with the community and problem solving. The following are some of the most notable achievements of police departments in the 1990s:

- The intellectual caliber of the police rose dramatically.
- Police began to use advanced management techniques and applied empirical data to their decision making.
- Standards of police conduct climbed. Despite well-publicized incidents of brutality, police tended to treat the public more fairly, more equitably, and more civilly than they did in the 1960s.
- Police became more diverse in race and gender.
- The work of the police became intellectually more demanding, requiring an array of new specialized knowledge about technology, forensic analysis, and crime.
- Police gradually accepted civilian review of police discipline.[19]

L06 Describe the major changes in law enforcement between 1970 and today

Policing and Law Enforcement Today

Contemporary law enforcement agencies are still undergoing transformation. There has been an ongoing effort to make police "user friendly" by decentralizing police departments and making them responsive to community needs. Police and law enforcement agencies are also adapting to the changing nature of crime: they must be prepared to handle terrorism, Internet fraud schemes, and identity theft, as well as rape, robbery, and burglary.[20]

Law enforcement duties are distributed across local, county, state, and federal jurisdictions. There are approximately 700,000 sworn law enforcement officers in the United States, employed in almost 20,000 different agencies.[21] Police and law enforcement agencies can be found in a variety of levels of government. There is no real hierarchy, and each branch has its own sphere of operations, though overlap may exist.

Federal Law Enforcement Agencies

The federal government has a number of law enforcement agencies designed to protect the rights and privileges of U.S. citizens; no single agency has unlimited jurisdiction, and each has been created to enforce specific laws and cope with particular situations. Federal agencies have no particular rank order or hierarchy of command or responsibility; each reports to a specific department or bureau.

Dozens of federal law enforcement agencies exist both inside and outside the cabinet-level departments. Here we focus on law enforcement agencies in two cabinet-level departments: the U.S. Justice Department and the Department of Homeland Security.

U.S. Justice Department Agencies The U.S. Justice Department houses four of the better-known federal law enforcement agencies.

FBI agents arrest a suspect during a mafia sweep. In conjunction with local authorities, agents arrested close to 130 people, including members of crime families from New York and New Jersey and several union officials, on charges including murder, racketeering, and extortion. Though homeland security is a top priority at the FBI these days, the agency still targets people who violate federal laws.

© Pool / The New York Times/Redux

- **Federal Bureau of Investigation (FBI)** The Federal Bureau of Investigation is an investigative agency with jurisdiction over all matters in which the United States is or may be an interested party. Its jurisdiction is limited, however, to federal laws, including all federal statutes not specifically assigned to other agencies. The FBI has approximately 30,000 employees, including more than 12,000 special agents and 17,000 support personnel who perform professional, administrative, technical, clerical, craft, trade, or maintenance operations. Since 9/11, the FBI has announced a reformulation of its priorities, making protecting the United States from terrorist attack its number one commitment. It is now charged with coordinating intelligence collection with the Border Patrol, the Secret Service, and the CIA. Among the agency's other activities are gathering crime statistics, running a comprehensive crime laboratory, and training local law enforcement officers.

- **Drug Enforcement Administration (DEA)** DEA agents assist local and state authorities in investigating illegal drug use and carrying out independent surveillance and enforcement activities to control the importation of narcotics. For example, DEA agents work with foreign governments in cooperative efforts aimed at destroying opium and marijuana crops at their source—hard-to-find fields tucked away in the interiors of Latin America, Asia, Europe, and Africa. Undercover DEA agents infiltrate drug rings and simulate buying narcotics to arrest drug dealers.

- **Bureau of Alcohol, Tobacco, Firearms, and Explosives (ATF)** The ATF helps control sales of untaxed liquor and cigarettes and, through the Gun Control Act of 1968 and the Organized Crime Control Act of 1970, has jurisdiction over the illegal sale, importation, and criminal misuse of firearms and explosives.

- **U.S. Marshals Service** The U.S. Marshals Service is America's oldest federal law enforcement agency and one of the most versatile. Its more than 3,000 deputy marshals and criminal investigators perform a number of functions, including judicial security, fugitive investigations, witness protection, prisoner transportation, prisoner services (the agency houses nearly 60,000 federal detainees each day), and administration of the U.S. Justice Department's Asset Forfeiture Program.

Homeland Security Agencies Soon after the 9/11 attacks on the Pentagon and the World Trade Center towers in New York City, President Bush proposed the creation of a new cabinet-level agency called the **Department of Homeland Security (DHS)**. On November 19, 2002, Congress passed legislation authorizing the creation of the DHS and assigned it the mission of providing intelligence analysis and infrastructure protection, strengthening the borders, improving the use of science and technology to counter weapons of mass destruction, and creating a comprehensive response and recovery division. Rather than working from the ground up, the DHS combined a number of existing agencies into a superagency that carries out a variety of missions, from border security to infrastructure protection. Two of the main law enforcement agencies housed within DHS are described in some detail below. We will revisit the work of the DHS in Chapter 14.

- **Customs and Border Protection (CBP)** After 9/11, the U.S. Border Patrol, portions of the U.S. Customs Service, the Immigration and Naturalization Service, and the Animal and Plant Health Inspection Service were combined into one office of Customs and Border Protection. The agency employs more than 40,000 personnel and is primarily responsible for protection of America's borders and ports of entry. The largest and most visible element of CBP is the Border Patrol. Its 10,000 agents combine to form one of the largest uniformed law enforcement agencies in the United States (see the Careers in Criminal Justice feature).

RealityCheck

MYTH OR REALITY? The core mission of the FBI is to enforce the criminal laws of the United States.

MYTH. Since 9/11, the FBI's priorities have changed. Now protection of the United States from terrorist attacks ranks near the top if its priority list.

To what extent does the FBI's decision to give priority to protection from terrorism affect its ability to fight other types of crime? Has America's law enforcement apparatus overreacted to the threat of terrorism?

Federal Bureau of Investigation (FBI)
The arm of the U.S. Justice Department that investigates violations of federal law, seeks to protect America from terrorist attacks, gathers crime statistics, runs a comprehensive crime laboratory, and helps train local law enforcement officers.

Drug Enforcement Administration (DEA)
The federal agency that enforces federal drug control laws.

Bureau of Alcohol, Tobacco, Firearms, and Explosives (ATF)
Federal agency with jurisdiction over the illegal sale, importation, and criminal misuse of firearms and explosives and the distribution of untaxed liquor and cigarettes.

U.S. Marshals Service
Federal agency whose jurisdiction includes protecting federal officials, transporting criminal defendants, and tracking down fugitives.

Department of Homeland Security (DHS)
Federal agency responsible for preventing terrorist attacks within the United States, reducing America's vulnerability to terrorism, and minimizing the damage and assisting in recovery from attacks that do occur.

Customs and Border Protection (CBP)
Federal agency responsible for the control and protection of America's borders and ports of entry. Its first priority is keeping terrorists and their weapons out of the United States.

Careers in Criminal Justice

BORDER PATROL AGENT

Duties and Characteristics of the Job

- The U.S. Border Patrol is the uniformed law enforcement arm of U.S. Customs and Border Protection (CBP). Its overall mission is to detect and prevent the illegal entry of aliens and terrorists into the United States, so the activities of all agents revolve around this mission.
- One of the key responsibilities of an agent is "line watch," which involves the detection, prevention, and apprehension of terrorists, undocumented aliens, and smugglers of aliens near the border.
- Border Patrol agents are also involved in farm and ranch check, traffic check, traffic observation, city patrol, transportation check, administrative, intelligence, and antismuggling activities.

Job Outlook

- Good benefits, a generous retirement policy, and the prestige associated with the position combine to make it highly desirable and thus very competitive.
- An early retirement policy ensures that there will always be job openings. Recruitment is ongoing, and the Border Patrol is always accepting applications.
- As concerns over border security, particularly at the U.S.–Mexico border, continue to increase, the Border Patrol will need to hire new agents.

Salary

- New agents are hired at a salary between $38,619 (GL-5) and $49,029 (GL-9), depending on education and experience. As in most federal government positions, there are excellent benefits.
- Salary varies according to the amount of overtime pay and where the agent is located.
- Agents promoted to supervisory positions earn higher pay, as do those who work in a geographical area where pay is higher in general.

Qualifications

- The Border Patrol wants applicants who are independent thinkers and can work alone, but also team players who work well with others.
- In order to apply to be an agent, it is necessary to be a U.S. citizen, to have no conviction for domestic violence, to have lived in the United States for the past three years, to have a valid driver's license at the time of appointment, and to be under age 40 at the time of appointment.
- Applicants must also pass a medical exam, drug testing, a physical fitness exam, and a background investigation.
- Candidates must be willing to travel wherever their assignments take them and be willing to move, particularly somewhere along the U.S.–Mexico border.

Education and Training

- To qualify for the GL-5 level salary, the applicant must have at least one year of work experience comparable in difficulty and responsibility to GL-4. This requirement is often met through a combination of work and educational experience. There is no degree requirement for joining the Border Patrol.
- If accepted, applicants spend several weeks at a training program in Artesia, New Mexico, where they learn necessary skills.
- After completion of this program at the academy, there is a two-year internship period, during which time formal training continues.

Word to the Wise

- Candidates must be willing to accept an initial assignment along the U.S. Southwest border with Mexico.
- It is necessary to work rotating shifts, often at night. Agents also work alone much of the time.
- Nine to ten hours of overtime are mandatory (called Administratively Uncontrolled Overtime). This is also a benefit, however, because it enables agents to make 25 percent over and above their base salary.
- Training and testing in Spanish proficiency are mandatory throughout training. A series of tests must be passed before an applicant can advance to agent status. Students interested in pursuing a Border Patrol career may wish to start taking Spanish courses if they have not already done so.
- Misdemeanor domestic violence and felony convictions are disqualifiers. Other misdemeanor convictions are not necessarily a barrier to employment, but full disclosure is required.
- Problems with bad credit and other background experiences that may imply poor character can lead to disqualification.

- **Secret Service** The U.S. Secret Service performs two main functions. The more visible of these is protection of national leaders, notably the president but also the vice president, the president-elect, the vice president–elect, the immediate families of these individuals, former presidents and their families, visiting heads of state, and other officials. The Secret Service was first established as a law enforcement entity in 1865 and was tasked with investigating the counterfeiting of U.S. currency. It continues this investigative function today. Since 1984, Secret Service investigative activities have been expanded to include the investigation of financial institution fraud, computer and telecommunications fraud, false identification documents, and other criminal activities.

Secret Service
Federal agency responsible for executive protection and for investigation of counterfeiting and various forms of financial fraud.

L07 Be familiar with the major federal law enforcement agencies

State Law Enforcement Agencies

Unlike municipal police departments, state police were legislatively created to deal with the growing incidence of crime in nonurban areas, a consequence of the increase in population mobility and the advent of personalized mass transportation in the form of the automobile. County sheriffs—elected officials with occasionally corrupt or questionable motives—had proved ineffective in dealing with the wide-ranging criminal activities that developed during the latter half of the nineteenth century. In addition, most local police agencies were unable to protect effectively against highly mobile lawbreakers who randomly struck at cities and towns throughout a state. In response to citizens' demands for effective and efficient law enforcement, state governors began to develop plans for police agencies that would be responsible to the state, instead of being tied to local politics and possible corruption.

The Texas Rangers, created in 1835, was one of the first state police agencies formed. Essentially a military outfit that patrolled the Mexican border, it was followed by the Massachusetts State Constables in 1865 and the Arizona Rangers in 1901. The states of Connecticut (1903) and Pennsylvania (1905) formed the first truly modern state police agencies.[22]

Today about 23 state police agencies have the same general police powers as municipal police and are territorially limited in their exercise of law enforcement regulations only by the state's boundaries. They provide investigative services to smaller communities when the need arises. The remaining state police agencies are primarily responsible for highway patrol and traffic law enforcement.

Some state police direct most of their attention to the enforcement of traffic laws. Others are restricted by legislation from becoming involved in the enforcement of certain areas of the law. For example, in some jurisdictions, state police are prohibited from becoming involved in strikes or other labor disputes, unless violence erupts.

The nation's 90,000 state police employees (about 60,000 officers and 30,000 civilians) carry out a variety of functions besides law enforcement and highway safety, including maintaining a training academy and providing emergency medical services.[23] State police crime laboratories aid local departments in investigating crime scenes and analyzing evidence. State police also provide special services and technical expertise in such areas as bomb-site analysis and homicide investigation. Some state police departments, such as California's, are involved in highly sophisticated traffic and highway safety programs, including the use of helicopters for patrol and rescue, the testing of safety devices for cars, and the conducting of postmortem examinations to determine the causes of fatal accidents.

State Law Enforcement and the War on Terror In the wake of the 9/11 attacks, a number of states have beefed up their intelligence-gathering capabilities and aimed them directly at homeland security. For example, California's

Sheriffs' departments, along with state and metropolitan law enforcement agencies, combine to make up the bulk of America's law enforcement apparatus. Here a sheriff's deputy accompanies accused killer Nicholas Sheley as he arrives at the Knox County Courthouse in Galesburg, Illinois, on July 11, 2008, for a hearing. Sheley was suspected of bludgeoning eight people to death and faced murder charges in Missouri and Illinois.

AP Images/*The Register-Mail*, Bill Gaither

Anti-Terrorism Information Center is a statewide intelligence system designed to combat terrorism. It divides the state into operational zones and links federal, state, and local information services in one system. Trained intelligence analysts operate within civil rights guidelines and use information in a secure communications system; information is analyzed daily.[24] The center combines machine intelligence with information coming from a variety of police agencies. The information is correlated and organized by analysts looking for trends. Rather than simply operating as an information-gathering unit, the center relies on a synthesizing process. It combines open-source public information with data on criminal trends and possible terrorist activities. Processed intelligence is designed to produce threat assessments for each area and to project trends outside the jurisdiction. The system attempts to process multiple sources of information to predict threats. By centralizing the collection and analytical sections of a statewide system, California's Department of Justice may have developed a method for moving offensively against terrorism.

County Law Enforcement Agencies

The county sheriff's role has evolved from that of the early English shire reeve, whose primary duty was to assist the royal judges in trying prisoners and enforcing sentences. From the time of the westward expansion in the United States until municipal departments were developed, the sheriff was often the sole legal authority over vast territories.

Today, sheriffs' offices contain about 330,000 full-time employees, including about 175,000 sworn personnel. Employment has risen an average of about 4 percent per year since 1990.[25] The duties of a sheriff's department vary according to the size and degree of development of the county. In some jurisdictions, sheriffs' offices provide basic law enforcement services such as performing routine patrols, responding to citizen calls for service, and investigating crimes.

Other standard tasks of a typical sheriff's department are serving civil process (summons and court orders), providing court security, and operating the county jail. Less commonly, sheriffs' departments may serve as coroners, tax collectors, overseers of highways and bridges, custodians of the county treasury, and providers of fire, animal control, and emergency medical services. In years past, sheriffs' offices also conducted executions. Typically, the law enforcement functions of a sheriff's department are restricted to unincorporated areas of a county, unless a city or town police department requests its help.

Some sheriffs' departments are exclusively law enforcement oriented; some carry out court-related duties only; some are involved solely in correctional and judicial matters and not in law enforcement. However, a majority are full-service programs that carry out judicial, correctional, and law enforcement activities. As a rule, agencies serving heavily populated areas (over 1 million) are devoted to maintaining county correctional facilities, whereas those in areas of smaller population are focused on law enforcement.

County Law Enforcement and the War on Terror A number of counties are now engaging in antiterror and homeland securities activities. For example, the Harris County, Texas, Office of Homeland Security and Emergency Management (OHSEM) is responsible for an emergency management plan that prepares for public recovery in the event of natural or manmade disasters, catastrophes, or attacks. It works in conjunction with the state, federal, and local authorities, including the city of Houston and other municipalities in the surrounding Harris County area when required. If needed, OHSEM activates an Emergency Operations Center to allow coordination of all support agencies to provide continuity of services to the public. OHSEM is responsible for advisement, notification, and assembly of services that are in the best interest of the citizens of Harris County. They prepare and distribute information and procedures governing the same.[26]

Similarly, in Montgomery County, Maryland, the Homeland Security Department plans, prevents, prepares, and protects against major threats that may harm, disrupt, or destroy the community, its commerce, and institutions. Its mission is to effectively manage and coordinate the county's unified response, mitigation, and recovery from the consequences of such disasters or events should they occur. It also serves to educate the public on emergency preparedness for all hazards and conducts outreach to diverse and special populations to protect, secure, and sustain critical infrastructures to ensure the continuity of essential services.[27]

Metropolitan Law Enforcement Agencies

Local police form the majority of the nation's authorized law enforcement personnel. Metropolitan police departments range in size from the New York City Police Department, with almost 40,000 full-time officers and 10,000 civilian employees, to rural police departments, which may consist of a single officer. At last count, nearly 13,000 local police departments nationwide had an estimated 600,000 full-time employees, including about 460,000 sworn personnel.[28] Metropolitan police departments are attracting applicants who value an exciting, well-paid job that also offers them an opportunity to provide valuable community service. Salaries in municipal police agencies are becoming more competitive.

Most TV police shows feature the crime-fighting efforts of big-city police officers, but the overwhelming majority of departments have fewer than 50 officers and serve a population of under 25,000. Recent data reveal that nearly three-quarters of all local police departments serve populations of under 10,000 people. Around 650 such agencies employ just one sworn officer.

Municipal police officers' responsibilities are immense, and they are often forced to make split-second decisions on life-and-death matters. At the same time, they must be sensitive to the needs of citizens who are often of diverse racial and ethnic backgrounds. What's more, local police perform multiple roles, including (but not limited to) investigating crimes, identifying suspects, and making arrests (see Exhibit 4.1).

LO8 Summarize the differences among state, county, and local law enforcement

Smaller agencies can have trouble carrying out many of the same functions as their big-city counterparts; the hundreds of small police agencies in each state often provide duplicate services. Whether consolidating smaller police agencies into "superagencies" would improve services is often debated among police experts. Smaller municipal agencies can provide important specialized services that might have to be relinquished if they were combined and incorporated into larger departments. Another approach has been to maintain smaller departments but to link them via computerized information sharing and resource management networks.[29]

Metropolitan Law Enforcement and the War on Terror

Federal and county law enforcement agencies are not alone in responding to the threat of terrorism. And, of course, nowhere is the threat of terrorism being taken more seriously than in New York City—one of the main targets of the 9/11 attacks—which has undertaken a number of antiterrorism initiatives, including the formation of its Counterterrorism Bureau.[30] Teams within the bureau have been trained to examine potential targets in the city and are now attempting to insulate those targets from possible attack. Viewed as prime targets are the city's bridges, the Empire State Building, Rockefeller Center, and the United Nations. Bureau detectives are assigned overseas to work with the police in several foreign cities, including cities in Canada and Israel. Detectives have been assigned as liaisons with the FBI and with Interpol in Lyon, France. The Intelligence Division has also been revamped, and agents are examining foreign newspapers and monitoring Internet sites. The department is also setting up several backup command centers in different parts of the city in case a terror attack puts headquarters out of operation. Several backup senior command teams have been created so that if people at the highest levels of the department are killed, individuals will already have been tapped to step into their jobs.

The Counterterrorism Bureau has assigned more than 100 city police detectives to work with FBI agents as part of a Joint Terrorist Task Force. In addition, the Intelligence Division's investigators now devote a substantial percentage of their resources to counterterrorism, up from about 2 percent before January 2002. The department is also drawing on the expertise of other institutions around the city. For example, NYPD SHIELD, one of the department's latest initiatives, is a public–private security partnership geared primarily toward equipping the private sector with information and training to effectively defend against terrorism.[31]

Private Policing

Supplementing local police forces has recently been a burgeoning private security industry. Private security service has become a multibillion-dollar industry with 10,000 firms and 1.5 million employees. Even federal police services have been privatized to cut expenses. Today, people employed in private policing outnumber public police by almost three to one.[32]

Some private security firms have become billion-dollar industries. The Wackenhut Corporation is the U.S.-based division of Group 4 Securicor, the world's second largest provider of security services. Among its clients are a number of Fortune 500 companies. It has a number of subsidiaries that work for the U.S. government. For example, Wackenhut Services Incorporated (WSI) is a primary contractor to NASA and the Army. Wackenhut also provides security and emergency response services to local governments—for example, helping them guard their public transport systems. Wackenhut helps the U.S. government protect nuclear reactors, guards the Trans-Alaska Pipeline System, and maintains security in secret government laboratories and facilities. It maintains a Custom Protection Officer Division, made up of highly trained uniformed security officers assigned to critical or complex facilities or situations requiring special skills in places such as government buildings and banks.

There will be more legal scrutiny as the private security business blossoms. A number of questions remain to be answered. One important issue is whether security guards are subject to the same search and seizure standards as police officers. For example, the U.S. Supreme Court has repeatedly stated that purely private search activities do not violate the Fourth Amendment's prohibitions. Is this cause for concern, considering that there are more private than public police in America?

Technology and Law Enforcement

Policing relies more and more frequently on modern technology to increase effectiveness, and there is little doubt that the influence of technology on policing will continue to grow. Police officers now trained to prevent burglaries may someday have to learn to create high-tech forensic labs that can identify suspects involved in theft of genetically engineered cultures from biomedical labs.[33] Criminal investigation is being enhanced by the application of sophisticated electronic gadgetry: computers, cell phones, and digital communication devices.

Police are becoming more sophisticated in their use of computer software to identify and convict criminals. Advanced computer software has helped in both the allocation of resources and the investigation of crime.

A number of other information technology techniques are now being used to increase police effectiveness and efficiency. For example, it is now recognized that there are geographic "hot spots" where a majority of predatory crimes are concentrated.[34] Computer mapping programs that can translate addresses into map coordinates allow departments to identify problem areas for particular crimes, such

■ Technology has and will continue to have a significant impact on law enforcement operations. This vehicle-mounted digital camera captures images of license plates and helps police identify suspects with outstanding warrants, stolen vehicles, and the like, all without the need to make a stop. What are the pros and cons of such devices?

© Sally Ryan/The New York Times/Redux

as drug dealing. Computer maps enable police to identify the location and time of day at which crimes occurred, as well as the linkage among criminal events, and to concentrate their forces accordingly.

Already in use, but not yet widespread, license plate recognition (LPR) technology employs cameras and computer software to discern the letters and numbers of vehicle license plates and then compares them with records contained in state and federal databases. New technology makes it possible to place the imaging cameras on the front or roof of a vehicle or in a patrol unit's light bar. Initially designed for use in parking lots (to record the time a vehicle entered), for access control (allowing authorized vehicles into a secure area), and for paying tolls, LPR technology recently has expanded into the realms of border control, identification of stolen vehicles, and traffic-fine enforcement (e.g., issuing tickets for running red lights), and vendors are marketing systems specifically for use by the law enforcement community.[35]

Some police departments are also using computerized imaging systems for criminal identification. Several software companies have developed identification programs that help witnesses create a composite picture of the perpetrator. A vast library of photographed or drawn facial features can be stored in computer files and accessed on a terminal screen. Witnesses can scan thousands of noses, eyes, and lips until they find those that match the perpetrator's. Eyeglasses, mustaches, and beards can be added; skin tones can be altered.

L09 Explain the role of technology in police work

Another technique is to digitize thousands of facial images. Police can then easily create a "photo lineup" of all suspects having a particular characteristic described by a witness. New computer software allows two-dimensional mug shots to be re-created on a three-dimensional basis. Effects on the three-dimensional image such as lighting and angles can also be changed to better reproduce the conditions that prevailed in the environment where a crime took place.[36]

DNA testing has become an invaluable tool for law enforcement. Here Theresa White, a forensic scientist at the New York State Police lab in Albany, New York, processes DNA samples. The Federal Bureau of Investigation and several states now collect DNA samples from those awaiting trial. The intent is to solve more crimes, but critics of the practice raise privacy concerns. Should authorities gather DNA samples from anyone charged (though not necessarily convicted) of a crime?

AP Images/Mike Groll

Fusion Centers

Many state and local law enforcement agencies have formed so-called fusion centers. What is a fusion center? According to the National Fusion Center Guidelines, it is "an effective and efficient mechanism to exchange information and intelligence, maximize resources, streamline operations, and improve the ability to fight crime and terrorism by analyzing data from a variety of sources." Fusion centers are typically set up for the purpose of sharing information and intelligence within specific jurisdictions and across levels of government. They often emphasize terrorism prevention and crime fighting with extensive use of technology. They frequently resemble a department's technological "nerve center" and are usually housed in a central location where information is collected and then shared with decision makers. There are four main goals for fusion centers:

- Support for a range of law enforcement activities, including anticrime operations and terrorism prevention
- Help for major incident operations and support for units charged with interdiction and criminal investigations
- Provide the means for community input, often through "tip lines"

- Assistance to law enforcement executives so they can make informed decisions about departmental priorities

Fusion centers are intended to provide a mechanism through which government agencies, law enforcement, and the private sector can work together for the common purpose of protecting the homeland and preserving public safety. They are premised on a model of collaboration. Collaboration between agencies and across levels of government has been lacking throughout history, but the events of 9/11 affirmed a need for change. The fusion center concept will continue to catch on and, in all likelihood, more will be developed as law enforcement comes to realize the benefits the fusion process can yield.

CRITICAL THINKING

1. *What additional strategies besides fusion centers are desirable for improving information sharing between law enforcement agencies and between law enforcement agencies and the public?*
2. *Are there any possible disadvantages associated with the fusion center concept? If so, what are they?*

The use of computerized automated fingerprint identification systems (AFIS) is growing as well. Using mathematical models, AFIS can classify fingerprints and identify up to 250 characteristics (minutiae) of the print. These automated systems use high-speed computer chips to plot each point of minutiae and count the number of ridge lines between that point and its four nearest neighbors. This substantially improves the speed and accuracy of fingerprint identification.

Advanced technology is also spurring new forensic methods of identification and analysis.[37] The most prominent technique is **DNA profiling**, a procedure that allows suspects to be identified on the basis of the genetic material found in hair, blood, and other bodily tissues and fluids. When DNA is used as evidence in a rape trial, DNA segments are taken from the victim, the suspect, and blood and semen found on the victim. A DNA match indicates a 4,000,000,000-to-1 likelihood that the suspect is the offender.

Many other technological advances have aided law enforcement with identifying, locating, and capturing criminals (see the Criminal Justice and Technology feature for another example). Most are beyond the scope of this text. New investigation techniques are constantly being developed, too. With each passing year, more and more high-tech devices and techniques are being added to the law enforcement toolkit.

DNA profiling
The identification of criminal suspects by matching DNA samples taken from their person with specimens found at the crime scene.

Ethical Challenge

FBI officials say they have developed surveillance cameras that can instantly compare people's "faceprints" against those of suspected terrorists and known criminals in a computerized database. This biometric facial recognition system uses measurable facial features, such as the distances and angles between geometric points on the face, to recognize a specific individual. This highly automated, computerized process can be installed at airports and train stations in order to constantly monitor people using transportation. Those who match photos can be called out, detained, and questioned.

Write an essay on the ethics of using this system. Is this use of technology cause for alarm? Is it an undesirable invasion of individual privacy, or does it represent a positive advance in security measures that generates benefits for society?

Summary

L01 **Describe how law enforcement developed in feudal England** The origin of U.S. police agencies traces to early English society. Under the pledge system, people were grouped into tithings and were entrusted with policing their own minor problems. Ten tithings were grouped into a hundred, supervised by a constable. Ten hundreds were organized into shires overseen by the shire reeve, the precursor to the modern sheriff.

L02 **Summarize characteristics of the first law enforcement agencies** Early thief takers were private police who apprehended criminals for reward payments. Henry Fielding's Bow Street Runners improved on the thief-taking system. The first organized police force was founded by Sir Robert Peel in London.

L03 **Discuss the development of law enforcement in the United States** Law enforcement in colonial America paralleled the British model. In the colonies, the county sheriff became the most important law enforcement agent. The first true U.S. police departments were formed in Boston, New York, and Philadelphia in the early nineteenth century.

L04 **Analyze the problems of early police agencies** Early American police were viewed as being dominated by political bosses who controlled their hiring practices and policies. In the nineteenth century, big-city police were still not respected by the public, were unsuccessful in their role as crime stoppers, and were not involved in progressive activities.

L05 **Discuss how reformers attempted to create professional police agencies** Reform movements begun in the 1920s culminated in the concept of professionalism.

Police professionalism was interpreted to mean tough, rule-oriented police work featuring advanced technology and hardware. The view that these measures would quickly reduce crime proved incorrect.

L06 **Describe the major changes in law enforcement between 1970 and today** The police experienced turmoil in the 1960s and 1970s, which led to reforms such as the hiring of women and members of minority groups. Questions about the effectiveness of law enforcement also led to the development of community policing. Police departments began to embrace new forms of policing that stressed cooperation with the community and problem solving.

L07 **Be familiar with the major federal law enforcement agencies** There are several major law enforcement agencies. At the federal level, the FBI is the largest federal agency. Other agencies include the Drug Enforcement Administration and the U.S. Marshals Service.

L08 **Summarize the differences among state, county, and local law enforcement** Most states maintain state police agencies, who investigate crimes and patrol the roadways. County-level law enforcement is provided by sheriffs' departments, who run jails and patrol rural areas. Local police agencies engage in patrol, investigative, and traffic functions, as well as many support activities.

L09 **Explain the role of technology in police work** Most police departments rely on advanced computer-based technology to prevent and control crime, identify suspects, and collate evidence. Examples include computerized crime mapping and automated fingerprint identification systems.

Review Questions

1. List the problems faced by today's police departments that were also present during the early days of policing.

2. Distinguish among the duties of the state police, sheriffs' departments, and local police departments.

3. Do you believe that the general public has greater respect for the police today than in the past? If so, why? If not, why not?

4. What are some of the technological advances that should help the police solve more crimes? What are the dangers of these advances?

5. Discuss the trends that will influence policing during the coming decade. What other social factors may affect police?

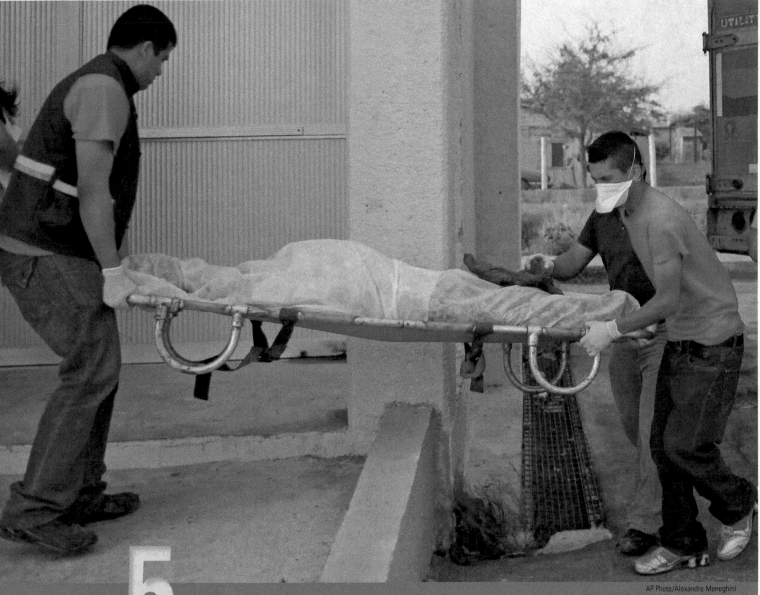

AP Photo/Alexandre Meneghini

5 The Police: Role and Function

Learning Objectives

LO1 Understand the organization of police departments

LO2 Articulate the complexities of the police role

LO3 Explain the limitations of patrol and methods for improving it

LO4 Summarize the investigation function

LO5 Explain what forensics is and what forensics experts do for police agencies

LO6 Understand the concept of community-oriented policing

LO7 Discuss the concept of problem-oriented policing

LO8 Be familiar with the various police support functions

In Juarez, Mexico, right across the border from El Paso, Texas, thousands of people have been killed as rival drug cartels fight among themselves and with Mexican government officials in an effort to protect lucrative drug trafficking routes. Unfortunately, there is evidence that some of the crime and violence once concentrated across the border has spread into the United States. In early 2010, prompted in part by the killing in Mexico of two U.S. citizens affiliated with the American consulate, Texas Senators Kay Bailey Hutchison and John Cornyn wrote to President Obama, asking for additional federal support at the border, arguing that "The spillover violence in Texas is real and it is escalating. Our border patrol agents and local law enforcement are more regularly engaged with gunmen associated with drug cartels, but our resources and personnel are limited."[1] ∎

Fortunately, it seems progress is being made. As of this writing, National Guard troops are being withdrawn from the region. Homeland Security Secretary Janet Napolitano said, "There is a perception that the border is worse now than it ever has been. That is wrong. The border is better now than it ever has been."[2]

Conventional crimes keep America's law enforcement agencies busy, but the added burden of coping with violence at the U.S.–Mexico border makes an already difficult job even tougher. Local police, along with federal officials, have to walk a thin line as they seek to improve conditions in the region. On the one hand, there is a need to enforce America's antidrug laws and block the supply of illicit substances. On the other hand, U.S. trade with Mexico exceeds $1 billion each day by some estimates, so any efforts to further curb border violence should be measured against a need to preserve legitimate trade; officials must be mindful of the possible public relations fallout that could result from aggressive enforcement.[3]

The police role is extremely varied and complex. Police officers are called on to deal with increasingly difficult and unpredictable situations. The crime problem continues to evolve in response to societal developments. Whether officers engage in preventive patrol, respond to calls for service, forge relationships with citizens, or even deal with spillover violence at our nation's borders, they have to be constantly vigilant and prepared. Anything less can give criminals the upper hand, something the public does not take kindly to.

This chapter describes the organization of police departments and their various operating branches: patrol, investigation, service, and administration. It discusses the realities and ambiguities of the police role and traces how the concept of the police mission has been changing radically. The chapter concludes with a brief overview of some of the most important administrative issues confronting today's U.S. law enforcement agencies.

The Police Organization

Most municipal police departments in the United States are independent agencies within the executive branch of government, operating without specific administrative control from any higher governmental authority. Although they often cooperate and participate in mutually beneficial enterprises, such as a joint task force with state and federal law enforcement agencies, local police agencies are functionally independent organizations with unique sets of rules, policies, procedures, norms, budgets, and so on.

Most local police departments are organized in a hierarchical manner, as illustrated in Figure 5.1. Within this organizational model, each element of the department normally has its own chain of command. In a large municipal department, there may be a number of independent investigation units headed by a captain who serves as the senior administrator, a lieutenant who oversees cases and investigations and acts as liaison with other police agencies, and sergeants and inspectors who carry out fieldwork. Smaller departments may have a captain or lieutenant as head of a particular branch or unit. Department size also affects the number of subunits. A department the size of New York's may contain several specialized investigative units, such as special victims or sex crimes, whereas many smaller departments do not employ detectives at all and rely on county or state police investigators to probe unsolved crimes. Regardless of its size, at the head of the organization is the **police chief**, who sets policy and has general administrative control over all the department's various operating branches.

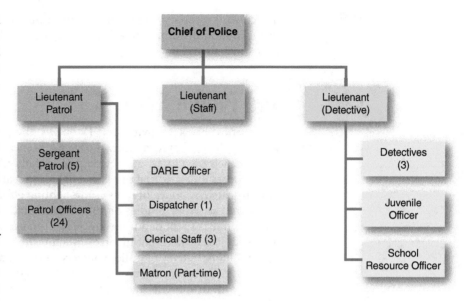

Figure 5.1 Vestal, New York, Police Department

Source: Town of Vestal, New York, www.vestalny.com/DeptPage .aspx?pID=10.

L01 Understand the organization of police departments

police chief
The top administrator of the police department, who sets policy and has general control over departmental policies and practices. The chief is typically a political rather than a civil service appointee and serves at the pleasure of the mayor.

time-in-rank system
For police officers to advance in rank, they must spend an appropriate amount of time, usually years, in the preceding rank—for example, to become a captain, an officer must first spend time as a lieutenant.

Pros and Cons of Police Organization

Police administrative organization has both its pros and cons. Because most departments are civil service organizations, administrators must rise through the ranks to get to command positions. To be promoted, they must pass a battery of tests, profiles, interviews, and so on. Most police departments employ a **time-in-rank system** for determining promotion eligibility. This means that before moving up the administrative ladder, an officer must spend a certain amount of time in the next lowest rank; a sergeant cannot become a captain without serving an appropriate amount of time as a lieutenant. This system has both benefits and shortcomings. On the plus side, it is designed to promote stability and fairness and to limit favoritism. The chief's favorite cannot be promoted over a more experienced officer who is better qualified. Once earned, a rank can rarely be taken away or changed if new management takes over. The rank system also protects police agencies from losing talented officers trained at public expense to other departments who offer more money or other incentives.

On the downside, the rank system restricts administrative flexibility. Unlike in the private sector, where the promotion of talented people can be accelerated in the best interests of the company, the time-in-rank system prohibits rapid advancement. A police agency would probably not be able to hire a computer systems expert with a Ph.D. and give her a command position in charge of its data-analysis section. The department would be forced to hire the expert as a civilian employee under the command of a ranking senior officer who might not be as technically proficient. Because senior administrators are promoted from within only after years of loyal service, time-in-rank may render some police agencies administratively conservative. Even when police executives adopt new programs, such as CompStat (see later in this chapter for more on CompStat), they are most likely to choose those elements that confer legitimacy on existing organizations, and on implementing them in ways that minimize disruption to existing organizational routines, rather than embracing truly innovative changes.[4]

The Police Role

In countless books, movies, and TV shows, the public has been presented with a view of policing that romanticizes police officers as fearless crime fighters who think little of their own safety as they engage in daily high-speed chases and shootouts. How close is this portrayal of a crime fighter to real life? Not very close, according to most research. A police officer's crime-fighting efforts are only a small part of his or her overall activities. Studies of police work indicate that a significant portion of an officer's time is spent handling minor disturbances, service calls, and administrative duties. Police work, then, involves much more than catching criminals. The most recent national survey of police contacts with civilians found that almost 44 million persons had at least one contact with police that year.[5]

More than half of the contacts are for traffic-related matters, and about 30 percent are to report problems or ask for assistance—for example, responding to a neighbor's complaint about music being too loud during a party, or warning kids not to shoot fireworks. This survey indicates that the police role is both varied and complex. These results are not surprising when Uniform Crime Report (UCR) arrest data are considered. Each year, about 700,000 local, county, and state police officers make about 14 million arrests, or about 20 each. Of these, about 2 million (approximately three per officer) are for serious Part I crimes. Given an even distribution of arrests, it is evident that the average police officer makes fewer than two arrests per month and fewer than a single felony arrest every four months.

These figures should be interpreted with caution because not all police officers are engaged in activities that allow them to make arrests, such as patrol or detective work. About one-third of all sworn officers in the nation's largest police departments are in such units as communications, antiterrorism, administration, and personnel. Even if the number of arrests per officer were adjusted by one-third, it would still amount to only 9 or 10 serious crime arrests per officer per year. So even though police handle thousands of calls each year, relatively few result in an arrest for a serious crime such as a robbery or burglary; in suburban and rural areas, years may go by before a police officer arrests someone for a serious crime.

The evidence, then, shows that unlike their TV and film counterparts, the police engage in many activities that are not related to crime. Police officers function in a variety of roles ranging from dispensers of emergency medical care to keepers of the peace on school grounds. Although officers in large urban departments may be called on to handle more felony cases than those in small towns, they too will probably find that most of their daily activities are not crime related. What are some of the most important functions of police?

LO2 Articulate the complexities of the police role

The Patrol Function

Regardless of style of policing, uniformed patrol officers are the backbone of the police department, usually accounting for about two-thirds of a department's personnel.[6] Patrol officers are the most highly visible components of the entire criminal justice system. The major purposes of patrol are to

- Deter crime by maintaining a visible police presence
- Maintain public order (peacekeeping) within the patrol area

- Enable the police department to respond quickly to violations of law or other emergencies
- Identify and apprehend law violators
- Aid individuals and care for those who cannot help themselves
- Facilitate the movement of traffic and people
- Create a feeling of security in the community[7]

Patrol Activities

Most experts agree that the great bulk of patrol efforts are devoted to what has been described as **order maintenance**, or **peacekeeping**: maintaining order and civility in their assigned jurisdiction.[8] Order-maintenance functions occupy the border between criminal and noncriminal behavior. The patrol officer's discretion often determines whether a noisy neighborhood dispute involves the crime of disturbing the peace or can be controlled by exercising street-corner diplomacy and sending the combatants on their way. Similarly, teenagers milling around in the shopping center parking lot may be brought in and turned over to the juvenile authorities or dispersed in a less formal and often more efficient manner.

The primary role of police seems to be "handling the situation." Police encounter many troubling incidents that need some sort of "fixing up."[9] Enforcing the law might be one tool a patrol officer uses; threat, coercion, sympathy, and understanding might be others. Most important is keeping things under control so that there are no complaints that the officer is doing nothing at all or doing too much. The real police role, then, may be as a community problem solver.

Police officers actually practice a policy of selective enforcement, concentrating on some crimes but handling the majority in an informal manner. A police officer is supposed to know when to take action and when not to, whom to arrest and whom to deal with by issuing a warning or some other informal action. If a mistake is made, the officer can come under fire from peers and superiors, as well as the media and the general public.

The effectiveness of patrol has been a topic of research for several decades. The Contemporary Issues in Criminal Justice feature summarizes the key findings in this area.

order maintenance (peacekeeping)
The order-maintenance aspect of the police role involves peacekeeping, maintaining order and authority without the need for formal arrest, "handling the situation," and keeping things under control by using threats, persuasion, and understanding.

Despite what the media might lead us to believe, police work does not always involve chasing down criminals and making arrests. The great bulk of patrol efforts are devoted to order maintenance and peacekeeping rather than to shootouts with dangerous criminals. Here Sacramento police officers Sara Butler and Mike Cooper talk with a homeless man as they hand out eviction notices to residents at a homeless tent city. Hundreds of residents living in a tent city along the American River were issued notices of eviction and were told to relocate to a nearby shelter. Their tent city was located on land belonging to the Sacramento Municipal Utility District.

© Justin Sullivan/Getty Images

Does Patrol Deter Crime? A Look at the Evidence

A primary goal of police patrol has been to deter criminal behavior. The visible presence of patrol cars on the street and the rapid deployment of police officers to the scene of a crime are viewed as effective methods of crime control. Is this view correct? The most widely heralded attempt at measuring patrol effectiveness was undertaken during the early 1970s in Kansas City, Missouri, where researchers divided 15 separate police districts into three groups: one group retained normal patrol; the second (proactive) set of districts were supplied with two to three times the normal amount of patrol forces; and the third (reactive) group had its preventive patrol eliminated, with police officers responding only when summoned by citizens to the scene of a particular crime. The Kansas City study found that these variations in patrol had little effect on the crime patterns in the 15 districts. The presence or absence of patrol officers did not seem to affect residential or business burglaries, motor vehicle thefts, larceny involving auto accessories, robberies, vandalism, or other criminal behavior, nor did they influence citizens' attitudes toward the police, their satisfaction with police, or their fear of future criminal behavior.

Since the Kansas City study findings were published, dozens of researchers have continued to seek an answer to the question of whether adding more police helps to bring down the crime rate. At one time, reviews of the existing research found that the actual number of law enforcement officers in a jurisdiction seemed to have little effect on area crimes. However, during the past decade, larger cities have expanded their police forces, and crime rates have plummeted—a trend that suggests that adding police may in fact reduce crime rates. The association between number of police personnel and crime rates has also been supported by a number of recent studies. Using a variety of methodologies, these studies have found that police presence may actually reduce crime levels and that adding police may bring crime levels down.

CRITICAL THINKING

The evidence is mixed on the deterrent effects of preventive patrol. This should not be taken to mean that patrol doesn't work. What can a police agency do to improve patrol? What methods are likely the most effective and why?

Improving Patrol

Police departments have in recent years initiated a number of programs and policies to try to improve patrol effectiveness. Some have proved more effective than others. Some are also more controversial than others.

Proactive Policing and Directed Patrol Although the mere presence of police may not be sufficient to deter crime, the manner in which they approach their task may make a difference. Police departments that use a proactive, aggressive law enforcement style may help reduce crime rates. Jurisdictions that encourage patrol officers to stop motor vehicles to issue citations and to aggressively arrest and detain suspicious persons also experience lower crime rates than jurisdictions that do not follow such proactive policies.[10] Departments that more actively enforce minor regulations, such as laws prohibiting disorderly conduct and traffic laws, are also more likely to experience lower felony rates.[11]

Pinpointing why **proactive policing** works so effectively is difficult. Proactive patrol efforts may help improve response time and increase the number of patrol cars that respond per crime.[12] It may have a **deterrent effect**: aggressive policing increases community perception that police arrest many criminals and that most violators get caught. Criminals may think twice about committing crimes in a town that has such an active police force! Proactive policing may also help control crime because it results in conviction of more criminals. Because aggressive police arrest more suspects, there are fewer left on the street to commit crime; fewer criminals produce lower crime rates.

Evidence also shows that targeting specific crimes through **directed patrol** can be successful. One aggressive patrol program, known as the Kansas City Gun Experiment, was directed at restricting the carrying of guns in high-risk places at high-risk times. Working with academics from the University of Maryland, the Kansas City Police Department focused extra patrol attention on a "hot spot" high-crime area identified by computer analysis of all gun crimes. Over a 29-week

proactive policing
A police department policy that emphasizes stopping crimes before they occur, rather than reacting to crimes that have already occurred.

deterrent effect
Stopping or reducing crime by convincing would-be criminals that they stand a significant risk of being apprehended and punished for their crimes.

directed patrol
A patrol strategy that involves concentrating police resources in areas where certain crimes are a significant problem.

period, the gun patrol officers conducted thousands of car and pedestrian checks and traffic stops and made over 600 arrests. Using frisks and searches, they found 29 guns; an additional 47 weapons were seized by other officers in the experimental area. There were 169 gun crimes in the target beat in the 29 weeks before the gun patrol but only 86 while the experiment was under way, a decrease of 49 percent.[13]

Strategies such as these have been a critical success. The downturn in the violent crime rate over the past decade has been attributed to aggressive police work in large cities such as New York aimed at controlling or eliminating lifestyle crimes: vandalism, panhandling, and graffiti.[14] Some commentators fear that aggressive policing will result in antagonism between proactive cops and the general public. However, recent research indicates that precinct-level efforts to ensure that officers are respectful of citizens helped lower the number of complaints and improved community relations.[15]

Making Arrests Can formal police action, such as an arrest, reduce crime? The evidence is mixed, but some studies suggest that contact with the police may cause some offenders to forgo repeat criminal behavior. Many first offenders will forgo criminal activity after undergoing arrest.[16] For example, an arrest for drunk driving reduces the likelihood of further driving while intoxicated.

Why do arrests deter crime? It is possible that news of increased and aggressive police arrest activity is rapidly diffused through the population and has an immediate impact on crime rates.[17] Arrests may also alter perceptions. An arrest for drunk driving may convince people that they will be rearrested if they drink and drive.[18] Consequently, as the number of arrests per capita increases, crime rates go down.

Rapid Response Improving response time may be one way of increasing police efficiency. Unfortunately, however, the research fails to support such assumptions. A National Institute of Justice study examined police response times in four cities. The authors found that rapid response had virtually no effect on crime.[19] Why? One explanation is that people tend to be slow when it comes to reporting crime. For example, a person may wake up in the morning and find that his or her car was vandalized. By then the trail has gone cold, making it nearly impossible to capture the perpetrator even if the police are summoned immediately upon discovery of the crime.

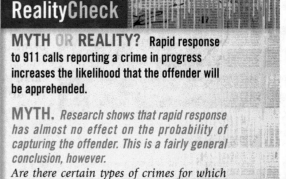

RealityCheck

MYTH OR REALITY? Rapid response to 911 calls reporting a crime in progress increases the likelihood that the offender will be apprehended.

MYTH. *Research shows that rapid response has almost no effect on the probability of capturing the offender. This is a fairly general conclusion, however.*
Are there certain types of crimes for which rapid response could work?

Broken Windows Policing A critical 1982 paper by George Kelling and James Q. Wilson advocated a new approach to improving police relations in the community, an approach that has come to be known as the **broken windows model**.[20] Kelling and Wilson made three points:

broken windows model
A term used to describe the role of the police as maintainers of community order and safety.

- *Neighborhood disorder creates fear.* Urban areas filled with street people, youth gangs, prostitutes, and the mentally disturbed are the ones most likely to maintain a high degree of crime.[21]
- *Neighborhoods give out crime-promoting signals.* A neighborhood filled with deteriorated housing, broken windows, and disorderly behavior gives out crime-promoting signals. Honest citizens live in fear in these areas, and predatory criminals are attracted to them.
- *Police need citizen cooperation.* If police are to reduce fear and successfully combat crime in these urban areas, they must have the cooperation, support, and assistance of the citizens.

According to the broken windows concept, a deteriorated neighborhood, whose residents are fearful, pessimistic, and despondent, is a magnet for crime. In contrast, neighborhoods where residents are civil to one another and where disorder is not tolerated send a different message: criminals are not wanted here, and criminal behavior will not be allowed. The broken windows approach holds that police administrators would be well advised to deploy their forces where they can encourage public confidence, strengthen feelings of safety, and elicit cooperation from citizens. Community preservation, public safety, and order maintenance—not crime fighting—should become the primary focus of patrol. Put another way, just as physicians and dentists practice preventive medicine and dentistry, police should help maintain an intact community structure rather than simply fighting crime. Does it work? In one of the most rigorous tests of broken windows theory in recent years, researchers identified 34 crime-ridden areas in Lowell, Massachusetts. Half (the treatment group) received broken windows policing; the other half (the control group) received the same levels of patrol as before. Results revealed substantial reductions in crime, disorder, and calls for service in the treatment areas, but not in the control areas.[22]

Using Technology Police departments have also relied on technology to help guide patrol efforts. The best-known program, **CompStat**, was begun in New York City as a means of directing police efforts in a more productive way.[23] William Bratton, who had been appointed NYC police chief, wanted to revitalize the department and break through its antiquated bureaucratic structures. He installed CompStat, a computerized system that gave local precinct commanders up-to-date information about where and when crime was occurring in their jurisdictions. Part of the CompStat program, twice-weekly "crime control strategy meetings," brought precinct commanders together with the department's top administrators, who asked them to report on crime problems in their precincts and tell what they were doing to turn things around. Those involved in the strategy sessions had both detailed data and electronic pin maps that showed how crime clustered geographically in the precinct and how patrol officers were being deployed. The CompStat program required local commanders to demonstrate their intimate knowledge of crime trends and develop strategies to address them effectively. When ideas were presented by the assembled police administrators, the local commanders were required to demonstrate, in follow-up sessions, how they had incorporated the new strategies in their patrol plan.

CompStat
A program originated by the New York City police that used carefully collected and analyzed crime data to shape policy and evaluate police effectiveness.

L03 **Explain the limitations of patrol and methods for improving it**

Broken windows theory claims that signs of disrepair, such as the graffiti and trash pictured here, invite serious crime. Evidence suggests there is a measure of truth to such claims. That being said, is graffiti always a bad thing? Some cities have gone so far as to approve areas for graffiti murals. Who is right?

© Bastar/iStockphoto

CompStat proved extremely successful and is generally credited with making a major contribution to the dramatic drop in New York City's crime rate during the past decade.

The Investigation Function

Fictional detectives in movies and on television shoot first and ask questions later. When they do conduct an interrogation, they think nothing of beating a confession out of the suspect. How accurate are these portrayals? Not very. The modern criminal investigator is likely to be an experienced civil servant, trained in investigatory techniques, knowledgeable about legal rules of evidence and procedure, and at least somewhat cautious about the legal and administrative consequences of his or her actions.[24]

Investigative services can be organized in a variety of ways. In New York, each borough or district has its own detective division that supervises investigators assigned to neighborhood police precincts (stations). Local squad detectives work closely with patrol officers to provide an immediate investigative response to crimes and incidents. (In some TV shows and movies, New York City detectives are shown barking commands at patrol officers and even snapping orders at uniformed sergeants and lieutenants; in reality, both branches are considered equal, so that would never happen. A patrol sergeant is the superior officer of a junior grade detective.) New York City also maintains specialized borough squads—homicide, robbery, and special victims—to give aid to local squads and help identify suspects whose crimes may have occurred in multiple locations. There are also specialty squads that help in areas such as forensics. In smaller cities, detective divisions may be organized into sections or bureaus, such as homicide, robbery, or rape (see Exhibit 5.1).

How Do Detectives Detect?

Detectives investigate the causes of crime and attempt to identify the individuals or groups responsible for committing particular offenses. They may enter a case after patrol officers have made the initial contact, such as when a patrol car interrupts a crime in progress and the offenders flee before they can be apprehended. Detectives can investigate a case entirely on their own, sometimes by following up on leads provided by informants. Sometimes detectives go undercover in order to investigate crime: a lone agent can infiltrate a criminal group or organization to gather information on future criminal activity. Undercover officers can also pose as victims to capture predatory criminals who have been conducting street robberies and muggings.[25]

In his study of investigation techniques, Martin Innes found that police detectives rely heavily on interviews and forensic evidence to create or manufacture a narrative of the crime, creating in a sense the "story" that sets out how, where, and why the incident took place.[26] To create their story, contemporary detectives typically use a three-pronged approach:[27]

- *Specific focus.* Interview witnesses, gather evidence, record events, and collect facts at the immediate crime scene.
- *General coverage.* (1) Canvass the neighborhood and make observations; (2) conduct interviews with friends, families, and associates; (3) contact coworkers or employers for information about victims and suspects; (4) construct victim/suspect timelines to outline their whereabouts prior to incident.
- *Informative.* Use modern technology to collect records of cell phones and pagers, computer hard drives (palm devices, laptops, notebooks, desktops, and servers), diaries, notes, and documents. This approach includes data that persons of interest in the investigation use, which, in turn, tell about their lives, interactions with others, and geographic connections.

Exhibit 5.1

Baton Rouge Police Detectives

Division I: Crimes against Persons

Homicide, Armed Robbery, Juvenile/Sex Crimes, Major Assaults/Missing Persons, Computer Crimes

- The **Homicide** division is responsible for investigating all criminal calls where a death or life-threatening injury has occurred, any officer-involved shooting, or the attempted murder of a police officer.
- The **Armed Robbery** division is responsible for investigating all criminal calls involving all degrees of robbery.
- The **Juvenile/Sex Crimes** division is responsible for maintaining juvenile investigation records, cases of child abuse, and all types of sex crimes.
- The **Major Assaults** division is responsible for investigating a wide range of non-life-threatening felony personal crimes and missing person cases.
- The **Computer Crimes** division investigates crimes committed against persons or computer systems using the Internet, email, or other electronic means.

Division II: Property Crimes

Burglary, Auto Theft/Impound, Forgery, Felony Theft

- The **Burglary** division is responsible for coordinating all follow-up investigations of burglaries, as well as the recovery of stolen property from local pawn shops.
- The **Auto Theft/Impound** division is responsible for conducting follow-up investigations of auto thefts and unauthorized use of movables. The unit also coordinates all records and information relating to vehicles stored and impounded by the department, and monitors local towing services to insure compliance with applicable standards and ordinances.
- The **Forgery** division is responsible for investigating all crimes involving thefts by fraudulent use of access cards, and forgeries of negotiable documents.
- The **Felony Theft** unit is responsible for all felony theft investigations that do not fall under the Auto Theft/Impound, Burglary, or Forgery divisions. The office is also responsible for felony damage to property cases. Priority is placed on business embezzlement incidents.

Division III: Investigative Support

Evidence, Crime Scene, Polygraph, Crime Stoppers

- The **Evidence** division is responsible for the collection, storage, cataloguing, and disposition of all evidence and property seized by, or turned in to, the department.
- The **Crime Scene** division is responsible for assisting in investigations by taking photographs, sketching major crime scenes, collecting and tagging evidence, and performing various scientific tests on suspects and/or evidence as needed.
- The **Polygraph** division conducts all polygraph, or lie detector, tests given to recruits, employees, or criminal suspects.
- The **Crime Stoppers** office coordinates all facets of the Crime Stoppers program with local news media, businesses, and the public.

Division IV: Special Operations

Narcotics, School Drug Task Force, State and Federal Liaisons

- The **Narcotics** division is responsible for investigating crimes involving illegal drugs as well as related vice crimes. This division administers the HIDTA and LSP Task Forces.
- The **School Drug** Task Force investigates crimes involving narcotics, explosives, and weapons in schools, school buses, and at school-sponsored events within the parish.
- **Liaison** detectives assigned to outside state and federal agencies work jointly with these agencies to participate in multijurisdictional investigations.

Source: Baton Rouge, Louisiana, Police Department, http://brgov.com/dept/brpd/criminal.htm (accessed June 2, 2011).

Detective work is an art as well as a science, based on experience and knowledge of human behavior gained on the job. As sociologist Robert Jackall found when he studied detectives in New York, the investigative branch has a unique culture and operating style. His observations are described in the Contemporary Issues in Criminal Justice feature.

Sting Operations

Another approach to investigation, commonly referred to as a **sting operation**, involves organized groups of detectives or patrol officers working in plain clothes who deceive criminals into openly committing illegal acts or conspiring to engage in criminal activity.

To sting criminals, some jurisdictions maintain **vice squads**, patrol officers working in plain clothes who focus on crimes of public morals such as prostitution or gambling. For example, female police officers may pose as prostitutes and arrest men who solicit their services.

Sting operations can be highly successful, but they are also open to criticism.[28] Covert police activities have often been criticized as violating the personal rights of citizens, while forcing officers into demeaning roles. Ironically, Mary Dodge and her associates found that rather than considering it demeaning, female officers find their sting work as make-believe prostitutes exciting; they also consider it a stepping-stone for promotion.[29]

sting operation
An undercover police operation in which police pose as criminals to trap law violators.

vice squad
Police officers assigned to enforce morality-based laws, such as those on prostitution, gambling, and pornography.

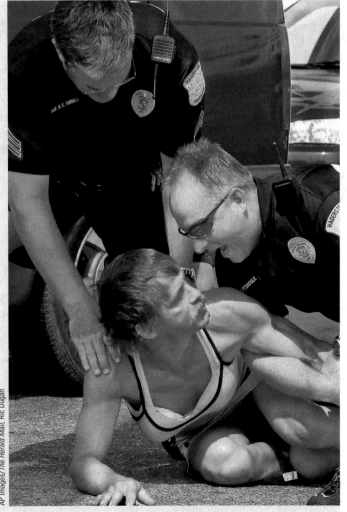

■ Sting operations are often helpful in combating drug and vice crimes. Here Martin Joe McDaniel is brought down by Hagerstown (Maryland) Police Department Sgt. Kevin Simmers, left, and Officer Martin Pitsnogle, right, during one of many prostitution stings. McDaniel was one of three men arrested in this particular operation. The department's frequent use of undercover sting operations won praise from the pastors of nearby churches, who had long complained about open solicitation in the area.

AP Images/*The Herald Mail*, Ric Dugan

By its very nature, a sting involves deceit by police agents that often comes close to entrapment. Sting operations may encourage criminals to commit new crimes because they have a new source for fencing stolen goods. Innocent people may damage their reputations by buying merchandise from a sting operation when they had no idea the items had been stolen. By putting the government into the fencing business, such operations blur the line between law enforcement and criminal activity.

Evaluating Investigations

Serious criticism has been leveled at the nation's detective forces for being bogged down in paperwork and relatively inefficient in clearing cases. One famous study of 153 detective bureaus by the RAND Corporation, a well-known think tank, found that a great deal of a detective's time was spent in unproductive work and that investigative expertise did little to solve cases; half of all detectives could be replaced without negatively influencing crime clearance rates.[30]

Although some question remains about the effectiveness of investigations, police detectives do make a valuable contribution to police work because their skilled interrogation and case-processing techniques are essential to eventual criminal conviction.[31] Detective work may be improved if investigators are able to spend more time on each case, allowing them to carefully collect physical evidence at the scene of the crime, identify witnesses, check departmental records, and use informants. Research shows that in more serious cases, especially homicide investigations, where detectives devote a lot of attention to a single crime, the likelihood increases that they will eventually identify and arrest the culprit.[32]

Nonetheless, a majority of cases that are solved are done so when the perpetrator is identified at the scene of the crime by patrol officers. Research shows that if a crime is reported while in progress, the police have about a 33 percent chance of making an arrest; the arrest probability declines to about 10 percent if the crime is reported 1 minute later, and to 5 percent if more than 15 minutes have elapsed. As the time between the crime and the arrest grows, the chances of a conviction are also reduced, probably because the ability to recover evidence is lost. Put another way, once a crime has been completed and the investigation is put in the hands of detectives, the chances of identifying and arresting the perpetrator diminish rapidly.[33]

One reason for investigation ineffectiveness is that detectives often lack sufficient resources to carry out a lengthy ongoing probe of any but the most serious cases. Research shows the following:

- *Unsolved cases.* Almost 50 percent of burglary cases are screened out by supervisors before assignment to a detective for a follow-up investigation. Of those assigned, 75 percent are dropped after the first day of the follow-up investigation. Although robbery cases are more likely to be assigned to detectives, 75 percent of them are also dropped after one day of investigation.
- *Length of investigation.* The vast majority of cases are investigated for no more than four hours stretching over three days. An average of 11 days elapses between the initial report of a crime and suspension of the investigation.
- *Sources of information.* Early in an investigation, the focus is on the victim; as the investigation is pursued, emphasis shifts to the suspect. The most critical information for determining case outcome is the name and description of the suspect and related crime information. Victims are most often the source of information; unfortunately, witnesses, informants, and members of the police department are consulted far less often. However, when these sources are tapped, they are likely to produce useful information.
- *Effectiveness.* Preliminary investigations by patrol officers are critical. In situations where the suspect's identity is not known immediately after the crime is committed, detectives make an arrest in less than 10 percent of all cases.[34]

LO4 Summarize the investigation function

Improving Investigation with Technology

In Chapter 4, the technological breakthroughs that have aided crime investigation were discussed in some detail. Information technology (IT) has revolutionized police work in many areas, including communications, criminal identification, and record storage. A number of tasks that used to involve painstaking labor by individuals are now being conducted with IT. Take, for instance, searching criminal histories. Police agencies are now using a program called CopLink to facilitate this time-consuming task. CopLink integrates information from different jurisdictions into a single database that detectives can access when working on investigations.[35] The CopLink program enables investigators to search the entire database of past criminal records and computes a list of possible suspects even if only limited data are available, such as first or last name, partial license plate numbers, vehicle type, vehicle color, location of crime, and/or weapon used.

Another technique that is improving investigation success is the use of DNA profiling. Using DNA in support of criminal investigations has increased both in the United States and around the world. The first national DNA database—the National DNA Database of England & Wales—is regarded by many police experts as the most important development in investigative technology since the adoption of fingerprint comparison early in the last century.[36] Still other strategies have been employed, such as the use of social networking. As the accompanying Criminal Justice and Technology feature attests, police have added Facebook and Twitter to their investigative toolkits.

Improving Investigations with Forensic Science

Investigations have improved along with advances in **forensic science**. The *CSI* television series and its various spin-offs have drawn attention to the developing field of forensics in police work, which uses a variety of sciences, mathematical principles, and problem-solving methods to identify perpetrators. Forensic

forensic science
The use of scientific techniques to investigate questions of interest to the justice system and solve crimes.

CRIMINAL JUSTICE AND **TECHNOLOGY**

Social Media and Investigations

Social networking has become quite popular, and police departments around the country have jumped on the bandwagon. In addition to maintaining department websites, many agencies have Facebook pages. Others report calls for service on Twitter, in real time, so concerned citizens can track crime trends and read details on what is happening in their communities—and where. In one case, a store owner helped detectives investigate the theft of a valuable collector jersey from his store. Detectives narrowed in on the store's Facebook friends list and quickly identified the four thieves because they were on the list. With successes like these, some departments have gone so far as to assign detectives to full-time monitoring of sites like Facebook and MySpace for leads on criminal activity.

People sometimes arrange for drug sales on Facebook. Sometimes they boast about their criminal exploits. Police have even used Facebook to combat underage drinking by narrowing in on incriminating photos posted by young people. And while it is true that Facebook

requires people to be confirmed as friends to view the details of a person's page, some people are less than diligent with their security settings and essentially post their information for the world to see. Also, it is not particularly difficult to become a person's Facebook friend. In one case, police worked with teenage volunteers to investigate cyber bullying. The volunteers would become friends with the suspects and then share information with police. One detective said, "We'd be foolish not to use [social networking] as an investigative tool."

CRITICAL THINKING

1. *Are there any downsides to the use of social networking in investigations?*
2. *To what extent should law enforcement personnel themselves be able to participate in social networking on their own personal time?*
3. *In what other creative ways could social networking be used by police to fight crime?*

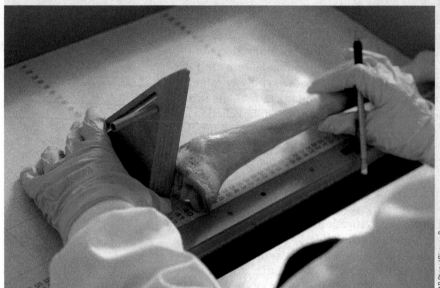

Forensic anthropologist Susan Myster measures a tibia belonging to an unidentified female at her lab located at the Midwest Medical Examiners office in Ramsey, Minnesota. Scientists like Myster are tasked with identifying human remains that are in advanced stages of decomposition or that are burned, mutilated, or otherwise unrecognizable. What other forensic science careers are available?

AP Photo/Pioneer Press, Chris Polydoroff

means "pertaining to the law," and forensic scientists perform comprehensive chemical and physical analyses on evidence submitted by law enforcement agencies. Although most forensic scientists focus on criminal cases (they are sometimes referred to as criminalists), others work in the civil justice system—for example, performing handwriting comparisons to determine the validity of a signature on a will. Today, forensic specialists can examine blood and other body fluids and tissues for the presence of alcohol, drugs, and poisons and can compare body fluids and hair for typing factors, including DNA analysis. Forensic scientists analyze trace physical evidence such as blood spatters, paint, soil, and glass to help reconstruct a crime scene and interpret how the crime was committed. In addition to forensics, investigation is being improved by information technology, which allows investigators to compare evidence found at the crime scene with material collected from similar crimes by other police agencies.

Forensic analyses involve the use of complex instruments and of chemical, physical, and microscopic examining techniques. In addition to analyzing crime scene investigations, forensic scientists provide testimony in a court of law when the case is brought to trial. Some forensic scientists are generalists, and others specialize in a particular scientific area, including toxicology, blood pattern analysis, crime scene investigation, impression evidence (e.g., footprints), trace evidence (e.g., hair left at a crime scene), and questioned documents. There is a forensics expert for nearly every conceivable type of evidence and criminal activity. See the Contemporary Issues in Criminal Justice feature for a somewhat different perspective on forensics. Are you interested in a career as a forensics expert? Read the Careers in Criminal Justice feature.

L05 Explain what forensics is and what forensics experts do for police agencies

Community-Oriented Policing

Police agencies have been trying for several decades to gain the cooperation and respect of the communities they serve. At first, efforts at improving the relationships between police departments and the public involved programs with the general title of police–community relations (PCR). Developed at the station house and departmental levels, these initial PCR programs were designed to make citizens more aware of police activities, alert them to methods of self-protection, and improve general attitudes toward policing.

"Forensics under the Microscope"

The *Chicago Tribune*'s "Forensics under the Microscope" series suggests that all is not well in the world of forensic sciences. Such concerns were echoed in a more recent National Academy of Sciences (NAS) report entitled *Strengthening Forensic Science in the United States: A Path Forward*. The authors of the report highlighted a series of problems with the forensic sciences, many of which are not well known to people on the outside—and particularly not to those who owe their knowledge of forensics and investigations to fictional television programs. Here are some of those problems.

- *Case backlog.* The NAS called attention to another report in which it was learned that federal, state, and local laboratories reported a backlog of nearly 500,000 requests for forensic analysis. This backlog has been made even more serious by requests for quick test results. Labs are having a difficult time keeping up.
- *DNA demands.* The ascendancy of DNA evidence and the opportunities to use it during investigations has further burdened crime labs. And even though the NAS, along with other experts and commissions, has heralded the advent of DNA testing as valuable for criminal investigation, there is only so much it can do. According to the NAS report, "DNA evidence comprises only about 10 percent of case work and is not always relevant to a particular case. Even if DNA evidence is available, it will assist in solving a crime only if it supports an evidential hypothesis that makes guilt or innocence more likely. For example, the fact that DNA evidence of a victim's husband is found in the house in which the couple lived and where the murder took place proves nothing. The fact that the husband's DNA is found under the fingernails of the victim who put up a struggle may have very different significance" (pp. 1–5 and 1–6).
- *Questionable evidence.* Now that DNA evidence is regarded as a gold standard in criminal investigations, this has started to cast doubt on convictions secured through other, more traditional types of evidence. According to the report, "The fact is that many forensic tests—such as those used to infer the source of tool marks or bite marks—have never been exposed to stringent scientific scrutiny. ... Even fingerprint analysis has been called into question" (p. 1–6).
- *Errors.* The NAS also called attention to several disturbing examples of errors and fraud in the forensic sciences. In one case, a state-mandated examination of

the West Virginia State Police laboratory revealed that the convictions of more than 100 people were in doubt. Another scandal involving the Houston Crime Laboratory came to light in 2003. An investigation revealed "routine failure to run essential scientific controls, failure to take adequate measures to prevent contamination of samples, failure to adequately document work performed and results obtained, and routine failure to follow correct procedures for computing statistical frequencies" (p. 1–8).

- *Incompatible fingerprint identification systems.* Law enforcement agencies around the country have developed and put in place automated fingerprint identification systems in an effort to solve crimes. The problem, according to the NAS, is that there is inadequate integration of these systems.
- *Lack of preparation for mass disasters.* According to the NAS, "Threats to food and transportation, concerns about nuclear and cyber security, and the need to develop rapid responses to chemical, nuclear, radiological, and biological threats underlie the need to ensure that there is a sufficient supply of adequately trained forensic specialists ... [but] public crime laboratories are insufficiently prepared to handle mass disasters" (p. 1–13).
- *The* CSI *effect.* The so-called "*CSI* effect," named for the popular television program, is concerned with the real-world implications of Hollywood's fictional spin on the forensic sciences and criminal investigations. The NAS found that some prosecutors believe they must make their in-court presentations as visually appealing as possible in an effort to please jurors who think they understand forensic work from having watched their favorite television programs. Attempts to satisfy such unrealistic expectations may possibly compromise the pursuit of justice. More attention will be given to the *CSI* effect in Chapter 8.

CRITICAL THINKING
Clearly there is room for improvement in the rapidly evolving forensic sciences. To what extent has the recent attention paid to wrongful convictions fueled calls for improvement, such as those in the NAS report? At the other extreme, what *improvements* have been made in recent years? The news cannot be all doom and gloom. Find out more on the National Academies Press website at www.nap.edu.

Although PCR efforts demonstrated the willingness of police agencies to cooperate with the public, some experts believed that law enforcement agencies needed to undergo a significant transformation to create meaningful partnerships with the public. In their view, community relations and crime control effectiveness cannot be the province of a few specialized units housed within a traditional police

Camden (New Jersey) police officer L. A. Sanchez walks a beat in a downtown shopping area. Police Chief Scott Thomson has said that even in the face of budget constraints and layoffs, he will realign his force in ways that the public won't notice. "The Camden Police Department will not abandon its community policing philosophy," says Chief Thomson.

community-oriented policing
Programs and strategies designed to bring police and the public closer together and create a more cooperative working environment between them.

foot patrol
Police patrols that take officers out of cars and put them on a walking beat in order to strengthen ties with the community.

department. Instead, the core police role must be altered if community involvement is to be won and maintained. This led to the development of **community-oriented policing**, a set of programs and strategies designed to bring police and the public closer together and create a more cooperative working environment between them.

Implementing Community-Oriented Policing

The community-oriented policing concept was originally implemented through a number of innovative demonstration projects.[37] Among the most publicized were experiments in **foot patrol**, which took officers out of cars and set them to walking beats in the neighborhood. Foot patrol efforts were aimed at forming a bond with community residents by acquainting them with the individual officers who patrolled their neighborhood and letting them know that police were caring and available. The first foot patrol experiments were conducted in cities in Michigan and New Jersey. An evaluation of foot patrol indicated that although it did not bring down the crime rate, residents in areas where foot patrol was added perceived greater safety and were less afraid of crime.[38]

Since the advent of these programs, hundreds of communities have adopted innovative forms of decentralized, neighborhood-based community-oriented policing models. The federal government has encouraged the growth of community-oriented policing by providing billions of dollars to hire and train officers through its Office of Community Oriented Policing Services (COPS) program, which has given local departments more than $10 billion in aid since its inception.[39] Recent surveys indicate that there has been a significant increase in community-oriented policing activities and that certain core programs, such as crime prevention, have become embedded in the police role.[40] Community-oriented policing (COP) programs have been implemented in large cities, suburban areas, and rural communities.[41]

Changing the Police Role

Community-oriented policing also emphasizes sharing power with local groups and individuals. A key element of the community-oriented policing philosophy is that

Careers in Criminal Justice

FORENSIC SCIENTIST

Duties and Characteristics of the Job

- Forensic scientists perform comprehensive chemical and physical analyses on evidence submitted by law enforcement agencies.
- Forensic scientists analyze the physical evidence they receive from police and then prepare reports describing the results of their analysis. Those documents, along with forensic scientists' expert testimony, can be important prosecutorial tools for convicting the accused. Therefore, their work is often instrumental in apprehending and convicting criminals.
- Although most forensic scientists focus on criminal cases and are sometimes called criminalists, others work in the civil justice system—performing duties such as comparing handwriting to determine the validity of a signature on a will.
- Forensic scientists perform two roles in their work. One is to analyze physical evidence found on a victim, at the scene. The other is to provide expert testimony in a court of law.
- Most forensic scientists work in crime laboratories run by city, county, or state governments; the next largest group work for federal agencies, including the Justice Department (FBI, DEA, and Secret Service) and the Treasury Department; a smaller number work in private labs and colleges and universities.
- Forensic scientists usually work a regular 40-hour week. Sometimes they have to travel and work long, irregular hours.
- They spend much time in laboratories analyzing evidence, but they also work in offices to record and draft reports on the results of their analyses.

Job Outlook

- Job opportunities are expected to increase as a result of the judicial system's continuing need for corroborating evidence in prosecutions.
- Forensic scientists can expect competition for jobs at the Departments of Justice, Treasury, and other federal law enforcement agencies.
- Job opportunities will be best for crime lab professionals who have an advanced degree or certification.
- The Bureau of Labor Statistics projects that there may be 17,000 positions for forensic scientists in 2016, so growth is anticipated.

Salary

- Experienced crime lab professionals can earn upwards of $100,000 a year.
- Lab directors earn in the low to mid-$100,000 range.

Qualifications

- Employment of most crime lab professionals is contingent upon satisfactory completion of a background investigation and random drug testing.
- Those who work in large labs may use technologically advanced equipment such as chromatographs to analyze drugs, alcohol, arson evidence, and fibers; spectrographs to identify chemicals; and computerized laboratory equipment.
- Crime lab professionals may be exposed to health or safety hazards when working in the lab or handling certain chemicals, but there is little risk if procedures are followed.

Education and Training

- Beginning forensic scientists usually must have at least a bachelor's degree in forensic science, chemistry, biology, physics, or physical anthropology.
- Several colleges and universities offer a bachelor's degree in forensic science; most also offer advanced degrees in specialized areas of forensic science.
- Whatever the major, required college courses include sciences such as biology, physics, chemistry, and pharmacology.
- A course in quantitative analysis and statistics is frequently required.
- Laboratory experience involving analytical instruments or blood sample analysis is helpful.
- Computer courses are also recommended, because employers prefer job applicants with computer skills to perform modeling and simulation tasks and to operate computerized laboratory equipment.

Word to the Wise

- A career in forensics is not what it is made out to be on television, in such programs as *CSI*, *Bones*, and *Criminal Minds*. Much time is spent in a laboratory, and little (if any at all) on the streets chasing down criminals.
- Forensics experts are often employed in criminal justice agencies, so certain criminal activities and convictions in one's past can serve as a bar to employment.

(continued)

- A degree in the social sciences is generally not enough for success as a forensic scientist. The very term "scientist" calls for training, and generally a degree, in the natural sciences.
- Compared to the nearly 700,000 sworn law enforcement personnel in the United States, there are very few forensic scientists (around 13,000).
- Most job opportunities will be found in and around large cities.

citizens must actively participate with police to fight crime. Such participation is essential because community climate is influenced by the informal social control created by a concerned citizenry coupled with effective policing.[42] Participation might involve providing information in areawide crime investigations or helping police reach out to troubled youths. The following are some other changes that have been linked to community-oriented policing initiatives.

neighborhood-oriented policing (NOP)
Community-oriented policing efforts aimed at individual neighborhoods.

- *Neighborhood orientation.* To achieve the goals of COP, some police agencies have tried to decentralize, an approach sometimes referred to as **neighborhood-oriented policing (NOP)**.[43] According to this view, problem solving is best done at the neighborhood level where issues originate, not at a far-off central headquarters. Because each neighborhood has its own particular needs, police decision making must be flexible and adaptive. For example, neighborhoods undergoing change in racial composition may experience high levels of racially motivated violence and require special police initiatives to reduce tensions.[44]
- *Changing management styles.* Community-oriented policing also means the redesign of police departments' administration and management. Management's role must be reinterpreted to focus on the problems of the community, not on the needs of the police department. The traditional vertical police organizational chart must be altered so that top-down management gives way to bottom-up decision making. The patrol officer becomes the manager of his beat and a key decision maker.
- *Changing recruitment and training.* Community-oriented policing means that police departments must alter their recruitment and training requirements. Future officers must develop community-organizing and problem-solving skills, along with traditional police skills. Their training must prepare them to succeed less on their ability to make arrests or issue citations and more on their ability to solve problems effectively.

Challenges of Community-Oriented Policing

The core concepts of police work are changing as administrators recognize the limitations and realities of police work in modern society. If they are to be successful, community-oriented policing strategies must be able to react effectively to some significant administrative problems.

Defining Community Critics believe that community-oriented policing works best in stable, affluent areas that are already characterized by a strong sense of community. The challenge of community is to reach out to all people in all neighborhoods, including young people and minorities, who may previously have been left out of the process.

Defining Roles Police administrators must also establish the exact role of community police agents. How should they integrate their activities with those of regular patrol forces? For example, should foot patrols have primary responsibility for policing in an area, or should they coordinate their activities with officers assigned to patrol cars?

Changing Supervisor Attitudes

Some supervisors are wary of community-oriented policing because it supports a decentralized command structure. Supervisors who learn to actively embrace community-oriented policing concepts are the ones best able to encourage patrol officers to follow suit.[45]

Reorienting Police Values

Research shows that police officers who have a traditional crime control orientation are less satisfied with community-oriented policing efforts than those who are public service oriented.[46] In some instances, officers holding traditional values may go as far as stigmatizing their own comrades assigned to community-oriented policing; their targets feel penalized by a lack of administrative support.[47] It is thus unlikely that community-oriented policing activities can be successful unless police line officers make a firm commitment to the values of community-oriented policing.[48]

Revise Training

Because the community-oriented policing model calls for an expansion of the police role from law enforcer to community organizer, police training must be revised to reflect this new mandate. If community-oriented policing is to be adopted on a wide scale, a whole new type of police officer must be recruited and trained in a whole new way. Training must prepare officers to succeed less on their ability to make arrests or issue citations and more on their ability to solve problems, prevent crime effectively, and deal with neighborhood diversity and cultural values.[49]

Reorient Recruitment

To make community-oriented policing successful, midlevel managers must be recruited and trained who are receptive to and can implement community-change strategies.[50] The selection of new recruits must be guided by a desire to find individuals with the skills and attitudes that support community-oriented policing.

Community-oriented policing calls for reorienting police values from crime control to more of a public service model. Though the need for crime control has not gone away, the logic behind a community philosophy is to rally the support of citizens so they will work collaboratively with law enforcement officials in an effort to prevent and report crime. Research has shown that it is not easy for agencies to reorient traditional values. What other aspects of community policing are difficult to implement?

© Greg Balfour Evans/Alamy

Community-Oriented Policing Effectiveness

There is empirical evidence that *some* community-oriented policing efforts can reduce disorder and impact the crime rate.[51] The most successful programs give officers time to meet with local residents to talk about crime in the neighborhood and to use personal initiative to solve problems. Although not all programs work (police–community newsletters and cleanup campaigns do not seem to do much good), the overall impression has been that patrol officers can actually reduce the level of fear in the community. Where it is used, citizens seem to like community-oriented policing, and those who volunteer and get involved in community crime prevention programs report higher confidence in the police force and its ability to create a secure environment.[52]

On the other hand, there is no clear-cut evidence that community-oriented policing is highly successful at reducing crime across the board. Crime rate reductions in cities that have used COP may be the result of an overall downturn in the nation's crime rate, rather than a result of community-oriented policing efforts. Researchers have also found that it is difficult to change the traditional values and attitudes of police officers involved in the programs.[53]

LO6 **Understand the concept of community-oriented policing**

Problem-Oriented Policing

problem-oriented policing
A style of police operations that stresses proactive problem solving, rather than reactive crime fighting.

Closely associated with, yet independent from, the community-oriented policing concept are **problem-oriented policing** strategies. Traditional police models focus on responding to calls for help in the shortest possible time, dealing with the situation, and then getting on the street again as soon as possible. In contrast, problem-oriented policing is proactive.

Problem-oriented policing (POP) requires police agencies to identify particular long-term community problems—street-level drug dealers, prostitution rings, gang hangouts—and develop strategies to eliminate them.[54] As with community-oriented policing, police departments must rely on local residents and private resources in order to be problem solvers. This means that police managers must learn how to develop community resources, design efficient and cost-effective solutions to problems, and become advocates as well as agents of reform.[55]

A significant percentage of police departments are now using special units to confront specific social problems. Problem-oriented policing models are supported by ample evidence that a great deal of urban crime is concentrated in a few hot spots.[56] A significant portion of all police calls in metropolitan areas typically radiate from a relatively few locations: bars, malls, the bus depot, hotels, and certain apartment buildings.[57] By implication, concentrating police resources on these **hot spots of crime** could reduce crime appreciably.[58]

hot spots of crime
Places from which a significant portion of all police calls originate. These hot spots include taverns and housing projects.

Problem-oriented strategies are being developed that focus on specific problem areas and/or specific criminal acts. For example, a POP effort in Sarasota, Florida, which was aimed at reducing prostitution, involved intensive, focused, high-visibility patrols to discourage prostitutes and their customers, undercover work to arrest prostitutes and drug dealers, and collaboration with hotel and motel owners to identify and arrest pimps and drug dealers.[59]

Another well-known program, Operation Ceasefire, is a problem-oriented policing intervention aimed at reducing youth homicide and youth firearms violence in Boston. According to evaluations of the program, Ceasefire produced significant reductions in youth homicide victimization and gun assault incidents in Boston that were not experienced in other communities in New England or elsewhere in the nation.[60]

Although programs such as these seem successful, the effectiveness of any street-level problem-solving effort must be interpreted with caution.[61] It is possible that the criminals will be displaced to other, "safer" areas of the city and will return shortly after the program is declared a success and the additional police forces have been pulled from the area.[62] Nonetheless, evidence shows that whereas merely saturating an area with police may not deter crime, focusing efforts on a particular problem may indeed have a crime-reducing effect.

L07 Discuss the concept of problem-oriented policing

Support Functions

As the model of a typical police department indicates (see again Figure 5.1), not all members of a department engage in what the general public regards as "real police work"—patrol, detection, and traffic control. Even in departments that are embracing community- and problem-oriented policing, a great deal of police resources are actually devoted to support and administrative functions. There are too many tasks to mention in detail, but the most important include those discussed next.

Many police departments maintain their own personnel service, which carries out such functions as recruiting new police officers, creating exams to determine the most qualified applicants, and handling promotions and transfers. Innovative selection techniques are constantly being developed and tested. For example, the Behavioral-Personnel Assessment Device (B-PAD) requires police applicants to view videotaped scenarios and respond as though they were officers handling the situation; reviews indicate that this procedure may be a reliable and unbiased method of choosing new recruits.[63]

Larger police departments often maintain an **internal affairs** branch charged with policing the police. Internal affairs units process citizen complaints of police corruption, investigate what may be the unnecessary use of force by police officers, and probe police participation in actual criminal activity, such as burglaries or narcotics violations. In addition, internal affairs divisions may assist police managers when disciplinary action is brought against individual officers. Internal affairs is a controversial function since investigators are feared and distrusted by fellow police officers. Nonetheless, rigorous self-scrutiny is the only way police departments can earn the respect of citizens. Because of these concerns, it has become commonplace for police departments to institute citizen oversight over police practices and to establish civilian review boards that have the power to listen to complaints and conduct investigations.

internal affairs
The branch of the police department that investigates charges of corruption or misconduct on the part of police officers.

The traffic patrol function is becoming ever more important as police departments struggle with budget cuts in cash-strapped cities across the country. Here, a Fairfax, Virginia, motorcycle officer aims his ProLaser III toward drivers who may be speeding.

© Paul J. Richards/AFP/Getty Images

Most police departments are responsible for the administration and control of their own budgets. This task includes administering payroll, purchasing equipment and services, planning budgets for future expenditures, and auditing departmental financial records.

Police departments include separate units charged with maintaining and disseminating information on wanted offenders, stolen merchandise, traffic violators, and so on. Modern data management systems enable police to use their records in a highly sophisticated fashion. For example, officers in a patrol car who spot a suspicious-looking vehicle can instantly receive a computerized rundown on whether it has been stolen. And if stolen property is recovered during an arrest, police using this sort of system can determine who reported the loss of the merchandise and arrange for its return.

Another important function of police communication is the effective and efficient dispatching of patrol cars. Again, modern computer technologies have been used to make the most of available resources.[64]

In many departments, training is continuous throughout an officer's career. Training usually begins at a police academy, which may be run exclusively for larger departments or may be part of a regional training center serving smaller and varied governmental units. More than 90 percent of all police departments require preservice training, including nearly all departments in larger cities (population over 100,000). The average officer receives more than 500 hours of preservice training, including 400 hours in the classroom and the rest in field training. Police in large cities receive over 1,000 hours of instruction divided almost evenly between classroom and field instruction.[65] Among the topics usually covered are law and civil rights, firearms handling, emergency medical care, and restraint techniques.[66]

After assuming their police duties, new recruits are assigned to field-training officers who break them in on the job. However, training does not stop here. On-the-job training is a continuous process in the modern police department and covers such areas as weapons skills, first aid, crowd control, and community relations. Some departments use roll call training, in which superior officers or outside experts address police officers at the beginning of the workday. Other departments allow police officers time off to attend annual training sessions to sharpen their skills and learn new policing techniques.

Police departments provide emergency aid to the ill, counsel youngsters, speak to school and community agencies on safety and drug abuse, and provide countless other services designed to improve citizen–police interactions.

Larger police departments maintain specialized units that help citizens protect themselves from criminal activity. They advise citizens on effective home security techniques or conduct Project ID campaigns—engraving valuables with an identifying number so that they can be returned if recovered after a burglary; police also work in schools teaching kids how to avoid drug use.[67] Police agencies maintain (or have access to) forensic laboratories that enable them to identify substances to be used as evidence and to classify fingerprints.

Ethical Challenge

The Middle City police force created Crime Control Teams—decentralized units relieved of routine, non-crime-related duties and given responsibility for controlling serious crime, apprehending offenders, conducting investigations, and increasing clearance rates on a neighborhood basis. Two team members, Officers Donald Libby and Karen Johnson, each of whom has more than 15 years on the force, were part of a team assigned to displace gangs of local teenagers who were constantly causing problems in the neighborhood. After a few months on the job, Libby and Johnson were the target of numerous complaints related to their treatment of neighborhood youths. They were charged with roughing up neighborhood kids, slapping some of them around, and being disrespectful. In the most serious incident, they used a nightstick on a 15-year-old whom they claim had resisted arrest after they found him smoking marijuana in the park. The youth suffered a broken arm and concussion and required hospitalization. When interviewed by the Internal Affairs bureau, the officers admitted they scuffled with the boy but claimed they were "only doing their job." Besides, they argued, community leaders had demanded results, and their aggressive style had helped lower the crime rate in the area by more than 20 percent. The boy and his parents have also filed suit, claiming that the amount of force used was unnecessary and violated his civil rights. As their defense attorney, you are asked to write an essay outlining their defense. Don't worry about legal rules. How would you defend the two officers?

LO8 Be familiar with the various police support functions

Planning and research functions include designing programs to increase police efficiency and strategies to test program effectiveness. Police planners monitor recent technological developments and institute programs to adapt them to police services.

Summary

LO1 **Understand the organization of police departments** Most municipal police departments in the United States are independent agencies within the executive branch of government. Most local police departments are organized in a hierarchical manner. Most police departments employ a time-in-rank system for determining promotion eligibility.

LO2 **Articulate the complexities of the police role** A police officer's crime-fighting efforts are only a small part of his or her overall activities. Studies of police work indicate that a significant portion of an officer's time is spent handling minor disturbances, service calls, and administrative duties. The police role involves many activities that are not crime related. The primary role of police seems to be "handling the situation."

LO3 **Explain the limitations of patrol and methods for improving it** Most experts agree that the great bulk of patrol efforts are devoted to what has been described as order maintenance, or peacekeeping: maintaining order and civility in the assigned jurisdiction. Evidence is mixed on the deterrent effect of patrol. Efforts to improve patrol have included proactive policing and directed patrol, targeting specific offenses for more arrests, rapid response, broken windows policing, and increased utilization of technology, including CompStat. Of these, rapid response has proven least effective.

LO4 **Summarize the investigation function** The first independent detective bureau was established by the London Metropolitan Police in 1841. Detectives investigate the causes of crime and attempt to identify the individuals or groups responsible for committing particular offenses. Police detectives make a valuable contribution to police work because their skilled interrogation and case-processing techniques are essential to eventual criminal conviction.

LO5 **Explain what forensics is and what forensics experts do for police agencies** Investigations have improved along with advances in forensic science. Forensic scientists perform comprehensive chemical and physical analyses on evidence submitted by law enforcement agencies.

LO6 **Understand the concept of community-oriented policing** Hundreds of communities have adopted innovative forms of decentralized, neighborhood-based community-oriented policing models. There is some empirical evidence that some community-oriented policing efforts can reduce disorder and reduce the crime rate.

LO7 **Discuss the concept of problem-oriented policing** Closely associated with, yet independent from, the community-oriented policing concept are problem-oriented policing strategies. Problem-oriented policing is proactive. Problem-oriented policing strategies require police agencies to identify particular long-term community problems (such as street-level drug dealers, prostitution rings, and gang hangouts) and to develop strategies to eliminate them.

LO8 **Be familiar with the various police support functions** Many police departments maintain their own personnel service, which carries out such functions as recruiting new police officers, creating exams to determine the most qualified applicants, and handling promotions and transfers. Larger police departments often maintain an internal affairs branch charged with "policing the police." Another important function of police communication is the effective and efficient dispatching of patrol cars. Again, modern computer technologies have been used to make the most of available resources.

Review Questions

1. Should the primary police role be law enforcement or community service? Explain.

2. Should a police chief be permitted to promote an officer with special skills to a supervisory position, or should all officers be forced to spend "time in rank"? Explain your answer.

3. Do the advantages of proactive policing outweigh the disadvantages? Explain.

4. Explain the concept of broken windows policing. Why might it be successful?

5. What are the problems facing investigators and forensics experts these days?

6. Can the police and the community ever form a partnership to fight crime? Why or why not? Does the community-oriented policing model remind you of early forms of policing? Explain.

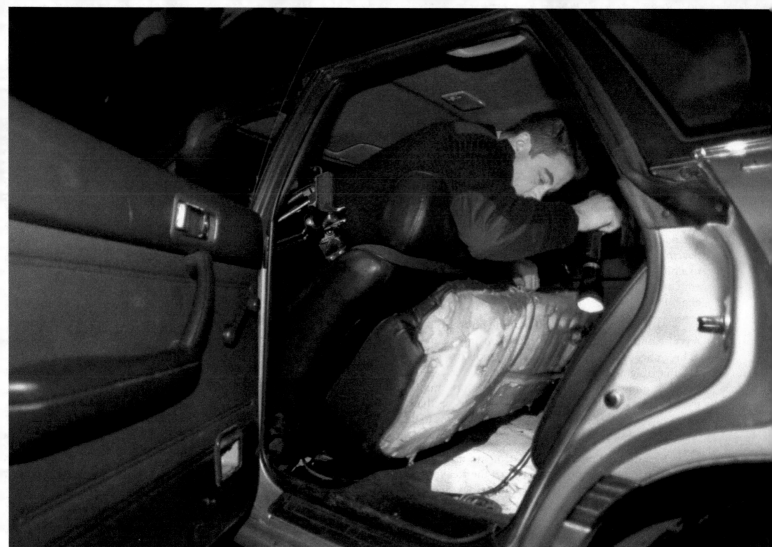

© Li-Hua Lan/*Syracuse Newspapers*/The Image Works

6 Issues in Policing: Professional, Social, and Legal

Learning Objectives

L01 Summarize demographic trends in policing
L02 Explain how minority and female officers act and are treated
L03 Explain police culture and personality
L04 Identify distinct policing styles
L05 Describe factors that affect police discretion
L06 Discuss four major problems of policing
L07 Distinguish between deadly and nondeadly force—and methods for controlling each
L08 Explain the importance of less-lethal weapons
L09 Be familiar with the Supreme Court's involvement with the police through its effort to control search and seizure and interrogation, and through establishment of the exclusionary rule

Rodney Gant was arrested for driving with a suspended license. After he was handcuffed and locked in the back seat of a police car, officers searched the passenger compartment of his car and found cocaine in the pocket of a jacket that was sitting on one of the seats. A trial court denied Gant's request to have the cocaine excluded at trial, but the Arizona Supreme Court reversed that decision, arguing that the search was unreasonable because, since Gant was locked up in the police car, there was no threat to officer safety or risk that the evidence would have been destroyed in the absence of an immediate search. The case then went to the U.S. Supreme Court, which held that the police can search the passenger compartment of a vehicle following a lawful arrest only when it is reasonable to believe that (1) the arrestee may have access to the vehicle at the time of the search or (2) the vehicle contains evidence of the offense of arrest.[1] In essence, the U.S. Supreme Court decided the search of Gant's car was unjustified and in violation of the Fourth Amendment. ■

The *Gant* decision altered the Supreme Court's earlier decision in *New York v. Belton*,[2] a case in which officers were essentially given carte blanche to search vehicle passenger compartments following lawful arrests. *Belton* was controversial, because even if an arrestee was locked up safely and did not pose any security threat, officers could still search the vehicle passenger compartment without probable cause. They were basically able to avoid the Fourth Amendment's probable cause requirement. Because *Gant* essentially overturned *Belton*, it has not been well received by the law enforcement community. Why exactly? It muddies the waters, because the Belton rule gave police clear authority to search, regardless of the offense in question or the arrestee's risk to the officers. Gant makes it more difficult for police to search. Supporters of the Gant decision, however, feel it honors Fourth Amendment rights and protects people from overreaching searches.

Court decisions like *Gant* are especially important in policing. Law enforcement officials need to know the legal landscape within which they operate. A lack of such understanding can make it difficult to secure criminal convictions, and it can even result in litigation. This chapter focuses not just on important legal issues like these, but also on a number of other social and professional issues facing police officers in the modern world. It begins by examining issues police face on the job, in court, and in society. Topics covered include diversity, police discretion, stress, fatigue, and use of force. This chapter concludes with a more careful look at law enforcement's legal environment.

Who Are the Police?

The composition of the nation's police forces is changing. Less than 50 years ago, police agencies were composed primarily of white males with a high school education who viewed policing as a secure position that brought them the respect of family and friends and took them a step up the social ladder. It was not

RealityCheck

MYTH OR REALITY?

- Male police officers believe that female police officers can perform the job as well as they can.
- Police officers feel that no one else understands what they do for a living.
- Veteran police officers receive the most citizen complaints.
- Thousands of people are fatally shot by police each year.
- The police are not required to advise all arrestees of their *Miranda* rights.
- Some warrantless searches are permissible as long as the police have probable cause.
- There are legal loopholes that enable guilty criminals to go free in alarming numbers.

uncommon to see police families in which one member of each new generation would enter the force. This picture has been changing and will continue to change. As criminal justice programs turn out thousands of graduates every year, an increasing number of police officers have at least some college education. In addition, affirmative action programs have slowly helped change the racial and gender composition of police departments to reflect community makeup. The following sections explore these changes in detail.

Demographic Makeup

With few exceptions, the personnel in most early police departments were white and male, a condition that persisted through most of the twentieth century. However, in most regions, the image of the police department as a bastion of white male dominance is either obsolete or rapidly changing. For more than 30 years, U.S. police departments have made a concerted effort to attract women and minority police officers, and there have been some impressive gains.[3] Today, about 13 percent of all officers are female, and about 25 percent are members of minority groups.[4]

The reasons behind this effort are varied. Viewed in its most positive light, diversity initiatives by police departments are intended to field a more balanced force that truly represents the communities they serve. A heterogeneous police force can be instrumental in gaining the confidence of the community by helping dispel the view that police departments are generally bigoted or biased organizations.[5] Furthermore, women and minority police officers possess special qualities that can serve to improve police performance. Spanish-speaking officers can facilitate investigations in Hispanic neighborhoods, and Asian officers are essential for undercover or surveillance work with Asian gangs and drug importers.

LO1 Summarize demographic trends in policing

Minority Police Officers

The earliest known date of when an African American was hired as a police officer was 1861 in Washington, D.C.; Chicago hired its first African American officer in 1872.[6] By 1890, an estimated 2,000 minority police officers were employed in the United States. At first, African American officers suffered a great deal of discrimination. Their work assignments were restricted, as were their chances for promotion. Minority officers were often assigned solely to patrolling African American neighborhoods, and in some cities they were required to call a white officer to make an arrest. Racial prejudice was common among white officers, and as late as the 1950s some refused to ride with African Americans in patrol cars.[7]

The experience of African American police officers has not been an easy one. In his classic 1969 book *Black in Blue*, Nicholas Alex pointed out that African American officers of the time suffered from what he called **double marginality**.[8] On the one hand, African American officers had to deal with the expectation that they would give members of their own race preferential treatment. On the other hand, black officers were the target of institutional racism. Alex found that African American officers adapted to these pressures in a range of ways, from denying that African American suspects should be treated differently from whites, to treating African American offenders more harshly than white offenders in order to prove their lack of bias.

Much has changed over the years. Minority police officers now seem as self-assured as white officers.[9] They may even be more willing than white officers to use their authority to take official action: the higher the percentage of black officers on the force, the higher the arrest rate for crimes such as assault.[10] Unfortunately, though, minority officers appear to be experiencing some of the same problems and issues encountered by white officers.[11] They report feeling similar rates of job-related stress and strain stemming from the same types of stressors, such as family conflict.[12] What is more, minority officers do report

double marginality
The social burden African American police officers carry by virtue of being both minority group members and law enforcement officers.

■ Miami Police Chief Miguel A. Exposito speaks during a press conference to announce "Operation Take Back Our Streets." His department launched the operation in response to shootings in the Model City and Little Haiti communities of Miami. The city has seen a number of shootings involving the use of high-powered assault weapons.

© Joe Raedle/Getty Images

more stress when they consider themselves "tokens" or marginalized within the department.[13]

Women in Policing

In 1910, Alice Stebbins Wells became the first woman to hold the title of police officer (in Los Angeles) and to have arrest powers.[14] For more than half a century, female officers endured separate criteria for selection, were assigned menial tasks, and were denied the opportunity for advancement.[15] Some relief was gained with the passage of the 1964 Civil Rights Act and its subsequent amendments. Courts have consistently supported the addition of women to police forces by striking down entrance requirements that eliminated almost all female candidates but could not be proved to predict job performance, such as criteria involving height and upper-body strength.[16] (Women do not do as well as men on strength tests and are much more likely to fail the entrance physical than male recruits; critics contend that many of these tests do not reflect the actual tasks of police on the job.[17]) Nonetheless, the role of women in police work is still restricted by social and administrative barriers that have been difficult to remove. Today, as we have noted, women make up more than 11 percent of officers, up from 7.6 percent in 1987.[18]

Studies of policewomen indicate that they are still struggling for acceptance, believe that they do not receive equal credit for their job performance, and report that it is common for them to be sexually harassed by their coworkers.[19] One reason for this may be that many male police officers tend to view policing as an overtly masculine profession that is not appropriate for women. Surveys of male officers show that many do not think women can handle the physical requirements of the job as well as men can.[20] Female police officers may also be targeted for more disciplinary action by administrators and, if cited, are more likely to receive harsher punishments than male officers—that is,

RealityCheck

MYTH OR REALITY? Male police officers believe that female police officers can perform the job as well as they can.

MYTH. *Although there are certainly exceptions, survey research reveals that male officers tend to view policing as mainly a masculine profession.*

Are these perceptions changing? What positive traits and characteristics do female officers bring to the job that male officers may not?

LO2 Explain how minority and female officers act and are treated

Careers in Criminal Justice

POLICE OFFICER

Duties and Characteristics of the Job

- Police officers are responsible for enforcing the written laws and ordinances of their jurisdiction.
- Police officers patrol within their jurisdiction and respond to calls wherever police attention is needed.
- Duties can be routine, such as writing a speeding ticket, or more involved, such as responding to a domestic disturbance or investigating a robbery.
- Nonpatrol duties include testifying in court and writing reports of their law enforcement actions.
- Some officers will choose or be chosen to work in specialized units such as the well-known special weapons and tactics (SWAT) or canine corps (K9).
- Police officers patrol jurisdictions of various sizes and have varying duties based on the nature of their jurisdiction. For example, sheriffs and their deputies enforce the laws within a county. State police primarily patrol state highways and respond to calls for backup from police units across their respective state. Institutions such as colleges and universities often have their own police forces as well, which enforce laws and rules in this specific area.
- Police work can be an intense and stressful job; it sometimes entails encounters with hostile and potentially violent people. Police are asked to put their lives on the line to preserve order and safety. Their actions are watched closely and reflect upon their entire department.
- Because the places that police protect must be watched at all times, police work shifts that may fall on weekends and holidays. Quite often it is the younger police officers who take these less desirable shifts. Additionally, police officers will often have to work overtime; 45-hour work weeks are common.

Job Outlook

- Government spending ultimately determines how many officers a department has.
- Overall opportunities in local police departments will be good for individuals who meet the psychological, personal, and physical qualifications. In addition to openings from employment growth, many openings will be created by the need to replace workers who retire and those who leave local agencies for federal jobs and private-sector security jobs.
- Police work is appealing to many because of the good benefits and retirement policies.
- For the better-paying positions, there may be more applicants than available positions. This competition means those with qualifications such as a college education will have better chances of being hired.
- After several years, those with a reputation for good work as well as the proper education can rise in the ranks of their department or be assigned to other desirable positions such as detective or investigator.

Salary

- Police patrol officers have median annual wages of more than $50,000. The middle 50 percent earn between $39,0000 and $65,000. The lowest 10 percent earned less than $30,000, and the highest 10 percent earned about $80,000.
- Median annual wages are $46,620 in federal government, $57,270 in state government, $51,020 in local government, and $43,350 in educational services.

Qualifications

- To be a police officer, you must be in good shape mentally and physically, as well as meet certain education requirements and pass written tests.
- New police officers go through rigorous training and testing—normally in the form of a local police academy for 12 to 14 weeks—before they go out on the streets.
- During training, new officers learn diverse skills that will be necessary for their job, such as knowledge of laws and individual rights, self-defense, and first aid. Applicants can also expect to be asked to pass lie detector and drug tests.
- Because of the enormous responsibility associated with being a police officer, certain personal qualities are considered key for future officers, such as responsibility, good communications skills, good judgment, and the ability to make quick decisions.

Education and Training	• In most cases, a high school diploma is required to be a police officer, but more and more jurisdictions are requiring at least some college education. • Although some college credits are enough to obtain a position on the police force, to be promoted and move up in rank, more education, generally in the form of a bachelor's degree in a relevant field, especially criminal justice, is necessary.
Word to the Wise	• There are generally more opportunities for employment in larger departments, usually in larger urban or suburban areas. • Not surprisingly, most opportunities exist in areas with comparatively higher crime rates or lower salaries.

a greater percentage receive punishments more severe than a reprimand.[21] Considering the sometimes hostile reception they get from male colleagues and supervisors, it may not come as a surprise that female officers report significantly higher levels of job-related stress than male officers.[22]

Despite these problems, the future of women in policing grows brighter every year.[23] Female officers want to remain in policing because it pays a good salary, offers job security, and is a challenging and exciting occupation.[24] These factors should continue to bring women to policing for years to come, but it is doubtful that we will see gender parity any time soon.[25]

Educational Characteristics

Even though most law enforcement agencies still do not require recruits to have a college degree, the number that require advanced education in the hiring and promotion process is growing. Today about one-third of all police departments require at least some type of college for new recruits, more than three times the number in 1990.[26]

What type of major are police departments looking for? About half the surveyed departments expressed a preference for criminal justice majors, most often because of their enhanced knowledge of the entire criminal justice system and of issues that arise in policing.

What are the benefits of higher education for police officers? Better communication with the public, especially minority and ethnic groups, is believed to be one benefit. Educated officers write better and more clearly and are more likely to be promoted. Police administrators believe that education enables officers to perform more effectively, generate fewer citizen complaints, show more initiative in performing police tasks, and generally act more professionally.[27] In addition, educated officers are less likely to have disciplinary problems and are viewed as better decision makers.[28] Higher education is also associated with greater self-confidence.[29]

The Police Profession

All professions have unique characteristics that distinguish them from other occupations and institutions. Policing is no exception. Police experts have long sought to understand the unique nature of the police experience and to determine how the challenges of police work shape the field and its employees. In this section, some of the factors that make policing unique are discussed in detail.

Police Culture

cynicism
The belief that most people's actions are motivated solely by personal needs and selfishness.

blue curtain
The secretive, insulated police culture that isolates officers from the rest of society.

Police experts have found that the experience of becoming a police officer and the nature of the job itself cause most officers to band together in a police subculture, characterized by **cynicism**, clannishness, secrecy, and insulation from others in society—the so-called **blue curtain**. Police officers tend to socialize with one another and believe that their occupation cuts them off from relationships with civilians. Joining the police subculture means always having to stick up for fellow officers against outsiders; maintaining a tough, macho exterior; and distrusting the motives and behavior of outsiders.[30] The code of silence demands that officers never turn in their peers, even if they engage in corrupt or illegal practices.[31]

Some police experts have described the following core beliefs as the heart of the police culture today:

- *Police are the only real crime fighters.* The public wants the police officer to fight crime; other agencies, both public and private, only play at crime fighting.
- *No one else understands the real nature of police work.* Lawyers, academics, politicians, and the public in general have little concept of what it means to be a police officer.
- *Loyalty to colleagues counts above everything else.* Police officers have to stick together, because everyone is out to get the police and make the job more difficult.
- *It is impossible to win the war against crime without bending the rules.* Courts have awarded criminal defendants too many civil rights.
- *Members of the public are basically unsupportive and unreasonably demanding.* People are quick to criticize police unless they themselves need police help.
- *Patrol work is the pits.* Detective work is glamorous and exciting.[32]

The forces that support a police culture are generally believed to develop out of on-the-job experiences. Most officers, both male and female, originally join police forces because they want to help people, fight crime, and have an interesting, exciting, prestigious career with a high degree of job security[33] Recruits often find that the social reality of police work does not mesh with their original career goals. They are unprepared for the emotional turmoil and conflict that accompany police work today.

Some experts fear that the police culture divides officers from the people they serve and creates an "us against the world" mentality, an independent police culture in which violations of the law may result in stigmatization of offenders and lead to a leveling of sanctions against those who occupy the "other" status.[34] Criminals are referred to as "terrorists" and "predators," terms that suggest they are evil individuals eager to prey upon the poor and vulnerable. This vision may encourage and promote violence and brutality.

At first glance, the existence of an independent police subculture seems damaging, but it may also have some benefits. Membership in the police culture helps recruits adjust to the rigors of police work and provides the emotional support needed for survival.[35] The culture encourages decisiveness in the face of uncertainty and the ability to make split-second judgments that may later be subject to extreme criticism. Officers who view themselves as crime fighters are the ones most likely to value solidarity and depend on the support and camaraderie of their fellow officers.[36] The police subculture encourages its members to draw a sharp distinction between good and evil. Officers, more than mere enforcers of the law, are warriors in the age-old battle between right and wrong.[37] Police officers perceive their working environment to be rife with danger, an outlook that reinforces cohesion among officers.[38] And because criminals—"predators"—represent a real danger, the police culture demands that its members be both competent and concerned with the safety of their peers and partners.[39]

In sum, the police culture has developed in response to the insulated, dangerous lifestyle of police officers. Policing is a dangerous occupation, and the unquestioned support and loyalty of their peers is not something officers could readily do without.[40] Although it is feared that an independent police culture may isolate police officers from the community and make them suspicious and mistrustful of the public they serve, it may also unify the police and improve the camaraderie and solidarity among fellow officers.

The Police Personality

To some commentators, the typical police personality can be described as dogmatic, authoritarian, and suspicious.[41] Cynicism has been found at all levels of policing (including chiefs of police) and throughout all stages of a police career.[42] These negative values and attitudes are believed to cause police officers to be secretive and isolated from the rest of society, weaving the blue curtain.[43]

How does cynicism develop? The police officer's working personality is shaped by constant exposure to danger and the need to use force and authority to defuse and control threatening situations.[44] Police feel suspicious of the public they serve and defensive about the actions of their fellow officers. There are two opposing viewpoints on the cause of this phenomenon. One is that police departments attract recruits who are by nature cynical, authoritarian, secretive, and so on.[45] Other experts maintain that socialization and experience on the police force itself cause these character traits to develop in officers. According to this view, as their experiences in the separate police culture develops, officers eventually embrace a unique set of personality traits that distinguishes them from the average citizen.[46]

Despite popular belief and some research support, efforts to find and identify a classic "police personality" have had mixed results. Although some research concludes that police values are different from those of the general adult population, other efforts reach an opposite conclusion: some have found that police officers are actually more psychologically healthy than the general population, less depressed and anxious, and more social and assertive.[47] Police officers have been found to value such personality traits as warmth, flexibility, and emotion; these qualities are far removed from rigidity and cynicism.[48] Because research has found evidence supportive of both viewpoints, it is not possible to determine how the police personality develops—or even whether one actually exists.

> **LO3** Explain police culture and personality

Policing Style

Part of the socialization of a police officer is developing a working attitude, or style, through which to approach policing. For example, some police officers may view the job as a well-paid civil service position that emphasizes careful compliance with written departmental rules and procedures. Other officers may see themselves as part of the "thin blue line" that protects the public from wrongdoers. They will use any means to get the culprit, even if it involves planting evidence on an obviously guilty person who has so far escaped arrest.

Several studies have attempted to define and classify police styles into behavioral clusters. An examination of this literature suggests that four styles of police work seem to fit the current behavior patterns of most police agents: the crime fighter, the social agent, the law enforcer, and the watchman. These are described in Exhibit 6.1. Although officers who embrace a particular style of policing may emphasize one area of law enforcement over another, their daily activities are likely to require them to engage in some police duties they consider trivial or unimportant.

> **LO4** Identify distinct policing styles

The Four Basic Styles of Policing

The Crime Fighter To the crime fighter, the most important aspects of police work are investigating serious crimes and apprehending criminals. Crime fighters focus on the victim and view effective police work as the only force that can keep society's "dangerous classes" in check. They are the thin blue line protecting society from murderers and rapists. They consider property crimes to be less significant and believe that such matters as misdemeanors, traffic control, and social service functions would be better handled by other agencies of government. The ability to investigate criminal behavior that poses a serious threat to life and safety, combined with the power to arrest criminals, separates a police department from other municipal agencies. Crime fighters see diluting these functions with minor social service and nonenforcement duties as harmful to police efforts to create a secure society.

The Social Agent The social agent believes that police should be involved in a wide range of activities without regard for their connection to law enforcement. Rather than viewing themselves as "criminal catchers," the social agents consider themselves as community problem solvers. They are troubleshooters who patch the holes that appear where the social fabric wears thin. They are happy to work with special-needs populations, such as the homeless, school kids, and those in need of emergency services. The social agent fits well in a community policing unit.

The Law Enforcer According to this view, duty is clearly set out in law. Law enforcers stress playing it "by the book." Since the police are specifically charged with apprehending all types of lawbreakers, they see themselves as generalized law enforcement agents. Although law enforcers may prefer working on serious crimes—because they are more intriguing and rewarding in terms of achievement, prestige, and status—they see the police role as one of enforcing all statutes and ordinances. They perceive themselves neither as community social workers nor as vengeance-seeking vigilantes: quite simply, they are professional law enforcement officers who perform the functions of detecting violations, identifying culprits, and taking the lawbreakers before a court. The law enforcer is devoted to the profession of police work and is the officer most likely to aspire to command rank.

The Watchman The watchman style is characterized by an emphasis on maintaining public order as the police goal, rather than law enforcement or general service. Watchmen choose to ignore many infractions and requests for service unless they believe that the social or political order is jeopardized. Juveniles are "expected" to misbehave and are best ignored or treated informally. Motorists will often be left alone if their driving does not endanger or annoy others. Vice and gambling are problems only when the currently accepted standards of public order are violated. Like the watchman of old, this officer takes action only when and if a problem arises. The watchman is the most passive officer, more concerned with retirement benefits than crime rates.

Sources: William Muir, *Police: Streetcorner Politicians* (Chicago; University of Chicago Press, 1977); James Q. Wilson, *Varieties of Police Behavior* (Cambridge, MA: Harvard University Press, 1968).

Police Discretion

discretion
The use of personal decision making and choice in carrying out operations in the criminal justice system. For example, police discretion can involve deciding whether to make an arrest; prosecutorial discretion can involve deciding whether to accept a plea bargain.

Police have the ability to deprive people of their liberty, arrest them and take them away in handcuffs, and even use deadly force to subdue them. A critical aspect of this professional responsibility is the personal **discretion** each officer has in carrying out his or her responsibilities. Discretion can involve selective enforcement of the law—as occurs, for instance, when a vice squad plainclothes officer decides not to take action against a tavern that is serving drinks after hours. Patrol officers use discretion when they decide to arrest one suspect for disorderly conduct but to escort another home.

The majority of police officers use a high degree of personal discretion in carrying out daily tasks, sometimes referred to as "low-visibility decision making" in criminal justice.[49] This terminology suggests that, unlike members of almost every other criminal justice agency, police are neither regulated in their daily procedures by administrative scrutiny nor subject to judicial review (except when their behavior clearly violates an offender's constitutional rights). The public recognizes the right of police to exercise discretion, even if it means using force to control an unruly suspect while treating a more cooperative one with deference and respect.[50]

The concept of **emotional intelligence** has important implications for the study of police discretion. Defined as the "ability to monitor one's own and others' feelings and emotions, to discriminate among them and to use this information to guide one's thinking and actions,"[51] emotional intelligence is critically important for police officers. Being in tune with one's emotions, being able to act in an emotionally mature fashion, and managing one's own mental state during difficult encounters can make all the difference in responding to the many situations that make policing a unique profession. Only recently has emotional intelligence training begun working its way into police training curricula.[52]

Researchers have identified a number of factors that affect police decision making.[53] The following sections describe the factors that influence police discretion and review suggestions for its control.

emotional intelligence
"The ability to monitor one's own and others' feelings and emotions, to discriminate among them and to use this information to guide one's thinking and actions."

Legal Factors

Police discretion is inversely related to the severity of the offense. This means police have far less personal discretion when they confront a suspect in a case involving murder or rape than when the offense is a simple assault or trespass.[54] For example, if a weapon is brandished or used, police are much more likely to respond with a formal arrest.[55] The likelihood of a police officer taking legal action, then, partly depends on how the individual officer views the severity of the offense.

Environmental Factors

The degree of discretion an officer will exercise is at least partially defined by the officer's living and working environment.[56] Police officers may work or dwell in a community culture that either tolerates eccentricities and personal freedoms or

■ Whether a police officer makes an arrest may depend on how the individual officer views offense severity. Here officer Deon Joseph waits for a squad car to transport Marco Rodriguez to a detox center in the Skid Row area of downtown Los Angeles, rather than to jail.

AP Images/Tracy Gitnick

expects extremely conservative, professional, no-nonsense behavior on the part of its civil servants. Communities that are proactive and include progressive governmental institutions also may influence a police officer's discretion. Police officers in communities that provide training in domestic violence prevention and maintain local shelters for battered women are more likely to take action in cases involving spousal abuse.[57]

Departmental Factors

Where and how the department operates also shape police practices. For example, officers are more likely to be proactive and use their arrest powers when they work in departments that are located in high-crime areas but have relatively few personnel.[58] In these departments, individual officers may believe they have to be proactive to compensate for the lack of resources. Departments also issue directives intended to influence police conduct, such as mandatory arrest policies for certain crimes.

Peer Factors

Police discretion is also subject to peer influence.[59] Police officers turn to their peers for both on-the-job advice and off-the-job companionship, essentially forming a subculture to provide a source of status, prestige, and reward. The peer group affects how police officers exercise discretion on two distinct levels. In an obvious, direct manner, other police officers dictate acceptable responses to street-level problems by providing or withholding approval in office discussions. Second, officers who take their job seriously and desire the respect and friendship of others will take their advice, abide by their norms, and seek out the most experienced and influential patrol officers on the force to adopt as behavior models.

Situational Factors

demeanor
The way in which a person outwardly manifests his or her personality.

Some research efforts find that police officers rely on **demeanor** (the attitude and appearance of the offender) in making decisions.[60] That is, if an offender is surly, talks back, or otherwise challenges the officer's authority, formal action is more likely to be taken.[61] Not everyone agrees, however. David Klinger, a police officer turned criminologist, maintains that demeanor may not be as much of a factor in shaping discretion as most others believe. Klinger believes that the average officer becomes used to surly demeanor and uncivil behavior, so it takes more than that to influence discretion.[62]

The way a crime or situation is encountered may also influence discretion. When a police officer stumbles on an altercation or break-in, the discretionary response may be different from the response when the officer is summoned by police radio. If an act has received official police recognition, such as the dispatch of a patrol car, police action must be taken or an explanation made as to why it was not. If a matter is brought to an officer's attention by a citizen observer, the officer can ignore the request and risk a complaint or take discretionary action.

Extralegal Factors

One oft-debated issue is whether police take race, class, and gender into account when making arrest decisions. Research results are mixed: Some studies show that the offender's age, gender, and racial characteristics are key determinants that shape the arrest process.[63] Others find that this unequal treatment is not a serious problem. For example, the gender gap in police arrests is closing; women are getting arrested for certain offenses (such as drunk driving) more than they ever have been in the past.[64]

Victim characteristics also appear to influence police action. For example, police are more willing to make an arrest when the victim is older, white, affluent, and

L05 Describe factors that affect police discretion

so on.[65] Neighborhood factors matter, as well. Related to this is the relationship between the parties. If the victim and the offender know one another, there is less of a chance that an arrest will be made.[66]

One significant issue is whether race plays a role in the decision to stop, question, and search motorists, a practice referred to as **racial profiling**. There is evidence that minorities are searched more often than whites.[67] Yet a number of researchers have found little to no evidence of racial profiling.[68] Some argue that it can even be beneficial. How could profiling be beneficial? Two Harvard scholars, Mathias Risse and Richard Zeckhauser, have argued that there is a significant correlation between membership in certain racial groups and the propensity to commit certain crimes.[69]

racial profiling
The practice of police targeting minority groups because of a belief that they are more likely to be engaged in criminal activity.

Problems of Policing

Law enforcement is not an easy job. The role ambiguity, social isolation, and threat of danger present in "working the street" are the police officer's constant companions. What effects do these strains have on police? This section discusses four of the most significant problems: job stress, fatigue, violence, and corruption.

Job Stress

The complexity of their role, the need to exercise prudent discretion, the threat of having to use violence and of having violence used against them, and isolation from the rest of society all take a toll on law enforcement officers. It is not surprising, then, that police officers experience tremendous stress, a factor that leads some to alcoholism, depression, and even suicide. There is evidence that police officers are all too often involved in marital disputes and even incidents of domestic violence that may be linked to stress.[70] These developments are not lost on police officers, many of whom feel significant amounts of job-related stress, a condition that may undermine their enthusiasm and commitment.[71] Stress and burnout become part of the job. Stress may not be constant, but at some time during their career (usually the middle years) most officers will feel the effects of stress.[72]

Causes of Stress A number of factors have been associated with job stress.[73] The pressure of being on duty 24 hours a day leads to stress and emotional detachment from both work and public needs. Policing is a dangerous profession, and officers are at risk for many forms of job-related accidental deaths. Stress has been related to internal conflict with administrative policies that deny officers support and a meaningful role in decision making. Some officers may become stressed when they are forced to adapt to the demands of community-oriented policing but are skeptical about the utility or effectiveness of this change in policy.[74] In addition, police suffer stress in their personal lives when they "bring the job home" or when their work hours are shifted, causing family disruptions.[75] Those who feel alienated from family and friends at home are more likely to feel stress on the job.[76]

Other stressors include poor training, substandard equipment, inadequate pay, lack of opportunity, job dissatisfaction, role conflict, exposure to brutality, and fears about competence, success, and safety.[77] Some officers may feel stress because they believe that the court system favors the rights of the criminal and handcuffs the police; others may be sensitive to a perceived lack of support from governmental officials and the general public.[78] Some officers even believe that their superiors care little about their welfare.[79]

The effects of stress can be shocking. Police work has been related to both physical and psychological ailments.[80] Police have a high rate of premature death caused by such conditions as heart disease and diabetes. They also experience a disproportionate number of divorces and other marital problems. Research indicates that police officers in some departments, but not all, have higher suicide rates than the general public.[81] Police who feel stress may not be open to adopting new ideas and programs such as community policing.[82]

Combating Stress Research efforts have shown that the more support police officers get in the workplace, the lower their feelings of stress and anxiety.[83] Consequently, departments have attempted to fight job-related stress by training officers to cope with its effects. Today stress training includes diet information, biofeedback, relaxation and meditation, and exercise. Many departments include stress management as part of an overall wellness program also designed to promote physical and mental health, fitness, and good nutrition.[84] Some programs have included family members; they may be better able to help the officer cope if they fully understand the difficulties of police work. Total wellness programming enhances the physical and emotional well-being of officers by emphasizing preventive physical and psychological measures.[85] And because police are aware of the many benefits of their job and enjoy the quality of life it provides, stress reduction programs can help officers focus on the positive aspects of police work.[86]

Fatigue

Nearly everyone has been tired at work from time to time. But whereas on-the-job sleepiness is inconsequential for many workers, it can lead to disaster for others. No one wants airline pilots to fall asleep, and the prospect of a truck driver sleeping behind the wheel is equally disturbing. What about a police officer? A police officer who is overly tired may be at a higher risk of acting inappropriately or being injured on the job.[87]

The problem of "tired cops"[88] has largely been overlooked, but it should not be.[89] Police officers often work lengthy shifts with unpredictable hours. The *Boston Globe* investigated one agency and found that 16 officers worked more than 80 hours in a week. One even worked 130 hours! Although it is difficult to fault anyone for seeking overtime pay, too much work can lead to disaster. Here are some examples:

- A Michigan police officer working nearly 24 hours straight crashes his cruiser while chasing a fleeing motorist. He is critically injured.
- In California, a sheriff's deputy working alone drifts off a deserted highway and is killed instantly when his patrol car crashes into a tree.

A tired police officer rests after a confrontation between demonstrators and police outside a convention center. Fatigue takes a toll in law enforcement, just as it does in a number of other professions. What unique features of police work make fatigue a problem? What can be done to address it?

AP Photo/Joe Cavaretta

- An officer in Florida, who has had trouble staying awake, runs a red light in her patrol car and crashes into a van driven by a deputy sheriff, injuring him severely.
- A police officer driving home from working in Ohio nods off at the wheel, begins swerving in and out of traffic, and runs off the road, striking and killing a man jogging down the sidewalk.

Controlling Fatigue What can be done to control police fatigue? One option is for administrators to make special efforts during scheduling to ensure that officers do not work too much overtime. Another is for administrators to adopt policies that place limitations on second jobs. Many officers moonlight as security guards, which may affect their on-the-job performance. A recent government report offered several other recommendations for limiting fatigue.

Violence and Brutality

There is evidence that only a small proportion of officers are continually involved in use-of-force incidents. Why do these cops continually get involved in violent confrontations? Aggressive cops may overreact to the stress of police work and at the same time feel socially isolated. They believe that the true source of their frustration is beyond their reach, so they take their frustrations out on readily available targets: vulnerable people in their immediate environment.[90]

What kind of police officer gets involved in problem behavior? Are some officers "chronic offenders"? Research seems to show that a few officers are in fact chronic offenders who account for a significant portion of all citizen complaints. The officers receiving the bulk of complaints tend to be young and less experienced.[91] Efforts to deal with these "problem cops" are now being undertaken in police departments around the nation.

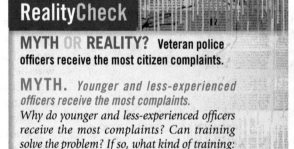

Curbing Violence Because incidents of brutality undermine efforts to build a bridge between police and the public, police departments around the United States have instituted specialized training programs to reduce them. A number of larger departments are instituting early warning systems to change the behavior of individual officers who have been identified as having performance problems. In most systems, problem officers are identified by their behavior profiles: citizen complaints, firearm discharge and use-of-force reports, civil litigation, incidents of resisting arrest, and high-speed pursuits and vehicular damage. The initial intervention generally consists of a review by the officer's immediate supervisor, who advises the officer of the sanctions he faces if problems continue; some cases are referred to counseling, training, or police psychologists. Evaluations of early warning programs indicate that they are quite successful.[92]

Some departments have developed administrative policies that emphasize limiting the use of force and containing armed offenders until specially trained backup teams are sent to take charge of the situation. Administrative policies have been found to be an effective control on use of deadly force, and their influence can be enhanced if they are clearly supported by the chief of police.[93]

Some cities are taking an aggressive, proactive stance to curb violent cops. Since 1977, the New York Police Department has been operating a Force-Related Integrity Testing program in which undercover officers pose as angry citizens in elaborate sting operations intended to weed out officers with a propensity for violence. In a typical encounter, officers responding to a radio call on a domestic dispute confront an aggressive husband who spews hatred at everyone around, including the police. The "husband" is actually an undercover officer from the internal affairs bureau, who is testing whether the officers, some of whom have a history of civilian complaints, will respond to verbal abuse with threats or violence. The NYPD conducts about 600 sting operations each year to test the integrity of its officers; several dozen are devoted to evaluating the conduct of officers with a history of abuse complaints.[94]

Perhaps the greatest factors in controlling the use of **police brutality** are the threat of civil judgments against individual officers who use excessive force, police chiefs who ignore or condone violent behavior, and the expectations that prevail in the cities and towns in which they are employed.

police brutality
Usually involves such actions as the use of abusive language, the unnecessary use of force or coercion, threats, prodding with nightsticks, stopping and searching people to harass them, and so on.

Corruption

corruption
Exercising legitimate discretion for improper reasons or using illegal means to achieve approved goals.

Ever since their creation, U.S. police departments have wrestled with the problem of controlling illegal and unprofessional behavior by their officers. **Corruption** pervaded the American police when the early departments were first formed. In the nineteenth century, police officers systematically ignored violations of laws related to drinking, gambling, and prostitution in return for regular payoffs. Some actually entered into relationships with professional criminals, especially pickpockets. Illegal behavior was tolerated in return for goods or information. Police officers helped politicians gain office by allowing electoral fraud to flourish; some senior officers sold promotions to higher rank in the department.[95] Although most police officers are not corrupt, the few who are dishonest bring discredit to the entire profession.

Varieties of Corruption Police deviance can include a number of activities. In a general sense, it involves misuse of authority by police officers in a manner designed to yield personal gain for themselves or others.[96] However, debate continues over whether a desire for personal gain is an essential part of corruption. Some experts argue that police misconduct also involves such issues as the unnecessary use of force, unreasonable searches, or an immoral personal life and that these should be considered just as serious as corruption motivated by economic gain.

Knapp Commission
A public body that led an investigation into police corruption in New York and uncovered a widespread network of payoffs and bribes.

Scholars have attempted to create typologies categorizing the forms that the abuse of police powers can take. When investigating corruption among police officers in New York City, the **Knapp Commission** classified abusers into two

Retired Tulsa, Oklahoma, Police Department Corporal Harold Wells, right, walks into a federal courthouse moments before he was found guilty in a police corruption trial. Two other officers, Nick DeBruin and Bruce Bohnam, were found not guilty of similar charges. A federal jury convicted Wells on charges he engaged in drug trafficking and stole federal money. It rejected prosecutors' claims that DeBruin and Bohnam were part of a corruption ring that left a blemish on the city police department and led to the release of more than 30 defendants.

AP Photo/The Tulsa World, Cory Young

categories: **meat eaters** and **grass eaters**. Meat eaters aggressively misuse police power for personal gain by demanding bribes, threatening legal action, or cooperating with criminals. In contrast, grass eaters accept payoffs when their everyday duties place them in a position to "look the other way."

Other police experts have attempted to create models to better understand police corruption. It may be possible to divide police corruption into four major categories. These are depicted in Exhibit 6.2.

Causes of Corruption No single explanation satisfactorily accounts for the various forms the abuse of power takes. One view holds that policing tends to attract individuals who do not have the financial means to maintain a coveted middle-class lifestyle. As they develop the cynical, authoritarian police personality, accepting graft seems an all-too-easy method of achieving financial security. A second view is that the wide discretion police enjoy, coupled with low visibility among the public and their own supervisors, makes them likely candidates for corruption. A third perspective holds that corruption is a function of society's ambivalence toward many forms of vice-related criminal behavior that police officers are sworn to control. Unenforceable laws governing moral standards promote corruption because they create large groups with an interest in undermining law enforcement. These include consumers who do not want to be deprived of their chosen form of recreation—people who gamble, wish to drink after the legal closing hour, or patronize prostitutes.

Control of Corruption How can police misconduct be controlled? One approach is to strengthen the internal administrative review process in police departments. A strong and well-supported internal affairs division has been linked to lowered corruption rates.[97] Another approach, instituted by then New York Commissioner Patrick Murphy in the wake of the Knapp Commission, is the *accountability system*. This holds that supervisors at each level are directly accountable for the illegal behaviors of the officers under them. Consequently, a commander can be demoted or forced to resign if someone under his or her command is found guilty of corruption.[98] Close scrutiny by a department, however, can lower officer morale and create the impression that the officers' own supervisors distrust them.

Another approach is to create outside review boards or special prosecutors, such as the Mollen Commission in New York and the Christopher Commission in Los Angeles, to investigate reported incidents of corruption. However, outside investigators and special prosecutors are often limited by their lack of intimate knowledge of day-to-day operations. As a result, they depend on the testimony of a few officers who are willing to cooperate, either to save themselves from prosecution or because they have a compelling moral commitment. Outside evaluators also face the problem of the blue curtain, which is quickly drawn when police officers feel their department is under scrutiny.

Some jurisdictions have even developed review boards that monitor police behavior and tactics and investigate civilian complaints. Although police agencies in some communities have embraced citizen reviews, others find them troublesome. Departmental opposition is most likely when oversight procedures represent outside interference, oversight staff lack experience with and understanding of police work, and/or oversight processes are unfair. Despite serious reservations about citizen oversight, many law enforcement administrators have identified positive outcomes from having a review board in place. These include improving community relations, enhancing an agency's ability to police itself, and (most important)

Exhibit 6.2

Varieties of Police Corruption

- *Internal corruption.* This corruption takes place among police officers themselves, involving both the bending of departmental rules and the outright performance of illegal acts.
- *Selective enforcement or nonenforcement.* This occurs when police abuse or exploit their discretion. If an officer frees a drug dealer in return for valuable information, that is considered a legitimate use of discretion; if the officer does so for money, that is an abuse of police power.
- *Active criminality.* This is participation by police in serious criminal behavior. Police may use their positions of trust and power to commit the very crimes they are entrusted with controlling.
- *Bribery and extortion.* This includes practices in which law enforcement roles are exploited specifically to raise money. Bribery is initiated by the citizen; extortion is initiated by the officer.

Source: Michael Johnston, *Political Corruption and Public Policy in America* (Monterey, CA: Brooks/Cole, 1982), p. 75.

meat eaters
A term for police officers who actively solicit bribes and vigorously engage in corrupt practices.

grass eaters
A term for police officers who accept payoffs when everyday duties place them in a position to "look the other way."

LO6 Discuss four major problems of policing

improving an agency's policies and procedures. Citizen oversight bodies can recommend changes in the way the department conducts its internal investigations into alleged misconduct and can also suggest ways to improve department policies governing officer behavior.[99]

Use of Force

How much force is being used by the police in the United States today?[100] Despite some highly publicized incidents that get a lot of media attention, research reveals that the use of force is not very common. A national survey on police contacts with civilians, sponsored by the federal government, sheds some light on this issue.[101] Among the survey's most important findings:

- An estimated 19 percent of U.S. residents age 16 or older had a face-to-face contact with a police officer.
- Contact between police and the public was more common among males, whites, and younger residents.
- Overall, about 9 out of 10 persons who had contact with police in 2005 felt the police acted properly.
- An estimated 2 percent of people stopped by police had force used or threatened against them during their most recent contact.
- Blacks and Hispanics experienced police use of force at higher rates than whites.

The data indicate that (a) relatively few contacts with police and the public involve physical force, but (b) there seem to be race and ethnic differences in the rate at which force is applied. As Table 6.1 shows, half of the force incidents involved more than scuffling or shouting. And even though African Americans (82%) were less likely than whites (91%) to feel that the police acted properly during a contact, the great majority of citizens of all races considered police behavior to be appropriate given the circumstances of the contact.

Deadly Force

deadly force
Force that is likely to cause death or serious bodily harm.

suicide by cop
A form of suicide in which a person acts in an aggressive manner with police officers in order to induce them to shoot to kill.

As it is commonly used, the term **deadly force** refers to the actions of a police officer who shoots and kills a suspect who flees from arrest, assaults a victim, or attacks an officer.[102] The justification for the use of deadly force can be traced to English common law, in which almost every criminal offense was a felony and bore the death penalty. The use of deadly force in the course of arresting a felon was considered expedient, saving the state the trouble of conducting a trial (the "fleeing-felon rule").[103]

Although the media depict hero cops in a constant stream of deadly shootouts in which scores of bad guys are killed, the actual number of people killed by the police each year is usually between 250 and 300.[104] And some of these shootings may even be precipitated by the target as a form of suicide.[105] This tragic event has become so common that the term **suicide by cop** has been coined to denote victim-precipitated killings by police.[106]

Although the police use of deadly force may not be as common as previously believed, it remains a central part of the police role. It is difficult to get an accurate figure, but at least 6,600 civilians have been killed by the police since 1976, and the true number is probably much higher.[107]

Controlling Deadly Force Because the police use of deadly force is such a serious issue, ongoing efforts have been made to control it. One of the most difficult issues in controlling the problem was the continued use of the fleeing-felon rule

TABLE 6.1 Police Response in Encounters with Citizens in which Use of Force was Reported	
Type of force used or threatened by police	Percent
Pushed or grabbed	43
Kicked or hit	9
Sprayed chemical/Pepper spray	3
Pointed gun	15
Used other force	10
Police threatened to use force	27
Shouted or cursed at by police	10
Type of force used or threatened was not reported	7

Source: Matthew Durose, Erica Smith, and Patrick Langan, *Contacts Between Police and the Public: Findings from the 2005 National Survey* (Washington, DC: Bureau of Justice Statistics, 2007), www.ojp.usdoj.gov/bjs/pub/pdf/cpp05.pdf. Percentages do not sum to 100 because some people reported, in cases where force was used, that officers used more than one type of force.

PART 2 ■ The Police and Law Enforcement

The term "deadly force" refers to the actions of a police officer who shoots and kills a suspect who is fleeing from arrest, assaults a victim, or attacks an officer. Here police assist a victim of an attempted robbery in Kokomo, Indiana. One man was wounded by police, and another was arrested following a four-hour standoff at a home, authorities said. Police said the standoff began about 3:30 P.M., when an officer on patrol was flagged down by a person reporting an armed robbery.

AP Images/*Kokomo Tribune*, Tim Bath

in a number of states. In 1985, the Supreme Court outlawed the indiscriminate use of deadly force with its decision in *Tennessee v. Garner*. In this case, the Court ruled that the use of deadly force against apparently unarmed and nondangerous fleeing felons is an illegal seizure of their person under the Fourth Amendment. Deadly force may not be used unless it is necessary to prevent an escape and the officer has probable cause to believe that the suspect poses a significant threat of death or serious injury to the officer or others. The majority opinion stated that where the suspect poses no immediate threat to the officer and no threat to others, the harm resulting from failing to apprehend the suspect does not justify the use of deadly force to do so: "A police officer may not seize an unarmed, nondangerous suspect by shooting him dead."[108]

Individual state jurisdictions still control police shooting policy. Some states have adopted statutory policies that restrict the police use of violence. Others have upgraded training in the use of force. The Federal Law Enforcement Training Center has developed the FLETC use-of-force model, illustrated in Figure 6.1, to teach officers the proper method to escalate force in response to the threat they face.

Reasonable officer's perception	Enforcement electives	Reasonable officer's response
Assaultive (serious bodily harm/death)	V	Deadly force
Assaultive (bodily harm)	IV	Defensive tactics
Resistant (active)	III	Compliance techniques
Resistant (passive)	II	Contact controls
Compliant (cooperative)	I	Verbal commands

Figure 6.1 The Federal Law Enforcement Training Center's Use-of-Force Model

Source: Franklin Graves and Gregory Connor, Federal Law Enforcement Training Center, Glynco, Georgia.

As the figure shows, resistance ranges from compliant and cooperative to assaultive with the threat of serious bodily harm or death. Officers are taught via lecture, demonstration, computer-based instruction, and training scenarios to assess the suspect's behavior and apply an appropriate and corresponding amount of force.[109]

Another way to control police shootings is through internal review and policy-making by police administrative review boards. For example, since 1972, the New York City Police Department has conducted an internal investigation any time an officer's weapon is discharged (within the exception of training situations). Several dispositions are possible. These can range from a conclusion that the shooting was in accordance with law and policy, all the way to termination and even criminal prosecution (if the prosecutor feels criminal charges are merited). The review board approach is controversial because it can mean that the department recommends that one of its own officers be turned over for criminal prosecution.[110]

Nondeadly Force

nondeadly force
Force that is unlikely to cause death or significant bodily harm.

Nondeadly force is force that is unlikely to cause death or significant bodily harm. Nondeadly force can range from the use of handcuffs and suspect compliance techniques to rubber bullets and stun guns. Officers resort to nondeadly force in a number of circumstances. They may begin with verbal commands and then escalate the force used when confronted with a resistant suspect. Researchers have found that the crime in question is strongly linked to the type of nondeadly force used and that officers are also influenced by past experience, the presence of other officers, and the presence and behavior of bystanders.[111] And even though nondeadly force is used more often than deadly force, it is still relatively rare— and at the lower end of the severity scale (e.g., grabbed by officer instead of hit). Researchers have estimated that police use or threaten to use nondeadly force in only 1.7 percent of all contacts and 20 percent of all arrests.[112]

LO7 Distinguish between deadly and nondeadly force— and methods for controlling each

Controlling Nondeadly Force In *Graham v. Connor*, the Supreme Court ruled that issues related to nondeadly force must be judged from the standpoint of a reasonable officer.[113] For example, say an officer is approached in a threatening manner by someone wielding a knife. The assailant fails to stop when warned and is killed by the officer, but it turns out later that the shooting victim was deaf and could not hear the officer's command. The officer would not be held liable if, at the time of the incident, he had no way of knowing the person's disability.

Less-Lethal Weapons

less-lethal weapons
Weapons designed to disable or immobilize rather than kill criminal suspects.

In the last few years, about a thousand local police forces have started using so-called **less-lethal weapons** to subdue certain suspects. Some of the most widely used less-lethal weapons are wood, rubber, or polyurethane bullets shot out of modified 37-mm pistols or 12-gauge shotguns. At short distances, officers use pepper spray and Tasers, which deliver electric shocks with long wire tentacles, producing intense muscle spasms. Other technologies still in development include guns that shoot giant nets, guns that squirt sticky glue, and lights that can temporarily blind a suspect. New weapons are being developed that shoot bags filled with lead pellets; the weapons have a range of 100 feet and pack the wallop of a pro boxer's punch.[114]

Recent research efforts indicate that less-lethal weapons may help reduce police use of force.[115] Greater effort must be made to regulate these less-lethal weapons and create effective policies for their use.[116]

LO8 Explain the importance of less-lethal weapons

Police and the Rule of Law

The police are charged with preventing crime and, when crime does occur, with investigating the case, identifying the culprit, and making an arrest, all the while gathering sufficient evidence to convict the culprit at trial. To carry out these tasks, police officers need to be able to search for evidence, to seize items such as guns and drugs, and to question suspects, witnesses, and victims, because at trial, they must provide prosecutors with sufficient evidence to prove guilt "beyond a reasonable doubt." This requirement means that soon after a crime is committed, they must make every effort to gather physical evidence, obtain confessions, and take witness statements that will stand up in court. Police officers also realize that evidence such as the testimony of a witness or a co-conspirator may evaporate before the trial begins. Then the outcome of the case may depend on some piece of physical evidence or a suspect's statement taken early during the investigation.

The need for police officers to gather evidence can conflict with the constitutional rights of citizens. For example, although police might prefer a free hand to search homes and cars for evidence, the Fourth Amendment restricts police activities by limiting searches and seizures to those deemed "reasonable." Likewise, when police wish to vigorously interrogate a suspect, they must honor the Fifth Amendment's prohibition against forcing people to incriminate themselves. The following sections address some key areas in which police operations have been restricted or curtailed by the courts.

Interrogation and Confessions

After an arrest is made, police want to interrogate suspects, hoping they will confess to a crime, name co-conspirators, or make incriminating statements that can be used against them in court. But the Fifth Amendment guarantees people the right to be free from self-incrimination. The courts have used this phrase to prohibit law enforcement agents from using physical or psychological coercion while interrogating suspects to get them to confess or give information. Confessions obtained from defendants through coercion, force, trickery, or promises of leniency are inadmissible because their trustworthiness is questionable.

The *Miranda* Rule In 1966, in the case of *Miranda v. Arizona*, the Supreme Court created objective standards for questioning by police after a defendant has been taken into custody.[117] Custody occurs when a person is not free to walk away, such as when an individual is arrested. The Court maintained that before the police can question a person who has been arrested or is in custody, they must inform the individual of her or his Fifth Amendment right to be free from self-incrimination. This is accomplished by the police issuing what is known as the ***Miranda* warning**, which informs the suspect that

- He has the right to remain silent.
- If he makes a statement, it can be used against him in court.
- He has the right to consult an attorney and to have the attorney present at the time of the interrogation.
- If he cannot afford an attorney, one will be appointed by the state.

If the defendant is not given the *Miranda* warning before the investigation, the evidence obtained from the interrogation cannot be admitted at trial. An accused person can waive his or her *Miranda* rights at any time. For the waiver to be effective, however, the state must first show that the defendant was aware of all the *Miranda* rights and must then prove that the waiver was made with the full knowledge of constitutional rights. People who cannot understand the *Miranda* warning because of their age, mental handicaps, or language problems cannot be legally questioned without their attorney present; if they *can* understand their rights and then waive them, they may be questioned.[118] The Supreme Court has decided a number of *Miranda*-related cases over the years. The key cases are summarized in Exhibit 6.3.

Miranda **warning**
The requirement that police officers inform suspects subjected to custodial interrogation that they have a constitutional right to remain silent, that their statements can later be used against them in court, that they can have an attorney present to help them, and that the state will pay for an attorney if they cannot afford to hire one.

RealityCheck

MYTH OR REALITY? The police are not required to advise all arrestees of their *Miranda* rights.

REALITY. Miranda *rights need be read only when custody (such as arrest) is coupled with interrogation.*

Police departments may adopt more restrictive policies, however, requiring Miranda warnings any time a person is arrested. Should the Miranda warnings be read every time a person is arrested?

Chicago Police Department Lieutenant Marty Ryczek shows off control panels to monitor video in the interview room at the police department's Area 1 headquarters. An Illinois law requires police to videotape homicide interrogations. The law was approved to help clean up a justice system haunted by wrongful convictions. Do you think video recordings of interrogations are beneficial? Why or why not?

AP Photo/Jeff Roberson

Exhibit 6.3

Important *Miranda*-related Decisions Over the Years

Fare v. Michael C. (1978) The *Miranda* warning applies only to the right to have an attorney present. The suspect cannot demand to speak to a priest, a probation officer, or any other official.[119]

New York v. Quarles (1984) A suspect can be questioned in the field without a *Miranda* warning if the information the police seek is needed to protect public safety. For example, in an emergency, suspects can be asked where they hid their weapons.[120] This is known as the public safety doctrine.

Oregon v. Elstad (1985) Admissions made in the absence of *Miranda* warnings are not admissible at trial, but post-*Miranda* voluntary statements (those made after the warnings are read) are admissible. A post-*Miranda* voluntary statement is admissible even if an initial incriminating statement was made in the absence of *Miranda* warnings.[121]

Colorado v. Connelly (1986) The admissions of mentally impaired defendants can be admitted in evidence as long as the police acted properly and there is a preponderance of the evidence that the defendants understood the meaning of *Miranda*.[122]

Moran v. Burbine (1986) An attorney's request to see the defendant does not affect the validity of the defendant's waiver of the right to counsel. Police misinformation to an attorney does not affect waiver of *Miranda* rights.[123] For example, a suspect's statements may be used if they are given voluntarily, even though his family has hired an attorney and the statements were made before the attorney arrived. Only the suspect can request an attorney, not his friends or family.

Colorado v. Spring (1987) Suspects need not be aware of all the possible outcomes of waiving their rights for the *Miranda* warning to be considered properly given.[124]

Minnick v. Mississippi (1990) When counsel is requested, interrogation must cease and cannot be resumed until an attorney is present.[125]

Arizona v. Fulminante (1991) The erroneous admission of a coerced confession at trial can be ruled a harmless error that would not automatically result in overturning a conviction.[126]

Davis v. United States (1994) A suspect who makes an ambiguous reference to an attorney during questioning, such as "Maybe I should talk to an attorney," is not protected under *Miranda*. The police may continue their questioning.[127]

Exhibit 6.3 (Continued)

Chavez v. Martinez (2003) Failure to give a suspect a *Miranda* warning is not illegal unless the case becomes a criminal issue.[128]

United States v. Patane (2004) A voluntary statement given in the absence of a *Miranda* warning can be used to obtain evidence that can be used at trial. Failure to give the warning does not make seizure of evidence illegal per se.[129]

Missouri v. Seibert (2004) *Miranda* warnings must be given before interrogation begins. The accused in this case was interrogated and confessed in the absence of *Miranda* warnings. *Miranda* rights were then read, at which point the accused "re-confessed." The pre-*Miranda* questioning was improper.[130]

Maryland v. Shatzer (2010) *Miranda* protections do not apply if a suspect is released from police custody for at least 14 days and then questioned. However, if the suspect is re-arrested, then *Miranda* warnings must be read.[131]

Florida v. Powell (2010) The *Miranda* warnings do not require that the suspect be advised that he or she has the right to have an attorney present during questioning. It is sufficient to advise the suspect that he or she has the right to talk with a lawyer before questioning and to consult a lawyer at any time during questioning.[132]

Berghuis v. Thompkins (2010) Unless a suspect asserts his or her *Miranda* rights, any subsequent voluntary statements given after the warnings are admissible in court. Simply remaining silent does not imply that a suspect has invoked *Miranda* protection.[133]

Miranda is now a police (and a prime-time television) institution. It is not surprising that today police administrators who in the past might have been wary of the restrictions forced by *Miranda* now actually favor its use.[134] Yet in spite of its acceptance, critics have called the *Miranda* decision incomprehensible and difficult to administer. How can one tell when a confession is truly voluntary or when it has been produced by pressure and coercion? Aren't all police interrogations essentially coercive?[135] To ensure that *Miranda* rules are being followed, many departments now routinely videotape interrogations.[136] Nonetheless, the *Miranda* decision continues to be an important one.

Search and Seizure

When conducting investigations, police officers want to collect evidence, seize it, and carry it away. They may wish to enter a suspect's home; look for evidence of a crime, such as bloody clothes, drugs, the missing money, or a weapon; seize the evidence; and store it in the evidence room so it can later be used at trial. The manner in which police may seize evidence is governed by the search-and-seizure requirements of the Fourth Amendment of the U.S. Constitution, which was designed by the framers to protect a criminal suspect from unreasonable searches and seizures. Under normal circumstances, no search or seizure undertaken without a search warrant is lawful.

A **search warrant** is a court order authorizing and directing the police to search a designated place for evidence of a crime. To obtain a search warrant, the following procedural requirements must be met: (1) the police officer must request the warrant from the court; (2) the officer must submit an affidavit establishing the proper grounds for the warrant; and (3) the affidavit must state the place to be searched and the property to be seized.

A warrant cannot be issued unless the presiding magistrate is presented with sufficient evidence to conclude that an offense has been or is being committed and that the suspect is the one who committed the offense; this is referred to as the **probable cause** requirement. In other words, the presiding judge must conclude

search warrant
An order issued by a judge, directing officers to conduct a search of specified premises for specified objects or persons and bring them before the court.

probable cause
The evidentiary criterion necessary to sustain an arrest or the issuance of an arrest or search warrant; less than absolute certainty or "beyond a reasonable doubt," but greater than mere suspicion or "hunch."

from the facts presented by the police that there is probable cause a crime has been committed and that the person or place to be searched is materially involved in that crime; there must be solid evidence of criminal involvement.

Searches must also be reasonable under the circumstances of the crime. Police would not be able to get a warrant to search a suspect's desk drawer for a missing piano! Nor could police obtain a warrant that allows them to tear down the walls of a person's house because it is suspected that they contain drugs. A search is considered unreasonable when it exceeds the scope of police authority or is highly invasive of personal privacy, even if it reveals incriminating evidence.

stop and frisk
The situation when police officers who are suspicious of an individual run their hands lightly over the suspect's outer garments to determine whether the person is carrying a concealed weapon. Also called a patdown or threshold inquiry, a stop and frisk is intended to stop short of any activity that could be considered a violation of Fourth Amendment rights.

Warrantless Searches To make it easier for police to conduct investigations and to protect public safety, the Supreme Court has ruled that under certain circumstances a valid search may be conducted without a search warrant. The six major exceptions are search incident to a valid arrest, stop and frisk, automobile search, consent search, plain-view search, and exigent circumstances.

- *Search incident to a valid arrest.* A warrantless search is valid if it is made incident to a lawful arrest. The reason for this exception is that the arresting officer must have the power to disarm the accused, protect himself or herself, preserve the evidence of the crime, and prevent the accused from escaping from custody. Because the search is lawful, the officer retains what he or she finds if it is connected with a crime. The officer is permitted to search only the defendant's person and the areas in the defendant's immediate physical surroundings that are under his or her control.[137]

- *Stop and frisk.* In the landmark *Terry v. Ohio* decision, the Supreme Court held that police officers can perform a **stop and frisk** when they have reasonable suspicion to believe criminal activity is afoot. For example, say the individual is found lurking behind a closed store. In such a case, the officer has a right to stop and question the individual and, if she or he has reason to believe that the person is carrying a concealed weapon, may frisk the subject—that is, pat down the person's outer clothing for the purpose of finding a concealed weapon. If an illegal weapon is found, then an arrest can be made and a search incident to the arrest performed.[138] Would it be legal to pat down a person merely because that person is standing in a high-crime neighborhood? Probably not. The Supreme Court suggests that an officer would need more suspicion—for example, if the person ran away when he spotted the police approaching.[139]

- *Automobile search.* An automobile may be searched without a warrant if there is probable cause to believe the car was involved in a crime.[140] Because automobiles are inherently mobile, there is a significant chance that evidence will be lost if the search is not conducted immediately; also, people should not expect as much privacy in their cars as in their homes.[141] Police officers who have legitimately stopped an automobile and who have probable cause to believe that contraband is concealed somewhere inside it may conduct a warrantless search of the vehicle that is as thorough as a magistrate could authorize by warrant.

  Because traffic stops can be dangerous, the Court has ruled that if a police officer perceives danger during a routine traffic stop, he can order the driver and passengers from the car without suspicion and conduct a limited search of their persons to ensure police officer safety.[142] Police officers can search the car and passengers after a traffic stop, as long as the search is reasonable and related to officer safety.[143] Usually, the search must be limited to the area under the driver's control or reach. Also reread this chapter's opening vignette for more on vehicle searches.

- *Consent search.* In a consent search, individuals waive their constitutional rights; therefore, neither a warrant nor probable cause need exist. For a consent search to be legal, the consent must be given voluntarily; threat or compulsion invalidates the search.[144] Although it has been held that voluntary consent is required, it has also been maintained that the police are under no obligation to inform individuals of their right to refuse the search.[145]
- *Plain-view search.* Even when an object is in a house or other areas involving an expectation of privacy, the object can be freely inspected if it can be seen by the general public. If a police officer looks through a fence and sees marijuana growing in a suspect's fields, no search warrant is needed for the property to be seized. The articles are considered to be in plain view, and therefore a search warrant need not be obtained to seize them.[146]
- *Exigent circumstances.* The Supreme Court has identified a number of exigent, or emergency, circumstances in which a search warrant might normally have been required, but because of some immediate emergency, police officers can search suspects and places without benefit of a warrant. These circumstances include hot pursuit, danger of escape, threats to evidence, and threats to others. In each situation, officers must have probable cause.[147] For example, as the Supreme Court recently decided in *Kentucky v. King*, it is constitutionally permissible for officers to forcibly enter a residence if they have probable cause that evidence is being destroyed within.[148]

The Exclusionary Rule

The **exclusionary rule** provides that all evidence obtained by unreasonable searches and seizures is inadmissible in criminal trials. Similarly, it excludes the use of illegal confessions under Fifth Amendment prohibitions.

After police agencies were created in the mid-nineteenth century, evidence obtained by unreasonable searches and seizures was admitted by state and federal governments in criminal trials. The only criteria for admissibility were whether the evidence was incriminating and whether it would help the judge or jury reach a verdict. Then, in 1914, the U.S. Supreme Court established the exclusionary rule in the case of *Weeks v. United States*, when it ruled that evidence obtained by unreasonable search and seizure must be excluded from a federal criminal trial.[149] In 1961, the Supreme Court made the exclusionary rule applicable to state courts in the landmark decision of *Mapp v. Ohio*.[150]

exclusionary rule
The principle that prohibits the use, in a trial, of evidence illegally obtained. Based on the Fourth Amendment "right of the people to be secure in their persons, houses, papers, and effects, against unreasonable searches and seizures." The rule is not a bar to prosecution, because legally obtained evidence may be available that may be used in a trial.

Controversy and Current Status When the exclusionary rule applies, valuable evidence may not be usable at trial because the police made an error or failed to obtain a proper warrant. This means that guilty defendants can go free when the police make mistakes, intentional or otherwise. What's more, because courts frequently decide in many types of cases (particularly those involving victimless offenses, such as gambling and drug use) that certain evidence should be excluded, the rule is believed to result in excessive court delays and to affect plea-bargaining negotiations negatively. In fact, however, the rule appears to result in relatively few case dismissals. Research

Ethical Challenge

Sgt. Jennifer Dorety is an eight-year veteran of the Midcity police force. On the morning of November 5, 2007, Paul C. Bessey, a city councilman, spots Dorety leaving a local restaurant without paying. When he queries the restaurant owner, she laughingly states that "Officer Jen" had been coming there for breakfast for two years and it's "always on the house." It is a mutual understanding they have because Dorety has been very helpful in keeping "riffraff" out of the place. In fact, she tells the councilman that she once called for her at the station house, and Officer Jen drove all the way across town to tell a troublemaker to leave.

The town has a strict policy prohibiting police officers from accepting or soliciting bribes or gratuities, so Councilman Bessey files a complaint against Dorety with the city's Civilian Review Board. There will be a hearing on the matter, and, if found liable, Dorety faces three possible penalties: suspension, suspension and loss of rank, or dismissal. Dorety asks you to act as her representative at the meeting.

Write an essay on how you would defend her actions before the board and what you believe is a fair outcome in the case.

good faith exception
The principle that evidence may be used in a criminal trial, even though the search warrant used to obtain it is technically faulty, if the police acted in good faith and to the best of their ability when they sought to obtain it from a judge.

efforts show that prosecutions are lost because of suppression rulings less than 1 percent of the time.[151]

Over time the Supreme Court has been diminishing the scope of the exclusionary rule. For example, evidence is admissible in court if the police officers acted in good faith by first obtaining court approval for their search, even if the warrant they received was deficient or faulty.[152] This has come to be known as the **good faith exception**.

Summary

L01 **Summarize demographic trends in policing** U.S. police departments have made a concerted effort to attract women and minority police officers, and today about 11 percent of all officers are female and about 23 percent are racial minorities.

L02 **Explain how minority and female officers act and are treated** Minority police officers now seem as self-assured as white officers. They may even be more willing to use their authority to take official action than white officers. Studies of policewomen indicate that they are still struggling for acceptance, believe that they do not receive equal credit for their job performance, and report that it is common for them to be sexually harassed by their coworkers. African American women, who account for less than 5 percent of police officers, occupy a unique status. They often incur the hostility of both white women and African American men, who feel threatened that these officers will take their place.

L03 **Explain police culture and personality** Experts have found that the experience of becoming a police officer and the nature of the job itself cause most officers to band together in a police subculture characterized by cynicism, clannishness, secrecy, and insulation from others in society—the blue curtain. The police officer's working personality is shaped by constant exposure to danger and the need to use force and authority to defuse and control threatening situations.

L04 **Identify distinct policing styles** Four styles of police work seem to fit the current behavior patterns of most police agents: the crime fighter, the social agent, the law enforcer, and the watchman.

L05 **Describe factors that affect police discretion** The majority of police officers use a high degree of personal discretion in carrying out daily tasks, a phenomenon sometimes referred to as "low-visibility decision making" in criminal justice. Several factors contribute to discretionary decision making: legal factors, environmental factors, departmental factors, peer factors, situational factors, and extralegal factors.

L06 **Discuss four major problems of policing** Police officers experience tremendous stress. Fatigue is also a problem in modern police agencies; officers often work long hours and can become overly tired from performance of their duties. Because incidents of brutality undermine efforts to build a bridge between police and the public, police departments around the United States have instituted specialized training programs to reduce it. Ever since their creation, U.S. police departments have wrestled with the problem of controlling illegal and unprofessional behavior by their officers.

L07 **Distinguish between deadly and nondeadly force—and methods for controlling each** Police officers are empowered to use force in the pursuit of their daily tasks. The term "deadly force" refers to the actions of a police officer who shoots and kills a suspect who flees from arrest, assaults a victim, or attacks an officer. "Nondeadly force" is that which is unlikely to cause death or significant bodily harm. Because the police use of force is such a serious issue, ongoing efforts have been made to control its use. Methods used to control police force include adhering to important court decisions and formulating appropriate policies.

L08 **Explain the importance of less-lethal weapons** Less-lethal weapons give police officers an opportunity to subdue certain suspects without the need for lethal force. The Taser is the most popular less-lethal weapon in use today.

L09 **Be familiar with the Supreme Court's involvement with the police through its effort to control search and seizure and interrogation, and through establishment of the exclusionary rule** The need for police officers to gather evidence can conflict with the constitutional rights of citizens. In the 1966 case of *Miranda v. Arizona*, the Supreme Court created objective standards for questioning by police after a defendant has been taken into custody. Under normal circumstances, no search or seizure undertaken without a search warrant is lawful. The Supreme Court has also ruled that under certain circumstances, a valid search may be conducted without a search warrant. The exclusionary rule provides that all evidence obtained by unreasonable searches and seizures is inadmissible in criminal trials.

1. Should male and female officers have the same duties in a police department? Explain your reasoning.

2. How can education enhance the effectiveness of police officers?

3. Do you think that an officer's working the street will eventually produce a cynical personality and distrust for civilians? Explain.

4. A police officer orders an unarmed person running away from a burglary to stop; the suspect keeps running and is shot and killed by the officer. Has the officer committed murder? Explain.

5. Would you like to live in a society that abolished police discretion and used a full enforcement policy? Why or why not?

6. Should illegally seized evidence be excluded from trial, even though it is conclusive proof of a person's criminal acts? Might there be another way to deal with police violation of the Fourth Amendment— for example, making them pay a fine?

7. Have criminals been given too many rights by the courts? Should courts be more concerned with the rights of victims or the rights of offenders? Have the police been "handcuffed" and prevented from doing their job in the most efficient manner?

COURTS AND ADJUDICATION

Numerous career options exist in the courts/adjudication arena. Perhaps the most sought-after positions are those of the prosecutor, the judge, and the defense attorney. Courtroom staff positions make attractive career options, too. One could pursue a career as a clerk, a courtroom reporter, or a court administrator. Court security and judicial support staff careers are also available, as are other positions that vary with the needs of the particular court.

Perhaps no other court career is as prestigious as that of a judge, but it takes time and hard work to become a judge.

- Judges are tasked with resolving legal matters that come before their courts.
- Judicial positions are available at various levels. Federal judgeships require presidential appointment; more attainable positions exist at the local level.
- In some jurisdictions, judges are elected officials.
- Though a law degree is not always listed as a job requirement, the vast majority of judges are attorneys. Many have served as prosecutors or defense attorneys, or both, earlier in their careers.
- Judges are held in high esteem, but they often have to sacrifice many of the financial benefits of a lucrative private practice.

Ruben Andres Martino's career highlights several of these realities. Judge Martino is the presiding judge of the Harlem Community Court, a problem-solving court that offers services, programs, and referrals in cases involving juvenile delinquents, parolees, and disputes between local residents. His typical day now involves conferencing cases, presiding over trials, reviewing motions, supervising staff and interns, and attending meetings related to the court and the community it serves.

Judge Martino believes that most people do not understand the tremendous responsibility judges have as they make decisions that directly impact people's lives.

We make these decisions with all of our human limitations. Often, we only have part of the information and hear conflicting versions of the situation. However, we try

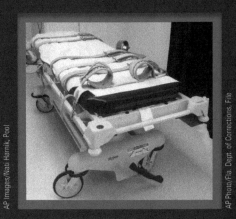

to do our best to make sure that justice is done and the integrity of our judicial system is upheld.

Every court must have a reporter, and the opportunities for employment as a court reporter are perhaps more realistic (at least in the short term) for most people than that of a judge.

- Court reporters create the official transcripts of legal proceedings—from pretrial conferences, plea hearing, sentencing hearings, preliminary hearings, during motions, and of course at trial.
- An associate's degree or higher is usually required.
- Court reporters are expected to have completed specialized training, typically in programs certified by the National Court Reporters Association.
- The median annual salary for court reporters is approximately $50,000. The highest paid court reporters can earn in excess of $80,000.

Carlos Martinez is a court reporter who works for the Sonoma County (California) superior courts. Before assuming his current position, Martinez was a deposition firm owner for seven years. He has been a court reporter for 15 years. The greatest technical challenges Martinez faces in a typical day are dealing with rapid speakers and technical jargon. On a more personal level, Martinez finds some cases, especially those involving murders, molestations, rapes, and abuse, difficult to listen to:

> You never get used to it and you never really forget. You just learn to live with it.

Part 3 of this text covers courts and adjudication. Chapter 7 provides an introduction to the court system as well as the roles of the prosecution and the defense. Chapter 8 covers pretrial and trial procedures. Pretrial topics include bail, charging the defendant, plea bargaining, and diversion. The trial section of Chapter 8 summarizes the trial process and the legal rights defendants enjoy. Chapter 9 looks at punishment and sentencing. The chapter begins with the history and goals of punishment, then it moves into specific types of sentences. Chapter 9 wraps up with a review of capital punishment and the controversies surrounding it.

> *"We make these decisions with all of our human limitations. Often, we only have part of the information and hear conflicting versions of the situation. However, we try to do our best to make sure that justice is done and the integrity of our judicial system is upheld."*
>
> Ruben Andres Martino

CHAPTER 7   **Courts, Prosecution, and the Defense**
CHAPTER 8   **Pretrial and Trial Procedures**
CHAPTER 9   **Punishment and Sentencing**

© Michael Matthews—Police Images/Alamy

7

Courts, Prosecution, and the Defense

Learning Objectives

LO1 Describe the varying structures of state court systems

LO2 Describe the federal court system

LO3 Summarize the selection procedure for and duties of the trial judge

LO4 Explain the role of the prosecutor

LO5 Describe prosecutorial discretion and summarize its pros and cons

LO6 Understand the role of the defense attorney in the justice process

LO7 Discuss the different forms of indigent defense

LO8 Summarize the pros and cons of private attorneys

LO9 Be familiar with the expanding role of technology in the court process

In 2008, police raided George Hayward's Baltimore house and found 1,024 pictures and nearly 200 videos of child pornography on his computer. Hayward was charged in federal court with multiple counts of sexual abuse of a minor, child rape, and sex offenses related to taking pictures and videos of naked children, some as young as 5 years old. He was convicted and, at age 72, sentenced to 20 years in federal prison, effectively a life sentence. But Maryland U.S. attorney Rod Rosenstein (the chief federal prosecutor for that jurisdiction) did not stop there. He also took Hayward's house, which he was authorized to do under federal forfeiture laws.

State and federal forfeiture statutes authorize law enforcement officials to seize and then assume ownership of property derived from or used to facilitate various crimes. Forfeiture has historically been used to target drug offenders' property, but it is increasingly being used against other types of offenders. In an effort to send a message to pedophiles, Rosenstein felt that it was necessary to do more than just sentence Hayward to prison. If offenders come to realize that their property can be taken, presumably they will be less inclined to break the law. ■

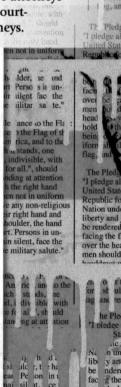

The criminal court is the setting in which many of the most important decisions in the criminal justice system are made. Eyewitness identification, bail, trial, plea negotiations, and sentencing all involve court decisions. The criminal court is a complex social agency with many independent but interrelated subsystems: administrator, prosecutor, defense attorney, judge, and probation department. The entire process—from filing of the initial complaint to final sentencing of the defendant—is governed by precise rules of law designed to ensure fairness. However, in today's crowded court system, such abstract goals are often impossible to achieve. The nation's court system is chronically underfunded, and recent economic downturns have not helped matters.

These constraints have a significant impact on the way courts carry out justice. Quite often, the U.S. court system is the scene of accommodation and "working things out," rather than an arena for a vigorous criminal defense. Plea negotiations and other nonjudicial alternatives, such as diversion, are far more common than the formal trial process. Consequently, U.S. criminal justice can be selective. Discretion accompanies defendants through every step of the process, determining what will happen to them and how their cases will be resolved. "Discretion" means that two people committing similar crimes may receive highly dissimilar treatment; most people convicted of homicide receive a prison sentence, but about 5 percent receive probation as a sole sentence; indeed, more murderers get probation than the death penalty.[1]

In this chapter, we examine the structure and function of the court system. The U.S. court system has evolved over the years into an intricately balanced legal process. To carry out this complex process, each state maintains its own state court organization and structure, and the federal court has an independent trial court system. These are described next.

State Courts

Every state maintains its own court system. States are free to create as many courts as they wish, to name courts what they like (in New York, felony courts are known as supreme courts!), and to establish specialized courts that handle a single type of legal matter, such as drug courts and domestic courts. Consequently, no two court organizations are exactly alike. State courts handle a wide variety of cases and regulate numerous personal behaviors ranging from homicide to property maintenance.

Courts of Limited Jurisdiction

state courts of limited jurisdiction
Courts that have jurisdiction over misdemeanors and conduct preliminary investigations of felony charges.

Depending on the jurisdiction in which they are located, **state courts of limited jurisdiction** are known by a variety of names—municipal courts, county courts, district courts, and metropolitan courts, to mention just a few. They are known as courts of limited jurisdiction because they are restricted to hearing minor or less serious civil and criminal cases.

Usually, courts of limited jurisdiction handle misdemeanor criminal infractions, violations of municipal ordinances, traffic violations, and civil suits where the damages involve less than a certain amount of money (usually $1,000 or less). In criminal matters, they hear cases involving misdemeanors such as shoplifting, disorderly conduct, and simple assault. Their sanctioning power is also limited. In criminal matters, punishments may be limited to fines, community sentencing, or incarceration in the county jail for up to a year. In addition to their trial work, limited jurisdiction courts conduct arraignments, preliminary, and bail hearings in felony cases (before they are transferred to superior courts).

The nation's approximately 13,500 independent courts of limited jurisdiction are the ones most often accused of providing assembly-line justice. Because the matters they decide involve minor personal confrontations and conflicts—family disputes, divorces, landlord–tenant conflicts, barroom brawls—the rule of the day is "handling the situation" and resolving the dispute.

Specialized Courts A growing phenomenon in the United States is the creation of specialty courts that focus on one type of criminal act, such as drug courts and mental health courts.[2] All cases within the jurisdiction that involve this particular type of crime are funneled to the specialty court, where presumably they will be resolved promptly. Examples of such courts include:

- *Drug courts.* The drug court movement began in Florida to address the growing problem of prison overcrowding due in large part to an influx of drug-involved

Janet Meredith, center, processes eggs during her shift at Prime Foods in Boonville, Indiana. Meredith, who is progressing through the Warrick County Drug Court system, started her job at Prime Foods about three months ago. Getting and keeping a steady job is one of the goals of the program. What other types of specialized courts have become popular in recent years?

AP Photo/mbr/*The Evansville Courier & Press,* Molly Bartels

offenders. Drug courts were created to have primary jurisdiction over cases involving substance abuse and trafficking. The aim is to channel nonviolent first offenders into intensive treatment programs rather than into jail or prison. Today there are more than 2,000 drug courts throughout the United States and its territories.[3]

- *Mental health courts.* Based largely on the organization of drug courts, mental health courts focus their attention on mental health treatment to help people with emotional problems reduce their chances of reoffending.[4] By focusing on the need for treatment, along with providing supervision and support from the community, mental health courts provide a venue for those dealing with mental health issues to avoid the trauma of jail or prison, where they will have little if any access to treatment.

There are now specialized courts for nearly every difficult problem confronting the criminal justice system. There are domestic violence courts, gang courts, gun courts, sex offender courts, homeless courts, parole reentry courts, community courts, and so on.

Courts of General Jurisdiction

Approximately 2,000 **courts of general jurisdiction** exist in the United States; they are variously called felony, superior, supreme, county, and circuit courts. Courts of general jurisdiction handle the more serious felony cases, such as murder, rape, and robbery, and civil cases where damages are over a specified amount, such as $10,000. Courts of general jurisdiction may also be responsible for reviewing cases on appeal from courts of limited jurisdiction.

Courts of general jurisdiction are typically organized in judicial districts or circuits, based on a political division such as a county or a group of counties. They then receive cases from the various limited courts located within the county or jurisdiction. Some general courts separate criminal and civil cases so that some specialize in civil matters while others maintain a caseload that is exclusively criminal.

State court systems now handle about 100 million new cases each year, a number that has increased more than 10 percent in the past decade. The great majority of these cases are traffic related, and about 20 million of these cases involve some form of criminal conduct.[5]

courts of general jurisdiction State or federal courts that have jurisdiction over felony offenses and more serious civil cases (that is, cases involving more than a dollar amount set by the legislature).

Appellate Courts

If defendants believe that the procedures used were in violation of their constitutional rights, they may ask an **appellate court** to review the trial process. Appellate courts do not try cases; they review the procedures of the case to determine whether an error was made by judicial authorities. In some instances, defendants can file an appeal if they believe that the law they were tried under was in violation of constitutional standards (for example, the crime they were charged with—say, "being a public nuisance"—was vague and ill defined) or if the procedures used in the case contravened principles of due process and equal protection or were in direct opposition to a constitutional guarantee (for example, they were denied the right to have competent legal representation).

It is the role of the appellate court to decide whether the trial judge made a legal error that influenced the outcome of the case, thereby denying the defendant a fair trial. Judicial error can include admitting into evidence illegally seized material, improperly charging a jury, allowing a prosecutor to ask witnesses improper questions, and so on. If, upon review, the appellate court decides that an error has been made, it can order a new trial or even allow the defendant to go free.

State criminal appeals are heard in one of the appellate courts in the 50 states and the District of Columbia. Each state has at least one **court of last resort**, usually called a state supreme court, which reviews issues of law and fact appealed from the trial courts; a few states have two high courts, one for civil appeals and the other for criminal cases.

appellate court A court that reconsiders a case that has already been tried in order to determine whether the measures used complied with accepted rules of criminal procedure and were in accordance with constitutional doctrines.

court of last resort A court that handles the final appeal on a matter. The U.S. Supreme Court is the official court of last resort for criminal matters.

LO1 Describe the varying structures of state court systems

Many people believe that criminal appeals clog the nation's court system because so many convicted criminals try to "beat the rap" on a technicality. Actually, criminal appeals represent a small percentage of the total number of cases processed by the nation's appellate courts. All types of appeals, including criminal ones, continue to inundate the courts, so most courts are having problems processing cases expeditiously.

Figure 7.1 illustrates the interrelationship of appellate and trial courts in a model state court structure. Each state's court organization, of course, may vary from this standard pattern. Though most states have a tiered court organization (lower, upper, and appellate courts), all vary in the way they delegate responsibility to a particular court system, and some have consolidated their courts into a single, unified system.

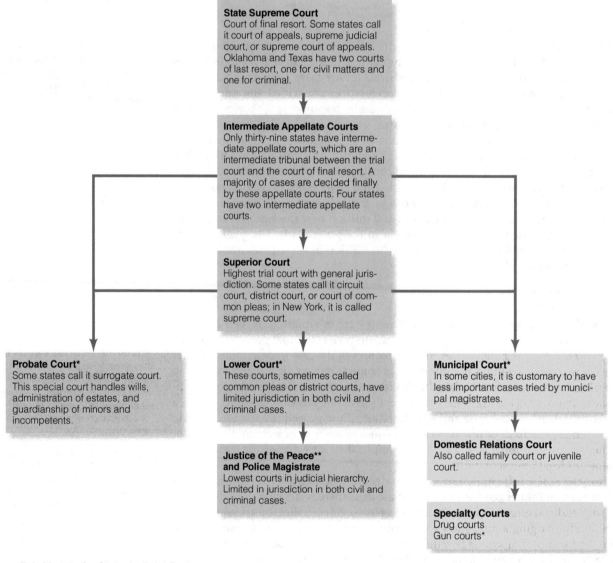

State Supreme Court
Court of final resort. Some states call it court of appeals, supreme judicial court, or supreme court of appeals. Oklahoma and Texas have two courts of last resort, one for civil matters and one for criminal.

Intermediate Appellate Courts
Only thirty-nine states have intermediate appellate courts, which are an intermediate tribunal between the trial court and the court of final resort. A majority of cases are decided finally by these appellate courts. Four states have two intermediate appellate courts.

Superior Court
Highest trial court with general jurisdiction. Some states call it circuit court, district court, or court of common pleas; in New York, it is called supreme court.

Probate Court*
Some states call it surrogate court. This special court handles wills, administration of estates, and guardianship of minors and incompetents.

Lower Court*
These courts, sometimes called common pleas or district courts, have limited jurisdiction in both civil and criminal cases.

Municipal Court*
In some cities, it is customary to have less important cases tried by municipal magistrates.

Justice of the Peace** and Police Magistrate**
Lowest courts in judicial hierarchy. Limited in jurisdiction in both civil and criminal cases.

Domestic Relations Court
Also called family court or juvenile court.

Specialty Courts
Drug courts
Gun courts*

Figure 7.1 Model of a State Judicial System

*Courts of special jurisdiction, such as probate, family, and juvenile courts, and the so-called inferior courts, such as common pleas and municipal courts, may be separate courts or part of the trial court of general jurisdiction.

**Justices of the peace do not exist in all states. Where they do exist, their jurisdictions vary greatly from state to state.

Source: American Bar Association, *Law and the Courts* (Chicago: ABA, 1974), p. 20; Bureau of Justice Statistics, State Court Organization–1998 (Washington, DC: Department of Justice, 2000).

Federal Courts

The legal basis for an independent federal court system is contained in Article 3, Section 1, of the U.S. Constitution, which provides that "the judicial power of the United States shall be vested in one Supreme Court, and in such inferior courts as Congress may from time to time ordain and establish." The important clauses in Article 3 indicate that the federal courts have jurisdiction over the laws of the United States and over treaties and cases involving admiralty and maritime jurisdiction, as well as over controversies between two or more states and citizens of different states.[6] This complex language generally means that state courts have jurisdiction over most common-law crimes but that the federal system maintains jurisdiction over violations of federal criminal statutes, civil suits between citizens of different states, and suits between a citizen and an agency of the federal government.

Within this authority, the federal government has established a three-tiered hierarchy of court jurisdiction that, in order of ascendancy, consists of the (1) U.S. district courts, (2) U.S. courts of appeals (circuit courts), and (3) the U.S. Supreme Court (see Figure 7.2).

U.S. District Courts

The trial courts of the federal system, U.S. district courts were organized by Congress in the Judicial Act of 1789. Today, 94 independent courts are in operation. Originally, each state was allowed one court; as the population grew, however, so did the need for courts, so now some states have multiple jurisdictions.

U.S. district courts have jurisdiction over cases involving violations of federal laws, including civil rights abuses, interstate transportation of stolen vehicles, and kidnappings. They may also hear cases on questions involving citizenship and the rights of aliens. The jurisdiction of the U.S. district court will occasionally overlap that of state courts. Citizens who reside in separate states and are involved in litigation of an amount in excess of $10,000 may choose to have their cases heard in

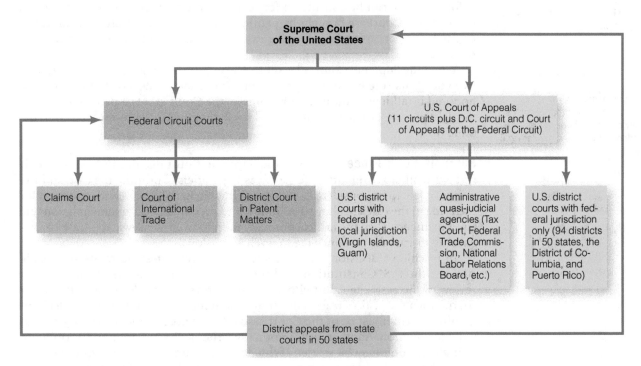

Figure 7.2 The Federal Judicial System

Source: American Bar Association, *Law and the Courts* (Chicago: ABA, 1974), p. 21; updated information provided by the Federal Courts Improvement Act of 1982 and West Publishing Company, St. Paul, MN.

either of the states or in the federal district court. Finally, federal district courts hear cases where one state sues a resident (or firm) in another state, where one state sues another, or where the federal government is a party in a suit.

U.S. Courts of Appeals

There are 13 judicial circuits, each with a court of appeals. Each circuit's Court of Appeals (formally called the "Court of Appeals for the [number] Circuit") is empowered to review federal and state appellate court cases on substantive and procedural issues involving rights guaranteed by the Constitution. Circuit courts do not actually retry cases, nor do they determine whether the facts brought out during trial support conviction or dismissal. Instead, they analyze judicial interpretations of the law, such as the charge (or instructions) to the jury, and reflect on the constitutional issues involved in each case they hear.

Although federal court criminal cases make up only a small percentage of appellate cases, they are still of concern to the judiciary. Steps have been taken to make appealing more difficult. The U.S. Supreme Court has tried to limit the number of appeals being filed by prison inmates, which often represent a significant number of cases appealed in the federal criminal justice system.

The U.S. Supreme Court

LO2 **Describe the federal court system**

writ of certiorari
An order of a superior court requesting that the record of an inferior court (or administrative body) be brought forward for review or inspection.

landmark decision
A decision handed down by the U.S. Supreme Court that becomes the law of the land and serves as a precedent for resolving similar legal issues.

The U.S. Supreme Court is the nation's highest appellate body and the court of last resort for all cases tried in the various federal and state courts. The Court is composed of nine members appointed for lifetime terms by the president, with the approval of Congress. The Court has discretion over most of the cases it will consider and may choose to hear only those it deems important, appropriate, and worthy of its attention. The Court chooses some 300 of the 5,000 cases appealed each year, and only about 100 of these receive full opinions.

When the Supreme Court decides to hear a case, it grants a **writ of certiorari**, requesting a transcript of the proceedings of the case for review. At least four of the nine justices sitting on the Court must vote to grant the writ of certiorari even before the case can be considered for review. More than 90 percent of the cases heard by the Court are brought by petition for a writ of certiorari. The Court has original jurisdiction for the remaining cases (e.g., those involving disputes between the states).

When the Supreme Court rules on a case, usually by majority decision (at least five votes), its rule becomes a precedent, or **landmark decision**, that must be honored by all lower courts. If, for example, the Court grants a particular litigant the right to counsel at a police lineup, all similarly situated clients must be given the same right.

Supreme Court Procedure After the Supreme Court decides to hear a case, it reviews written arguments (referred to as legal briefs) outlining the case and the points of law to be considered. After the written material is reviewed, attorneys for each side in the case are allowed 30 minutes to present an oral argument before the court members. Then the justices normally meet in what is known as a "case conference" to discuss the case and vote to reach a decision.

In reaching a decision, the Supreme Court reevaluates and reinterprets state statutes, the U.S. Constitution, and previous case decisions. On the basis of its review of the case, the Court either affirms or reverses the decision of the lower court. When the justices reach a decision, and in the event that the Court's decision is split, the chief justice of the Court assigns a member of the majority group to write the opinion. Another justice normally writes a dissent, or minority, opinion; a single opinion may be written if the decision is unanimous. When the case is finished, it is submitted to the public and becomes the law of the land. The decision represents the legal precedents that add to the existing body of law on a given subject, change it, and guide its future development.

The Supreme Court hears a select number of cases appealed from the lower courts. Often it lets the lower-court decision stand because there are simply too many cases. Here members of the Narragansett Indian Tribe sit in Washington County District Court in South Kingstown, Rhode Island, where they pleaded not guilty to criminal charges stemming from a 2003 Rhode Island State Police raid on a smoke shop on tribal land in 2007. The raid was challenged, but the U.S. Supreme Court let a lower-court ruling stand, thus allowing the criminal proceeding to get under way.

AP Images/Joe Giblin

The Judiciary

The judge is the senior officer in a court of criminal law. Judges' duties are quite varied and far more extensive than might be expected.

- Their primary duty is to oversee the trial process. This means that during trials, judges control the appropriateness of conduct, settle questions of evidence and procedure, and guide the questioning of witnesses.
- In a **jury trial**, the judge must instruct jurors on which evidence it is proper to examine and which should be ignored. The judge also formally charges the jury by instructing its members on what points of law and evidence they must consider to reach a decision of either guilty or not guilty.
- When a jury trial is waived, in a bench trial, the judge must decide whether the defendant is guilty as charged. If a defendant is found guilty, the judge must decide on the sentence (in some cases, this is legislatively determined), which includes choosing the type of sentence, its length, and, in the case of probation, the conditions under which it may be revoked.
- The judge controls and influences court agencies: probation, the court clerk, the police, and the district attorney's office. Probation and the clerk may be under the judge's explicit control. In some courts, the operations, philosophy, and procedures of these agencies are within the magistrate's administrative domain. In others—where a state agency controls the probation department—the attitudes of the county or district court judge greatly influence the way a probation department is run and how its decisions are made.

While carrying out their duties, judges must be wary of the legal controls placed on the trial process by the appellate court system. If an error is made, the judge's decision may be reversed, causing (at the very least) personal embarrassment. Some experts believe that fear of reversal may shape judicial decision making, but research shows that judges may be more independent than previously believed. Judges relish using their judicial power as a policymaking tool to influence important social policies such as affirmative action or privacy.[7]

Of course, judges do not wield their power in isolation. They work together with prosecutors and defense attorneys, whose work is featured shortly. They are also

jury trial
The process of deciding a case by a group of persons selected and sworn in to serve as jurors at a criminal trial, often as a 6- or 12-person jury.

■ Judge Lael Montgomery, center, talks with attorneys at the bench during a trial at the Boulder County Justice Center in Boulder, Colorado. Colorado and other states are increasingly using performance reviews to hold judges more accountable without resorting to term limits or taking other measures that some fear would threaten the judiciary's independence.

assisted by a number of courtroom personnel, including clerks, court administrators, security personnel, court reporters, and other support staff. See Exhibit 7.1 for additional details.

The Judge and the Justice System

Judicial attitudes and philosophy have a major impact on how the justice system operates. Judicial attitudes may extend way beyond the courtroom. Police policies may be directly influenced by the judge, whose sentencing discretion affects the arrest process. If a local judge usually imposes minimal sentences—such as a fine—for a particular offense, the police may be reluctant to arrest offenders for that crime, knowing that doing so will basically be a waste of time. Similarly, if a judge is known to have a liberal attitude toward police discretion, the local department may be more inclined to engage in practices that border on entrapment or to pursue cases through easily obtained wiretaps. However, a magistrate oriented toward strict use of due process guarantees would stifle such activities by dismissing all cases involving apparent police abuses of personal freedoms.

The district attorney's office may also be sensitive to judicial attitudes. The district attorney might forgo indictments in cases that the presiding magistrate expressly considers trivial or quasi-criminal and in which the judge has been known to take only token action, such as the prosecution of pornographers.

Finally, the judge considers requests by prosecutors for leniency (or severity) in sentencing. The judge's reaction to these requests is important if the police and the district attorney are to honor the bargains they may have made with defendants to secure information, cooperation, or guilty pleas. When police tell informers that they will try to convince the judge to go easy on them to secure required information, they will often discuss the terms of the promised leniency with representatives of the court. If a judge ignores police demands, the department's bargaining power is severely diminished, and communication within the criminal justice system is impaired.

Judicial Qualifications and Selection

Judicial qualifications and selection vary between the federal and state levels. In general, there are fewer formal qualifications and more *informal* qualifications at the federal level. The opposite is often true at the state level.

Exhibit 7.1

Court Staff

The most visible courtroom personnel include the judge, the prosecutor, and the defense attorney. But there are many other important court personnel and staff persons. The typical large jurisdiction probably has a mix of the following personnel working in the courtroom or courthouse at any given time.

Clerk Court clerks are responsible for a wide range of duties. Their main responsibilities include maintaining court records; receiving, processing, and maintaining judgments; issuing process, such as summonses, subpoenas, and wage garnishments; preserving the court seal; swearing in witnesses, jurors, and grand jurors; collecting fees and fines; handling inquiries from attorneys and other parties; and printing and distributing opinions of the court.

Court administrator There are two general types of court administrators. The first is a state employee. In each state, these individuals are part of the state administrative office of the court, which is usually under the direction of the state supreme court. Court administrators help develop and implement policies and services for the judicial branch throughout the state. They also conduct research and determine whether judicial needs are identified and incorporated into long-term plans. They establish priorities for the courts, address financial problems and budgeting issues, and manage the use of technology within a state's judicial branch.

The second type of court administrator is a local court administrator. These individuals manage the daily operations of the court, usually under the direction of the presiding judge. They provide administrative support for court programs, help the court establish new programs and evaluate them, and manage purchasing and accounts payable, among other responsibilities.

Court security The marshal or bailiff for the court is responsible for courthouse security. In some states, such as California, court security is provided by sheriff's deputies who screen people entering the building, provide security during trials, and transport suspects to court from jail. Depending on the jurisdiction, court security personnel may take on additional responsibilities, including some investigation, bond supervising, community service monitoring, and making arrests as needed.

Legal staff The larger and more powerful the court, the more likely it will have a variety of legal staff. These personnel can include legal counsel (prosecutors and defense attorneys), staff attorneys, research attorneys, and law clerks. Law clerks are not to be confused with court clerks. Unlike court clerks, law clerks are often recent law school graduates who assist judges with researching issues before the courts and writing opinions. U.S. Supreme Court law clerks are the cream of the crop, having graduated from many of the nation's top law schools.

Judicial support staff A judge's support staff may include executive assistants, administrative assistants, secretaries, or a mix of all three. Support staff edit and type judicial opinions, create and arrange files, coordinate meetings, coordinate travel arrangements, answer telephone and email inquiries, mail correspondence, and serve as an intermediary between the judge and other outside parties.

Court reporter The court reporter records judicial proceedings word for word. See the Careers in Criminal Justice box in Chapter 8 for more on court reporters.

Jury staff Many courts have dedicated jury personnel who maintain and review lists of prospective jurors. They may also determine who is eligible to serve, determine the number of jurors needed, issue summonses for jury service, and handle requests by jurors for dismissal, exemption, or disqualification. These individuals may also meet with prospective jurors to explain the process, tell them where to go, and dismiss them from service at the end of the day.

Other officers Many courts have representatives on site from other criminal justice agencies. There may be juvenile officers who are vested with the authority to take charge of children who come under the jurisdiction of the juvenile or family court. Representatives from probation may assist judges by performing pre-sentence investigations that can be used during sentencing. In some states, the probation department is part of the judiciary and is thus more closely connected with the court than probation departments in other states.

Federal Level Federal judges are appointed by the president with the advice and consent of the Senate. Senate confirmation of federal judiciary appointees, especially those chosen to serve on the U.S. Supreme Court, can be a contentious process. One exception to this process exists for the appointment of a **U.S. magistrate judge**. Magistrate judges are federal trial judges appointed by district court judges who preside over various civil cases with the consent of the parties and over certain misdemeanor cases.

Interestingly, there are almost no formal qualifications for federal judges. The Constitution and federal law are silent on judicial qualifications. There are no exams that must be passed, and there is not even a requirement that a federal judge be a lawyer. Even so, positions in the federal judiciary are very prestigious and sought-after. They thus attract highly qualified, seasoned attorneys.

State Level The qualifications for appointment to one of the existing 30,000 judgeships vary from state to state and court to court. Most often, the potential judge must be a resident of the state, licensed to practice law, a member of the state bar association, and at least 25 years and less than 70 years of age. However, a significant degree of diversity exists in the basic qualifications, depending on the level of court jurisdiction. Although almost every state requires judges to have a law degree if they are to serve on appellate courts or courts of general jurisdiction, it is not uncommon for municipal or town court judges to lack a legal background, even though they have the power to incarcerate criminal defendants for petty crimes such as vandalism.

Many methods are used to select judges, depending on the level of court jurisdiction. In some jurisdictions, judges are appointed officials, most often appointed by the state governor. In some states, in an effort to remove politics from judicial appointments, the governor's recommendations must be confirmed by the state senate, the governor's council, a special confirmation committee, an executive council elected by the state assembly, or an elected review board. Some states employ a judicial nominating commission that submits names to the governor for approval.

Another form of judicial selection is popular election. Judges may run as members of the Republican, Democratic, or other parties, or without party affiliation. Although this practice is used in a majority of states, each state sets its own terms of appointment. In some states judges are elected to 15-year terms, in others to 4-year terms.[8] See Figure 7.3 for a map of judicial selection methods by state.

The state of Missouri pioneered a nonpartisan method of selecting judges. This **Missouri Plan** is now used in some manner in the majority of states. The plan consists of three parts:

1. A judicial nominating commission selects and nominates potential candidates for the bench. In Missouri, the judicial commission is composed of the chief justice of the state supreme court, three lawyers elected by the Missouri bar (the organization of all lawyers licensed in this state), and three citizens selected by the governor.
2. An elected official (usually from the executive branch, such as the governor) makes appointments from the list submitted by the commission.
3. Subsequent nonpartisan and noncompetitive elections take place, in which incumbent judges run on their records and voters can choose either to retain or to dismiss them.[9]

The quality of the judiciary is a concern. Although merit plans, screening committees, and popular elections are designed to ensure a competent judiciary, it has often been charged that many judicial appointments are made to pay off political debts or to reward cronies and loyal friends. Also not uncommon are charges that

U.S. magistrate judge
A federal trial judge who is appointed by a district court judge and who presides over various civil cases with the consent of the parties and over certain misdemeanor cases.

Missouri Plan
A way of picking judges through nonpartisan elections as a way to ensure that judges adhere to high standards of judicial performance.

LO3 Summarize the selection procedure for and duties of the trial judge

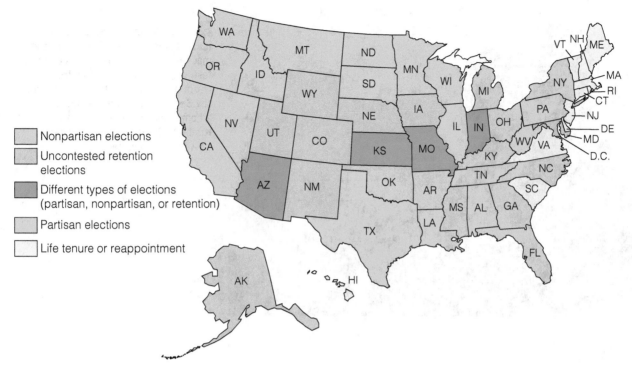

Figure 7.3 Selection Methods by State for General Jurisdiction Trial Court Judges

Source: American Bar Association, www.americanbar.org/content/dam/aba/migrated/leadership/fact_sheet.authcheckdam.pdf (accessed June 8, 2011)

Legend:
- Nonpartisan elections
- Uncontested retention elections
- Different types of elections (partisan, nonpartisan, or retention)
- Partisan elections
- Life tenure or reappointment

those who wish to be nominated for judgeships are required to make significant political contributions.

The Prosecutor

Depending on the level of government and the jurisdiction in which he or she functions, the prosecutor may be known as a district attorney, county attorney, state's attorney, or U.S. attorney. Whatever the title, the **prosecutor** is the people's attorney, who is responsible for representing the public in criminal matters.

Because they are the chief law enforcement officers of a particular jurisdiction, their jurisdiction spans the entire justice system process from the time when search and arrest warrants are issued or a grand jury is impaneled to the final sentencing decision and appeal. These are some of the general duties of a prosecutor:

- Provides advice to law enforcement officers during investigation to determine whether criminal charges should be filed
- During the pretrial stage, represents the state in plea negotiations, pretrial motions, and bail hearings
- Represents the state at hearings, criminal trials, and appeals
- Acts as legal advisor to county commissioners and other elected officials

In addition to these duties, local jurisdictions may create specific programs directed by local prosecutors. One example is career-criminal prosecution programs, which involve identifying dangerous adult and juvenile offenders who commit a high number of crimes, so that prosecutors can target them for swift prosecution. Many jurisdictions have developed protection programs so that victims of domestic violence can obtain temporary court orders (and, after a hearing, more long-term court orders) protecting them from an abusive spouse; research indicates that protection orders can reduce the incidence of repeat violence.[10]

RealityCheck

MYTH OR REALITY? Elected state judges can be affiliated with a political party.

REALITY. *This is not true in all states, but some states permit partisan judicial elections. This means a judge can run as a Democrat, a Republican, an independent, or a member of any other political party.*
Should judges be allowed to run on political platforms? Why or why not?

prosecutor
Representative of the state (executive branch) in criminal proceedings; advocate for the state's case—the charge—in the adversary trial. Examples include the attorney general of the United States, U.S. attorneys, the attorneys general of the states, district attorneys, and police prosecutors. The prosecutor participates in investigations both before and after arrest, prepares legal documents, participates in obtaining arrest or search warrants, and decides whether to charge a suspect and, if so, with which offense. The prosecutor argues the state's case at trial, advises the police, participates in plea negotiations, and makes sentencing recommendations.

New Hampshire State Police investigator Steve Puckett shows the machete presented as evidence during testimony in Steve Spader's trial in Nashua, New Hampshire. Prosecutors say Spader wielded a machete during a home invasion, killing 42-year-old Kimberly Cates and maiming her 11-year-old daughter.

AP Photo/Don Himsel, Pool

Types of Prosecutors

In the federal system, prosecutors are known as U.S. attorneys and are appointed by the president. They are responsible for representing the government in federal district courts. The chief prosecutor is usually an administrator, and assistants normally handle the actual preparation and trial work. Federal prosecutors are professional civil service employees with reasonable salaries and job security.

On the state and county levels, the attorney general and the district attorney, respectively, are the chief prosecutorial officers. Again, the bulk of the criminal prosecution and staff work is performed by scores of full- and part-time attorneys, police investigators, and clerical personnel. Most attorneys who work for prosecutors at the state and county levels are political appointees who earn low salaries, handle many cases, and (in some jurisdictions) maintain private law practices. Many young lawyers take these staff positions to gain the trial experience that will qualify them for better opportunities.

In urban jurisdictions, the structure of the district attorney's office is often specialized, with separate divisions for felonies, misdemeanors, and trial and appeal assignments. In rural offices, chief prosecutors handle many of the criminal cases themselves. Where assistant prosecutors are employed, they often work part time, have limited professional opportunities, and depend on the political patronage of chief prosecutors for their positions.

The personnel practices, organizational structures, and political atmosphere of many prosecutors' offices often restrict their effectiveness in investigating and prosecuting criminal offenses. For many years, prosecutors have been criticized for bargaining justice away, using their positions as stepping stones to higher political office, and often failing to investigate or simply dismissing criminal cases. Lately, however, the prosecutor's public image has improved. Violations of federal laws, such as white-collar crime, drug peddling, and corruption, are being more aggressively investigated by the 94 U.S. attorneys and the nearly 2,000 assistant U.S. attorneys. Aggressive federal prosecutors have also made extraordinary progress in the war against insider trading and securities fraud on Wall Street. There have been a number of highly publicized indictments alleging that some corporate managers abused their power to loot company assets.

Today, there are about 2,400 state court prosecutors' offices, which employ about 79,000 attorneys, investigators, and support staff to handle felony cases in the state

Careers in Criminal Justice

PROSECUTOR

Duties and Characteristics of the Job

- Prosecutors represent the public in criminal trials and are responsible for proving in court that the accused is guilty of the charges brought against him or her.
- Prosecutors work at the municipal, state, and federal levels of government. During a trial, a prosecutor is opposed by a defense attorney, who represents the interests of the accused offender.
- To convince the judge or jury of the defendant's guilt, the prosecutor questions witnesses and gives statements, using evidence collected during the investigative phase of the case.
- Prosecutors also decide which cases to bring to trial and have the authority to settle cases out of court. Even though they represent the people, prosecutors often meet with victims of crime and present the case from their point of view when in court.
- Victims of crime and their families, community members, and law enforcement depend on the prosecutor to prove the guilt of an alleged offender to a jury or judge and achieve a conviction.
- Prosecutors may work long hours, especially during trials. In general, prosecutors tend to be paid less than their counterparts in private practice, but many report high personal satisfaction from seeing that justice is served.

Job Outlook

- Crime rates and budgets dictate the number of job openings. In light of recent budget crises, prosecutors offices have scaled back on hiring.
- Opportunities should open up on a regular basis, because the position has a high turnover rate.
- There are opportunities for advancement in larger offices, especially in urban areas. A state prosecutor may also wish to seek a position as a federal prosecutor.
- After leaving their position, former prosecutors might open up their own private practice, possibly with the intent of running a lucrative defense attorney business.
- Prosecutors can also seek appointments to prestigious and well-paying judge positions or choose to leave the practice of law for a political career.

Salary

- Prosecutors working at federal and state offices tend to earn more than those working at county and municipal levels.
- In larger cities, pay will be higher. The average prosecutor salary is around $62,000 per year. Senior prosecutors often earn in excess of $100,000 per year.

Qualifications

- Like other lawyers, prosecutors need to be comfortable and practiced at public speaking, and they also need well-developed analytical skills.
- There is something of a political aspect to gaining this position, because in some areas one must be elected or appointed to it.

Education and Training

- A bachelor's degree with an emphasis on writing, analytical, and research skills is necessary.
- A law degree is also required.
- Law school graduates must pass the state bar exam in order to practice law.

Word to the Wise

- Entry into law school is very competitive, and the educational requirements are challenging.
- Prosecutors are government employees. As such, they do not earn as much as some attorneys in the private sector.
- Most criminal cases never make it to trial, so prosecutors with ambitions of doing nothing but argue jury trials may be disappointed.
- For cases that *do* go to trial, there is a great deal of behind-the-scenes preparation. A successful prosecutor is a detail-oriented person, not just a skilled orator.
- There is high turnover, partly as a result of prosecutors "burning out" after a few years. This can be attributed to the relatively low-pay, high-volume work, and to dealing with unpleasant criminal cases.

trial courts. Usually, the most active prosecutors are employed in larger counties with populations of over 500,000.

Prosecutors, like other justice system professionals, are now confronting issues related to cyber crime and terrorism and the use of technology both to commit crimes and to solve them once they occur. According to the most recent federal survey of prosecutors,

- At least two-thirds of state court prosecutors had litigated a computer-related crime such as credit card fraud (80%), identity theft (69%), or transmission of child pornography (67%).
- One-quarter (24%) of the offices participated in a state or local task force for homeland security; one-third reported that an office member attended training on homeland security issues.
- Most prosecutors (95%) relied on state-operated forensic laboratories to perform DNA analysis, with about a third (34%) also using privately operated DNA labs.[11]

The Careers in Criminal Justice feature examines the job of the prosecutor more closely.

L04 Explain the role of the prosecutor

Prosecutorial Discretion

The prosecutor decides whether to bring a case to trial or to dismiss it outright. Even if the prosecutor decides to pursue a case, the charges may later be dropped if conditions are not favorable for a conviction; this is referred to as *nolle prosequi*. This recently happened in the case of Dominique Strauss-Kahn, former International Monetary Fund (IMF) chief. Strauss-Kahn was arrested on May 14, 2011, for sexual assault, but prosecutors later decided to drop charges against him because of doubts about the credibility of the supposed victim.

The courts have protected the prosecutor's right to exercise discretion over processing of legal cases, maintaining that prosecutorial decision making can be controlled or overturned only if a defendant can prove that the prosecutor let discrimination guide his or her decision making.[12] Even in felony cases, the prosecutor ordinarily exercises much discretion in deciding whether to charge the accused with a crime.[13] After a police investigation, the prosecutor may be asked to review the sufficiency of the evidence to determine whether a criminal complaint should be filed. In some jurisdictions, this may involve presenting the evidence at a preliminary hearing. In other cases, the prosecutor may decide to seek a criminal complaint through the grand jury or other information procedure.

There is little question that prosecutors exercise a great deal of discretion in even the most serious cases. In a now classic study, Barbara Boland examined the flow of felony cases through three jurisdictions in the United States: Golden, Colorado; the borough of Manhattan in New York City; and Salt Lake City, Utah.[14] Although procedures were different in the three districts, prosecutors used their discretion to dismiss a high percentage of the cases before trial. When cases were forwarded for trial, very few defendants were actually acquitted, indicating that the prosecutorial discretion was exercised to screen out the weakest cases. In addition, of those cases accepted for prosecution, a high percentage ended with the defendant pleading guilty. All the evidence here points to the conclusion that prosecutorial discretion is used to reduce potential trial cases to a minimum.

The prosecutor may also play a limited role in exercising discretion in minor offenses. This role may consist of simply consulting with the police after their investigation results in a complaint being filed against the accused. In such instances, the decision to charge a person with a crime may be left primarily to the discretion of the law enforcement agency. The prosecutor may decide to enter this type of case after an arrest has been made and a complaint filed with the court, and she may subsequently determine whether to adjust the matter or proceed to trial.

Factors Influencing Prosecutorial Discretion

Research indicates that a wide variety of factors influence prosecutorial discretion in invoking criminal sanction. These include legal issues, victim issues, extralegal issues, and resource issues.

Legal Issues Legal issues can include the characteristics of the justice system, the crime, the criminal, and the victim. The quality of police work and the amount and relevance of the evidence the police gather are critical legal variables that a prosecutor considers in deciding whether to bring a case forward to trial.[15] A defendant who is a known drug user, has a long history of criminal offending, and caused the victim extensive physical injuries is more likely to be prosecuted than one who is a first offender, does not use drugs, and did not seriously injure a victim.[16] Crime seriousness certainly influences discretion. As might be expected, prosecutors are much more likely to use their discretion in minor incidents than in more serious ones.[17]

Victim Issues In some instances, the victim's behavior may influence charging decisions. Some victims may become reluctant to press charges, especially if the offender is a parent or spouse. Domestic violence cases are often difficult to prosecute (see the Contemporary Issues in Criminal Justice feature for more on this). Some victims are unlikely to encourage or work with prosecutors even after the police get involved. Victim cooperation is a key factor in the decision to prosecute cases: The odds of a case being prosecuted are seven times greater when victims are considered cooperative.[18]

Extralegal Issues Extralegal factors include the offender's race, gender, and ethnic background. Of course, due process considerations demand that these personal characteristics have no bearing on the use of prosecutorial discretion. Nonetheless, some research efforts have found that the race of the offender or victim influences

CONTEMPORARY ISSUES IN CRIMINAL JUSTICE

No-Drop Prosecution: Does It Work?

Over time, prosecutors have been faced with a high rate of dismissals in domestic violence cases. The key problem is that victims often refuse to participate in the process and testify against their abusers. It sometimes proves difficult for prosecutors to secure convictions without the testimony from victims. In response to this problem, some jurisdictions have enacted so-called "no-drop prosecution" policies, also called "evidence-based" prosecution. These policies *require* prosecutors to bring charges against domestic abusers regardless of whether the victim participates. Calling them evidence-based means that if there is enough evidence (such as police reports and accounts of witnesses), then the prosecutor will bring charges even without the victim's testimony. No-drop prosecution policies have since "caught on," but do they work? Unfortunately, the evidence is not encouraging.

In a recent evaluation, researchers compared the rearrest rates of abusers in two different jurisdictions in New York: the Bronx and Brooklyn. In the Bronx, domestic violence cases are usually not pursued if the victim does not wish to participate. In Brooklyn, the opposite is true; if there is an arrest, charges are filed, regardless of the victim's wishes. After following defendants for six months, the researchers found basically no difference in rearrest rates. They cautiously concluded that no-drop prosecution does not lead to dramatic reductions in arrest patterns among offenders, and it is important to note that there is not much research in this area because the strategy is relatively new. The researchers *did* find that victims offered some support for evidence-based prosecution because it put the onus for taking a case forward on the prosecutor, not the victim: "Many of those who preferred that their cases not be prosecuted would not have minded if the prosecution proceeded without them; they wanted to avoid confronting the abusers in court and were wary of assuming the responsibility for ensuring that the abusers experienced penalties for their crimes."

CRITICAL THINKING
1. Should a domestic violence prosecution proceed even if it is against the will of the victim?
2. What are the advantages and disadvantages of basically removing the victim from the criminal process in the way no-drop prosecution often does?

prosecutorial discretion, but others show that decisions are relatively unbiased.[19] Proving racial influence is difficult. In order to establish bias, a defendant must produce credible evidence that similarly situated defendants of other races could have been prosecuted but were not.

L05 Describe prosecutorial discretion and summarize its pros and cons

Resource Issues Resource issues that influence prosecutorial discretion include the availability of treatment and detention facilities, the size of caseloads, and the number of prosecutors available. In some drug cases, prosecutors may decline to bring the case to trial because preparing it for prosecution would demand costly forensic analysis, expert witnesses, and forensic accountants.[20] Some research efforts have concluded that the availability of resources may be a more critical factor in shaping prosecutorial discretion than either legal or extralegal factors. In a world of tight government budgets, a prosecutor's office may be forced to accept plea bargains simply because it lacks the resources and personnel to bring many cases to trial.[21]

The Pros and Cons of Prosecutorial Discretion

Regardless of its source, the proper exercise of prosecutorial discretion can improve the criminal justice process by preventing the rigid implementation of criminal law. Discretion allows the prosecutor to consider alternative decisions and humanize the operation of the criminal justice system. If prosecutors had little or no discretion, they would be forced to prosecute all cases brought to their attention. As Judge Charles Breitel put it, "If every policeman, every prosecutor, every court, and every postsentence agency performed his or its responsibility in strict accordance with rules of law, precisely and narrowly laid down, the criminal law would be ordered but intolerable."[22]

On the other side, too much discretion can lead to abuses that result in the abandonment of law. Prosecutors are political creatures. Although they are charged with serving the people, they also must keep their reputations in mind; losing too many high-profile cases may jeopardize their chances of reelection. They therefore may be unwilling to prosecute cases where the odds of conviction are low; they are worried about convictability.[23]

Prosecutorial Ethics

Although the prosecutor's primary duty is to enforce criminal law, the fundamental obligation is to seek justice. If the prosecutor discovers facts suggesting that the accused is innocent, he or she must bring this information to the attention of the court.

In carrying out their stated duties, prosecutors are sometimes caught in an ethical conundrum. They are compelled by their supervisors to do everything possible to obtain a guilty verdict, all the while acting as public officials concerned to ensure that justice is done. Sometimes this conflict can lead to prosecutorial misconduct. According to some legal authorities, unethical prosecutorial behavior is often motivated by the desire to obtain a conviction and by the fact that such misbehavior is rarely punished by the courts.[24] Some prosecutors may conceal evidence, or misrepresent it, or influence juries by impugning the character of opposing witnesses. Even where a court may instruct a jury to ignore certain evidence, a prosecutor may attempt to sway the jury or the judge by simply mentioning the tainted evidence.

Prosecutorial Misconduct

Because prosecutorial misconduct is a serious matter, the courts have reviewed such prosecutorial behavior as making disruptive statements in court, failing to adhere to sentence recommendations pursuant to a plea bargain, making public statements harmful to the state's case that are not constitutionally protected under the First Amendment, and withholding evidence that might exonerate a defendant.

Courts have also been more concerned about prosecutors who use their discretion in a vindictive manner to punish defendants who exercise their legal rights. Three cases illustrate controls placed on "vindictive" prosecutors:

- **North Carolina v. Pearce.** In this case, the U.S. Supreme Court held that a judge in a retrial cannot impose a sentence more severe than that originally imposed. In other words, a prosecutor cannot seek a stricter sentence for a defendant who succeeds in getting her first conviction set aside.[25]
- **Blackledge v. Perry.** The U.S. Supreme Court found that imposing a penalty on a defendant for having successfully pursued a statutory right of appeal is a violation of due process of law and amounts to prosecutorial vindictiveness.[26]
- **Bordenkircher v. Hayes.** In this case, the Court allowed the prosecutor to carry out threats of increased charges made during plea negotiations when the defendant refused to plead guilty to the original charge.[27]

These decisions provide the framework for the "prosecutorial vindictiveness" doctrine: Due process of law may be violated if the prosecutor retaliates against a defendant and there is proof of actual vindictiveness. The prosecutor's legitimate exercise of discretion must be balanced against the defendant's legal rights.

The Defense Attorney

The defense attorney is the counterpart of the prosecuting attorney in the criminal process. The accused has a constitutional right to counsel, and when the defendant cannot afford an attorney, the state must provide one. The accused may obtain counsel from the private bar if he can afford to do so; if the defendant is indigent, private counsel or a **public defender** may be assigned by the court (see the discussion on the defense of the indigent later in this chapter).

The Role of the Criminal Defense Attorney

The defense counsel is an attorney as well as an officer of the court. As an attorney, the defense counsel is obligated to uphold the integrity of the legal profession and to observe the requirements of the American Bar Association's Code of Professional Responsibility in the defense of a client.

Defense attorneys are viewed as the prime movers in what is essentially an **adversarial procedure**: the procedure used to determine truth in the adjudication of guilt, in which the defense (advocate for the accused) is pitted against the prosecution (advocate for the state), with the judge acting as arbiter of the legal rules. Under the adversary system, the burden is on the state to prove the charges beyond a reasonable doubt. The defense uses all means at its disposal to refute the state's case. This system of having the two parties publicly debate, though imperfect, is thought to be the most effective method of arriving at the truth in a criminal case.

As a member of the legal profession, however, the defense counsel must be aware of her role as an officer of the court. The defense counsel is obligated to uphold the integrity of the legal profession and to rely on constitutional ideals of fair play and professional ethics to provide adequate representation for a client.

The Right to Counsel

The **Sixth Amendment** to the U.S. Constitution allows for provision of counsel at trial. But what about the **indigent** criminal defendant who cannot afford to retain an attorney?

In the 1963 landmark case of *Gideon v. Wainwright*, the U.S. Supreme Court took the first major step on the issue of right to counsel by holding that state courts must provide counsel to indigent defendants in felony prosecutions.[28] Almost 10 years later, in the 1972 case of *Argersinger v. Hamlin*, the Court extended the obligation to provide counsel to all criminal cases where the penalty includes imprisonment—regardless of whether the offense is a felony or a misdemeanor.[29] These two

public defender
An attorney usually employed (at no cost to the accused) by the government to represent poor persons accused of a crime.

adversarial procedure
The process of publicly pitting the prosecution and the defense against one another in pursuit of the truth.

L06 Understand the role of the defense attorney in the justice process

Sixth Amendment
The U.S. constitutional amendment containing various criminal trial rights, such as the right to public trial, the right to trial by jury, and the right to confrontation of witnesses.

indigent
Without the means to hire an attorney.

Gideon v. Wainwright
The 1963 U.S. Supreme Court case that granted counsel to indigent defendants in felony prosecutions.

■ Casey Anthony sobs in the arms of defense attorney Dorothy Clay Sims after graphic photos showing the bones of Caylee Anthony are displayed during day 15 of her first-degree murder trial at the Orange County Courthouse, in Orlando, Florida, June 10, 2011. Celebrity medical examiner Dr. Jan Garavaglia testified that bones scattered in the woods near Casey Anthony's home were positively identified as those of her 2-year-old daughter Caylee. The trial jury was not convinced and found Anthony not guilty of the murder charges. She was, however, found guilty of lying to the police.

major decisions are related to the Sixth Amendment right to counsel as it applies to the presentation of a defense at the trial stages of the criminal justice system.

In numerous Supreme Court decisions since *Gideon v. Wainwright*, the states have been required to provide counsel for indigent defendants at virtually all other stages of the criminal process, beginning with arrest and concluding with the defendant's release from the system. Today, the Sixth Amendment right to counsel and the Fifth and Fourteenth Amendments' guarantee of due process of law have been judicially interpreted together to provide the defendant with counsel by the state in all types of criminal proceedings.

Areas remain in the criminal justice system where the courts have not required that the assistance of counsel be provided for the accused. These include pre-indictment lineups; booking procedures, including the taking of fingerprints and other forms of identification; grand jury investigations; appeals beyond the first review; disciplinary proceedings in correctional institutions; and revocation hearings after release. Nevertheless, the general rule of thumb is that no person can be deprived of freedom or lose a "liberty interest" without representation by counsel.

Legal Services for the Indigent

To satisfy the constitutional requirements that indigent defendants be provided with the assistance of counsel at various stages of the criminal process, the federal government and the states have had to evaluate and expand criminal defense services. Today, about 3,000 state and local agencies are providing indigent legal services in the United States.

Providing legal services for the indigent offender is a huge and costly undertaking. And although most states have a formal set of rules to signify who is an indigent, and many require indigents to repay the state for at least part of their legal services (known as "recoupment"), indigent legal services still cost over $1.5 billion annually.

Programs providing counsel assistance to indigent defendants can be divided into three major categories: public defender systems, **assigned counsel** systems, and **contract systems** (see Exhibit 7.2). Other approaches to the delivery of legal services include the use of mixed systems, such as representation by both the public defender and the private bar, law school clinical programs, and prepaid legal services. Although many jurisdictions have a combination of these programs, statewide public defender programs seem to be on the increase.[30]

In general, the attorney list/assigned counsel system is used in less populated areas, where case flow is minimal and a full-time public defender is not needed. Public defenders are usually found in larger urban areas with high case flow rates. So although a proportionately larger area of the country is served by the assigned counsel system, a significant proportion of criminal defendants are represented by public defenders.

The Private Bar

Although most criminal defendants are represented by publicly supported lawyers, there are also private attorneys who specialize in criminal practice. Because most lawyers are not prepared in law school for criminal work, their skill often results from their experience in the trial courts. Some nationally known criminal defense attorneys represent defendants for large fees in celebrated and widely publicized cases, but this occurs rather infrequently.

Besides this limited group of well-known criminal lawyers, some lawyers and law firms serve as house counsel for such professional criminals as narcotics dealers,

assigned counsel
A lawyer appointed by the court to represent a defendant in a criminal case because the person is too poor to hire counsel.

contract system (attorney)
Providing counsel to indigent offenders by having attorneys under contract to the county handle all (or some) such cases.

Exhibit 7.2

The Forms of Indigent Defense

- *Public defender.* A salaried staff of full-time or part-time attorneys who render indigent criminal defense services through a public or private nonprofit organization, or as direct government-paid employees. The first public defender program in the United States opened in 1913 in Los Angeles. Public defenders can be part of a statewide agency, county government, the judiciary, or an independent nonprofit organization or other institution.
- *Assigned counsel.* The appointment is from a list of private bar members who accept cases on a judge-by-judge, court-by-court, or case-by-case basis. This may include an administrative component and a set of rules and guidelines governing the appointment and processing of cases handled by the private bar members. There are two main types of assigned counsel systems. In the first, which makes up about 75 percent of all assigned counsel systems, the presiding judge appoints attorneys on a case-by-case basis; this is referred to as an ad hoc assigned counsel system. The second type is referred to as a coordinated assigned counsel system, in which an administrator oversees the appointment of counsel and sets up guidelines for the administration of indigent legal services. The fees awarded to assigned counsels can vary widely, depending on the nature of the case. Restructuring the attorney fee system is undoubtedly needed to maintain fair standards for the payment of such legal services.
- *Contract.* Nonsalaried private attorneys, bar associations, law firms, consortiums or groups of attorneys, or nonprofit corporations contract with a funding source to provide court-appointed representation in a jurisdiction. In some instances, an attorney is given a set amount of money and is required to handle all cases assigned. In other jurisdictions, contract lawyers agree to provide legal representation for a set number of cases at a fixed fee. A third system involves representation at an estimated cost per case until the dollar amount of the contract is reached. At that point, the contract may be renegotiated, but the lawyers are not obligated to take new cases.

Source: Carol J. DeFrances, *State-Funded Indigent Defense Services, 1999* (Washington, DC: Bureau of Justice Statistics, 2001).

gamblers, prostitutes, and even big-time burglars. These lawyers, however, constitute a very small percentage of the private bar practicing criminal law.

A large number of criminal defendants are represented by lawyers who often accept many cases for small fees. These lawyers may belong to small law firms or work alone, but a sizable portion of their practice involves representing those accused of crime. Other private practitioners occasionally take on criminal matters as part of their general practice. A lawyer whose practice involves a substantial proportion of criminal cases is often considered a specialist in the field. And there is little question that having a preeminent private attorney can help clients achieve a favorable outcome ("not guilty" verdict).

Does the Type of Lawyer Matter?

Do criminal defendants who hire their own private lawyers do better in court than those who depend on legal representatives provided by the state? Is one type of defense attorney for the indigent better than another?

Public vs. Private Attorneys Although there are some advantages to private counsel, national surveys indicate that state-appointed attorneys do quite well in court. According to data compiled by the federal government:

- Conviction rates for indigent defendants and for those with their own lawyers were about the same in federal and state courts. About 90 percent of the federal defendants and 75 percent of the defendants in the most populous counties were found guilty regardless of which type of attorneys represented them.
- Of those found guilty, however, those represented by publicly financed attorneys were incarcerated at a higher rate than those defendants who paid for their own legal representation.
- On average, sentence lengths for defendants sent to jail or prison were shorter for those with publicly financed attorneys than for those who hired counsel. In federal district court, those with publicly financed attorneys were given just under five years on average, and those with private attorneys just over five years. In large state courts, those with publicly financed attorneys were sentenced to an average of two and a half years, and those with private attorneys to three years.[31]

The Competence of Defense Attorneys

Inadequacy of counsel may occur in a variety of instances. The attorney may refuse to meet regularly with the client, fail to cross-examine key government witnesses, or fail to investigate the case properly. A defendant's plea of guilty may be based on poor advice, where the attorney may misjudge the admissibility of evidence. When co-defendants have separate counsel, conflicts of interest between the defense attorneys may arise. On an appellate level, the lawyer may decline to file a brief, instead relying on a brief submitted for one of the co-appellants.

The U.S. Supreme Court defined the concept of attorney competence in the 1984 case of *Strickland v. Washington*.[32] The case established the two-pronged test for determining effectiveness of counsel:

1. The defendant must show that the counsel's performance was deficient and that such serious errors were made as to essentially eliminate the presence of counsel guaranteed by the Sixth Amendment.
2. The defendant must also show that the deficient performance prejudiced the case to such an extent that the defendant was deprived of a fair trial.

Determining whether defense counsel is ineffective is a subjective decision. The Supreme Court has ruled that an attorney can be effective even when he admits a client's guilt before the trial is over, as long as doing so is part of a reasonable defense strategy, such as gaining sympathy from the jury.[33] For a defense attorney

Luis Munuzuri-Harris, 31, converses with his attorneys, assistant public defender Chuck Traina and public defender Maria Pavlidis, as tears roll down his face. Harris was accused of posing as a police officer to pull over and rape a 28-year-old woman. He later fired his attorneys and represented himself at trial. Needless to say, it was rather uncomfortable for the rape victim to be questioned at trial by the man who allegedly raped her! A jury found Munuzuri-Harris guilty on January 21, 2011. Should defendants be allowed to represent themselves?

© O'Rourke, Skip/ZUMA Press/Corbis

to be considered incompetent, he or she would have to miss filings, fail to follow normal trial procedure, and/or fail to use defense tactics that the average attorney would be sure to follow, such as using expert witnesses or mentioning past behaviors that might mitigate guilt.

Court Administration

In addition to qualified personnel, there is a need for efficient management of the judiciary system. The need for efficient management techniques in an ever-expanding criminal court system has led to the recognition that improving court administration is one way to relieve court congestion. Management goals include improving the organization and scheduling of cases, devising methods to allocate court resources efficiently, administering fines and monies due the court, preparing budgets, and overseeing personnel.

The federal courts have led the way in creating and organizing court administration. In 1939, Congress passed the Administrative Office Act, which established the Administrative Office of the United States Courts. Its director was charged with gathering statistics on the work of the federal courts and preparing the judicial budget for approval by the Conference of Senior Circuit Judges. One clause of the act created a judicial council with general supervisory responsibilities for the district and circuit courts.

Unlike the federal government, the states have experienced slow and uneven growth in the development and application of court management principles. The first state to establish an administrative office was North Dakota in 1927. Today, all states employ some form of central administration.

Using Technology in Court Management

In most jurisdictions today, centralized court administrative services perform numerous functions with the help of sophisticated computers that free the judiciary to fulfill their roles as arbiters of justice. Rapid retrieval and organization of data are now being used for such functions as these:

- Maintaining case histories and statistical reporting
- Monitoring and scheduling cases

Technology will become ever more present in the courtrooms of the future. The courtroom featured here contains flat screen televisions throughout, including one in front of each juror. Courts like this one rely on computer technology and the Internet to bring together witnesses, lawyers, judges, and the jury.

AP Images/Gary C. Knapp

- Preparing documents
- Indexing cases
- Issuing summonses
- Notifying witnesses, attorneys, and others of required appearances
- Selecting and notifying jurors
- Preparing and administering budgets and payrolls

Computer technology is also being applied in the courts in such areas as videotaped testimonies, new court reporting devices, information systems, and data processing systems to handle such functions as court docketing and jury management. In 1968, only 10 states had state-level automated information systems; today all states employ such systems for a variety of tasks and duties. Other developing areas of court technology include the following:[34]

Communications Court jurisdictions are also cooperating with police departments in the installation of communications gear that makes it possible to arraign defendants over closed-circuit television while they are in police custody. Closed-circuit television has been used for judicial conferences and scheduling meetings. Some courts are using voice-activated cameras to record all testimony during trials; these are the sole means of keeping trial records.

Videoconferencing About 400 courts across the country have videoconferencing capability. It is now being employed for juvenile detention hearings, expert witness testimony at trial, oral arguments on appeal, and parole hearings. More than 150 courts use two-way live, televised remote linkups for first appearance and arraignment. In the usual arrangement, defendants appear from a special location in the jail where they can see and hear, and be seen and heard by, the presiding magistrate.

Evidence Presentation High-tech courtrooms are now equipped for real-time transcription and translation, audio-video preservation of the court record, remote witness participation, computer graphics displays, television monitors for jurors, and computers for counsel and judge.

LO9 Be familiar with the expanding role of technology in the court process

Case Management In the 1970s, municipal courts installed tracking systems, which used databases to manage court data. These older systems were limited and could not process the complex interrelationships that pervade information about persons, cases, time, and financial matters in court cases. Contemporary relational databases now provide the flexibility to handle complex case management.

Internet Utilization The Internet has found its way into the court system. In the federal system, J-Net is the judiciary's intranet website. J-Net makes it easier for judges and court personnel to find important information in a timely fashion. The federal court's Administrative Office also sends official correspondence by email, which provides instantaneous communication of important information.

Information Sharing Technology has been harnessed to make it easier for courts to share information within and between states. This helps cut down on costs and accelerates the criminal justice process.

The computer cannot replace the judge, but it can be used to help speed up the trial process by identifying backlogs and bottlenecks that can be eradicated with intelligent managerial techniques. Just as a manager must know the type and quantity of goods on hand in a warehouse, so an administrative judge must have available information about those entering the judge's domain, what happens to them once they are in it, and how they fare after judgment has been rendered.

Ethical Challenge

You are a defense attorney whose newest client is on trial for a burglary. During an interview held in confidence, your client admits to killing three people and burying their bodies near where he lives. He takes you to the gravesites to prove his claims. The police and prosecutor seem totally unaware of these crimes.

Write an essay describing how you would or should handle this disclosure: keep it confidential, call the cops, send an anonymous tip, or whatever. Consider the legal, moral, and practical issues associated with your decision. Would it make a difference if your client told you that if he were set free, he might kill again?

Summary

L01 **Describe the varying structures of state court systems** State courts handle a wide variety of cases and regulate numerous personal behaviors ranging from homicide to property maintenance. Courts of limited jurisdiction are restricted in the types of cases they may hear. Courts of general jurisdiction handle the more serious felony cases (such as murder, rape, and robbery) and civil cases in which damages are over a specified amount, such as $10,000. Appellate courts do not try cases; they review the procedures of the case to determine whether an error was made by judicial authorities.

L02 **Describe the federal court system** The federal government has established a three-tiered hierarchy of court jurisdiction that, in order of ascendancy, consists of the U.S. district courts, the U.S. courts of appeals (circuit courts), and the U.S. Supreme Court.

L03 **Summarize the selection procedure for and duties of the trial judge** The judge is the senior officer in a court of criminal law. His or her primary duty is to oversee the trial process. The qualifications for appointment to one of the existing 30,000 judgeships vary between the federal and state level—and from state to state. Most typically, the potential judge must be a resident of the state, must be licensed to practice law, must be a member of the state bar association, and must be at least 25 years of age and less than 70 years of age. Selection methods vary, too, and include election, appointment, and combinations of each.

L04 **Explain the role of the prosecutor** In the federal system, prosecutors are known as U.S. attorneys and are appointed by the president. On the state and county levels, the attorney general and the district attorney, respectively, are the chief prosecutorial officers. Whatever the title, the prosecutor is the people's attorney, who is responsible for representing the public in criminal matters. Even if the prosecutor decides to pursue a case, the charges may later be dropped, if conditions are not favorable for a conviction, in a process called *nolle prosequi*.

L05 **Describe prosecutorial discretion and summarize its pros and cons** Regardless of its source, the proper exercise of prosecutorial discretion can improve the criminal justice process by preventing the rigid implementation of criminal law. Although the prosecutor's primary duty is to enforce criminal law, his or her fundamental obligation as an attorney is to seek justice, as well as to convict those who are guilty.

L06 **Understand the role of the defense attorney in the justice process** The defense attorney is the counterpart of the prosecuting attorney in the criminal justice process. In the 1963 landmark case of *Gideon v. Wainwright*, the Supreme Court took the first major step on the issue of right to counsel by holding that state courts must provide indigent defendants in felony prosecutions with private counsel or a public defender.

L07 **Discuss the different forms of indigent defense** To satisfy the constitutional requirements that indigent defendants be provided with the assistance of counsel at various stages of the criminal process, the federal government and the states have had to provide indigent defense services. Most criminal defendants are represented by publicly supported lawyers (e.g., public defenders), but there are also private attorneys who specialize in criminal practice.

L08 **Summarize the pros and cons of private attorneys** Even though there are some advantages to private counsel, national surveys indicate that state-appointed attorneys do quite well in court. The *Strickland v. Washington* case established the two-pronged test for determining effectiveness of counsel.

L09 **Be familiar with the expanding role of technology in the court process** Technology is important to the administration and management of courts. High-tech courtrooms are now equipped for real-time transcription and translation, audio-video preservation of the court record, remote witness participation, computer graphics displays, television monitors for jurors, and computers for counsel and judge. Contemporary relational databases now provide the flexibility to handle complex case management.

Review Questions

1. Specialized courts (e.g., drug courts) are popping up all over the country. What is your assessment of this trend? Why do you feel this way?

2. Should defense attorneys cooperate with a prosecutor if it means their clients will go to jail?

3. Should a prosecutor have absolute discretion over which cases to proceed on and which to drop?

4. Should clients be made aware of an attorney's track record in court?

5. Does the assigned counsel system present an inherent conflict of interest, inasmuch as attorneys are hired and paid by the institution they are to oppose?

6. Should victims play a role in the application of prosecutorial discretion? Before you answer, consider how that system might harm some defendants and benefit others.

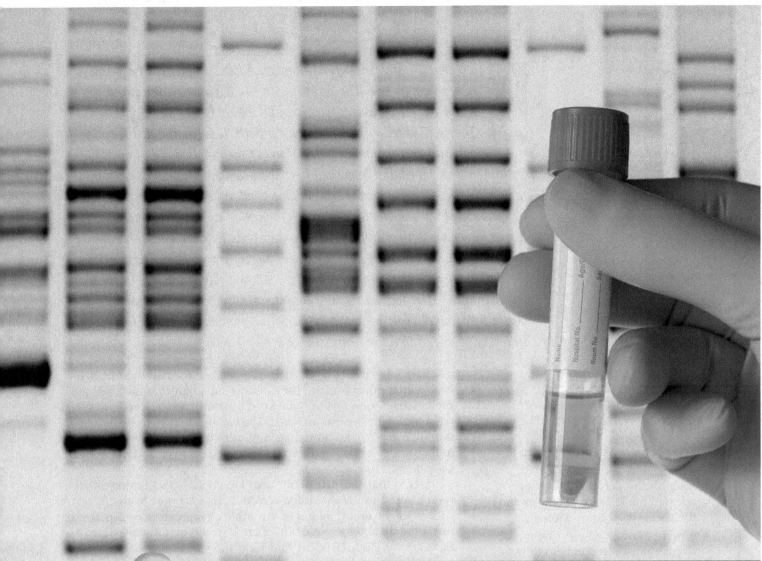
© Zmeel/iStockphoto

8 Pretrial and Trial Procedures

Learning Objectives

LO1   Summarize the bail process

LO2   Discuss the main issues associated with bail

LO3   Differentiate between the two main mechanisms for charging defendants (grand jury indictment and prosecutor's information)

LO4   Summarize the pleas available to a criminal defendant

LO5   Explain the issues involved in plea bargaining

LO6   Describe the plea bargaining process

LO7   Explain the purpose of pretrial diversion

LO8   Describe the goals and purpose of the trial process

LO9   Explain the legal rights of the accused at trial

LO10   Summarize the trial process

Two men driving through Anchorage, Alaska, approached a prostitute, soliciting sex. The prostitute, K.G., agreed to a price and got in the car. The three drove around, looking for a place to park. They settled on a quiet area near a park. K.G. demanded cash in advance, but the men refused. One of them pulled a gun on K.G. Both men then raped and assaulted her. She was then ordered to get out of the car and lie face down in the snow. She tried to flee, but the passenger jumped out of the vehicle, beat her with a wooden axe handle, and shot her in the head. Both men tried to cover her body with snow and left her for dead. But K.G. did not die. The bullet merely grazed her head, and she was able to find her way to a nearby road and flag down a motorist for assistance. After recovering, she accompanied police to the crime scene, where they found a spent shell casing, the axe handle, some of K.G.'s blood-stained clothing, and a used condom. ■

Six days later, police stopped Dexter Jackson for flashing his high-beams at another vehicle. They discovered a gun that matched the shell casing found earlier—and several items that K.G. reported carrying the night she was attacked. The car also matched the description K.G. gave to the police. Jackson admitted being the driver and told police that William Osborne was the passenger. K.G. identified Osborne in a lineup.

Prior to trial, the state performed "DQ Alpha" DNA testing on the sperm found in the discarded condom. This form of testing is not particularly accurate and has an error rate of approximately 5 percent (meaning that in a group of 100 men, it would identify five of them as suspects). Both Osborne and Jackson were convicted. Osborne received the harsher sentence, because the DNA testing identified him as the perpetrator. He challenged his conviction, claiming that he was entitled to a more accurate form of DNA testing. The case recently came before the U.S. Supreme Court, which held that there is no constitutional right for a convicted individual to access the state's evidence to perform additional DNA testing, even if he or she pays for it.[1] The Court explained in a 5-to-4 decision that legislatures should set rules governing access to DNA evidence for testing. Nearly all the states (but not Alaska, as of the date the Supreme Court reached its decision in this case) had done so, and the Court felt it was not its responsibility to change that.

This chapter reviews the pretrial and trial process, beginning with the pretrial procedures. **Pretrial procedures** are important components of the justice process because the vast majority of criminal cases are resolved informally at this stage and never come before the courts. Although the media like to focus on the elaborate jury trial with its dramatic elements and impressive setting, formal criminal trials are relatively infrequent. Consequently, understanding the events that take place during the pretrial period is essential to grasping the reality of the criminal justice process.

Bail

A cash bond or some other security provided to the court to ensure the appearance of the defendant at every subsequent stage of the criminal justice process, especially trial, is known as **bail**. Its purpose is to obtain the release from custody of a person charged with a crime. Once the amount of bail is set by the court, the defendant is

required to deposit all or a percentage of the entire amount in cash or security (or to pay a professional bonding agent to submit a bond). If the defendant is released on bail but fails to appear in court at the stipulated time, the bail deposit is forfeited. A defendant who fails to make bail is confined in jail until the court appearance.

Right to Bail

The Eighth Amendment to the U.S. Constitution does not guarantee a right to bail but rather prohibits "excessive bail." Because many state statutes place no precise limit on the amount of bail a judge may impose, many defendants who cannot make bail are placed in detention while awaiting trial. It has become apparent over the years that the bail system is discriminatory because defendants who are financially well off can make bail, whereas indigent defendants languish in **pretrial detention** in the county jail. In addition, keeping a person in jail imposes serious financial burdens on local and state governments—and, in turn, on taxpayers—who must pay for the cost of confinement. These factors have given rise to bail reform programs that depend on the defendant's personal promise ("recognizance") to appear in court for trial, rather than on her or his financial ability to make bail.

The Eighth Amendment restriction on excessive bail may also be interpreted to mean that the sole purpose of bail is to ensure that the defendant returns for trial; bail may not be used as a form of punishment, nor may it be used to coerce or threaten a defendant. In most cases, a defendant has the right to be released on reasonable bail. Many jurisdictions also require a bail review hearing by a higher court when the initial judge has set what might be considered excessive bail.

In *Stack v. Boyle*, the Supreme Court found bail to be a traditional right to freedom before trial that permits unhampered preparation of a defense and prevents the criminal defendant from being punished prior to conviction.[2] The Court held that bail is excessive when it exceeds an amount reasonably calculated to ensure that the defendant will return for trial. To meet this criterion, bail should be in the amount that is generally set for similar offenses. Higher bail can be imposed when evidence supporting

pretrial procedures
Critical pretrial processes and decisions, including bail, arraignment, and plea negotiation.

bail
The monetary amount for or condition of pretrial release, normally set by a judge at the initial appearance. The purpose of bail is to ensure the return of the accused at subsequent proceedings.

pretrial detention
Holding an offender in secure confinement before trial.

RealityCheck

MYTH OR REALITY? There is no constitutional right to bail.

REALITY. *The Eighth Amendment only prohibits excessive bail (and cruel and unusual punishment).*
The prohibition against excessive bail does not extend to everyone, because the Supreme Court has not required that the states honor this part of the Eighth Amendment. Nearly every state constitution has some sort of prohibition against excessive bail, but there can still be considerable variability in what is considered "excessive."

Frederick Scott Salyer walks out of the Sacramento County jail with his attorney Malcolm Segal. The 54-year-old agribusiness mogul, whose tomato-products empire collapsed amid a years-long federal probe that resulted in charges of racketeering, bribery, obstruction of justice, and antitrust violations, was released on bail. As of this writing, the trial is scheduled for April 17, 2012.

© Leslie Sterling, *Sacramento Bee*/MCT/Landov

the increase is presented at a hearing at which the defendant's constitutional rights can be protected. Although *Stack* did not mandate an absolute right to bail, it did set guidelines for state courts to follow: if a crime is bailable, the amount set should not be frivolous, unusual, or beyond a person's ability to pay.

Bail Release Mechanisms

When and how are bail decisions made? Bail in a felony case is typically considered at a court hearing conducted shortly after a person has been taken into custody. At the hearing, such issues as type of crime, flight risk, and dangerousness are considered before a bail amount is set. In jurisdictions with pretrial release programs, program staff often interview arrestees detained at the jail before the first hearing, verify their background information, and present recommendations to the court at arraignment. Prior record is an important factor: less than half of defendants with an active criminal justice status (such as parole or probation) at the time of arrest are released, compared to more than two-thirds of those with no active status. Some jurisdictions have developed bail schedules to make amounts uniform based on crime and criminal history.

Bail is typically granted during a court hearing in felony cases, but in less serious cases, bail may be handled in a variety of ways:

- *Police field citation release.* An arresting officer releases the arrestee on a written promise to appear in court, at or near the actual time and location of the arrest. This procedure is commonly used for misdemeanor charges and is similar to the issuance of a traffic ticket.
- *Police station house citation release.* The determination of an arrestee's eligibility and suitability for release and the actual release of the arrestee are deferred until after he or she has been removed from the scene of an arrest and brought to the station house or police headquarters.
- *Police/pretrial jail citation release.* The determination of an arrestee's eligibility and suitability for citation release and the actual release of the arrestee are deferred until after he or she has been delivered by the arresting department to a jail or other pretrial detention facility for screening, booking, and admission.
- *Direct release programs.* To streamline release processes and reduce the length of stay in detention, pretrial program courts may authorize pretrial programs to release defendants without direct judicial involvement.
- *Police/court bail schedule.* An arrestee can post bail at the station house or jail according to amounts specified in a bail schedule. The schedule is a list of all bailable charges and a corresponding dollar amount for each. Schedules vary widely from jurisdiction to jurisdiction.

In practice, a significant majority of criminal defendants are released on bail prior to trial.[3] The most recent surveys of pretrial release practices show that about two-thirds of felony defendants were released before the final disposition of their case. Defendants charged with the most serious violent offenses were less likely to be released than those charged with less serious public-order or drug offenses. Nonetheless, more than half of all violent criminals are released before trial. As might be expected, defendants charged with murder are the least likely to be released prior to case disposition (about 8% are released on pretrial bail), followed by defendants whose most serious arrest charge was robbery (about 42% are released on bail), motor vehicle theft (44% bail release rate), burglary (49%), or rape (55%).

Types of Bail

There are a variety of ways or mechanisms to secure bail, depending on the jurisdiction, the crime, and the defendant.

- *Full cash bail.* The defendant pays the full bail amount out of pocket. In some jurisdictions, property can be pledged instead of cash.

- *Deposit bail.* The defendant deposits a percentage of the bail amount, typically 10 percent, with the court. When the defendant appears in court, the deposit is returned, sometimes minus an administrative fee. If the defendant fails to appear, he or she is liable for the full amount of the bail.
- *Surety bail.* The defendant pays a percentage of the bond, usually 10 percent, to a bonding agent who posts the full bail. The fee paid to the bonding agent is not returned to the defendant if he or she appears in court. The bonding agent is liable for the full amount of the bond should the defendant fail to appear. Bonding agents often require posting collateral to cover the full bail amount. This is the most common form of bail.
- *Conditional bail.* The defendant is released after promising to obey some specified conditions in lieu of cash, such as attending a treatment program before trial.
- *Unsecured bond.* The defendant is released with no immediate requirement of payment. However, if the defendant fails to appear, he or she is liable for the full amount.
- *Release on recognizance.* According to the **release on recognizance (ROR)** concept, eligible defendants are released without bail upon their promise to return for trial.

release on recognizance (ROR) A nonmonetary condition for the pretrial release of an accused individual; an alternative to monetary bail that is granted after the court determines that the accused has ties in the community, has no prior record of default, and is likely to appear at subsequent proceedings.

L01 Summarize the bail process

Bail Issues

Whether a defendant can be expected to appear for his or her trial is a key issue in determining bail.[4] Bail cannot be used to punish an accused, nor can it be denied or revoked at the whim of the court. Nonetheless, for the following reasons, critics argue that money bail is one of the most objectionable aspects of the criminal justice system.

- It is discriminatory because it works against the poor.
- It is costly because the government must pay to detain those offenders who cannot make bail but who would otherwise remain in the community.
- It is unfair because a higher proportion of detainees receive longer sentences than people released on bail.
- It is dehumanizing because innocent people who cannot make bail suffer in the nation's deteriorated jail system.

There is also the problem of racial and ethnic disparity in the bail process. Some research efforts show that the decision whether to grant bail may be racially or ethnically biased; black and Latino defendants receive less favorable treatment than whites charged with similar offenses.[5] Although these results are troubling, it is often difficult to gauge racial/ethnic disparity in the bail process because differences in income, community ties, family support, and criminal record, rather than judicial bias, may account for any observed differences in the bail process.

Despite these drawbacks, the bail system remains in place to ensure that defendants return for trial and that the truly dangerous can be kept in secure confinement pending their court proceedings.

Bondsmen and Bounty Hunters When bailees abscond before trial, bondsmen routinely hire skip tracers, enforcement agents, or bounty hunters to track them down. Each year an estimated 400 full-time bail enforcement agents catch some 25,000 fugitives in the United States.[6] Although organizations such as the National Institute of Bail Enforcement attempt to provide training, some untrained and/or unprofessional bounty hunters may use brutal tactics that can end in tragedy. Consequently, efforts have been made to reform and even eliminate money bail and reduce the importance of bonding agents.

Pretrial Detention Conditions The criminal defendant who is not eligible for bail or ROR is subject to pretrial detention in the local county jail. The jail has long been a trouble spot for the criminal justice system. Conditions tend to be poor, and

■ Duane "Dog" Chapman, star of the A&E reality TV series *Dog the Bounty Hunter*, listens to his lawyers on a speaker phone in his home in Honolulu, Hawaii, in 2007. Chapman was told all charges stemming from his 2003 arrest of serial rapist Andrew Luster were dropped. Duane Chapman, his son Leland Chapman, and team member of the TV series Tim Chapman were arrested by federal agents in their Hawaii homes on behalf of the Mexican government in 2006, on charges relating to deprivation of liberty, for extradition back to Mexico. To what extent does the A&E series capture the reality of bounty hunters' work?

rehabilitation is a low priority. Hundreds of jails are overcrowded, and many are under court orders to reduce their populations and improve conditions.

What happens to people who do not get bail or who cannot afford to put up bail money? Traditionally, these individuals are more likely to be convicted and then to get longer prison sentences than those who commit similar crimes but who were released on bail. A federally sponsored study of case processing in the nation's largest counties found that about 63 percent of all defendants granted bail were convicted; in contrast, 78 percent of detainees were convicted.[7] Detainees are also more likely than releasees to be convicted of a felony offense and, therefore, are eligible for a long prison sentence instead of the much shorter term of incarceration given misdemeanants.

Bail Reform Critics believe that the bail system is discriminatory because defendants who are financially well off can make bail, whereas indigent defendants languish in pretrial detention in the county jail—and then get convicted at higher rates. This has led to a number of bail-related reforms. The first such reform program was pioneered by the Vera Institute of Justice in an experiment called the **Manhattan Bail Project**, which began in 1961 with the cooperation of the New York City criminal courts and local law students.[8] The project found that if the court had sufficient background information about the defendant, it could make a reasonably good judgment about whether the accused would return to court. When release decisions were based on such information as the nature of the offense, family ties, and employment record, most defendants who were released on their

Manhattan Bail Project
The innovative experiment in bail reform that introduced and successfully tested the concept of release on recognizance.

own recognizance returned to court. The results of the Vera Institute's initial operation showed a default rate of less than 0.7 percent.

The success of ROR programs in the early 1960s resulted in bail reforms that culminated with the enactment of the federal Bail Reform Act of 1966, the first change in federal bail laws since 1789.[9] This legislation sought to ensure that release would be granted in all noncapital cases in which there was sufficient reason to believe that the defendant would return to court. The law clearly established the presumption of ROR that must be overcome before money bail is required, authorized 10 percent **deposit bail**, introduced the concept of conditional release, and stressed the philosophy that release should be under the least restrictive conditions necessary to ensure court appearance.

During the 1970s and early 1980s, the pretrial release movement was hampered by public pressure over pretrial increases in crime. As a result, the more recent federal legislation, the **Bail Reform Act of 1984**, mandated that no defendants shall be kept in pretrial detention simply because they cannot afford money bail, established the presumption for ROR in all cases in which a person is bailable, and formalized restrictive preventive detention provisions (these are explained later in this chapter). The 1984 act required that community safety, as well as the risk of flight, be considered in the release decision. Consequently, such criminal justice factors as the seriousness of the charged offense, the weight of the evidence, the sentence that may be imposed upon conviction, court appearance history, and prior convictions are likely to influence the release decisions of the federal court.

Preventive Detention Bail reform acts have made it easier for some people to secure pretrial release, but they have also helped keep defendants who are considered dangerous behind bars before trial without the possibility of bail—a practice known as **preventive detention**. These laws require that certain dangerous defendants be confined before trial for their own protection and that of the community. Preventive detention is an important manifestation of the crime control perspective on justice, because it favors the use of incapacitation to control the future behavior of suspected criminals. Critics, however, are concerned that preventive detention amounts to punishment before trial.

The most striking use of preventive detention can be found in the federal Bail Reform Act of 1984.[10] Although the act does contain provisions for ROR, it also allows judges to order preventive detention if they determine "that no condition or combination of conditions will reasonably assure the appearance of the person as required and the safety of any other person and the community."[11]

A number of state jurisdictions have incorporated elements of preventive detention into their bail systems. Although most of the restrictions do not constitute outright preventive detention, they serve to narrow the scope of bail eligibility. These provisions include three main features: (1) exclusion of certain crimes from bail eligibility, (2) definition of bail to include appearance in court and community safety, and (3) the limitations on right to bail for those previously convicted.

Pretrial Services In our overburdened court system, it is critical to determine which defendants can safely be released on bail pending trial.[12] In many jurisdictions, specialized pretrial services help courts deal with this problem. Hundreds of pretrial bail programs have been established in rural, suburban, and urban jurisdictions; they are typically operated in probation departments, court offices, and local jails and through independent county contractors. These programs provide a number of critical services:

- Gathering and verifying information about arrestees—including criminal history, current status in the criminal justice system, address, employment, and drug and alcohol use history—which judicial officers can then take into account in making release/detention decisions

RealityCheck

MYTH OR REALITY? A significant percentage of those released on bail never show up for their scheduled court dates.

MYTH. *Research suggests otherwise. The Manhattan Bail Project found that less than 1 percent of those released default.*
Official statistics tell a similar story; relatively few people released before their trial dates reoffend, get arrested, or fail to show up when they are required to do so. Could the same be expected with release on recognizance programs?

deposit bail
The monetary amount set by a judge at a hearing as a condition of pretrial release; the percentage of the total bond required to be paid by the defendant.

Bail Reform Act of 1984
Federal legislation that provides for both greater emphasis on release on recognizance for nondangerous offenders and preventive detention for those who present a menace to the community.

preventive detention
The practice of holding dangerous suspects before trial without bail.

- Assessing each arrestee's likelihood of failure to appear and chances of being rearrested
- Monitoring released defendants' compliance with conditions of release designed to minimize pretrial crime, including curfews, orders restricting contact with alleged victims and possible witnesses, home confinement, and drug and alcohol testing
- Providing direct "intensive" supervision for some categories of defendants by using program staff and collaborating with the police, other agencies, and community organizations

Some pretrial services programs are now being aimed at special needs. One type focuses on defendants suffering from mental illness; almost three-quarters of pretrial services programs now inquire about mental health status and treatment as a regular part of their interview, and about one-quarter report having implemented special supervision procedures for defendants with mental illness. Another area of concern is domestic violence. About one-quarter of all pretrial programs have developed special risk-assessment procedures for defendants charged with domestic violence offenses, and about one-third have implemented special procedures to supervise defendants charged with domestic violence offenses.

LO2 **Discuss the main issues associated with bail**

Charging the Defendant

Charging a defendant with a crime is a process that varies somewhat, depending on whether it occurs via a grand jury or a preliminary hearing.

The Indictment Process and the Grand Jury

The grand jury was an early development of the English common law. Under the Magna Carta (1215), no freeman could be seized and imprisoned unless he had been judged by his peers. To determine fairly who was eligible to be tried, a group of freemen from the district where the crime was committed would be brought together to examine the facts of the case and determine whether the charges had merit. Thus, the grand jury was created as a check against arbitrary prosecution by a judge who might be a puppet of the government.

The concept of the grand jury was brought to the American colonies by early settlers and later incorporated into the Fifth Amendment of the U.S. Constitution, which states that "no person shall be held to answer for a capital, or otherwise infamous crime, unless on presentment or indictment of a grand jury." What is the role of the grand jury today? First, the grand jury has the power to act as an independent investigating body. In this capacity, it examines the possibility of criminal activity within its jurisdiction. These investigative efforts may be directed toward general rather than individual criminal conduct—for example, organized crime or insider trading. After an investigation is completed, a report called a **presentment** is issued. The presentment contains not only information concerning the findings of the grand jury but also, usually, a recommendation of indictment.

The grand jury's second and better-known role is to act as the community's conscience in determining whether the accusation of the state (the prosecution) justifies a trial. The grand jury relies on the testimony of witnesses called by the prosecution through its subpoena power. After examining the evidence and the testimony of witnesses, the grand jury decides whether probable cause exists for prosecution. If it does, an **indictment**, or true bill, is affirmed. If the grand jury fails to find probable cause, a **no bill** (meaning that the indictment is ignored) is passed. In some states, a prosecutor can present evidence to a different grand jury if a no bill is returned; in other states, this action is prohibited by statute.

Critiquing the Grand Jury The grand jury usually meets at the request of the prosecution, and hearings are closed and secret. Neither the defense attorney nor the defendant is allowed to attend, and grand jury hearings are not open to the public.

presentment
The report of a grand jury investigation, which usually includes a recommendation of indictment.

indictment
The action by a grand jury when it finds that probable cause exists for prosecution of an accused suspect.

no bill
The action by a grand jury when it votes not to indict an accused suspect.

The prosecuting attorney presents the charges and calls witnesses who testify under oath to support the indictment. This process has been criticized as being a "rubber stamp" for the prosecution, because the presentation of evidence is shaped by the district attorney, who is not required by law to reveal information that might exonerate the accused.[13] An alternative is to open the grand jury room to the defense and hold the government to the same types of constitutional safeguards to protect defendants that are now used at trial.[14]

The Information Process and the Preliminary Hearing

In about half the states, a prosecutor's **information** is the charging mechanism of choice. When a person is charged in this fashion, a **preliminary hearing** is necessary. The purposes of the preliminary hearing and the grand jury hearing are the same—to establish whether probable cause is sufficient to merit a trial. The procedures differ between the two, however.

The preliminary hearing is conducted before a magistrate or lower-court judge and, unlike the grand jury hearing, is open to the public unless the defendant requests otherwise. Present at the preliminary hearing are the prosecuting attorney, the defendant, and the defendant's counsel, if one has already been retained. The prosecution presents its evidence and witnesses to the judge. The defendant or the defense counsel then has the right to cross-examine witnesses and to challenge the prosecutor's evidence.

information
A written accusation submitted to the court by a prosecutor, alleging that a particular individual committed the offense in question.

preliminary hearing
A hearing that occurs in lieu of a grand jury hearing, when the prosecutor charges via information. Three issues are decided: whether a crime was committed, whether the court has jurisdiction over the case, and whether there is sufficient probable cause to believe the defendant committed the alleged crime.

■ Justin Cooper, 11, wears his father's mining hard hat during a candlelight vigil for the 25 coal miners who were killed and four who, at the time this picture was taken, were still unaccounted for in the Upper Big Branch Mine explosion in Whitesville, West Virginia, April 7, 2010. Rescue workers were unable to enter the mine due to noxious gases and, sadly, the other four trapped miners were also killed. As of this writing, two men have been indicted in the case and a federal grand jury is deciding whether to charge other individuals who may have been responsible for the accident.

© Roger L. Wollenberg/UPI/Landov

After hearing the evidence, the judge decides whether there is sufficient probable cause to believe that the defendant committed the alleged crime. If so, the defendant is bound over for trial, and the prosecuting attorney's information (described earlier; it is similar to an indictment) is filed with the superior court, usually within 15 days. If the judge does not find sufficient probable cause, the charges are dismissed and the defendant is released from custody.

A unique aspect of the preliminary hearing is the defendant's right to waive the proceeding, a procedure that has advantages (and disadvantages) for both the prosecutor and the defendant. For the prosecutor, waiver helps avoid the need to reveal evidence to the defense before trial. Defense attorneys may waive the preliminary hearing for three possible reasons: (1) when the defendant has already decided to plead guilty, (2) in order to speed the criminal justice process, and/or (3) to avoid the negative publicity that might result from the hearing. On the other hand, a preliminary hearing may have some advantage to the defendant who believes that it will result in a dismissal of the charges. In addition, the preliminary hearing gives the defense an opportunity to learn what evidence the prosecution has.

Figure 8.1 outlines the significant differences between the grand jury and the preliminary hearing processes.

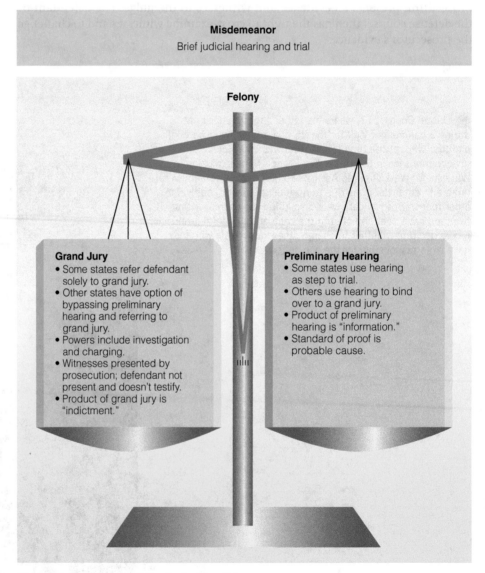

Misdemeanor
Brief judicial hearing and trial

Felony

Grand Jury
- Some states refer defendant solely to grand jury.
- Other states have option of bypassing preliminary hearing and referring to grand jury.
- Powers include investigation and charging.
- Witnesses presented by prosecution; defendant not present and doesn't testify.
- Product of grand jury is "indictment."

Preliminary Hearing
- Some states use hearing as step to trial.
- Others use hearing to bind over to a grand jury.
- Product of preliminary hearing is "information."
- Standard of proof is probable cause.

Figure 8.1 Charging the Defendant with a Crime

Note the difference between the grand jury and the preliminary hearing.

Arraignment

After an indictment or information is filed following a grand jury or preliminary hearing, an arraignment takes place before the court that will try the case. At the arraignment, the judge informs the defendant of the charges against her and appoints counsel if one has not yet been retained. According to the Sixth Amendment of the U.S. Constitution, the accused has the right to be informed of the nature and cause of the accusation; thus, the judge at the arraignment must make sure that the defendant clearly understands the charges.

After the charges are read and explained, the defendant is asked to enter a plea. If a plea of not guilty or not guilty by reason of insanity is entered, a trial date is set. When the defendant pleads guilty or *nolo contendere*, a date for sentencing is arranged. The magistrate then either sets bail or releases the defendant on personal recognizance.

The Plea

Ordinarily, a defendant in a criminal trial will enter one of three pleas: guilty, not guilty, or *nolo contendere*.

Guilty Most defendants appearing before the courts plead guilty prior to the trial stage. A guilty plea has several consequences. It functions not only as an admission of guilt but also as a surrender of the entire array of constitutional rights designed to protect a criminal defendant against unjustified conviction, including the right to remain silent, the right to confront witnesses against him or her, the right to a trial by jury, and the right to have an alleged offense proven beyond a reasonable doubt. Once a plea is made, it cannot be rescinded or withdrawn after sentencing, even if there is a change in the law that might have made conviction more problematic.[15]

As a result, judges must follow certain procedures when accepting a plea of guilty. First, the judge must clearly state to the defendant the constitutional guarantees that he or she automatically waives by entering this plea. Second, the judge must believe that the facts of the case establish a basis for the plea and that the plea is made voluntarily. Third, the defendant must be informed of the right to counsel during the pleading process. In many felony cases, the judge will insist on the presence of defense counsel. Finally, the judge must inform the defendant of the possible sentencing outcomes, including the maximum sentence that can be imposed.

After a guilty plea has been entered, a sentencing date is arranged. In a majority of states, a guilty plea may be withdrawn and replaced with a not-guilty plea at any time prior to sentencing, if good cause is shown.

Not Guilty At the arraignment or before the trial, a not-guilty plea is entered in one of two ways: (1) it is verbally stated by the defendant or the defense counsel, or (2) it is entered for the defendant by the court while the defendant stands mute before the bench.

Once a plea of not guilty is recorded, a trial date is set. In misdemeanor cases, trials take place in the lower-court system, whereas felony cases are normally transferred to the superior court. At this time, a continuance or issuance of bail is once again considered.

Nolo Contendere With this plea (which means "no contest"), the defendant does not accept or deny responsibility for the crime(s) charged but agrees to accept punishment. Even though *nolo contendere* is essentially a plea of guilty, it may not be held against the defendant as proof in a subsequent legal matter, such as a civil lawsuit, because technically there has been no admission of guilt. This plea is accepted at the discretion of the trial court and must be voluntarily and intelligently made by the defendant.

RealityCheck

MYTH OR REALITY? A person arraigned on criminal charges must plead either guilty or innocent.

MYTH. *There are three pleas: guilty, not guilty, and* nolo contendere.
The media routinely get it wrong, claiming that so-and-so pleaded innocent. There is no such plea! What is the difference between "not guilty" and "innocent"?

L04 Summarize the pleas available to a criminal defendant

Plea Bargaining

plea bargaining
Nonjudicial settlement of a case in which the defendant exchanges a guilty plea for some consideration, such as a reduced sentence.

Plea bargaining is the exchange of prosecutorial and judicial concessions for pleas of guilty. Normally, a bargain can be made between the prosecutor and the defense attorney in one of four ways:

● The initial charges may be reduced to those of a lesser offense, thus automatically reducing the sentence imposed.
● In cases where many counts are charged, the prosecutor may reduce the number of counts.
● The prosecutor may promise to recommend a lenient sentence, such as probation.
● When the charge imposed has a negative label attached (e.g., child molester), the prosecutor may alter the charge to a more "socially acceptable" one (such as assault) in exchange for a plea of guilty.

There is little question that these methods result in lesser sentences, especially when defendants are in states whose sentencing policies limit judicial discretion. Pleading guilty to reduced charges may help replace the absence of judicial leniency.[16]

Plea bargaining is one of the most common practices in the criminal justice system and a cornerstone of the informal justice system. Today more than 90 percent of criminal convictions are the result of negotiated pleas of guilty. Even in serious felony cases, plea bargaining can be an option.

Plea bargaining is actually a relatively recent development, which took hold late in the nineteenth century. During the first 125 years after the nation's birth, the trial by jury was viewed as the fairest and most reliable method of determining the truth in a criminal matter. However, plea bargaining became more attractive at the turn of the twentieth century, when the mechanization of manufacture and transportation prompted a flood of complex civil cases; this event persuaded judges that criminal cases had to be settled quickly lest the court system break down.[17]

Pros and Cons of Plea Negotiation

Because of excessive criminal court caseloads and the personal and professional needs of the prosecution and the defense (to reach disposition of the case in the least possible time), plea bargaining has become an essential yet controversial part

Mel Gibson at the Los Angeles Courthouse Airport branch after entering into a plea agreement on March 11, 2011, in Los Angeles, California. Gibson entered a plea of no contest to a charge of misdemeanor battery against ex-girlfriend Oksana Grigorieva and was placed on probation.

of the administration of justice. Proponents contend that plea bargaining actually benefits both the state and the defendant in the following ways:

- The overall costs of the criminal prosecution are reduced.
- The administrative efficiency of the courts is greatly improved.
- The prosecution can devote more time to more serious cases.
- The defendant avoids possible detention and an extended trial and may receive a reduced sentence.
- Resources can be devoted more efficiently to cases that need greater attention.[18]

Those who favor plea bargaining believe it is appropriate to enter into plea discussions when the interests of the state in the effective administration of justice will be served.

Opponents of the plea bargaining process believe that the negotiated plea should be eliminated for the following reasons:

- It encourages defendants to waive their constitutional right to trial.
- Plea bargains allow dangerous offenders to receive lenient sentences. Jesse Timmendequas, a previously convicted sex offender, was given a 10-year plea-bargained sentence for child rape. Upon his release, he raped and killed 7-year-old Megan Kanka in one of the nation's most notorious crimes.[19]
- Plea bargaining also raises the danger that an innocent person will be convicted of a crime if he or she is convinced that the lighter treatment ensured by a guilty plea is preferable to the risk of conviction and a harsher sentence following a formal trial.
- Prosecutors are given a free hand to induce or compel defendants to plea bargain, thus circumventing law.[20]
- It is possible that innocent persons will admit guilt if they believe that the system is biased and that they have little chance of being acquitted.
- A guilty-plea culture has developed among defense lawyers. Elements of this attitude include the belief that most of their clients are dishonest people who committed the crime with which they have been charged and that getting a "sentence discount" for them is the best and only way to go.[21]

Legal Issues in Plea Bargaining

The U.S. Supreme Court has reviewed the propriety of plea bargaining in several decisions and, while imposing limits on the practice, has upheld its continued use. The Court has ruled in several key cases that:

- Defendants are entitled to the effective assistance of counsel to protect them from pressure and influence.[22]
- Pleas must be made voluntarily and without pressure. However, a prosecutor can tell defendants that they may be facing the death penalty if they go to trial.[23]
- Any promise made by the prosecutor during the plea negotiations must be kept after the defendant admits guilt in open court. A prosecutor who promises leniency in private negotiations must stick to that position in court.[24]
- Defendants must also keep their side of the bargain to receive the promised offer of leniency.[25] For example, if they agree to testify against a co-defendant, they must give evidence at trial or forfeit the bargain.
- A defendant's due process rights are not violated when a prosecutor threatens to reindict the accused on more serious charges—for example, as a habitual offender—if the defendant does not plead guilty to a lesser offense.[26]
- Accepting a guilty plea from a defendant who maintains his or her innocence is valid.[27]
- Statements made during a plea bargain may be used under some circumstances at trial if the negotiations break down. Statements made during a plea negotiation can be used if the defendant (a) admits to a crime during the bargaining process but then (b) later testifies in open court that he or she did not do the act and (c) is innocent of the charges.[28]

L05 Explain the issues involved in plea bargaining

Plea Bargaining Decision Making

The plea bargaining process is largely informal, lacking in guidelines, and discretionary. Research shows that prosecutorial discretion rather than defendant characteristics controls plea negotiations.[29] Yet studies also show that plea bargaining reflects a degree of cooperation between prosecutors and defense attorneys; in the vast majority of cases, they work together to achieve a favorable outcome.[30]

Research on plea negotiation indicates that the process is rather complex. Offender, case, and community characteristics also weigh heavily on the negotiation process.[31] Such factors as the offense, the defendant's prior record and age, and the type, strength, and admissibility of evidence are important in the plea bargaining decision as well. The attitude of the complainant is also an important factor in the decision-making process. In victimless cases, such as heroin possession, the attitude of the police is most often considered, whereas in victim-related crimes, such as rape, the victim's attitude is a primary concern. Even the prosecutor's ego or political objectives can factor in. The list of factors that can affect plea agreements is practically endless.

The Role of the Defense Counsel Although the prosecutor formulates and offers the deal, the defense counsel—a public defender or a private attorney—is required to play an advisory role in plea negotiations. The defendant's counsel is expected to be aware of the facts of the case and familiar with the law and to advise the defendant of the alternatives available. The defense attorney is basically responsible for making certain that the accused understands the nature of the plea bargaining process and the guilty plea. This means that the defense counsel should explain to the defendant that by pleading guilty, he is waiving certain rights that would be available if he were to go to trial. In addition, the defense attorney has the duty to keep the defendant informed of developments and discussions with the prosecutor regarding plea bargaining. While doing so, the attorney for the accused cannot misrepresent evidence or mislead the client into making a detrimental agreement. The defense counsel is not just ethically but also constitutionally required to communicate all plea bargaining offers to a client, even if counsel believes the offers to be unacceptable.[32]

The Role of the Judge The leading national legal organization, the ABA, is opposed to judicial participation in plea negotiations.[33] According to ABA standards, judges should not be a party to arrangements for the determination of a sentence, whether as a result of a guilty plea or a finding of guilty based on proof. According to this view, judicial participation in plea negotiations (a) creates the impression in the mind of defendants that they cannot receive a fair trial, (b) lessens the ability of the judge to make an objective determination of the voluntary nature of the plea, (c) is inconsistent with the theory behind the use of pre-sentence investigation reports, and (d) may induce innocent defendants to plead guilty because they are afraid to reject the disposition desired by the judge.[34] How, then, are judges involved in plea bargaining? Judges must approve plea agreements.

The Role of the Victim What role should victims play in plea bargaining? Some suggest that the system today is too "victim driven" and that prosecutors too often seek approval for the plea from a victim or family member. Others maintain that the victim plays an almost secondary role in the process. In reality, the victim is not "empowered" at the pretrial stage of the criminal process. Statutes do not require that the prosecutor defer to the victim's wishes, and there are no legal consequences of ignoring the victim in a plea bargaining decision.

Plea Bargaining Reform

In recent years, efforts have been made to convert plea bargaining into a more visible, understandable, and fair dispositional process. Safeguards and guidelines have been developed to ensure that innocent defendants do not plead guilty under coercion. For example, the judge questions the defendant about the facts of the guilty plea before accepting the plea; the defense counsel is present and can advise the defendant

LO6 Describe the plea bargaining process

■ Plea bargains are used in some of the most notorious violent cases. Here, on November 5, 2003, Gary Leon Ridgway initials his plea agreement in the King County Courthouse in Seattle, where he pleaded guilty to 48 murders. Ridgway added a confession read out by the prosecutor in open court: "I killed so many women I have a hard time keeping them straight." The plea agreement spared Ridgway his life, but he was sentenced to 48 life sentences with no possibility of parole.

© Elaine Thompson/Reuters/Pool/Landov

of his or her rights; the prosecutor and the defense attorney openly discuss the plea; and full and frank information about the defendant and the offenses is made available at this stage of the process. In addition, judicial supervision ensures that plea bargaining is conducted in a fair manner.

Negotiation Oversight Some jurisdictions have established guidelines to provide consistency in plea bargaining cases. Guidelines define the kinds and types of cases and offenders that may be suitable for plea bargaining. Guidelines cover such aspects as avoiding overindictment and controlling unprovable indictments, reducing felonies to misdemeanors, and bargaining with defendants.[35]

Banning Plea Bargaining What would happen if plea bargaining were banned outright, as its critics advocate? Numerous jurisdictions throughout the United States have experimented with bans on plea bargaining. In 1975, Alaska eliminated the practice. Honolulu has also attempted to abolish plea bargaining. Other jurisdictions, including Iowa, Arizona, Delaware, and the District of Columbia, have sought to limit the use of plea bargaining.[36] In theory, eliminating plea bargains means that prosecutors in these jurisdictions make no concessions to a defendant in exchange for a guilty plea.

In reality, however, in these and most jurisdictions, sentence-related concessions, charge-reduction concessions, and alternative methods for prosecution continue to be used in one way or another.[37] Where plea bargaining is limited or abolished, the number of trials may increase, the sentence severity may change, and more questions about the right to a speedy trial may arise. Discretion may also be shifted further up the system. Instead of spending countless hours preparing for and conducting a trial, prosecutors may dismiss more cases outright or decide not to prosecute them after initial action has been taken.

Pretrial Diversion

Another important feature in the early court process is placing offenders into noncriminal **diversion** programs before their formal trial or conviction. The first pretrial diversion programs were established more than 40 years ago to reduce the stigma created by the formal trial process. To avoid stigma and labeling, diversion programs suspend

diversion
A noncriminal alternative to trial, usually featuring counseling, job training, and educational opportunities.

criminal proceedings so that the accused can participate in a community treatment program under court supervision. Diversion programs give the client an opportunity to:

- Avoid the stigma of a criminal record
- Continue to work and support his or her family
- Continue pursuing educational goals
- Access rehabilitation services, such as anger management, while remaining in the community
- When needed, make restitution to the victim of crime or pay back the community through volunteer services

Diversion also enables the justice system to reduce costs and alleviate prison crowding.

Diversion programs can take many forms. Some are run by separate, independent agencies that were originally set up with federal funds but are now being continued with county or state assistance. Others are organized as part of a police, prosecutor, or probation department's internal structure. Still others represent a joint venture between the county government and a private, nonprofit organization that carries out the treatment process.

LO7 Explain the purpose of pretrial diversion

First viewed as a panacea that could reduce court congestion and help treat minor offenders, diversion programs soon came under fire when national evaluations concluded that they are no more successful at avoiding stigma and reducing recidivism than traditional justice processing.[38] There was also the suspicion that diversion might *widen the net of the justice system*. By this, critics meant that the people placed in diversion programs were the ones most likely to have otherwise been dismissed after a brief hearing with a warning or small fine.[39] Now they were receiving more treatment than they would have if the program had not been in place. Those who would ordinarily have received a more serious sentence were not eligible for diversion anyway. Thus, rather than limiting contact with the system, the diversion programs actually increase its grasp.

Of course, not all justice experts agree with this charge, and some programs have shown great promise. Recent evaluations indicate that given the proper treatment, some types of offenders, such as drug offenders, who are offered a place in pretrial programs can significantly lower their rates of recidivism.[40]

The Trial

The criminal trial is an open and public hearing designed to examine the facts of the case brought by the state against the accused. Criminal trials are relatively rare events (most cases are settled by a plea bargain during the pretrial stage), but they are an important and enduring fixture in the criminal justice system. By its very nature, the criminal trial is a symbol of the moral authority of the state. It is the symbol of the administration of objective and impartial justice.

bench trial
The trial of a criminal matter by a judge only. The accused waives any constitutional right to trial by jury.

adjudication
The determination of guilt or innocence; a judgment concerning criminal charges. The majority of offenders charged plead guilty; of the remainder, some cases are adjudicated by a judge and a jury, some are adjudicated by a judge without a jury, and others are dismissed.

Most formal trials are heard by a jury, although some defendants waive their constitutional right to a jury trial and request a **bench trial**, in which the judge alone renders a verdict. In this situation, which occurs daily in the lower criminal courts, the judge may initiate a number of formal or informal dispositions, including dismissing the case, finding the defendant not guilty, finding the defendant guilty and imposing a sentence, or even continuing the case indefinitely. The decision the judge makes often depends on the seriousness of the offense, the background and previous record of the defendant, and the judgment of the court about whether the case can be properly dealt with in the criminal process. The judge may simply continue the case without a finding, in which case the verdict is withheld without a finding of guilt to induce the accused to improve her behavior in the community; if the defendant's behavior does improve, the case is ordinarily closed within a specific amount of time.

LO8 Describe the goals and purpose of the trial process

This section reviews some of the institutions and processes involved in **adjudication** and trial. We begin with a discussion of the legal rights that structure the trial process.

Legal Rights during Trial

Underlying every trial are constitutional principles, complex legal procedures, rules of court, and interpretations of statutes—all designed to ensure that the accused will receive a fair trial.

The Right to an Impartial Judge Even though the Constitution does not say so, every criminal defendant enjoys the right to a trial by an impartial judge. The Supreme Court ruled as much way back in the 1927 case of *Tumey v. Ohio*. In that case, a municipal court judge was also the mayor, an executive official. What's more, he received fines and fees that he ordered against defendants who were convicted in his courtroom. The Supreme Court held that it is a violation of due process when a judge "has a direct, personal, substantial pecuniary interest in reaching a conclusion against [a defendant] in his case."[41]

What if a judge is not impartial? How can such a judge be removed? Generally, the judge will excuse him or herself if there is a conflict of interest. Judicial codes of ethics provide the guidelines judges need to make such decisions. Some jurisdictions, however, permit peremptory removal of judges.[42] These are like the peremptory challenges used in jury selection (covered later in this chapter). When this occurs, one of the attorneys can move to have the judge removed, and another judge will come on board. Usually the peremptory removal can occur only once.

The Right to Be Competent at Trial To stand trial, a criminal defendant must be considered mentally competent to understand the nature and extent of the legal proceedings. If a defendant is considered mentally incompetent, his trial must be postponed until treatment renders him capable of participating in his own defense.

Can state authorities force a mentally unfit defendant to be treated so that he can be tried? In *Riggins v. Nevada* (1992), the U.S. Supreme Court ruled that forced treatment does not violate a defendant's due process rights if it was medically appropriate and, considering less intrusive alternatives, was essential for the defendant's own safety or the safety of others.[43]

The Right to Confront Witnesses The Sixth Amendment states that "In all criminal prosecutions, the accused shall enjoy the right . . . to be confronted with the witnesses against him." The accused enjoys this right not just by being able to confront witnesses in person, but by being allowed to participate in his or her trial. That is, trials cannot be conducted without the accused being afforded the right to appear in person. This right can be waived or forfeited through misconduct. The accused may choose not to show up,[44] which is constitutionally permissible, and he or she may forfeit the right to appear by acting out and causing a significant distraction in the courtroom.[45] There are also some exceptions, such as in child abuse cases, where it is felt that child victims would suffer irreparable harm by being forced to appear before their abusers.[46]

The **confrontation clause** is essential to a fair criminal trial because it restricts and controls the admissibility of **hearsay evidence**. Hearsay evidence is akin to secondhand evidence; rather than being told firsthand, it consists of information related by a second party (it is what one person hears and then says—hence the term "hearsay"). The Framers of the Constitution sought face-to-face accusations in which the defendant has a right to see and cross-examine all witnesses. The idea that it is always more difficult to tell lies about people to their face than behind their back underlies the confrontation clause.

confrontation clause
A part of the Sixth Amendment that establishes the right of a criminal defendant to see and cross-examine all the witnesses against him or her.

hearsay evidence
Testimony that is not firsthand but, rather, relates information told by a second party.

The Right to Compulsory Process The Sixth Amendment says, in part, that the accused shall "have compulsory process for obtaining witnesses in his favor." **Compulsory process** means to compel the production of witnesses via a subpoena. A subpoena is an order requiring a witness to appear in court at a specified time and place. The Supreme Court decided that compulsory process is a fundamental right in the case of *Washington v. Texas* (1967).[47]

compulsory process
Compelling the production of witnesses via a subpoena.

The Right to an Impartial Jury It is no accident that of all the rights guaranteed to the people by the Constitution, only the right to a jury trial in criminal cases appears in both the original Constitution (Article III, Section 2) and the Bill of Rights (the Sixth Amendment). Although they may have disagreed on many points, the Framers did not question the wisdom of the jury trial.

Today, the criminal defendant has the right to choose whether the trial will be before a judge or a jury. Although the Sixth Amendment guarantees the defendant the right to a jury trial, the defendant can and often does waive this right. A substantial proportion of defendants, particularly those charged with misdemeanors, are tried before the court without a jury.

The major legal issue surrounding jury trial has been whether all defendants—those accused of misdemeanors as well as those accused of felonies—have an absolute right to a jury trial. Although the Constitution says that the right to a jury trial exists in *"all criminal prosecutions,"* the U.S. Supreme Court has restricted this right. In *Baldwin v. New York* (1970), the Supreme Court decided that a defendant has a constitutional right to a jury trial when facing a possible prison sentence of six months or more, regardless of whether the crime committed was a felony or a misdemeanor.[48] When the possible sentence is six months or less, the accused is not entitled to a jury trial unless it is authorized by state statute. In most jurisdictions, the more serious the charge, the greater likelihood of trial—and of a trial by jury.

The Right to Counsel at Trial Recall from previous chapters that the defendant has a right to counsel at numerous points in the criminal justice process. Today, state courts must provide counsel at trial to indigent defendants who face even the possibility of incarceration.[49] The threat of incarceration need not be immediate. Even if the defendant might be sentenced to probation in which a prison or jail term is suspended, or might receive any other type of sentence containing a threat of future incarceration, he is afforded the right to counsel at trial.[50]

What if a defendant wants to serve as his or her own attorney? As a result of a 1975 Supreme Court decision, defendants are now permitted to proceed *pro se*, or for themselves.[51] Today, when defendants ask to be permitted to represent themselves and are found competent to do so, the court normally approves their requests. However, these defendants are nearly always cautioned by the court against self-representation. When *pro se* defendants' actions are disorderly and disruptive, the court can terminate their right to represent themselves.

pro se
"For oneself"; presenting one's own defense in a criminal trial; self-representation.

The Right to a Speedy Trial The tactics employed by wary defense attorneys (pretrial motions, complex plea negotiations, delay tactics during trial), along with inefficiencies in the court process (such as the frequent granting of continuances, poor scheduling procedures, and the abuse of time by court personnel), have made delay in criminal cases a serious and constitutional issue. As the American Bar Association states in the *Standards Relating to Speedy Trial*, "Congestion in the trial courts of this country, particularly in urban centers, is currently one of the major problems of judicial administration."[52] Delays in the trial process conflict with the Sixth Amendment's guarantee of a right to a speedy trial.[53]

The Right to a Public Trial The Sixth Amendment refers to a "public trial." This simply means that all trials must be open to the public. The right to a public trial is generally unrestricted. Anyone who wants to see a criminal trial can do so.

Sometimes having a trial open to the public can cause problems. In the 1966 case of *Sheppard v. Maxwell*, the courtroom was packed with people, including members of the media, for all nine weeks of the trial. Reporters handled evidence and took pictures throughout the trial. The Supreme Court eventually reversed the defendant's conviction, citing the "carnival atmosphere." The case did not lead to the exclusion of cameras from the courtroom, but some judges require that they be kept out. This is why one sometimes sees sketches of a case instead of actual photos.

Adverse pretrial publicity can prevent a defendant from getting a fair trial. The release of premature evidence by the prosecutor, extensive and critical reporting by

■ Members of the public line up for seats outside the Orange County courtroom to hear opening statements in the Casey Anthony murder trial in Orlando, Florida, May 24, 2011. After 33 days of testimony by more than 90 witnesses and presentation to the jurors of more than 400 pieces of evidence, Anthony was found not guilty of murder. Do you agree with the verdict? Why or why not?

© Reuters/Scott Audette/Landov

the news media, and vivid and uncalled-for details in indictments can all prejudice a defendant's case. Press coverage can begin early in a criminal case and can even affect the outcome.

As a general rule, pretrial publicity and reporting cannot be controlled. However, judges may bar the press from some pretrial legal proceedings and hearings, such as preliminary hearings, when police officers make an arrest, or when a warrant is being served, if their presence will infringe on the defendant's right to a fair trial.[54] Other steps can be taken as well. These include changes of venue (moving the trial to another jurisdiction, where there is less press coverage and hence less contamination of the pool of potential jurors) and gag orders (restrictions on what the parties or the media can report), among others.

The Right to Be Convicted by Proof Beyond a Reasonable Doubt The standard required to convict a defendant charged with a crime at the adjudicatory stage of the criminal process is **proof beyond a reasonable doubt**. This requirement dates back to early American history and over the years has become the accepted measure of persuasion needed by the prosecutor to convince the judge or jury of the defendant's guilt. Many twentieth-century U.S. Supreme Court decisions have reinforced this standard by making "beyond a reasonable doubt a due process and constitutional requirement."[55] In *Brinegar v. United States* (1949), for instance, the Supreme Court stated:

> Guilt in a criminal case must be proven beyond a reasonable doubt and by evidence confined to that which long experience in the common-law tradition,

proof beyond a reasonable doubt
The standard of proof needed to convict in a criminal case. The evidence offered in court does not have to amount to absolute certainty, but it should leave no reasonable doubt that the defendant committed the alleged crime.

to some extent embodied in the Constitution, has crystallized into rules of evidence consistent with that standard. These rules are historically grounded rights of our system, developed to safeguard men from dubious and unjust convictions with resulting forfeitures of life, liberty, and property.[56]

The reasonable doubt standard is an essential ingredient of the criminal justice process. It is the prime instrument for reducing the risk of convictions based on factual errors.[57] The underlying premise of this standard is that it is better to release a guilty person than to convict someone who is innocent. Because the defendant is presumed innocent until proven guilty, this standard forces the prosecution to overcome this presumption with the highest standard of proof. Unlike the civil law, where a mere **preponderance of the evidence** is the standard, the criminal process requires proof beyond a reasonable doubt for each element of the offense.[58] The various evidentiary standards of proof are analyzed and compared in Exhibit 8.1.

preponderance of the evidence The level of proof in civil cases; more than half the evidence supports the allegations of one side.

The Trial Process

The trial of a criminal case is a formal process conducted in a specific and orderly fashion in accordance with rules of criminal law, procedure, and evidence. Unlike what transpires in popular TV programs involving lawyers—where witnesses are often asked leading and prejudicial questions and where judges go far beyond their supervisory role—the modern criminal trial is a complicated and often time-consuming, technical affair. It is a structured adversarial proceeding in which both prosecution and defense follow specific procedures and argue the merits of their cases before the judge and jury. Each side seeks to present its case in the most favorable light.

Exhibit 8.1

Evidentiary Standards of Proof: Degrees of Certainty

Standard	Definition	Ruling
Absolute certainty	No possibility of error; 100% certainty	Not used in civil or criminal law
Beyond reasonable doubt; moral certainty	Conclusive and complete proof, without leaving any reasonable doubt about the innocence or guilt of the defendant; allows the defendant the benefit of any possibility of innocence	Criminal trial
Clear and convincing	Prevailing and persuasive to the trier of fact	Civil commitments, insanity defense evidence
Preponderance of the evidence	Greater weight of evidence in terms of credibility; more convincing than an opposite point of view	Civil trial
Probable cause	U.S. constitutional standard for arrest and search warrants, requiring existence of facts sufficient to warrant that a crime has been committed	Arrest, preliminary hearing, motions
Sufficient evidence	Adequate evidence to reverse a trial court	Appellate review
Reasonable suspicion	Rational, reasonable belief that facts warrant investigation of a crime on less than probable cause	Police investigations
Less than probable cause	Mere suspicion; less than reasonable belief to conclude criminal activity exists	Prudent police investigation where safety of an officer or others is endangered

---

Although each jurisdiction in the United States has its own trial procedures, all jurisdictions conduct criminal trials in a generally similar fashion. The basic steps of the criminal trial, which proceed in an established order, are described in this section and outlined in Figure 8.2.

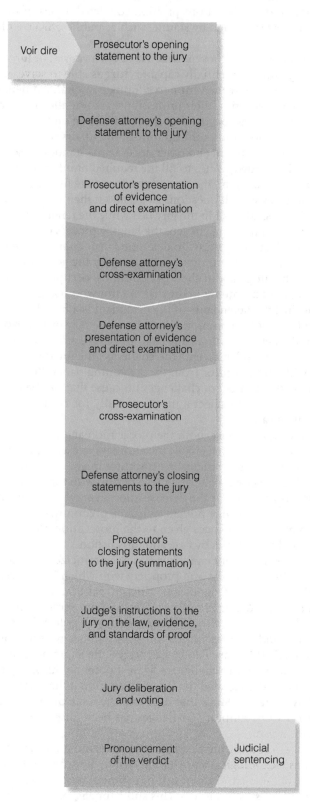

Figure 8.2 The Steps in a Jury Trial

Source: Marvin Zalman and Larry Siegel, *Criminal Procedure: Constitution and Society* (St. Paul, MN: West, 1991), p. 655.

Jury Selection In both civil and criminal cases, jurors are selected randomly from licensing or voter registration lists within each court's jurisdiction. Few states impose qualifications on those called for jury service, although most mandate a residency requirement.[59] There is also little uniformity in the amount of time served by jurors; the term ranges from one day to months, depending on the nature of the trial. In addition, most jurisdictions prohibit convicted felons from serving on juries, as well as others exempted by statute, such as public officials, physicians, and attorneys.

The initial list of persons chosen, which is called a **venire**, or jury array, provides the state with a group of potentially capable citizens able to serve on a jury. Many states, by rule of law, review the venire to eliminate unqualified persons and to exempt those who, by reason of their professions, are not allowed to be jurors. The actual jury selection process begins with those remaining on the list.

The court clerk, who handles the administrative affairs of the court—including the processing of the complaint and other documents—randomly selects what he or she believes will be enough names to fill the required number of places on the jury. After reporting to a courtroom, the prospective jurors are first required to swear that they will truthfully answer all questions asked about their qualifications to serve. A group of 12 will be asked to sit in the jury box while the remaining group stands by.

Once prospective jurors are chosen, the lengthy process of **voir dire** (from the French for "to tell the truth") starts. To determine their appropriateness to sit on the jury, prospective jurors are examined under oath by the government, the defense, and sometimes the judge about their backgrounds, occupations, residences, and possible knowledge of or interest in the case. A juror who acknowledges any bias for or prejudice against the defendant—if the defendant is a friend or relative, or if the juror has already formed an opinion about the case—may be removed by either the prosecution or the defense with a **challenge for cause** asking the judge to dismiss the biased juror. If the judge accepts the challenge, the juror is removed for cause and replaced with another juror from the remaining panel. Because normally no limit is placed on the number of challenges for cause that can be exercised, it often takes considerable time to select a jury, especially for controversial and highly publicized criminal cases.

Besides challenges for cause, both the prosecution and the defense are allowed **peremptory challenges**, which enable the attorneys to excuse jurors for no particular reason or for undisclosed reasons. A prosecutor might not want a bartender as a juror in a drunk-driving case, believing that a person with that occupation would be sympathetic to the accused. Or the defense attorney might excuse a male prospective juror because the attorney prefers to have a predominantly female jury. The number of peremptory challenges given to the prosecution and defense is limited by state statute and often varies by case and jurisdiction.

The peremptory challenge has been criticized by legal experts who question the fairness and propriety with which it has been used.[60] Historically, the most significant criticism was that it was used by the prosecution to exclude African Americans from serving on juries in which the defendant was also African American—a policy that seemed to allow legally condoned discrimination against minority group members. In the landmark 1986 case *Batson v. Kentucky*, the Supreme Court held that the use of peremptory challenges against potential jurors by prosecutors in criminal cases violated the U.S. Constitution if the challenges were based solely on race.[61] Since that decision, the issue of race discrimination in the use of peremptory challenges has been raised by defendants in numerous cases.

It is becoming increasingly difficult to find impartial jurors, especially in this technological age. Heinous crimes have always been broadcast all over the news, and the result has sometimes been to contaminate the pool of prospective jurors. This still happens, of course, but such crimes are the exception rather than the rule. But now jurors are able to turn

venire
The group called for jury duty from which jury panels are selected.

voir dire
The process in which a potential jury panel is questioned by the prosecution and the defense in order to select jurors who are unbiased and objective.

challenge for cause
A request that a prospective juror be removed because he or she is biased or has prior knowledge about a case, or for other reasons that demonstrate the individual's inability to render a fair and impartial judgment in a particular case.

peremptory challenge
The dismissal of a potential juror by either the prosecution or the defense for unexplained, discretionary reasons.

RealityCheck

MYTH OR REALITY? There is nothing inherently wrong with a black jury deciding the fate of a white defendant.

REALITY. *The Sixth Amendment requires an "impartial jury of the state." If a black jury can be impartial with respect to a white defendant, there is no problem. The reverse is also true. The problem is one of appearances. Also, and very important, if it can be shown that prospective jurors were excluded because of race, then the resulting jury will not conform to Sixth Amendment requirements.*

to their BlackBerrys and iPhones to seek information about *any* case. By searching the Internet and sharing information (such as on Facebook), they often learn more about cases than is presented in court, which they are expressly forbidden to do. As one article recently noted, this practice is "wreaking havoc on trials around the country, upending deliberations and infuriating judges."[62] Although there is no official tally of the number of cases compromised by jurors' Internet research, the number is certainly growing. For example, a Florida case involving a man accused of illegally selling prescription drugs was upended because one juror researched the case on her own and was able to discover information not presented at trial. After her actions came to light, the judge had no choice but to declare a mistrial.

Opening Statements Once the jury has been selected and the criminal complaint has been read to the jurors by the court clerk, the prosecutor and the defense attorney may each make an opening statement about the case. The purpose of the prosecutor's statement is to acquaint the judge and jury with the particular criminal charges, to outline the facts, and to describe how the government will prove the defendant guilty beyond a reasonable doubt. The defense attorney reviews the case and indicates how the defense intends to show that the accused is not guilty.

Typically, the prosecutor is entitled to offer an opening statement, which is followed by the defense's opening statement. Both sides use the statement to give the jury a concise overview of the evidence that is to follow. Neither attorney is allowed to make prejudicial remarks or inflammatory statements or to mention irrelevant facts. Both are free, however, to identify what they will eventually prove by way of evidence, which includes witnesses, physical evidence, and the use of expert testimony. The opening statements are important because they give both sides an opportunity to sway the jury before the trial begins.

Prosecution's Case Following the opening statements, the government begins its case by presenting evidence to the court through its witnesses. Numerous types of evidence are presented at trial (see Exhibit 8.2). Those called as witnesses—such as police officers, victims, or experts—provide testimony via direct examination. During **direct examination**, the prosecutor questions the witness to reveal the facts believed pertinent to the government's case. Testimony involves what the witness actually saw, heard, or touched; it does not include opinions. However, a witness's opinion can be given in certain situations, such as when describing the motion of a vehicle or indicating whether a defendant appeared to act intoxicated or insane. Witnesses may also qualify to give opinions because they are experts on a particular subject relevant to the case. For example, a psychiatrist may testify about a defendant's mental capacity at the time of the crime.

direct examination
The questioning of one's own (prosecution or defense) witness during a trial.

Upon completion of the prosecutor's questioning, the defense usually conducts a **cross-examination** of the witness. During this exchange, the defense attorney may challenge elements of the testimony, such as the witness's accuracy in reporting what was seen or heard. The right to cross-examine witnesses is an essential part of a trial, and unless extremely unusual circumstances exist (such as a person's being hospitalized), witness statements will not be considered unless they are made in court and are open for question. If desired, the prosecutor may seek a second direct examination after the defense attorney has completed cross-examination; this allows the prosecutor to ask additional questions about information brought out during cross-examination. Finally, the defense attorney may then question, or re-cross-examine, the witness once again. All witnesses for the trial are sworn in and questioned in the same basic manner.

cross-examination
The process in which the defense and the prosecution interrogate witnesses for the other side during a trial.

directed verdict
The right of a judge to direct a jury to acquit a defendant because the state has not proved the elements of the crime or otherwise has not established guilt according to law.

The Criminal Defense Once the prosecutor has provided all the government's evidence against a defendant, he will inform the court that he rests the people's case. The defense attorney at this point may enter a motion for a **directed verdict**. This is a procedural device in which the defense attorney asks the judge to order the jury

Exhibit 8.2

Types of Evidence Presented at Trial

In general, the primary test for the admissibility of evidence in a criminal proceeding is its relevance; that is, the court must consider whether the gun, tool, or bottle has relevant evidentiary value in determining the issues in the case. Ordinarily, evidence that establishes an element of the crime is acceptable to the court. In a prosecution for possession of drugs, evidence that shows the defendant to be a known drug user might be relevant. In a prosecution for bribery, photos of the defendant receiving a package from a co-conspirator would clearly be found relevant to the case. There are four main types of evidence:

- *Testimonial evidence.* Given by police officers, citizens, and experts, this is the most basic form of evidence. The witness must state, under oath, what he or she heard, saw, or experienced.
- *Real evidence.* Exhibits that can be taken into the jury room for review by the jury constitute real evidence. A revolver that may have been in the defendant's control at the time of a murder, tools in the possession of a suspect charged with a burglary, and a bottle allegedly holding narcotics are examples of real, or physical, evidence. Photographs, maps, diagrams, and crime scene displays are other types of real evidence.
- *Documentary evidence.* This type of evidence includes writings, government reports, public records, business or hospital records, fingerprint identification, and DNA profiling.
- *Circumstantial evidence.* In trial proceedings, circumstantial (indirect) evidence is often inferred or indirectly used to prove a fact in question. For example, in a murder case, evidence that carpet fibers found on the body match the carpet in the defendant's home may be used at trial to link the two, even though they do not provide direct evidence that the suspect actually killed the victim.

to return a verdict of not guilty. Depending on the weight of the prosecution's case, the judge may either sustain or overrule this motion. In essence, the defense attorney argues in the directed verdict that the prosecutor's case against the defendant is insufficient to support the legal elements needed to prove the defendant guilty beyond a reasonable doubt. If the court sustains the motion, the trial is terminated. If it rejects the motion, the defense begins to legally rebut the prosecution's case.

The defense attorney has the option of presenting many, some, or no witnesses on behalf of the defendant. The burden of proving guilt is on the prosecution, and if the defense team believes that the burden has not been met, they may feel there is no need to present witnesses of their own. In addition, the defense attorney must decide whether the defendant should take the stand and testify in his own behalf. In a criminal trial, the defendant is protected by the Fifth Amendment right to be free from self-incrimination, which means that a person cannot be forced by the state to testify against himself. However, defendants who choose voluntarily to tell their side of the story can be subject to cross-examination by the prosecutor.

The defense attorney is charged with putting on a vigorous defense in the adversary system of justice. She presents her own witnesses and introduces evidence to refute the prosecution's allegations. After the defense concludes its case, the government may then present rebuttal evidence. If the judge grants permission, this involves bringing forward evidence to refute, counteract, or disprove evidence introduced by the defense. A prosecutor may not go into new matters or present evidence that further supports or reinforces his own case. At the end of rebuttal, the defense may be allowed surrebuttal—presenting witnesses to respond to issues that were raised for the first time in the prosecutor's rebuttal case. The defense cannot restate its case or introduce new issues during surrebuttal evidence.

Closing Arguments In closing arguments, the attorneys review the facts and evidence of the case in a manner favorable to their respective positions. At this stage of the trial, both prosecution and defense are permitted to draw reasonable inferences and to show

The *CSI* Effect

When *CSI: Crime Scene Investigation,* debuted, it was a surprise television hit. At one point, it was labeled the most popular show in the world. Its spinoff programs, *CSI: Miami* and *CSI: New York,* were also popular. Together, the *CSI* programs are the most-watched drama series in the world.

The criminal investigations genre is but the latest to evolve in the long history of television programming that has featured (and sensationalized) criminal investigations and courtroom proceedings. More than most other shows, though, *CSI* and its progeny may have started to blur the lines between reality and fiction. And this effect may be enhanced by the popularity of crime magazine shows such as *48 Hours Mystery, American Justice,* and (sometimes) *Dateline NBC,* which feature real cases. But it's *not* because these entertainment programs portray the criminal justice system so accurately that they seem more realistic than fictional. Read on.

Many attorneys, judges, and journalists have started to claim that *CSI*-like programs have influenced jurors' expectations. Some have alleged that jurors sometimes acquit defendants when no scientific evidence is presented. Others have alleged that jurors have developed unrealistic expectations about just what information scientific investigations can bring to bear on a case. As one prosecutor put it, "Jurors now expect us to have a DNA test for just about every case. They expect us to have the most advanced technology possible, and they expect it to look like it does on television."

DOES A *CSI* EFFECT REALLY EXIST?

Donald Shelton, a judge, and his colleagues, criminology professors at Eastern Michigan University, surveyed 1,000 prospective jurors in an effort to determine whether there is a real "*CSI* effect." They asked questions concerning expectations and demands for scientific evidence and the television programs that the respondents regularly watched. The respondents were asked about several crime types and then asked to report what scientific evidence they would expect to see presented at trial. Choices for the latter ranged from eyewitness testimony and circumstantial evidence to DNA, ballistics, and fingerprint evidence. They were even asked how likely they would be to find the defendant guilty or not guilty based on the evidence presented by the prosecution. What did the researchers find?

- 46 percent expected to see scientific evidence presented in *every* criminal case.
- 22 percent expected to see DNA evidence in *every* criminal case.
- 36 percent expected to see fingerprint evidence in *every* criminal case.
- 32 percent expected to see ballistic or other firearms evidence in *every* criminal case.

What do the percentages mean? Are expectations unrealistic? In one-third of all criminal cases, it is virtually impossible to gather fingerprint evidence. It appears, indeed, that the respondents' expectations were driven somewhat by their television-watching habits. For all the categories of evidence, *CSI* viewers tended to have higher expectations for being presented with scientific evidence. This suggests there is evidence of a *CSI* effect, but Shelton and his colleagues also found that respondents were only somewhat likely to alter their verdicts based on the presence or absence of scientific evidence in a trial. They found, for example, that

- *CSI* viewers were more likely than their non-*CSI*-viewing counterparts to convict without scientific evidence if eyewitness testimony was available.
- In rape cases, *CSI* viewers were less likely to convict if DNA evidence was not presented.
- In breaking-and-entering and theft scenarios, victim or other testimony was sufficient to convict.

Shelton and his colleagues concluded, in short, that there *is* a *CSI* effect, but it may not be as influential as was previously thought. Not everyone agrees, however. The National Academy of Sciences report presented in the Contemporary Issues in Criminal Justice feature "Forensics under the Microscope" in Chapter 5 revealed that a number of prosecutors are concerned about a supposedly real *CSI*-like effect.

CRITICAL THINKING

It is said that life imitates art. As the popularity of the crime scene investigator profession grows, more students will probably be drawn into forensics, and more police and law enforcement agencies are likely to use forensic specialists in their daily operations. Do you think that crime is better solved in the lab or on the beat?

---

how the facts prove or refute the defendant's guilt. Often both attorneys have a free hand in arguing about the facts, issues, and evidence, including the applicable law. They cannot comment on matters not in evidence, however, or on the defendant's failure to testify in a criminal case. Normally, the prosecutor makes a closing statement first, followed by the defense, and many jurisdictions allow the prosecution an opportunity for rebuttal. Either party can elect to forgo the right to make a final summation to the jury.

Instructions to the Jury In a criminal trial, the judge will instruct, or charge, the jury members on the principles of law that ought to guide and control their decision on the defendant's innocence or guilt. Included in the charge will be information about the elements of the alleged offense, the type of evidence needed to prove each element, and the burden of proof that must be met to obtain a guilty verdict. Although the judge commonly provides this instruction, he or she may ask the prosecutor and the defense attorney to submit instructions for consideration; the judge will then exercise discretion in determining whether to use any of their instructions. The instructions that cover the law applicable to the case are extremely important because they may serve as the basis for a subsequent appeal. The Contemporary Issues in Criminal Justice feature discusses the "*CSI* effect," a relatively recent phenomenon that judges need to be aware of as they instruct the jury on how to go about its business.

Deliberation and Verdict Once the charge is given to the jury members, they retire to deliberate on a verdict. In highly publicized and celebrated cases, the judge may sequester the jury, preventing them from having contact with the outside world. This process is discretionary, and most judges believe that sequestering or "locking up a jury" is needed only in sensational cases.

A review of the case by the jury may take hours or even days. The jurors always meet privately during their deliberations, and in certain lengthy and highly publicized cases, they are kept overnight in a hotel until the verdict is reached. In less sensational cases, the jurors may be allowed to go home, but they are cautioned not to discuss the case with anyone.

If a verdict cannot be reached, the trial may result in a hung jury, after which the prosecutor must bring the defendant to trial again if the prosecution desires a conviction. If found not guilty, the defendant is released from the criminal process. If the defendant is convicted, the judge will normally order a pre-sentence investigation by the probation department before imposing a sentence. Before sentencing, the defense attorney will probably submit a motion for a new trial, alleging that legal errors occurred in the trial proceedings. The judge may deny the motion and impose a sentence immediately, a practice quite common in most misdemeanor offenses. In felony cases, however, the judge will set a date for sentencing, and the defendant will either be placed on bail or held in custody until that time.

Although jurors are required by law to base their decision on the facts of the case and on the judge's legal instructions, they are sometimes asked by the defense to ignore both and render decisions based on emotion and personal preference.[63] This strategy, called **jury nullification**, has been in practice since 1735 when

jury nullification
A defense tactic that consists of suggesting that the jury acquit a defendant, despite evidence that he actually violated the law, by maintaining that the law was unjust or not applicable to the case.

■ A judge's instructions to the jury are among the most important parts of the trial process. Flawed instructions can form the basis of an appeal. Here, Gage County District Court judge Paul Korslund briefs members of the jury during the trial of Richard Griswold at the Gage County Court, in Beatrice, Nebraska, on May 19, 2008. Griswold, 43, of Beatrice, was charged with first-degree murder and use of a weapon to commit a felony in the death of 49-year-old Connie Eacret. In what is believed to have been a first for the state, media cameras were being allowed in the courtroom for a criminal trial.

AP Images/Nati Harnik, Pool

John Peter Zenger, editor of the *New York Weekly Journal*, was charged with printing libelous statements about the governor of the Colony of New York, William Cosby. Despite the fact that Zenger clearly printed the alleged libels and the trial judge gave the jury clear instructions for a finding of guilt, the jury found Zenger not guilty on all charges. The Zenger case remains one of the most famous examples of jury nullification in the nation's history.

Supporters of jury nullification argue that it is an important safeguard against government oppression and that the function of the jury is to serve as a safety valve against the unjust application of the law. Critics, however, see jury nullification as an abuse of power. Would it be fair if jurors, motivated by racial bias, found a person accused of a hate crime not guilty despite overwhelming evidence of guilt?[64]

The Sentence Imposing the criminal sentence is normally the responsibility of the trial judge. In some jurisdictions, the jury may determine the sentence or make recommendations involving leniency for certain offenses. Often, the sentencing decision is based on information and recommendations given to the court by the probation department after a pre-sentence investigation of the defendant. The sentence itself is determined by the statutory requirements for the particular crime as established by the legislature; in addition, the judge ordinarily has a great deal of discretion in reaching a sentencing decision. The different criminal sanctions available include fines, probation, imprisonment, and even commitment to a state hospital. The sentence may be a combination of all these.

Appeals Once a verdict has been rendered and a defendant found guilty, the defense may petition an appellate court to review the procedures used during trial. Defendants have two main avenues to challenge such procedures: appeals and habeas corpus. These both give the convicted person an opportunity to appeal to a higher state or federal court on the basis of an error that affected the conviction in the trial court. Extraordinary trial court errors, such as denial of the right to counsel or inability to provide a fair trial, are subject to the plain error rule of the federal courts.[65] Harmless errors, such as the use of innocuous identification procedures or the denial of counsel at a noncritical stage of the proceeding, would not necessarily result in the overturning of a criminal conviction.

A postconviction **appeal** is a request for an appellate court to examine a lower court's decision in order to determine whether proper procedures were followed. It is important to note that appeals do not give the convicted an opportunity to try the case a second time, only to challenge procedural matters (such as a judge's decision to exclude a witness's testimony). Most defendants benefit from at least one direct appeal. Direct appeals are guaranteed by law; the result is that most defendants get to appeal at least once, even if they cannot afford it.[66] Discretionary appeals are also possible. It is up to the appellate court to decide whether it will hear a discretionary appeal. There is no restriction on the number of discretionary appeals that can be filed.

Through objections made at the pretrial and trial stages of the criminal process, the defense counsel will reserve specific legal issues on the record as the basis for appeal. A copy of the transcript of these proceedings will serve as the basis on which the appellate court will review any errors that may have occurred during the lower-court proceedings. The Careers in Criminal Justice feature describes the work of the court reporter, the person who prepares these transcripts.

A **writ of *habeas corpus*** is the primary means by which state prisoners have their convictions or sentences reviewed in the federal court. A writ of *habeas corpus* (which means "you may have the body") seeks to determine the validity of a detention by asking the court to release the person or give legal reasons for the incarceration.

appeal
A request for an appellate court to examine a lower court's decision in order to determine whether proper procedures were followed.

writ of *habeas corpus*
A judicial order requesting that a person who detains another person produce the body of the prisoner and give reasons for his or her capture and detention. *Habeas corpus* is a legal device used to request that a judicial body review the reasons for a person's confinement and the conditions of confinement. *Habeas corpus* is known as "the great writ."

LO10 Summarize the trial process

Careers in Criminal Justice

COURT REPORTER

Duties and Characteristics of the Job

- Court reporters create the official transcripts of legal proceedings such as trials and depositions.
- These transcripts include all the dialogue as well as other important details, such as emotional reactions.
- Court reporters use voice writers that make an audio record of the proceedings.
- Some use audio equipment to tape an event and then supplement this recording later with notes taken during the proceedings.
- The commonly used recording method in legal and courtroom settings is stenographic machines that transcribe spoken words. A court reporter can press multiple keys simultaneously to represent words, sounds, or even phrases.
- Although the primary responsibility of court reporters is to record courtroom legal proceedings, when requested they also provide this information from the official record.
- Court reporters can advise lawyers on legal procedure when necessary.

Job Outlook

- The number of jobs available for court reporters is greater than the number of trained professionals entering the field.
- The job outlook is favorable for entry-level court reporters, especially those who are certified.
- Court reporters are always needed in courtrooms and lawyers' offices across the country, although jobs may be more plentiful in urban areas.
- They often freelance for extra income at attorneys' offices or as closed-captioners and/or real-time translators.
- Other court reporters work for court reporting agencies or freelance full time.
- Agency workers and freelancers enjoy the flexibility of setting their own schedules.

Salary

- Pay will depend on several factors, including method of transcription, region of the United States, type of employer, amount of previous work experience, and level of certification.
- The median annual salary for court reporters is around $50,000. The majority of court reporters earn between $35,390 and $67,430. At the extremes, a small percentage of court reporters earn $25,360 and the highest paid earn $83,500 or more.

Qualifications

- The qualifications one must have to be a practicing court reporter vary by state.
- In some states, court reporters are required to be notary publics; in others, an individual must become a certified court reporter (CCR) by passing a state certification test.
- Court reporters must continually study and practice their skills.

Education and Training

- At the minimum, a court reporter needs an associate's degree, although requiring a bachelor's degree is more common.
- In addition to general education, training programs are available at vocational or technical schools.
- There are 70 programs approved by the National Court Reporters Association in the United States and Canada.

Word to the Wise

- Because a court reporter must create a record of events as they occur, the ability to listen carefully and work quickly is key. Familiarity with legal terms and practices is necessary, as is a thorough knowledge of grammar, spelling, and vocabulary.
- Court reporters must become intimately familiar with stenotype machines. As one reporter said, "Your wrists will become your worst enemy if you don't show them some love."
- Despite the seemingly simple training requirements, many people drop out, partly as a consequence of the high speed required (around 225 words per minute, far in excess of the speed at which skilled typists can type).
- There can be considerable stress in the job because of the constant pressure to be fast and accurate.
- The future is somewhat uncertain; digital audio recorders could well replace court reporters some day.

Summary

L01 **Summarize the bail process** The purpose of bail is to obtain the release from custody of a person charged with a crime. The Eighth Amendment to the U.S. Constitution does not guarantee a right to bail but, rather, prohibits "excessive bail." Bail is typically granted during a court hearing, but there are other stages in the system in which bail may be granted, depending on the jurisdiction, the crime, and the defendant. In practice, a majority of criminal defendants are released on bail prior to trial.

L02 **Discuss the main issues associated with bail** Bail is a controversial practice, but it serves a valuable function. Bonding agents are available to assist defendants who do not have sufficient resources with pretrial release. Those who cannot make bail often wait in jail until trial. Jail conditions are often unpleasant and crowded. Jailed defendants are also convicted at higher rates than those released on bail. In light of these issues, various bail reforms have been enacted over the years, ranging from release on recognizance to preventive detention. Pretrial services are also provided for certain defendants.

L03 **Differentiate between the two main mechanisms for charging defendants (grand jury indictment and prosecutor's information)** The grand jury's role is to act as the community's conscience in determining whether the accusation of the state (the prosecution) justifies a trial. If the grand jury believes charges are merited, an indictment will be issued. If not, a "no bill" is passed. The charging mechanism used in about half the states, as an alternative to the grand jury, is a prosecutor's information. An information is a written accusation submitted to the court by a prosecutor, alleging that a particular individual committed the offense in question

L04 **Summarize the pleas available to a criminal defendant** The defendant in a criminal trial will enter one of three pleas: guilty, not guilty, or *nolo contendere*. The pleas of guilty and not guilty are self-explanatory. *Nolo contendere* is essentially a plea of guilty, but it may not be held against the defendant as proof in a subsequent legal matter, such as a civil lawsuit

L05 **Explain the issues involved in plea bargaining** Plea bargaining is one of the most common practices in the criminal justice system today and is a cornerstone of the informal justice system. Today, more than 90 percent of criminal convictions are estimated to result from negotiated pleas of guilty. Some critics of plea bargaining believe that defendants are treated with leniency as a result of the practice. Supporters of plea bargaining point out that all parties benefit from the practice (the prosecutor gets a conviction, the defense gets leniency, and the court saves the costs of a trial). Various Supreme Court decisions place constraints on plea bargaining.

L06 **Describe the plea bargaining process** The plea bargaining process is largely informal, lacking in guidelines, and discretionary. The prosecutor typically presents the defendant with an offer of a reduced charge or favorable sentencing recommendation. Defense counsel is required to play an advisory role in plea negotiations. Judges should not be a party to arrangements for the determination of a sentence, whether as a result of a guilty plea or as a result of a finding of guilty based on proof. The victim is not empowered at the pretrial stage of the criminal process to influence a plea bargaining decision. Recently, efforts have been made to convert plea bargaining into a more visible, understandable, and fair process.

L07 **Explain the purpose of pretrial diversion** Another important feature in the early court process is placing offenders into noncriminal diversion programs before their formal trial or conviction. Pretrial diversion helps the accused avoid the stigma of a criminal conviction.

L08 **Describe the goals and purpose of the trial process** The criminal trial is an open and public hearing designed to examine the facts of the case brought by the state against the accused. The trial is an important and enduring fixture in the criminal justice system. By its very nature, it is a symbol of the moral authority of the state and impartial justice. Most formal trials are heard by a jury, although some defendants waive their constitutional right to a jury trial and request a bench trial, in which the judge alone renders a verdict.

L09 **Explain the legal rights of the accused at trial** Legal rights at trial include the right to an impartial judge, the right to be competent at trial, the right to confront witnesses, the right to compulsory process, the right to an impartial jury, the right to counsel, the right to a speedy trial, the right to a public trial, and the right to be convicted by proof beyond a reasonable doubt.

L010 **Summarize the trial process** The criminal trial is a formal process conducted in a specific and orderly fashion in accordance with rules of criminal law, procedure, and evidence. Once the jury has been selected, the prosecutor and the defense attorney may each make an opening statement about the case. Following the opening statements, the government begins its case by presenting evidence to the court through its witnesses. Once the prosecution has provided all the government's evidence against a defendant, it will inform the court that it rests the people's case. Closing arguments are used by the attorneys to review the facts and evidence of the case in a manner favorable to their respective positions. The judge will then instruct, or charge, the jury members on the principles of law that ought to guide and control their decision on the defendant's innocence or guilt. Imposing the criminal sentence (if a "guilty" verdict is reached) is normally the responsibility of the trial judge.

Review Questions

1. Should those accused of violent acts be subjected to preventive detention instead of bail, even though they have not been convicted of a crime? Is it fair to the victim to have the alleged attacker running around loose?

2. Should criminal defendants be allowed to bargain for a reduced sentence in exchange for a guilty plea? Should the victim always be included in the plea bargaining process?

3. What purpose does a grand jury or preliminary hearing serve in adjudicating felony offenses? Should one of these methods be abandoned, and if so, which one?

4. Do criminal defendants enjoy too many rights at trial? Why or why not?

5. Should people be denied the right to serve as jurors without explanation or cause? In other words, should the peremptory challenge be maintained?

6. "In the adversary system of criminal justice, the burden of proof in a criminal trial to show that the defendant is guilty beyond a reasonable doubt is on the government." Explain the meaning of this statement.

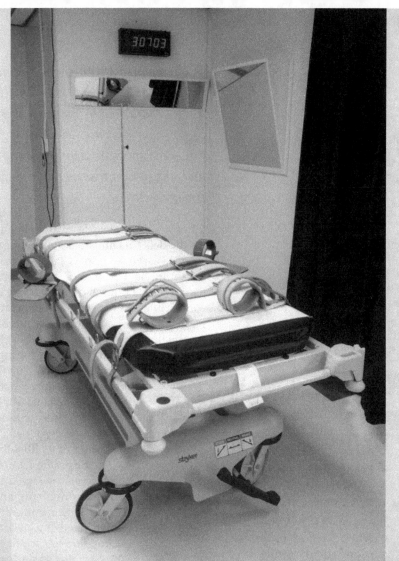

AP Photo/Fla. Dept. of Corrections, File

9 Punishment and Sentencing

Learning Objectives

LO1 Outline the historical development of punishment

LO2 List the major goals of contemporary sentencing

LO3 Distinguish among general and specific deterrence, incapacitation, and retribution

LO4 Compare rehabilitation with just deserts

LO5 Identify various sentencing models

LO6 Explain how sentences are imposed

LO7 Summarize factors associated with sentencing decisions

LO8 List the arguments for and against capital punishment

LO9 Be familiar with the legal issues associated with capital punishment

*I*n early 2009, the Supreme Court decided whether it should hear an appeal from William Johnson, a man who had been on death row in Florida for 32 years.[1] In seeking to have the Court hear his case, Johnson argued that the lengthy amount of time he spent on death row, not the sentence itself, amounted to cruel and unusual punishment, in violation of the U.S. Constitution's Eighth Amendment. ■

Johnson's argument was creative, but it lacked merit because he was partly responsible for the delay, having filed many appeals over the years. Calling Johnson out on this, Justice Clarence Thomas said, "I remain unaware of any support in the American constitutional tradition or in this Court's precedent for the proposition that a defendant can avail himself of the panoply of appellate and collateral procedures and then complain when his execution is delayed." On the other hand, something is at least partially awry when a person spends 32 years waiting for a sentence to be carried out. Although he supported the Court's decision not to grant review, Justice John Paul Stevens said, "[O]ur experience during the past three decades has demonstrated that delays in state-sponsored killings are inescapable and that executing defendants after such delays is unacceptably cruel. This inevitable cruelty, coupled with the diminished justification for carrying out an execution after the lapse of so much time, reinforces my opinion that contemporary decisions to retain the death penalty as a part of our law are the product of habit and inattention rather than an acceptable deliberative process."

The Supreme Court elected *not* to hear Johnson's case, but its decision sent a signal that there is some concern about the delays between sentencing and execution in capital cases. And although delays like those in Johnson's case are rare, the death penalty is not administered quickly for *any* offenders. According to the Death Penalty Information Center, in 1990 the average time between sentencing and execution was seven years. That grew to over 12 years in 2008.[2] By all accounts, delays continue to lengthen, prompting death penalty critics to complain about the costs of a drawn-out appeals process. Supporters also express disdain over delays, claiming instead that they undermine the retributive force of death and compromise the penalty's deterrent effect. Both parties agree something must be done.

The death penalty is the most extreme form of punishment, and it is used relatively rarely, but it raises fundamental questions about the nature and extent of punishment: Should the most serious of criminals be executed? What options, if any, are preferable to capital punishment? Is contemporary punishment too harsh or too lenient? Regardless of the penalty in question, is sentencing fair? Is there discrimination in sentencing based on race, gender, or social class? How often are mistakes made? These are but a few of the most significant questions in the realm of punishment and sentencing.

This chapter first examines the history of punishment and then focuses on incarceration and capital punishment, the two most traditional and punitive forms of criminal sanctions used today. Chapter 10 reviews alternative sentences that have been developed to reduce the strain on the overburdened correctional system; these sentences provide intermediate sanctions designed to control people whose behavior and personality make incarceration unnecessary. Such sanctions include probation and other forms of community correction.

RealityCheck

MYTH OR REALITY?

- **Rehabilitating criminals is the primary goal of contemporary sentencing.**
- **Theft can result in life in prison.**
- **When it comes to sentencing, there is one standard rule: If you commit a serious crime, you serve a lot of time.**
- **The United States is one of the few countries that still retains the death penalty.**
- **The death penalty deters homicide.**

The History of Punishment

The punishment and correction of criminals has changed considerably through the ages, reflecting custom, economic conditions, and religious and political ideals.[3]

From Exile to Fines, Torture to Forfeiture

In early Greece and Rome, the most common state-administered punishment was banishment, or exile. Only slaves were commonly subjected to harsh physical punishment for their misdeeds. Interpersonal violence, even attacks that resulted in death, were viewed as a private matter. These ancient peoples typically used economic punishments, such as fines, for such crimes as assault on a slave, arson, and housebreaking.

During the Middle Ages (the fifth to fifteenth centuries), there was little law or governmental control. Offenses often sparked blood feuds carried out by the families of the injured parties. When possible, the Roman custom of settling disputes by fine or an exchange of property was adopted as a means of resolving interpersonal conflicts with a minimum of bloodshed. After the eleventh century, during the feudal period, forfeiture of land and property was common punishment for persons who violated law and custom or who failed to fulfill their feudal obligations to their lord. The word "felony" has its origins in the twelfth century, when the term "felonia" referred to a breach of faith with one's feudal lord.

During this period, the main emphasis of criminal law and punishment was on maintaining public order. If in the heat of passion or while intoxicated a person severely injured or killed his neighbor, freemen in the area would gather to pronounce a judgment and make the culprit do penance or pay compensation called *wergild* (literally, "man payment"). The purpose of the fine was to pacify the injured party and ensure that the conflict would not develop into a blood feud and anarchy. The inability of the peasantry to pay a fine led to the use of corporal punishment, such as whipping or branding, as a substitute penalty.

The development of the common law in the eleventh century brought some standardization to penal practices. However, corrections remained an amalgam of fines and brutal physical punishments. The criminal wealthy could buy their way out of punishment and into exile, but capital and corporal punishment were used to control the criminal poor, who were executed and mutilated at ever-increasing rates. Execution, banishment, mutilation, branding, and flogging were inflicted on

■ In earlier times, punishment was often quite severe. Even kings, such as Charles I of England, were not immune to death by beheading.

© The Granger Collection, New York

a whole range of offenders, from murderers and robbers to vagrants and Gypsies. Punishments became unmatched in their cruelty, featuring a gruesome variety of physical tortures, often administered as part of a public spectacle, presumably so that the horrific sanctions would act as deterrents. But the variety and imagination of the tortures inflicted on even minor criminals before their death suggest that retribution, sadism, and spectacle were more important than any presumed deterrent effect.

Public Work and Transportation to the Colonies

By the end of the sixteenth century, the rise of the city and overseas colonization provided tremendous markets for manufactured goods and spurred the need for labor. Punishment of criminals changed to meet the demands created by these social conditions. Instead of being tortured or executed, many offenders were made to do hard labor for their crimes. "Poor laws," developed at the end of the sixteenth century, required that the poor, vagrants, and vagabonds be put to work in public or private enterprises. Houses of correction were developed to make it convenient to assign petty law violators to work details. In London, a workhouse was developed at Brideswell in 1557; its use became so popular that by 1576 Parliament ordered a Brideswell-type workhouse to be built in every county in England. Many convicted offenders were pressed into sea duty as galley slaves. Galley slavery was considered so loathsome a fate that many convicts mutilated themselves rather than submit to servitude on the high seas.

The constant shortage of labor in the European colonies also prompted authorities to transport convicts overseas. In England, an Order in Council of 1617 granted a reprieve and stay of execution to people convicted of robbery and other felonies who were strong enough to be employed overseas. Similar measures were used in France and Italy to recruit galley slaves and workers.

Transporting convicts to the colonies became popular: it supplied labor, cost little, and was actually profitable for the government, because manufacturers and plantation owners paid for the convicts' services. The Old Bailey Court in London supplied at least 10,000 convicts between 1717 and 1775. Convicts would serve a period as workers and then become free again.

The American Revolution ended the transportation of felons to North America, but it continued in Australia and New Zealand. Between 1787 and 1875, when the practice was finally abandoned, over 135,000 felons were transported to Australia.

Although transportation in lieu of a death sentence might at first glance seem merciful, transported prisoners endured terrible hardships. Those who were sent to Australia suffered incredible physical abuse, including severe whippings and mutilation. Many of the British prison officials placed in charge of the Australian penal colonies could best be described as sociopaths or sadists.

The Rise of the Prison

Between the American Revolution in 1776 and the first decades of the nineteenth century, the European and U.S. populations increased rapidly. Transportation of convicts to North America was no longer an option. The increased use of machinery made industry capital intensive, not labor intensive. As a result, there was less need for unskilled laborers in England, and many workers could not find suitable employment.

The gulf between poor workers and wealthy landowners and merchants widened. The crime rate rose significantly, prompting a return to physical punishment and increased use of the death penalty. In England during the later part of the eighteenth century, 350 types of crimes were punishable by death. Although many people sentenced to death for trivial offenses were spared the gallows, the use of capital punishment was common in England during the mid-eighteenth century. Prompted by the excessive use of physical and capital punishment, legal philosophers argued that physical punishment should be replaced by periods of confinement and incapacitation. Jails and workhouses were thus used to hold petty offenders, vagabonds, the homeless, and debtors. However, these institutions were not meant for hard-core criminals. One solution to imprisoning a growing criminal population was to keep prisoners in abandoned ships anchored in rivers and harbors throughout England. In 1777, the degrading conditions under which prisoners lived in these ships inspired John Howard, the sheriff of Bedfordshire, to write *The State of the Prisons in England and Wales*, which led to Parliament's passage of legislation mandating the construction of secure and sanitary structures to house prisoners.

By 1820, long periods of incarceration in walled institutions called reformatories or **penitentiaries** began to replace physical punishment in England and the United States. These institutions were considered to represent liberal reform at a time when harsh physical punishment and incarceration in filthy holding facilities were the norm. The history of correctional institutions will be discussed further in Chapter 11. Incarceration has remained the primary mode of punishment for serious offenses in the United States since it was introduced in the early nineteenth century. Ironically in our high-tech society, some of the institutions developed soon after the Revolutionary War are still in use today. In contemporary society, prison as a method of punishment has been supplemented by a sentence to community supervision for less serious offenders, and the death penalty is reserved for those considered the most serious and dangerous.

penitentiary
A state or federal correctional institution for the incarceration of felony offenders for terms of one year or more.

LO1 Outline the historical development of punishment

The Goals of Modern Sentencing

When we hear about a notorious criminal receiving a long prison sentence or the death penalty for a particularly heinous crime, each of us has a distinct reaction. Some of us are gratified that a truly evil person "got just what he deserved"; many people feel safer because a dangerous person is now "where he can't harm any other innocent victims"; others hope the punishment serves as a warning to potential criminals that "everyone gets caught in the end"; some may actually feel sorry for the defendant—"he got a raw deal, he needs help, not punishment"; and still others hope that "when he gets out, he'll have learned his lesson." And when an offender is forced to pay a large fine, we say, "What goes around comes around."

Each of these sentiments may be at work when criminal sentences are formulated. After all, sentences are devised and implemented by judges, many of whom are elected officials and share the general public's sentiments and fears. The objectives of criminal sentencing today can usually be grouped into five distinct areas: deterrence (both general and specific), incapacitation, retribution/just desert, rehabilitation, and equity/restitution.

LO2 List the major goals of contemporary sentencing

Deterrence

Deterrence is one of the most popular goals of sentencing. There are two types of deterrence: general and specific. According to the concept of **general deterrence**, people will be too afraid to break the law if they believe that they will be caught and punished severely. The more certain and severe the punishment, the greater the deterrent effect. However, punishment cannot be so harsh that it seems disproportionate and unfair. If it were, people would believe they had nothing to lose, and their crimes might escalate in frequency and severity. Thus, if the crime of rape were punished by death, rapists might be encouraged to kill their victims to dispose of the one person who could identify them at trial. Because they would already be facing the death penalty for rape, they would have nothing more to lose by committing murder as well.

Some justice experts believe that the recent decline in the crime rate is a result of increasing criminal penalties. Once arrested, people have a greater chance of being convicted today than they did in the past. This phenomenon is referred to as "expected punishment," defined as the number of days in prison a typical criminal can expect to serve per crime.[4] Despite rising recently, expected punishment

general deterrence
A crime control policy that depends on the fear of criminal penalties. General deterrence measures, such as long prison sentences for violent crimes, are aimed at convincing the *potential law violator* that the pains associated with paying for the crime outweigh the benefits.

specific deterrence
A crime control policy suggesting that punishment should be severe enough to convince *convicted offenders* never to repeat their criminal activity.

rates are actually still quite low because (a) crime clearance rates remain well under 50 percent, (b) many cases are dropped at the pretrial and trial stages (*nolle prosequi*), and (c) about one-third of convicted felons are given probationary rather than prison sentences.

Take the crime of burglary. About 2 million burglaries are reported to the police each year, about 200,000 burglars are arrested, 100,000 are convicted, and about 40,000 are sent to prison. Therefore, for every 50 reported burglaries, only one burglar is incarcerated. (Keep in mind that some burglars commit many crimes per year, so we are not talking about 2 million individual burglars but 2 million burglaries!) Such inefficiency limits the deterrent effect of punishment.

Because the justice system is still inefficient, the general deterrent effect of punishment is less than desired. The percentage of convicted offenders who now receive a prison sentence has actually declined during the past decade, and the estimated average prison sentence received by violent felony offenders in state courts decreased from nearly 10 years in 1994 to about 7.5 years today. If this trend continues, the deterrent effect of punishments may decline, and crime rates may increase as a result. Note, however, that the actual time served per sentence has increased somewhat, meaning that inmates are spending more of their sentence behind bars before they are released. This may help neutralize the effect of lighter sentences.[5]

In contrast to general deterrence, the goal of **specific deterrence** is to convince offenders that the pains of punishment are greater than the benefits of crime; hence they will not repeat their criminal offending. The experience of suffering punishment should inhibit future law violations.

Claims for a specific deterrent effect are weakened by data showing that most inmates (more than 80%) who are released from prison have had prior convictions, and the great majority (68%) will reoffend soon after their release. A prison stay seems to have little effect on reoffending.[6] Despite these sketchy results, the goal of specific deterrence remains a fundamental part of sentencing. Some judges and policymakers maintain that a "taste of the bars" should reduce the desire for repeat offending.[7]

Incapacitation

incapacitation
The policy of keeping dangerous criminals in confinement to eliminate the risk of their repeating their offense in society.

Because criminals will not be able to repeat their criminal acts while they are under state control, **incapacitation** of criminals is another goal of sentencing. For some offenders, this means a period in a high-security state prison where behavior is closely monitored. Keeping dangerous criminals behind bars prevents them, during this period of incapacitation, from repeating their illegal activities.

Does incapacitating criminals help reduce the crime rate? The evidence is mixed. Between 1990 and 2009, the prison population more than doubled (from 700,000 to more than 1.4 million) and the crime rate dropped dramatically, indicating a significant incarceration effect. However, there have been periods, such as between 1980 and 1990, when the prison population increased and so did the crime rate. This indicates that incarceration trends may influence crime rates but that reductions in crime may also be related to other factors, such as population makeup, police effectiveness, declining drug use, and the economy.[8]

It is also possible that incarceration has a short-term effect that diminishes as more and more people are put in prison and the incarceration benefit of incarcerating each new inmate decreases. Think of it this way: If the country had only a single prison cell and only one person could be locked up at a time, chances are that person would be the nation's most dangerous, violent chronic offender. The crime reduction benefit of locking up just that single person would be significant. If we could incarcerate only two, the second inmate would be slightly less dangerous. Each time a person is added to the prison population, the crime reduction benefit is somewhat less than that achieved by imprisoning the inmate who came before. We now have 1.4 million people behind bars. The millionth-plus inmate is far less dangerous than the first, and the incarceration benefits of locking him up are significantly less, yet the *cost* of incarcerating each new inmate remains the same as that of locking up the first![9] Thus, by definition, using incapacitation to reduce crime rates always yields diminishing returns.[10]

Retribution/Just Desert

According to the retributive goal of sentencing, the essential purpose of the criminal process is to punish offenders—fairly and justly—in a manner that is proportionate to the gravity of their crimes.[11] Offenders are punished simply and solely because they *deserve* to be disciplined for what they have done: "the punishment should fit the crime."[12] It would be wrong to punish people to set an example for others or to deter would-be criminals, as the general deterrence goal demands. Punishment should be no more or less than the offender's actions deserve; it must be based on how **blameworthy** the person is. This is referred to as the concept of **just desert**.[13]

According to this view, punishments must be equally and fairly distributed to all people who commit similar illegal acts. However, determining just punishments can be difficult, because there is generally little consensus about the treatment of criminals, the seriousness of crimes, and the proper response to criminal acts. Consequently, there has been an ongoing effort to calculate fair and just sentences and to apply them in an equitable way.

Rehabilitation

Some sentences are based on the need to treat and/or rehabilitate criminal offenders. Because society has failed them, many offenders have been forced to grow up in disorganized neighborhoods, have been the target of biased police officers, and are disadvantaged at home, at school, and in the job market. To compensate for these deprivations, the justice system is obligated to help these unfortunate people and not simply punish them for their misdeeds.[14] Advocates of **rehabilitation** believe that if the proper treatment is applied, an offender will present no further threat to society.[15] It is not surprising, then, that the general public supports the treatment goal of sentencing and prefers it to policies based on punishment and incarceration.[16]

Equity/Restitution

Because criminals benefit from their misdeeds, it seems both fair and just to demand that they reimburse society for the losses their crimes have caused. In the early common law, *wergild* and fines represented the concept of creating an equitable solution to crime by requiring the convicted offender to make restitution to both the victim and the state. Today, judges continue to require that offenders compensate victims for their losses.

The **equity** goal of punishment means that convicted criminals should pay back their victims for their loss, the justice system for the costs of processing their case, and society for any disruption they may have caused. In a so-called victimless crime such as drug trafficking, the social costs might include the expense of drug enforcement efforts, drug treatment centers, and care for infants born to drug-addicted mothers. The costs of violent crimes might include the services of emergency room doctors, lost workdays and productivity, and treatment for long-term psychological problems. To help defray these costs, convicted offenders might be required to pay a fine, forfeit the property they acquired through illegal gain, do community service work, make financial restitution to their victim, and reimburse the state for the costs of the criminal process. And because the criminals' actions helped expand their personal gains, rights, and privileges at society's expense, justice demands that they lose rights and privileges to restore the social balance.

LO3 Distinguish among general and specific deterrence, incapacitation, and retribution

blameworthy
Culpable or guilty of participating in a particular criminal offense.

just desert
The philosophy of justice asserting that those who violate the rights of others deserve to be punished. The severity of punishment should be commensurate with the seriousness of the crime.

RealityCheck

MYTH OR REALITY? Rehabilitating criminals is the primary goal of contemporary sentencing.

MYTH. *Rehabilitation remains one of many sentencing goals.*
Sentencing has multiple goals, including deterrence, incapacitation, and restitution. Which do you think is the primary goal of sentencing and why?

rehabilitation
The strategy of applying proper treatment so an offender will present no further threat to society.

equity
The action or practice of awarding each person what is due him or her; sanctions based on equity seek to compensate individual victims and society in general for their losses due to crime.

LO4 Compare rehabilitation with just deserts

Many offenders are ordered to pay restitution, often in conjunction with other penalties. Larry McClure, standing here next to one of his winning cars in the Morgan-McClure Motorsports shop in Abingdon, Virginia, was sentenced to 18 months in prison and ordered to pay more than $125,000 in restitution, fines, and investigative costs for tax evasion. The government claimed he accepted bags of cash in order to avoid paying taxes on his profits.

AP Images/Bristol Herald Courier, Andre Teague

Sentencing Models

When a convicted offender is sentenced to prison, the statutes of the jurisdiction in which the crime was committed determine what penalties the court may impose. Over the years, a variety of sentencing structures have been used in the United States. They include indeterminate sentences, determinate sentences, and mandatory sentences.

Indeterminate Sentences

indeterminate sentence
A term of incarceration with a stated minimum and maximum length, such as a sentence to prison for a period of from 3 to 10 years. The prisoner would be eligible for parole after the minimum sentence has been served. Based on the belief that sentences should fit the criminal, indeterminate sentences allow individualized sentences and provide for sentencing flexibility. Judges can set a high minimum to override the purpose of the indeterminate sentence.

In the 1870s, prison reformers Enoch Wines and Zebulon Brockway and others called for creation of **indeterminate sentences** tailored to fit individual needs. Offenders, the argument went, should be placed in confinement only until they are rehabilitated and then released on parole. Criminals were believed to be "sick" rather than bad; they could be successfully treated in prison. Rather than holding that "the punishment should fit the crime," reformers believed that "the treatment should fit the offender."

The indeterminate sentence is still the most widely used type of sentence in the United States. Convicted offenders are typically given a "light" minimum sentence that must be served and a lengthy maximum sentence that is the outer boundary of the time that can be served. For example, the legislature might set a sentence of a minimum of 2 years and a maximum of 20 years for burglary; the convicted offender must be sentenced to no less than 2 years but no more than 20 years in prison. Under this scheme, the actual length of time served by the offender is controlled by both the judge and the correctional agency. A judge could sentence a burglar to 5–15; the inmate then may be paroled from confinement soon after serving the minimum sentence *if* the correctional authorities believe that she is ready to live in the community. If the inmate accumulates good time, she could be released in as little as 30 months; a troublesome inmate, however, would be forced to do all 15 years.

The basic purpose of the indeterminate sentence is to individualize each sentence in the interests of rehabilitating the offender. This type of sentencing allows for flexibility not only in the type of sentence to be imposed but also in the length of time to be served.

Most jurisdictions that use indeterminate sentences employ statutes that specify minimum and maximum terms but allow judicial discretion to fix the actual sentence within those limits. The typical minimum sentence is at least one year; a few state jurisdictions require at least a two-year minimum sentence for felons.[17]

Determinate Sentences

Dissatisfaction with the disparities and uncertainty of indeterminate sentencing has prompted some states and the federal government to abandon it in favor of determinate sentencing models or structured sentencing models, aimed at curbing judicial discretion.

Determinate sentences offer a fixed term of years, the maximum set in law by the legislature, to be served by the offender sentenced to prison for a particular crime. If the law provides for a sentence of up to 20 years for robbery, the judge might sentence a repeat offender to a 15-year term; another, less-experienced felon might receive a more lenient sentence of 5 years.

In order to regulate the length of determinate sentences and curb judicial discretion, most jurisdictions that employ them have developed methods to structure and control the sentencing process and make it more rational. To accomplish this task, **sentencing guidelines** have been implemented by determinate-sentencing states and the federal government. Guidelines give judges a recommended sentence based on the seriousness of a crime and the background of an offender: The more serious the crime and the more extensive the offender's criminal background, the longer the prison term recommended by the guidelines. For example, guidelines might recommend a sentence of five years for robbery if the offender had no prior offense record and did not use excessive force or violence. For a second offense, the recommended sentence would increase to seven years; those who used force and had a prior record would have three years added to their sentence, and so on. Guidelines are designed to reduce racial and gender disparity by eliminating judicial discretion.[18]

The Future of Guidelines Several states use some form of structured sentencing. Until recently some states used voluntary/advisory sentencing guidelines (sometimes called descriptive guidelines), which merely suggest rather than mandate sentences, whereas others used presumptive sentencing guidelines (sometimes called prescriptive guidelines), which required judges to use the guidelines to shape their sentencing decisions.[19]

Two Supreme Court cases have placed a moratorium on the use of presumptive guidelines and put their future in doubt. First, in *Blakely v. Washington*, the Court found that Washington State's sentencing guidelines were a violation of a defendant's Sixth Amendment rights because they allowed a judge to consider aggravating factors that would enhance the sentence.[20] The Court ruled that this amounts to a finding of fact without the benefit of a jury trial or personal admission. In *Blakely*, the sentencing judge, acting alone, had decided that the offense involved "deliberate cruelty" and enhanced Blakely's sentence. Proving a state of mind such as "deliberate cruelty" must be determined by a jury "beyond a reasonable doubt" and not by a judge applying guidelines. Then, in *United States v. Booker*, the Court ruled that the federal guidelines were unconstitutional, allowing that judges should consider the guideline ranges but must also be permitted to alter sentences in consideration of other factors; sentences could then be subject to appellate review if they were unreasonable.[21] Since these cases were decided, guidelines have been used in an advisory capacity alone.

Even before *Blakely* and *Booker* limited their use, presumptive guidelines had been criticized as being rigid, harsh, overly complex, and disliked by the judiciary.[22] They substantially increased correctional populations, especially when they were used in a haphazard fashion and were not tied to the availability of correctional resources.[23]

These cases did not in essence outlaw guidelines but, rather, ruled that changes were needed in the way they are administered. State and federal courts

determinate sentence
A fixed term of incarceration, such as three years' imprisonment. Many people consider determinate sentences too restrictive for rehabilitative purposes; the advantage is that offenders know how much time they have to serve—that is, when they will be released.

sentencing guidelines
A set of standards that define parameters for trial judges to follow in their sentencing decisions.

are now addressing these issues and creating mechanisms for proper administration of the guidelines, especially if the case involves sentencing enhancement. Since these cases were decided, the future of guidelines seems hazy. However, a recent (2006) report by the Federal Sentencing Commission found that even though federal courts interpreted the *Booker* decision in different ways, the majority of cases continue to be sentenced within the range of existing sentencing guidelines. So even though the guidelines are now advisory rather than mandatory, they still have a great deal of impact on sentencing decisions.[24] Sentencing guidelines are still being used in this new advisory fashion in Minnesota and other states.

Mandatory Sentences

mandatory sentence
A statutory requirement that a certain penalty shall be set and carried out in all cases upon conviction for a specified offense or series of offenses.

Another effort to limit judicial discretion and at the same time get tough on crime has been development of the **mandatory sentence**. Some states have passed legislation prohibiting people convicted of certain offenses, such as violent crimes or drug trafficking, from being placed on probation; they must serve at least some time in prison. Other statutes are aimed at chronic recidivists. Mandatory-sentencing legislation may impose minimum and maximum terms, but usually it requires a fixed prison sentence.

Mandatory sentencing generally limits the judge's discretionary power to impose any disposition but that authorized by the legislature. On the one hand, it limits individualized sentencing and restricts sentencing disparity. On the other hand, the discretion taken from judges does not disappear. Studies show that mandatory-sentencing laws give prosecutors considerable power, because they can decide whether or not a particular defendant should be charged under a mandatory-sentencing statute.[25]

The majority of states have already replaced discretionary sentencing with fixed-term mandatory sentences for such crimes as the sale of hard drugs, kidnapping, gun possession, and arson. The results have been mixed. Mandatory sentences have helped increase the size of the correctional population to record levels. Because of mandatory sentences, many offenders who in the past might have received probation are being incarcerated. Mandatory sentences have also failed to eliminate racial disparity from the sentencing process.[26]

Three-Strikes Laws Three-strikes (and-you're-out) laws are perhaps the most widely known form of determinate sentencing. They provide lengthy prison terms, usually 25 years to life, for any person convicted of three felony offenses. Approximately half the states have three-strikes laws, but nearly all of them require that the third felony be a serious one. In California, however, any third felony can result in life in prison.

Three-strikes laws have undeniable political appeal to legislators being pressured by their constituents to "do something about crime." Yet even if they may possibly be effective against crime, any effort to deter criminal behavior through tough laws is not without costs. Criminologist Marc Mauer, a leading opponent of the three-strikes law, finds that the approach may satisfy the public's hunger for retribution but that it makes little practical sense.[27] First, many "three-time losers" are on the brink of aging out of crime; locking them up for life should have little effect on the crime rate. In addition, current sentences for chronic violent offenders are already severe, and yet their punishment seems to have had little efficacy in reducing national violence rates. A three-strikes policy also suffers because criminals typically underestimate their risk of apprehension, while overestimating the rewards of crime.

Three-strikes laws, particularly California's, have prompted a number of studies seeking to determine whether they deter crime. Although a handful of studies report a deterrent effect, the vast majority show that three-strikes laws have little or no effect on crime.[28] The authors of two studies even found that there is more homicide in

Inmate Anthony Turner, 46, who is serving 25 years to life for a three-strikes offense, sits in his cell at the California Institution for Men state prison in Chino, California, June 3, 2011. The California Supreme Court ordered the state to release more than 30,000 inmates over the next two years or take other steps to ease overcrowding in its prisons to prevent "needless suffering and death." Whether Turner's sentence will be affected by the court's decision is unclear. In all likelihood it will not, given that he is a repeat offender. Should three-time felons be sentenced to prison for life?

© Lucy Nicholson/Reuters/Landov

three-strikes states, which suggests that those who face life in prison have a powerful incentive not to go down without a fight.[29]

Three-strikes laws have also been challenged on constitutional grounds. For example, on March 6, 2003, the Supreme Court upheld the three-strikes sentence of Leandro Andrade, a man sentenced to prison in California for 50 years for stealing $153 worth of videotapes.[30] It also upheld the conviction of Gary Ewing, who appealed a prior 25-year sentence for stealing a set of golf clubs.[31] In both cases the Court ruled that the challenged sentences were not so grossly disproportionate as to violate the Eighth Amendment's prohibition against cruel and unusual punishment.

Truth in Sentencing

As you may recall, although criminal sentences are getting shorter, people are spending more of their sentence behind bars. One reason is the "get tough" measure known as *truth in sentencing*, which is designed to fight a rising crime rate. These laws require offenders to serve a substantial portion of their prison sentence behind bars.[32] Parole eligibility and good-time credits are restricted or eliminated. The movement was encouraged by the Violent Offender Incarceration and Truth-in-Sentencing Incentive Grants Program, part of the federal government's 1994 crime act, which offered funds to help offset the state costs involved with creating longer sentences. To qualify for federal funds, states must require persons convicted of a violent felony crime to serve not less than 85 percent of their prison sentence. The provision is already having an effect: violent offenders released from prison in 1996 served slightly more than half of their prison sentence, or 45 months. Under truth-in-sentencing laws, violent inmates entering prison today will serve an average of 88 months behind bars. Today, more than half the states and the District of Columbia have met the federal Truth-in-Sentencing Incentive Grants Program eligibility criteria, and another 13 have adopted some form of truth-in-sentencing program.

RealityCheck

MYTH OR REALITY? Theft can result in life in prison.

REALITY. *If you have two felony convictions in the state of California, theft can result in life in prison, provided it is grand theft.*

Grand theft is theft of objects exceeding a certain value, such as $400. Should a third-time felon get life in prison for theft of something valued at less than $1,000? Why?

L05 Identify various sentencing models

Imposing the Sentence

In most felony cases, except where the law provides for mandatory prison terms, sentencing is usually based on a variety of information available to the judge. Some jurisdictions allow victims to make impact statements that are considered at sentencing hearings. Most judges also consider a pre-sentence investigation report by the probation department as they make a sentencing decision. This report is a social and personal history, as well as an evaluation of the defendant's chances for rehabilitation within the community. Judges may also issue credit for time already served, such as during pretrial detention.

Concurrent vs. Consecutive Sentences

In some instances, when an accused is convicted of two or more charges, the judge must decide whether to impose consecutive or **concurrent sentences**. If the sentences are concurrent, they begin the same day and are completed when the longest term has been served. For example, say a defendant is convicted of burglarizing an apartment and assaulting its occupant. He is sentenced to 3 years on a charge of assault and 10 years for burglary, with the sentences to be served concurrently. After 10 years in prison, the sentences would be completed.

In contrast, receiving a **consecutive sentence** means that upon completion of the sentence for one crime, the offender begins serving time for the second of multiple crimes. If the defendant in the previous example had been sentenced consecutively, he would serve 3 years on the assault charge and then 10 years for the burglary. Therefore, the total term on the two charges would be 13 years. Concurrent sentences are the norm; consecutive sentences are requested for the most serious criminals and for those who are unwilling to cooperate with authorities. Figure 9.1 shows the difference between a consecutive and a concurrent sentence.

The Effect of Good Time

When judges impose an incarceration sentence, they know and take into account the fact that the amount of time spent in prison is reduced by the implementation of "time off for good behavior." This concept was first used in 1817 in New York, and it was quickly adopted in most other jurisdictions. Good time is still in use today; inmates can accrue standard good time at a rate ranging from 10 to 15 days per month. In addition, some correctional authorities grant earned sentence reductions to inmates who participate in treatment programs, such as educational and vocational training, or who volunteer for experimental medical testing programs. In some jurisdictions more than half of a determinate sentence can be erased by accumulating both standard and earned good time.

Good-time laws enable inmates to calculate their release date at the time they enter prison by subtracting the expected good time from their sentence. However,

Example: In state X
1. Rape is punishable by 10 years in prison
2. Possession of a handgun by 3 years
3. Possession of heroin by 4 years

Consecutive sentence	**Concurrent sentence**
Rape + possession of a handgun + possession of heroin	Rape + possession of a handgun + possession of heroin
10 + 3 + 4 = 17 years	10 years
(each sentence must be served individually)	(all sentences served simultaneously)

Figure 9.1 Consecutive vs. Concurrent Sentences

good time can be lost if inmates break prison rules, get into fights, or disobey correctional officers. In some jurisdictions, former inmates can be returned to prison to serve the balance of their unexpired sentence when their good time is revoked for failing to conform to conditions set down for their release (for example, by not reporting to a postrelease supervisor or by abusing drugs).

How People Are Sentenced

The federal government conducts surveys on sentencing practices in state and federal courts.[33] The most recent survey found that more than 1 million adults are convicted of felonies in a single year. What happens after convictions? About 70 percent of all felons convicted in state courts were sentenced to a period of confinement—40 percent to state prisons and 30 percent to local jails.[34] The remaining 30 percent were sentenced to straight probation with no jail or prison time to serve. Felons sentenced to a state prison had an average sentence of four and a half years but were likely to serve only half of that sentence before release. Besides being sentenced to incarceration or probation, about one-third of all sentenced offenders are typically expected to pay a fine, pay victim restitution, receive treatment, perform community service, or comply with some other additional penalty. As Table 9.1 shows, violent offenders who are given a prison sentence average about eight years, whereas property offenders are typically sentenced to about four years. If they receive a jail sentence, their period of confinement is considerably less.

The number of convicted offenders being sent to prison today is actually lower than a decade ago, illustrating the increasing popularity of cost-effective community

Many prison sentences carry with them a provision for the possibility of good time, which takes time off the sentence for good behavior. Here Nick Hogan, son of the famous wrestler Hulk Hogan, hugs his sister, Brooke Hogan, as he leaves the Pinellas County Jail after serving five months behind bars for being involved in the car crash that seriously injured Marine John Graziano. He had been sentenced to serve eight months but was released early for good behavior.

© Tim Boyles/Getty Images

TABLE 9.1 Lengths of Felony Sentences Imposed by State Courts

Most serious conviction offense	Mean Sentence Length in State Courts for Felons Sentenced to Incarceration or Probation			
	Total Prison (months)	Jail (months)		Straight probation (months)
All offenses	38	59	6	38
Violent offenses	71	96	7	44
Property offenses	30	47	6	38
Drug offenses	31	50	5	37
Weapon offenses	32	48	6	37
Other offenses	24	41	5	36

Note: Means exclude life sentences and death sentences.

Source: Sean Rosenmerkel and Matthew Durose, *Felony Sentences in State Courts, 2006* (Washington, DC: Bureau of Justice Statistics, 2009), http://bjs.ojp.usdoj.gov/content/pub/pdf/fssc06st.pdf (accessed June 26, 2011).

LO6 Explain how sentences are imposed

sentencing. However, because of tough sentencing laws requiring people to spend more time behind bars, the average time served per offense has not decreased substantially.

What Factors Affect Sentencing?

What factors influence judges when they decide on criminal sentences? As already mentioned, crime seriousness and the offender's prior record are certainly considered. State sentencing codes usually include various factors that can legitimately influence the length of prison sentences, including the following:

- The severity of the offense
- The offender's prior criminal record
- Whether the offender used violence
- Whether the offender used weapons
- Whether the crime was committed for money

Research does in fact show a strong correlation between these legal variables and the type and length of sentence received. Judges sentence more severely in cases involving the most serious criminal charges, such as terrorism, while tempering the severity of sentencing in less egregious offenses.[35] As Figure 9.2 shows, people with prior felony convictions are much more likely to receive prison time than those convicted of misdemeanors and those who have no prior convictions.

Besides these legally appropriate factors, sentencing experts suspect that judges may also be influenced by the defendant's social class, gender, age, and race—and even by victim characteristics. Consideration of such variables would be a direct violation of constitutional due process and equal protection, as well as of federal statutes, such as the Civil Rights Act. Limiting judicial bias is one reason why states have adopted determinate and mandatory sentencing statutes.

Social Class Evidence supports an association between social class and sentencing outcomes: members of the lower class may expect to get longer prison sentences than more affluent defendants. Not all research efforts have found a consistent relationship between social class and

RealityCheck

MYTH OR REALITY? When it comes to sentencing, there is one standard rule: If you commit a serious crime, you serve a lot of time.

MYTH. *It would be ideal if justice were blind, but judges are human and, whether consciously or unconsciously, base their decisions in part on other factors, many of which are not related to the crime in question. Scores of studies bear this out.*

Factors such as class, race, gender, and age have been shown to influence sentencing. What are the consequences of this? Can anything be done to limit the influence of such extralegal factors on sentencing?

Percent of defendants convicted of a violent felony

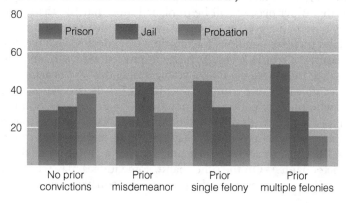

Percent of defendants convicted of a nonviolent felony

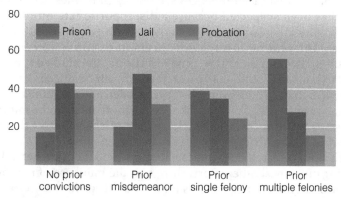

Figure 9.2 Sentence by Prior Record

Source: Thomas H. Cohen and Tracey Kyckelhahn, *Felony Defendants in Large Urban Counties, 2006* (Washington, DC: Bureau of Justice Statistics, 2010), p. 14, http://bjs.ojp.usdoj.gov/content/pub/pdf/fdluc06.pdf (accessed June 26, 2011).

sentence length. The relationship may be more robust for some crime patterns than for others. Nonetheless, the consensus is that affluent defendants are more likely than the indigent to receive lenient sentences.[36]

Gender Does a defendant's gender influence how he or she is sentenced? Some theorists believe that women benefit from sentence disparity because the criminal justice system is dominated by men who have a paternalistic or protective attitude toward women; this is referred to as the **chivalry hypothesis**. In contrast, others argue that female criminals can be the victim of bias because their law breaking violates what men view as "proper" female behavior.[37]

Which position is true? Most research indicates that women receive more favorable outcomes the further they go in the criminal justice system: they are more likely to receive preferential treatment from a judge at sentencing than they are from the police officer making the arrest or the prosecutor seeking the indictment.[38] This favoritism crosses both racial and ethnic lines, benefiting African American, white, and Hispanic women.[39] Gender bias may be present because judges perceive women as better risks than men. Women have been granted more lenient pretrial release conditions and lower bail amounts than men; women are also more likely to spend less time in pretrial detention.[40] Ironically, mandatory and structured sentences, designed originally to limit bias and discretion, have resulted in harsher sentences for women. Because these methods are "gender neutral," they reverse any advantage women may have had in sentencing decisions. Some women who were peripherally involved in drug trafficking through association with boyfriends and husbands have received very long sentences.[41]

chivalry hypothesis
The view that the low rates of female crime and delinquency are a reflection of the leniency with which police and judges treat female offenders.

Age Another extralegal factor that may play a role in sentencing is age. It should be expected that older people will be punished more harshly than younger ones, because they have had a greater opportunity to accumulate a criminal record and most state laws increase penalties for multiple offenders. Of course, this creates a dilemma: because of crimes he might have committed years ago, an older offender may be punished more severely than a younger offender who is actually more dangerous or is committing more crimes in the present.[42] This association of more severe punishment with older offenders does not always hold, however. Some judges may instead be more lenient with older defendants and more punitive toward younger ones.[43] Although sentencing leniency may be a result of judges' perception that the elderly pose little risk to society, such practices are a violation of the civil rights of younger defendants.[44] On the other hand, some judges may wish to protect the youngest defendants, sparing them the pains of a prison experience.[45]

Race No issue concerning personal factors in sentencing is more important than the suspicion that race influences sentencing outcomes. Racial disparity in sentencing has been suspected because a disproportionate number of African American inmates are in state prisons and on death row. Minorities—especially those who are indigent or unemployed—seem to receive longer sentences than Caucasians.[46] Shawn Bushway and Anne Morrison Piehl studied sentencing outcomes in Maryland and found that, on average, African Americans have 20 percent longer sentences than whites, even when age, gender, and recommended sentence length are held constant.[47] Young black men are more likely to be imprisoned for drug offenses, a practice (says sentencing expert Michael Tonry) that places the entire cohort of young African American males in jeopardy.[48]

Although some research does indicate that a defendant's race has a direct effect on sentencing outcomes, other efforts show that the influence of race on sentencing is less clear-cut than anticipated. As John Wooldredge found, in some contexts minority group members actually get more lenient sentences than whites.[49] It is possible, the counterargument goes, that the disproportionate number of minority group members in prison is not a function of racial bias by judges but, rather, reflects actual racial and ethnic differences in the crime rate: minority group members go to prison more often simply because they commit more crime.

Race may also affect sentencing in other ways. Research indicates that it is the victim's race, rather than the offender's, that structures sentencing outcomes.[50] Minority defendants are sanctioned more severely if their victim is white than if their target is a fellow minority group member; minority defendants who kill whites are more likely to get the death penalty than are those who kill other minorities.[51]

In sum, although the true association between race and sentencing is complex, there is little question that the defendant's race helps shape the contours of justice. Whatever the cause, the effects can be devastating. As Bruce Western warns, whole communities are being destabilized by the marginalizing and incarcerating of so many African American men. And doing prison time can turn minor offenders into hardened criminals, which removes any chance of rehabilitation. Indeed, the prison boom "may be a self-defeating strategy for crime control."[52]

Victim Characteristics Victim characteristics may also influence sentencing. Victims may be asked or allowed to make a **victim impact statement** before the sentencing judge, which gives them the opportunity to tell of their experiences and describe their ordeal. In a murder case, the surviving family can recount the effect the crime has had on their lives and well-being.[53] The effect of victim and witness statements on sentencing has been the subject of some debate. Some research suggests that victim statements result in a higher rate of incarceration, but other efforts find that the effects of victim and witness statements are insignificant.[54]

A victim's personal characteristics may influence sentencing. Sentences may be reduced when victims have "negative" personal characteristics or qualities. For example, people convicted of raping prostitutes or substance abusers receive much shorter sentences than those who assault women without these negative characteristics.[55]

victim impact statement
A postconviction statement by the victim of crime that may be used to guide sentencing decisions.

L07 Summarize factors associated with sentencing decisions

Historically, victims had little to no involvement in the criminal process. Today, they often make victim impact statements, which gives the judge an opportunity to hear their side of the story. Here Sandra Burke, oldest daughter of murder victim Lloyd Ford, reads a victim impact statement to Fourth District Court judge Darla Williamson on March 20, 2009, during the sentence hearing for Judy Gough, far right, in Boise, Idaho. Gough, who admitted to killing her husband in 1980 with a deer rifle and burying his body in the backyard of her Boise home, was sentenced to 10 years in prison.

AP Photo/The Idaho Statesman, Darin Oswald

Capital Punishment

The most severe sentence used in the United States is capital punishment, or execution. More than 14,500 confirmed executions have been carried out in America under civil authority, starting with the execution of Captain George Kendall in 1608. Most of these executions have been for murder and rape. However, federal, state, and military laws have conferred the death penalty for other crimes, including robbery, kidnapping, treason (offenses against the federal government), espionage, and desertion from military service.

In recent years, the Supreme Court has limited the death penalty to first-degree murder and only then when aggravating circumstances, such as murder for profit or murder using extreme cruelty, are present.[56] The federal government still has provisions for imposing the death penalty for espionage by a member of the armed forces, treason, and killing during a criminal conspiracy, such as drug trafficking. Some states have laws permitting capital punishment for crimes besides first-degree murder, but those laws continue to come under scrutiny. Figure 9.3 provides a perspective on executions from 1930 to the present. Figure 9.4 presents a map of the death-penalty states and non-death-penalty states.

No issue in the criminal justice system is more controversial or emotional than implementation of the death penalty. Opponents and proponents have formulated a number of powerful arguments in support of their positions; these arguments are reviewed in the following sections.

Arguments for the Death Penalty

The death penalty has long been one of the most controversial aspects of the justice system, and it will probably continue to be a source of significant debate.[57] Let's first consider the views supporting availability of the death penalty.

Deterrence Proponents of capital punishment argue that executions serve as a strong deterrent for serious crimes. From a specific deterrent standpoint, an offender who is dead can no longer commit crime! From a general deterrent standpoint, proponents maintain that an execution can produce a substantial decline in the murder rate.[58] They argue, for example, that homicide rates increased dramatically in the 1960s and 1970s, when executions were halted by the courts and death penalty laws

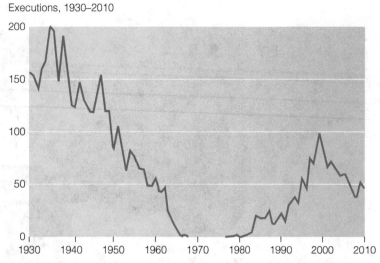

Executions, 1930–2010

Figure 9.3 Executions, 1930–Present

- In 2009, 52 inmates were executed, 15 more than 2008.
- Of the 52 executions that took place in 2009, 24 were in Texas, 6 were in Alabama, 5 were in Ohio, 3 each were in Virginia, Georgia, and Oklahoma, 2 each were in Florida, South Carolina, and Tennessee, and 1 each were in Indiana and Missouri.
- Of the 52 persons executed in 2009, 23 were white, 22 were black, and 7 were Hispanic.
- All 52 inmates executed in 2009 were male.
- Lethal injection was used in 51 executions in 2009; 1 execution was by electrocution.

Sources: Death Penalty Information Center, http://www.deathpenaltyinfo.org/executions (accessed June 27, 2011); Bureau of Justice Statistics, *Capital Punishment*, http://bjs.ojp.usdoj.gov/index.cfm?ty=tp&tid=18#key_facts (accessed June 27, 2011).

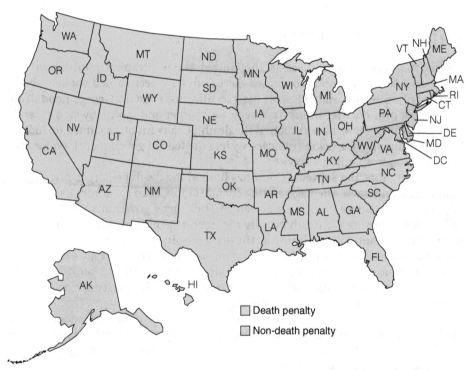

Figure 9.4 Death-Penalty and Non-Death-Penalty States with Executions Since 1976

Source: Death Penalty Information Center, www.deathpenaltyinfo.org/states-and-without-death-penalty (accessed June 27, 2011).

were subsequently abolished. It is not a coincidence, they argue, that murder rates have dropped since the death penalty was reinstated; murder rates would actually be much higher if capital punishment were not being used.[59] The death penalty scares would-be criminals, and not surprisingly, homicide rates drop after a well-publicized execution.[60]

Morally Correct Death penalty supporters often argue that such a harsh punishment is morally correct. After all, it is mentioned in the Bible and other religious works. And although the U.S. Constitution forbids "cruel and unusual punishments," it does not prohibit the death penalty, as it was widely used at the time the Constitution was drafted. The "original intent" of the founding fathers was to allow the states to use the death penalty. Supporters also argue that the death penalty is morally correct because it provides the greatest justice for the victim and helps alleviate the psychic pain of the victim's family and friends. In sum, the death penalty makes a moral statement: there is behavior that is so unacceptable to a community of human beings that one who engages in such behavior forfeits his right to live.[61]

Proportional to the Crime Putting dangerous criminals to death also conforms to the requirement that the punishment must be proportional to the seriousness of the crime. We use a system of escalating punishments, so it follows that the most serious punishment should be used to sanction the most serious crime. Before the brutality of the death penalty is considered, the cruelty with which the victim was treated should not be forgotten.

RealityCheck

MYTH OR REALITY? The United States is one of the few countries that still retains the death penalty.

REALITY. *According to Amnesty International, 139 countries have abolished the death penalty in law or practice, or for certain crimes, leaving 58 "retentionist countries."* Few of the retentionist countries are what we would call industrialized, advanced, or close allies of the United States. Why does the United States retain the death penalty when the majority of the industrialized countries in the world have abolished it?

Reflects Public Opinion Supporters also argue that death penalty is justified because it represents the will of the people. A majority of the general public believe that criminals who kill innocent victims should forfeit their own lives. Public opinion polls show that Americans favor the use of the death penalty by a wide majority.[62] Public approval rests on the belief that the death penalty is an important instrument of social control, can deter crime, and is less costly than maintaining a murderer in prison for life.[63] Research by Alexis Durham and his associates found that almost everyone (95%) would give criminals the death penalty under some circumstances, and the most heinous crimes are those for which the public is most likely to approve capital punishment.[64]

Unlikely Chance of Error The many legal controls and appeals currently in use make it almost impossible for an innocent person to be executed or for the death penalty to be used in a racist or capricious manner. Although some unfortunate mistakes may have been made in the past, the current system makes it virtually impossible to execute an innocent person. Federal courts closely scrutinize all death penalty cases and rule for the defendant in an estimated 60 to 70 percent of the appeals. Such judicial care should ensure that only those who are both unquestionably guilty and deserving of death are executed.

Arguments Against the Death Penalty

Arguments for the death penalty are countered as follows by those who support its abolition.

Possibility of Error The recent use of scientific evidence based on DNA has also resulted in numerous exonerations of wrongfully convicted death row inmates. One study found that an average of 42 exonerations of death row inmates occurred each year between 1989 and 2003.[65] Such research reveals that even today, there is grave risk of an innocent person's being executed.[66]

This recent attention to exonerations has both prompted and been influenced by an "innocence movement." In the early 1990s, only two organizations existed to take on cases of prisoners claiming to be factually innocent—that is, they claimed they played no role in the crime of which they were convicted. Today more than 50 of these innocence projects exist. Collectively, they screen claims of innocence, work to exonerate the factually innocent, promote policies to reduce errors of justice, and provide support for exonerees.

Why so many errors? There are several reasons. As many as 25 percent of all eyewitness identifications may be wrong; many of these errors are caused by suggestive police lineups. Once a person is misidentified, police may develop "tunnel vision"—an unshakeable belief that the suspect is the real criminal. Tunnel vision can lead police to become overly aggressive during interrogations, causing innocent persons to confess simply in order to escape the enormous psychological strain of high-pressure interrogation. This is a special problem with suspects who are more easily manipulated, such as teenagers and mentally challenged suspects. Police often rely on informants, especially jailhouse snitches claiming that a suspect confessed. These snitches may be pathological liars willing to say anything to get a break in their cases.

Police are also not required to include exculpatory evidence—evidence that favors innocence—in their investigative reports. Even if they do, many prosecutors fail to turn over exculpatory evidence to defense lawyers, although they are required to do so by law. Overworked or incompetent defense attorneys often fail to provide a thorough defense. Judges and appellate courts tend to favor the prosecution and in a large proportion of cases simply overlook serious errors. In a number of cases, junk science, substandard forensic laboratories, or fraudulent forensic scientists have presented juries with completely erroneous conclusions.

Because of the chances of error in death penalty cases, a number of states have even placed a moratorium on executions until the issue of errors in the process can be adequately addressed.[67] Because errors may occur, some commentators have called for a new evidentiary standard of "absolute certainty" to replace "beyond a reasonable doubt" in death penalty cases (others argue that this standard would put an end to guilty verdicts because at least one juror would always have some uncertainty).[68]

Unfair Use of Discretion Critics of the death penalty also frown on the tremendous discretion used in seeking the death penalty and the arbitrary manner in which it is imposed. Of the approximately 10,000 persons convicted each year on homicide charges, only 250 to 300 are sentenced to death, while an equal number receive a sentence of probation or community supervision only. It is true that many convicted murderers do not commit first-degree murder and therefore are ineligible for execution, but it is also likely that many serious criminals who could have received the death penalty are not sentenced to death because of prosecutorial discretion. Some escape death by cooperating or giving testimony against their partners in the crime. A person who commits a particularly heinous crime and knows full well that he will receive the death penalty if convicted may be the one most likely to plea bargain to avoid capital punishment. Is it fair to spare the life of a dangerous killer who cooperates with the prosecutor, while executing another who does not?

Misplaced Vengeance Although critics acknowledge that the general public approves of the death penalty, they maintain that prevailing attitudes reflect a primitive desire for revenge and not "just desert." Public acceptance of capital punishment has been compared to the approval of human sacrifices practiced by the Aztecs in Mexico 500 years ago.[69] Just because the public approves does not make it morally correct. It is ironic, critics suggest, that many death penalty advocates oppose abortion on the grounds that it is the taking of human life.[70] The desire to be vengeful and punitive outweighs their scruples about taking life.

At least 30 states now have a sentence of life in prison without the possibility of parole, and many argue that this sentence can be as harsh as execution. Being locked up in prison without any chance of release (barring a rare executive reprieve) may be a worse punishment than a painless death by lethal injection. If vengeance is the goal, life without parole may eliminate the need for capital punishment.

Weak Public Support Although the majority of Americans approve of the death penalty, there is evidence that their approval has declined over the past decade.[71] Also, when surveys give respondents a choice of punishments, such as life without parole, support for the death penalty declines to the 50 percent level.[72] Well-publicized cases of innocent people being sentenced to death have also helped erode support for capital punishment.[73] So although a majority of the public still support the death penalty in principle, a substantial proportion lack confidence in its use and believe that executions should be halted until the justice system can be made foolproof.[74]

There is also evidence that support for the death penalty is influenced by such factors as the personal characteristics of the offender and the circumstances of the offense.[75] People who generally support the death penalty may not want to see it used with juveniles, the mentally challenged, or the mentally ill.[76] And even if a majority support capital punishment, their motives must be closely examined: is it possible that support for the death penalty is a function of racist attitudes and the belief that capital punishment helps control and restrain the minority population?[77]

Little Deterrent Effect Considerable empirical research has been carried out on the effectiveness of capital punishment as a deterrent. In particular, studies have tried to determine whether the death sentence serves as a more effective deterrent than life imprisonment for capital crimes such as homicide. Three methods have been used:

- *Immediate-impact studies*, which calculate the effect that a well-publicized execution has on the short-term murder rate
- *Time-series analysis*, which compares long-term trends in murder and capital punishment rates
- *Contiguous-state analysis*, which compares murder rates in states that have the death penalty with murder rates in a similar state that has abolished capital punishment

Using these three methods over a 60-year period, most researchers have failed to show any deterrent effect of capital punishment.[78] Most of the studies show that murder rates do not seem to rise when a state abolishes capital punishment, nor do they decrease when the death penalty is adopted. The murder rates are also quite similar in states that use the death penalty and in neighboring states that have abolished capital punishment. Finally, little evidence shows that executions can lower the murder rate. One test of the deterrent effect of the death penalty in Texas found no association between the frequency of execution and murder rates during the years 1984 to 1997.[79]

A few studies have found that the long-term application of capital punishment may actually reduce the murder rate.[80] However, these have been disputed by researchers who questioned the methodology used and maintain that the deterrent effects the studies uncovered are an artifact of the statistical techniques used in the research.[81]

The general consensus among death penalty researchers today is that the threat of capital punishment has little effect on murder rates. It is still not known why capital punishment fails as a deterrent, but the cause may lie in the nature of homicide. As noted earlier, murder is often a crime of passion involving people who know each other, and many murders are committed by people under the influence of drugs and alcohol—more than 50 percent of all people arrested for murder test positive for drug use. People caught up in intense conflict with friends, acquaintances, and family members and people under the influence of drugs and alcohol are not likely to take into account the threat of the death penalty.

Despite the less-than-conclusive empirical evidence, many people still insist on the efficacy of the death penalty as a crime deterrent, and recent U.S. Supreme Court decisions seem to justify its use. And some researchers still continue to find that the death penalty can deter crime, although their findings are the exception.[82] Of course, even if the death penalty were no greater a deterrent than a life sentence, some people would still advocate its use on the grounds that it is the only way to permanently rid society of particular dangerous criminals who deserve to die.

RealityCheck

MYTH OR REALITY? The death penalty deters homicide.

MYTH. *The vast majority of the research on this subject has shown that the death penalty does little, if anything, to deter homicide.*

Why are most researchers convinced the death penalty fails to deter homicide? Clearly it is effective from a specific deterrent standpoint, but why might would-be killers not be deterred by the threat of capital punishment?

No Hope of Rehabilitation The death sentence rules out any hope of offender rehabilitation. There is evidence that convicted killers frequently make good parole risks; convicted murderers are often model inmates and, once released, commit fewer crimes than other parolees. It is possible that the general public, including people who sit on juries, overestimate the dangerousness of people who commit murder. In reality, those people given a life sentence for capital murder have *much less than a 1 percent* (0.2%) chance of committing another homicide over a 40-year term; the risk of their committing an assault is about 16 percent.[83]

Race, Gender, and Other Bias Capital punishment may be tarnished by gender, racial, ethnic, and other biases. More people are sentenced to death, and the death penalty is used more often, in nations with a large minority population. This phenomenon has led to formulation of what is referred to as the "minority-group-threat hypothesis"—that the use of extreme punishment is related to the regulation of groups that are racially, culturally, or ethnically different.[84] Let's look at some of the evidence:

- There is evidence that homicides with male offenders and female victims are more likely to result in a death sentence than homicides involving female offenders and male victims.[85]
- Homicides involving strangers are more likely to result in a death sentence than homicides involving nonstrangers or acquaintances.
- Prosecutors are more likely to recommend the death sentence for people who kill white victims than they are in any other racial combination of victim and criminal.[86] Prosecutors are less likely to seek the death penalty if the victim is a minority group member.[87] A male minority group member killing a white female is more likely to result in the death penalty than any other race/gender combination.[88]

Ever since the death penalty was first instituted in the United States, disproportionate numbers of minorities have been executed. Charges of racial bias are supported by the disproportionate numbers of African Americans who have received the death sentence, who are currently on death row, and who have been executed (53.5% of all executions). Racism was particularly blatant when the death penalty was invoked in rape cases: of those receiving the death penalty for rape, 90 percent in the South and 63 percent in the North and West were African American.[89] Today, about 40 percent of the inmates on death row are African American, a number disproportionate to the minority representation in the population. When a black criminal kills a white victim, the likelihood of the death penalty being invoked is far greater than when a white criminal kills a black victim.[90]

Causes More Crime than It Deters Some critics fear that the introduction of capital punishment will encourage criminals to escalate their violent behavior, consequently putting police officers at risk. A suspect who kills someone during a botched robbery may be inclined to "fire away" upon encountering police rather than to surrender peacefully. The killer faces the death penalty already, so what does he have to lose? Geoffrey Rapp studied the effect of capital punishment on the killings of police and found that, all other things being equal, the greater the number of new inmates on death row, the greater the number of police officers killed by citizens.[91] Rapp concluded that what the death penalty seems to do is create an extremely dangerous environment for law enforcement officers, because it does not deter criminals and may lull officers into a false sense of security, leading them to believe that the death penalty will deter violence directed against them and causing them to let their guard down.

The death penalty may also produce more violence than it prevents—the so-called **brutalization effect**.[92] Executions may increase murder rates because they raise the general violence level in society and because people prone to violence actually identify with the executioner, not with the target of the death penalty. When

brutalization effect
An outcome of capital punishment that enhances, rather than deters, the level of violence in society. The death penalty reinforces the view that violence is an appropriate response to provocation.

someone gets in a conflict with such violence-prone individuals or challenges their authority, these individuals may "execute" them, just as the state executes people who violate its rules.[93] There is evidence that the brutalization effect does influence murder rates: stranger homicides increase after an execution.[94] People may be more inclined to settle conflicts with violence after a state executes a criminal—"If they can do it, why can't I?"[95]

Cruel and Inhuman Abolitionists believe that executions are unnecessarily cruel and inhuman and come at a high moral and social cost. Even death by lethal injection, which is considered relatively humane by advocates, has been challenged because it may cause extreme pain and can take much longer to cause death than was originally believed.[96] Our society does not punish criminals by subjecting them to the same acts they themselves committed. Rapists are not sexually assaulted, and arsonists do not have their houses burned down. Why, then, should murderers be killed?

Robert Johnson has described the execution process as a form of torture in which the condemned are first tormented psychologically by being made to feel powerless and alone while on death row; suicide is a constant problem among those awaiting death.[97] The execution itself is a barbaric affair marked by the smell of burning flesh and stiffened bodies. The executioners suffer from delayed stress reactions, including anxiety and a dehumanized personal identity.

Most Developed Countries Have Abandoned It According to the Death Penalty Information Center, over half the countries in the world have abolished the death penalty in law or in practice. Just since 1990, more than 45 countries have abolished the death penalty for all crimes. Even China has recently revised its criminal law to eliminate the death penalty for certain crimes. According to LiYing Li, "This signifies a leap forward in China's legal reforms and an effort by China to move closer to the international norms."[98]

It Is Expensive Some people complain that they do not want to support "some killer in prison for 30 years." Abolitionists counter that legal appeals drive the cost of executions far higher than the cost of years of incarceration. If the money spent on the judicial process were invested, the interest would more than pay for the lifetime upkeep of death row inmates. Because of numerous appeals, the median time between conviction by a jury, sentencing by a judge, and execution can be rather lengthy. For example, recent data show that the average inmate sentenced to death has been on death row for over 12 years.[99] Several states have begun to explore abolishing the death penalty to save money in light of the recession.

Morally Wrong The death penalty is brutal and demeaning, according to critics. They argue that even if the general public voices approval of the death penalty, "social vengeance by death is a primitive way of revenge which stands in the way of moral progress."[100] And although early religious leaders accepted the death penalty, today many (such as the Catholic Church) condemn the practice of execution.[101]

In his book *The Contradictions of American Capital Punishment*, Franklin Zimring links America's obsession with the death penalty—unique among developed nations—with its vigilante tradition, in which people on the frontier took justice into their own hands, assuming that their targets were always guilty as charged.[102] The death penalty was widely practiced against slaves, and at one time mass executions were a brutal and common practice to stifle any thought of escapes and/or revolts.[103]

While the debate continues, there seems to be little question that the public's support for the death penalty has weakened, and concomitantly, the number of death sentences being handed down is in sharp decline (see Figure 9.5).[104] Whether these developments portend the demise of capital punishment remains to be seen.

L08 List the arguments for and against capital punishment

Debbie Coluter, a certified nurse's assistant, assists an elderly inmate with Alzheimer's disease to his cell at the California Medical Facility in Vacaville, California. Older and terminally ill inmates cost two to three times as much to incarcerate as younger prisoners, straining state prisons and costing taxpayers billions of dollars.

AP Photo/Rich Pedroncelli

Legal Issues in Capital Punishment

The constitutionality of the death penalty has been a major concern to both the nation's courts and its social scientists. In 1972, the U.S. Supreme Court in *Furman v. Georgia* decided that the discretionary imposition of the death penalty was cruel and unusual punishment under the Eighth and Fourteenth Amendments of the U.S. Constitution.[105] The Supreme Court did not completely rule

Prisoners on death row, 1953–2009

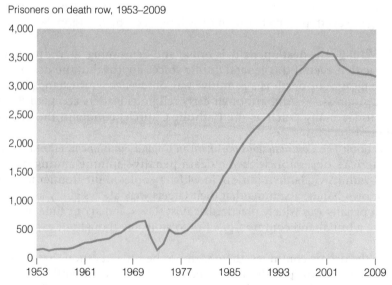

Figure 9.5 Prisoners on Death Row

Source: Bureau of Justice Statistics, *Capital Punishment,* http://bjs.ojp.usdoj.gov/content/glance/dr.cfm (accessed June 27, 2011).

out the use of capital punishment as a penalty; rather, it objected to the arbitrary and capricious manner in which it was imposed. After *Furman*, many states changed statutes that had allowed jury discretion in imposing the death penalty. Then, in July 1976, the Supreme Court ruled on the constitutionality of five state death penalty statutes. In the first case, *Gregg v. Georgia*, the Court found valid the Georgia statute holding that a finding by the jury of at least 1 "aggravating circumstance" out of 10 is required in pronouncing the death penalty in murder cases.[106] In the *Gregg* case, the jury imposed the death penalty after finding beyond a reasonable doubt two aggravating circumstances: (1) the offender was engaged in the commission of two other capital felonies, and (2) the offender committed the offense of murder for the purpose of receiving money and other financial gains (specifically, an automobile).[107] The *Gregg* decision signaled the return of capital punishment as a sentencing option.

Although the Court has supported the legality of the death penalty, it has also placed significant limitations on its use. Rulings have promoted procedural fairness in the capital sentencing process. For example, in *Ring v. Arizona*, the Court found that juries, not judges, must make the critical findings that send convicted killers to death row. The Court reasoned that the Sixth Amendment's right to a jury trial would be "senselessly diminished" if it did not allow jurors to decide whether a person deserves the death penalty.[108] A number of other legal restrictions have also been put in place. We cannot list them all here, but some of the more important ones include:

- The Court has limited the crimes for which the death penalty can be employed by ruling that it is not permissible to punish rapists, even those who rape children, with death.[109] Only people who commit intentional or felony murder may be executed.
- The mentally ill may not be executed.[110] In a 2002 case, *Atkins v. Virginia*, the Court also ruled that execution of mentally challenged criminals is "cruel and unusual punishment" prohibited by the Eighth Amendment.[111]
- In *Roper v. Simmons* (2005), the Court set a limit of 18 years as the age of defendants who could be sentenced to death.[112] The Court said that executing young teens violates "the evolving standards of decency that mark the progress of a maturing society" and that American society regards juveniles as less responsible than adult criminals. Prior to *Simmons*, nineteen states had laws allowing the execution of teenagers under 18 years old.

Ethical Challenge

Carla B. is a 36-year-old white female convicted of killing her husband of 12 years, Jack B., a wealthy and prominent attorney. The police report shows that in order to inherit his substantial trust fund, Carla gave her husband a large dose of a sleeping sedative and, when he felt uncomfortable and dizzy, offered to take him to the emergency room at the local hospital. After he passed out in the car, she slid the comatose man into the driver's seat and then rolled the vehicle down an embankment. After watching the car burst into flames, she walked to her own car, which she had hidden earlier, and drove home. When police came to report the accident, she told the officers that Jack had gone to get some groceries and she was wondering why he had taken so long. At first she expressed shock over his death and burst into tears. Later, forensic evidence and an eyewitness to the event helped investigators unravel her plot.

This is Carla B.'s first conviction. She is a highly educated woman with a degree in French literature from an Ivy League university. She comes from a loving and devoted family. Her parents and sisters, though in shock, are willing to stand beside her. She has two young children who are currently living with relatives; they also seem devoted to their mother. She has done charitable work and is well liked. She has no prior history of violence, mental instability, or the like. Psychiatric reports show that she is unlikely to commit further crimes.

At the sentencing hearing, Carla is filled with remorse and states that her greed overcame her reasoning. She is currently on a suicide watch at the county jail because she has told her counselor that she "does not deserve to live"; her anguish seems genuine.

As a member of the jury during the capital sentencing stage, you hold her fate in your hands. You can recommend death, life in prison, a prison sentence, or even probation. State law requires that each jury member provide a written document stating the reasons for his or her sentencing decision. Please state them here.

L09 Be familiar with the legal issues associated with capital punishment

Summary

L01 **Outline the historical development of punishment** Historically, people who violated the law were considered morally corrupt and in need of strong discipline. In early Greece and Rome, the most common state-administered punishment was banishment, or exile. During the Middle Ages, people found guilty of crime faced a wide range of punishments, including physical torture, branding, whipping, and for most felony offenses, death. The development of the common law in the eleventh century brought some standardization to penal practices. By the end of the sixteenth century, many offenders were made to do hard labor for their crimes. In England, transporting convicts to the colonies became popular.

L02 **List the major goals of contemporary sentencing** The goals of criminal sentencing today can be grouped into six distinct areas: general deterrence, incapacitation, specific deterrence, retribution/just desert, rehabilitation, and equity/restitution.

L03 **Distinguish among general and specific deterrence, incapacitation, and retribution** According to the concept of general deterrence, people will be too afraid to break the law if they believe that they will be caught and punished severely. The purpose of specific deterrence, another goal of punishment, is to convince offenders that the pains of punishment are greater than the potential benefits of crime. Because criminals will not be able to repeat their criminal acts while they are under state control, incapacitation of criminals is another goal of sentencing. According to the retributive goal of sentencing, the essential purpose of the criminal process is to punish offenders—fairly and justly—in a manner that is proportionate to the gravity of their crimes.

L04 **Compare rehabilitation with just deserts** Some sentences are based on the need to treat and/or rehabilitate criminal offenders. Because criminals profit from their misdeeds, it seems both fair and just to demand that they reimburse society for losses it has sustained because of their crimes.

L05 **Identify various sentencing models** Indeterminate sentences are tailored to fit individual needs. Convicted offenders are typically given a "light" minimum sentence that must be served and a lengthy maximum sentence that is the outer boundary of the time that can be served. Determinate sentences offer a fixed term of years, the maximum set in law by the legislature, to be served by the offender sentenced to prison for a particular crime. Sentencing guidelines have been implemented to provide judges with a recommended sentence based on the seriousness of a crime and the background of an offender. Some states have passed mandatory sentence legislation (e.g., three-strikes) prohibiting people convicted of certain offenses, such as violent crimes or drug trafficking, from being placed on probation; they must serve at least some time in prison.

L06 **Explain how sentences are imposed** In some instances, when an accused is convicted of two or more charges, the judge must decide whether to impose consecutive or concurrent sentences. When judges impose an incarceration sentence, they know and take into account the fact that the amount of time spent in prison is reduced by the implementation of "time off for good behavior."

L07 **Summarize factors associated with sentencing decisions** State sentencing codes usually include various factors that can legitimately influence the length of prison sentences, including the severity of the offense, the offender's prior criminal record, whether the offender used violence, whether the offender used weapons, and whether the crime was committed for money. Evidence supports an association between social class and sentencing outcomes: members of the lower class may expect to get longer prison sentences than more affluent defendants. Most research indicates that women receive more favorable outcomes the further they go in the criminal justice system. The same is often true with the elderly. Minorities also seem to receive longer sentences than Caucasians, especially those who are indigent or unemployed.

L08 **List the arguments for and against capital punishment** Proponents of capital punishment feel that executions serve as a strong deterrent for serious crimes. They also argue that capital punishment is morally correct, is proportional to the crime, reflects public opinion, can be implemented with little to no chance of error. Critics of capital punishment cite the potential for error and the supposed unfair use of discretion in sentencing people to death (some offenders get death sentences while others do not). They also claim that capital punishment represents misplaced vengeance and that there is not enough public support for the death penalty. Finally, critics argue the death penalty does not deter crime; that it abandons all hope for offender rehabilitation; is biased against certain demographics; amounts to immoral, cruel, and inhuman punishment; may cause crime to increase; is expensive; and has been abandoned in most developed nations.

L09 **Be familiar with the legal issues associated with capital punishment** The constitutionality of the death penalty has been a major concern to both the nation's courts and its social scientists. Though the Supreme Court has upheld the death penalty for the most serious offenders, it has prohibited it as a sentence for certain crimes, notably rape—even child rape. Juveniles cannot be sentenced to death, nor can the mentally retarded.

1. Discuss the sentencing dispositions in your jurisdiction. What are the pros and cons of each?

2. Compare the various types of incarceration sentences. What are the similarities and differences? Why are many jurisdictions considering the passage of mandatory sentencing laws?

3. Discuss the issue of capital punishment. In your opinion, does it serve as a deterrent? What new rulings has the Supreme Court made on the legality of the death penalty?

4. Why does the problem of sentencing disparity exist? Do programs exist that can reduce the disparity of sentences? If so, what are they? Should all people who commit the same crime receive the same sentence? Explain.

5. Should convicted criminals be released from prison when correctional authorities are convinced they are rehabilitated? Why or why not?

PART 4

CORRECTIONS AND ALTERNATIVE SANCTIONS

There are many possible careers in corrections, some in the community and others within secure facilities such as prisons or jails. One of the most sought-after jobs in community corrections is the probation officer.

- Probation officers monitor offenders' behavior through personal contact with the offenders and their families.
- The number of cases a probation officer has depends on both the counseling needs of offenders and the risks they pose to society.
- Educational requirements for probation officers vary by state, but a bachelor's degree in social work or criminal justice is usually required.
- Some states require probation officers to have one year of work experience in a related field or one year of graduate study in criminal justice, social work, or psychology.

Many probation officers gain personal satisfaction from counseling members of their community and helping them become productive citizens. Median annual earnings of probation officers is about $36,130. Officers and specialists who work in urban areas usually have higher earnings than those working in rural areas.

Typical of probation officers, Ann Beranis first got interested in the justice system while working on her master's degree at the Illinois School of Professional Psychology. Having been a probation officer for the past ten years, she finds the job both challenging and rewarding. The job becomes a challenge when clients are resistant to change and it becomes difficult finding the necessary resources to help convince them to make positive changes. Her greatest reward on the job is "seeing a client turn their life around, and leave probation with confidence in themselves and hope for the future." It is also rewarding, she says, knowing that the hard work she puts into a case helps crime victims and protects the community from further victimization.

Another popular career, this one in secure corrections, is that of correctional counselor, who reviews and evaluates prison inmates and determines the most effective method of rehabilitation.

- Correctional counselors are asked to create, enact, manage, and sometimes evaluate programs designed to improve the psychosocial functioning of offenders.

- They provide educational sessions, survey the needs of offenders, and prepare reports for court.
- There is a growing need for correctional counselors, and the counselors can choose a specialization, such as substance abuse or juvenile rehabilitation.
- The median salary is $47,350, but positions at the federal level will generally pay a higher salary.
- Those with graduate-level education and special qualifications such as expertise working with drug addicts are also more likely to have higher salaries and greater opportunities for advancement.

How do correctional counselors enjoy their job? Gina Curcio is a correctional counselor at the Essex County House of Corrections in Middleton, Massachusetts. She finds that her job can be a mystery to people and that most civilians have no idea what a correctional facility is like and what kind of programs and services it offers. Her friends think that the jail only holds offenders who commit minor offenses, such as DUI or nonpayment of child support. But in reality Essex County also holds pretrial detainees who in many cases are federal inmates charged with very serious offenses, including murder, drug trafficking, and rape. Why are they being held in a local jail? The corrections department is paid a daily fee to detain and house federal inmates until they can be tried and sentenced.

Curcio likes her job and finds the greatest rewards are the sense of camaraderie and teamwork, the experience in criminal justice, some great job-related benefits (health insurance and all kinds of incentives, including physical fitness and education), and tuition reimbursement. She works hard to gain respect, which as a young female officer is something she feels she has to do. Someday she hopes to teach criminal justice and use the experience and knowledge she has gained on the job.

Part 4 contains three chapters that cover the correctional process in all the various forms it currently takes. Chapter 10 surveys community-based corrections, including probation, and alternative sanctions ranging from fines to electronic monitoring and home confinement. Chapter 11 introduces the history of corrections and also reviews the various forms of secure corrections being used today. Finally, Chapter 12 looks at the prison experience, covering such topics as prison culture, sexual assault, treatment programs, and prisoners' rights. There are also sections on leaving prison, parole, and the re-entry process.

> *"A criminal justice education offers an understanding of the key components of this field—the legal system, law enforcement as it applies to offender supervision, and social work/counseling skills and issues."*
>
> Ann Beranis

© Phil McCarten/Reuters/Landov

10 Community Sentences: Probation, Intermediate Sanctions, and Restorative Justice

Learning Objectives

LO1   **Be familiar with the concept of community sentencing**

LO2   **Know the history of community sentences**

LO3   **Recognize the different types of probation sentences**

LO4   **Be familiar with the rules of probation**

LO5   **Know about the organization and administration of probation services**

LO6   **List and discuss the elements of a probation department's duties**

LO7   **Be familiar with the legal rights of probationers**

LO8   **Debate the effectiveness of probation**

LO9   **Know what is meant by intermediate sanctions**

LO10   **Define restorative justice and discuss its merits**

On August 23, 2007, celebrity Lindsay Lohan pleaded guilty to misdemeanor cocaine use and driving under the influence and was sentenced to one day's imprisonment and 10 days' community service, and ordered to pay fines, complete an alcohol education program, and spend three years on probation. In 2010, she violated her probation order by failing to attend substance abuse classes and was jailed for 90 days (though she served only 23 behind bars). On April 22, 2011, media outlets trumpeted another chapter in her sad tale. Lindsay was ordered to spend 120 days behind bars for another breach in her probation: she was accused of taking a necklace from a local jewelry store. Lindsay is not alone as a celebrity probationer. Some of the other famous or near famous serving community sentences include:

- After he pleaded guilty in January 2011 to sexual misconduct and patronizing an underage prostitute, former New York Giants great Lawrence Taylor was sentenced to six years on probation. The former all-star linebacker was also required to register as a sex offender.[1]
- In 2011, movie star Mel Gibson was sentenced to three years' probation and ordered to undergo a year of counseling after pleading no contest to a charge of simple misdemeanor battery for attacking his girlfriend Oksana Grigorieva during a heated argument in January 2010.[2]
- Rappers and pop stars routinely get probation. Lil Wayne, whose real name is Dwayne Michael Carter, Jr., received probation after he pleaded guilty to one count of possession of a dangerous drug. Three other drug and weapons charges were dismissed after his arrest at a U.S. Border Patrol checkpoint. Not to be outdone, Eminem received a year of probation on weapons charges stemming from an argument he had with an associate of the group Insane Clown Posse. And of course, in 2009, Chris Brown was sentenced to five years of probation and 180 days of community service after a plea bargain in his felony assault case for beating his girlfriend Rihanna.[3] ■

Are these people being given special treatment simply because they are celebs? Would the average person be sent to prison for possessing drugs, threatening someone with a gun, or having sex with an underage girl? Probably not. Probation and other community sentencing venues are the most commonly used means of correction today and are hardly reserved for the rich and famous; millions of people are on probation for these and similar crimes.

As the term is used today, **probation** is a criminal sentence that suspends or delays a correctional term in a prison or jail so that, instead of being incarcerated, offenders are returned to the community for a period in which they must (a) abide by certain conditions set forth by the court and (b) be supervised by a probation officer. It is the most commonly used means of dispensing correctional treatment to convicted offenders.

RealityCheck

MYTH OR REALITY?

- Only celebrities get probation for serious crimes.
- Probation was begun in England and brought over to the United States with the colonists.
- Violent offenders who commit murder, rape, or assault are barred from probation.
- Probation rules cannot force offenders to take polygraph tests to determine whether they have engaged in illegal behavior; this would be a violation of their privacy rights.
- Probation officers can search a probationer's home without a warrant if they suspect foul play or criminal activity.
- Married probationers are more likely to succeed than their single or divorced peers.
- Convicted criminals can be forced to forfeit their homes and cars.
- A person can be required to spend time in prison as part of his or her probation sentence.
- It is permissible to force people to remain in their homes under house arrest.
- Some jurisdictions encourage face-to-face meetings between offenders and victims and allow victims to participate in justice decision making.

LO1 Be familiar with the concept of community sentencing

probation
A sentence entailing the conditional release of a convicted offender into the community under the supervision of the court (in the person of a probation officer), subject to certain conditions for a specified time.

judicial reprieve
The common-law practice that allowed judges to suspend punishment so that convicted offenders could seek a pardon, gather new evidence, or demonstrate that they had reformed their behavior.

recognizance
The medieval practice of allowing convicted offenders to go unpunished if they agreed to refrain from any further criminal behavior.

sureties
During the Middle Ages, people responsible for the behavior of an offender released before trial.

The fact that probation is used so often rests on the belief that most convicted criminals are neither dangerous nor a menace to society and can be reformed if given a second chance. Probation provides offenders with the opportunity to prove themselves while being closely supervised in the community by trained personnel who can help them reestablish proper forms of behavior. Even felony offenders can be successfully rehabilitated if given the proper balance of community supervision, treatment, and control. And importantly, during tough economic times, probation is a cost-effective alternative to incarceration. So it's not just celebrities who get probation: an overwhelming majority of convicted offenders also get a "second chance" via probation.[4]

This chapter reviews community-based criminal sanctions. It begins with a brief history of community sentencing. It then discusses the role of traditional probation as a community-based correctional practice. Next it focuses on so-called alternative or intermediate sanctions such as intensive supervision, house arrest, and electronic monitoring. Finally, the chapter turns to a discussion of the concept of restorative justice and programs based on its principles.

The History of Probation and Community Sentencing

Where did the idea of community supervision and control begin? During medieval times, the practice of **judicial reprieve** allowed judges to suspend punishment so that convicted offenders could seek a pardon, gather new evidence, or demonstrate that they had reformed their behavior. Another practice, called **recognizance**, enabled convicted offenders to go unpunished if they agreed to refrain from further criminal behavior. Sometimes **sureties** were required—these were people who made themselves responsible for the behavior of an offender after the offender's release.

John Augustus and the Creation of Probation

John Augustus of Boston is usually credited with originating community sentencing.[5] As a private citizen, Augustus began in 1841 to supervise offenders released to his custody by a Boston judge. Over an 18-year period, Augustus supervised close to 2,000 convicted offenders and helped them get jobs and establish themselves in the community. Augustus had an amazingly high success rate, and few of his charges became involved in crime again.

In 1878, Augustus's work inspired the Massachusetts legislature to pass a law authorizing the appointment of a paid probation officer for the city of Boston. In 1880, probation was extended to other jurisdictions in Massachusetts, and by 1898, the probation movement had spread to the superior (felony) courts.[6] The Massachusetts experience was copied by Missouri (1887) and Vermont (1898) and, soon after, by most other states. In 1925, the federal government established a probation system for the U.S. district courts. The probation concept soon became the most widely used correctional mechanism in the United States.[7]

Probation Today

There are now approximately 2,000 adult probation agencies in the United States. Slightly more than half are associated with a state-level agency, whereas the remainder are organized at the county or municipal level of government. About 30 states combine probation and parole supervision into a single agency.

The adult probation population grew about 2 percent per year between 1995 and 2008 until more than 4 million people were on probation. Then in 2009 the number of people on probation slowly began to decline. While growth in the probation population has slowed, more than 4 million people are still on probation and more than 2 million people are still being placed on probation annually. Without probation, the correctional system would rapidly become even more overcrowded, overly expensive, and unmanageable.

Awarding Probation

Most probation orders involve a contract between the court and the offender in which a prison or jail term is suspended and the probationer promises to obey a set of **probation rules**, or conditions mandated by the court. If the rules are violated, or if the probationer commits another criminal offense, probation may be revoked. **Revocation** means that the community sentence is terminated and the original sentence of incarceration is enforced. If an offender on probation commits a second offense that is more serious than the first, he or she may also be indicted, tried, and sentenced to prison on the second offense.

Today, probationary sentences may be granted by state and federal district courts and state superior (felony) courts. In most jurisdictions, although juries can recommend probation, judges have the final say in the matter of discretion. Most states have attempted to shape judicial discretion by creating guidelines for granting probation, directing them to look at such factors as the manner in which the crime was carried out, whether pain was inflicted on a vulnerable victim such as a child. In contrast, probation may be recommended when the defendant is youthful or when they were pressured by a co-defendant into committing the crime. A recent Supreme Court case, *Gall v. United States*, held that granting a probationary sentence to a deserving defendant was not unreasonable even though the Federal Sentencing Guidelines called for a prison sentence. Gall had voluntarily withdrawn from a drug ring three years before indictments were handed down. He moved to another state, opened a business, and started a new life. The judge decided to give him a break and handed down a probation-only sentence. When the prosecution appealed, the Court held that it is appropriate for the sentencing judge to consider all the elements in the case when deciding whether a probation sentence is appropriate.[8]

More than half of all cases involve a direct sentence to probation for a fixed period of time. In about one-quarter of probation sentences, the judge will formulate a prison sentence and then suspend it if the offender agrees to obey the rules of probation while living in the community (a **suspended sentence**).[9] If the offender completes the probation term without further trouble, their sentence is considered served. Some offenders (about 10 percent) receive some form of split sentence in which they must first serve a jail term before being released on probation. In the remaining cases, the imposition of the sentence is suspended and the case continued without a finding until further notice.

For misdemeanors, probation usually extends for the entire period of the jail sentence, whereas felonies are more likely to warrant probationary periods that are actually shorter than the suspended prison sentences. The typical felony probation sentence is a little more than three years.[10]

Probation Eligibility

Although originally conceived as a way to provide a second chance for young offenders who committed nonserious crimes, probation today is also a means of reducing the population overload in an overcrowded and underfunded correctional system. Many serious criminal offenders are therefore given probation sentences, including people with prior felony convictions; more than 30 percent of first-time felons are sentenced to probation, and about 15 percent of repeat felony offenders are given community sentences![11] This means that 15 percent of criminal defendants receive probation even though the current offense was at least their second conviction for a felony offense. Nor are violent criminals exempt from receiving a community sentence: about 20 percent of all people convicted of violent felonies receive probation. So there are two distinct

L02 Know the history of community sentences

probation rules
Conditions or restrictions mandated by the court that must be obeyed by a probationer.

revocation
An administrative act performed by a parole authority that removes a person from parole, or a judicial order by a court removing a person from parole or probation, in response to a violation on the part of the parolee or probationer.

suspended sentence
A prison term that is delayed while the defendant undergoes a period of community treatment. If the treatment is successful, the prison sentence is terminated.

L03 Recognize the different types of probation sentences

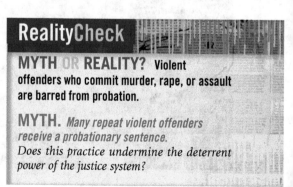

RealityCheck

MYTH OR REALITY? Violent offenders who commit murder, rape, or assault are barred from probation.

MYTH. *Many repeat violent offenders receive a probationary sentence.*
Does this practice undermine the deterrent power of the justice system?

sides to probation: (1) the treatment and rehabilitation of nondangerous offenders deserving of a second chance, and (2) the supervision and control of criminals who might otherwise be incarcerated if probation were not available.

Conditions of Probation

When granting probation, the court sets down certain conditions or rules of behavior that the probationer is bound to obey. Although probation officers themselves can later set some conditions, courts have typically ruled that the most restrictive ones must be approved by the sentencing judge and that probation officers cannot require the defendant to adhere to new requirements of supervision about which he or she did not have reasonable notice.[12]

Some conditions are standard and are applied in every probation case (e.g., "Do not leave the jurisdiction"), but the sentencing judge usually has broad discretion to set specific conditions on a case-by-case basis. Sometimes an individual probationer is given specific rules related to his or her particular circumstances, such as the requirement to enroll in an anger management or drug treatment program, make a personal apology to the victim, or have no contact with his or her ex-spouse.[13] A presiding judge may not impose capricious or cruel conditions, of course, such as requiring an offender to make restitution out of proportion to the seriousness of the criminal act.[14] Judges may, however, legally impose restrictions tailored to fit the probationer's individual needs and/or to protect society from additional harm. For example, they can force sex offenders to register with state authorities and require probationers to take periodic polygraph tests to determine whether they have engaged in illegal behavior.[15] Community supervision may be revoked if probationers fail to comply with the conditions of their probation and do not obey the reasonable requests of the probation staff to meet their treatment obligations.[16]

LO4 Be familiar with the rules of probation

Administration of Probation Services

Probation services are organized in a variety of ways, depending on the state and the jurisdiction in which they are located. Some states have an independent statewide probation service, and in others, probation is controlled by local courts. Thirty-five

In some jurisdictions, probation and parole services have been combined so that probation officers may be called upon to supervise parolees. Here, Lucinda Carroll, probation officer with Washington County, Oregon, checks on the household of a man on parole for a domestic violence charge. With her is Chelsea Klostreich, also a probation and parole officer with Washington County. The officers travel in pairs for safety.

© Torsten Kjellstrand/*The Oregonian*/Landov

states combine probation and parole supervision services in a single unit situated within the department of corrections or organized as an independent agency; about one-quarter of probationers are supervised in these joint operations. Some departments combine juvenile and adult probation departments, whereas others maintain these departments separately.

Regardless of how probation services are organized, probation officers (POs) are typically assigned to a department situated in a single court district, such as a juvenile, superior, district, or municipal court. The relationship between the department and court personnel (especially the judge) is extremely close.

In the typical department, the chief probation officer (CPO) sets policy, supervises hiring, determines training needs, and may personally discuss with or recommend sentencing to the judge. The probation staff carries out the actual monitoring and treatment of offenders.

An officer's working style is influenced by both personal values and the department's general policies and orientation toward the goals of probation.[17] Some POs view themselves as "social workers" and maintain a treatment orientation; their goal is to help offenders adjust in the community. Others are "law enforcers" who are more concerned with supervision, control, and public safety; some jurisdictions require that probation officers carry guns if they make home visits.[18] For more on a career as a probation officer, see the Careers in Criminal Justice feature.

L05 Know about the organization and administration of probation services

Elements of Probation

Probation officers engage in five primary tasks: investigation, intake, diagnosis/risk classification, supervision, and treatments.

Pre-sentence Investigation In the investigative stage, the supervising probation officer accumulates important information on the background and activities of the offender being considered for probation. This **pre-sentence investigation** serves as the basis for sentencing and controls whether the convicted defendant will be granted community release or sentenced to secure confinement. In the event that the offender is placed on probation, the investigation becomes useful as a tool to shape treatment and supervision efforts.

pre-sentence investigation
An investigation performed by a probation officer attached to a trial court after the conviction of a defendant.

The style and content of pre-sentence investigations may vary among jurisdictions and also among individual POs within the same jurisdiction. Some departments require voluminous reports covering every aspect of the defendant's life. Other departments require that officers stick to the basic facts, such as the defendant's age, race, sex, and previous offense record.

At the conclusion of most pre-sentence investigations, a recommendation is made to the presiding judge that reflects the department's sentencing posture on the case at hand. This is a crucial aspect of the report, because the sentencing judge usually follows the probation department's recommendation. Numerous factors may contribute to a recommendation of community treatment; among the most critical are the investigator's conclusion that the defendant is someone probation officers can work with and effectively treat. Equally important is the belief that the perspective probationer will be able to abide by both legal and institutional rules.[19]

Intake Probation officers who conduct **intake** interviews may be looking to settle the case without the necessity of a court hearing. The probation officer will work with all parties involved in the case—offender, victim, police officer, and so on—to design an equitable resolution of the case. If the intake process is successful, the probation officer may settle the case without further court action, recommend restitution or other compensation, or recommend unofficial or informal probation. If an equitable solution cannot be found, the case would be filed for a court hearing.

intake
The process in which a probation officer settles cases at the initial appearance before the onset of formal criminal proceedings; also, the process in which a juvenile referral is received and a decision is made to file a petition in the juvenile court, release the juvenile, or refer the juvenile elsewhere.

Diagnosis/Risk Classification In order to select appropriate treatment modes, probation officers analyze the client's character, attitudes, and behavior. An effective diagnosis integrates all that has been learned about the individual, organized

Careers in Criminal Justice

PROBATION OFFICER

Duties and Characteristics of the Job

- Probation officers monitor offenders behavior through personal contact with the offenders and their families.
- Another part of the probation officer's job involves working in the courts.
- The number of cases a probation officer has depends on both the counseling needs of offenders and the risks they pose to society.
- Probation officers may find their jobs stressful because they work with convicted criminals and interact with many other individuals who may be angry, upset, or uncooperative, including family members and friends of their clients.
- Although stress makes these jobs difficult at times, the work also can be rewarding. Many probation officers gain personal satisfaction from counseling members of their community and helping them become productive citizens.

Job Outlook

- Jobs for probation officers are more plentiful in urban areas.
- There are also more jobs in states that have numerous men and women on probation.
- Employment of probation officers is projected to grow during the next few years.
- Overcrowding in prisons also has swelled the probation population as judges and prosecutors search for alternative forms of punishment, such as electronic monitoring and day reporting centers.
- Other openings will result from the need to replace workers who leave the occupation permanently—including the large number expected to retire over the next several years.

Salary

- Median annual earnings of probation officers is about $36,130. The middle 50 percent earned between $29,260 and $44,890.
- The lowest 10 percent earned less than $24,310, and the highest 10 percent earned more than $54,810.
- Officers and specialists who work in urban areas usually have higher earnings than those working in rural areas.

Qualifications

- Prospective probation officers must be in good physical condition and must be emotionally stable.
- Most agencies require applicants to be at least 21 years old and, for federal employment, not older than 37. Those convicted of felonies may not be eligible for employment in these occupations.
- Probation officers need strong writing skills because of the large number of reports they must prepare.
- Familiarity with computers is often required.
- Job candidates also should be knowledgeable about laws and regulations pertaining to corrections.

Education and Training

- Educational requirements for probation officers vary by state, but a bachelor's degree in social work or criminal justice is usually required.
- Some states require probation officers to have one year of work experience in a related field or one year of graduate study in criminal justice, social work, or psychology.
- Most probation officers must complete a training program and work as trainees for about six months.
- Candidates who successfully complete the training period obtain a permanent position.
- Some states require applicants to take a certification test during or after training.
- Applicants usually must also pass written, oral, psychological, and physical examinations.

Word to the Wise

- Probation can be challenging but it is also quite rewarding. Although an advanced degree is not a requirement, it may be the key to advancement in larger departments. Budget cutbacks may mean tougher cases entering community corrections rather than more expensive custodial placements.

in such a way as to facilitate the establishment of future treatment goals. Based on the risk level diagnosis, some clients may receive frequent (intensive) supervision in which they are contacted by their supervising probation officer almost every day, whereas those considered low risk are assigned to minimum monitoring. A number of **risk classification** approaches are now used, but most employ such objective measures as the offender's age, employment status, drug abuse history, prior felony convictions, and number of address changes in the year prior to sentencing. Some departments are using standardized tests to predict failure and assign treatment such as the Level of Service Inventory—Revised (or LSI-R).[20]

risk classification
Classifying probationers so that they may receive an appropriate level of treatment and control.

Developing effective risk assessment has taken on greater importance because probation is now routinely employed with felons who have been convicted of violent crimes such as rape and murder.[21] Nonetheless, some critics have complained that the emergence of standardized diagnostic tools and tests has diminished the probationer officer's individual role in classification, thereby eliminating the human element from diagnosis and treatment.[22]

Supervision An important part of the probation officer's duties is monitoring clients in the community, making sure they obey their probation orders, and helping them to stay out of trouble. In some cases, this can mean giving random drug tests, monitoring the family situation, and keeping in touch with employers. Some officers have a control orientation, believe in strict supervision, and are quick to sanction offenders who violate rules. Others are more treatment oriented and question the effectiveness of punitive sanctions and strict supervision. Recent research has identified a new breed of younger probation officers who are actually more inclined to control and punish rule violators than their older counterparts,

One reason for this turn to closer and more punitive supervision is the threat of litigation. Failure to supervise probationers adequately can result in the officer and the department being held legally liable for civil damages. For example, probation departments have been sued by a rape victim when her attacker was a probationer with a history sexual assault and still on the street despite repeatedly violating his probation orders.[23]

Several newly developed technologies are now being used to aid supervision, and some can provide probation officers with tools to better manage their caseloads. For example, sleep pattern analysis technology, already used by some jurisdictions, provides preliminary indications of substance abuse that creates identifiable sleep disruption patterns. The technology consists of a small device, secured to an offender's wrist with a tamper-evident band, that measures sleep quality by recording gross motor activity. Some departments are now monitoring probationers forbidden to drive with ankle bracelets that collect data on the unique patterns of movement associated with foot-to-brake, foot-to-gas pedal, and acceleration and deceleration of a motor vehicle.[24]

Treatment Probation staff are assigned to carry out a program of therapy designed to help the client deal with the problems that are suspected of being the cause of her or his antisocial behavior. In years past, the probation staff had primary responsibility for supervision and treatment, but today's large caseloads limit opportunities for hands-on treatment; most probation treatment efforts rely on community resources.

Treatment protocols may vary according to client needs. Some of those who have a drinking problem may be asked to participate in a community-based 12-step program; others might spend time in a residential detoxification center. A spousal abuser may be required to enroll in an anger management program. A probation officer may work with teachers and other school officials to develop a program designed to help a young probationer reduce his or her truancy and avoid becoming a dropout.

As part of the treatment process, probation officers use community services to help their clients adjust and improve their lives. Jacquess Scott, left, speaks with Diana Hanks-Hasan, a workforce manager with Gateway Constructors in St. Louis, during the Partnership for Success Job Fair at the University of Missouri–St. Louis. About 500 men and women who had been convicted for local, state, and federal crimes showed up for the job fair, organized by the U.S. Probation Office for the Eastern District of Missouri.

motivational interviewing
A technique that increases the probationer's awareness of his potential problems by asking him to visualize a better future and learn strategies to reach his goals.

L06 **List and discuss the elements of a probation department's duties**

A number of innovative techniques are now being used with probationers. One popular technique called **motivational interviewing** assumes that disinterested probationers forced into treatment will lack the will to change. Motivational interviewing therefore attempts to increase the probationer's awareness of their potential problems, and acknowledge the risks they face if they fail to change their behavior. Clients are asked to visualize a better future and learn strategies to reach their goals. While the technique seems promising, results have been mixed.[25]

Another popular client-centered approach, cognitive behavioral therapy, is discussed in the Contemporary Issues in Criminal Justice feature.

Legal Rights of Probationers

What are the legal rights of probationers? How has the U.S. Supreme Court set limits on the probation process? A number of important legal issues surround probation, one set involving the civil rights of probationers and another involving the rights of probationers during the revocation process.

Civil Rights The Court has ruled that probationers have a unique status and therefore are entitled to fewer constitutional protections than other citizens.

- *Minnesota v. Murphy* (1984).[26] The probation officer–client relationship is not confidential, as are physician–patient and attorney–client relationships. If a probationer admits to committing a crime to his or her probation supervisor, the information can be passed on to the police or district attorney. The *Murphy* decision held that a probation officer could even use trickery or psychological pressure to get information and turn it over to the police.
- *Griffin v. Wisconsin* (1987).[27] *Griffin* held that a probationer's home may be searched without a warrant because probation departments "have in mind the welfare of the probationer" and must "respond quickly to evidence of misconduct."
- *United States v. Knights* (2001).[28] The warrantless search of a probationer's home for the purposes of gathering criminal evidence is legal under some circumstances—for example, if (a) the search was based on a reasonable suspicion that the probationer

Treating Probationers with Cognitive Behavioral Therapy

Cognitive behavioral therapy (CBT) is a correctional treatment approach that focuses on patterns of thinking and the beliefs, attitudes, and values that underlie thinking. The therapy assumes that most people can become conscious of their own thoughts and behaviors and then make positive changes. A person's thoughts are often the result of experience, and behavior is often influenced and prompted by these thoughts. In addition, thoughts may sometimes become distorted and fail to reflect reality accurately.

When a probationer is placed in a CBT program, the goal is to restructure distorted thinking and perception, which in turn changes a person's behavior for the better. Characteristics of distorted thinking may include immature or developmentally arrested thoughts; poor problem solving and decision making; an inability to consider the effects of one's behavior; a hampered ability to reason and accept blame for wrongdoing; or an inability to manage feelings of anger. These distorted thinking patterns can lead to making poor decisions and engaging in antisocial behavior to solve problems.

Recently Patrick Clark reviewed the existing literature on cognitive behavior to assess its effectiveness. He found that, unlike other approaches, CBT places responsibility in the hands of clients while supplying them with the tools to solve their problems, focusing on the present rather than the past. People taking part in CBT learn specific skills that can be used to solve the problems they confront all the time as well as skills they can use to achieve legitimate goals and objectives. CBT first concentrates on developing skills to recognize distorted or unrealistic thinking when it happens, and then on changing that thinking or belief to mollify or eliminate problematic behavior.

PROGRAM EFFECTIVENESS

CBT is one of the few treatment approaches that has been broadly validated with research. Unlike other traditional and popular therapies, CBT has been the subject of more than 400 clinical trials involving a broad range of conditions and populations. For example, Sesha Kethineni and Jeremy Braithwaite found excellent results when they evaluated a CBT program used with juvenile probationers. CBT has shown to be reliably effective with a wide variety of personal problems and behaviors, including substance abuse, antisocial and aggressive behavior, and mood disorders, all of which have been linked to criminality.

Evidence of the treatment's effectiveness has been produced by Mark Lipsey, who examined the effectiveness of various approaches to intervention with offenders. His review analyzed the results of 548 studies from 1958 to 2002 that assessed intervention policies, practices, and programs. Lipsey found that interventions based on punishment and deterrence actually increased recidivism. On the other hand, therapeutic approaches based on counseling, skill building, and multiple services had the greatest impact in reducing further problem behavior. In a recent review of correctional treatment, Lipsey, along with Nana Landenberger, found that CBT significantly reduced recidivism. The greatest effects were found among more serious offenders, perhaps because CBT's enabling, self-help approach increases program participation and is therefore most effective with clients who shun or resist other approaches. The therapy is also more effective in reducing further criminal behavior when clients simultaneously receive other support, such as supervision, employment, education and training, and other mental health counseling.

CRITICAL THINKING

If changing or altering disruptive thinking patterns is key to changing behavior, does that mean that crime is more of an individual problem than a result of poverty, social inequality, and disorganization? Is the logical conclusion, then, that if crime is more common in poor neighborhoods and communities, affluent people have better cognitive skills than the poor?

---

had committed another crime while on probation and (b) submitting to searches was part of the probation order. The government's interest in preventing crime, combined with *Knights*'s diminished expectation of privacy, required only a *reasonable suspicion* to make the search fit within the protections of the Fourth Amendment.

Revocation Rights During the course of a probationary term, violating the rules or terms of probation or committing a new crime can result in probation being revoked, at which time the offender may be placed in an institution. Revocation is not often an easy decision, because it conflicts with the treatment philosophy of many probation departments.

If revocation is a possibility, the offender is notified, and a formal hearing is scheduled to look into the matter. If the charges against the probationer are upheld, the offender can either be maintained on probation or have his probation revoked and be forced to serve the remainder of his sentence behind bars.

RealityCheck

MYTH OR REALITY? Probation officers can search a probationer's home without a warrant if they suspect foul play or criminal activity.

REALITY. *Probationers have fewer expectations of privacy than the average citizen and their home can be searched without a warrant if there is cause.*

Do you think that probationers should have the same civil rights as anyone else living in the community?

In some significant decisions, the U.S. Supreme Court provided procedural safeguards to apply at proceedings to revoke probation (and parole):

- *Mempa v. Rhay* (1967). A probationer is constitutionally entitled to counsel in a revocation-of-probation proceeding where the imposition of sentence had been suspended.[29]
- *Morrissey v. Brewer* (1972). *Morrissey*, a parole case, established that an informal inquiry must be held to determine whether there is probable cause that a parolee has violated the conditions of parole. If so, a formal revocation hearing is required before parole can be revoked. Because the revocation of probation and that of parole are similar, the standards in *Morrissey* are applied to the probation process as well.[30]
- *Gagnon v. Scarpelli* (1973). *Gagnon* established that both probationers and parolees have a constitutionally limited right to legal counsel in revocation proceedings.[31] A judge may deny counsel under some circumstances, such as when probation will be continued despite the violation.
- *Beardon v. Georgia* (1983) In *Beardon*, the U.S. Supreme Court ruled that a judge cannot revoke a defendant's probation for failure to pay a fine and/or make restitution The state may not thereafter imprison a defendant solely because he or she lacks the resources to pay, because this would be a violation of a probationer's right to equal protection.[32]
- *United States v. Granderson* (1994). The *Granderson* ruling helped clarify what can happen to a probationer whose community sentence is revoked. Granderson was eligible for a 6-month prison sentence but instead was given 60 months of probation. When he tested positive for drugs, his probation was revoked. The statute he was sentenced under required that he serve one-third of his original sentence in prison. When the trial court sentenced him to 20 months, he appealed. Was his original sentence 6 months or 60 months? The Supreme Court found that it would be unfair to force a probationer to serve more time in prison than he would have served if originally incarcerated and ruled that the proper term should have been one-third of the 6 months, or 2 months.[33]

LO7 Be familiar with the legal rights of probationers

How Successful Is Probation?

Probation is the most commonly used alternative sentence for a number of reasons: it is humane, it helps offenders maintain community and family ties, and it is cost effective. Incarcerating an inmate typically costs over $25,000 per year, whereas probation costs about $2,000 per year.

Although unquestionably inexpensive, is probation successful? If most probation orders fail, the costs of repeated criminality would certainly outweigh the cost savings of a probation sentence. National data indicate that about 60 percent of probationers successfully complete their probationary sentence, whereas about 40 percent are rearrested, violate probation rules, or abscond; about 18 percent find themselves behind bars.[34]

Most revocations occur for technical violations during the first three months of the probation sentence.[35] Ironically, many revocations stem from failure to attend required treatment programs that were originally created to help probationers kick their drug habits, stay out of trouble, and succeed on probation.[36]

Studies of federal probationers show even better results (30 percent failure rate).[37] Although a 30 to 40 percent failure rate may seem high, even the most serious criminals who receive probation are less likely to recidivate than those who are sent to prison or jail for committing similar crimes.[38]

Probation may work because it is easier to treat offenders in their home environment than in a closed institution. When Christopher Krebs and his associates carefully compared treatment outcomes of large groups of drug-involved offenders in the state of Florida they found that institutional treatment in jail or prison cost three times as much as community-based treatment, but was actually less successful; inmates showed no particular improvement after attending institutional drug treatment programs, while those on probation achieved positive results.

The conclusion: the use of community-based treatment can increase public safety while costing a lot less than locking up offenders.[39] Even clients with the most serious personal problems, such as mental illness, seem to do better on probation than in closed institutions.[40]

How Successful Is Felony Probation?

Are probationers convicted of serious felonies more likely to recidivate than minor offenders who receive probation? Is it possible that the success of probation reflects the fact that probationers are far less dangerous and incorrigible than offenders sentenced to prison? One way to determine the real success of probation is to disaggregate felons from misdemeanants and see how the former group does on community sentencing. In a now-famous study, Joan Petersilia and her colleagues at the RAND Corporation, a private think tank, traced the outcomes of 1,672 men convicted of felonies who had been granted probation in Los Angeles and Alameda counties in California.[41] The crimes these probationers committed were indistinguishable from those of offenders sentenced to prison.

Petersilia found that 1,087 (65 percent) of the felony probationers were soon rearrested; of those rearrested, 853 (51 percent) were convicted; and of those convicted, 568 (34 percent) were sentenced to jail or prison. Of the probationers who had new charges filed against them, 75 percent were charged with burglary, theft, robbery, and other predatory crimes; 18 percent were convicted of serious, violent crimes.

These data indicate that many people given prison sentences could have been granted community sentences, and vice versa. This is a disturbing finding when so many felons granted community sentences fail to complete their probationary period.

Although the failure rate found by Petersilia seems disturbingly high, her findings still support the continued use of probation, given the fact that felons who receive probation are less likely to recidivate than felons who are sent to prison for committing similar crimes.[42]

> **L08** Debate the effectiveness of probation

Who Fails on Probation and Who Succeeds?

Who is most likely to fail on probation? Many probationers have grown up in troubled households in which family members are or have been incarcerated and/or drug abusers. Others have lived part of their lives in foster homes or state institutions and have suffered high rates of physical and sexual abuse. This sort of deprived background often makes it difficult for probationers to comply with the rules of probation and forgo criminal activity. Surveys indicate that almost 20 percent of probationers suffer from mental illness and that those with a history of instability are most likely to be rearrested.[43]

Prior record is also related to probation success: clients who have a history of criminal behavior, prior probation, and previous incarceration are the most likely to fail.[44] Also, as probation sentences have become more common, caseloads now contain significant numbers of serious repeat offenders, a group that is difficult to treat and control.[45]

In contrast, probationers who are married with children, have lived in the area for two or more years, and are adequately employed are the most likely to be successful on probation.[46] Among female probationers, those who have stable marriages, are better educated, and are employed are more likely to complete probation orders successfully than male or female probationers who are single, less educated, and unemployed.

The Future of Probation

Some critics are worried that probation is now undergoing a shift from traditional casework methods that featured diagnosis and treatment to an emphasis on risk assessment and control.[47] To improve

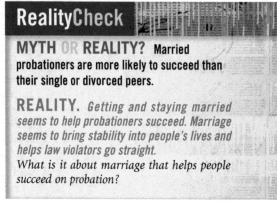

RealityCheck

MYTH OR REALITY? Married probationers are more likely to succeed than their single or divorced peers.

REALITY. *Getting and staying married seems to help probationers succeed. Marriage seems to bring stability into people's lives and helps law violators go straight.*

What is it about marriage that helps people succeed on probation?

the effectiveness of probation even more, in a process that leading expert Joan Petersilia calls "reforming, reinvesting, and restructuring," several steps appear to be necessary, including providing more financial resources and implementing quality programming for appropriate probation target groups.[48] A number of initiatives that are now ongoing or being suggested may help shape the future of probation:

- *Making probationers pay.* At least 25 states now impose some form of fee on probationers to defray the cost of community corrections. Massachusetts initiated **day fees**, which are based on the probationer's wages (the usual fee is between one and three days' wages each month).[49] Texas requires judges to impose supervision fees unless the offender is truly unable to pay; fees make up more than half the probation department's annual budget.[50]

- *Making probation more effective.* Legislatures are instituting policies that reward the most effective and efficient local departments. In 2008, the Arizona legislature established an incentive system that rewards departments with up to 40 percent of any cost savings in each county resulting from a reduction in probation revocations. The money can then be used to fund substance abuse treatment, community supervision services, and victim services.[51]

- *HotSpot probation.* HotSpot probation initiatives involve police officers, probation agents, neighbors, and social service professionals in community supervision teams. Using a team approach, they provide increased monitoring of offenders through home visits and drug testing. They also work with the offenders to ease reentry through offender creation of work crews that participate in community cleanups, work on vacant houses, and participate in other projects.[52]

- *Area needs.* Some experts suggest that probation caseloads be organized around area needs rather than client needs. Research shows that probationers' residences are concentrated in certain locations. In the future, probation officers may be assigned cases on the basis of where they live so that they can acquire a working knowledge of community issues and develop expertise on how best to serve their clients' interests and needs.[53]

- *Specialized probation.* Some probation departments are experimenting with focused or specialized probation, in which teams of probation officers take on clients convicted of one specific type of crime, such as drug offenses or domestic violence, rather than treating a mixed bag of offenders. Focusing on specialized caseloads enables probation officers to develop specific treatment and control skills.[54] In some instances, probation officers collaborate with other social service agencies such as public health to provide a range of services to treat special needs clients.[55]

- *Private probation.* Used in at least 10 states, including Colorado and Missouri, private probation involves contracting with companies that, for a fee, engage in many typical probation activities from supervision to giving periodic breathalyzer tests.[56] By utilizing private probation for low-risk offenders, state probation departments can commit more resources to high-risk offenders.[57]

- *Swift and sure punishment.* The threat of swift and sure punishment that is somewhat less than a full revocation may help reduce rule violations. Hawaii has been experimenting with a system that provides immediate punishment for any probationers found in violation of their court orders. Probationers are warned during a court hearing that if they violate the conditions of probation, they will be immediately arrested, will appear in court within hours, and will have the terms of their supervision modified to include a short stay in jail. The jail terms imposed are usually only a few days, but sentence length increases for successive violations. The program appears to be highly successful in reducing violations.[58] Delaware's Step'n Out program is designed for offenders who fail drug tests. Participants are then given drug tests once or twice a week. Continued drug use progressively leads to mandated treatment, more frequent testing, curfew, and incarceration sanctions. Those who are drug free are reclassified and move to standard community supervision.[59]

Probation is unquestionably undergoing dramatic changes. In many jurisdictions, traditional probation is being supplemented by **intermediate sanctions**, which are penalties that fall between traditional community supervision and confinement in jail or prison. These new correctional services are discussed in the following section.

intermediate sanctions
Punishments that fall between probation and prison ("probation plus"). Community-based sanctions, including house arrest and intensive supervision, serve as alternatives to incarceration.

Intermediate Sanctions

He may be willing to take a grenade for us, but will he do community service? Just a few days after winning the Grammy for "Best Male Pop Vocal Performance" Bruno Mars pleaded guilty to cocaine possession at a court in Las Vegas court but was spared going to jail. His punishment: probation, a $2,000 fine, 200 hours of community service at a nonprofit organization, and eight hours with a drug counselor in Los Angeles.

Bruno Mars's sentence reflects the growing trend to add sanctions to traditional probation sentences; in his case, the sanctions were monetary fines and community service. These programs can be viewed as "probation plus," because they add restrictive penalties and conditions to traditional community service orders, which feature treatment and rehabilitation over control and restraint.[60] These newer forms of community sentences have the potential to become reasonable alternatives to treatment and rehabilitation alone, and thus to help address many of the economic and social problems faced by correctional administrators. Here are some of the advantages of intermediate sanctions:

- They are less costly than jail or prison sentences.
- They help the offender maintain family and community ties.
- They can be structured to maximize security and maintain public safety.
- They can be scaled in severity to correspond to the seriousness of the crime.
- They can feature restoration and reintegration rather than punishment and ostracism.
- By siphoning off offenders from the secure correctional system, they reduce the need for future prison and jail construction.
- Intermediate sanctions help meet the need to develop community sentences that are fair, equitable, and proportional.[61]
- They can be designed to increase control over probationers whose serious or repeat crimes make a straight probation sentence inappropriate, yet for whom a prison sentence would be unduly harsh and counterproductive.[62]
- Intermediate sanctions can potentially be used as halfway-back strategies for offenders who violate the conditions of their community release. Rule violators can be placed under increasingly more intensive supervision before actual incarceration is required.

Intermediate sanctions include programs that are usually administered by probation departments: intensive probation supervision, house arrest, electronic monitoring, restitution orders, shock probation or split sentences, and residential community corrections.[63] Some experts also include high-impact shock incarceration, or boot camp experiences, within the definition of intermediate sanctions, but these programs are usually operated by correctional departments and are therefore discussed separately in Chapter 11. Intermediate sanctions also involve sentences that may be administered independently of probation: fines and forfeiture, pretrial programs, and pretrial and post-trial residential programs. Intermediate sanctions therefore range from the barely intrusive, such as restitution orders, to the highly restrictive, such as house arrest accompanied by electronic monitoring and a stay in a community correctional center.

As Figure 10.1 illustrates, intermediate sanctions can form the successive steps of a meaningful "ladder" of scaled punishments outside of prison, thereby restoring fairness and equity to nonincarceration sentences.[64] Forgers may be ordered to make restitution to their victims, and rapists can be placed in a community facility and

Figure 10.1 Punishment Ladder

■ Peter Hernandez, aka Bruno Mars, center, appears in court to waive an evidentiary hearing for a felony cocaine possession charge and receive a date in state court for a plea, on February 4, 2011, in Las Vegas. He pleaded guilty as a first offender to a charge that will be dismissed if he stays out of trouble for a year, completes community service and drug counseling, and pays a $2,000 fine. Agreeing to perform these intermediate sanctions helped Mars "dodge a grenade," i.e., stay out of prison.

receive counseling at a local clinic. This feature of intermediate sanctions enables judges to fit the punishment to the crime without resorting to a prison sentence.

The forms of intermediate sanctions currently in use are more thoroughly discussed in the following sections.

Fines

fine
A money payment levied on offenders to compensate society for their misdeeds.

Monetary payments, or **fines**, can be imposed on offenders as an intermediate punishment for their criminal acts. They are a direct offshoot of the early common-law practice of requiring that compensation (*wergild*) be paid to the victim and the state for criminal acts. Fines are still commonly used in Europe, where they are often the sole penalty, even in cases involving chronic offenders who commit fairly serious crimes.[65]

In the United States, fines are most commonly used in cases involving misdemeanors and lesser offenses. Fines are also frequently used in felony cases where the offender benefited financially.

Fines may be used as a sole sanction but are typically combined with other punishments, such as probation. Judges commonly levy other monetary sanctions along with fines, such as court costs, public defender fees, probation and treatment fees, and victim restitution, to increase the force of the financial punishment. However, there is evidence that many offenders fail to pay fines and that courts are negligent in their efforts to collect unpaid fees.[66]

In most jurisdictions, little guidance is given to the sentencing judge directing the imposition of the fine. Judges often have inadequate information on the offender's ability to pay, and this results in defaults and contempt charges. Because the standard sanction for nonpayment is incarceration, many offenders held in local jails are confined for nonpayment of criminal fines. Even though the U.S. Supreme Court in *Tate v. Short* (1971) recognized that incarcerating a person who is financially unable to pay a fine discriminates against the poor, many judges continue to incarcerate offenders for noncompliance with financial orders.[67] To compensate for this disparity, some jurisdictions have experimented with **day fines** geared to an offender's net daily income. Used in Europe, day fines are designed to be equitable and fairly distributed, by being weighted by a daily-income value taken from a chart similar to an income tax table; the number of the offender's dependents is also taken into account. The day fine concept means that the severity of punishment is geared to the offender's ability to pay.[68]

day fine
A fine geared to the average daily income of the convicted offender in an effort to bring equity to the sentencing process.

Forfeiture

Another intermediate sanction with a financial basis is criminal (*in personam*) and civil (*in rem*) **forfeiture**. Both involve the seizure of goods and instrumentalities related to the commission or outcome of a criminal act. The difference is that criminal forfeiture proceedings target criminal defendants and can only follow a criminal conviction. In contrast, civil forfeiture proceedings target property used in a crime and do not require that formal criminal proceedings be initiated against a person or that the person be proved guilty of a crime.[69] For example, federal law provides that after arresting drug traffickers, the government may seize the boats they used to import the narcotics, the cars they used to carry the drugs overland, the warehouses in which the drugs were stored, and the homes paid for with the drug profits; on conviction, the drug dealers lose permanent ownership of these "instrumentalities" of crime.

Forfeiture is not a new sanction. During the Middle Ages, "forfeiture of estate" was a mandatory result of most felony convictions. The Crown could seize all of a felon's real and personal property. Forfeiture derived from the common-law concept of "corruption of blood," or "attaint," which prohibited a felon's family from inheriting or receiving his property or estate. The common law mandated that descendants could not inherit property from a relative who might have obtained the property illegally: "[T]he Corruption of Blood stops the Course of Regular Descent, as to Estates, over which the Criminal could have no Power, because he never enjoyed them."[70]

Forfeiture was reintroduced to U.S. law with the passage of the Racketeer Influenced and Corrupt Organization (RICO) Act and the Continuing Criminal Enterprises Act, both of which allow the seizure of any property derived from illegal enterprises or conspiracies. Although these acts were designed to apply to ongoing criminal conspiracies, such as drug or pornography rings, they are now being applied to a far-ranging series of criminal acts, including white-collar crimes. More than 100 federal statutes use forfeiture of property as a punishment.

Although law enforcement officials at first applauded the use of forfeiture as a hard-hitting way of seizing the illegal profits of drug law violators, the practice has been criticized because the government has often been overzealous in its application. For example, million-dollar yachts have been seized because someone aboard possessed a small amount of marijuana; this confiscatory practice is referred to as **zero tolerance**. This strict interpretation of the forfeiture statutes has come under fire because it is often used capriciously, the penalty is sometimes disproportionate to the crime involved, and it makes the government a "partner in crime."[71] It is also alleged that forfeiture unfairly targets a narrow range of offenders. For example, it is common for government employees involved in corruption to forfeit their pensions, but employees of public companies are exempt from such punishment.[72] There is also the issue of conflict of interest: because law enforcement agencies can use forfeited assets to supplement their budgets, they may direct their efforts to cases that promise the greatest "payoff" rather than to cases that have the highest law enforcement priority.[73]

Restitution

Another popular intermediate sanction is **restitution**, which can take the form of requiring offenders either to pay back the victims of crime (**monetary restitution**) or to serve the community to compensate for their criminal acts (**community service restitution**).[74] Restitution programs offer offenders a chance to avoid a jail or prison sentence or a lengthier probation period. The programs may help them develop a sense of allegiance to society, better work habits, and some degree of gratitude for being given a second chance. Restitution serves many other purposes, including giving the community something of value without asking it to foot the bill for an incarceration, and helping victims regain lost property and income.

forfeiture
The seizure of personal property by the state as a civil or criminal penalty.

RealityCheck

MYTH OR REALITY? Convicted criminals can be forced to surrender their homes and cars.

REALITY. *Under forfeiture programs, people can be forced to surrender the instrumentalities of their criminal behavior. Should someone convicted of DWI for the third time forfeit her vehicle?*

zero tolerance
The practice of seizing all instrumentalities of a crime, including homes, boats, and cars. It is an extreme example of the law of forfeiture.

restitution
A condition of probation in which the offender repays society or the victim of crime for the trouble and expense the offender caused.

monetary restitution
A sanction requiring that convicted offenders compensate crime victims by reimbursing them for out-of-pocket losses caused by the crime. Losses can include property damage, lost wages, and medical costs.

community service restitution
An alternative sanction that requires an offender to work in the community at such tasks as cleaning public parks or working with disabled children in lieu of an incarceration sentence.

If a defendant is sentenced to pay monetary restitution as part of her probation order, a determination of victim loss is made and a plan for paying fair compensation developed. To avoid the situation in which a wealthy offender can fill a restitution order by merely writing a check, judges will sometimes order that compensation be paid out of income derived from a low-paid social service or public works job.

Community service orders usually require duty in a public nursing home, shelter, hospital, drug treatment unit, or works program; some young vandals may find that they must clean up the damage they caused to the school or the park. Judges and probation officers have embraced the concept of restitution because it appears to benefit the victim, the offender, the criminal justice system, and society.[75] Financial restitution is inexpensive to administer, helps avoid stigma, and provides some compensation for victims of crime. Helping offenders avoid a jail sentence can mean saving the public thousands of dollars that would have gone to maintaining them in a secure institution, frees up needed resources, and gives the community the feeling that equity has been restored to the justice system.

Does restitution work? Most reviews rate it as a qualified success. One recent evaluation of community service in Texas found that nearly three-fourths of offenders with community service orders met their obligations and completed community service work.[76] The Texas experience is not atypical; most restitution clients successfully complete their orders and have no subsequent contact with the justice system.[77]

Shock Probation and Split Sentencing

Shock probation and **split sentences** are alternative sanctions designed to allow judges to grant offenders community release only after they have sampled prison life. These sanctions are based on the premise that if offenders get a taste of incarceration sufficient to shock them into law-abiding behavior, they will be reluctant to violate the rules of probation or commit another crime.

In a number of states and in the Federal Criminal Code, a jail term can actually be a condition of probation, an arrangement known as split

shock probation
A sentence in which offenders serve a short prison term before they begin probation, to impress them with the pains of imprisonment.

split sentence
A practice that requires convicted criminals to spend a portion of their sentence behind bars and the remainder in the community.

Nicole Polizzi, left, better known as "Snooki" from the MTV show *Jersey Shore* sits with Mary Cozzolino in court on September 8, 2010, in Seaside Heights, New Jersey, waiting to face charges of being a public nuisance and annoying others on the Seaside Heights beach in July. Calling her "a Lindsay Lohan wannabe," Judge Damian G. Murray fined Polizzi $500 and ordered her to perform community service after she pleaded guilty to disturbing others. Snooki has gone on to fame and fortune, illustrating the effectiveness of community sanctions, at least for celebrities.

AP Photo/Mel Evans

sentencing. About 10 percent of probationers are now given split sentences. The shock probation approach involves resentencing an offender to probation after a short prison stay. The shock comes because the offender originally received a long maximum sentence but is then eligible for release to community supervision at the discretion of the judge (usually within 90 days of incarceration).

Some states have linked the short prison stay with a boot camp experience, referred to as shock incarceration, in which young inmates undergo a brief but intense period of military-like training and hard labor designed to impress them with the rigors of prison life.[78] (Boot camp programs are discussed in greater detail in Chapter 11.) Shock probation and split sentencing have been praised as ways to limit prison time, reintegrate the client quickly into the community, maintain family ties, and reduce prison populations and the costs of corrections.[79] An initial jail sentence probably makes offenders more receptive to the conditions of probation, because it amply illustrates the problems they will face if probation is violated.

But split sentences and shock probation programs have been criticized by those who believe that even a brief period of incarceration can interfere with the purpose of probation, which is to provide the offender with nonstigmatizing, community-based treatment. Even a short-term commitment subjects probationers to the destructive effects of institutionalization, disrupts their life in the community, and stigmatizes them for having been in jail.

> **RealityCheck**
>
> **MYTH OR REALITY?** A person can be required to spend time in prison as part of their probation sentence.
>
> **REALITY.** *Split sentences that require a stay in prison are a common form of probation sentencing.*
>
> *Does a jail or prison stay defeat the core purpose of probation: helping people avoid the stigma and pain of imprisonment?*

Intensive Probation Supervision

Intensive probation supervision (IPS) programs, also referred to as intensive supervision programs, have been implemented in some form in about 40 states and today include more than 100,000 clients. IPS programs involve small caseloads of 15 to 40 clients who are kept under close watch by probation officers. IPS programs typically have three primary goals:

- *Decarceration.* Without intensive supervision, clients would normally be sent to already overcrowded prisons or jails.
- *Control.* High-risk offenders can be maintained in the community under much closer security than traditional probation efforts can provide.
- *Reintegration.* Offenders can maintain community ties and be reoriented toward a more productive life, while avoiding the pains of imprisonment.

In general, IPS programs rely on a great degree of client contact to achieve the goals of decarceration, control, and reintegration. Most programs have admissions criteria based on the nature of the offense and the offender's criminal background. Some programs exclude violent offenders; others will not take substance abusers. In contrast, some jurisdictions do not exclude offenders based on their prior criminal history.

IPS programs are used in several ways. In some states, IPS is a direct sentence imposed by a judge; in others, it is a postsentencing alternative used to divert offenders from the correctional system. A third practice is to use IPS as a case management tool to give the local probation staff flexibility in dealing with clients. Other jurisdictions use IPS in all three ways, in addition to applying it to probation violators to bring them halfway back into the community without resorting to a prison term.

intensive probation supervision (IPS)
A type of intermediate sanction involving small probation caseloads and strict monitoring on a daily or weekly basis.

Evaluations of IPS IPS programs are a mixed bag. Some show IPS clients have a higher rearrest rate than other probationers, while others suggest that these failure rates are about equal.[80] More encouraging is evidence that IPS clients have better records than similar offenders who suffer incarceration.[81]

It should come as no surprise that IPS clients have a high failure rate; after all, they are more serious criminals who might otherwise have been incarcerated. Probation officers may also be more willing to revoke the probation of IPS clients because they believe these clients pose a greater risk to the community. Why risk the program to save a few "bad apples"?

Although national evaluations of the program have not been encouraging, IPS seems to work better for some offenders than for others. Those with good employment records seem to do better than the underemployed or unemployed.[82] Younger offenders who commit petty crimes are the most likely to fail on IPS; ironically, people with these characteristics are the ones most likely to be included in IPS programs.[83]

IPS may also be more effective when it is combined with particular treatment modalities such as cognitive-behavioral treatment, which stresses such life skills as problem solving, social skills, negotiation skills, management of emotion, and values enhancement.[84]

House Arrest

When Martha Stewart was released from prison in 2005, she was required to serve a five-month term of house arrest in which she could not leave home for more than 48 hours at a time and had to wear an electronic tracking device. Her sentence was not unique—except for the fact that her estate is so big that walking to the edges of the property put her out of range of her tracking device.

House arrest requires convicted offenders to spend extended periods of time in their own home as an alternative to an incarceration sentence. For example, persons convicted on a drunk-driving charge might be sentenced to spend between 6:00 PM Friday and 8:00 AM Monday and every weekday after 5:30 PM in their home for six months. According to current estimates, more than 10,000 people are under house arrest.

As with IPS programs, there is a great deal of variation in house arrest initiatives. Some are administered by probation departments, and others are simply judicial sentences monitored by surveillance officers. Some check clients 20 or more times a month, whereas others do only a few curfew checks. Some use 24-hour confinement; others allow offenders to attend work or school.

No definitive data indicate that house arrest is an effective crime deterrent, nor is there sufficient evidence to conclude that it has utility as a device to lower the recidivism rate. What data exist show that IPS recidivism rates are almost identical to a matched sample of inmates.[85] Although these findings are troublesome, the advantages of house arrest in reducing costs and overcrowding in the correctional system probably make further experimentation inevitable.

Electronic Monitoring

For house arrest to work, sentencing authorities must be assured that arrestees are actually at home during their assigned times. Random calls and visits are one way to check on compliance with house arrest orders. However, one of the more interesting developments in the criminal justice system has been the introduction of **electronic monitoring (EM)** devices to manage offender obedience to home confinement orders.[86] Some use continuous signaling devices that are battery-powered and transmit a radio signal two or more times per minute. They are placed on the offender's wrist or ankle with a tamper-resistant strap and must be worn at all times. A receiver detects the transmitter's signals and conveys a message via telephone report to a central computer when either it stops receiving the radio frequency or the signal resumes. When installed in a typical home environment, receivers can detect transmitter signals from a distance of 150 feet or more.

Newer electronic monitoring systems now feature automatic tracking devices that limit offenders' movements to acceptable areas. Some rely on global positioning satellite (GPS) technology that enables authorities to monitor geographic locale and conditions of release. For example, the system can be programmed to indicate a violation whenever a known sex offender approaches a school or a day care center.[87] Some of these

house arrest
A form of intermediate sanction that requires the convicted offender to spend a designated amount of time per week in his or her own home—such as from 5:00 PM Friday until 8:00 AM Monday.

electronic monitoring (EM)
Requiring convicted offenders to wear a monitoring device as part of their community sentence. Typically part of a house arrest order, this enables the probation department to ensure that offenders are complying with court-ordered limitations on their freedom.

employ victim notification systems that alert the victim when the offender is approaching that person's residence. A transmitter is worn by both the offender and the victim, and a receiver is placed at both residences. Another innovation is the field monitoring device, or "drive-by" units, another type of continuous signaling technology. Probation or parole officers or other authorities use a portable device that can be handheld or used in a vehicle with a roof-mounted antenna. When within 200 to 800 feet of an offender's ankle or wrist transmitter, the portable device can detect the radio signals of the offender's transmitter.[88] These services are particularly important in domestic violence cases, where victims may not feel safe in their own home and are forced to flee to shelters.[89]

Electronic monitoring supporters claim EM has the benefits of relatively low cost and high security, while helping offenders avoid the pains of imprisonment in overcrowded, dangerous state facilities. Because offenders are monitored by computers, an initial investment in hardware eliminates the need for hiring many more supervisory officers to handle large numbers of clients. Because of its low cost and assumed effectiveness, EM is now being used with a wide variety of offenders, even those who have committed serious felony sex offenses.[90]

There is some evidence that EM can be effective. When Kathy Padget and her associates evaluated data on more than 75,000 offenders placed on home confinement in Florida, they found that EM significantly reduces the likelihood of technical violations, reoffending, and absconding.[91] However, some critics argue that the evidence that EM can lower recidivism rates is thin and that it may not work well as a stand-alone program. Instead, EM can improve public safety when it is combined with some other treatment modality, such as social interventions and counseling.[92] A follow-up study by William Bales and his associates found strong empirical evidence that EM is an effective correctional strategy to divert offenders from prison and can also be used effectively as a form of post-prison supervision. They conclude that the recent growth in the use of EM is beneficial and reduces threats to public safety, especially when combined with GPS tracking technology.[93]

Residential Community Corrections

The most secure intermediate sanction is a sentence to a **residential community corrections (RCC)** facility. Such a facility has been defined as "a freestanding nonsecure building that is not part of a prison or jail and houses pretrial and adjudicated adults. The residents regularly depart to work, to attend school, and/or [to] participate in treatment activities and programs."[94]

Traditionally, the role of community corrections was played by the nonsecure halfway house, which was designed to reintegrate soon-to-be-paroled prison inmates into the community. Inmates spend the last few months of their sentence in the halfway house, acquiring suitable employment, building up cash reserves, obtaining an apartment, and developing a job-related wardrobe.

The traditional concept of community corrections has expanded. Today, the community correctional facility is a vehicle to provide intermediate sanctions as well as a prerelease center for those about to be paroled from the prison system. RCC has been used as a direct sentencing option for judges who believe particular offenders need a correctional alternative halfway between traditional probation and a stay in prison. Placement in an RCC center can be used as a condition of probation for offenders who need a nonsecure community facility that provides a more structured treatment environment than traditional probation. It is commonly used in the juvenile justice system for youths who need a more secure environment than can be provided by traditional probation yet are not deemed a threat to the community and do not require a secure placement.

More than 2,000 state-run community-based facilities are in use today. In addition, up to 2,500 private, nonprofit RCC programs operate in the United States. About half also house inmates who have been released from prison and use the RCC placement as a way to ease back into society. The remainder are true intermediate sanctions, including about 400 federally sponsored programs.

residential community corrections (RCC)
A nonsecure facility, located in the community, that houses probationers who need a more secure environment. Typically, residents are free during the day to go to work, school, or treatment, and they return in the evening for counseling sessions and meals.

day reporting center (DRC)
A nonresidential community-based treatment program.

Day Reporting Centers One recent development in community corrections has been the use of RCC facilities as **day reporting centers (DRCs)**.[95] These provide a single location to which a variety of clients can report for supervision and treatment. They can be used as a step up in security for probationers who have failed in the community and as a step down in security for jail or prison inmates.[96]

Evaluations show that DRCs can be successful at reducing recidivism.[97] DRCs seem to work better with certain types of offenders, such as those who are older and more experienced, than with others, such as younger offenders.[98] DRC participants with alcohol problems, criminal companions, and poor living situations are also more likely to fail. In contrast, those who receive counseling seem to do better.[99]

Concept Summary 10.1 sets out the goals and problems of the various forms of intermediate sanctions.

L09 **Know what is meant by intermediate sanctions**

Restorative Justice Programs

Some critics and specialists in criminal justice believe that the new alternative and intermediate sanctions add a punitive aspect to community sentencing that can hinder rehabilitation efforts. Instead, the advocates of **restorative justice** suggest a policy based on restoring the damage caused by crime and creating a system of justice that includes all the parties harmed by the criminal act: the victim, the offender, the community, and society.[100]

restorative justice
A view of criminal justice that focuses on crime as an act against the community rather than the state. Justice should involve all parties affected by crime—victims, criminals, law enforcement, and the community.

Restorative justice models are consistent with the thought of Australian justice expert John Braithwaite, who argues that crime control today involves shaming and stigmatizing offenders. This helps set them apart from normative society and undermines their potential for change. Instead he calls for a policy of "reintegrative shaming." Here disapproval is limited to the offender's evil deeds. Law violators must be brought to realize that although their actions have caused harm, they are still valuable people—people who can be reaccepted by society. A critical element of reintegrative shaming occurs when the offenders themselves begin to understand and recognize their wrongdoing and shame. To be reintegrative, shaming must be brief and controlled, and it must be followed by ceremonies of forgiveness, apology, and repentance.[101] Braithwaite's work is at the core of the restorative justice movement.

Concept Summary 10.1

Intermediate Sanctions

Sanction	Goal	Problems
Fines	Monetary sanction	Overburdens the poor
Forfeiture	Monetary sanction, equity	Can be overreaching
Restitution	Pay back victim	Does not reduce recidivism
Shock incarceration and split sentence	"Taste of bars" as a deterrent	Can cause labeling and stigma
Intensive probation	Small caseloads, more supervision	High failure rate
House arrest	Avoids jail	Lacks treatment possibility
Electronic monitoring	Supervision by computer	Technology-dependent, no treatment
Residential community	Less secure than prison	Expensive, high failure rate

A Florida Parishes Juvenile Detention Center detainee works in the center's garden in Goodbee, Louisiana. Detainees give back to the community by harvesting the produce and donating it to a local food pantry. Juvenile detainees are learning restorative justice with programs like these that teach new skills and encourage them to give back to the community.

AP Images/Daily Star/Kari Wheeler

The Concept of Restoration

According to the restorative view, crimes bring harm to the community in which they occur. The traditional justice system has done little to involve the community in the justice process. What has developed is a system of coercive punishments administered by bureaucrats that is inherently harmful to offenders and reduces the likelihood that they will ever again become productive members of society. This system relies on punishment, stigma, and disgrace. What is needed instead is a justice policy that repairs the harm caused by crime and involves all parties that have suffered from that harm, including the victim, the community, and the offender. Exhibit 10.1 sets out the principles of the restorative justice approach.

An important aspect of achieving these goals is that offenders must accept accountability for their actions and responsibility for the harm their actions caused. Only then can they be restored as productive members of their community. Restoration involves turning the justice system into a "healing" process rather than a distributor of retribution and revenge.

Most people involved in offender–victim relationships actually know one another or were related in some way before the criminal incident took place. Instead of treating one of the involved parties as a victim deserving sympathy and the other as a criminal deserving punishment, it is more productive to address the issues that produced the conflict between these people. Rather than taking sides and choosing whom to isolate and punish, society should try to reconcile the parties involved in conflict.[102] The effectiveness of justice ultimately depends on the stake a person has in the community (or a particular social group). If a person does not value her membership in the group, she will be unlikely to accept responsibility, show remorse, or repair the injuries caused by her actions.

Restoration Programs

Restoration programs try to include all the parties involved in a criminal act: the victim, the offender, and the community. Although processes differ in structure and style, they generally include the following:

- Recognition by offenders that they have caused injury to personal and social relations, and a determination and acceptance of responsibility (ideally accompanied by a statement of remorse)
- A commitment to both material reparation (e.g., monetary restitution) and symbolic reparation (e.g., an apology)
- A determination of community support and assistance for both victim and offender

The intended result of the process is to repair injuries suffered by the victim and the community, while ensuring reintegration of the offender.

Negotiation, mediation, consensus building, and peacemaking have been part of the dispute resolution process in European and Asian communities for centuries.[103] Native American people and members of Canada's First Nations have long used the type of community participation in the adjudication process (in sentencing circles, sentencing panels, and panels of elders) that restorative justice advocates are now embracing.[104]

In some Native American communities, people accused of breaking the law meet with community members, victims (if any), village elders, and agents of the justice system in a **sentencing circle**. All members of the circle express their feelings about the act that was committed and raise questions or concerns. The accused can express regret about his or her actions and a desire to change the harmful behavior. People may suggest ways in which the offender can make things up to the community and those who were harmed. A treatment program, such as Alcoholics Anonymous, may be suggested, if appropriate.

sentencing circle
A type of sentencing in which victims, family members, community members, and the offender participate in an effort to devise fair and reasonable sanctions that are ultimately aimed at reintegrating the offender into the community.

Restoration in Practice

Restorative justice policies and practices are now being adapted around the world. Restorative justice is being embraced on many levels in the justice system.

Schools Some schools have employed restorative justice practices to avoid more punitive measures such as expulsion in dealing with students involved in drug and alcohol abuse. Schools in Minnesota, Colorado, and elsewhere are trying to involve students in "relational rehabilitation" programs, which strive to improve offenders' relationships with key figures in the community who may have been harmed by their actions.[105]

Police Programs Restorative justice has also been implemented when police first encounter crime. The new community policing models can be viewed as an attempt to incorporate restorative concepts into law enforcement. Restorative justice relies on criminal justice policymakers listening to and responding to the needs of those who will be affected by their actions, and community policing relies on policies established with input and exchanges between officers and citizens.[106] The technique is also being used by police around the world. In England, police are using a format called restorative cautioning. After an arrest is made, police in England and Wales traditionally had four alternative procedures they could follow: (1) take no further action; (2) give an informal warning; (3) administer a formal police caution; or (4) decide to prosecute by sending the case to the Crown Prosecution Service. English police forces are now experimenting with a form of restorative cautioning. In this approach, a trained police facilitator uses a script to encourage an offender to take responsibility for repairing the harm caused by the offense. Sometimes the victim is present, in which case the meeting is called a restorative conference; usually, however, the victim is not present. Traditional cautioning, by contrast, lasts only a few minutes, requires no special training, and focuses on the officer explaining the possible consequences of future offending. Even though the police report that the new system seems to be working quite well (crime rates are down as much as 30 percent), some experts have questioned whether restorative cautioning can produce the results being claimed.[107]

Pretrial Programs Some jurisdictions have instituted restorative justice programs as a form of diversion from the court process. One program is called conferencing; its aim is to divert offenders from the justice system by offering them the opportunity to attend a conference to discuss and resolve the offense instead of being charged and appearing in court.[108] Conferencing is not offered when offenders wish to contest their guilt. Those who do not are referred to the conference, which normally lasts one to two hours and is attended by the victims and their supporters, the offenders and their supporters, and other relevant parties. The conference coordinator focuses the discussion on condemning the act without condemning the character of the actor. Offenders are asked to explain what happened, how they have felt about the crime, and what they think should be done. The victims and others are asked to describe the physical, financial, and emotional consequences of the crime. This discussion may lead the offenders, their families, and their friends to experience the shame of the act, prompting an apology to the victim. A plan of action is developed and signed by key participants. The plan may include the offender paying compensation to the victim, doing work for the victim or the community, or any other undertaking the participants may agree on. It is the responsibility of the conference participants to determine the outcomes that are most appropriate for these particular victims and these particular offenders.

Court Programs In the court system, restorative programs usually involve diverting the offender from the formal court process. Instead, these programs encourage meeting and reconciling the conflicts between offenders and victims via victim advocacy, mediation programs, and sentencing circles, in which crime victims and their families are brought together with offenders and their families in an effort to formulate a sanction that addresses the needs of each party. Victims are given a chance to tell their stories, and offenders can help compensate them financially or provide some service (such as repairing damaged property).[109] Again, the goal is to enable offenders to appreciate the damage they have caused, to make amends, and to be reintegrated into society. Restorative justice has found a niche all over the world. It is even being used to resolve cases in the Middle East involving Arabs and Israelis![110]

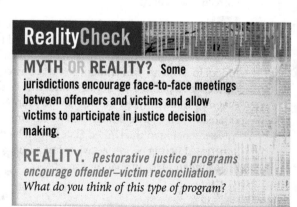

RealityCheck

MYTH OR REALITY? Some jurisdictions encourage face-to-face meetings between offenders and victims and allow victims to participate in justice decision making.

REALITY. *Restorative justice programs encourage offender–victim reconciliation. What do you think of this type of program?*

The Challenge of Restorative Justice

Although restorative justice holds great promise, there are also some concerns.[111] One issue is whether programs reach out to all members of the community. Research indicates that entry into these programs may be tilted toward white offenders and more restrictive to minorities, a condition that negates the purpose of the restorative movement.[112]

Restorative justice programs must be especially aware of cultural and social differences, which can be found throughout America's heterogeneous society.[113] What may be considered restorative in one subculture may be considered insulting and damaging in another.[114] Similarly, so many diverse programs call themselves restorative that evaluating them is difficult. Each one may be pursuing a unique objective. In other words, no single definition of restorative justice has been arrived at.[115]

Possibly the greatest challenge to restorative justice is the difficult task of balancing the needs of offenders with those of their victims. If programs focus solely on responding to the victim's needs, they may risk ignoring the offender's needs and increasing the likelihood of reoffending. Advocates of restorative justice may falsely assume that relatively brief interludes of public shaming will change deeply rooted criminal predispositions.[116] But is it reasonable to include any form of punishment or sanction in a "restorative"-based program?[117]

In contrast, programs focusing on the offender may turn off victims and their advocates. Many victims do want an apology, if it is heartfelt and genuine. But some want, even more urgently, to put the traumatic incident behind them, to retrieve stolen property being held for use at trial, and to be assured that the offender will receive treatment he is thought to need if he is not to victimize someone else. For victims such as these, restorative justice processes can seem unnecessary at best.[118]

Ethical Challenge

You are a district court judge. Before you is the case of a famous 26-year-old party-girl-model-hotel-heiress who was arrested for reckless driving at 2:00 AM, even though she was under a probation order forbidding any misbehavior and imposing an 11:00 PM curfew. The sentencing judge had warned her against any further violations and made it clear that violating the conditions of probation would not be tolerated. How would you deal with the case? Should she be jailed for her behavior, or are alternative sanctions available? How do you justify your decision, and on what theory or view of justice is it based?

Summary

LO1 Be familiar with the concept of community sentencing Community sentencing relies on the belief that the typical offender can be successfully treated while remaining in the community and, given the proper care and services, is unlikely to recidivate. There are now a great variety of community sentences, ranging from traditional probation to house arrest and placement in community correctional centers.

LO2 Know the history of community sentences The roots of community sentencing can be traced to the English common-law practice of judicial reprieve, which allowed judges to suspend punishment so that convicted offenders could seek a pardon, gather new evidence, or demonstrate that they had reformed their behavior. John Augustus of Boston is usually credited with pioneering community sentencing in the United States when he voluntarily supervised young people convicted of crime, a practice that led to the modern probation concept.

LO3 Recognize the different types of probation sentences Probationary sentences may be granted by state and federal district courts and state superior (felony) courts. Some are to a straight term of probation, while others involve a suspended sentence, a delayed sentence, or a mixed sentence involving a jail or prison stay.

LO4 Be familiar with the rules of probation When granting probation, the court sets down certain conditions or rules of behavior that the probationer is bound to obey. Rules can set curfews, prohibit behaviors such as drinking and owning a gun, and/or mandate that the probationer hold a job and not leave the jurisdiction without permission. Probation may be revoked if clients fail to comply with rules and disobey reasonable requests to meet their treatment obligations.

LO5 Know about the organization and administration of probation services Some states have a statewide probation service, but each court jurisdiction controls its local department. Other states maintain a strong statewide authority with centralized control and administration.

L06 **List and discuss the elements of a probation department's duties** Staff officers in probation departments are usually charged with five primary tasks: investigation, intake, diagnosis/risk classification, supervision, and treatment. As part of clients' entry into probation, an assessment is made about how much risk they pose to the community and themselves. On the basis of this assessment, offenders are assigned to a specific supervision level.

L07 **Be familiar with the legal rights of probationers** The U.S. Supreme Court has ruled that probationers have a unique status and therefore are entitled to fewer constitutional protections than other citizens. During the course of a probationary term, violating the rules or terms of probation or committing a new crime can result in probation being revoked.

L08 **Debate the effectiveness of probation** Probation is cost-effective. Although the failure rate seems disturbingly high, even the most serious criminals who receive

probation are less likely to recidivate than those who are sent to prison for committing similar crimes. Young males who are unemployed or who have a very low income, a prior criminal record, and a history of instability are most likely to be rearrested.

L09 **Know what is meant by intermediate sanctions** Intermediate sanctions add some other community sanction to a probation sentence, such as a fine, electronic monitoring, or house arrest. They offer effective alternatives to prisons and jails. They also have the potential to save money; although they are more expensive than traditional probation, they are far less costly than incarceration.

L010 **Define restorative justice and discuss its merits** Restorative programs stress healing and redemption rather than punishment and deterrence. Restoration means that offenders accept accountability for their actions and responsibility for the harm their actions caused. Restoration programs are now being used around the nation and involve mediation, sentencing circles, and similar non-punitive treatment efforts.

Review Questions

1. What is the purpose of probation? Identify some conditions of probation and discuss the responsibilities of the probation officer.

2. Discuss the procedures involved in probation revocation. What are the rights of the probationer? Is probation a privilege or a right?

3. Should a convicted criminal make restitution to the victim? When is restitution inappropriate? Could it be considered a bribe?

4. Should offenders be fined on the basis of the seriousness of what they did or in terms of their ability to pay? Is it fair to base day fines on wages?

Should offenders be punished more severely because they are financially successful?

5. Does house arrest involve a violation of personal freedom? Does wearing an ankle bracelet smack of "Big Brother"? Would you want the government monitoring your daily activities?

6. Do you agree that criminals can be restored through community interaction? Considering the fact that recidivism rates are so high, are traditional sanctions a waste of time and restorative ones the wave of the future?

Sheriff's Department of Wyandotte County, Kansas

11 Corrections: History, Institutions, and Populations

Learning Objectives

LO1 Understand the meaning of the term *new penology*

LO2 Be able to explain how the first penal institutions developed in Europe

LO3 Explain how William Penn revolutionized corrections

LO4 Compare the New York and Pennsylvania prison models

LO5 Chart the development of penal reform

LO6 Know how parole developed

LO7 List the purposes of jails and be familiar with the makeup of jail populations

LO8 Be familiar with the term *new-generation jail*

LO9 Classify the different types of federal and state penal institutions

LO10 Discuss prison population trends

Keaira Brown was just 13 years old when she was charged with murder and became the youngest person in Wyandotte County, Kansas, ever to be tried as an adult. Her family life was close but troubled. Her mother, Cheryl Brown, had three other children, two enrolled in local colleges. Keaira was involved in after-school activities, including playing the violin. But when her mom went to prison on a drug charge, things began to spiral downhill for Keaira, and when she was only 10 she attempted suicide. On July 23, 2008, at about 4:00 PM, Keaira was supposed to be at a summer program at the Boys and Girls Club in Kansas City. Instead, she was involved in a carjacking of Scott Sappington, Jr., a junior at Sumner Academy, who had just dropped his siblings off at their grandmother's house. When he returned to his car, neighbors heard him yell, "Hey, hey," then there was a struggle inside the car, and he was shot in the head. An investigation led to a 6-year-old who told police that a young girl told a group of children to get rid of her bloody clothes. Police distributed pictures of the bloody clothes to the media, and soon after, the clothes were traced back to Keaira Brown. ■

Prosecutors thought the murder was a result of a carjacking that went wrong, while Keaira's family claimed that she was an innocent pawn for area gang members who thought she would not be prosecuted because of her age. They were incorrect. In April, almost a year after the crime, a Wyandotte County judge ruled that Keaira should face trial as an adult. On November 9, 2010, Keaira Brown was found guilty of first-degree murder and attempted aggravated robbery. She will have to serve 20 years before being eligible for parole.

Stories such as that of Keaira Brown are certainly not unique. The Supreme Court has ruled that it is quite legal to incarcerate a juvenile in adult prison for life if they commit a capital crime.[1] So Keaira is now one of the millions of inmates in a vast correctional system that has branches in the federal, state, and county levels of government. Felons may be placed in state or federal penitentiaries (prisons), which are usually isolated, high-security structures. Misdemeanants are housed in local county jails, reformatories, or houses of correction. Juvenile offenders have their own institutions called schools, camps, ranches, or homes; these are typically nonsecure facilities that provide both confinement and rehabilitative services for young offenders. However, not all juveniles are confined in separate institutions. Some who commit serious crimes can be transferred to the adult court and serve their sentence in an adult prison with older, more experienced criminals.

The contemporary correctional system, then, encompasses a wide range of institutions ranging from nonsecure camps that house white-collar criminals to super-maximum-security institutions, such as the federal prison in Florence, Colorado, where the nation's most dangerous felons are confined.

One of the great tragedies of our time is that "correctional" institutions—whatever form they may take—do not seem to "correct," and many former inmates recidivate soon after reentering society. It can be reasonably estimated that more than half of all inmates will be back in prison within six years of their release; this means that each year about 250,000 former inmates return to prison because they failed on parole.[2]

RealityCheck

MYTH OR REALITY? The correctional system is not as effective as was hoped: recidivism rates remain unacceptably high.

REALITY. *More than half of all released inmates return to prison.*
What is it about the prison experience that causes people to fail on parole?

prison
A state or federal correctional institution for incarceration of felony offenders for terms of one year or more.

jail
A place to detain people awaiting trial, to serve as a lockup for drunks and disorderly individuals, and to confine convicted misdemeanants serving sentences of less than one year.

LO1 Understand the meaning of the term *new penology*

There has been an ongoing debate over the true role of secure corrections. Some penal experts maintain that **prisons** and **jails** should be used to keep dangerous offenders apart from society, dispensing "just deserts" for their crimes.[3] Under this model, correctional effectiveness is measured in terms of such outcomes as physical security, length of incapacitation, and inmates who return to society fearing criminal sanctions. An opposing view is that the purpose of corrections is treatment and that, when properly funded and effectively directed, correctional facilities can provide successful offender rehabilitation.[4] Numerous examples of successful treatment programs flourish in prisons. Educational programs enable inmates to get college credits, vocational training has become more sophisticated, counseling and substance abuse programs are almost universal, and every state maintains early-release and community correctional programs of some sort.

Today the desert/incapacitation model, sometimes called the *new penology*, holds sway. Rather than administer individualized treatment, decision makers rely on actuarial tables and tests to make decisions; indeed, they seem more concerned with security and "managing" large inmate populations than with treating individual offenders.[5] Critics charge that this policy has resulted in a rapidly increasing prison population that is bereft of the human touch; defenders counter that it is effective because the crime rate has declined as the number of people under lock and key has risen. The connection between a declining crime rate and a rising prison population is not lost on politicians who are eager to energize their political campaigns by advocating a "get tough" policy toward crime.[6] Nonetheless, even though the new penology dominates, correctional rehabilitation is still an important element of the justice system, and there are numerous opportunities for careers in such positions as corrections counselor, described in the Careers in Criminal Justice feature.

In this chapter, we explore the correctional system, beginning with the history and nature of correctional institutions. Then, in Chapter 12, we will examine institutional life in some detail.

The History of Correctional Institutions

The original legal punishments were typically banishment or slavery, restitution, corporal punishment, and execution. The concept of incarcerating convicted offenders for long periods of time as a punishment for their misdeeds did not become the norm of corrections until the nineteenth century.[7]

Although the use of incarceration as a routine punishment began much later, some early European institutions were created specifically to detain and punish criminal offenders. Penal institutions were constructed in England during the tenth century to hold pretrial detainees and those waiting for their sentence to be carried out.[8] During the twelfth century, King Henry II constructed a series of county jails to hold thieves and vagrants before the disposition of their sentence. In 1557, the workhouse in Brideswell was built to hold people convicted of relatively minor offenses who would work to pay off their debt to society. Those who had committed more serious offenses were held there pending execution.

Le Stinche, a prison in Florence, Italy, was used to punish offenders as early as 1301.[9] Prisoners were enclosed in separate cells, classified on the basis of gender, age, mental state, and seriousness of their crime. Furloughs and conditional release were permitted, and—perhaps for the first time—a period of incarceration replaced corporal punishment for some offenses. Although Le Stinche existed for 500 years, relatively little is known about its administration or whether this early example of incarceration was unique to Florence.

Jail conditions were deplorable because jailers ran them for personal gain. The fewer services provided, the greater their profit. Early jails were catchall institutions that held not only criminal offenders awaiting trial but also vagabonds, debtors, the mentally ill, and assorted others.

Careers in Criminal Justice

CORRECTIONS COUNSELOR

Duties and Characteristics of the Job
- Review the situation of individual offenders and determine the most effective method of rehabilitation.
- Create, enact, manage, and sometimes evaluate programs designed to improve the psychosocial functioning of offenders.
- Provide counseling and educational sessions, survey the needs of offenders, and prepare reports for court.
- Counselors can choose a specialization, such as substance abuse or juvenile rehabilitation.
- Corrections counselors most often work in an office setting.
- Counseling can be a stressful job, considering the population being served, the often serious nature of their problems, and the pressure for immediate results.

Job Outlook
- The employment of counselors is expected to grow at a faster than average rate in the near future.
- The expansion of the prison system means that opportunities for employment as a corrections counselor are good.
- The need for correctional counselors should remain strong, especially if violent crime rates trend upward and courts mandate treatment for all inmates.

Salary
- Median salary is about $48,000. Positions at the federal level will generally pay a higher salary. Those with graduate-level education are also more likely to have higher salaries and greater opportunities for advancement.

Qualifications
- Special qualifications such as expertise working with drug addicts or violent offenders can lead to a higher-paying position.
- In addition to educational requirements, for many entry-level jobs some previous work experience will be necessary, such as substance abuse counseling or corrections casework.
- The ability to speak a second language is also an advantage.
- Personality characteristics and skills such as the desire to help others and the ability to communicate effectively are important.
- Due to the settings and populations that counselors work with, a future counselor will need to pass a background check and gain security clearance at the appropriate level. Additionally, certain states require certification before a corrections counselor can work in that state.

Education and Training
- Future corrections counselors should have a bachelor's degree in a field such as social work, criminal justice, or psychology.
- Additional education at the master's level in these fields may be necessary to advance in the field or to achieve certain positions. Qualifications for higher-paid positions are more demanding.
- Counselors' education and work experience should familiarize them with the criminal justice system and prepare them for determining how to reduce a client's chances of recidivism as well as how to deal with unwilling clients.
- For some positions, clinical training can take the place of experience.

Word to the Wise
- Counselors should be prepared to work with needy, troubled people. Burnout can be a problem. It is important not to personalize the work or take it home.

From 1776 to 1785, a growing inmate population that could no longer be transported to North America forced the English to house prisoners on **hulks**—abandoned ships anchored in harbors.

The hulks became infamous for their degrading conditions and brutal punishments but were not abandoned until 1858. The writings of John Howard, the reform-oriented sheriff of Bedfordshire, drew attention to the squalid conditions in British penal institutions. His famous book *The State of the Prisons* (1777) condemned the lack of basic care given English inmates awaiting trial or serving sentences.[10] Howard's efforts to create humane standards in the British penal system resulted in the Penitentiary Act, by which Parliament established a more orderly penal system, with periodic inspections, elimination of the fee system, and greater consideration for inmates.

hulks
Abandoned ships anchored in harbors and used in eighteenth-century England to house prisoners.

LO2 Be able to explain how the first penal institutions developed in Europe

The Origin of Corrections in the United States

Although Europe had jails and a variety of other penal facilities, correctional reform was first instituted in the United States. The first American jail was built in James City in the Virginia colony in the early seventeenth century. However, the modern American correctional system had its origin in Pennsylvania under the leadership of William Penn.

At the end of the seventeenth century, Penn revised Pennsylvania's criminal code to forbid torture and the capricious use of mutilation and physical punishment. These penalties were replaced with imprisonment at hard labor, moderate flogging, fines, and forfeiture of property. All lands and goods belonging to felons were to be used to make restitution to the victims of their crimes, with restitution being limited to twice the value of the damages. Felons who owned no property were assigned by law to the prison workhouse until the victim was compensated.

Penn ordered that a new type of institution be built to replace the widely used public forms of punishment—stocks, pillories, gallows, and branding irons. Each county was instructed to build a house of corrections similar to today's jails. County trustees or commissioners were responsible for raising money to build the jails and providing for their maintenance, although they were operated by the local sheriff. Penn's reforms remained in effect until his death in 1718, at which time the criminal penal code was changed back to open public punishment and harsh brutality.

One of the first American penal institutions was Newgate Prison, which opened in 1773 in Connecticut on the site of an abandoned copper mine and was in use until the 1820s.[11] In 1785, Castle Island prison was opened in Massachusetts and operated for about 15 years. The origin of the modern correctional system is usually traced to eighteenth-century developments.

The Development of Prisons

Why did prisons develop at this time? One reason was that during this period of enlightenment, a concerted effort was made to alleviate the harsh punishments and torture that had been the norm. The interest of religious groups, such as the Quakers, in prison reform was prompted in part by humanitarian ideals. Another factor was the economic potential of prison industry, which was viewed as a valuable economic asset in times of short labor supply.[12]

In 1776, these trends led Pennsylvania once again to adopt William Penn's code, and in 1787 a group of Quakers led by Benjamin Rush formed the Philadelphia Society for Alleviating the Miseries of Public Prisons. The aim of the society was to bring some degree of humane and orderly treatment to the growing penal system. The Quakers' influence on the legislature resulted in limiting the use of the death penalty to cases involving treason, murder, rape, or arson. Their next step was to reform the institutional system so that the prison could serve as a suitable alternative to physical punishment.

The only models of custodial institutions at that time were the local county jails that Penn had established. These facilities were designed to detain offenders, to securely incarcerate convicts awaiting other punishment, or to hold offenders who were working off their crimes. The Pennsylvania jails placed men, women, and children of all ages indiscriminately in one room. Liquor was often freely sold.

Under pressure from the Quakers to improve these conditions, the Pennsylvania legislature in 1790 called for the renovation of the prison system. The eventual result was the creation of a separate wing of Philadelphia's **Walnut Street Jail** to house convicted felons (except those sentenced to death). Prisoners were placed in solitary cells, where they remained in isolation and did not have the right to work.[13] Quarters that contained the solitary or separate cells were called the **penitentiary house**, as was already the custom in England.

L03 Explain how William Penn revolutionized corrections

Walnut Street Jail
An eighteenth-century institution that housed convicted criminals in Philadelphia.

penitentiary house
Term used for early prisons, so named because inmates were supposed to have penitence for their sins.

The first execution by electrocution, of William Kemmler, for murder, at Auburn Prison, New York, August 6, 1890. While at first considered efficient and "humane," the electric chair has been replaced by lethal injection. Do you consider that an improvement?

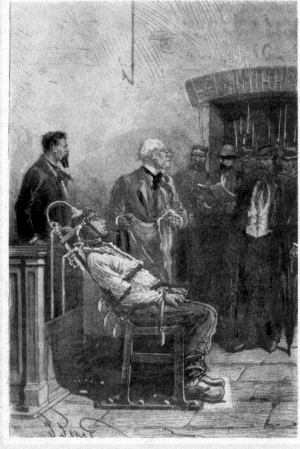

The New York and Pennsylvania Systems

As the nineteenth century got under way, both the Pennsylvania and the New York prison systems were experiencing difficulties maintaining the ever-increasing numbers of convicted criminals. Initially, administrators dealt with the problem by increasing the use of pardons, relaxing prison discipline, and limiting supervision.

In 1816, New York built a new prison at Auburn, hoping to alleviate some of the overcrowding at Newgate. The Auburn Prison design became known as the **congregate system** because most prisoners ate and worked in groups. In 1819, construction began on a wing of solitary cells to house unruly prisoners. Three classes of prisoners were then created. One group remained continually in solitary confinement as a result of breaches of prison discipline, the second group was allowed labor as an occasional form of recreation, and the third and largest class worked together during the day and was separated only at night.

The philosophy of the Auburn prison system was crime prevention through fear of punishment and silent confinement. The worst felons were to be cut off from all contact with other prisoners, and although they were treated and fed relatively well, they had no hope of pardon to relieve their solitude or isolation. For a time, some of the worst convicts were forced to remain alone and silent during the entire day. This practice, which led to mental breakdowns, suicides, and self-mutilations, was abolished in 1823. The solution adopted at Auburn was to keep convicts in

congregate system
Prison system first used in New York that allowed inmates to engage in group activities such as work, meals, and recreation.

MYTH OR REALITY? The first correctional institutions were actually considered a "liberal" reform.

REALITY. *Although they might be considered a harsh form of punishment today, prisons were originally considered a humanitarian reform sponsored by religious groups.*

Considering that recidivism rates are so high, should we embrace the treatment and rehabilitation elements of incarceration rather than focusing on prison as a means of dispensing punishment?

Pennsylvania system
The correctional model used in Pennsylvania that isolated inmates from one another so they would be prevented from planning escapes, make them easy to manage and give them time to experience penitence.

LO4 Compare the New York and Pennsylvania prison models

separate cells at night but allow them to work together during the day under enforced silence.

Regimentation became the standard mode of prison life. Convicts did not simply walk from place to place; instead, they went in close order and single file, each looking over the shoulder of the preceding person, faces inclined to the right, feet moving in unison. The lockstep prison shuffle was developed at Auburn and is still used in some institutions today.[14] The inmates' time was regulated by bells telling them when to wake up, sleep, and work. The system was so like the military that many of its early administrators were recruited from the armed services.

In 1818, Pennsylvania took the radical step of establishing a prison that placed each inmate in a single cell for the duration of his sentence. Classifications were abolished because each cell was intended as a miniature prison that would prevent the inmates from contaminating one another. The new Pennsylvania state prison, called the Western Penitentiary, had an unusual architectural design. It was built in a semicircle, with the cells positioned along its circumference. Built back to back, some cells faced the boundary wall, and others faced the internal area of the circle. Its inmates were kept in solitary confinement almost constantly, being allowed out for about an hour a day for exercise. In 1829, a second, similar penitentiary using the isolate system was built in Philadelphia and was called the Eastern Penitentiary.

Supporters of the **Pennsylvania system** believed that the penitentiary was truly a place to do penance. By removing the sinner from society and allowing the prisoner a period of isolation in which to consider the evils of crime, the Pennsylvania system reflected the influence of religion and religious philosophy on corrections. Its supporters believed that solitary confinement with in-cell labor would make work so attractive that upon release, the inmate would be well suited to resume a productive existence in society.

The Pennsylvania system eliminated the need for large numbers of guards or disciplinary measures. Isolated from one another, inmates could not plan escapes or collectively break rules. When discipline was a problem, however, the whip and the iron gag were used.

Advocates of the Auburn system believed that theirs was the cheapest and most productive way to reform prisoners and that solitary confinement as practiced in Pennsylvania was cruel and inhumane. In contrast, advocates of Pennsylvania's isolation model argued that their system was quiet, efficient, humane, and well ordered, yielding the ultimate correctional facility.[15] They considered the Auburn system a breeding place for criminal associations, because it allowed inmates to get to know one another.

New York's congregate model eventually prevailed and spread throughout the United States. Many of its features are still used today. Its innovations included congregate working conditions, the use of solitary confinement to punish unruly inmates, military regimentation, and discipline. Concept Summary 11.1 describes the differences between these two prison systems.

Concept Summary 11.1

Early Correctional Systems

Prison	Structure	Living Conditions	Activities	Discipline
Auburn system	Tiered cells	Congregate	Group work	Silence, harsh punishment
Pennsylvania system	Single cells set in semicircle	Isolated	In-cell work, Bible study	Silence, harsh punishment

Corrections in the Nineteenth Century

The prison of the nineteenth century was remarkably similar to that of today. The congregate system was adopted in all states except Pennsylvania. Prisons were overcrowded, and the single-cell principle was often ignored. Although the prison was viewed as an improvement over capital and corporal punishment, it quickly became the scene of depressed conditions. Inmates were treated harshly and routinely whipped and tortured. Prison brutality flourished in these institutions, which had originally been devised as a more humane correctional alternative. In these early penal institutions, brutal corporal punishment was doled out indoors where, hidden from public view, it could become even more savage.[16]

Prison industry developed and became the predominant theme around which institutions were organized. Some prisons used the **contract system**, in which officials sold the labor of inmates to private businesses. Sometimes the contractor supervised the inmates inside the prison itself. Under the **convict-lease system**, the state leased its prisoners to a business for a fixed annual fee and gave up supervision and control. Finally, some institutions had prisoners produce goods for the prison's own use.[17]

The development of prison industry quickly led to the abuse of inmates, who were forced to work for almost no wages, and to profiteering by dishonest administrators and business owners. During the Civil War era, prisons were major manufacturers of clothes, shoes, boots, furniture, and the like. Beginning in the 1870s, opposition by trade unions sparked restrictions on interstate commerce in prison goods. The prison, like the police department, became the scene of political intrigue and of efforts by political administrators to control the hiring of personnel and dispensing of patronage.

contract system
The practice of correctional officials selling the labor of inmates to private businesses.

convict-lease system
The practice of leasing inmates to a business for a fixed annual fee.

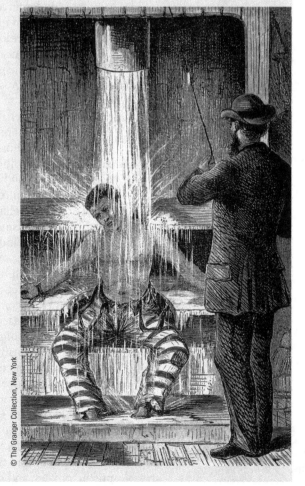

Prison in the late nineteenth century was a brutal place. This line engraving from 1869 shows an inmate undergoing a water torture in New York's Sing Sing Prison.

© The Granger Collection, New York

Reform Efforts The National Congress of Penitentiary and Reformatory Discipline, held in Cincinnati in 1870, heralded a new era of prison reform. Organized by penologists Enoch Wines and Theodore Dwight, the congress provided a forum for corrections experts from around the nation to call for the treatment, education, and training of inmates. By 1870, Zebulon Brockway, warden of the Elmira Reformatory in New York, advocated individualized treatment, the indeterminate sentence, and parole. The reformatory program initiated by Brockway included elementary education for illiterates, designated library hours, lectures by faculty members of the local Elmira College, and a group of vocational training shops. From 1888 to 1920, Elmira administrators used military-like training to discipline the inmates and organize the institution. The military organization could be seen in every aspect of the institution: schooling, manual training, sports, supervision of inmates, and even parole decisions.[18] The cost to the state of the institution's operations was to be held to a minimum.

L05 **Chart the development of penal reform**

RealityCheck

MYTH OR REALITY? Educating inmates began in the 1960s during the Kennedy administration.

MYTH. *The first attempts to educate inmates actually were developed during the nineteenth century.*

Is it fair to provide inmates with college courses, while many nonoffenders struggle to pay tuition?

The Development of Parole In the early seventeenth century, English judges began to spare the lives of offenders by banishing them to the newly formed overseas colonies. In 1617, the Privy Counsel of the British Parliament standardized this practice by passing an order granting reprieves and stays of execution to convicts willing to be transported to the colonies. Transportation was viewed as an answer to labor shortages caused by war, disease, and the opening of new commercial markets.

In 1717, the British Parliament passed legislation embodying the concept of *property in service*, which transferred control of prisoners to a contractor or shipmaster until the expiration of their sentences. When the prisoners arrived in the colonies, their services could be resold to the highest bidder. After sale, an offender's status changed from convict to indentured servant.

Transportation quickly became the most common sentence for theft offenders. In the American colonies, property in service had to be abandoned after the revolution. Thereafter, Australia, claimed as a British colony in 1770, became the destination for most transported felons. From 1815 to 1850, large numbers of inmates were shipped to Australia to serve as indentured servants working for plantation owners, in mines, or on sheep stations.

The English Penal Servitude Act of 1853 all but ended transportation and substituted imprisonment as a punishment. Part of this act made it possible to grant a *ticket-of-leave* to those who had served a sufficient portion of their prison sentence. This form of conditional release permitted former prisoners to be at large in specified areas. The conditions of their release were written on a license that the former inmates were required to carry with them at all times. Conditions usually included sobriety, lawful behavior, and hard work. Many releasees violated these provisions, prompting criticism of the system. Eventually, members of prisoner aid societies helped supervise and care for releasees.

The concept of parole spread to the United States. As early as 1822, volunteers from the Philadelphia-based Society for Alleviating the Miseries of Public Prisons began to help offenders once they were released from prison. In 1851, the society appointed two agents to work with inmates discharged from Pennsylvania penal institutions. Massachusetts appointed an agent in 1845 to help released inmates obtain jobs, clothing, and transportation.

In the 1870s, using a carefully weighted screening procedure, Zebulon Brockway selected rehabilitated offenders from Elmira Reformatory for early release under the supervision of citizen volunteers known as *guardians*. The guardians met with the parolees at least once a month and submitted written reports on their progress. The parole concept spread rapidly. Ohio created the first parole agency in 1884. By 1901, as many as 20 states had created some type of parole agency. By 1927, only three states (Florida, Mississippi, and Virginia) had not established some sort of parole release. Parole had become institutionalized as the primary method of release for prison inmates, and half of all inmates released in the United States were paroled.[19]

L06 **Know how parole developed**

Prisons in the Twentieth Century

The early twentieth century was a time of contrasts in the U.S. prison system.[20] At one extreme were those who advocated reform, such as the Mutual Welfare League, led by Thomas Mott Osborne. Prison reform groups proposed better treatment for inmates, an end to harsh corporal punishment, the creation of meaningful prison industries, and educational programs. Reformers argued that prisoners should not be isolated from society and that the best elements of society—education, religion, meaningful work, and self-governance—should be brought to the prison. Osborne went so far as to spend a week in New York's notorious Sing Sing Prison to learn firsthand about its conditions.

In time, some of the more rigid prison rules gave way to liberal reform. By the mid-1930s, few prisons required inmates to wear the red-and-white-striped convict suit; nondescript gray uniforms were substituted. The code of silence ended, as did the lockstep shuffle. Prisoners were allowed "the freedom of the yard" to mingle and exercise an hour or two each day.[21] Movies and radio appeared in the 1930s. Visiting policies and mail privileges were liberalized.

A more important trend was the development of specialized prisons designed to treat particular types of offenders. In New York, for example, the prisons at Clinton and Auburn were viewed as industrial facilities for hard-core inmates, Great Meadow was an agricultural center for nondangerous offenders, and Dannemora was a facility for the criminally insane. In California, San Quentin housed inmates considered salvageable by correctional authorities, and Folsom was reserved for hard-core offenders.[22]

Prison industry also evolved. Opposition by organized labor helped put an end to the convict-lease system and forced inmate labor. By 1900, a number of states had restricted the sale of prisoner-made goods on the open market. The worldwide Great Depression, which began in 1929, prompted industry and union leaders to further pressure state legislators to reduce competition from prison industries. A series of ever more restrictive federal legislative initiatives led to the Sumners-Ashurst Act (1940), which made it a federal offense to transport interstate commerce goods made in prison for private use, regardless of the laws of the state receiving the goods.[23] The restrictions imposed by the federal government helped to severely curtail prison industry for 40 years. Private entrepreneurs shunned prison investments because they were no longer profitable. The result was inmate idleness and make-work jobs.[24]

Despite some changes and reforms, the prison in the mid-twentieth century remained a destructive total institution. Although some aspects of inmate life improved, severe discipline, harsh rules, and solitary confinement were the way of life in prison.

Contemporary Correctional Institutions

The modern era has been a period of change and turmoil in the nation's correctional system. Three trends stand out. First, between 1960 and 1980, came the prisoners' rights movement. After many years of indifference (the so-called hands-off doctrine), state and federal courts ruled in case after case that institutionalized inmates had rights to freedom of religion and speech, medical care, procedural due process, and proper living conditions. Inmates won rights unheard of in the nineteenth and early twentieth centuries. Since 1980, however, an increasingly conservative judiciary has curtailed the growth of inmate rights.

Second, violence within the correctional system became a national concern. Well-publicized riots at New York's Attica Prison and the New Mexico State Penitentiary drew attention to the potential for death and destruction that lurks in every prison. Prison rapes and killings have become commonplace. The locus of control in many prisons has shifted from the correctional staff to violent inmate gangs. In reaction, some administrators have tried to improve conditions and provide innovative programs that give inmates a voice in running the institution. Another reaction has been to tighten discipline and build new super-maximum-security prisons

One of the most dramatic incidents in corrections history took place at the Attica State Prison in Attica, New York, in September 1971, when inmates rioted and seized control of the prison. During the following four days of negotiations, authorities agreed to 28 of the prisoners' demands, but they would not agree to demands for complete amnesty from criminal prosecution for those involved in the prison takeover, or to demands for the removal of Attica's superintendent. Under orders from Governor Nelson Rockefeller, state police took back control of the prison, using shotguns and tear gas. By the time the uprising was put down, more than 43 people had been killed, including 10 correctional officers and civilian employees, some of whom died from "friendly fire."

AP Photo

medical model

A correctional philosophy grounded on the belief that inmates are sick people who need treatment rather than punishment in order to help them reform.

to control the most dangerous offenders. The problem of prison overcrowding has made efforts to improve conditions extremely difficult.

Third, the view that traditional correctional rehabilitation efforts have failed prompted many penologists to reconsider the purpose of incarcerating criminals. Between 1960 and 1980, it was common for correctional administrators to cling to the **medical model**, which viewed inmates as sick people who were suffering from some social malady that prevented them from adjusting to society. Correctional treatment could help cure them and enable them to live productive lives once they returned to the community. In the 1970s, efforts were also made to help offenders become reintegrated into society by providing them with new career opportunities that relied on work-release programs. Inmates were allowed to work outside the institution during the day and return in the evening. Some were given extended furloughs in the community. Work-release became a political issue when, in a famous incident, Willie Horton, a furloughed inmate from Massachusetts, raped a young woman. Criticism of the state's "liberal" furlough program helped Vice President George H. W. Bush defeat Massachusetts Governor Michael S. Dukakis for the U.S. presidency in 1988. In the aftermath of the Horton case, a number of states, including Massachusetts, restricted their furlough policies.

Prisons have come to be viewed as places for control, incapacitation, and punishment, instead of sites for rehabilitation and reform. Advocates of the "no-frills," or penal harm, movement believe that if prison is a punishing experience, would-be criminals will be deterred from committing crimes and current inmates will be encouraged to go straight. Nonetheless, efforts to use correctional institutions as treatment facilities have not ended, and such innovations as the development of private industries on prison grounds have kept the rehabilitative ideal alive.

The pressure on correctional institutions caused by overpopulation and the burden of constantly increasing correctional costs have prompted the development of alternatives to incarceration, such as intensive probation supervision, house arrest, and electronic monitoring (see Chapter 10). What has developed is a dual correctional policy: keep as many nonviolent offenders out of the correctional system as possible by means of community-based programs; incarcerate dangerous, violent offenders for long periods of time.[25] These efforts have been compromised by a growing get-tough stance in judicial and legislative sentencing policy, accented by mandatory minimum sentences for gun crimes and drug trafficking. Despite the development of alternatives to incarceration, the number of people under lock and key has remained stubbornly high.

The following sections review the most prominent types of correctional facilities in operation today.

Jails

The nation's jails are institutional facilities with five primary purposes:

- They detain accused offenders who cannot make or are not eligible for bail prior to trial.
- They hold convicted offenders who are awaiting sentence.
- They serve as the principal institution of secure confinement for offenders convicted of misdemeanors.
- They hold probationers and parolees picked up for violations and waiting for a hearing.
- They house felons when state prisons are overcrowded.

A number of formats are used to jail offenders. About 15,000 local jurisdictions maintain short-term police or municipal lockups that house offenders for no more than 48 hours before a bail hearing can be held; thereafter, detainees are kept in the county jail.

Jail Populations and Trends

After rising for more than a decade, the number of people being held in jail began to decline in 2009, and by 2010 there were about 750,000 jail inmates.[26] This is more than 242 inmates for every 100,000 U.S. residents, down from peak in 2009 of about 260. This recent downward trend in jail population may be a reflection of a declining U.S. crime rate and greater reliance on alternatives to incarceration such as probation, electronic monitoring, and house arrest.

Who goes to jail? Almost 9 out of every 10 jail inmates are adult males, and although whites make up more than 40 percent of the jail population, a disproportionate number of jail inmates are minority group members, a finding that reflects the social and economic disparities in our nation. African Americans are nearly five times more likely than whites, nearly three times more likely than Hispanics, and over nine times more likely than persons of other races to have been in jail; this pattern has not changed for the past decade. Disproportionate minority representation in jail may be responsible, in part, for race-based disparity in the ability to obtain bail, a practice that can have long-term consequences: pretrial detainees tend to get longer prison sentences and are more likely to be incarcerated than those released on bail. Minority over-representation in jail may be the first step to subsequent over-representation in prison.

At one time many thousands of minor children were held in jails as runaways, truants, and so on. The number of juveniles held in adult jails has been in decline since 1995, a result of ongoing government initiatives to remove juveniles from adult facilities; nonetheless, about 7,500 minors are still being held in adult jails each day, a number that has remained stable for the past decade.

Jail Conditions

Jails are usually a low-priority item in the criminal justice system. Because they are often administered on a county level, jail services have not been sufficiently regulated nor has a unified national policy been developed to mandate what constitutes adequate jail conditions. Consequently, jails in some counties are physically deteriorated, holding dangerous and troubled people, many of whom suffer emotional problems that remain untreated. It is not surprising, then, that although the suicide rate has declined significantly, the percentage of jail inmates who take their own lives is still higher than that of the general population. In a recent (2010) survey, the National Center on Institutions and Alternatives (NCIA) found a dramatic decrease in the rate of suicide in county jails during the past 20 years. The suicide rate in county jails was calculated to be 38 deaths per 100,000 inmates, which was approximately three times greater than that in the general population of the United States (at 11 deaths per 100,000 citizens), but about a 70 precent decrease from the 107 suicides per 100,000 inmates 20 years ago.[27] Why have jail suicides declined? One reason may be greater recognition of the problem and efforts to provide services to the jail population, a significant portion of which have psychological and substance abuse problems and a history of past suicide attemts. Another possible answer may be found in the development of new-generation jails, discussed below.

RealityCheck

MYTH OR REALITY? Many jail inmates suffer from social and mental problems.

REALITY. *Jail inmates suffer from severe social and psychological problems, including mental illness.*

What can be done to address this problem, or can nothing be accomplished?

New-Generation Jails

To relieve overcrowding and improve effectiveness, a jail-building boom has been under way. Many of the new jails are using modern designs referred to as "new-generation jails."[28] Traditional jails are constructed and use what is referred to as the linear/intermittent surveillance model. Jails using this design are rectangular, with corridors leading to either single- or multiple-occupancy cells arranged at right angles to the corridor. Correctional officers must patrol to see into cells or housing areas, and when they are in a position to observe one cell they cannot observe others; unobserved inmates are essentially unsupervised.

In contrast, new-generation jails allow for continuous observation of residents. There are two types: direct-supervision and indirect-supervision jails. Direct-supervision jails contain a cluster of cells surrounding a living area or "pod," which has tables, chairs, televisions, and other material. A correctional officer is stationed within the pod. The officer can observe the inmates continuously and is able to relate to them on a personal level. Placing the officer in the pod achieves an increased awareness of the behaviors and needs of the inmates. This results in a safer environment for both staff and inmates. Because interaction between inmates is constantly and closely monitored, dissension can be quickly detected before it escalates. During the day, inmates stay in the open area (dayroom) and typically are not permitted to go into their rooms except with permission of the officer in charge. The officer controls door locks to cells from the control panel. In

Former Boston University medical student Philip Markoff stands with his attorney John Salsberg during his arraignment in Suffolk Superior Court on June 22, 2009, in Boston. Markoff, the so-called Craigslist Killer, was later found dead of apparent suicide in his jail cell on August 15, 2010. Jail suicides are common but not unexpected considering that the population is troubled, volatile, and often involved in substance and alcohol abuse. Do you think the format and structure of the new-generation jails help reduce suicide?

AP Photo/Bizuayehu Tesfaye, Pool

case of trouble or if the officer leaves the station for an extended period of time, command of this panel can be switched to a panel at a remote location, known as central control. The officer usually wears a device that permits immediate communication with central control, and the area is also covered by a video camera monitored by an officer in the central control room. Indirect-supervision jails are similar in construction, but the correctional officer's station is located inside a secure room. Microphones and speakers inside the living unit permit the officer to hear and communicate with inmates.

LO8 Be familiar with the term *new-generation jail*

Prisons

The Federal Bureau of Prisons and every state government maintain closed correctional facilities, also called prisons, penitentiaries, or reformatories. The most recent government figures show federal, state, and local governments spent close to $70 billion on corrections in a single year, up from about $12 billion in 1986; this amounts to an annual cost of about $125 per year for every American citizen.[29]

The prison is the final repository for the most troubled criminal offenders. Many come from distressed backgrounds and have little hope or opportunity; all too many have emotional problems and grew up in abusive households. A majority are alcohol and drug dependent at the time of their arrest. Those considered both dangerous and incorrigible may find themselves in super-maximum-security prisons, where they spend most of their days confined to their cells.

Types of Prisons

There are more than 1,700 public adult correctional facilities housing state prisoners. In addition, there are about 100 federal prisons and more than 400 privately run institutions. Usually, prisons are organized or classified on three levels—maximum, medium, and minimum security—and each has distinct characteristics.

Maximum-Security Prisons Housing the most notorious criminals, and often the subject of films and stories, **maximum-security prisons** are probably the institutions most familiar to the public. Famous "max prisons" have included Sing Sing, Joliet, Attica, Walpole, and the most fearsome prison of all, the now-closed federal facility on Alcatraz Island known as the Rock.

A typical maximum-security facility is fortress-like, surrounded by stone walls with guard towers at strategic places. These walls may be 25 feet high, and sometimes inner and outer walls divide the prison into courtyards. Barbed wire or electrified fences are used to discourage escape. High security, armed guards, and stone walls give the inmate the sense that the facility is impregnable and reassure the citizens outside that convicts will be completely incapacitated. Because they fear that violence may flair up at any minute, prison administrators have been quick to adapt the latest high-tech measures to help them maintain security, a topic covered in the Criminal Justice and Technology feature.

Inmates live in interior, metal-barred cells that contain their own plumbing and sanitary facilities and are locked securely either by key or by electronic device. Cells are organized in sections called blocks, and in large prisons, a number of cell blocks make up a wing. During the day, the inmates engage in closely controlled activities: meals, workshops, education, and so on. Rule violators may be confined to their cells, and working and other shared recreational activities are viewed as privileges.

The byword of the maximum-security prison is "security." Correctional workers are made aware that each inmate may be a dangerous criminal or violent, and as a result, the utmost security must be maintained. These prisons are designed to eliminate hidden corners where people can congregate, and passages are constructed so that they can be easily blocked off to quell disturbances.

Super-Maximum-Security Prisons Some states have constructed **super-maximum-security prisons** (supermax prisons) to house the most predatory criminals. These

maximum-security prison
A correctional institution that houses dangerous felons and maintains strict security measures, high walls, and limited contact with the outside world.

super-maximum-security prison
The newest form of a maximum-security prison that uses high-level security measures to incapacitate the nation's most dangerous criminals. Most inmates are in lockdown 23 hours a day.

CRIMINAL JUSTICE AND TECHNOLOGY

Technocorrections: Contemporary Correctional Technology

Technical experts have identified numerous areas of correctional management that can be aided by information technology (IT), including reception and commitment; sentence and time accounting; classification; caseload management; security; discipline; housing/bed management; medical services; grievances; programs; scheduling; investigations/gang management; property; trust accounting; visitation; release and discharge; and community supervision. Because there are so many areas where IT can be applied within correctional establishments, prison administrators have begun to take advantage of the potential offered by the new technologies. How has IT been applied within prison walls? A few examples follow.

GROUND-PENETRATING RADAR

Ground-penetrating radar (GPR) can locate tunnels that inmates use to escape. GPR works almost like an old-fashioned Geiger counter, but instead of detecting metal, the system detects changes in ground composition, including voids such as those created by a tunnel.

HEARTBEAT MONITORING

Now it is possible to prevent escapes by monitoring inmates' heartbeats! The Advanced Vehicle Interrogation and Notification System (AVIAN) detects the presence of persons trying to escape by hiding in vehicles. Using the data from seismic sensors that are placed on the vehicle, the AVIAN reads the shock wave generated by the beating heart, which couples to any surface or object with which the body is in contact. It collects the data and analyzes it using advanced signal-processing algorithms to detect a person hiding in a vehicle such as a large truck in less than two minutes. The system works by accounting for all the frequencies of movement in the vehicle, such as the expansion and contraction of an engine or rain hitting the roof.

BACKSCATTER IMAGING SYSTEM FOR CONCEALED WEAPONS

This system uses a backscatter imager to detect weapons and contraband. The primary advantage of this device over current walk-through portals is that it can detect nonmetallic as well as metallic weapons. It uses low-power x-rays equal to about five minutes of exposure to the sun at sea level. Although these x-rays penetrate clothing, they do not penetrate the body.

BODY-SCANNING SCREENING SYSTEM

This is a stationary screening system to detect nonmetallic weapons and contraband in the lower body cavities. It uses simplified magnetic resonance imaging (MRI) as a noninvasive alternative to x-ray and physical body cavity searches. The stationary screening system makes use of first-generation medical MRI.

PERSONAL ALARM LOCATION SYSTEM

It is now possible for prison employees to carry a tiny transmitter linking them with a computer in a central control room. In an emergency, they can hit an alarm button and transmit to a computer that automatically records whose distress button has been pushed. An architectural map of the facility instantly appears on screen, showing the exact location of the staff member in need of assistance.

BIOMETRIC RECOGNITION

A new biometric system uses facial recognition by matching more than 200 individual points on the human face with a digitally stored image. The system is used to control access in buildings and rooms inside buildings. It is now available and will become much more common in the near future.

CRITICAL THINKING

1. *Some elements of technocorrections intrude on the privacy of inmates. Should the need for security outweigh an inmate's right to privacy?*
2. *Should probationers and parolees be monitored with modern technology? Do they deserve more privacy than incarcerated inmates?*

high-security institutions can be independent correctional centers or locked wings of existing prisons.[30] Some supermax prisons lock inmates in their cells 22 to 24 hours a day, never allowing them out unless they are shackled.[31]

The 484-bed facility in Florence, Colorado, has the most sophisticated security measures in the United States, including 168 video cameras and 1,400 electronically controlled gates. Inside the cells, all furniture is unmovable; the desk, bed, and TV stand are made of cement. All potential weapons, including soap dishes, toilet seats, and toilet handles, have been removed. The cement walls are 5,000-pound quality, and steel bars crisscross every eight inches inside the walls. Cells are angled so that inmates can see neither each other nor the outside. This cuts down on communication and denies inmates a sense of location, to prevent escapes.

A number of experts have given supermax prisons mixed reviews. Although they can achieve correctional benefits by enhancing security and quality of life, critics believe that they infringe directly on the right of inmates to due process because they deprive them of such basic rights such as human contact; they also eliminate any opportunity for rehabilitation.[32]

Some recent research by Daniel Mears and his colleagues on supermax prisons yielded mixed results. Mears, along with Jamie Watson, conducted surveys of correctional officials and found that, on the one hand, supermax prisons may actually enhance the quality of life of inmates and consequently improve their mental health. They increase privacy, reduce danger, and even provide creature comforts (such as TV sets) that are unavailable in general-population prisons. Staff report less stress and fear because they have to contend with fewer disruptive inmates.

On the other hand, Mears and Watson found that supermax prisons also have some unintended negative consequences. Staff may have too much control over inmates—a condition that damages staff–inmate relationships. Long hours of isolation may be associated with mental illness and psychological disturbances. Supermax inmates seem to have a more difficult time readjusting upon release. A stay in a supermax prison inhibits reintegration into other prisons, communities, and families. In another study, Mears and Jennifer Castro surveyed wardens and found that even though they seem to favor supermax prisons, they also expressed concern that the general public consider supermax institutions inhumane, that they drain limited funds from state budgets, and that they produce increases in litigation and court interventions, as well as increased recidivism and reentry failure among released inmates.[33]

RealityCheck

MYTH OR REALITY? Super-maximum-security prisons are highly effective.

MYTH. *Although supermax prisons provide high security, they also produce maladjusted residents who have high failure rates upon release.*

Would you use supermax prisons if you were the head of the state corrections department?

Medium-Security Prisons Although they are similar in appearance to maximum-security prisons, in **medium-security prisons** the security and atmosphere are neither so tense nor so vigilant. Medium-security prisons are also surrounded by walls, but there may be fewer guard towers or other security precautions; visitations with personal contact may be allowed. Although most prisoners are housed in cells, individual honor rooms in medium-security prisons are used to reward those who make exemplary rehabilitation efforts. Finally, medium-security prisons promote greater treatment efforts, and the relaxed atmosphere allows freedom of movement for rehabilitation workers and other therapeutic personnel.

medium-security prison
A less secure institution that houses nonviolent offenders and provides more opportunities for contact with the outside world.

Minimum-Security Prisons Operating without armed guards or perimeter walls, **minimum-security prisons** usually house the most trustworthy and least violent offenders; white-collar criminals may be their most common occupants. Inmates are allowed a great deal of personal freedom. Instead of being marched to activities by guards, they are summoned by bells or loudspeaker announcements, and they assemble on their own. Work furloughs and educational releases are encouraged, and vocational training is of the highest level. Dress codes are lax, and inmates are allowed to grow beards or mustaches and to demonstrate other individual characteristics.

minimum-security prison
The least secure institution, which houses white-collar and nonviolent offenders, maintains few security measures, and has liberal furlough and visitation policies.

Minimum-security facilities may have dormitories or small private rooms for inmates. Prisoners are allowed to own personal possessions that might be deemed dangerous in a maximum-security prison, such as radios.

Minimum-security prisons have been criticized for being like "country clubs"; some federal facilities for white-collar criminals even have tennis courts and pools (they are derisively called "Club Fed"). Yet they remain prisons, and the isolation and loneliness of prison life deeply affect the inmates.

Alternative Correctional Institutions

In addition to prisons and jails, a number of other correctional institutions are operating within the United States. Some have been in use for quite some time, whereas others have been developed more recently as part of innovative or experimental programs.

There are many different types of prisons, and some cater to special populations. The Eloy Detention Center in Eloy, Arizona, is used for undocumented aliens only. Any undocumented alien from the southern United States who is found, after apprehension, to have a criminal record is brought to this prison. People from over 50 countries have been incarcerated at Eloy, and at least 30 countries are usually represented in the inmate population at any given time. Inmates are allowed outdoor recreation every day.

© Scott Goldsmith/Aurora

Prison Farms and Camps

Prison farms and camps are used to detain offenders. These types of facilities are found primarily in the South and the West and have been in operation since the nineteenth century. Today, about 40 farms, 40 forest camps, 80 road camps, and more than 60 similar facilities (vocational training centers, ranches, and so on) exist in the nation. Prisoners on farms produce dairy products, grain, and vegetable crops that are used in the state correctional system and other governmental facilities, such as hospitals and schools. Forestry camp inmates maintain state parks, fight forest fires, and do reforestation work. Ranches, primarily a western phenomenon, employ inmates in cattle raising and horse breeding, among other activities. Road gangs repair roads and state highways.

Shock Incarceration in Boot Camps

boot camp
A short-term militaristic correctional facility in which inmates undergo intensive physical conditioning and discipline.

Another correctional innovation that gained popularity in the 1980s and 1990s, the **boot camp**, involves youthful, first-time offenders in military discipline and physical training. The concept is that short periods (90 to 180 days) of high-intensity exercise and work will "shock" the inmate into going straight. Tough physical training is designed to promote responsibility and improve decision-making skills, build self-confidence, and teach socialization skills. Inmates are treated with rough intensity by drillmasters who may call them names and punish the entire group for the failure of one member.[34]

Some programs also include educational and training components, counseling sessions, and treatment for special-needs populations, whereas others devote little or no time to therapeutic activities. Some receive program participants directly from court sentencing; others choose potential candidates from the general inmate population. Some allow voluntary participation and others voluntary termination.[35]

shock incarceration
A short prison sentence served in boot camp–type facilities.

Is **shock incarceration** a correctional panacea or another fad doomed to failure? Those who advocate shock incarceration portray it as a lower-cost alternative to overcrowded prisons. Both staff and inmates report benefiting from the experience.[36] The costs of boot camps are no lower than those of traditional prisons on a daily basis, but because sentences are shorter, they provide long-term savings. A number of states, including Georgia and New York, make extensive use of shock incarceration facilities.

Despite such support, empirical research has not supported boot camp effectiveness.[37] There is little evidence that boot camps can significantly lower recidivism rates. Because of these sketchy results, the future of the boot camp approach is uncertain. The federal government, among other correctional authorities, has announced the closing of its boot camp program.[38]

Community Correctional Facilities

Community correctional facilities called **halfway houses** hold inmates just before their release. These facilities are designed to bridge the gap between institutional living and the community. Specialized treatment may be offered, and the residents use the experience to cushion the shock of reentering society.

Halfway houses can look like residential homes and in many instances were originally residences; in urban centers, older apartment buildings can be adapted for the purpose. Usually, these facilities have a central treatment theme—such as group therapy or reality therapy—that is used to rehabilitate and reintegrate clients.

Despite the encouraging philosophical concept presented by the halfway house, evaluation of specific programs has not led to a definite endorsement of this type of treatment.[39] One significant problem has been a lack of support from community residents, who fear the establishment of an institution housing "dangerous offenders" in their neighborhood. Court actions have been brought and zoning restrictions imposed in some areas to foil efforts to create halfway houses.[40] As a result, many halfway houses are located in decrepit neighborhoods in the worst areas of town—certainly a condition that must influence the attitudes and behavior of the inmates. Furthermore, the climate of control exercised in most halfway houses, where rule violation can be met with a quick return to the institution, may not be one that the average inmate can distinguish from his former high-security penal institution.

Private Prisons

Correctional facilities are now being run by private firms as business enterprises, and their growth has outstripped that of public facilities; more than 400 are now in operation around the United States.

halfway house
A community-based correctional facility that houses inmates before their outright release so they can become gradually acclimated to conventional society.

■ Kameron Fair, 6, kisses his baby sister, Madison Barnett, 1, while visiting the Nova House, a halfway house in Dayton, Ohio. Kameron met his sister for the first time when his mom, Renee Poling, was released from the Ohio Reformatory for Women. Madison spent the first year of her life in the prison with her mother. Does keeping children with incarcerated parents help their life chances?

AP Photo/*Columbus Dispatch*, Renee Sauer

In some instances, a private corporation will finance and build an institution and then contract with correctional authorities to provide services for convicted criminals. Sometimes the private concern will finance and build the institution and then lease it outright to the government. This model has the advantage of allowing the government to circumvent the usually difficult process of getting voters to approve a bond issue and raising funds for prison construction. Another common form of private involvement is specific service contracts; for example, a private concern might be hired to manage the prison health-care system, food services, or staff training.

On January 6, 1986, the U.S. Corrections Corporation opened the first private state prison in Marion, Kentucky—a 300-bed minimum-security facility for inmates who are within three years of parole. Today, CCA houses approximately 75,000 offenders and detainees in more than 60 facilities, 44 of which are company-owned, with a total bed capacity of more than 80,000. CCA currently partners with all three federal corrections agencies (the Federal Bureau of Prisons, the U.S. Marshals Service, and Immigration and Customs Enforcement), nearly half of all states, and more than a dozen local municipalities.[41] A competitor, the GEO Corporation, oversees 116 correctional, detention, and residential treatment facilities, which total approximately 80,000 beds.[42] Nor are private prisons a uniquely American institution; they also play an important correctional role in Australia and the United Kingdom.[43]

Do Private Prisons Work? The most thorough evaluations of differences in recidivism rates between private and public facilities find little difference between the recidivism rates of inmates released from the two different types of institutions.[44] There is some evidence that inmates released from private prisons who do reoffend may commit less serious offenses than those released from public institutions, and although private and state institutions cost about the same to operate, private prisons seem cheaper to construct.[45]

Although these findings help support the concept of the private correctional institution, some experts question reliance on private prisons, believing that their use raises a number of vexing problems. Will private providers be able to evaluate programs effectively, knowing that a negative evaluation might cause them to lose their contract? Will they skimp on services and programs in order to reduce costs? Might they not skim off the "easy" cases and leave hard-core inmates to the state's care? And will the need to keep business booming require widening the net to fill empty cells? Must private providers maintain state-mandated liability insurance to cover inmate claims?[46] Some private service providers have been sued because their services were inadequate, causing harm to inmates.[47]

Private corrections firms also run into opposition from existing state correctional staff and management, who fear the loss of jobs and autonomy. Moreover, the public may be skeptical about an untested private concern's ability to provide security and protection. Private corrections also faces administrative problems. How will program quality be controlled? To compete on price, a private facility may have to cut corners to beat the competition. Determining accountability for problems and mishaps will be difficult when dealing with a corporation whose managers and officers are protected legally from personal responsibility for their actions.

LO9 Classify the different types of federal and state penal institutions

Inmate Populations

This vast correctional system, with more than 2,000 public and private institutions, now contains more than 1.6 million inmates. The imprisonment rate—the number of sentenced prisoners per 100,000 residents—is now 506 per 100,000, up from 475 per 100,000 U.S. residents in 2000.[48] During Ronald Reagan's first term as president, 1 in every 77 adults was under the control of the correctional system in the United States. Now it is 1 in 31, or 3.2 percent of all adults. And the costs of this incarceration binge is high: 1 day in prison costs more than 10 days on parole or 22 days on probation.[49]

LO10 Discuss prison population trends

Who makes up this population? Prison inmates are disproportionately young, male (90%), minority, and poor. A recent report (2010) by the Pew Foundation, found these racial disparities in the inmate population:

- One in 87 working-aged white men is in prison or jail, compared with 1 in 36 Hispanic men and 1 in 12 African American men.
- More young (age 20 to 34) African American men without a high school diploma or GED are currently behind bars (37 percent) than employed (26 percent).[50]

Many inmates suffer from multiple social problems: they are undereducated, underemployed, and come from abusive homes.[51] Recent research found that a significant number, about 9 percent, had experienced homelessness (living on the street or in a homeless shelter) and other related social problems, including mental illness, substance abuse, and unemployment; this is four to six times the estimated rate in the general U.S. adult population.[52]

It is not surprising, then, that surveys show that inmates suffer from serious psychological and emotional problems, including psychosis and major depression.[53]

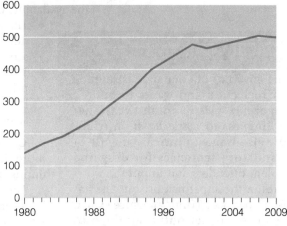

Imprisonment rate, 1980–2009
Number of offenders per 100,000 population

Figure 11.1 Imprisonment Rate 1980–2009

Source: Correctional Populations in the United States, 2009, and Prisoners in 2009, http://bjs.ojp.usdoj.gov/content/glance/incrt.cfm (accessed July 28, 2011).

Growth Trends

The prison population skyrocketed between 1980 and 2006, when it finally began to stabilize (Figure 11.1). There has been a slight decline in the number of prisoners per 100,000 population, and today there are about 500 inmates for every 100,000 citizens.

Why has the prison population remained high during the past decade even though the crime rate has fallen dramatically? There are a number of reasons for this trend.

- Many people who are released from prison soon return after failing on parole and other forms of early release. Hence, a significant portion of the prison population are re-entries. About 250,000 new inmates, or one-third of the people now entering prison, are parole violators.[54]

RealityCheck

MYTH OR REALITY? The inmate population is now decreasing because the crime rate is down.

MYTH. *The prison population has remained stable, even though the crime rate is down.* Tougher prison sentences, coupled with longer stays before release, have resulted in a growing prison population. Nonetheless, the rate of growth seems to be slowing. Why?

■ Despite the crime drop, the inmate population has not declined, and this has resulted in overcrowding in some institutions. Here, inmates in the reception housing area of the California State Prison in Los Angeles County are jammed into a building that has been turned into a dormitory. California prison officials, grappling with severe overcrowding, are considering moving more long-term inmates to the only state prison in Los Angeles County at Lancaster. State officials, overseen by a federal court judge, are juggling 171,000 prisoners within a prison system built for fewer than half that many inmates. Lancaster residents are worried that additional permanent inmates would mean that their relatives would flock to the area, bringing gang members and a criminal element to a region already hard hit by the recession.

© Ted Soqui/Corbis

- Tough criminal legislation, including mandatory-minimum sentencing laws, increases the chances that a convicted offender will be incarcerated and limits the availability of early release via parole.[55]
- The amount of time served in prison has increased because of such developments as truth-in-sentencing laws that require inmates to serve at least 85 percent of their sentences behind bars.[56]
- There is a significant association among drug use, drug arrests, and prison overcrowding.[57] The drug epidemic in the 1980s and 1990s helped swell prison populations with people serving very long sentences.

Given these trends, about 5 percent of the current population, or more than 13 million people, will serve a prison sentence sometime during their lives.[58]

The nation's prison population may be "maxing out" because the long-term effects of the crime rate drop may finally be taking effect. Tight state budgets may convince law makers to utilize community alternatives that are far cheaper than prisons. As costs skyrocket, some states are now spending more on prisons than on higher education. It would not be surprising if the voting public begins to question the wisdom of a strict incarceration policy, especially if crime is no longer a heated and highly debated political issue.

Ethical Challenge

The governor of your state is running for reelection and wants to build a supermax prison to showcase her willingness to crack down on crime. She also wants to increase the use of mandatory sentences for drug and violent offenders and to put the worst ones in the supermax prison. She has asked you, as a criminal justice expert, to write a paper outlining the pros and cons (no pun intended) of this correctional policy and to come up with alternative models if you disapprove of her plan. What would you say to her?

Summary

L01 **Know the meaning of the term** *new penology* The new penology refers to the fact that today's correctional system relies on the use of actuarial tables and tests in decision making. Administrators seem more concerned with security and "managing" large inmate populations than with treating individual offenders.

L02 **Be able to explain how the first penal institutions developed in Europe** Although the routine use of incarceration as a criminal punishment began in the late eighteenth and early nineteenth centuries, some early European institutions were created specifically to detain and punish criminal offenders.

L03 **Explain how William Penn revolutionized corrections** The "modern" American correctional system had its origins in Pennsylvania under the leadership of William Penn. Philadelphia's Walnut Street Jail was used to house convicted felons, except those sentenced to death.

L04 **Compare the New York and Pennsylvania prison models** In 1816, New York built a new prison at Auburn that used the congregate system, in which most prisoners ate and worked in groups. In contrast, Pennsylvania established a prison that placed each inmate in a single cell for the duration of his sentence. By the late nineteenth century, the congregate system was adopted in all states except Pennsylvania.

L05 **Chart the development of penal reform** The National Congress of Penitentiary and Reformatory

Discipline, held in Cincinnati in 1870, heralded a new era of prison reform. Another important trend was the development of specialized prisons designed to treat particular types of offenders.

L06 **Know how parole developed** The forerunner of parole began in Ireland in the 1850s, when penitentiary inmates spent the last portion of their sentences living in an intermediate institution and working in the outside community. In 1822, volunteers from the Philadelphia-based Society for Alleviating the Miseries of Public Prisons began to help offenders once they were released from prison. In 1851, the society appointed two agents to work with inmates discharged from Pennsylvania penal institutions. Massachusetts appointed an agent in 1845 to help released inmates obtain jobs, clothing, and transportation.

L07 **List the purposes of jails and be familiar with the makeup of jail populations** The nation's jails are institutional facilities used to detain accused offenders who cannot make or are not eligible for bail prior to trial and to hold convicted offenders awaiting sentence. They serve as the principal institution of secure confinement for offenders convicted of misdemeanors.

L08 **Be familiar with the term** *new-generation jail* New-generation jails allow for continuous observation of residents. In the direct supervision version, officers are stationed within pods and get to interact with and monitor inmates. Indirect-supervision jails have correctional officers stationed inside a secure room. Microphones and speakers inside the living unit permit the officer to hear and communicate with inmates.

L09 **Classify the different types of federal and state penal institutions** Maximum-security prisons housing the most notorious criminals are fortress-like, surrounded by stone walls with guard towers at strategic places. Some states have constructed super-maximum-security prisons (supermax prisons) to house the most predatory criminals. Similar in appearance to maximum-security prisons, medium-security prisons are characterized by less vigilant security provisions and a less tense atmosphere. Operating without armed guards or perimeter walls, minimum-security prisons usually house the most trustworthy and least violent offenders.

L010 **Discuss prison population trends** The inmate population has finally stabilized. One reason for the large number of inmates despite the nation's crime drop is that tough new criminal legislation, including mandatory sentencing laws, increases the chances that a convicted offender will be incarcerated and limits the availability for early release via parole.

Review Questions

1. Would you allow a community correctional center to be built in your neighborhood?

2. Should pretrial detainees and convicted offenders be kept in the same institution?

3. What can be done to reduce overcrowding in correctional facilities?

4. Should private companies be allowed to run correctional institutions?

5. What are the drawbacks to shock incarceration?

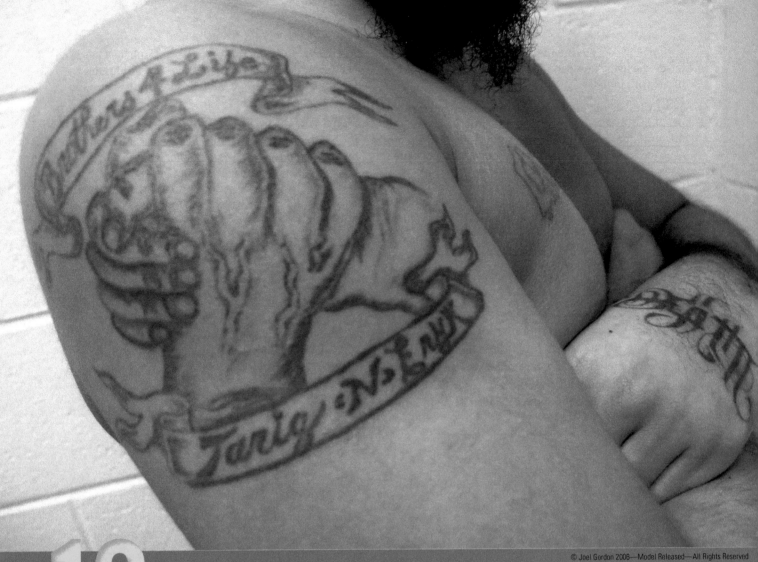

12 Prison Life: Living in and Leaving Prison

Learning Objectives

LO1 Discuss the problems of the adult correctional system

LO2 Know what is meant by the term *total institution*

LO3 Be familiar with the problem of sexual coercion in prison and what is being done to help

LO4 Chart the prisonization process and the development of the inmate social code

LO5 Compare the lives and cultures of male and female inmates

LO6 Be familiar with the different forms of correctional treatment

LO7 Discuss the world of correctional officers

LO8 Understand the causes of prison violence

LO9 Know what is meant by prisoners' rights, and discuss some key privileges that have been granted to inmates

LO10 Be knowledgeable about the parole process and the problems of prisoner reentry

Kevin James grew up in South Central Los Angeles and became a member of the 76th Street Crips gang. In 1997, at the age of 21, James was convicted on a robbery charge and began serving a 10-year sentence at the California State Prison in Tehachapi. While in prison, James dabbled in religion, became involved with the Nation of Islam, and later drifted into a fringe group of Sunni Muslims known as Jam'iyyat Ul-Islam Is-Saheed (the Assembly of Authentic Islam) or JIS. James soon began preaching to new inmates that it was the duty of Muslims to violently attack the enemies of Islam, including the U.S. government. He eventually took control of JIS and began distributing a handwritten document called the "JIS Protocol," which described his personal beliefs, including his justification for killing "infidels." He used his old gang contacts to spread the word and in 2003, when he was transferred to the maximum-security California State Prison in Sacramento (New Folsom Prison), he continued his mission of converting other inmates to the cause. One of his followers, 25-year-old Levar Washington, who was about to be paroled, was instructed to recruit five people without felony records from the community, including some who knew about bomb-making and explosives, and attack a target symbolic of the Iraq war: a U.S. Army recruiting office.

The group researched targets and prepared a document called "Modes of Attack." The document listed as possible targets "LAX and consulate of Zion," "military targets," "army recruiting centers throughout the county," "military base in Manhattan Beach" and "campsite of Zion."

After police investigators linked Washington and his group to a gas station robbery, a crime committed to fund their terrorist activities, various Jihadist documents were found at a South Los Angeles apartment where they lived. In addition to the "Modes of Attack" document, investigators discovered a document titled "Notoriety Moves," which contained a James-authored statement to be given to the media after a deadly attack. The proposed press statement read, in part, "This incident is the first in a series of incidents to come in a plight to defend and propagate traditional Islam in its purity." The document also warns "sincere Muslims" to avoid a series of targets, including "Those Jewish and non-Jewish supporters of an Israeli state."

For their efforts, Washington was sentenced to 22 years in prison and Kevin James, the mastermind behind the plots, received 16 additional years to his sentence.[1] ■

RealityCheck

MYTH OR REALITY?

- The correctional system has failed to live up to its promise because so many inmates recidivate.
- Prison rapes are common, and most inmates are sexually assaulted soon after they arrive in prison.
- Prisons are total institutions with unique social codes and value systems.
- There are significant gender-based differences between the prison experiences of men and women.
- Despite negative publicity that "nothing works," many prison rehabilitation efforts are actually effective.
- Inmates lose all civil rights once they enter a high-security correctional facility.
- Most released inmates fail on parole.

Kevin James and his followers are not unique. Not only do inmates join prison gangs, many are now being indoctrinated into radical groups. The sad truth is that a majority of inmates return to prison soon after their release, helping to swell the number of people behind bars. During the past 25 years, as the prison population increased in size, corrections officials responded by constructing new facilities at a record pace. The number of state facilities increased from just under 600 to over 1,000.[2] These facilities take on a variety of forms, including prisons, prison hospitals, prison farms, and boot camps; centers for reception, classification, or alcohol and drug treatment; and work release centers.[3] Not all prisons are brand new: 25 were built before 1875, 79 between 1875 and 1924, and 141 between 1925 and 1949. In fact, some of the first prisons ever constructed, such as the Concord Reformatory in Massachusetts, are still in operation.

More than half of all inmates are held in large, fortress-like maximum-security institutions; prison overcrowding is a significant problem. The prison system now holds about 1.5 million people, and some institutions are operating above stated capacity. Meaningful treatment efforts are often wishful thinking, and recidivism rates are shockingly high; about half of all inmates return within three years of being released on parole.[4] It is not surprising that many inmates are resentful of the deteriorated conditions or that correctional officers fear the consequences of inmate unrest. Rather than deterring people from future criminality, a prison stay may actually reinforce and/or encourage their criminal offending.[5] The typical prison has been described as a "school for crime" in which young offenders are taught by older cons to become sophisticated criminals.

This chapter presents a brief review of some of the most important issues confronting the nation's correctional system, including inmate life, treatment strategies, inmate legal rights, and release from prison.

RealityCheck

MYTH OR REALITY? The correctional system has failed to live up to its promise because so many inmates recidivate.

REALITY. *Most inmates return to prison, either by committing new crimes or by violating the terms of their parole release.*

Do you think this situation reflects the type of people who go to prison or the prison experience itself?

Men Imprisoned

total institution
A regimented, dehumanizing institution such as a prison, in which inmates are kept in social isolation, cut off from the world at large.

Prisons in the United States are **total institutions**. This means that inmates locked within their walls are segregated from the outside world, kept under constant surveillance, and forced to obey strict official rules to avoid facing formal sanctions. Their personal possessions are taken from them, and they must conform to institutional norms of dress and personal appearance. Many human functions are strictly curtailed; heterosexual sex, friendships, family relationships, education, and participation in group activities become privileges of the past.

An inmate's first experience occurs in a classification or reception center, where inmates are given a series of psychological and other tests and evaluated on the basis of their personality, background, offense history, and treatment needs. On the basis of the classification they are given, they are assigned to a permanent facility. Hardcore, repeat, and violent offenders will go to the maximum-security unit; offenders with learning disabilities may be assigned to an institution that specializes in educational services; mentally disordered offenders will be held in a facility that can provide psychiatric care; and so on. Today, sophisticated classification instruments are being used to maximize the effectiveness of placements, thereby cutting down on the cost of incarceration.[6]

When they arrive at prison, inmates are stripped, searched, shorn, and assigned living quarters. They quickly learn what the term *total institution* really means. Inmate turned author James A. Paluch, Jr., calls his cell a "cold coffin . . . leaving a chilling effect on anyone forced to live inside them."[7]

Newcomers swiftly discover that all previous concepts of personal privacy and dignity are soon forgotten. Inmates in large, inaccessible prisons may find themselves physically cut off from families, friends, and associates. Visitors may find it difficult to travel great distances to see them; mail is censored and sometimes destroyed. And while incarcerated, inmates are forced to associate with a peer group afflicted with a disproportionate share of mental and physical problems. Various communicable diseases are commonly found, such as hepatitis C virus, HIV, and syphilis. Not surprisingly, inmate health is significantly worse than that of the general population.[8] Personal losses include the deprivation of liberty, goods and services, heterosexual relationships, autonomy, and security.[9] Inmates may be subject to verbal and physical attack and threats, with little chance of legal redress. Overcrowded prisons are filled with young, aggressive men who are responsible for the majority of inmate-on-inmate assaults.[10]

Inmates may find that some prisoners have formed cliques, or groups, based on ethnic backgrounds or personal interests; they are also likely to encounter Mafia-like or racial terror groups that must be dealt with. Inmates may find that power in the prison is shared by correctional officers and inmate gangs; the only way to avoid being beaten and raped may be to learn how to beat and rape.

Some prisoners, especially the most vulnerable, become the target of charismatic leaders seeking to recruit them to some cause or group. Angry and embittered by their circumstances, alienated from their families, these vulnerable inmates are looking for meaning and identity. Some may start attending Christian services in the chapel and then convert to a fringe group such as the Black Hebrew Israelism. Some, like Kevin James and Levar Washington, eventually get recruited into terror cells and are groomed to engage in militant activity on the outside. Some inmates are so alienated from social life that they fall prey to anti-government groups that have their own hierarchy, code of conduct, secret communication system, and collective identity.[11]

But not all inmates are radicalized or have what it takes to join radical cells. If they are weak and unable to defend themselves, new inmates may find that they are considered "punks"; if they ask a guard for help, they are labeled a "snitch." Those most likely to be targets of sexual assaults may spend their sentence in protective custody, sacrificing the "freedom of the yard" and rehabilitation services for personal protection.[12]

LO2 Know what is meant by the term *total institution*

Coping in Prison

Despite all these hardships, many inmates learn to adapt to the prison routine. Each prisoner has his own method of coping. He may stay alone, become friends with another inmate, join a group, or seek the advice of treatment personnel. Inmates soon learn that their lifestyle and activities can contribute to their being victimized by more aggressive inmates. The more time they spend in closely guarded activities, the less likely they are to become the victims of violence. The more they isolate themselves from others who might protect them, the greater their vulnerability to attack. The more visitors they receive, the more likely they are to be attacked by fellow inmates jealous of their relationships with the outside world.[13]

Some learn how to fight back to prove they are not people who can be bullied. Older, more experienced men are better able to cope with the prison experience; younger inmates, especially juveniles sent to adult prisons, are more likely to participate in violent episodes.[14]

Men who viewed violence as an acceptable method of settling disputes before entering prison are the ones most likely to use violence while they are inmates.[15] Inmates who have a history of pre-arrest drug use and have been incarcerated for violent crimes are the ones most likely to get involved in assaults and drug/alcohol offenses while they are incarcerated.[16] Survival in prison may depend on one's ability to identify troubled inmates and avoid contact.

Sexual Coercion

It is a commonly held belief that rape and sexual coercion are customary prison behaviors. Some inmates will demand regular sexual access in exchange for protection from even more violent rape and beatings. In his shocking memoir *Fish*, T. J. Parsell writes about how he was sent to prison at age 17 for a robbery (with a toy gun). Parsell was raped on his first night by four older inmates, who then flipped a coin to decide who would "own" him for the rest of his sentence.[17]

Who are the targets of prison sexual violence? Younger inmates, gay men, and bisexual men are selected most often to be targets of sexual assaults.[18] Young males may be raped and kept as sexual slaves by older, more aggressive inmates. When these "slave holders" are released, they often sell their "prison wives" to other inmates.[19] Some inmates will request that regular sexual payments be made to them in exchange for protection from even more violent inmates who threaten rape and beatings.[20] These weaker inmates are called "punks" and put at the bottom of the inmate sexual hierarchy. Straight inmates are more likely to respect "true" homosexuals because they were gay before entering prison and are therefore "true to themselves," while punks are despised because they are weak: they did not want to have sex with other men, but were too weak to resist or not brave enough to stand up to sexual predators. Even "queens," inmates who look and act as women, get more respect than punks because they chose their lifestyle and did not have it forced upon them by others.[21]

How Common Is Prison Rape? While these stories are both common and frightening, it is still unclear how much rape and sexually violent activity occurs in prisons, mainly because most prison rape goes unreported. The victims are either too embarrassed to tell anyone or may fear harassment by other inmates and further retaliation by their attackers.[22] Many inmates refuse to report rape, and others may misunderstand what constitutes a rape—that is, they don't consider verbal coercion a form of sexual assault. Some refuse to report rape because they believe nothing can be done. It is not surprising that some research efforts indicate that rape is very rare, whereas others find that nearly half of all inmates experience some form of sexual coercion.[23] A recent (2009) national survey of sexual coercion in prison sponsored by the Bureau of Justice Statistics found:

- About 1.9 percent of male prison inmates reported an incident involving another inmate.
- About 2.9 percent of prison inmates reported having had sex or sexual contact with staff.
- About 80,000 inmates are subject to sexual coercion each year.[24]

This survey shows that prison rape may be less common than previously believed and that inmates are more likely to experience sexual coercion from staff than other inmates.[25] Again, these data may underreport the problem: most inmates say they are aware of sexual coercion in prison, and about 9 percent say they know an inmate who has been raped.[26]

Regardless of the extent of prison rape, Congress enacted the Prison Rape Reduction Act of 2003, which established three programs in the Department of Justice:

- A program dedicated to collecting national prison rape statistics, interpreting data, and conducting research
- A program dedicated to the dissemination of information and procedures for combating prison rape
- A program to assist in funding state programs[27]

The Inmate Social Code

For many years, criminal justice experts maintained that inmates formed their own world with a unique set of norms and rules, known as the **inmate subculture**.[28] A significant aspect of the inmate subculture was a unique **inmate social code**—unwritten guidelines that expressed the values, attitudes, and type of behavior that older inmates demanded of young ones. Passed on from one generation of

RealityCheck

MYTH OR REALITY? Prison rapes are common, and most inmates are sexually assaulted soon after they arrive in prison.

MYTH. It is difficult to get an accurate measure, but national studies indicate that many inmates are able to avoid sexual coercion and abuse.

Do you think only certain types of inmates are targeted? If so, who is most at risk?

inmate subculture
The loosely defined culture that pervades prisons and has its own norms, rules, and language.

inmate social code
An unwritten code of behavior, passed from older inmates to younger ones, that serves as a guideline to appropriate inmate behavior within the correctional institution.

inmates to another, the inmate social code represented the values of interpersonal relations in the prison.

National attention was first drawn to the inmate social code and subculture by Donald Clemmer's classic book *The Prison Community*, in which he presented a detailed sociological study of life in a maximum-security prison.[29] Clemmer was able to identify a unique language, or argot, that prisoners use. He found that prisoners tend to group themselves into cliques on the basis of such personal criteria as sexual preference, political beliefs, and offense history. He found complex sexual relationships in prison and concluded that many heterosexual men turn to homosexual relationships when faced with long sentences and the loneliness of prison life.

Clemmer's most important contribution may have been his identification of the **prisonization** process. This he defined as the inmate's assimilation into the existing prison culture through acceptance of its language, sexual code, and norms of behavior. Those who become the most "prisonized" are the least likely to reform on the outside.

Using Clemmer's work as a jumping-off point, a number of prominent sociologists have set out to explore more fully the various roles in the prison community. The most important principles of the dominant inmate culture are listed in Exhibit 12.1.

Although some inmates violate the code and exploit their peers, the "right guy" is someone who uses the inmate social code as his personal behavior guide. He is always loyal to his fellow prisoners, keeps his promises, is dependable and trustworthy, and never interferes with inmates who are conniving against the officials.[30] The right guy does not go around looking for a fight, but he never runs away from one; he acts "like a man."

The effects of prisonization may be long-term and destructive. Many inmates become hostile to the legal system, learning to use violence as a means of solving problems and to value criminal peers.[31] For some this change may be permanent; for others it is temporary, and they may revert to their "normal" life after release.

The New Inmate Culture

The importation of outside values into the inmate culture has had a dramatic effect on prison life. Although the old inmate subculture may have been harmful because its norms and values insulated the inmate from change efforts, it also helped create order in the institution and prevented violence among the inmates. People who violated the code and victimized others were sanctioned by their peers. An understanding developed between guards and inmate leaders: the guards would let the inmates have things their own way, and the inmates would not let things get out of hand and draw the attention of the administration.

The old system may be dying or already dead in most institutions. The change seems to have been precipitated by the black power movement in the 1960s and 1970s. Black inmates were no longer content to play a subservient role and challenged the power of established white inmates. As the black power movement gained prominence, racial tension in prisons created divisions that severely altered the inmate subculture. Older, respected inmates could no longer cross racial lines to mediate disputes. Predatory inmates could victimize others without fear of retaliation. Consequently, more inmates than ever are now assigned to protective custody for their own safety.

Exhibit 12.1

Elements of the Inmate Social Code

1. *Don't interfere with inmates' interests.* Within this area of the code are maxims related to serving the least amount of time in the greatest possible comfort. For example, inmates are warned never to betray another inmate to authorities; in other words, grievances must be handled personally. Other aspects of the noninterference doctrine include "Don't be nosy," "Don't have a loose lip," "Keep off the other inmates' backs," and "Don't put another inmate on the spot."

2. *Don't lose your head.* Inmates are also cautioned to refrain from arguing, quarreling, or engaging in other emotional displays with fellow inmates. The novice may hear such warnings as "Play it cool," and "Do your own time."

3. *Don't exploit inmates.* Prisoners are warned not to take advantage of one another: "Don't steal from cons," "Don't welsh on a debt," and "Be right."

4. *Be tough and don't lose your dignity.* Although Rule 2 forbids conflict, once it starts, an inmate must be prepared to deal with it effectively and thoroughly. Maxims include "Don't cop out," "Don't weaken," and "Be tough; be a man."

5. *Don't be a sucker.* Inmates are cautioned not to make fools of themselves or support the guards or prison administration over the interest of the inmates: "Be sharp."

Source: Gresham Sykes, *The Society of Captives* (Princeton, NJ: Princeton University Press, 1958).

---

prisonization
Assimilation into the separate culture in the prison that has its own set of rewards and behaviors, as well as its own norms, rules, and language. The traditional prison culture is now being replaced by a violent gang culture.

L04 Chart the prisonization process and the development of the inmate social code

---

RealityCheck

MYTH OR REALITY? Prisons are total institutions with unique social codes and value systems.

REALITY. *Prisons are a world in themselves, with a unique set of values, attitudes, and behaviors.*

Can you think of another type of living arrangement that may be comparable? Hint: Do you live in a dorm?

In the new culture, African American and Latino inmates are much more cohesively organized than whites.[32] Their groups sometimes form out of religious or political affiliations, such as the Black Muslims; out of efforts to combat discrimination in prison, such as the Latino group La Nuestra Familia; or from street gangs, such as the Vice Lords or Gangster Disciples in the Illinois prison system and the Crips in California. Where white inmates have successfully organized, it is in the form of a neo-Nazi group called the Aryan Brotherhood. Racially homogeneous gangs are so cohesive and powerful that they are able to replace the original inmate code with one of their own.

Women Imprisoned

At the turn of the twentieth century, female inmates were viewed as morally depraved people who flouted conventional rules of female behavior. The treatment of white and African American women differed significantly. In some states, white women were placed in female-only reformatories designed to improve their deportment; black women were placed in male prisons, where they were put on chain gangs and were subject to beatings.[33]

Female Institutions

Women's prisons tend to be smaller than those housing male inmates. Although some female institutions are strictly penal, with steel bars, concrete floors, and other security measures, the majority are nonsecure institutions similar to college dormitories and group homes in the community. Women's facilities, especially those in the community, commonly offer inmates a great deal of autonomy and allow them to make decisions affecting their daily lives.

However, like men's prisons, women's prisons suffer from a lack of adequate training and of health, treatment, and educational facilities. Psychological counseling often takes the form of group sessions conducted by laypeople, such as correctional officers. Many female inmates are mothers and had custody of their children before incarceration, but little effort is made to help them develop better parenting skills. Although most female (and male) inmates have at least one child, less than a quarter actually get an annual visit. Who takes care of these children while their mothers are incarcerated? Most children of incarcerated women are placed with their father, a grandparent, another relative, or a family friend. About 10 percent wind up in foster homes or state facilities.[34]

Job-training opportunities are also a problem. Where vocational training exists, it is in areas that offer limited financial reward, which hinders adjustment upon release. Female inmates, many of whom were on the economic margin before their incarceration began, find little opportunity for improvement during their prison experience.[35] Surveys also indicate that the prison experience does little to prepare women to reenter the workforce after they complete their sentence. Gender stereotypes still shape vocational opportunities.[36] Female inmates are still being trained for "women's roles," such as child rearing, and are not given the preparation they need to make successful adjustments in the community.[37]

Female Inmates

Like their male counterparts, female inmates are young (most are under age 30), minority group members, unmarried, undereducated (more than half are high school dropouts), and either unemployed or underemployed. The typical woman behind bars is a poor, unskilled woman of color with small children, has health problems, has a history of abuse, and is incarcerated for low-level drug or property offenses.[38] It is not surprising that these conditions also produce high suicide rates in the female prison population.[39]

Incarcerated women also have had a troubled family life. Significant numbers were at-risk children, products of broken homes and the welfare system; over half have received welfare at some time during their adult lives. Many claim to have been physically or sexually abused at some point in their lives. This pattern continued in adult life: Many female inmates were victims of domestic violence. It is not surprising that many display psychological problems.[40]

A significant number of female inmates report having substance abuse problems. About three-fourths have used drugs at some time in their lives, and almost half were involved with addictive drugs, such as cocaine, heroin, or PCP. The incarceration of so many women who are low criminal risks yet face a high risk of exposure to HIV (human immunodeficiency virus, which causes AIDS) and other health threats because of their prior history of drug abuse presents a significant problem. One study of incarcerated women found that one-third of the sample reported that before their arrest, they had traded sex for money or drugs; 24 percent of the women reported trading sex for money or drugs "weekly or more often."[41] Such risky behavior significantly increases the likelihood of their carrying the AIDS virus or other sexually transmitted diseases.

The picture that emerges of the female inmate is troubling. After a lifetime of emotional turmoil, physical and sexual abuse, and drug use, it seems improbable that overcrowded, underfunded correctional institutions can forge a dramatic turnaround in the behavior of at-risk female inmates. Many have lost custody of their children, a trauma that is more likely to afflict those who are already substance abusers and suffer from depression.[42] It should come as no surprise that many female inmates feel strain and conflict, which are psychological conditions related to violent episodes.[43]

Sexual Violence in Women's Prisons There are also numerous reports of female prisoners being sexually abused and exploited by male correctional workers who either use brute force or psychological coercion to gain sexual control over inmates. The recent national survey on sexual abuse found that 4.7 percent of female inmates report being abused by another inmate and 2.1 percent by a staff member.[44] Staff-on-inmate sexual misconduct covers a wide range of behaviors, from lewd remarks to voyeurism, to assault and rape. Few if any of these incidents are reported, and perpetrators rarely go to trial. Institutional workers cover for each other, and women who file complaints are offered little protection from vengeful guards.[45] Because the situation persists, more than 40 states and the District of Columbia have been forced to pass laws criminalizing some types of staff sexual misconduct in prisons.[46] However, not all sexual liaisons in women's prisons are unwanted and when Rebecca Trammell conducted interviews with former female inmates, she found that some inmates fight over correctional officers as the only men in their lives. The "relational violence" which may occur is similar to what is commonly described as adolescent behavior.[47]

Adapting to the Female Institution

Daily life in women's prisons differs somewhat from that in male institutions. For one thing, unlike male inmates, women usually do not present an immediate physical danger to staff and fellow inmates. Relatively few engage in violent behavior, and incidents of inmate-initiated sexual aggression, so common in male institutions, are rare in women's prisons.[48] Few female inmates experience the violent atmosphere common in male institutions or suffer the same racial and ethnic conflict and divisiveness.[49] But even though female inmates may experience less discomfort than males, that does not mean their experience is a bed of roses. Many still experience fear and are forced to undergo a process of socialization fraught with danger and volatile situations.[50] However, female inmates seem to receive more social support from both internal sources (e.g., inmate peers, correctional staff) and external sources (e.g., families, peers)—a factor that may lessen the pains of prison life, help them adjust, and improve the social climate within female institutions.[51]

The rigid, anti-authority inmate social code found in many male institutions does not exist in female institutions.[52] Confinement for women, however, may

LO5 Compare the lives and cultures of male and female inmates

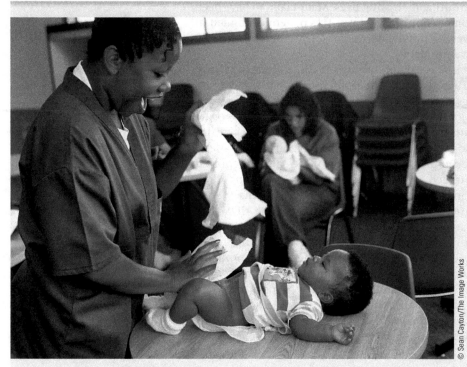

Many female inmates are moms, and keeping them involved with their children can be a challenge. Here a mother changes the diaper on her year-and-a-half-old son, as another mother visits with her newborn baby at the visitor's center inside the Colorado Women's Correctional Facility in Canon City, Colorado. The two incarcerated mothers get to visit with their children for three hours each week through the New Horizon Ministries, a Mennonite prison ministry that cares for the children and, later, reunites them with their parents.

make-believe family
In female institutions, the substitute family group—including faux father, mother, and siblings—created by some inmates.

produce severe anxiety and anger because of separation from families and loved ones and the inability to function in normal female roles. Unlike men, who direct their anger outward, female prisoners may turn to more self-destructive acts to cope with their problems. Female inmates are more likely than males to mutilate their own bodies and to attempt suicide. For example, one common practice among female inmates is self-mutilation, or "carving." This ranges from simple scratches to carving on their body the name of their boyfriend or even complex statements or sentences ("To mother, with hate").[53]

Another form of adaptation to prison used by women is the **make-believe family**. This group contains masculine and feminine figures acting as fathers and mothers; some even act as children and take on the role of brother or sister. Formalized marriages and divorces may be conducted. Sometimes one inmate plays multiple roles, such that a "sister" in one family may "marry" and become the "wife" of another inmate. It is estimated that about half of all female inmates are members of make-believe families.

Correctional Treatment

Almost every prison facility uses some mode of treatment for inmates. This may come in the form of individual or group therapy programs or educational or vocational training. This section presents a number of therapeutic methods that have been used nationally in correctional settings and identifies some of their more salient features.

Individual and Group Treatment

Prison inmates typically suffer from a variety of cognitive and psychosocial deficits, such as poor emotional control, social skills, and interpersonal problem solving; these deficits are often linked to long-term substance abuse. Modern counseling programs help inmates to control emotions (e.g., understanding why they feel the

RealityCheck

MYTH OR REALITY? There are significant gender-based differences between the prison experiences of men and women.

REALITY. *Women are less violent than men in prison, and the culture of the female prison has spawned nurturing "make-believe" families and other pseudo-family groups, whereas male institutions are dominated by violent prison gangs.*

Do you think this is because women are naturally less violent?

way they do, dealing with nervousness or anxiety, solving their problems creatively); to communicate with others (e.g., understanding what people tell them, communicating clearly when they write); to deal with legal concerns (e.g., keeping out of legal trouble, avoiding breaking laws); to manage general life issues (e.g., finding a job, dealing with difficult coworkers, being a good parent); and to develop and maintain social relationships (e.g., having good relations with others, making others happy, making others proud).[54]

To achieve these goals, correctional systems use a variety of intensive individual and group techniques, including behavior modification, aversive therapy, milieu therapy, reality therapy, transactional analysis, and responsibility therapy. Some programs use traditional techniques such as group therapy while others employ nontraditional artistic and spiritual activities, such as visual and performance arts, meditation, and yoga.[55]

Anger Management Anger and lack of self-control have been linked to violent criminal behavior both in the institution and, upon release, in the community. As a result, **anger management** programs may be the form of group therapy most frequently offered within prison settings.[56] Anger management is often combined with other group techniques as part of drug treatment and sex offender treatment programs. Cognitive-behavioral approaches are frequently used as a means of helping inmates find ways to control their anger. Anger management or violence programs have also been implemented in other countries; for example, violence management programs are widely used in Australia.[57]

Faith-Based Programs Research has shown that inmates involved in religious programs and education do better following release than those in comparison groups but that the differences quickly erode.[58] Nonetheless, under the George W. Bush administration, faith-based rehabilitation efforts flourished.[59] In 2003, then-governor Jeb Bush dedicated the first faith-based prison in the United States, a 750-bed medium-security facility for men in Lawtey, Florida.[60] Missouri and Florida also opened facilities for youthful offenders based on faith-based principles.[61] Today there are hundreds in operation around the United States.

While these programs are based on faith or spiritual principles, the study of religious texts or materials and participation in religious services or rituals are not viewed as their central focus. Instead, faith-based programs are more often involved in secular activities such as helping clients gain skills or training, building support networks, and creating a supportive relationship between staff, volunteers, and clients.[62]

Faith-based programs seem to work better with some inmates than others, and those who enter such programs with feelings of self-worth are more likely to complete the course than those with less confidence.[63]

Drug Treatment Most prisons have programs designed to help inmates suffering from alcohol and substance abuse. The most recent data suggest that about 30 percent of all inmates are provided with some form of services.[64]

Numerous drug programs rely on inmate self-help through twelve-step groups such as Narcotics or Alcoholics Anonymous. Others rely on traditional counseling programs such as cognitive behavioral counseling. Another approach is to provide abusers with methadone as a substitute for heroin; some evaluations have shown this method to be effective.[65] Because substance abuse is so prevalent among correctional clients, some correctional facilities have been reformulated into **therapeutic communities** that apply a psychosocial, experiential learning process and rely on positive peer pressure within a highly structured social environment. The community itself, including staff and program participants, becomes the primary method of change. They work together as members of a "family" in order to create a culture where community members confront each other's negative behavior and attitudes and establish an open, trusting, and safe environment. The TC approach, then, relies on mutual self-help. It also encourages personal disclosure rather than the isolation of the general prison culture.[66]

therapeutic communities
Institutions that rely on positive peer pressure within a highly structured social environment in order to create positive inmate change.

Treating substance-abusing offenders has proven difficult. Even such highly touted programs such as cognitive behavioral therapy and the therapeutic community approach have yielded mixed results: some evaluations have found clients in these programs are just as likely to recidivate as those in the general population.[67] Nonetheless, success rates may be masked by the way individual programs are administered and the effectiveness of treatment delivery. For example, there is evidence that those inmates who successfully complete TC programs have significantly lower recidivism rates than nonattendees and are more likely to seek treatment once they return to the community. In addition, when run correctly TC programs seem effective in reducing rearrest and reincarceration rates.[68]

HIV/AIDS Treatment The AIDS-infected inmate has been the subject of great concern. Two groups of people at high risk of contracting HIV are intravenous drug users who share needles and males who engage in same-sex relations—two behaviors common in prison. Because drug use is common and syringes scarce, many high-risk inmates share drug paraphernalia, increasing the danger of HIV infection.[69]

Although the numbers are constantly changing, the rate of HIV infection among state and federal prisoners has stabilized at around 2 percent, and there are about 25,000 HIV-infected inmates.

Correctional administrators have found it difficult to arrive at effective policies to confront AIDS. Although all state and federal jurisdictions do some AIDS testing, only the federal Bureau of Prisons and relatively few states conduct mass screenings of all inmates. Most states test inmates only if there are significant indications that they are HIV-positive.

Most correctional systems are now training staff about AIDS. Educational programs for inmates are often inadequate because administrators are reluctant to give them information on safe sex and the proper cleaning of drug paraphernalia (both sexual relations and drug use are forbidden in prison).

Educational Programs

Besides programs stressing personal growth through individual analysis or group therapy, inmate rehabilitation is also pursued through vocational and educational training. Although these two kinds of training sometimes differ in style and content, they can also overlap when, for example, education involves practical, job-related study.

The first prison treatment programs were in fact educational. A prison school was opened at the Walnut Street Jail in 1784. Elementary courses were offered in New York's prison system in 1801 and in Pennsylvania's in 1844. An actual school system was established in Detroit's House of Corrections in 1870, and the Elmira Reformatory opened a vocational trade school in 1876. Today, most institutions provide some type of educational program. At some prisons, inmates can obtain a high school diploma or a general educational development (GED) certificate through equivalency exams. Other institutions provide an actual classroom education, usually staffed by certified teachers employed full time at the prison or by part-time teachers who also teach full time at nearby public schools.

Educational programs vary in quality and intensity. Some are full-time programs employing highly qualified and concerned educators, whereas others are part-time programs without any real goals or objectives. In some institutions, programs have been designed to circumvent the difficulties inherent in the prison structure. They encourage volunteers from the community and local schools to tutor willing and motivated inmates. Some prison administrators have arranged flexible schedules for inmate students and actively encourage their participation in these programs. In several states, statewide school districts serving prisons have been created. Forming such districts can make better-qualified staff available and provide the materials and resources necessary for meaningful educational programs.

Most research indicates that participation in correctional education programs has benefits both in and out of prisons. Karen Lahm found that inmates who take part in GED, high school, vocational, and/or college programs report much fewer rule violations while incarcerated than those who ignore educational opportunities.[70] Participation in prison-based education produces higher postrelease earnings and employment rates, especially for minority inmates.[71] However, the results of prison education on recidivism are a mixed bag: some studies show a positive effect while others find little or no relationship.[72]

Vocational Programs

Every state correctional system also has some job-related services for inmates. Some have elaborate training programs inside the institution, whereas others have instituted prerelease and postrelease employment services. Inmates who hope to obtain parole need to participate in prison industry. Documenting a history of stable employment in prison is essential if parole agents are to convince prospective employers that the ex-offender is a good risk, and postrelease employment is usually required for parole eligibility.[73]

A few of the more important work-related services are discussed in the following sections.

Vocational Training Most institutions provide vocational training programs. On the federal level, the Federal Prison Industries, which is more commonly known as UNICOR, teaches inmates to produce goods and services for government use such as clothing and textiles, industrial products, and office furniture. UNICOR sales average about $800 million a year and yield a profit of $120 million a year—making UNICOR the most profitable line of business in the United States.[74]

Despite the promising aspects of such programs, they have also been seriously criticized. Inmates often have trouble finding skill-related, high-paying jobs upon their release. Equipment in prisons is often secondhand, obsolete, and hard to come by. Some programs are thinly disguised excuses for prison upkeep and maintenance, and unions and other groups resent the intrusion of prison labor into their markets.

Work Release To supplement programs stressing rehabilitation via in-house job training or education, more than 40 states have attempted to implement **work release** or **furlough** programs. These allow deserving inmates to leave the institution and hold regular jobs in the community.

work release
A prison treatment program that allows inmates to be released during the day to work in the community and returned to prison at night.

furlough
A correctional policy that allows inmates to leave the institution for vocational or educational training, for employment, or to maintain family ties.

On June 3, 2009, Michael R. Harris, editor-in-chief of the *San Quentin News*, hands out copies of the newspaper to visiting criminal justice students from San Diego State University. Like journalists everywhere, the staff of the *San Quentin News* cover news, sports, and the local arts scene. But these reporters are truly "pen men": The paper is written for and by inmates of the San Quentin State Prison in California. Working on the paper provides inmates with both educational and vocational training.

AP Images/Eric Risberg

Inmates enrolled in work release may live at the institutions at night while working in the community during the day. However, security problems (for instance, contraband may be brought in) and the usual remoteness of prisons often make this arrangement difficult. More typical is the extended work release, where prisoners are allowed to remain in the community for significant periods of time. To help inmates adjust, some states operate community-based prerelease centers where inmates live while working. Some inmates may work at their previous jobs, whereas others seek new employment.

Like other programs, work release has its good and bad points. On the one hand, inmates are sometimes reluctantly received in the community and find that certain areas of employment are closed to them. Citizens are often concerned about prisoners "stealing" jobs or working for lower than normal wages; consequently, such practices are prohibited by Public Law 89-176, which controls the federal work release program.

On the other hand, inmates gain many benefits from work release, including the ability to maintain work skills, maintain community ties, and make an easier transition from prison to the outside world. For those who have learned a skill in the institution, work release offers an excellent opportunity to try out a new occupation. For others, the job may be a training situation in which new skills are acquired. A number of states have reported that few work release inmates abscond while in the community.

Private Prison Enterprise The federal government helped put private industry into prisons when it approved the Free Venture Program in 1976. Seven states, including Connecticut, South Carolina, and Minnesota, were given grants to implement private industries inside prison walls.

Today, private prison industries have used a number of models. One approach, the state-use model, makes the correctional system a supplier of goods and services that serves state-run institutions[75] In another approach, the free-enterprise model, private companies set up manufacturing units on prison grounds or purchase goods made by inmates in shops owned and operated by the corrections department. In the corporate model, a semi-independent business is created on prison grounds, and its profits go to the state government and inmate laborers.

Postrelease Programs Vocational programming also involves helping inmates obtain jobs before they are released and keep them once they are on the outside. A number of correctional departments have set up employment services designed to ease the transition between institution and community. Employment program staff assess inmates' backgrounds to determine their abilities, interests, goals, and capabilities. They also help them create job plans essential to receiving early release (parole) and successfully reintegrating into the community. Some programs maintain community correctional placements in sheltered environments that help inmates bridge the gap between institutions and the outside world. Services include job placement, skill development, family counseling, and legal and medical assistance.

Can Rehabilitation Work?

Despite the variety and number of treatment programs in operation, questions remain about their effectiveness. In an oft-cited research effort, Robert Martinson and his associates (1975) found that a majority of treatment programs were failures, giving birth to the cry that "nothing works" in prison rehabilitations.[76] Martinson's work created considerable debate over the effectiveness of correctional treatment. Even some of the most carefully crafted treatment efforts, using the most up-to-date rehabilitation modalities (such as cognitive-behavioral therapy), failed to have a positive impact on inmates returning to the community, a finding that supports the "nothing works" mantra.[77]

Treatment proponents have dismissed the "nothing works" philosophy as exaggerated and, using sophisticated data analysis techniques, have found evidence that

L06 Be familiar with the different forms of correctional treatment

correctional rehabilitation can be effective.[78] When Paul Gendreau and Robert Ross reviewed the published work on correctional rehabilitation programs, they found that many intervention programs reported success.[79] More recently, Mark Lipsey and Francis Cullen's comprehensive review of the studies of correctional rehabilitation found consistently positive effects on reducing recidivism. Success seems to rely on the type of treatment, its implementation, and the nature of the offenders to whom it is applied.[80]

Guarding the Institution

Controlling a prison is a complex task. On the one hand, a tough, high-security environment may meet the goals of punishment and control but fail to reinforce positive behavior changes. On the other hand, too liberal an administrative stance can lower staff morale and place inmates in charge of the institution. For many years, prison guards were viewed as ruthless people who enjoyed their power over inmates, fought rehabilitation efforts, were racist, and had a "lock psychosis" developed from years of counting, numbering, and checking on inmates. This view has changed in recent years. Correctional officers are now viewed as public servants who are seeking the security and financial rewards of a civil service position.[81] Most are in favor of rehabilitation efforts and do not harbor any particular animosity toward the inmates.[82] The correctional officer has been characterized as a "people worker" who must be prepared to deal with the problems of inmates on a personal level and also as a member of a complex bureaucracy who must be able to cope with its demands. Mike Vuolo and Candace Kruttschnitt found that correctional officers can have a sizable impact on prisoners' ability to adjust to prison life. Correctional staff members who conduct themselves professionally and gain the respect and cooperation of the inmates are able to have a very positive influence on their later readjustment to society. In contrast, those who fail miserably on both counts may be contributing the nation's high recidivism rates.[83]

The greatest problem faced by correctional officers is probably the stress created by the duality of their role: maintainers of order and security *and* advocates of treatment and rehabilitation. Eric Lambert and his associates found that the stress of the prison experience can lead to emotional exhaustion, a powerful dimension of job burnout, which if left unchecked is associated with high levels of turnover and absenteeism and general job dissatisfaction.[84]

However, those who have high levels of job satisfaction, good relations with their coworkers, and high levels of social support seem to be better able to deal with the stress of the correctional setting.[85] For more on the work of a correctional officer, read the Careers in Criminal Justice feature.

Female Correctional Officers

Women now work side by side with male guards in almost every state, performing the same duties. Research indicates that discipline has not suffered because of the inclusion of women in the guard force. Sexual assaults have been rare, and more negative attitudes have been expressed by the female guards' male peers than by inmates. Most commentators believe that the presence of female guards can have an important beneficial effect on the self-image of inmates and can improve the guard–inmate working relationship.

Ironically, female correctional officers may find that an assignment to a male institution can boost their career. Recent restrictions on male staff in female institutions, in the wake of well-publicized sex scandals, have forced administrators to assign women officers to the dormitory areas, the least desirable areas in which to work. Women officers are not similarly restricted in male-only facilities.[86]

LO7 Discuss the world of correctional officers

Careers in Criminal Justice

CORRECTIONAL OFFICER

Duties and Characteristics of the Job

- The primary job of a correctional officer is to supervise individuals who are serving time in prison after being convicted.
- Their duties include supervising and submitting reports on inmate behavior, maintaining order within the population by enforcing institutional rules and policies, and ensuring order in the institution by searching for contraband or settling disputes between inmates.
- Although correctional officers tend to work a standard five-day, 40-hour work week, odds are they will work overtime on weekends, holidays, and nights as well, because jails and prisons must be staffed at all hours.

Job Outlook

- Opportunities exist for employment at the local level, but a majority of correctional officer positions are at state and federal prisons. A smaller number of jobs are available with private institutions.
- Thanks to a growing demand for correctional officers, combined with high rates of turnover within the field, prospects for employment are very good.
- A good correctional officer with the proper education and training has the potential to be promoted to correctional sergeant and to other administrative and supervisory positions.

Salary

- Median annual salary for a correctional officer is about $36,000.
- Median annual earnings in the public sector were recently $47,750 in the federal government, $36,140 in state government, and $34,820 in local government.
- Correctional officers usually are provided with uniforms or a clothing allowance to purchase their own uniforms. Their retirement coverage entitles correctional officers to retire at age 50 after 20 years of service or at any age with 25 years of service.

Qualifications

- Exact qualifications vary depending on what level of government and what type of setting the position is in.
- A majority of correctional institutions look for several characteristics in potential employees: correctional officers should be U.S. citizens, be at least 18 to 21 years old, and be able to pass a background check and a drug test.
- Correctional officers must also be in good physical and mental health, meet education requirements, and be able to work in a challenging environment where good judgment and quick thinking are necessary.
- Tests may be administered to judge whether an applicant meets these qualifications.

Education and Training

- Although only a high school diploma may be necessary to become a correctional officer, a bachelor's degree (especially in a field such as criminology, sociology, or criminal justice) will make career advancement easier and can greatly increase annual salary.
- After hiring and training, there may be a period of on-the-job training with an experienced officer.
- At the federal level, a bachelor's degree or three years of experience in a related occupation is necessary for employment.
- Federal corrections officers will have at least 200 hours of on-the-job training and a period of training at the federal Bureau of Prisons.

Word to the Wise

- Correctional officers are forced to routinely deal with, and sometimes restrain, people who suffer from HIV, hepatitis B and C, tuberculosis, and other contagious diseases.
- Officers are in danger of physical harm from prison-made weapons.
- When conducting body or cell searches, correction officers are in danger of being jabbed or cut by a piece of contraband.
- Officers must control mentally ill inmates.
- Officers are subject to taunts and verbal harassment.

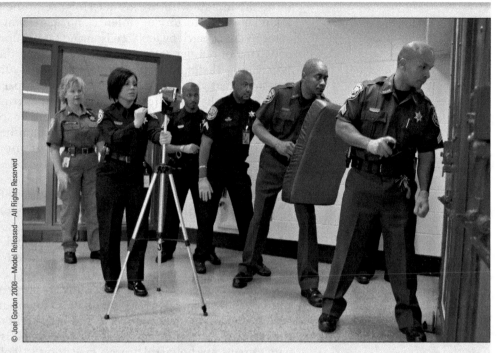

■ It is common for women to be employed in male prisons. Here, corrections officers are attempting to have an inmate moved to another cell. After he refuses to move, corrections officers are prepared to extract the inmate from the cell by force. Two officers are operating a still camera and videotaping during this cell extraction; another officer is holding blue blocking pads as the captain watches the procedure from the back.

Prison Violence

Conflict, violence, and brutality are sad but ever-present facts of institutional life. Violence can involve individual conflict: inmate versus inmate, inmate versus staff, staff versus inmate. Nonsexual assaults may stem from an aggressor's desire to shake down the victim for money and personal favors, may be motivated by racial conflict, or may simply be used to establish power within the institution. For example, on March 28, 2008, a riot at the federal penitentiary in Three Rivers, Texas, left one prisoner dead and 22 others injured. Intelligence sources said they believe the riot began when tensions over prison leadership developed between Mexican American inmates who consider themselves Chicanos and inmates who have closer ties to Mexico.[87]

Violence can also involve large groups of inmates, such as the infamous Attica riot in 1971, which claimed 39 lives, or the New Mexico State Penitentiary riot of February 1980, in which the death toll was 33. More than 300 prison riots have occurred since the first one in 1774, 90 percent of them since 1952.[88]

What Causes Violence?

What are the causes of prison violence? There is no single explanation for either collective or individual violence, although theories abound.[89] However, recent research by Benjamin Steiner shows that factors related to prison administration, inmate population characteristics, and the racial makeup of inmates and staff can influence violence levels.[90] Some of the factors related to individual and collective violence, respectively, are discussed in some detail below.

Individual Violence

● *History of prior violence.* Before they were incarcerated, many inmates were violence-prone individuals who always used force to get their own way. Some are former gang members who join inmate gangs as soon as they enter the institution.[91] In many instances, street gangs maintain prison branches that unite the inmate with his former violence-prone peers.[92] While the association between a history of violence and aggression behind bars is significant, some recent research by Jon Sorenson and Mark Cunningham found that people convicted of murder are no more violent than other members of the inmate population. Their finding is important because it runs counter to the argument that murderers are dangerous people with a "propensity for murder." Sorenson and Cunningham's conclusion that a murder conviction is not any greater predictor of prison violence than a conviction for some other offense counters an important argument for the use of capital punishment.[93]

- *Age.* Younger inmates, those with a record of prior incarceration, and those who have suffered pre-arrest drug use are the ones most likely to engage in disruptive behavior in prison, especially if they are not active participants in institutional treatment programs.[94] Sadly, juvenile offenders who are sentenced to adult institutions have significantly higher violence rates than the adult inmate population.[95] While it may be puzzling to some that inmates convicted of murder seem no more violent behind bars than the next inmate, it is possible that these may be older inmates who have learned from experience to "do their own time."[96]

- *Psychological factors.* Many inmates suffer from personality disorders. Recent research shows that among institutionalized offenders, psychopathy is the strongest predictor of violent recidivism and indifferent response to treatment.[97] In the crowded, dehumanizing world of the prison, it is not surprising that people with extreme psychological distress may resort to violence to dominate others.[98]

- *Prison conditions.* The prison experience itself causes people to become violent. Inhuman conditions, including overcrowding, depersonalization, and the threat of sexual assault, are violence-producing conditions.[99] Even in the most humane prisons, life is a constant put-down, and prison conditions are a threat to the inmates' sense of self-worth; violence is an expected consequence of these conditions. Violence levels are not much different between high-security and low-security prisons, suggesting that the prison experience itself, and not the level of control, produces violence.[100] The converse is also true: effective interventions can help reduce violence in even the most disruptive inmates, especially those who begin to realize that repeat violent incidents are punished by long-term stays in segregation and other negative consequences.[101]

- *Lack of dispute resolution mechanisms.* Many prisons lack effective mechanisms for handling inmate grievances against either prison officials or other inmates fairly and equitably. Prisoners who complain about other inmates are viewed as "rats" or "snitches" and are marked for death by their enemies. Similarly, inmates' complaints or lawsuits filed against the prison administration may result in their being placed in solitary confinement—"the hole."

- *Basic survival.* Inmates resort to violence in order to survive. The lack of physical security, the dearth of adequate mechanisms for resolving complaints, and the code of silence promote individual violence by inmates who might otherwise be effectively controlled.

Collective Violence

- *Inmate-balance theory.* Riots and other forms of collective violence occur when prison officials make an abrupt effort to take control of the prison and limit freedoms. Crackdowns occur when officials perceive that inmate leaders have too much power and take measures to control their illicit privileges, such as gambling or stealing food.[102]

- *Administrative-control theory.* Collective violence is caused by prison mismanagement, lack of strong security, and inadequate control by prison officials. Poor management may inhibit conflict management and set the stage for violence. Repressive administrations give inmates the feeling that nothing will ever change, that they have nothing to lose, and that violence is the only means for change.

Some prison violence is collective, involving mass riots, vandalism, and arson. Here, on February 5, 2009, plumes of smoke rise from the yard and recreation building of the Reeves County Detention Center unit I in Pecos, Texas. These fires came five days after inmates set fire to other parts of the RCDC units I and II during a riot spurred by complaints about inadequate health care and food. This remote West Texas county secured its finances and kept jobs at home by turning over its sprawling prison to private management, but two inmate riots have led to increased scrutiny of the facility.

AP Images Pecos Enterprise, Smokey Briggs

Despite these problems, both the suicide rate and the homicide rate in prisons have been in sharp decline. Although it is difficult to determine the cause of this drop in violence directed at self and others, more advanced security measures coupled with improved prison administration may be responsible.

LO8 Understand the causes of prison violence

Prisoners' Rights

Before the early 1960s, it was accepted that upon conviction, an individual forfeited all rights not expressly granted by statutory law or correctional policy; in other words, inmates were civilly dead. The U.S. Supreme Court held that convicted offenders should expect to be penalized for their misdeeds and that part of their punishment was the loss of freedoms that law-abiding citizens take for granted.

One reason why inmates lacked rights was that state and federal courts were reluctant to intervene in the administration of prisons unless the circumstances of a case clearly indicated a serious breach of the Eighth Amendment protection against cruel and unusual punishment. This judicial policy is referred to as the **hands-off doctrine**.

As the 1960s drew to a close, the hands-off doctrine was eroded. Federal district courts began seriously considering prisoners' claims about conditions in the various state and federal institutions and used their power to intervene on behalf of the inmates. In some ways, this concern reflected the spirit of the times, which saw the onset of the civil rights movement, and subsequently emerged in the areas of student rights, public welfare, mental institutions, juvenile court systems, and military justice.

Beginning in the late 1960s, such activist groups as the NAACP Legal Defense Fund and the American Civil Liberties Union's National Prison Project began to search for appropriate legal vehicles to bring prisoners' complaints before state and federal courts. The most widely used device was the federal Civil Rights Act, 42 U.S.C. 1983:

> Every person who, under color of any statute, ordinance, regulation, custom, or usage of any State or Territory subjects, or causes to be subjected, any citizen of the

hands-off doctrine
The legal practice of allowing prison administrators a free hand to run the institution, even if correctional practices violate inmates' constitutional rights; ended with the onset of the prisoners' rights movement in the 1960s.

United States or other person within the jurisdiction thereof to the deprivation of any rights, privileges, or immunities secured by the Constitution and laws shall be liable to the party injured in an action at law, suit in equity, or other proper proceeding for redress.

The legal argument went that, as U.S. citizens, prison inmates could sue state officials if their civil rights were violated—for example, if they were the victims of racial or religious discrimination.

The subsequent prisoners' rights crusade, stretching from 1964 to 1980, paralleled the civil rights and women's movements. Battle lines were drawn between prison officials, who hoped to maintain their power and resented interference by the courts, and inmate groups and their sympathizers, who used state and federal courts as a forum for demanding better living conditions and personal rights.

To slow down prison litigation which had been clogging the federal courts, Congress passed the Prison Litigation Reform Act in 1996.[103] The most important provision of the Act requires prisoners to exhaust all internal administrative grievance procedures before they can file a civil rights case in federal court. It also bars litigation if a prisoner has not suffered a physical injury in addition to a violation of his or her constitutional rights. There is a limitation on the number of times an appeal can be filed: if a judge decides that it is frivolous, malicious, or does not state a proper claim it counts as a "strike." After you get three strikes, another lawsuit cannot be filed unless the inmate is willing to pay the entire court filing fee up-front. The U.S. Supreme Court has upheld the provisions of the Act in two cases—one dealing with a request for monetary relief and the other with allegations of excessive use of force—*Booth v. Churner* (2001) and *Porter v. Nussle* (2002), in which the Court ruled that it is constitutional to require that an inmate go through all administrative processes before a case can be brought to the courts.[104] Civil rights groups believe that the Reform Act has a chilling affect on inmate litigation and has asked Congress to amend its provisions.[105]

While the prisoner's movement may have slowed, it has not ended. Below, some of the most important substantive and procedural rights of inmates are discussed.

Substantive Rights

Through a slow process of legal review, the courts have granted inmates a number of **substantive rights** that have significantly influenced the entire correctional system. The most important of these rights are discussed in the following sections.

Access to Courts, Legal Services, and Materials Courts have held that inmates are entitled to have legal materials available and must be provided with assistance in drawing up and filing complaints. Inmates who help others, so-called **jailhouse lawyers**, cannot be interfered with or harassed by prison administrators.

Freedom of the Press and of Expression Courts have consistently ruled that only when a compelling state interest exists can prisoners' First Amendment rights be modified; correctional authorities must justify the limiting of free speech by showing that granting it would threaten institutional security. If prison administrators believe that correspondence undermines prison security, the First Amendment rights of inmates can be curtailed.[106]

Freedom of Religion In general, the courts have ruled that inmates have the right to assemble and pray in the religion of their choice but that religious symbols and practices that interfere with institutional security can be restricted. Administrators can draw the line if responding to religious needs becomes cumbersome or impossible for reasons of cost or security. Granting special privileges can also be denied on the grounds that they will cause other groups to make similar demands that cannot be met within the institution.

Medical Rights In early prisons, inmates' right to medical treatment was restricted through the "exceptional circumstances doctrine." Using this policy, the courts would hear only those cases in which the circumstances revealed utter disregard for human dignity, while denying hearings to less serious cases. The cases that were allowed access to the courts usually entailed total denial of medical care.

To gain their medical rights, prisoners have resorted to class action suits (suits brought on behalf of all individuals affected by similar circumstances—in this case, poor medical attention). In the most significant case, *Newman v. Alabama* (1972), the entire Alabama prison system's medical facilities were declared inadequate.[107] The Supreme Court cited the following factors as contributing to inadequate care: insufficient physician and nurse resources, reliance on untrained inmates for para-medical work, intentional failure in treating the sick and injured, and failure to con-form to proper medical standards. The *Newman* case forced corrections departments to upgrade prison medical facilities.

It was not until 1976, in *Estelle v. Gamble*, that the Supreme Court clearly affirmed inmates' right to medical care.[108] Gamble had hurt his back in a Texas prison and filed suit because he contested the type of treatment he had received and questioned the lack of interest that prison guards had shown in his case. The Supreme Court said, "Deliberate indifference to serious medical needs of prisoners constitutes the 'unnecessary and wanton infliction of pain,' proscribed by the Eighth Amendment."[109] The *Gamble* ruling mandated that inmate health care reflect what is available to citizens in the general community. Consequently, correctional admin-istrators must consider access, quality, and cost of health care as part of the prison regime.[110]

Cruel and Unusual Punishment The concept of **cruel and unusual punishment** is founded in the Eighth Amendment of the Constitution. The term itself has not been specifically defined by the Supreme Court, but the Court has held that treat-ment constitutes cruel and unusual punishment when it does the following:

- Degrades the dignity of human beings[111]
- Is more severe than (is disproportional to) the offense for which it has been given[112]
- Shocks the general conscience and is fundamentally unfair[113]
- Is deliberately indifferent to a person's safety and well-being[114]
- Punishes people because of their status, such as race, religion, and mental state[115]
- Is in flagrant disregard of due process of law, such as punishment that is capriciously applied[116]

State and federal courts have placed strict limits on disciplinary methods that may be considered inhumane. Corporal punishment all but ended after the practice was condemned in *Jackson v. Bishop* (1968).[117] Although the solitary confinement of disruptive inmates continues, its prolonged use under barbaric conditions has been held to be in violation of the Eighth Amendment. Courts have found that inmates placed in solitary have the right to adequate personal hygiene, to exer-cise, mattresses, and ventilation, and to rules specifying how they can earn their release.

Racial Segregation In the 2005 case *Johnson v. California*, the Supreme Court ruled that the segregation of prison inmates based on race, in their cells or anywhere on prison grounds, is an inappropriate form of racial classification.[118] However, it left it open for lower courts to decide, using a standard of *strict scrutiny*, when segregation is inappropriate and unconstitutional. *Johnson* focused on the policy of segregating inmates upon their arrival at a prison. However, the Court's ruling seemed to sug-gest that if racial segregation was allowed for incoming inmates, there is a danger that it might also be used "in the dining halls, yards, and general housing areas." Segregation should only be allowed, the judges reasoned, if a prison administra-tor could prove that it served a compelling interest to promote prison safety. The Court recognized that "prisons are dangerous places, and the special circumstances they present may justify racial classifications in some contexts." Because the Chino

cruel and unusual punishment Physical punishment or punishment that is far in excess of that given to people under similar circum-stances and is therefore banned by the Eighth Amendment. The death penalty has so far not been considered cruel and unusual if it is administered in a fair and nondiscriminatory fashion.

This photo, taken in 2009, shows inmates Tim Heffernan, left, and Daniel Mabson talking from their adjacent bunks at the Sierra Conservation Center in Jamestown, California. Despite efforts by California prison officials to end one of the nation's last vestiges of institutionalized, government-mandated racial segregation, powerful race-based gangs violently oppose attempts to desegregate prison housing units. Blacks, whites, and Hispanics are willing to sleep side by side in bunk beds spaced an arm's length apart, but would brawl and risk longer sentences rather than accept an inmate of another race in a bed above or below them in the same bunk-bed stack. Does housing inmates according to race violate their civil rights? The photo also illustrates the problems of overcrowding and the housing of four inmates in a cell designed for a single person.

AP Photo/Rich Pedroncelli

RealityCheck

MYTH OR REALITY? Inmates lose all civil rights once they enter a high-security correctional facility.

MYTH. *Inmates retain many civil rights, even behind prison walls.*

Do you agree? Should inmates maintain all civil rights, including the right to vote or to give press interviews, while in prison?

LO9 **Know what is meant by prisoners' rights, and discuss some key privileges that have been granted to inmates**

parole
The early release of a prisoner from imprisonment, subject to conditions set by a parole board.

riot occurred after California began to integrate prison entry centers, it is possible that future efforts to racially integrate prisons will be frustrated. It is possible that state courts, even when using a strict scrutiny standard, may conclude that racial integration, in some instances, is just too dangerous.

Overall Prison Conditions Prisoners have long had the right to the minimal conditions necessary for human survival, such as the food, clothing, shelter, and medical care necessary to sustain human life. A number of attempts have been made to articulate reasonable standards of prison care and to make sure that officials adhere to them. Courts have held that although people are sent to prison for punishment, it does not mean that prison should be a punishing experience.[119] In the 1994 case of *Farmer v. Brennan*, the court ruled that prison officials are legally liable if, knowing that an inmate faces a serious risk of harm, they disregard that risk by failing to take measures to avoid or reduce it. Furthermore, prison officials should be able to infer the risk from the evidence at hand; they need not be warned or told.[120]

Although inmates retain the right to reasonable care, if there is a legitimate purpose for the use of governmental restrictions, those restrictions may be considered constitutional. Thus, it might be possible to restrict reading material, allow strip searches, and prohibit inmates from receiving packages from the outside if the restrictions are legitimate security measures. If overcrowded conditions require it, inmates may be double-bunked in cells designed for a single inmate.[121]

Leaving Prison: Parole

At the expiration of their prison term, most inmates return to society and try to resume their lives. For some inmates, their reintegration into society comes by way of **parole**—the planned community release and supervision of incarcerated offenders before the expiration of their full prison sentences. Once on parole, former inmates have to live by a strict set of rules that mandate they stay out of trouble, stay drug and alcohol free, be employed, and attend counseling. Parolees are monitored by their case officers who may administer random drug tests and use GPS tracking devices to keep tabs on their whereabouts.[122]

In some states parole is granted by a parole board, a duly constituted body of men and women who review inmate cases and determine whether offenders have reached a rehabilitative level sufficient to deal with the outside world. The board also dictates what specific parole rules parolees must obey. Most boards are independent agencies that consist of members appointed by the governor; the rest are affiliated with the Department of Corrections. A majority have the authority to make final release decisions; most require interviews with parole-eligible offenders prior to release. A majority of parole boards also set the rules of parole and are given the power to revoke parole when these rules are violated or the parolee commits another crime.[123]

In a number of jurisdictions, discretionary parole has been abandoned, and the amount of time a person must remain in prison is a predetermined percentage of the sentence, assuming there are no infractions or escape attempts. In this "mandatory parole release" approach, the inmate is released when the unserved portion of the maximum prison term equals his or her earned good time (minus time served in jail awaiting trial). In some states, sentences can be reduced by more than half with a combination of statutory and earned good time. If the conditions of their release are violated, mandatory releasees can have their good time revoked and be returned to the institution to serve the remainder of their unexpired term. The remaining inmates are released for a variety of reasons, including expiration of their term, commutation of their sentence, and court orders to relieve overcrowded prisons. The use of discretionary parole has been in steep decline, while the number of inmates released on mandatory parole has increased significantly. There are more than 800,000 people currently on parole, and each year about 500,000 inmates are granted parole and slightly more exit or complete parole, so the total population on parole has finally begun (2009) a downward trend, reversing years of increases upward.[124]

Parole Effectiveness

Despite all efforts to treat, correct, and rehabilitate incarcerated offenders, many return to prison shortly after their release. Persons released from prison face a multitude of difficulties. They remain largely uneducated, unskilled, and usually without solid family support systems—then add to this the burdens of a prison record. Not surprisingly, most parolees fail, and rather quickly; rearrests are most common in the first six months after release.[125]

A recent (2011) report by the influential Pew Foundation found nearly 43 percent of prisoners released in 2004 and 45 percent of those released in 1999 were reincarcerated within three years of their release, either for committing a new crime or for violating the terms of their supervised release. Not all states had the same failure rates. The more successful ones made important correctional decisions—such as the types of offenders sentenced to prison, how inmates are selected for release, how long they are under supervision—using carefully drawn empirical evidence. Which strategies were the most successful? States that made extensive use of probation for petty offenders had relatively higher inmate recidivism rates, since only the most hard-core inmates were actually sent to prison. Parole was more successful in states that employed programs that target motivated offenders to stay crime- and drug-free through a combination of swift and certain sanctions for prison violations and rewards for obeying correctional rules.[126]

The Problem of Reentry

Parole failure is still a significant problem, and a growing portion of the correctional population consists of parolees who failed on the outside. Why has the phenomenon of parole failure remained so stubborn and hard to control? Why is it so difficult to reenter society?

One reason may be the very nature of the prison experience itself. The psychological and economic problems that lead offenders to recidivism are rarely addressed by a stay in prison. Despite rehabilitation efforts, the typical ex-convict is still the same undereducated, unemployed, substance-abusing, lower-socioeconomic-status male he was when arrested. Being separated from friends and family, not sharing in conventional society, associating with dangerous people, and adapting to a volatile lifestyle probably have done little to improve the offender's personality or behavior. It seems naïve to think that incarceration alone can help someone overcome these lifelong disabilities. By their very nature, prisons seek to impose and maintain order and conformity rather than to help inmates develop skills such as independence and critical thinking—factors that may be essential once the inmate is forced to cope outside the prison walls.[127]

It is also possible that reentry problems are related to the releasee's own lifelong personal deficits. Most research efforts indicate that recidivates are young men and women who have managed to accumulate a long history of drug abuse and criminal behavior in a short time.[128] They may have an antisocial personality and childhood experiences with family dysfunction; many have suffered from a lifetime of substance abuse or dependence disorder.[129] It is not surprising that releasees who maintain criminal peer associations, carry weapons, abuse alcohol, and harbor aggressive feelings are the most likely to fail upon reentry.[130]

Once the parolee is on the outside, these problems do not easily subside. Some ex-inmates may feel compelled to prove that the prison experience has not changed them; taking drugs or being sexually aggressive may show friends that they have not lost their "heart."[131] In contrast, parolees who have had a good employment record in the past and who maintain jobs after their release are the most likely to avoid recidivating.[132]

RealityCheck

MYTH OR REALITY? **Most released inmates fail on parole.**

REALITY. *More than half of all released inmates return to prison shortly after their release.*

If you ran the correctional system, what would you do to reverse this trend?

Why Do People Fail on Parole?

Why do so many inmates fail in the community? A number of social, economic, and personal factors interfere with reentry success.

Reentry risks can be tied to legal changes in how people are released from prison. Changes in sentencing laws have resulted in the growth of mandatory release and limits on discretionary parole. Inmates may be discouraged from seeking involvement in rehabilitation programs because they no longer affect the chance of parole. The lack of incentive means that fewer inmates leaving prison have participated in programs to address deficiencies in the areas of employment, education, and substance use. Many of those being released have therefore not received adequate treatment and are unprepared for life in conventional society.[133]

Nor does the situation improve upon release. Many inmates are not assigned to supervision caseloads once they are back in the community. About 200,000 released inmates go unsupervised each year, three-quarters of whom have been released after completing their maximum sentence and are therefore not required to be supervised. A number of research efforts indicate that supervision can be valuable. When Michael Osterman looked at the records of those released from prison in New Jersey he found that after three years those released with parole supervision were generally less involved in new crimes when compared with those who were released unconditionally.[134] Of course, inmates who "max out" or otherwise go unsupervised may be the more serious offenders whose survival in the community would be lower even if they were supervised. If these differences are controlled, the effect of supervision is neutralized.[135] So the actual effect of supervision after release is still open to debate.[136]

Regardless of how they are released, the risks the flood of newly released inmates present to the community include increases in child abuse, family violence, the spread of infectious diseases, homelessness, and community disorganization. Many have no way to cope and wind up in homeless shelters.[137] These problems take a heavy toll on communities and also limit reentry success.

Economic Problems Prison takes a heavy economic toll on former inmates. Most people leave prison with no savings, no immediate entitlement to unemployment benefits, and few employment prospects, especially in this era of high unemployment.[138] The Pew Foundation found that serving time significantly reduces economic status and prospects:

- Serving time reduces hourly wages for men by approximately 11 percent, annual employment by 9 weeks, and annual earnings by 40 percent.
- By age 48, the typical former inmate will have earned $179,000 less than if he had never been incarcerated.

A prison experience locks people onto the lowest rung of the economic ladder and significantly reduces their chances for upward economic mobility. A year after release, as many as 60 percent of former inmates are not employed in the regular labor market, and employers are increasingly reluctant to hire ex-offenders. Ex-offenders are commonly barred from working in the fields in which most jobs are being created, such as child care, education, security, nursing, and home health care. More jobs are also now unionized, and many unions exclude ex-offenders. Parolees who had a good employment record before their incarceration and who are able to find jobs after their release are the ones most likely to avoid recidivating.[139] Another bit of good news comes from a recent four-state survey conducted by Paul Hirschfield and Alex Piquero which found that though some people regard ex-offenders as dangerous and dishonest, many reject these stereotypes, and a majority say that they would be willing to work and associate with people who were previously incarcerated. Even people who believe in harsh punishment may be willing to work alongside people who paid their debt to society. If more people were acquainted with ex-offenders, the more willing they would be to hire them and give them the economic opportunities to succeed.[140]

Family Problems Inmates with strong social support and close family ties have a better chance of making it on the outside.[141] But prison can take its toll on social relationships, and being a former inmate can devastate family economic and social functioning. Poor inmates and their families may be no longer welcome in subsidized

On February 16, 2009, Eugene Nater and Sonya Blevins, who were recently released from prison, prepare salad for customers at Salad Creations at the Westfield Annapolis mall in Annapolis, Maryland. McQucio Moore, a former parole officer in Washington, D.C., and the owner of Salad Creations, hired the two just before Christmas. It is the first time he has ever hired offenders. Having a job is one key step toward successful rehabilitation after reentry into society.

AP Images / The Annapolis Capital, Joshua McKerrow

■ Former sex offenders often have a tough time adjusting in the community. In this photo, Kenneth Barillas is interviewed under a sign attached to his home, near the residence of sex offender Donald Robinson. After being locked away for 25 years for sex crimes, Robinson, then 57 years old, moved to a little block of unassuming homes in East Palo Alto, California. The timing was particularly bad. The day before, Philip Garrido's arrest for allegedly kidnapping 11-year-old Jaycee Lee Dugard and keeping her for 18 years made headlines around the world. The spotlight was on sex offenders. And Robinson, who had spent 12 years after his 1997 release from prison in a state mental hospital for recidivist sex offenders, remained under state-sponsored treatment as an outpatient. How would you feel if someone like Robinson moved next door to you? Would you hang out a sign like Barillas did or welcome him to the neighborhood?

public housing complexes. This is a consequence of the U.S. Department of Housing and Urban Development's "one strike and you're out" policy, whereby all members of the household are evicted if one member is involved in crime.[142] Without government subsidies, former inmates' families may not have the economic means to find affordable housing. The Pew Foundation found that family income averaged over the years a father is incarcerated is 22 percent lower than family income was the year before the father was incarcerated. Even in the year after the father is released, family income remains 15 percent lower than it was the year before incarceration.[143]

Kids are hurt educationally, socially, and financially if a parent is a former inmate. The Pew Foundation found that children with fathers who have been incarcerated are significantly more likely than other children to be expelled or suspended from school (23 percent compared with 4 percent). Children of incarcerated and released parents may suffer confusion, sadness, and social stigma, and these feelings often result in difficulties in school, low self-esteem, aggressive behavior, and general emotional dysfunction. One reason is that mothers released from prison have difficulty finding services such as housing, employment, and child care, and this causes stress for them and their children.

Another problem is that if the parents are negative role models, children fail to develop positive attitudes about work and responsibility. Children of incarcerated parents are five times more likely to serve time in prison than children whose parents are not incarcerated.

Community Problems Parole expert Richard Seiter notes that when there were only a few hundred thousand prisoners and a few thousand releasees per year, the issues surrounding the release of offenders did not overwhelm communities.[144] Families could house ex-inmates, job-search organizations could find them jobs, and community social service agencies could respond to their individual needs for mental health or substance abuse treatment. Today, the sheer number of reentering inmates has taxed the communities to which they are returning.[145]

Community characteristics can also influence the way parole violations are handled. Parolees returning to communities with high unemployment rates—a factor considered by parole board members to be an unstable environment—are more likely to have their parole revoked.[146] Similarly, parolees living in areas with concentrated disadvantage and social disorder, where bars are plentiful and liquor stores abundant, also suffer higher rates of recidivism. Clearly the neighborhood plays a significant role in parole success. Communities that can provide social and mental health services also influence parole success. For example, many former inmates need mental and psychological services that some communities simply cannot provide. Even when public mental health services are available, many mentally ill individuals fail to use them because they fear institutionalization, deny they are mentally ill, or distrust the mental health system. The situation will become more serious as more and more parolees are released into the same disorganized communities where deteriorated conditions may have motivated their original crimes. Having mental health services nearby seems to have a significant effect on parole board decision making.[147] The further parolees live from social service providers, the more likely they will be returned to prison.

Recognizing that some communities experience high rates of incarceration and reentry, some have created coalitions of community organizations to interact with every person returning home from prison. In New York City, the NYC Justice Corps provides transitional employment for young adults returning home from prison and jail in two neighborhoods most impacted by incarceration and reentry. In each location, a local organization brings together young people with their community to identify community improvement projects the NYC Justice Corps members can execute while developing hard skills that ready them for the labor market.[148]

Legal Problems Ex-inmates may also find that going straight is an economic impossibility. Many employers are reluctant to hire people who have served time. Even if a criminal record does not automatically prohibit employment, why would an employer hire an ex-con when other applicants are available? If ex-offenders lie about their prison experience and are later found out, they will be dismissed for misrepresentation. Research shows that former inmates who gain and keep meaningful employment are more likely to succeed on parole than those who are unemployed or underemployed.[149] One reason why ex-inmates find it so difficult to make it on the outside is the legal restrictions they are forced to endure. These may include prohibitions on certain kinds of employment, limits on obtaining licenses, and restrictions on their freedom of movement.[150]

Improving Chances on Reentry

Can something be done to ease reentry? Now that the scope of the problem has been recognized, both the federal and state governments have devoted energy to improving success at reentry. On April 9, 2008, the Second Chance Act was signed into law. This federal legislation authorized various grants to government agencies and nonprofit groups to provide a variety of services (including employment assistance, housing, substance abuse treatment, and family programming) that can help to reduce reoffending and violations of probation and parole.

State correctional agencies have made an effort to help inmates take advantage of these services. Take, for instance, the state of Maryland. In order to inform soon-to-be-released inmates of these services and help them to better prepare for reentry, the Maryland Correctional Education Libraries acquired two mobile units in April 2007. Equipped with computers and other educational tools, the mobile units are able to serve all the prerelease centers in Maryland.[151] Another prerelease program designed to help inmates solve the problems of reentry is discussed in the Contemporary Issues in Criminal Justice feature.

L10 Be knowledgeable about the parole process and the problems of prisoner reentry

Getting Ready Program

The Getting Ready Program is Arizona's common-sense approach to prerelease preparation designed to reduce postrelease recidivism. It is aimed at giving inmates better coping skills that can help them ease the shock of reentry.

The program begins on day one of incarceration and continues to the conclusion of every inmate's sentence. Getting Ready redefines the officer–offender relationship, shifting many responsibilities from the staff to the inmates and empowering both groups to function at substantively high levels. For example, officers do not tell inmates when to get up and when to go to sleep. Getting Ready does not just preach about what you ought to be doing when you get back to the real world. It brings the real world—what they call a "Parallel Universe"—into prison so that inmates in every custody level acquire and practice basic life skills from the first to the last day of their incarceration. In a sense, it makes prison life resemble life in the community. One example is health care. Because health care costs are rising, Getting Ready helps inmates to lower their medical costs upon release. It teaches then healthy habits—not smoking, eating healthy foods, exercising, and complying with medical directions—activities that will result in a lower co-pay on the outside. The Parallel Universe model has also been applied to inmates' work assignments. The program uses U.S. Department of Labor's *Dictionary of Occupational Titles* to determine job categories and salaries and revises inmate pay to reflect what someone could expect to receive proportionately for performing this work in the community.

The same principle was applied to education. An inmate is not required to complete or further his education, but until he earns a GED—assuming he is academically able, which encompasses the vast majority of the population—he can be employed only in entry-level jobs, earning entry-level wages.

Like in the real world, once they earn a GED, many other employment opportunities open up. In Getting Ready, a GED becomes a prerequisite to job training, better work assignments, and higher wages.

Getting Ready uses a three-tiered earned incentive system that changes the traditional paradigm. This system recognizes good behavior—greater acceptance of responsibility and better decision-making—with rewards or incentives that can be earned over time, are appropriate to each custody level, and are prized by the population. For example, in Getting Ready, an inmate has to work very hard to earn a visit in which family members are allowed to bring food, and not all inmates in every custody level are eligible. Similarly, inmates who do well have the possibility of eating their meals in a less regimented setting, followed by watching a TV show or televised sports event, and the opportunity to buy snacks not ordinarily sold in the commissary.

Evaluations of the program indicate that since it was implemented violence has been reduced, with inmate-on-inmate assaults decreasing 46 percent, inmate-on-staff assaults down 33 percent, suicides down 67 percent, and sexual assaults down 61 percent. The average one-year return rate for all releases in the two years before and after Getting Ready started improved 2.75 percent. Within this group of releases were 1,500 inmates who completed Getting Ready in its entirety. This group has done considerably better, as much as two years after release, than inmates of comparable risk who were not in the program.

CRITICAL THINKING

What life skills do you think would help inmates make it on the outside? What about conjugal visits? Should married inmates be allowed to have overnight visits with their spouses to maintain a family life, critical to adjustment on the outside? What problems might this cause?

Ethical Challenge

Some prison administrators and politicians believe that prisoners are being coddled and have too many privileges. They want to adopt a no-frills policy designed to convince inmates never to repeat their criminal acts. Prisons, they believe, are places of confinement and nothing more. They want to take away privileges, reduce treatment programs, increase punishment for infractions, and reduce the quality of prison life (i.e., no dessert at meals!). The argument is that prisoners have it too easy, and if prison was a punishing experience they would not dare return.

Write an essay that challenges these beliefs. You may want to refer to the sections on rehabilitation and treatment to point out that successful programs do exist, and to the sections on prisoners' rights to show that certain kinds of care may be a legal right of inmates, rather than a privilege. *Note:* If you prefer to support aspects of the no-frills policy, please do so, but be sure to acknowledge the information provided in the sections mentioned here.

In addition, some programs provide postrelease counseling and support. One promising Virginia program, Women Inspired to Transform (WIT), uses volunteers to teach female returnees about anger management, job interviewing, communication, relationships, and parenting.[152] Some programs enroll inmates in education, substance abuse, and other institutional programs that are customized to address their individual needs and ease their reentry, while providing follow-up postrelease treatment programming, including social service assistance (such as substance abuse and mental health treatment) and vocational development (such as training, education, and resume development necessary.[153]

Summary

L01 **Discuss the problems of the adult correctional system** A significant number of facilities are old and in ill repair. Institutions are overcrowded, and meaningful treatment efforts are often a matter of wishful thinking. The typical prison is often described as a "school for crime." Recidivism rates are shockingly high.

L02 **Know what is meant by the term** *total institution* Prisons in the United States are total institutions which limit individuality and demand obedience. Inmates locked within their walls are segregated from the outside world. They have to learn to cope with their new environment or risk injury or even death.

L03 **Be familiar with the problem of sexual coercion in prison and what is being done to help** Young males may be raped and kept as sexual slaves by older, more aggressive inmates. The Prison Rape Reduction Act of 2003 established three programs to reduce rape in prison. However, many inmates refuse to report rape and others may misunderstand what constitutes a rape, so the true extent of prison rape may never be known.

L04 **Chart the prisonization process and the development of the inmate social code** Part of living in prison involves learning to protect oneself and developing survival instincts. Inmates form their own world, with a unique set of norms and rules, known as the inmate subculture. Those who become the most "prisonized" will be the least likely to avoid criminal activity on the outside.

L05 **Compare the lives and cultures of male and female inmates** Women's prisons tend to be smaller than those housing male inmates, but female inmates may suffer from a lack of adequate job training and from inferior health, treatment, and educational facilities. Unlike male inmates, women usually do not present an immediate physical danger to staff and fellow inmates. Make-believe family groups contain masculine and feminine figures acting as fathers and mothers; some even act as children and take on the role of brother or sister.

L06 **Be familiar with the different forms of correctional treatment** Counseling programs help inmates to control their emotions, communicate with others, deal with legal concerns, manage general life issues, control substance abuse, and develop and maintain social relationships. Inmate rehabilitation is also pursued through vocational and educational training.

L07 **Discuss the world of correctional officers** Correctional officers are now viewed as dedicated public servants. Most are in favor of rehabilitation efforts, so that the typical correctional officer has been characterized as a "people worker." There are few gender differences in the behavior of correctional officers.

L08 **Understand the causes of prison violence** Violence can involve individual conflict: inmate versus inmate, inmate versus staff, or staff versus inmate. Prison violence is associated with overcrowding, lack of effective dispute resolution mechanisms, individual history of violence, and poor prison conditions.

L09 **Know what is meant by prisoners' rights, and discuss some key privileges that have been granted to inmates** Today inmates have the right to medical care, freedom from cruel and unusual treatment, the right to an attorney, and the right to practice their religion. Inmates can sue the prison administration if their rights have been violated—for example, if they are denied proper medical care.

L010 **Be knowledgeable about the parole process and the problems of prisoner reentry** Most inmates are paroled either by mandatory release or parole board vote. Parole is generally viewed as a privilege granted to deserving inmates on the basis of their good behavior while in prison. More than half of all parolees return to prison shortly after their release. Recidivism may be a by-product of the disruptive effect a prison experience has on personal relationships.

Review Questions

1. Considering the dangers that men face during their prison stay, should nonviolent inmates be placed in separate institutions to protect them from harm?

2. Should women be allowed to work as guards in men's prisons? What about male guards in women's prisons?

3. Should prison inmates be allowed a free college education while noncriminals are forced to pay tuition?

4. Which would be more effective: telling inmates that they have to earn the right to be paroled, or giving inmates their parole date in advance and telling them they will lose it for misbehavior?

5. What is the role of the parole board?

6. Should a former prisoner enjoy all the civil rights afforded the average citizen?

7. Should former inmates lose their right to vote?

PART 5

CONTEMPORARY ISSUES IN AMERICAN CRIMINAL JUSTICE

Although many people are drawn to mainstream careers in law enforcement, courts, and corrections, there are other areas of criminal justice with good job potential. One such area is juvenile probation. Juvenile probation officers, like adult probation officers, must fulfill a number of obligations, including:

- Monitoring offenders through personal contacts
- Developing a relationship with the monitored juvenile and serving as a positive role model
- Preparing and delivering reports to the court and recommending treatment options
- Scheduling drug testing and searches of the monitored juvenile's property
- Ensuring that juveniles are held accountable through their actions and comply with probation conditions

Kevin Kellems, an intensive juvenile probation officer in Calhoun County, Michigan, performs these functions and more. Kellems's career, like others in criminal justice, can be challenging:

> The stress comes from working with a population of young people and their families who are often highly chaotic and dysfunctional. Continued budget cuts also increase stress by reducing the services available to the children and families who need them. It can be disappointing to see the same youth return to court time after time without making any changes—or caring to.

> Yet Kellems also finds being a juvenile probation officer rewarding:

> The greatest rewards on this job are often very small baby steps that a family or client makes that you cannot really appreciate until you stop and look back on the case after closing it.

This section of *Essentials of Criminal Justice* also features a chapter on recent developments and cutting edge problems in criminal justice. Among them is terrorism. In the wake of the September 11, 2001, attacks, a number of homeland security careers have been created. By all accounts, this is an area in which the federal government will see continued growth.

Mark O. is a special agent for the Department of Homeland Security. He works for the Immigration and Customs (ICE) Office of Investigations conducting criminal investigations into suspected, alleged, and/or known violations of federal law. Because of the secure nature of his work, we cannot reveal his real name or publish his photo. Why did he become a criminal investigator? Upon graduating from college with a degree in psychology, he began working in a psychiatric hospital. A New York City native, he was personally affected by the terrorist attacks on 9/11, and felt compelled to do something to help protect his country. Very shortly thereafter, he applied for and was offered his first federal law enforcement position. Eventually, he moved into the area of antiterrorism and counterterrorism.

Although he loves his job, Mark believes that the general public holds many misconceptions about investigative work. Unlike what is often portrayed on television, investigations take time. Sometimes it may be several years before a single arrest is made. Often, solving a case depends not on the discovery of a single "smoking gun" but, rather, on the painstaking accumulation of evidence. Consequently, investigation requires a great deal of patience. Answers aren't always clear-cut, so an investigator must maintain a high level of alertness, flexibility, and focus. Yet the rewards are great. Mark gets to work alongside many dedicated colleagues who share a deep desire to do something to help their fellow citizens.

> "As a teenager, I ended up hanging around a much older and hard-core crowd. This led to more than a few brushes with law enforcement. Seeing that the future only held jail and prison if I continued on my path, I decided to change my course. In so doing, I wanted to help others do the same."
>
> Kevin Kellems

Part 5 contains two chapters that cover these special issues in criminal justice. Chapter 13 looks at the history of juvenile justice and current issues such as transfer to the adult court and juvenile sentencing issues. Chapter 14 looks at emerging issues the justice system must learn to confront: cyber crime, global crime, green crime, and corporate crime.

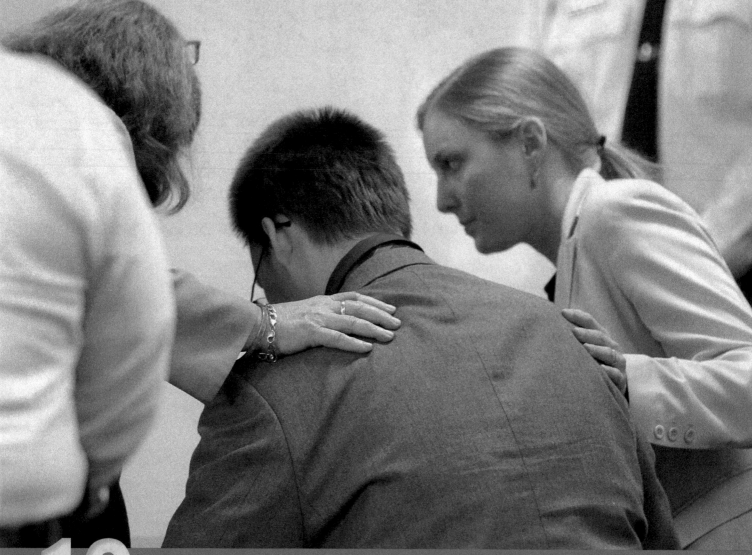

AP Photo/Pat Greenhouse, Pool

13 Juvenile Justice in the Twenty-First Century

Learning Objectives

LO1 Describe the history of juvenile justice

LO2 Discuss the establishment of the juvenile court

LO3 Describe the changes in juvenile justice that began in the 1960s and continue today

LO4 Summarize police processing of juvenile offenders

LO5 Describe the juvenile court process

LO6 Explain the concept of waiver

LO7 Explain the importance of *In re Gault*

LO8 Describe the juvenile correctional process

*I*t was a case that shook the Commonwealth of Massachusetts to its core. Sixteen-year-old John Odgren followed James Alenson, a young boy he had never met, into the bathroom at Lincoln-Sudbury Regional High School, drew a knife, and stabbed him to death. Because he was 16 at the time, Massachusetts law required that Odgren be charged as an adult, and he was tried on a charge of first-degree murder before a jury in Middlesex Superior Court. Odgren's attorney, Jonathan Shapiro, defended him by suggesting that he was delusional and psychotic at the time of the murder: "Why did a geeky, uncoordinated, awkward 16-year-old who had never been in any trouble with the law suddenly and without provocation ferociously stab to death a 15-year-old classmate who he did not even know?" Shapiro asked. The defense also argued that Odgren suffered from attention-deficit/hyperactivity disorder, depression, anxiety, bipolar disorder, and even Asperger syndrome, a form of autism whose symptoms include significant difficulties in social interaction, repetitive patterns of behavior, physical clumsiness, and atypical use of language. Odgren was reportedly obsessed with the number 19, and the fact that he committed his crime on the 19th day of the month was not viewed as a coincidence. The prosecution did not deny that Odgren had a history of mental illness but maintained that his condition was not serious enough to be considered legal insanity. The jury heard that Odgren had a history of secretly bringing knives to school and enjoying violent novels, as if he were carefully planning "the perfect murder." The jurors rejected the defense argument that Odgren was criminally insane when he murdered Alenson and convicted him of first-degree murder. Odgren's conviction was upheld by the State Supreme Judicial Court.[1] ∎

RealityCheck

MYTH OR REALITY?

- *Parens patriae* is the guiding philosophy of juvenile justice today.
- All juveniles fall under the jurisdiction of the adult court at age 18.
- Juveniles enjoy different rights than adults.
- Juvenile trials are different from adult trials.
- Youths are more violent and criminally dangerous today than they were in the past.

The Odgren case is representative of the difficult choices that agents of the juvenile justice system are continually asked to make: How should troubled children be treated? What can be done to treat dangerous young offenders? Should youthful law violators be given special treatment because of their age, or should they be treated in a similar fashion to adults committing the same crimes?

Independent of (yet interrelated with) the adult criminal justice system, the juvenile justice system is primarily responsible for dealing with juvenile and youth crime, as well as with incorrigible and truant children and runaways. Conceived at the turn of the twentieth century, the juvenile justice system was viewed as a quasi-social welfare agency that was to act as a surrogate parent in the interests of the child; this is referred to as the *parens patriae* philosophy. Many people who work in the system still hold to the original social welfare principles of the juvenile justice system. In contrast, those who adopt a crime control orientation suggest that the juvenile justice system's *parens patriae* philosophy is outdated. They point to nationally publicized incidents of juvenile violence, such as the shootings at Columbine High School in Colorado, as indicators that serious juvenile offenders should be punished and disciplined rather than treated and rehabilitated. "Why should we give special treatment to violent young juveniles?" they ask. "After all, juveniles commit almost 9 percent of all the murders in the United States and about 15 percent of all rapes."[2]

It remains to be seen whether the juvenile justice system will continue on its path toward deterrence, punishment, and control or return to its former role as a treatment-dispensing agency. This chapter reviews the history of juvenile justice and discusses the justice system's processing of youthful offenders.

The History of Juvenile Justice

The modern practice of legally separating adult criminals and juvenile offenders can be traced back to two developments in English custom and law that occurred centuries ago: the development of Elizabethan-era poor laws and the creation of the English chancery court. Both of these innovations were designed to allow the state to take control of the lives of needy but not necessarily criminal children.[3]

- *Poor laws.* As early as 1535, the English passed statutes known as **poor laws**, which (among other things) mandated the appointment of overseers who placed destitute or neglected children with families who then trained them in agricultural, trade, or domestic services; this practice was referred to as *indenture*. The Elizabethan poor laws of 1601 created a system of church wardens and overseers who, with the consent of the justices of the peace, identified vagrant, delinquent, and neglected children and took measures to put them to work. Often this meant placing them in poorhouses or workhouses or, more commonly, apprenticing them until their adulthood.
- *Chancery courts.* English chancery courts provided judicial relief to those who had no legal standing or could expect no legal relief because of the corruption and inadequacy of other common-law courts. People who felt their rights were being violated could take their cases to the chancery court for review. In this capacity, the chancery court protected the property rights and welfare of more minor children who could not care for themselves—children whose position and property were of direct concern to the monarch. The courts dealt with issues of guardianship and the use and control of property. Thus, if the guardian of an orphaned child wished to sell off his ward's inheritance, the chancery court might be asked to review the proceedings and determine whether the sale was in the child's best interest.

Care of Children in Early America

Poor laws and chancery courts were brought from England to colonial America. Poor laws were passed in Virginia in 1646, and in Connecticut and Massachusetts in 1678, and continued in force until the early nineteenth century. They mandated care for wayward and destitute children. However, those youths who committed serious criminal offenses continued to be tried in the same courts as adults.

To accommodate dependent youths, local jurisdictions developed almshouses, poorhouses, and workhouses. Crowded and unhealthy, these shelters accepted the poor, the insane, the diseased, and vagrant and destitute children. Middle-class civic leaders, who referred to themselves as **child savers**, began to develop organizations and groups to help alleviate the burdens of the poor and immigrants by sponsoring shelter care for youths, educational and social activities, and the development of settlement houses. In retrospect, their main focus seems to have been on extending governmental control over a whole range of youthful activities that previously had been left to private or family control, including idleness, drinking, vagrancy, and delinquency.[4]

Boys on the steps of an abandoned tenement building in New York City, about 1889. The child savers were concerned that, if left alone, children like these would enter a life of crime. They created the House of Refuge to care for poor and neglected kids. Critics accused them of class and race bias.

© The Granger Collection, New York

The Child-Saving Movement

The child savers were responsible for creating a number of programs for indigent youths, including the New York House of Refuge, which began operations in 1825.[5] Its charter was to protect indigent youths who were at risk of crime by taking them off the streets and reforming them in a family-like environment.[6]

The New York House of Refuge, actually a reformatory, opened on January 1, 1825, with only six boys and three girls, but within the first decade of its operation, 1,678 children were sent there because of vagrancy and petty crimes. Once an adolescent was a resident, his or her daily schedule was devoted for the most part to supervised labor, which was regarded as beneficial to education and discipline. Male inmates worked in shops that produced brushes, cane chairs, brass nails, and shoes. The female inmates sewed uniforms, did laundry, and carried out other domestic work. The reformatory had the authority to bind out inmates through indenture agreements to private employers; most males so bound out were farm workers, and most females were domestic laborers.

The Refuge Movement Spreads

When the House of Refuge opened, critics complained that the institution was run like a prison, with strict discipline and absolute separation of the sexes. Such a harsh program drove many children to run away, and the House of Refuge was forced to take a more lenient approach. Despite criticism, the concept enjoyed expanding popularity. In 1826, for example, the Boston City Council founded the House of Reformation for juvenile offenders.[7]

The child savers also influenced state and local governments to create independent correctional institutions to house minors. The first of these reform schools opened in Westboro, Massachusetts, in 1848 and in Rochester, New York, in 1849. Children lived in congregate conditions and spent their days working at institutional

Children's Aid Society
A child-saving organization begun by Charles Loring Brace; it took children from the streets in large cities and placed them with farm families on the prairie.

LO1 Describe the history of juvenile justice

juvenile court
A court that has original jurisdiction over persons defined by statute as juveniles and alleged to be delinquents or status offenders.

jobs, learning a trade where possible, and receiving some basic education. They were racially and sexually segregated, discipline was harsh and often involved whipping and isolation, and the physical care was of poor quality.

In 1853, New York philanthropist Charles Loring Brace helped develop the **Children's Aid Society** as an alternative for dealing with neglected and delinquent youths. Brace proposed rescuing wayward youths from the harsh environment of the city and providing them with temporary shelter and care. He then sought to place them in private homes in rural communities where they could engage in farming and agricultural work beyond the influence of the city. Although some placements proved successful, others resulted in the exploitation of children in a strange environment with few avenues of escape.

Establishment of the Juvenile Court

As the nation expanded, it became evident that private charities and public organizations were not caring adequately for the growing number of troubled youths. The child savers lobbied for an independent, state-supported **juvenile court**, and their efforts prompted the development of the first comprehensive juvenile court in Illinois in 1899. The Illinois Juvenile Court Act set up an independent court to handle criminal law violations by children under 16 years of age, as well as to care for neglected, dependent, and wayward youths. The act also created a probation department to monitor youths in the community and to direct juvenile court judges to place serious offenders in secure schools for boys and industrial schools for girls. The ostensible purpose of the act was to separate juveniles from adult offenders and to provide a legal framework in which juveniles could get adequate care and custody. By 1925, most states had developed juvenile courts.

The Development of Juvenile Justice

The juvenile court movement quickly spread across the United States. In its early form it provided youths with quasi-legal, quasi-therapeutic, personalized justice. The main concern was the "best interests of the child," not strict adherence to legal doctrine, constitutional rights, or due process of law. The court was paternalistic, rather than adversarial. Attorneys were not required; hearsay evidence, inadmissible in criminal trials, was commonly employed in the adjudication of juvenile offenders. Children were encouraged to admit their "guilt" in open court (in violation of their Fifth Amendment rights). Verdicts were based on a "preponderance of the evidence," instead of being "beyond a reasonable doubt." Juvenile courts then functioned as quasi-social service agencies.

Reform Schools Youngsters who were found delinquent in juvenile court could spend years in a state training school. Although they prided themselves on being nonpunitive, these early reform schools attempted to exercise control based on the concept of reform through hard work and discipline. In the second half of the nineteenth century, the emphasis shifted from massive industrial schools to the cottage system. Juvenile offenders were housed in a series of small cabins, each one holding 20 to 40 children, run by "cottage parents," who attempted to create a homelike atmosphere. The first cottage system was established in Massachusetts, the second in Ohio. The system was generally applauded for being a great improvement over the industrial training schools.[8] By the 1950s, psychological treatment was introduced in juvenile corrections. Group counseling techniques became standard procedure in most juvenile institutions.

Legal Change In the 1960s and 1970s, the U.S. Supreme Court radically altered the juvenile justice system when it issued a series of decisions that established the

LO2 Discuss the establishment of the juvenile court

Exhibit 13.1

Important Juvenile Justice Cases

- *Kent v. United States* (1966) determined that a child has the right to an attorney at any hearing to decide whether his or her case should be transferred to juvenile court (waiver hearings).
- *In re Gault* (1967) ruled that a minor has basic due process rights at trial, including: (1) notice of the charges, (2) right to counsel, (3) right to confront and cross-examine witnesses, (4) privilege against self-incrimination, and (5) the right to a transcript of the trial record.
- *In re Winship* (1970) determined that the level of evidence for a finding of "juvenile delinquency" is proof beyond a reasonable doubt.
- *McKeiver v. Pennsylvania* (1971) held that trial by jury in a juvenile court's adjudicative stage is not a constitutional requirement.
- *Breed v. Jones* (1975) ruled that a child has the protection of the double-jeopardy clause of the Fifth Amendment and cannot be tried twice for the same crime.
- *Fare v. Michael C.* (1979) held that a child has the protection of the *Miranda* decision: the right to remain silent during a police interrogation and to request that a lawyer be provided to protect his or her interests.
- *Schall v. Martin* (1984) allowed for the placement of children in preventive detention before their adjudication.
- *New Jersey v. T.L.O.* (1985) determined that although the Fourth Amendment protection against unreasonable search and seizure applies to children, school officials can legally search kids who violate school rules (e.g., smoking on campus), even when there is no evidence that the student violated the law.
- *Vernonia School District v. Acton* (1995) held that the Fourth Amendment's guarantee against unreasonable searches is not violated by drug testing all students choosing to participate in interscholastic athletics.
- *Roper v. Simmons* (2005) determined that juveniles who commit murder before they turn 18 cannot be sentenced to death.
- *Graham v. Florida* (2010) prohibited life imprisonment for juveniles convicted for non-homicide offenses.

Sources: *Kent. v. United States*, 383 U.S. 541 (1966); *In re Gault*, 387 U.S. 1 (1967); *In re Winship*, 397 U.S. 358 (1970); *McKeiver v. Pennsylvania*, 403 U.S. 528 (1971); *Breed v. Jones*, 421 U.S. 519 (1975); *Fare v. Michael C.*, 442 U.S. 707 (1979); *Schall v. Martin*, 467 U.S. 253 (1984); *New Jersey v. T.L.O.*, 469 U.S. 325 (1985); *Vernonia School District v. Acton*, 515 U.S. 646 (1995); *Roper v. Simmons*, 543 U.S. 551 (2005); *Graham v. Florida*, 560 U.S. ___ (2010).

right of juveniles to due process of law. The Court established that juveniles had the same rights as adults in important areas of trial process, including the right to confront witnesses, notice of charges, and the right to counsel. Exhibit 13.1 lists some of the legal cases that were most important in bringing procedural due process to the juvenile justice process.

Besides the legal revolution brought about by the Supreme Court, Congress passed the Juvenile Justice and Delinquency Prevention Act of 1974 (JJDP Act) and established the federal Office of Juvenile Justice and Delinquency Prevention (OJJDP).[9] This legislation was enacted to identify the needs of youths and to fund programs in the juvenile justice system. Its main goal was to separate wayward, nondangerous youths from institutions housing delinquents and to remove adolescents from institutions housing adult offenders. In 1988, the act was amended to address the issue of minority overrepresentation in the juvenile justice system, and in 1996, in a move reflecting the growing national frustration with serious delinquent offenders, the act was again amended to make it easier to hold delinquents in adult penal institutions. The various stages in the history of juvenile justice are set out in Concept Summary 13.1.

Juvenile Justice Today

juvenile delinquency
Participation in illegal behavior by a minor who falls under a statutory age limit.

status offender
A juvenile who engages in behavior legally forbidden to minors, such as running away, truancy, or incorrigibility.

Today, the juvenile justice system has jurisdiction over two distinct categories of offenders: delinquents and status offenders.[10] **Juvenile delinquency** is a term applied to children who fall under a jurisdictional age limit, which varies from state to state, and who commit an act in violation of the penal code. **Status offenders** commit acts forbidden to minors, which include truancy and being a habitually disobedient and ungovernable child (see Figure 13.1). They are commonly characterized in state statutes as persons or children in need of supervision (PINS or CHINS). Most states distinguish such behavior from delinquent conduct to reduce the effect of any stigma on children, although in most jurisdictions, status offenders can be placed on probation much as delinquent offenders can. They are, however, in most instances barred from being placed in secure facilities that hold delinquent offenders. In addition, juvenile courts generally have jurisdiction over situations involving conduct directed at (rather than committed by) juveniles, such as parental neglect, deprivation, abandonment, and abuse.

The states have also set different maximum ages below which children fall under the jurisdiction of the juvenile court. Many states include all children under 18 years of age, others set the limit at 17, and still others at 16.

Some states exclude certain classes of offenders or offenses from the juvenile justice system. Those youths who commit serious violent offenses such as rape or murder may be automatically excluded from the juvenile justice system and treated as adults on the premise that they stand little chance of rehabilitation within the confines of the juvenile system. Juvenile court judges may also transfer, or waive, to adult court repeat offenders whom they deem untreatable by the juvenile authorities.

Another trend has been to create family courts, which include a broad range of family- and child-related issues within their jurisdictions. Family courts are in use or are being considered in more than half of all U.S. states. They are designed to provide more individualized, client-focused treatment than traditional juvenile courts and to bring a holistic

RealityCheck

MYTH OR REALITY? All juveniles fall under the jurisdiction of the adult court at age 18.

MYTH. *There is considerable variation from state to state in terms of who is considered an adult for purposes of criminal prosecution. In Connecticut, New York, and North Carolina, the oldest age for juvenile court jurisdiction in delinquency matters is 15. This means that youths 16 or older are tried as adults in those states. And there are exceptions to these rules. Sometimes younger individuals can be "waived" to adult court—a topic taken up later in the chapter.*

At what age should a person be considered an adult for purposes of criminal prosecution? Can you conceive of a situation in which someone who is 10 years old or less should be prosecuted for a crime?

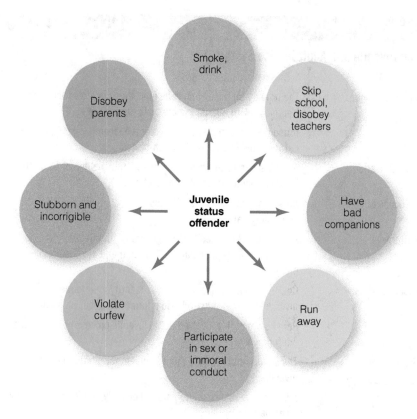

Figure 13.1 Examples of Status Offenses

approach to helping kids and their families, rather than focusing on punishing and/ or controlling delinquency.[11]

The juvenile justice system has evolved into a parallel yet independent system of justice with its own terminology and rules of procedure. Exhibit 13.2 describes the basic similarities and differences between the juvenile and adult justice systems. Exhibit 13.3 points out how the language used in the juvenile court differs from that used in the adult system.

Today, the juvenile justice system is responsible for processing and treating almost 2 million cases of youthful misbehavior annually. Each state's system is unique, so it is difficult to give a precise accounting of the justice process. Moreover, depending on local practice and tradition, case processing often varies from community to community within a single state. Keeping this in mind, the following sections provide a general description of some key processes and decision points in juvenile justice. Figure 13.2 presents a model of the juvenile justice process.

L03 Describe the changes in juvenile justice that began in the 1960s and continue today

Police Processing of the Juvenile Offender

According to the Uniform Crime Reports, police officers arrest more than one million juveniles under age 18 each year.[12] Most large police departments have detectives who handle only juvenile delinquency cases and focus their attention on the problems of youth. In addition to conducting their own investigations, they typically take control of cases after an arrest is made by a uniformed officer.

Most states do not have specific statutory provisions distinguishing the arrest process for children from that for adults. Some jurisdictions, however, give broad arrest powers to the police in juvenile cases by authorizing the officer to make an arrest whenever he or she believes the child's behavior falls within the jurisdiction of

Exhibit 13.2

Similarities and Differences between Juvenile and Adult Justice Systems

Similarities	Differences
Discretion used by police officers, judges, and correctional personnel.	The primary purpose of juvenile procedures is protection and treatment; with adults, the aim is to punish the guilty.
Right to receive Miranda warning.	Jurisdiction is determined by age in the juvenile system, by the nature of the offense in the adult system.
Protection from prejudicial lineups or other identification procedures.	Juveniles can be apprehended for acts that would not be criminal if committed by an adult (status offenses).
Procedural safeguards when making an admission of guilt.	Juvenile proceedings are not considered criminal; adult proceedings are.
Advocacy roles of prosecutors and defense attorneys.	Juvenile court proceedings are generally informal and private; adult court proceedings are more formal and are open to the public.
Right to counsel at most key stages of the court process.	Courts cannot release to the press identifying information about a juvenile, but they must release information about an adult.
Availability of pretrial motions.	Parents are highly involved in the juvenile process but not in the adult process.
Plea negotiation/plea bargaining.	The standard of arrest is more stringent for adults than for juveniles.
Right to a hearing and an appeal.	Juveniles are released into parental custody; adults are generally given bail.
Standard of proof beyond a reasonable doubt.	Juveniles have no constitutional right to a jury trial; adults do. Some states extend this right to juveniles by statute.
Pretrial detention possible.	Juveniles can be searched in school without probable cause or a warrant.
Detention without bail if considered dangerous.	A juvenile's record is generally sealed when the age of majority is reached; an adult's record is permanent.
Probation as a sentencing option.	A juvenile court cannot sentence juveniles to county jails or state prisons, which are reserved for adults.
Community treatment as a sentencing option.	The U.S. Supreme Court has declared that the Eighth Amendment prohibits the death penalty for juveniles under age 18.

Exhibit 13.3

Comparison of Terms Used in Adult and Juvenile Justice Systems

	Juvenile Terms	Adult Terms
The person and the act	Delinquent child	Criminal
	Delinquent act	Crime
Preadjudicatory stage	Take into custody	Arrest
	Petition	Indictment
	Agree to a finding	Plead guilty
	Deny the petition	Plead not guilty
	Adjustment	Plea bargain
	Detention facility; child-care shelter	Jail

Exhibit 13.3 *Continued*

Adjudicatory stage	Substitution	Reduction of charges
	Adjudicatory or fact-finding hearing	Trial
	Adjudication	
Postadjudicatory stage	Dispositional hearing	Sentencing hearing
	Disposition	Sentence
	Commitment	Incarceration
	Youth development center; treatment center; training school	Prison
		Halfway house
	Residential child-care facility	Parole
	Aftercare	

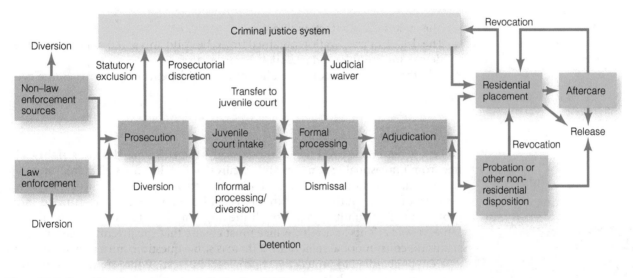

Figure 13.2 Case Flow through the Juvenile Justice System

Sources: Office of Juvenile Justice and Delinquency Prevention, http://ojjdp.ncjrs.org/ojstatbb/structure_process/case.html (accessed April 12, 2011).

the juvenile court. Consequently, police may arrest youths for behavior considered legal for adults, including running away, curfew violations, and being in possession of alcohol.

Use of Discretion

When a juvenile is found to have engaged in delinquent or incorrigible behavior, police agencies are charged with the decision to release or to detain the child and refer her to juvenile court. Because of the state's interest in the child, the police generally have more discretion in the investigatory and arrest stages of the juvenile process than they do when dealing with adult offenders.

This discretionary decision—to release or to detain—is based not only on the nature of the offense but also on police attitudes and the child's social and personal conditions at the time of the arrest. The following is a partial list of factors believed to be significant in police decision making about juvenile offenders:

- The type and seriousness of the child's offense
- The ability of the parents to be of assistance in disciplining the child

Anthony Caravella, who spent almost 26 years in prison on rape and murder charges, gets a hug from his lawyer, Diane Cuddihy, at the Broward County (Florida) Courthouse after he was exonerated. Caravella was 15 when he was arrested. Prosecutors initially sought the death penalty, but the jury voted 11–1 for a life prison sentence. How extensive a problem are wrongful convictions?

© Used with permission of the *Sun Sentinel*, copyright 2011. Amy Beth Bennett, *Sun Sentinel*

- The child's past contacts with police
- The degree of cooperation obtained from the child and parents, along with their demeanor, attitude, and personal characteristics
- Whether the child denies the allegations in the petition and insists on a court hearing[13]

Legal Rights

Once a juvenile has been taken into custody, the child has the same right to be free from unreasonable searches and seizures as an adult does. Children in police custody can be detained prior to trial, interrogated, and placed in lineups. However, because of their youth and inexperience, children are generally afforded more protections than adults. Even though the Supreme Court has given juveniles the same *Miranda* rights as adults, police must ensure that the juvenile suspect understands his constitutional rights and, if there is some question, must provide access to a parent or guardian to protect the child's legal interests. Police should interrogate a juvenile without an adult present only if they are sure that the youth is unquestionably mature and experienced enough to understand his legal rights.[14]

LO4 **Summarize police processing of juvenile offenders**

The Juvenile Court Process

RealityCheck

MYTH OR REALITY? Juveniles enjoy different rights than adults.

REALITY. *The Supreme Court has over the years extended more and more protections to juveniles (see Exhibit 13.1), but there are still rights that juveniles do not enjoy. One is the right to a jury trial.*

Should juveniles have access to trial by jury? Why or why not? Juvenile proceedings are also usually closed to the public, unlike adult criminal trials. Is this advantageous or disadvantageous to the juvenile?

After the police have determined that a case warrants further attention, they will bind it over to the prosecutor's office, which then has the responsibility for channeling the case through the juvenile court. In addition, cases may be petitioned to the court from non–law enforcement sources, such as when educational authorities ask the court to intervene in cases of truancy or when parents directly petition the court asking that their child be considered a status offender. The juvenile court plays a major role in controlling juvenile behavior and delivering social services to children in need.

U.S. juvenile courts process an estimated 1.6 million delinquency cases each year. The juvenile court delinquency caseload today is four times as large as it was in 1960.

The Intake Process

After police processing, the juvenile offender is usually remanded to the local juvenile court's intake division. At this juncture, court intake officers or probation personnel review and initially screen the child and the family to determine whether the child needs to be handled formally or the case can be settled without the need for costly and intrusive official intervention. Their report helps the prosecutor decide whether to handle the case informally or bind it over for trial. The intake stage represents an opportunity to place a child in informal programs both within the court and in the community. The intake process also is critically important because more than half of the referrals to the juvenile courts never go beyond this stage.

The Detention Process

After a juvenile is formally taken into custody, either as a delinquent or as a status offender, the prosecutor usually makes a decision to release the child to the parent or guardian or to detain the child in a secure shelter pending trial.

Detention has always been a controversial area of juvenile justice. Far too many children have been routinely placed in detention while awaiting court appearances. Status offenders and delinquents have been held in the same facility, and in many parts of the country, adult county jails were used to detain juvenile offenders. The Juvenile Justice Act of 1974 emphasized reducing the number of children placed in inappropriate detention facilities. Although the act was largely effective, there are places where the practice continues.

detention
The temporary care of a child alleged to be a delinquent or status offender who requires secure custody, pending court disposition.

Despite such measures, hundreds of thousands of youths, most of whom are already living under difficult circumstances, are placed in pretrial detention each year. Many have suffered long histories of abuse and mental health problems.[15] The detention decision may reflect a child's personal characteristics and the quality of his or her home life rather than dangerousness or flight risk.[16] Detention is widely misapplied, according to the report by the Justice Policy Institute, a Washington, D.C.–based group, because even though detention facilities are meant to temporarily house those youths who are likely to reoffend before their trial or who are unlikely to appear for their court date, many of the youths in this country's detention centers do not meet these criteria. Seventy percent of youths in detention are held for nonviolent charges. More than two-thirds are charged with property offenses, public order offenses, technical probation violations, or status offenses (such as running away or breaking curfew).[17]

Legal Issues Most state statutes ordinarily require a hearing on the appropriateness of detention if the initial decision is to keep the child in custody. At this hearing, the child has a right to counsel and may be given other procedural due process safeguards, notably the privilege against self-incrimination and the right to confront and cross-examine witnesses. Most state juvenile court acts provide criteria to support a decision to detain the child. These include (a) the need to protect the child, (b) whether the child presents a serious danger to the public, and (c) the likelihood that the juvenile will return to court for adjudication. Whereas in adult cases most offenders are released if they can afford bail, juveniles may be detained for a variety of reasons, including their own protection. Normally, the finding of the judge that the child should be detained must be supported by factual evidence. In the 1984 case of *Schall v. Martin*, the U.S. Supreme Court upheld the right of the states to detain a child before trial to protect that child's welfare and the public safety.[18]

Reforming Detention There has been an ongoing effort to reform detention. The most important reform has been the successful effort to remove status offenders from lockups containing delinquents. After decades of effort, nearly all states have passed laws requiring that status offenders be placed in nonsecure shelters, rather than secure detention facilities, thereby reducing their contact with more dangerous delinquent youths.

Another serious problem is the detention of youths in adult jails. This practice is common in rural areas where there are relatively few separate facilities for young offenders.[19] The OJJDP has given millions of dollars in aid to encourage the

■ Youthful offenders are often required to attend classes while in detention. Here Robert Harris, 17, left, listens to Fulton County Superior Court Judge Marvin Arrington, right, during Harris's high school graduation ceremony at the Metro Regional Youth Detention Center on May 15, 2009, in Atlanta. Harris is the first youth to graduate at the 11-year-old facility and has been accepted to enter Georgia Military College.

AP Images/Erik S. Lesser

removal of juveniles from adult lockups. These grants have helped jurisdictions develop intake screening procedures, specific release or detention criteria, and alternative residential and nonresidential programs for juveniles awaiting trial. By 1980, amendments to the act mandating the absolute removal of juveniles from jails had been adopted. Despite such efforts, many states are not complying with the removal provisions and still detain juveniles in adult jails. Adding to their numbers are youths who commit nonserious acts—such as runaways—but are apprehended in rural areas where there are no juvenile facilities. There are also states that define the age limit for delinquency as 16 or 17 and therefore treat minors of that age as legal adults. At the time of the last available jail census, more than 7,000 persons under age 18 were housed in adult jails. Jail stays are generally of short duration, so it is likely that hundreds of thousands of minors are held in adult jails each year.

Whatever the actual number jailed today, placing young offenders in adult jails continues to be a significant problem in the juvenile justice system. Juveniles detained in adult jails often live in squalid conditions and are subject to physical and sexual abuse. The practice is widely condemned, but eliminating the confinement of juveniles in adult institutions remains a difficult task.

Bail

If a child is not detained, the question of bail arises. Federal courts have not found it necessary to rule on the issue of a juvenile's constitutional right to bail, because liberal statutory release provisions act as appropriate alternatives. Although only a few state statutes allow release on money bail, many others have juvenile code provisions that emphasize the release of the child to the parents as an acceptable substitute. A constitutional right to bail that on its face seems to benefit a child may have unforeseen results. The imposition of money bail might create a serious economic strain on the child's family, while conflicting with the protective and social concerns of the juvenile court. Considerations of economic liabilities and other procedural inequities have influenced the majority of courts that have confronted this question to hold that juveniles do not have a right to bail.

Kayla Hassall, 16, one of five teenagers accused of beating fellow teen Victoria N. Lindsay, weeps as she apologizes to the victim's mother Talisa Lindsay outside the courtroom on February 4, 2009, in Bartow, Florida. The attack was recorded on video and seen around the world via the Internet and television. Kayla pleaded no contest to misdemeanor battery. In exchange for her plea, prosecutors agreed to drop a related felony charge.

AP Images/Michael Wilson, Pool

Plea Bargaining

Before trial, prosecutors in the juvenile courts may attempt to negotiate a settlement to the case. For example, if the offender admits to the facts of the petition, she may be offered placement in a special community-based treatment program in lieu of a term in a secure state facility. Or a status offense petition may be substituted for one of delinquency so that the adolescent can avoid being housed in a state training school and instead be placed in a more treatment-oriented facility.

If a bargain can be reached, the child will be asked to admit in open court that he did in fact commit the act of which he stands accused. State juvenile courts tend to minimize the stigma associated with the use of adult criminal standards by using other terminology, such as "agree to a finding" or "accept the petition" rather than "admit guilt." When the child makes an admission, juvenile courts require the following procedural safeguards: the child knows of the right to a trial, the plea or admission is made voluntarily, and the child understands the charges and consequences of the plea.

Waiver of Jurisdiction

Before development of the first modern juvenile court in Illinois in 1899, juveniles were tried for violations of the law in adult criminal courts. The consequences were devastating; many children were treated as criminal offenders and often sentenced to adult prisons. Although the subsequent passage of state legislation creating juvenile courts eliminated this problem, the juvenile justice system did recognize that certain forms of conduct require that children be tried as adults. Today, most American jurisdictions provide by statute for **waiver**, or transfer, of juvenile offenders to the criminal courts. Waiver is also widely used in juvenile courts in Europe and Great Britain.[20]

In its most basic form, the decision of whether to waive a juvenile to the adult, or criminal, court is made in a **transfer hearing**. The decision to transfer a juvenile to the criminal court is often based on statutory criteria established by the state's juvenile court act, so waiver provisions vary considerably among jurisdictions. Most

LO5 Describe the juvenile court process

waiver (juvenile)
A practice in which the juvenile court waives its jurisdiction over a juvenile and transfers the case to adult criminal court for trial. In some states, a waiver hearing is held to determine jurisdiction, whereas in others, juveniles may be automatically waived if they are accused of committing a serious crime such as murder.

transfer hearing
The hearing in which a decision is made to waive a juvenile to the criminal court. Waiver decisions are based on such criteria as the child's age, her or his prior offense history, and the nature of the offense.

commonly considered are the child's age and the nature of the offense alleged in the petition. Some jurisdictions require that children be over a certain age (typically, 14) before they can be waived. Others mandate that the youth be charged with a felony before being tried as an adult, whereas others permit waiver of jurisdiction to the criminal court regardless of the seriousness of the offense when a child is a chronic offender. In about 30 states, certain offenses, such as murder, have been excluded from juvenile court jurisdiction, creating a mandatory waiver provision for children who have committed those crimes.

Legal Controls Because of the nature of the waiver decision and its effect on the child in terms of status and disposition, the Supreme Court has imposed procedural protections for juveniles in the waiver process. In *Kent v. United States* (1966), the Court held that the waiver proceeding is a critically important stage in the juvenile justice process and that juveniles must be afforded minimum requirements of due process of law at such proceedings, including the right to legal counsel.[21] Then in *Breed v. Jones* (1975), the Court held that the prosecution of juveniles as adults in the California Superior Court violated the double jeopardy clause of the Fifth Amendment if they had previously been tried on the same charge in juvenile court.[22] The Court concluded that jeopardy attaches when the juvenile court begins to hear evidence at the adjudicatory hearing; this requires that the waiver hearing take place before any adjudication.

Youth in Adult Courts Today, all states allow juveniles to be tried as adults in criminal courts in one of four ways:

- *Direct file waiver.* The prosecutor has the discretion of filing charges for certain legislatively designated offenses in either juvenile or criminal court. About 15 states have this provision.
- *Excluded offense waiver.* State laws exclude from juvenile court jurisdiction certain offenses that are either very minor, such as traffic or fishing violations, or very serious, such as murder. About 29 states now have such laws for certain crimes.
- *Judicial waiver.* After a formal hearing at which both prosecutor and defense attorney present evidence, a juvenile court judge may decide to waive jurisdiction and transfer the case to criminal court. This procedure is also known as "binding over" or "certifying" juvenile cases to criminal court.
- *Reverse waiver.* State laws mandate that certain offenses be tried in adult court. Once the case is heard in the adult court, the trial judge may decide that the offender would be better served by the juvenile court and order a reverse waiver. About 25 states have this provision for certain circumstances.[23]

Every state has provisions for handling juveniles in adult criminal courts, and the trend is to make the waiver broader.[24] In 31 states, once a juvenile is tried in adult court, she is no longer eligible for juvenile justice on any subsequent offense.

The Effect of Waiver The problem of youths processed in adult courts is a serious one. About 8,000 juvenile delinquency cases are now being transferred to the adult courts each year. Supporters view the waiver process as a sound method of getting the most serious juvenile offenders off the streets. Kids are most likely to be transferred to criminal court if they have injured someone with a weapon or if they have a long juvenile court record.[25]

Waiver has its advocates, but many experts question its utility, arguing that it does more harm than good. One great fear is that juveniles will be forced to serve time in adult prisons, where they will be exposed to experienced criminals in what are essentially "schools for crime." In addition, children may be targets of adult predators if they are confined to adult institutions:

- Youths held in adult prisons and jails are five times more likely to be victims of attempted sexual attacks or rapes than those held in juvenile institutions.
- The suicide rate for juveniles in adult prisons and jails is nearly eight times higher than that for juveniles in youth detention centers.[26]

Sixteen-year-old Emily Ball, left, wipes away tears during a sentencing hearing for her involvement in the 2009 murder of Travis White, in Covington, Kentucky. Ball, who was 14 at the time of the crime, admitted luring White to a house in Covington where two men beat him to death. Judge Martin Sheehan sentenced her to 15 years incarceration on charges of conspiracy to commit first-degree assault, unlawful imprisonment, and tampering with physical evidence.

AP Photo/The Cincinnati Enquirer, Patrick Reddy

Although some youths who are transferred to adult court never spend a day in an adult prison, thousands do, and many of them become enmeshed in the daily life of an adult correctional facility. They miss out on being housed in juvenile facilities that are smaller, have much lower inmate-to-staff ratios, and place greater emphasis on treatment, counseling, education, and mentoring of inmates. Although some adult facilities do provide easy access to education and treatment, young inmates lose out on developing the relatively more supportive, mentoring-focused style of staff–inmate interactions that a juvenile facility provides.[27]

What is accomplished by treating juveniles as adults? Studies of the impact of the recent waiver statutes have yielded several interesting—and conflicting—results. Some recent (2006) research by Benjamin Steiner and Emily Wright on the effect of direct waiver laws found that they have little effect on juvenile violent crime rates in the states that have adopted them.[28] Other studies have found that juveniles waived to adult court receive harsher punishment and may be viewed as dangerous and incapable of being rehabilitated.[29] Waived juveniles may also spend more time in juvenile detention awaiting trial. In the end, what began as a get-tough measure has had the opposite effect, while costing taxpayers more money.[30]

Transfer decisions are not always carried out fairly or equitably, and evidence indicates that minorities are waived to adult court at a rate that is greater than their representation in the population.[31] About 40 percent of all waived youths are African Americans, even though they represent less than a third (31 percent) of the juvenile court population.[32] No area of juvenile justice has received more attention recently than efforts to redefine the jurisdiction of the juvenile court.[33]

The Adjudication

There are often three judicial hearings in the juvenile court process. The first, typically called an **initial appearance**, is similar to the arraignment in the adult system. The child is informed of the charges against him, attorneys are appointed, bail is

LO6 Explain the concept of waiver

initial appearance
A juvenile's first appearance before the juvenile court judge, in which the charges are reviewed and an effort is made to settle the case without a trial. If the child does not have legal counsel, an attorney is appointed.

disposition
For juvenile offenders, the equivalent of sentencing for adult offenders. The theory is that disposition is more rehabilitative than retributive. Possible dispositions include dismissing the case, releasing the youth to the custody of his or her parents, placing the offender on probation, or sending him or her to a state correctional institution.

commitment
Decision of judge ordering an adjudicated and sentenced juvenile offender to be placed in a correctional facility.

treatment
The rehabilitative method used to effect a change of behavior in the juvenile offender, in the form of therapy, or educational or vocational programs.

reviewed, and in many instances cases are settled with an admission of the facts, followed by a community sentence. If the case cannot be settled at this initial stage, it is bound over for trial.

The second is the adjudicatory hearing (often called the fact-finding hearing in juvenile proceedings). In it, the court hears evidence on the allegations stated in the delinquency petition. In its early development, the juvenile court did not emphasize judicial rule making similar to that of the criminal trial process. Absent were such basic requirements as the standard of proof, rules of evidence, and similar adjudicatory formalities. Proceedings were to be nonadversarial, informal, and noncriminal. Gradually, however, the juvenile trial process became a target of criticism because judges were handing out punishments to children without affording them legal rights. This changed in 1967 when the Supreme Court's landmark *In re Gault* decision radically altered the juvenile justice system.[34] In *Gault*, the Court ruled that the concept of fundamental fairness is applicable to juvenile delinquency proceedings. The Court granted critical rights to juvenile defendants, most important among them the notice of the charges, the right to counsel, the right to confront and cross-examine witnesses, the privilege against self-incrimination, and the right to a transcript of the trial record.

The *Gault* decision completely altered the juvenile trial process. Instead of dealing with children in a benign and paternalistic fashion, the courts were forced to process juvenile offenders within the framework of appropriate constitutional procedures. And although *Gault* was technically limited to the adjudicatory stage, it has spurred further legal reform throughout the juvenile system. Today, the right to counsel, the privilege against self-incrimination, the right to treatment in detention and correctional facilities, and other constitutional protections are applied at all stages of the juvenile process, from investigation through adjudication to parole. *Gault* ushered in an era of legal rights for juveniles.

Once an adjudicatory hearing has been completed, the court is normally required to enter a judgment against the child. This may take the form of declaring the child delinquent or a ward of the court or possibly even suspending judgment to avoid the stigma of a juvenile record. After a judgment is entered, the court can begin its determination of possible **dispositions** for the child.

Some alternatives to the juvenile court trial are now in operation, and one of the more popular ones, the teen court, is discussed in the Contemporary Issues in Criminal Justice feature.

Disposition and Treatment

At the dispositional hearing, the third step in juvenile adjudication, the judge imposes a sentence on the juvenile offender based on her offense, prior record, and family background. Normally, the judge has broad discretionary power to issue a range of dispositions from dismissal to institutional **commitment**. In theory, the dispositional decision is an effort by the court to serve the best interests of the child, the family, and the community. In many respects, this postadjudicative process is the most important stage in the juvenile court system, because it represents the last opportunity for the court to influence the child and control her behavior.

To ensure that only relevant and appropriate evidence is considered by the court during adjudication, most jurisdictions require a separate hearing to formulate an appropriate disposition. The bifurcated hearing process ensures that the adjudicatory hearing is used solely to determine the merits of the allegations, whereas the dispositional hearing determines whether the child is in need of rehabilitation.

In theory, the juvenile court seeks to provide a disposition that represents an individualized **treatment** plan for the child. This decision is normally based on the pre-sentence investigation of the probation department, reports from social agencies, and possibly a psychiatric evaluation. The judge generally has broad discretion

Are Teen Courts Effective?

To relieve overcrowding and provide an alternative to traditional forms of juvenile courts, teen courts (also called youth courts) are now in operation around the United States. According to the National Association of Youth Courts, there are over 1,000 teen court programs in operation in 49 states and the District of Columbia.

Teen courts differ from other juvenile justice programs because in most instances young people, not adults, determine the disposition in a case. Cases handled in these courts typically involve young juveniles (ages 10 to 15), with no prior arrest records, who are being charged with minor law violations (such as shoplifting, vandalism, and disorderly conduct). Typically, young offenders are asked to volunteer to have their case heard in a teen court instead of the more formal court of the traditional juvenile justice system.

As in a regular juvenile court, teen court defendants may go through an intake process, a preliminary review of charges, a court hearing, and sentencing. In a teen court, however, other young people are responsible for much of the process. Charges may be presented to the court by a 15-year-old "prosecutor." Defendants may be represented by a 16-year-old "defense attorney." Other youths may serve as jurors, court clerks, and bailiffs. In some teen courts, a youth "judge" (or panel of youth judges) may choose the best disposition or sanction for each case. In a few teen courts, youths even determine whether the facts in a case have been proven by the prosecutor (similar to a finding of guilt). Offenders are often ordered to pay restitution or perform community service. Some teen courts require offenders to write formal apologies to their victims; others require offenders to serve on a subsequent teen court jury. Many courts use other innovative dispositions, such as requiring offenders to attend classes designed to improve their decision-making skills, enhance their awareness of victims, and deter them from future illegal acts.

Although decisions are made by juveniles, adults are also involved in teen courts. They often administer the programs, and they are usually responsible for essential functions such as budgeting, planning, and personnel. In many programs, adults supervise the courtroom activities, and they often coordinate the community service placements, where youths work to fulfill the terms of their dispositions. In some programs, adults act as the judges while teens serve as attorneys and jurors.

Are teen courts effective? The evidence is mixed. Evaluations by Kevin Minor and his associates of teen courts in Kentucky and by Paige Harrison and her colleagues in New Mexico indicate that recidivism levels range from 25 percent to 30 percent. In contrast, the Urban Institute's Evaluation of Teen Courts Project, which was based on four teen court programs (in Alaska, Maryland, Arizona, and Missouri), found that after six months, recidivism ranged from 6 percent to 9 percent, whereas cases sent to juvenile courts had an 18 percent recidivism rate. Considering that these cases typically involve offenses of only moderate seriousness, the findings do not suggest that the program can play a significant role in reducing teenage crime rates.

CRITICAL THINKING

1. Could teen courts be used to try serious criminal acts such as burglary and robbery?
2. Is a conflict of interest created when teens judge the behavior of other teens? Does the fact that they themselves may one day become defendants in a teen court influence such judges' decision making?

---

in dispositional matters but is limited by the provisions of the state's juvenile court act. The following are typical juvenile court dispositions:

- Suspended judgment
- Probation
- Placement in a community treatment program
- Commitment to the state agency responsible for juvenile institutional care

In addition, the court may place the child with parents or relatives, make dispositional arrangements with private youth-serving agencies, or order the child committed to a mental institution.

Disposition Outcomes In dispositional hearings, juvenile court judges must determine the most appropriate sanction for delinquent youths. Disposition options include commitment to an institution or another residential facility; probation; and a variety of other dispositions, such as referral to an outside agency or treatment program, community service, fines, or restitution. Very often the court imposes some combination of these sanctions. What have been the trends in juvenile disposition? The number of adjudicated delinquency cases resulting in residential placement has increased significantly during the past decade, and today about 10 percent of all cases petitioned to juvenile court get some form of residential treatment. An additional 400,000 kids are put on probation each year.

Juvenile Sentencing Reform

Over the past decade, juvenile justice experts and the general public have become aroused about the serious juvenile crime rate in general and about violent acts committed by children in particular. As a result, some law enforcement officials and conservative legislators have demanded that the juvenile justice system take a more serious stand with dangerous juvenile offenders. Many state legislatures have responded by toughening their juvenile codes. Some jurisdictions have passed mandatory or determinate incarceration sentences for juveniles convicted of serious felonies. Not all jurisdictions have abandoned rehabilitation as a primary dispositional goal, however, and some still hold to the philosophy that placements should be based on the least detrimental alternative. This view requires that judges employ the least intrusive measures possible to safeguard a child's growth and development.[35]

A second reform has been the concerted effort to remove status offenders from the juvenile justice system and restrict their entry into institutional programs. Because of the development of numerous diversion programs, many children involved in truancy and incorrigible behavior who ordinarily would have been sent to a closed institution are now being placed in community programs. There are far fewer status offenders in detention or institutions than ever before.

A third reform effort has been to standardize dispositions in juvenile court. As early as 1977, Washington passed one of the first determinate sentencing laws for juvenile offenders, resulting in other states adopting similar statutes.[36] All children found to be delinquent are evaluated on a point system based on their age, prior juvenile record, and type of crime committed. Minor offenders are handled in the community. Those committing more serious offenses are placed on probation. Children who commit the most serious offenses are subject to standardized institutional penalties. As a result, juvenile offenders who commit such crimes as rape or armed robbery are being sentenced to institutionalization for two, three, and four years. This approach is different from indeterminate sentencing, under which children who have committed a serious crime might be released from institutions in less than a year if correctional authorities believe they have been rehabilitated.

The Juvenile Correctional Process

After disposition in juvenile court, delinquent offenders may be placed in some form of correctional treatment. Although many are placed in the community, more than 100,000 are now in secure facilities.

Probation

The most commonly used formal sentence for juvenile offenders is probation, and many states require that a youth fail on probation before being sent to an institution (unless the criminal act is quite serious). Probation involves placing the child under the supervision of the juvenile probation department for the purpose of community treatment. A juvenile may also be required to follow special rules, such as maintaining a curfew or attending substance abuse meetings. Alternative sanctions such as community service or monetary restitution may be ordered. Serious offenders can be placed in intensive supervision or under house arrest. Just as in the adult system, probation can be revoked if the rules are not followed, and the court may impose stricter sanctions.

Juvenile probation is an important component of the juvenile justice system. It is the most widely used method of community treatment in juvenile court. Similar in form and function to adult probation, supervising juveniles in the community combines elements of treatment and control. Some probation officers maintain a social work orientation and want to provide needy kids with an effective treatment plan, but others maintain a law enforcement orientation, believing that their clients are offenders who need close monitoring.[37]

Institutionalization

The most severe of the statutory dispositions available to the juvenile court involves commitment of the child to an institution. The committed child may be sent to a state training school or private residential treatment facility. These are usually minimum-security facilities with small populations and an emphasis on treatment and education. Some states, however, maintain facilities with populations over 1,000.

State statutes vary in terms of the length of the child's commitment. Traditionally, many jurisdictions committed the child up to majority, which usually meant 21 years of age. This normally deprived the child of freedom for an extensive period of time—sometimes longer than an adult sentenced for the same offense would be confined. As a result, some states have passed legislation under which children are committed for periods ranging from one to three years.

To better handle violent juvenile offenders, some states have created separate or intermediate juvenile systems. Under such statutes, 14- to 17-year-olds charged with certain violent felonies are treated as adults and, if convicted, are sentenced to new intermediate prisons, separated from both adult and regular juvenile offenders, for terms of two to five years.

Today more than 100,000 juveniles are being held in either privately run or publicly managed juvenile correctional facilities.[38] About 35 percent are held for person-oriented offenses; the rest are held for property offenses (25 percent), drug offenses (9 percent), public order offenses (11 percent), technical violations (16 percent), and status offenses (5 percent).[39] The efforts made in recent years to keep status offenders out of institutions seem to have paid off.

The typical resident of a juvenile facility is a 15- to 16-year-old white male incarcerated for an average stay of five months in a public facility or six months in a private facility. Private facilities tend to house younger teens, whereas public institutions provide custodial care for older youths, including a small percentage of youths between 18 and 21 years of age.

Deinstitutionalization

Some experts in delinquency and juvenile law question the policy of institutionalizing juvenile offenders. Many believe that large institutions are too costly to operate and only produce more sophisticated criminals. This dilemma has produced a number of efforts to remove youths from juvenile facilities and replace large institutions with smaller, community-based facilities. The Commonwealth of Massachusetts closed all its state training schools more than 20 years ago (subsequently, however, public pressure caused a few secure facilities to be reopened). Many other states have established small residential facilities operated by juvenile-care agencies to replace larger units.

Despite the daily rhetoric on crime control, public support for community-based programs for juveniles still exists. Although such programs are not panaceas, many experts still recommend more treatment and less incarceration for juvenile offenders. Utah, Maryland, Vermont, and Pennsylvania, for example, have dramatically reduced their reform school populations while setting up a wide range of intensive treatment programs for juveniles. Many large, impersonal, and expensive state institutions with unqualified staff and ineffective treatment programs have been eliminated.

Aftercare

Aftercare marks the final stage of the formal juvenile justice process. Its purpose is to help youths make the transition from residential or institutional settings back into the community. Effective aftercare programs provide adequate supervision and support services to help juvenile offenders avoid criminal activity. Examples of programs include electronic monitoring, counseling, treatment and community service referrals, education, work training, and intensive parole supervision.

Most juvenile aftercare involves parole. A juvenile parole officer provides the child with counseling, school referral, vocational training, and other services. Children who violate the conditions of parole may have their parole revoked and be returned to the institution. Unlike the adult postconviction process, where the Supreme Court has imposed procedural protections in probation and parole revocations, juveniles do not have such due process rights. State courts have also been reluctant to grant juveniles rights in this area, and those that have granted them generally refuse to require that the whole array of rights be made available, as they are to adult offenders. Since the *Gault* decision, however, many states have adopted administrative regulations requiring juvenile agencies to incorporate due process, such as proper notice of the hearing and the right to counsel in postconviction proceedings.

Preventing Delinquency

Although the juvenile justice system has been concerned with controlling delinquent behavior, important efforts are now being made to prevent delinquency before it occurs. "Delinquency prevention" refers to intervening in young people's lives before they engage in delinquency in the first place—that is, preventing any involvement in delinquency at all. In the past, delinquency prevention was the responsibility of treatment-oriented agencies such as day care providers, YMCA and YWCA, Boys and Girls Clubs of America, and other private and public agencies. Today, there are many community-based treatment programs involving a combination of juvenile justice and treatment agencies. Some programs focus on the educational experience and attempt to help kids maintain their bond to society by strengthening their attachments to school. Much of these efforts are conducted by social workers whose specialty is working with troubled youths.

Comprehensive community-based delinquency prevention programs are taking a systematic approach or using a comprehensive planning model to develop preventive interventions. This includes analyzing the delinquency problem, identifying resources available in the community, prioritizing delinquency problems, and

If juvenile delinquency can be prevented from occurring in the first place, young people stand the best chance of leading productive, law-abiding lives. Here Judge Alison Nelson Floyd, right, helps student Samuel Jordan, 10, from the W.E.B. Dubois Leadership Academy, navigate his way through his responsibilities as a judge in a mock trial in the courtroom of Judge Charles Patton at the Justice Center in Cleveland, Ohio, on March 21, 2009. Floyd, a juvenile court judge, volunteered to teach the boys, ages 10–13 years, about the workings of the criminal justice system.

© Lisa DeJong/The Plain Dealer/Landov

identifying successful programs in other communities and tailoring them to local conditions and needs.[40] Not all comprehensive community-based prevention programs follow this model, but evidence suggests that this approach will produce the greatest reductions in juvenile delinquency.[41]

L08 Describe the juvenile correctional process

Problems of Juvenile Justice

Even those experts who want to retain an independent juvenile court have called for its restructuring.[42] Crime control advocates want to reduce the court's jurisdiction over juveniles charged with serious crimes and liberalize the prosecutor's ability to try them in adult courts. Opponents feel that the traditional *parens patriae* philosophy of juvenile justice ought to prevail.

In *Bad Kids: Race and the Transformation of the Juvenile Court*, legal expert Barry Feld makes the rather controversial suggestion that the juvenile court system should be discontinued and replaced by an alternative method of justice.[43] In Feld's words, the juvenile court has become a "deficient second-rate criminal court." The welfare and rehabilitative purposes of the juvenile court have been subordinated to its role as law enforcement agent, so there is little purpose for retaining it in its current state. Feld's beliefs have been substantiated by research showing that at least in some jurisdictions, the focus of juvenile justice has shifted from individual needs to the seriousness of the crime, enhancing the prosecution's power to make decisions and the system's reliance on the adversarial process at the expense of *parens patriae*.[44]

Not all experts agree with Feld that the juvenile court has become redundant. Some, such as John Kerbs, believe that the get-tough approach will force the criminal courts to provide harsher sentences and tougher treatment—and that the brunt of these draconian sentences will fall squarely on the shoulders of minority youths. Research efforts routinely show that African American adults are unduly punished in adult courts. Sending juvenile offenders to these venues is likely to enmesh them further in a system that is already unfair.[45]

Minority Overrepresentation in Juvenile Justice

In addition to controversies over its goals and values, another significant and enduring problem in juvenile justice is the overrepresentation of minority youths in the system and the inequitable treatment they receive. Minority youths accused of delinquent acts are less likely than white youths to be diverted from the court system into informal sanctions and are more likely to receive sentences involving incarceration. Nationally, the ratio of minority custody to white custody is 2.6 to 1, meaning that there are 2.6 members of minority groups in custody for every white juvenile in custody.[46] In some states, the ratio is greater than 4 to 1.[47]

Not only is the disproportionate minority representation in juvenile correctional facilities a very serious matter, but it also reflects the racial disparity that occurs at every stage of the juvenile justice process. A disproportionate number of minority youths suffer arrest, detention, waivers, and so on. A report by the National Council on Crime and Delinquency highlights this problem. The council's "Treatment of Youth of Color in the Justice System" describes how minority youths receive differential treatment at every stage of the justice process.[48] Among the findings from the council's report are these:

- Although African American youths are 16 percent of the adolescent population in the United States, they are 38 percent of the almost 100,000 youths confined in local detention and state correctional systems. They were overrepresented in all offense categories.
- Youths of color make up the majority of young people held in both public and private facilities.

Ethical Challenge

You are a juvenile court judge. John has been arrested for robbery and rape. His victim, a young neighborhood girl, was seriously injured in the attack and needed extensive hospitalization; she is now in counseling. Because the charges are serious, John can be waived to the adult court and tried as an adult even though he is only 14 years old. Under existing state law, a hearing must be held to determine whether there is sufficient evidence that John cannot be successfully treated in the juvenile justice system and therefore warrants transfer to the adult system. The final decision on the matter is yours alone.

At the waiver hearing, you discover that John is the oldest of three siblings living in a single-parent home. He has had no contact with his father for more than 10 years. His psychological evaluations show hostility, anger toward females, and great feelings of frustration. His intelligence is above average, but his behavioral and academic records are poor. John is a loner with few friends. This is his first formal involvement with the juvenile court. Previous contact was limited to an informal complaint for disorderly conduct at age 13, which was dismissed by the court's intake department. During the hearing, John verbalizes what you interpret to be superficial remorse for his offenses.

Write an essay discussing whether you would waive John to the adult court or treat him as a juvenile. Give the reasons for your decision.

- Youths of color, especially Latino youths, are a much larger proportion of the young in public facilities than in private facilities, which tend to be less harsh environments.
- Although they represent just 34 percent of the U.S. population, youths of color represent 62 percent of young people in detention, 66 percent of those committed to public facilities, and 55 percent of those committed to private facilities.
- Nationwide, youths of color were overrepresented in the detained population at 3.1 times the rate of white youths, among commitments to public facilities at 2.9 times the rate of white youths, and among private commitments at 2.0 times the rate of white youths.
- Overall, custody rates were four times greater for African American youths than for white youths. Custody rates for Latino and Native American youths were 1.8 and 2.6 times the custody rate for white youths, respectively.

Summary

L01 **Describe the history of juvenile justice** The modern practice of legally separating adult and juvenile offenders can be traced back to the development of Elizabethan-era poor laws and the creation of the English chancery court. Poor laws mandated care for wayward and destitute children. Chancery courts protected the rights and welfare of children who could not care for themselves. Juvenile justice was also influenced by the child-saving movement. The child savers were responsible for creating a number of programs for indigent youths, including the New York House of Refuge, which began operations in 1825. The child savers also influenced state and local governments to create independent correctional institutions to house minors.

L02 **Discuss the establishment of the juvenile court** The child savers lobbied for an independent, state-supported juvenile court. Their efforts prompted the development of the first comprehensive juvenile court in Illinois in 1899. The main concern was the "best interests of the child," not strict adherence to legal doctrine, constitutional rights, or due process of law. Youngsters who were found delinquent in juvenile court could spend years in a state training school.

L03 **Describe the changes in juvenile justice that began in the 1960s and continue today** In the 1960s and 1970s, the U.S. Supreme Court radically altered the juvenile justice system when it rendered a series of decisions that established the right of juveniles to due process of law. The term *juvenile delinquency* now refers to children who fall under a jurisdictional age limit, which varies from state to state, and who commit an act in violation of the penal code. Status offenders commit acts forbidden to minors, which include truancy, running away, and being a habitually disobedient and ungovernable child. Another trend has been to create family courts, which include a broad range of family- and child-related issues within their jurisdictions.

L04 **Summarize police processing of juvenile offenders** Most states do not have specific statutory provisions distinguishing the arrest process for children from that for adults. Some jurisdictions give broad arrest powers to the police in juvenile cases by authorizing the officer to make an arrest whenever she or he believes that the child's behavior falls within the jurisdiction of the juvenile court. Police may arrest youths for behavior considered legal for adults, including running away, violating curfew, and being in possession of alcohol. When a juvenile is found to have engaged in delinquent or incorrigible behavior, police agencies are charged with the decision to release or to detain the child and refer her to juvenile court.

L05 **Describe the juvenile court process** After a juvenile is formally taken into custody, either as a delinquent or as a status offender, the prosecutor usually decides whether to release the child to the parent or guardian or to detain the child in a secure shelter pending trial. There are often three judicial hearings in the juvenile court process. The first, typically called an initial appearance, is similar to the arraignment in the adult system. The adjudicatory hearing (often called the fact-finding hearing) is the second. In it, the court hears evidence on the allegations stated in the delinquency petition. At a later dispositional hearing, the juvenile court judge imposes a sentence on the juvenile offender based on the offense, the youth's prior record, and his or her family background.

L06 **Explain the concept of waiver** Today, most U.S. jurisdictions provide by statute for waiver, or transfer, of juvenile offenders to the criminal courts. In *Kent v. United States* (1966), the Supreme Court held that the waiver proceeding is a critically important stage in the juvenile justice process and that juveniles must be afforded minimum requirements of due process of law at such proceedings, including the right to legal counsel. Waiver

does not seem to influence crime rates or recidivism rates; one reason may be that juveniles whose cases are waived to criminal court are sentenced more leniently than they would have been in juvenile court.

L07 **Explain the importance of *In re Gault*** *In re Gault* granted critical rights to juvenile defendants, the most important of these rights being notice of the charges, the right to counsel, the right to confront and cross-examine witnesses, the privilege against self-incrimination, and the right to a transcript of the trial record.

L08 **Describe the juvenile correctional process** Probation is the most commonly used formal sentence for juvenile offenders, and many states require that a youth fail on probation before being sent to an institution (unless the criminal act is quite serious). The most severe of the statutory dispositions available to the juvenile court involves commitment of the child to an institution. Some experts in delinquency and juvenile law question the policy of institutionalizing juvenile offenders.

Review Questions

1. Should status offenders be treated by the juvenile court? Explain. Should they be placed in confinement for such acts as running away or cutting school? Why or why not?

2. Should a juvenile ever be waived to adult court with the possible risk that the child will be incarcerated with adult felons? Why or why not?

3. Do you support the death penalty for children? Explain.

4. Should juveniles be given mandatory incarceration sentences for serious crimes, as adults are? Explain.

5. Is it fair to deny juveniles a jury trial? Why or why not?

6. Do you think the trend toward treating juveniles like adult offenders is desirable? Explain.

14 Crime and Justice in the New Millennium

Learning Objectives

*I*n 2010, Americans became very familiar with a previously unknown website called WikiLeaks, an international organization that publishes classified and secret documents that are submitted by unnamed and anonymous sources.

Launched in 2006 and run by Julian Assange, an Australian computer hacker who emigrated to Sweden, WikiLeaks has supporters around the globe. In April 2010, the site began to post videos and documents that had been illegally appropriated from U.S. diplomatic and military computers by unknown hackers. For example, one video showed a 2007 incident in which Iraqi civilians and journalists were killed by U.S. forces. It also leaked more than 76,000 classified war documents from Afghanistan. In November 2010, it released U.S. State Department cables. In the aftermath of the leaks, Army Specialist Bradley Manning, 22, was arrested after an informant told federal authorities that he had overheard him bragging about giving WikiLeaks a video of a helicopter assault in Iraq plus more than 260,000 classified U.S. diplomatic cables taken from government computers. ■

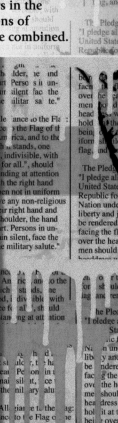

RealityCheck

MYTH OR REALITY?

- Corporate criminals rarely go to jail.
- Worries about illegal logging are the overblown fantasies of a group of trouble-making tree huggers.
- Illegally dumping old computers is a global problem.
- The porn industry is booming and adult film actors are getting rich.
- It is perfectly legal to buy a stock, post online info telling people to buy the stock because its profits are jumping, and then sell it once the price goes up.
- A cyber attack against Iran derailed its nuclear program.
- There are more drug users in the world than the populations of England, Italy, and France combined.

At the time of this writing, Assange has been accused of sexual misconduct and is currently out on bail fighting extradition to Sweden; no charges have been filed against him for the WikiLeaks disclosures.[1] In July 2010, Manning was sent to the Marine Corps Brig, Quantico, Virginia, where he was held in "maximum custody" solitary confinement. Civil rights groups raised an alarm over his harsh treatment, declaring that it violated his constitutional rights. Bowing to pressure, the Pentagon transferred Manning to the general population in the federal prison in Fort Leavenworth, Kansas, on April 20, 2011.

Just a few years ago, complex global incidents involving leaking classified documents could not have been contemplated, let alone transacted. Innovation brings change and with it new opportunities to commit crime and new challenges for the criminal justice system. The technological revolution has provided new tools to misappropriate funds, damage property, sell illicit material, or conduct warfare, espionage, and terror. The technological revolution has broadened the scope of crime and increased the demands on the justice system. It is now routine for offenders to use complex and technologically sophisticated methods to secure illegal profits and provide criminal services. Criminal conspiracies may not only be national in scope, but can also be transnational criminal enterprises that involve criminal gangs whose activities cross nations and continents.

In some instances this new brand of crime can involve a single individual who engages in a complex criminal enterprise, such as the multi-billion-dollar fraud perpetrated by financier Bernard Madoff (more on him later). It can also involve people acting in transnational organized crime syndicates, such as those that actively traffic in contraband, such as narcotics and weapons, and even humans for pornography and prostitution.

In this chapter, we review four independent yet interrelated emerging criminal activities that are presenting challenges for the criminal justice system: **corporate enterprise crime**, green crime, cyber crime, and transnational organized crime. While distinct and independent, these emerging crime types often overlap. Transnational criminals may use cyberspace to conduct fraud schemes and then seek

corporate enterprise crime
Conspiracies that involve bending the rules of legitimate business and commerce to make illegal profits in the marketplace. Enterprise crimes involve the violation of law in the course of an otherwise legitimate occupation.

legitimate enterprises to launder money, diversify their sources of income, increase their power and influence, and gain and enhance respectability.[2] Transnational criminal gangs may appropriate marketing concepts from legitimate business enterprise. Otherwise legitimate corporate enterprise executives may turn to green crimes such as illegally dumping hazardous waste products to get around government regulations and increase their profits.[3]

Corporate Enterprise Crime

One new crime trend facing the justice system is corporate enterprise crimes, which now amount to hundreds of billions of dollars, far outstripping the expense of any other type of crime. The FBI is currently pursuing more than 500 corporate fraud cases, several of which involve losses to public investors that individually exceed $1 billion. Business people such as Bernard Madoff and Robert Allen Stanford, owner of Stanford Financial Group and other affiliated companies, have been convicted on charges of scamming people out of their life savings.[4] These large-scale financial crimes have involved subprime lending institutions, brokerage houses, home-building firms, hedge funds, and financial institutions. Trillions of dollars in shareholder value have been lost, several prominent companies (such as Bear Stearns and Lehman Brothers) have gone out of business, several prominent banks (including IndyMac Bank and Washington Mutual) have failed, and the federal government has provided over a trillion dollars in relief to keep other companies from failing (American Insurance Group, General Motors, and Citigroup).[5] Government enforcement agencies such as the FBI and New York State Attorney General's office are currently involved in investigating accounting schemes designed to deceive both investors and government auditors about the true financial condition of a corporation in an attempt to inflate share prices based on fictitious performance indicators. This practice not only can result in financial losses to investors, but has done immeasurable damage to both the states and U.S. economy.[6]

LO1 Discuss the impact of criminal enterprise crime

Fraud on Wall Street

The creation of global capital markets has created unprecedented opportunities for U.S. businesses to access capital and investors to diversify their portfolios. This large-scale investment growth, however, has also led to significant growth in the amount of fraud and misconduct seen on Wall Street. Investment firms have engaged in deceptive schemes to defraud clients. Investment counselors and insurance agents use their positions to cheat individual clients by misleading them on the quality of their investments. Financial organizations have cheated their clients by promoting risky investments as being iron-clad safe.

Perhaps the greatest of these crimes was pulled off by financier Bernard Madoff, who had operated Bernard L. Madoff Investment Securities. Madoff Investments became one of Wall Street's largest "specialist" trading firms, dedicated to investment management and advice. Managing billions in assets, Madoff was a member of the jet set and a trusted advisor to many wealthy people, including director Steven Spielberg, as well as sophisticated financial managers and investors. At first Madoff promised and delivered healthy returns, helping to draw in a constant flow of investors. Things went south when the market crashed and people wanted their money back, only to find there was none available. It turns out that Madoff's asset management firm was a giant **Ponzi scheme** (see Exhibit 14.1). Madoff had not invested any of the money he had taken in from investors but instead deposited it in various banks, using the interest and principal to pay off investors when they wanted to take money out of their accounts. At first few did because they were making such fantastic paper profits that they kept reinvesting dividends and capital gains. Madoff, of course, convinced them to keep their profits in the account rather than ask for a distribution. When the market turned and people began asking for their principal, his house of cards fell apart.

Ponzi scheme
An investment fraud that involves the payment of purported returns to existing investors from funds contributed by new investors.

LO2 Describe a Ponzi scheme

When Madoff realized he could never catch up to the paper profits, he finally told his sons what he had done and they contacted the FBI. Madoff later claimed that he merely wanted to satisfy the expectations of high returns his clients demanded and which simply could not be met by legal means. Instead, he resorted to an illegal scheme involving false trading activities, illegal foreign transfers, and false SEC filings. He hoped that clients would simply reinvest their gains without requesting withdrawals until he could figure a way out of investing the money and actually making a profit! When finally caught, Madoff admitted he knew his day of reckoning was inevitable.

Madoff's Ponzi scheme has been estimated to cost clients an estimated *$65 billion*, maybe the largest criminal conspiracy in history. On March 12, 2009, he pleaded guilty to an 11-count criminal complaint, charged with violations of the antifraud provisions of the Securities Act of 1933, the Securities Exchange Act of 1934, and the Investment Advisers Act of 1940.[7] On June 29, 2009, Madoff was sentenced to 150 years in prison, a life sentence.

The Subprime Mortgage Scandal

During 2008–2009, the nation was rocked by another form of Wall Street fraud that threatened to destroy the financial system and the real estate market and create a 1929-style depression: the collapse of the subprime mortgage system. A subprime mortgage is a home loan given to borrowers who, because of their income, would not ordinarily qualify for bank loans. Once the subprime loans have been issued, the vendors typically bundle

Exhibit 14.1

What Is a Ponzi Scheme?

A Ponzi scheme is an investment fraud that involves the payment of purported returns to existing investors from funds contributed by new investors. Ponzi scheme organizers often solicit new investors by promising to invest funds in opportunities claimed to generate high returns with little or no risk. In many Ponzi schemes, the fraudsters focus on attracting new money to make promised payments to earlier-stage investors and to use for personal expenses, instead of engaging in any legitimate investment activity. With little or no legitimate earnings, the schemes require a consistent flow of money from new investors to continue. Ponzi schemes tend to collapse when it becomes difficult to recruit new investors or when a large number of investors ask to cash out.

Why are they called "Ponzi schemes"? The term comes from one Charles Ponzi, who duped thousands of New England residents into investing in a postage stamp speculation scheme back in the 1920s. At a time when the annual interest rate for bank accounts was 5 percent, Ponzi promised investors that he could provide a 50 percent return in just 90 days. Ponzi initially bought a small number of international mail coupons in support of his scheme, but quickly switched to using incoming funds to pay off earlier investors.

Source: "Ponzi Schemes," Securities and Exchange Commission, www.sec.gov/answers/ponzi.htm (accessed July 4, 2011).

Bernard L. Madoff, the accused mastermind of a $50 billion Ponzi scheme, leaves federal court in New York, January 14, 2009. Madoff later received a life sentence for his crimes.

AP Photo/Stuart Ramson

securitization
The process in which vendors take individual subprime loans and bundle them into large pools and sell them as securities.

them into large pools and sell them as securities, a process known as **securitization**. Because they carry risk, these securities typically pay a higher interest rate than normal securities, making them attractive to investors. By 2006, subprimes had grown to 20 percent of the mortgage market, up from 2 percent a decade earlier; this means an estimated $1.3 trillion, of the total $4.5 trillion total mortgage loans outstanding, is subprime.

While subprime mortgages can help first-time home buyers of limited means, they also have been the source of fraud by both borrowers and lenders. Borrowers have provided false information to the mortgage broker and/or lender, enabling them to get loans for which they were not qualified. Those involved in mortgage lending—including mortgage brokers, lenders, appraisers, underwriters, accountants, real estate agents, settlement attorneys, land developers, investors, builders, bank account representatives, trust account representatives, investment banks, and credit rating agencies—have gotten involved in criminal fraud to maintain or increase their current standard of living. In addition to traditional industry conspirators, there have been instances involving various organized criminal groups and gang members involved in mortgage fraud activity.[8]

Subprime lenders made risky loans assuming that real estate values would always be increasing, allowing borrowers to refinance or sell their properties before going into default. However, when sales slowed down in the housing market, loan defaults increased and the securities lost value. As a result, mortgage companies experienced financial distress and bankruptcy.[9]

Desperate for funds, some subprime lenders, in order to stave off regulators, engaged in false accounting entries and fraudulently inflated assets and revenues. Some manipulated their reported loan portfolio risks and used various accounting schemes to inflate their financial reports. And in some cases, before these subprime lenders' stocks rapidly declined in value, executives with insider information sold their equity positions and profited illegally. As a result of these practices, some subprime lenders are being investigated by federal agencies for corporate fraud and insider trading.

LO3 Be familiar with the mortgage fraud scandal

Billion-Dollar Management Fraud

Sometimes executives in large corporations take advantage of their position to engage in management frauds, which typically involve falsifying financial information for their own financial benefit. Managers may engage in false transactions and accounting entries, bogus trades, insider trading, kickbacks, backdating of executive stock options, and misuse or misappropriation of company property. Retaining one's present position within the company by manipulating accounts and concealing unacceptable performance from stockholders would also be included in management fraud.

While management fraud is not a recent phenomenon, multi-billion-dollar schemes have threatened the nation's financial system. Management fraud has involved some of the nation's largest companies and richest people. Take for example the infamous Enron case. Executives of the oil and gas trading firm, once one of the largest companies in the United States, engaged in a massive fraud scheme that caused the company to go bankrupt. Chairman Kenneth L. Lay was charged with conspiracy, securities fraud, wire fraud, bank fraud, and making false statements. Enron CEO Jeffrey K. Skilling and former Enron Chief Accounting Officer Richard Causey were also charged with money laundering and conspiracy. The government claimed that executives oversaw a massive conspiracy to delude investors into believing that Enron was a growing company when, in fact, it was undergoing business setbacks. Why did they do it: greed. Between 1998 and 2001, Lay, who died in 2006, received approximately $300 million from the sale of Enron stock options and restricted stock and made over $217 million in profit; he was also paid more than $19 million in salary and bonuses.[10]

Criminalizing Corporate Enterprise Crime

What efforts have been made to bring violators of the public trust to justice? Though law enforcement agencies and the courts have traditionally been reluctant to throw corporate executives in jail, a number of well-publicized cases (such as Bernard Madoff) indicate that the gloves are off and the government is willing to punish high-profile corporate criminals with long prison sentences. Because the Madoff, Enron, and other scandals have deprived so many people of their life savings and caused such disruptions in the financial markets, both justice system personnel and the general public now consider corporate crimes as more serious offenses than common-law theft offenses and perpetrators deserving of severe punishment.[11] Penalties have been increasing, and long prison sentences are being routinely handed out for corporate crimes.[12] In fact, punishing corporate criminals with prison terms has become so routine and punishments so severe, that some commentators now argue that the government may actually be going overboard.[13]

Corporate Crime Law Enforcement The detection and enforcement of large scale corporate crime are primarily in the hands of administrative departments and agencies with investigation arms to police the areas of commerce that are their responsibility. The Securities and Exchange Commission (SEC) has been given the responsibility for overseeing the nation's capital markets. It is assigned the task of protecting investors; maintaining fair, orderly, and efficient markets; and facilitating capital formation.

If SEC investigators detect inappropriate behavior in the financial system, they may decide either to bring a case in federal court or before an administrative law judge, depending upon the type of sanction or relief that is being sought. For example, if the commission seeks to bar or remove someone from acting as a corporate officer, they must take the case to a federal district court. During the proceeding, the SEC will ask the judge to issue a court order, called an injunction, prohibiting any further acts or practices that violate the law or commission rules. An injunction can also require audits and accounting for frauds. In addition to barring or suspending the individual from serving as a corporate officer or director, the SEC can seek civil monetary penalties or the return of illegal profits (called disgorgement). A person who violates the court's order may be found in contempt and be subject to additional fines or imprisonment.

The decision to pursue criminal rather than civil violations usually is based on both the seriousness of the case and the perpetrator's intent, actions to conceal the violation, and prior record. Any evidence of criminal activity is then sent to the Department of Justice or the FBI for investigation. Some other federal agencies, such as the Environmental Protection Agency (EPA) and the U.S. Postal Service, have their own investigative arms. Enforcement generally is reactive (generated by complaints) rather than proactive (involving ongoing investigations or the monitoring of activities). Investigations are carried out by the various federal agencies and the FBI. If criminal prosecution is called for, the case will be handled by attorneys from the criminal, tax, antitrust, and civil rights divisions of the Justice Department. If insufficient evidence is available to warrant a criminal prosecution, the case will be handled civilly or administratively by some other federal agency. For example, the Federal Trade Commission can issue a cease and desist order in antitrust or merchandising fraud cases.

State Level Enforcement Responding to the threat of large-scale corporate fraud, a number of states have created special task forces and prosecution teams to crack down on fraudulent schemes and bring perpetrators to justice. In addition, state legislatures have passed a spate of new laws aimed directly at easing prosecution for corporate crimes. For example, Florida has created the Mortgage Fraud Task Force to address the issues of mortgage and foreclosure rescue fraud. The task force investigates cases in which false or misleading documents are filed to fool lenders into making mortgage loans to people who cannot hope to pay them back or on properties whose values have been grossly inflated.[14]

Workers clean oil residue from the rocks that form a jetty protecting a Gulfport, Mississippi, boat ramp on September 28, 2010, soon after the BP oil spill. At nearby Ken Combs Pier, Secretary of the Navy Ray Mabus announced his plan for Gulf Coast restoration. Should people be held criminally liable for environmental disasters caused by their negligence, or is this a civil matter?

© Amanda McCoy/Biloxi Sun Herald/MCT/Landov

green crime
Criminal activity that involves violation of rules and laws designed to protect the environment, including illegal dumping, polluting, fishing, logging and so on.

Green Crime

On April 20, 2010, an explosion occurred on the *Deepwater Horizon* oil rig, killing 11 platform workers and injuring 17 others.[15] The rig was built by Hyundai Heavy Industries of Korea, owned by the Transocean Drilling Corporation, the drilling overseen by Halliburton, and leased by BP (formerly British Petroleum), in order to drill a deepwater (5,000 feet below the surface) rig in the Gulf of Mexico. At first, estimates of the spill were 5,000 barrels a day, but they quickly rose to 60,000. While company officials frantically tried to stem the flow with a variety of failed schemes, millions of barrels of escaping oil created a slick that covered thousands of square miles, devastating wildlife and causing one of the greatest natural disasters in the nation's history. BP, facing civil fines, offered to place $20 billion in an escrow account to cover damages. The leak was finally stopped in August 2010.

On June 1, 2010, the Obama administration announced that it had launched a criminal probe in order to "prosecute to the fullest extent of the law" any persons or companies that broke the law in the time leading up to the spill.[16] Under federal environmental laws, a company may be charged with a misdemeanor for negligent conduct or a felony if there is evidence that company personnel knowingly engaged in conduct risking injury. It would be a criminal act if, for example, employees of BP or its subcontractors, Transocean and Halliburton:

- Lied in the permit process for obtaining a drilling license
- Tried to cover up the severity of the spill
- Knowing of negligence in construction, chose to ignore the danger it imposed
- Engaged in or approved of unsafe, risky, or dangerous methods to remove the drill, knowing that such methods could injure those on board

To prove a felony, and potentially put BP executives in prison, the government would have to show that company officials knew in advance that its actions would lead to the explosion and oil spill but chose to ignore the danger; a misdemeanor requires only mere negligence. But even a misdemeanor conviction would amp up the loss to the company, because the Federal Alternative Fines Act allows the government to request monetary fines that are twice the loss associated with an offense.[17] This provision can also have a devastating effect on employees, because fines imposed on individuals under the act may *not* be paid by their employer.[18] Adding all legal fees and damage claims, a criminal conviction would cost BP more than $60 billion. It would also mean that the company would be prevented from having future sales contracts with the government, a penalty that would cost BP additional billions each year. Finally, lying to the government during the investigation could bring additional common-law charges of making false statements, obstruction of justice, and conspiracy. As of this writing, criminal charges have yet to be filed, and it seems unlikely they ever will.

Green crimes are violations of existing criminal laws designed to protect people, the environment or both. They include crimes against workers such as occupational health and safety crimes, as well as laws designed to protect nature and the environment (the Clean Air Act, Clean Water Act, and so on). Oil spills are just part of the growing green crime problem that is facing the justice system. Green crimes involve a wide range of actions and outcomes that harm the environment and that stem from decisions about what is produced, where it is produced, and how it is produced.[19] Global warming, overdevelopment, population growth, and other changes will continue to bring these issues front and center, and they will soon become a major focus of the criminal justice system.[20]

Forms of Green Crime

Green crime can take many different forms, ranging from deforestation and illegal logging to violations of worker safety. A few of the most damaging green crimes are set out below.

Illegal Logging Illegal logging involves harvesting, processing, and transporting timber or wood products in violation of existing laws and treaties.[21] It is a universal phenomenon, occurring in major timber-producing countries, especially in the third world where enforcement is lax. Logging violations include taking trees in protected areas such as national parks, going over legally prescribed logging quotas, processing logs without acquiring licenses, and exporting logs without paying export duties. By sidestepping the law, loggers can create greater profits than those generated through legal methods. The situation is serious because illegal logging can have severe environmental and social impact: illegal logging exhausts forests, destroys wildlife, and damages its habitats. It causes ruinous damage to the forests, including deforestation and forest degradation worldwide. The destruction of forest cover can cause flash floods and landslides that have killed thousands of people.[22]

RealityCheck

MYTH OR REALITY? Worries about illegal logging are the overblown fantasies of a group of trouble-making tree huggers.

MYTH. *Illegal logging is a $15 billion industry that is threatening the ecological balance in many areas around the globe.*

If the flow of illegal drugs cannot be contained, how can we control the illegal harvesting of trees?

While the scale of illegal logging is difficult to estimate, it is believed that more than half of all logging activities in the most vulnerable forest regions—southeast Asia, central Africa, South America, and Russia—may be conducted illegally. Worldwide estimates suggest that illegal activities may account for over a tenth of the total global timber trade, representing products worth at least $15 billion per year.

Illegal Fishing Unlicensed and illegal fishing practices are another billion-dollar green crime. It can take on many forms and involve highly different parties, ranging from huge factory ships operating on the high seas that catch thousands of tons of fish on each voyage, to smaller, locally operating ships that confine themselves to national waters. Illegal fishing occurs when these ships sign on to their home nation's rules but then choose to ignore their scope and boundary, or operate in a country's waters without permission or on the high seas without a flag. Because catches remain clandestine and are not reported, their illegal fishing can have a detrimental effect on species as government regulators have no idea how many are being caught. As a result, stocks become depleted and species endangered. For example, Patagonian toothfish (*Dissostichus eleginoides*), popular in restaurants as "Chilean sea bass," is endangered because nearly half

Illegal loggers load the wood they cut from a mangrove forest before they were detained by Malaysia's State of Selangor Forestry Department in Port Klang on June 22, 2011. Selangor has lost 100 million ringgit ($33 million) worth of logs to illegal logging over the last 10 years, proving that illegal logging is a growing global problem.

those caught are victims of illegal fishing methods. Because of the relatively long time it takes toothfish to mature, illegal fishing means that many are caught before they have a chance to reproduce. Illegal fishing reduces the number of new adults that can replace those lost from fishing, and the ability of populations to replenish themselves is quickly lost.[23]

Illegal Dumping Some green-criminals want to skirt local, state, and federal restrictions on dumping dangerous substances in the environment. Rather than pay expensive processing fees, they may secretly dispose of hazardous wastes in illegal dump sites. Illegally dumped wastes can either be hazardous or nonhazardous materials that are discarded in an effort to avoid either disposal fees or the time and effort required for proper disposal. Materials dumped range from used motor oil to waste from construction sites.

One of the largest and fastest growing problems is the disposal of 7 million tons of obsolete high-tech electronics, called e-waste, such as televisions, computers and computer monitors, laptops, VCRs, and so on.[24] A considerable amount of e-waste is now being sent abroad to developing nations for recycling, often in violation of international laws restricting such commerce. All too often, the material overwhelms recycling plants and is instead dumped in local villages near people and water sources.

Illegal Polluting Criminal environmental pollution is defined as the intentional or negligent discharge of a toxic or contaminating substance into the biosystem that is known to have an adverse effect on the natural environment or life. Individuals and companies may commit this crime to save processing and dumping fees, thereby adding to profits. Illegal pollution schemes may involve the ground release of toxic chemicals such as kepone, vinyl chloride, mercury, PCBs, and asbestos. Illegal and/or controlled air pollutants include hydrochlorofluorocarbons (HCFCs), aerosols, asbestos, carbon monoxide, chlorofluorocarbons (CFCs), criteria air pollutants, lead, mercury, methane, nitrogen oxides (NO_x), radon, refrigerants, and sulfur oxides (SO_2). Water pollution is defined as the dumping of a substance that degrades or alters the quality of the waters to an extent that is detrimental to their use by humans or by an animal or a plant that is useful to humans. This includes the disposal into rivers, lakes, and streams of toxic chemicals.[25]

RealityCheck

MYTH OR REALITY? Illegally dumping old computers is a global problem.

REALITY. *As strange as it seems, it is difficult and costly to get rid of old computer parts which may contain toxic substances, hence a growing demand for illegal overseas dump sites in third-world nations.*

As the use of computers grows, this problem may increase. Is it possible that tablets such as the iPad may reduce the dumping of computer parts?

LO4 Be familiar with the various forms of green crime

Enforcing Environmental Laws

The United States and most sovereign nations have passed laws making it a crime to pollute or damage the environment. For example, among environmental laws in the U.S. are the following:

- *Clean Water Act (1972).* Establishes and maintains goals and standards for U.S. water quality and purity. It was amended in 1987 to increase controls on toxic pollutants, and in 1990 to more effectively address the hazard of oil spills.
- *Emergency Planning and Community Right-to-Know Act (1986).* Requires companies to disclose information about toxic chemicals they release into the air and water and dispose of on land.
- *Endangered Species Act (1973).* Designed to protect and recover endangered and threatened species of fish, wildlife, and plants in the United States and beyond. The law works in part by protecting species habitats.
- *Oil Pollution Act (1990).* Enacted in the aftermath of the *Exxon Valdez* oil spill in Alaska's Prince William Sound, this law streamlines federal response to oil spills by requiring oil storage facilities and vessels to prepare spill-response plans and provide for their rapid implementation. The law also increases polluters' liability for cleanup costs and damage to natural resources.

The major enforcement arm against environmental crimes is the Environmental Protection Agency, which was given full law enforcement authority in 1988. The EPA has successfully prosecuted significant violations across all major environmental statutes, including data fraud cases (for instance, private laboratories submitting false environmental data to state and federal environmental agencies); indiscriminate hazardous waste dumping that resulted in serious injuries and death; industry-wide ocean dumping by cruise ships; oil spills that caused significant damage to waterways, wetlands, and beaches; international smuggling of CFC refrigerants that damage the ozone layer and increase skin cancer risk; and illegal handling of hazardous substances such as pesticides and asbestos that exposed children, the poor, and other especially vulnerable groups to potentially serious illness.[26] Its Criminal Investigation Division (EPA CID) investigates allegations of criminal wrongdoing prohibited by various environmental statutes.

Cyber Crime

Cyber crime, another challenge for the contemporary justice system, typically involves the theft and/or destruction of information, resources, or funds via computer networks, and/or the Internet. This relatively new category of crimes presents a compelling challenge for the justice system and the law enforcement community because (a) it is rapidly evolving, with new schemes being created daily, (b) it is difficult to detect through traditional law enforcement channels, and (c) to control it, agents of the justice system must develop technical skills that match those of the perpetrators.[27] It is even possible that the recent decline in crime is actually a result of cyber crime replacing traditional street crime. Instead of robbing a bank at gunpoint, a new group of contemporary thieves find it easier to hack into accounts and transfer funds to offshore banks. Instead of shoplifting from a brick-and-mortar store, the contemporary cyber thief devises clever schemes to steal from etailers.

There are actually three forms of cyber crime (summarized in Concept Summary 14.1). Some cyber criminals use modern technology to accumulate goods and services. **Cyber theft** schemes range from illegally copying material under copyright protection to using technology to commit traditional theft-based offenses such as larceny and fraud. Other cyber criminals are motivated less by profit and more by the urge to commit **cyber vandalism**, or technological destruction. They aim their malicious attacks at disrupting, defacing, and destroying technology

cyber crime
The theft and/or destruction of information, resources, or funds via computers, computer networks, or the Internet.

cyber theft
The use of computer networks for criminal profits. Illegal copyright infringement, identity theft, and Internet securities fraud are examples of cyber theft.

cyber vandalism
Malicious attacks aimed at disrupting, defacing, and destroying technology.

Concept Summary 14.1

Typology of Cyber Crimes

Crime	Definition	Examples
Cyber theft	Use of cyberspace to distribute illegal goods and services or to defraud people for quick profits	Illegal copyright infringement, identity theft, Internet securities fraud, warez
Cyber vandalism	Use of cyberspace for revenge, for destruction, or to achieve malicious ends	Website defacement, worms, viruses, cyber stalking, cyber bullying
Cyber war	An effort by enemy forces to disrupt the intersection where the virtual electronic reality of computers meets the physical world	Use of logic bombs to disrupt or destroy "secure" systems or networks, use of the Internet to communicate covertly with agents around the world

cyber war
Politically motivated attacks designed to compromise the electronic infrastructure of the enemy and to disrupt its economy.

they find offensive. Finally, **cyber war** consists of acts aimed at undermining the social, economic, and political system of an enemy nation by destroying its electronic infrastructure and disrupting its economy. This can range from stealing secrets from foreign nations (cyber espionage) to destroying an enemy's Web-based infrastructure.

Cyber Theft: Cyber Crimes for Profit

The Internet enables criminals to operate in a more efficient and effective manner. Cyber thieves now have the luxury of remaining anonymous, living almost anywhere on the planet, conducting their business during the day or at night, and working alone or in a group, while at the same time reaching a much greater number of potential victims than ever before. No longer are con artists and criminal entrepreneurs limited to fleecing victims in a particular geographic locale; the whole world can be their target. And the technology revolution has opened up novel avenues of attack for cyber theft—ranging from the unlawful distribution of computer software to Internet security fraud—that heretofore were nonexistent.

Cyber thieves conspire to use cyberspace either to distribute illegal goods and services or to defraud people for quick profits. Some of the most common methods are described below.

Computer Fraud Computer fraud is not a unique offense but rather a common-law crime committed using contemporary technology. Consequently, many computer crimes are prosecuted under such traditional criminal statutes as those prohibiting larceny and fraud. However, not all computer crimes fall under common-law statutes, because the property stolen may be intangible—that is, electronic and/or magnetic impulse. Such crimes include:

- *Theft of information.* This is the unauthorized obtaining of information from a computer (for example, hacking), including software that is copied for profit.
- *The "salami slice" fraud.* The perpetrator carefully "slices" small sums from the balances of a large number of accounts in order to bypass internal controls and escape detection.
- *Software theft.* The comparative ease of making copies of computer software has led to a huge illegal market, depriving authors of very significant revenues.[28]

Internet Pornography The IT revolution has revitalized the porn industry. The Internet is an ideal venue for selling and distributing adult material; the computer is an ideal device for storing and viewing it. While it is difficult to estimate the extent of the industry, it is estimated that the revenue generated from adult sites each year is greater than all movie box office sales. The number of visits to pornographic sites (mostly by men, though women make up about 30 percent of the viewers) surpasses those made to Internet search engines; some individual sites report as many as 50 million hits per year.[29] Revenue from Internet porn comes from a number of sources: paid subscriptions, advertisements for other porn sites, fees for diverting web traffic to other sites, sale of sex-related products, and providing auxiliary services such as age verification services. Nonetheless, industry sales are in decline: free Internet content has cut into paid services. As a result producers, actors and actresses in the domestic adult film industry have found their income substantially declining.[30]

Because many porn sites are located in foreign lands, enforcement has proven difficult. However, law enforcement agencies here and abroad are now cracking down on the distribution of sexual material involving juveniles (kiddie porn). To give an example of the extent of this problem: Europol, the European Union police agency, recently cracked the website of a kiddie porn ring and developed intelligence reports on 4,200 participants in 35 countries, 670 of whom are suspected of downloading illegal images of child abuse or engaging in illegal acts with minors. More than 180 arrests were made and 230 children saved from the pornographers.[31]

RealityCheck

MYTH OR REALITY? The porn industry is booming and adult film actors are getting rich.

MYTH. *Free Internet content has hurt the industry's profits and film stars have experienced a significant drop in income.*
Has the Internet destroyed the novelty and allure of adult films?

Denial-of-Service Attack A denial-of-service attack is an attempt to extort money from legitimate users of an Internet service by threatening to interfere with the user's access to that service.[32] Examples include attempts to "flood" a computer network, thereby preventing access by legitimate network traffic; attempts to disrupt connections within a computer network, thereby interrupting access to a service; attempts to prevent a particular individual from accessing a service; and attempts to disrupt service to a specific system or person.

denial-of-service attack
Extorting money from an Internet service user by threatening to prevent the user having access to the service.

Copyright Infringement It is now common for groups of individuals to plan and work together to obtain software illegally and then "crack" or "rip" its copyright protections before posting it on the Internet for other members of the group to use. Its criminal purveyors refer to this pirated material as **warez** (pronounced like "wares," as in "software"). Frequently, these new pirated copies reach the Internet days or weeks before the legitimate product is commercially available.

warez
Copyrighted software illegally downloaded and sold by organized groups without license to do so.

Internet Securities Fraud Internet securities fraud involves using the Internet to intentionally manipulate the securities marketplace for profit. Three major types of Internet securities fraud are common today.

- *Market manipulation.* Stock market manipulation occurs when an individual tries to control the price of stock by interfering with the natural forces of supply and demand. There are two principal forms of this crime: the "pump and dump" and the "cyber smear." In a pump and dump scheme, erroneous and deceptive information is posted online to get unsuspecting investors interested in a stock while those spreading the information sell previously purchased stock at an inflated price. The cyber smear is a reverse pump and dump: negative information is spread online about a stock, driving down its price and enabling people to buy it at an artificially low price before rebuttals by the company's officers reestablish the legitimate price.[33]
- *Fraudulent offerings of securities.* Some cyber criminals create websites specifically designed to sell securities fraudulently. To make the offerings look more attractive than they are, assets may be inflated, expected returns overstated, and risks understated. In these schemes, investors are promised abnormally high profits on their investments. No investment is actually made. Early investors are

paid returns with the investment money received from the later investors. The system usually collapses, and the later investors do not receive dividends and lose their initial investment.

- *Illegal touting.* This crime occurs when individuals make securities recommendations and fail to disclose that they are being paid to disseminate their favorable opinions.

identity theft
Using the Internet to steal someone's identity and/or impersonate the victim in order to conduct illicit transactions, such as committing fraud using the victim's name and identity.

phishing
Also known as carding and spoofing, phishing consists of illegally acquiring personal information, such as bank passwords and credit card numbers, by masquerading as a trustworthy person or business in what appears to be an official electronic communication, such as an email or an instant message. The term *phishing* comes from the lures used to "fish" for financial information and passwords.

etailing fraud
Using the Internet to illegally buy or sell merchandise.

Identity Theft These thieves use the Internet to steal someone's identity and/or impersonate the victim to open a new credit card account or conduct some other financial transaction.[34] **Identity theft** can destroy a person's life by manipulating credit records or depleting bank accounts. Some identity thieves create false emails and/or websites that look legitimate but are designed to gain illegal access to a victims' personal information; this is known as **phishing** (and also as *carding* and *spoofing*).

Phishing emails and websites have become even more of a problem now that cyber criminals can easily copy brand names, the names of corporate personnel, and their insignia directly into the email. The look is so authentic that victims believe the email comes from the advertised company. Most phishers send out spam emails to a large number of recipients, knowing that some of those recipients will have accounts with the company they are impersonating. Some phishing schemes involve job offers. Once the unsuspecting victims fill out the "application," answering personal questions and including their Social Security number, the phisher has them in his grasp.[35]

Etailing Fraud New fraud schemes are evolving to exploit the fact that billions of dollars of goods are sold on the Internet each year. **Etailing fraud** can involve both illegally buying and selling merchandise on the Internet. Some etailing scams involve failure to deliver on promised purchases or services, and others involve the substitution of cheaper or used material for higher-quality purchases.

Illegal Drug Distribution The Internet has become a prime purveyor of prescription drugs, some of which can be quite dangerous when they are used to excess or fall into the hands of minors. There are thousands of websites advertising or offering controlled prescription drugs for sale. Many require no prescription from a patient's physician, while others simply ask that the prescription be faxed—increasing the risk of multiple use of one prescription or other fraud.[36]

Cyber Vandalism: Cyber Crime with Malicious Intent

Some cyber criminals may be motivated not by greed or profit but by the desire for revenge, to inflict wanton destruction, and/or to achieve a malicious intent. Cyber vandalism involves such crimes as sending destructive viruses and worms to attack important computer networks. Cyber vandals are motivated more by malice than by greed:

- Some cyber vandals target computers and networks, seeking revenge for some perceived wrong.
- Some desire to exhibit their technical prowess and superiority.
- Some wish to highlight the vulnerability of computer security systems.
- Some want to spy on other people's private financial and personal information ("computer voyeurism").
- Some want to destroy computer security because they believe in open access to all systems and programs.[37]

Some of the most common forms of cyber vandalism are discussed in detail below.

Viruses and Worms A computer virus is one type of malicious software program (also called *malware*) that disrupts or destroys existing programs and networks, causing them to perform the task for which the virus was designed.[38] The virus is then spread from one computer to another when a user sends out an infected file through email or may even hack into a network. Computer worms are similar to viruses, but they use computer networks or the Internet to self-replicate and "send themselves" to other users, generally via email without the aid of the operator.

Trojan Horses Some hackers may introduce a Trojan horse program into a computer system. The Trojan horse looks like a benign application, but it contains illicit codes that can damage the system operations. Sometimes hackers with a sense of irony will install a Trojan horse and claim that it is an antivirus program. When it is opened, it spreads viruses in the computer system. Trojan horses do not replicate themselves as viruses do, they can be just as destructive.

Web Defacement Cyber vandals may target the websites of their victims. Web defacement is a type of cyber vandalism that occurs when a computer hacker intrudes on another person's website by inserting or substituting codes that expose visitors to the site to misleading or provocative information.

Cyber Stalking Traditional stalking involves repeated harassing or threatening behavior, such as following a person, appearing at a person's home or place of business, making harassing phone calls, leaving written messages or objects, or vandalizing a person's property. **Cyber stalking** is the use of the Internet, email, or other electronic communications devices to stalk another person.[39] Some cyber stalkers pursue minors through online chat rooms, establish a relationship with a child, and later ask to make contact. Today, Internet predators are more likely to meet, develop relationships with, and beguile at-risk adolescents and underage teenagers, rather than using coercion and violence.[40]

cyber stalking
Using the Internet, email, or other electronic communications devices to stalk or harass another person.

Cyber Bullying In cyberspace, physical distance is no longer a refuge from the frequency and depth of harm doled out by a bully to his or her victim.[41] Cyber bullying is willful and repeated harm inflicted through the medium of electronic text. Like their real-world counterparts, cyber bullies are malicious and cowardly aggressors who seek pleasure or profit through the mistreatment of other individuals.

◼ Cyber bullying has been the cause of more than one teen suicide attempt. Mourners gather outside the funeral for 17-year-old Alexis Pilkington, March 25, 2010, in Babylon, New York. Pilkington was a popular athlete, a well-liked soccer star who had already landed a scholarship to college. But none of that stopped the teenager from becoming the target of nasty online comments. Even after the Long Island girl killed herself, the harassing Internet messages kept on coming, posted on a page meant to stand as a tribute.

AP Photo/David Goldman, FILE

Although power in traditional bullying might be physical (stature) or social (competency or popularity), online power may simply stem from net proficiency. Cyber bullies who are able to navigate the Net and utilize technology in a way that enables them to harass others are in a position of power relative to a victim.[42]

Cyber War In 2010, Iran announced that the computers at its nuclear facility in Natanz were under attack by an outside enemy, presumably the United States. It turned out to be the Stuxnet computer worm, a destructive program that wiped out roughly a fifth of Iran's nuclear centrifuges and helped delay for years—though not destroy—Tehran's ability to make its first nuclear arms. It was the most effective use of cyber war to date.

RealityCheck

MYTH OR REALITY? A cyber attack against Iran derailed its nuclear program.

REALITY. *The Stuxnet worm wiped out a fifth of the centrifuges Iran was using to make fissionable material.*

In what ways could cyber war be waged against a nation's infrastructure?

Cyber war has been defined as "the premeditated, politically motivated attack against information, computer systems, computer programs, and data which result in violence against noncombatant targets by subnational groups or clandestine agents."[43] It involves an effort by covert forces to disrupt the intersection where the virtual electronic reality of computers intersects with the physical world.[44] Cyberwar may involve the use of computer network tools to shut down critical national infrastructures or to coerce or intimidate a government or civilian population.[45]

Even though they may come from a region where computer databases and the Internet are not widely used, terrorist organizations are beginning to understand the damage that cyber crime can inflict on their enemies. Terrorist organizations are now adapting IT into their arsenal, and agencies of the U.S. justice system have to be ready for a sustained attack on the nation's electronic infrastructure.

LO5 Discuss the various forms of cyber crime

One form of attack is cyber espionage. This involves hacking secure computer networks at the enemy's most sensitive military bases, defense contractors, and aerospace companies in order to steal important data or to assess their defenses. Infrastructure attacks can also be aimed at water treatment plants, electric plants, dams, oil refineries, and nuclear power plants. These industries all provide vital services to society by allowing people to go about their daily lives. Terrorist computer hackers could make a dam overflow or cause real property damage to oil refineries or nuclear plants by shutting down safeguards in the system to prevent catastrophic accidents.[46]

Controlling Cyber Crime

The proliferation of cyber crimes has created the need for new laws and enforcement processes. Because technology evolves so rapidly, enforcement presents challenges that are particularly vexing. Numerous organizations have been set up to provide training and support for law enforcement agents. In addition, federal and state laws have been aimed at particular areas of high-tech crimes.[47] What are some of the legislative initiatives designed to limit or control cyber crime?

Software Piracy The government has actively pursued members of the warez community, and some have been charged and convicted under the Computer Fraud and Abuse Act (CFAA), which criminalizes accessing computer systems without authorization to obtain information.[48] The Digital Millennium Copyright Act (DMCA) makes it a crime to circumvent antipiracy measures built into most commercial software and also outlaws the manufacture, sale, or distribution of code-cracking devices used to copy software illegally.[49]

Copyright Infringement The United States Criminal Code provides penalties for a first-time illegal copyright offender of five years of incarceration and a fine of $250,000.[50] Infringing copies and all equipment used to make those copies are also subject to forfeiture and destruction.[51]

Identity Theft To meet this increasing threat, Congress passed the Identity Theft and Assumption Deterrence Act of 1998 (the Identity Theft Act) to make it a federal crime when anyone knowingly transfers or uses, without lawful authority, a means of identification of another person with the intent to commit, or to aid or abet, any unlawful activity that constitutes a violation of federal law, or that constitutes a felony under any applicable state or local law.[52] Violations of the act are investigated by federal investigative agencies such as the U.S. Secret Service, the FBI, and the U.S. Postal Inspection Service. In 2004, the Identity Theft Penalty Enhancement Act was signed into law. The act increases existing penalties for the crime of identity theft, establishes aggravated identity theft as a criminal offense, and establishes mandatory penalties for aggravated identity theft. According to this law, anyone who knowingly "transfers, possesses, or uses, without lawful authority" someone else's identification will be sentenced to an extra prison term of two years with no possibility of parole. Individuals committing identity fraud while engaged in crimes associated with terrorism—such as aircraft destruction, arson, airport violence, or kidnapping top government officials—will receive a mandatory sentence enhancement of five years.

Internet Pornography As noted previously, it is difficult to detect and control Internet pornography. Opponents of any controls warn that the right of free speech may be violated. Congress has struggled to create legislation that will restrict objectionable use without violating First Amendment freedoms. Fearing the proliferation of kiddie porn over the Internet, Congress enacted the Child Pornography Prevention Act of 1996 (CPPA) that outlawed sexually related material that used or *appeared to use* children under 18 engaging in sexual conduct. In *Ashcroft v. The Free Speech Coalition*, the Supreme Court ruled that sexually related material in which an actual child appears is illegal, but possessing "virtual" pornography is legal. The Court reasoned that real children are not harmed with a virtual child.[53] In response to the Court's decision, Congress passed the PROTECT (Prosecutorial Remedies and Other Tools to end the Exploitation of Children Today) Act of 2003, which outlawed virtual kiddie porn that makes it almost impossible to distinguish the difference between a real child and a morphed or created image.[54] The Supreme Court reviewed this law in a 2008 case, *United States v. Williams*, which held that the government can legitimately outlaw sale of child pornography even if the images are computer-generated, if those who purchased the images *thought they were buying images of real children*. The Court noted that offers to engage in illegal transactions are excluded from First Amendment protection, so that the "speech" of an individual claiming to be in possession of child pornography is therefore not protected by the First Amendment.[55] So possessing virtual child pornography may be legal, but selling it is a crime.

Computer Crimes Congress has treated computer-related crimes as distinct federal offenses since passage of the Counterfeit Access Device and Computer Fraud and Abuse Law in 1984.[56] The 1984 act protected classified United States defense and foreign relations information, financial institution and consumer reporting agency files, and access to computers operated for the government. The act was supplemented in 1996 by the National Information Infrastructure Protection Act (NIIPA), which significantly broadens the scope of the law.

Enforcing Cyber Laws

How has the justice system responded to cyber crime? Most of the efforts are being made at the federal level. The government is now operating a number of organizations that are coordinating efforts to control cyber fraud. One approach is to create working groups that coordinate the activities of numerous agencies involved in investigating cyber crime. The Interagency Telemarketing and Internet Fraud Working Group brings together representatives of numerous United States Attorneys' offices, the FBI, the Secret Service, the Postal Inspection Service, the Federal Trade Commission, the Securities and Exchange Commission, and other law enforcement and regulatory agencies to share information about trends and patterns in Internet fraud schemes. One of the most successful federal efforts is the New York Electronic Crimes Task Force (NYECTF), a partnership between the U.S. Secret Service and a host of other public safety agencies and private corporations. Its success has prompted Boston, Miami, Charlotte, Chicago, Las Vegas, San Francisco, Los Angeles, and Washington, D.C., to set up similar task forces.[57]

Transnational Crime

globalization
The process of creating a global economy through transnational markets and political and legal systems.

The new global economy is a particular vexing development for agents of the criminal justice system because it vastly expands the reach of criminal organizations while at the same time creating new opportunities for criminal conspiracies. **Globalization** refers to the process of creating transnational markets and political and legal systems and has shifted the focus of crime from a local to a world perspective.

Globalization began when large companies decided to establish themselves in foreign markets by adapting their products or services to the local culture. The process took off with the fall of the Soviet Union, which opened new European markets. The development of China into a super industrial power encouraged foreign investors to take advantage of China's huge supply of workers. As the Internet and communication revolution unfolded, companies were able to establish instant communications with their far-flung corporate empires, a technological breakthrough that further aided trade and foreign investments.

While globalization can improve the standard of living in third-world nations by providing jobs and training, it can also be a device for criminal cartels to avoid prosecution and regulation, while expanding their markets and profits.[58]

It is not surprising then that globalization has created a fertile ground for contemporary criminal organizations. By expanding the reach of both criminal and non-criminal organizations, globalization also increases the vulnerability of indigenous people with a traditional way of life.[59] With money and power to spare, criminal enterprise groups can recruit new members, bribe government officials, and even fund private armies. International organized crime has globalized its activities for the same reasons as legitimate multinational corporations have expanded around the world: new markets bring new sources of profits. Illicit enterprises are able to expand to take advantage of these new economic circumstances thanks to the communications and international transportation revolution.[60] Technological advances such as efficient and widespread commercial airline traffic, improvements in telecommunications (ranging from global cell phone connectivity to the Internet), and the growth of international trade have all aided the growth in illicit transnational activities. These changes have facilitated the cross-border movement of goods and people, conditions exploited by criminals who now use Internet chat rooms to plan their activities. On a cultural level, globalization brings with it an ideology of free markets and free trade. The cultural shift means less intervention and regulation, conditions exploited by crime groups to cross unpatrolled borders and to expand their activities to new regions of the world. **Transnational crime** groups freely exploit this new freedom to travel to regions where they cannot be extradited, base their operations in countries with ineffective or corrupt law enforcement, and launder their money in countries with bank secrecy or few effective controls. Globalization has allowed both individual offenders and criminal gangs to gain tremendous operational benefits while reducing risks of apprehension and punishment. In other words, crime has gone global.

transnational crime
Use of illegal tactics to gain profit in the global marketplace, typically involving the cross-border sale and distribution of illegal commodities.

Types of Transnational Crimes

The globalization of crime involves traditional crimes such as the distribution of pornography and developing criminal activities such as cyber crime. Other criminal activities with a global reach include human trafficking, migrant smuggling, drug smuggling, arms dealing, maritime piracy, and trafficking in environmental resources and counterfeit goods.[61]

The global gangs exploit instability to set up operations in areas that are beyond the reach of the law. Criminal gangs then create even more instability so that the local population becomes dependent on criminal activity for their economic survival. Would a local farmer involved in drug production in a rural area of Bolivia dare to take on the criminal gang—which he not only depends on for his livelihood but which promises deadly reprisals for disloyalty—knowing that he is beyond the protection of the law?

Global gangs take advantage of the latest technological developments to distribute illegal materials. An example of a traditional crime that has been revolutionized by global communications is child pornography. The Internet has enabled cheap and instant global distribution to millions of customers from concealed origins, usually situated in countries where prosecution is unlikely. In the past, the images would have had to be processed, printed and the hard copies distributed via mail or retail outlets.[62]

The trade in human organs—especially kidneys—is substantial and demand appears to be growing. Desperate victims in developing countries are exploited as their kidneys are purchased for low prices; others sell their body parts when traffickers use coercive means, such as force or threats of force to secure the removal of the victim's organs. These crimes would not be possible without global transportation means available today.[63]

The profits from transnational criminal enterprise can be immense. The United Nations estimates that immigrant smugglers earn about $7 billion per year smuggling an estimated 3 million people (though some may be smuggled more than once). There are between 170–250 million drug users in the world and up to 38 million may be routine or problem users; more than 4 million are in treatment; the illegal drug trade brings in about $350 billion per year. Human trafficking, another activity of transnational gangs, is discussed in the Contemporary Issues in Criminal Justice feature.

Transnational Crime Groups

Transnational crime networks may locate themselves in nations whose governments are too weak to present effective opposition. If they believe that the government may be interfering with their illegal activities that bring them immense profits, such as drug trafficking, they will carry out a terror campaign, killing police officials and using bribery, violence, or terror to achieve their goals. The political turmoil of the 21st century coupled with advances in telecommunications and computer technology have had the unintended effect of providing avenues for the rapid expansion of transnational organized crime activities.[64]

Asian Gangs Asian groups are involved in a number of global criminal conspiracies ranging from extortion and smuggling to arms dealing and human trafficking. Among the best-known groups are:

- *Yakuza*. A Japanese criminal group often involved in multinational criminal activities, including human trafficking, gambling, prostitution, and undermining licit businesses.
- *Fuk Ching*. A Chinese organized criminal group in the United States involved in smuggling, street violence, and human trafficking.
- *Triads*. Underground criminal societies based in Hong Kong that control secret markets and bus routes and are often involved in money laundering and drug trafficking.
- *Heijin*. Taiwanese gangsters who are often executives in large corporations. They are often involved in white-collar crimes, such as illegal stock trading and bribery, and sometimes run for public office.
- *Jao Pho*. Organized crime group in Thailand involved in illegal political and business activity.
- *Red Wa*. Gangsters from Thailand involved in manufacturing and trafficking methamphetamine.[65]

RealityCheck

MYTH OR REALITY? There are more drug users in the world than the populations of England, Italy, and France combined.

REALITY. *And you can throw in Spain and Holland as well.*

With an estimated 250 million users, the profits from illegal drug trafficking are immense. What possible incentives (or punishments) could dissuade traffickers to choose another line of work?

LO8 Understand the concept of transnational crime

Global Sex Trafficking

Human trafficking has become a global problem. How great a problem? The International Labor Organization (ILO)—the United Nations agency charged with addressing labor standards, employment, and social protection issues—estimates that there are at least 12 million adults and children in forced labor, bonded labor, and commercial sexual servitude at any given time. Of these victims, the ILO estimates that at least 1.39 million, 56 percent female, are victims of commercial sexual servitude, both transnational and within countries.

Every year, hundreds of thousands of women and children—primarily from Southeast Asia and Eastern Europe—are lured by the promise of good jobs and then end up forced into brothels or as circuit travelers in labor camps. Most go to wealthy industrialized countries. Japan now has more than 10,000 commercial sex establishments with 150,000 to 200,000 foreign girls trafficked into the country each year. India has experienced a large influx of foreign sex workers who are believed to be the source of the HIV epidemic that is sweeping the country. Traffickers import up to 50,000 women and children every year into the United States despite legal prohibitions (in addition to prostitution, some are brought in to work in sweatshops).

Global trafficking gangs use force, fraud, or coercion to exploit a person for profit. Victims are subjected to labor and/or sexual exploitation. Gangs prey on the weak, targeting vulnerable men, women, and children. They use creative and ruthless ploys designed to trick, coerce, and win the confidence of potential victims. Very often these ruses involve promises of a better life through employment, educational opportunities, or marriage.

Trafficking for labor exploitation—the form of trafficking claiming the greatest number of victims—includes traditional slavery, forced labor, and holding people in bondage until they can pay off debts. Trafficking for sexual exploitation may include involvement in prostitution or pornographic films. The use of force or coercion can be direct and violent or psychological. Women may be kidnapped, beaten, raped, and led to believe they can never return home. If they still won't cooperate, their families and friends may be threatened or attacked.

Trafficking gangs are located in Latin America, Asia, and Eastern European nations such as Bulgaria and Russia. The UN report found that sex traffickers are often women, many of whom began as sex workers themselves. They are encouraged by their recruiter/trafficker to return home and recruit other women, often under the scrutiny of people working for the trafficker to make sure they don't try to escape.

Because it is a global enterprise, there is a great deal of cooperation in trafficking, so that in Eastern Europe a single gang may include Russians, Moldavians, Egyptians, and Syrians. Cooperation allows sex slaves to be trafficked not only to neighboring countries but all around the globe. The UN found that victims from East Asia were detected in more than 20 countries in regions throughout the world, including Europe, the Americas, the Middle East, Central Asia, and Africa.

COMBATING TRAFFICKING

Recently, the United States made stopping the trafficking of women a top priority. In 1998, the "Memorandum on Steps to Combat Violence Against Women and the Trafficking of Women and Girls" was issued, which directed the secretary of state, the attorney general, and the president's Interagency Council on Women to expand their work against violence against women to include work against the trafficking of women.

In the former Soviet Union, prevention education projects are aimed at potential victims of trafficking, and nongovernmental organizations have established hotlines for victims or women seeking information about the risks of accepting job offers abroad.

The UN found that the number of convictions for human trafficking is increasing, especially in a handful of countries. Nonetheless, most countries' conviction rates rarely exceed 1.5 per 100,000 people, which is even below the level normally recorded for rare crimes like kidnapping.

CRITICAL THINKING

1. If put in charge, what would you do to slow or end the international sex trade? Before you answer, remember the saying that prostitution is the oldest profession, which implies that curbing it may prove quite difficult.

2. Should men who hire prostitutes who are obviously involved in the sex trade against their will be punished more severely in order to deter them from getting involved in the exploitation of these vulnerable young women? Or is it unfair to expect someone to know the reasons their sex partner was involved in prostitution?

Russian Transnational Crime Groups Since the collapse of the Soviet Union in 1991, criminal organizations in Russia and other former Soviet republics such as the Ukraine have engaged in a variety of crimes: drugs and arms trafficking, stolen automobiles, trafficking in women and children, and money laundering.[66] No area of the world seems immune to this menace, especially not the United States. America is the land of opportunity for unloading criminal goods and laundering dirty money.

Russian criminals make extensive use of the state governmental apparatus to protect and promote their criminal activities. For example, most businesses in

Russia—legal, quasi-legal, and illegal—must operate with the protection of a *krysha* (roof). The protection is often provided by police or security officials employed outside their "official" capacities for this purpose. In other cases, officials are "silent partners" in criminal enterprises that they, in turn, protect. The criminalization of the privatization process has resulted in the massive use of state funds for criminal gain. Valuable properties are purchased through insider deals for much less than their true value and then resold for lucrative profits. Criminals have been able to directly influence the state's domestic and foreign policy to promote the interests of organized crime, either by attaining public office themselves or by buying public officials.

In the United States, Russian criminal groups are extensively engaged in a broad array of frauds and scams, including health care fraud, insurance scams, stock frauds, antiquities swindles, forgery, and fuel tax evasion schemes.[67] Russians are believed to be the main purveyors of credit card fraud in the United States. Legitimate businesses, such as the movie business and textile industry, have become targets of criminals from the former Soviet Union, and they are often used for money laundering and extortion.

Mexican Drug Cartels Mexican drug cartels have become large-scale suppliers of narcotics, marijuana, and methamphetamines In addition, an estimated 90 percent of cocaine entering the United States transits Mexico. Mexican drug gangs routinely use violence, and fighting for control of the border regions has affected U.S. citizens: more than 60 Americans have been kidnapped and Mexican drug cartel members have threatened to kill U.S. journalists covering drug violence in the border region. And, as a result of their immense profits, Mexican cartels are the leading wholesale launderers of drug money from the United States.[68]

There are numerous drug cartels operating in Mexico, the main ones being Gulf, Tijuana, Sinaloa, Juárez, Millennium, Oaxaca, and Colima. Some are dominant in local regions, while the major gangs—Gulf, Sinaloa, and Juárez—are present throughout all of Mexico. In recent years, new cartels have formed and others have become allies, in a constantly shifting landscape of drug activity. Recently, for example, the Tijuana cartel formed an alliance with the Gulf cartel and several cartels (Sinaloa, Juárez, and Valencia cartels) have also formed an alliance known as "The Federation."

> **LO9** Be familiar with some of the most important transnational crime groups

Controlling Transnational Crime

Efforts to combat transnational organized crime are typically in the hands of federal agencies. One approach is to form international working groups to collect intelligence, share information, and plot unified strategies among member nations. The FBI belongs to several international working groups aimed at combating transnational gangs in various parts of the world. For example, to combat the influence and reach of Eurasian organized crime, the FBI is involved in the following groups and activities:

- *Eurasian Organized Crime Working Group.* Established in 1994, it meets to discuss and jointly address the transnational aspects of Eurasian organized crime that impact member countries and the international community in general. The member countries are Canada, Great Britain, Germany, France, Italy, Japan, the U.S., and Russia.
- *Central European Working Group.* This group is part of a project that brings together the FBI and Central European law enforcement agencies to discuss cooperative investigative matters covering the broad spectrum of Eurasian organized crime. A principal concern is the growing presence of Russian and other Eurasian organized criminals in Central Europe and the United States. The initiative works on practical interaction between the participating agencies to establish lines of communication and working relationships, to develop strategies and tactics to address transnational organized crime matters impacting the region, and to identify potential common targets.

- *Southeast European Cooperative Initiative.* This is an international organization intended to coordinate police and customs regional actions for preventing and combating transborder crime. It is headquartered in Bucharest, Romania, and has 12 fully participating member countries. The United States has been one of 14 countries with observer status since 1998. The initiative's center serves as a clearinghouse for information and intelligence sharing, allowing the quick exchange of information in a professional and trustworthy environment. The initiative also supports specialized task forces for countering serious transborder crime such as the trafficking of people, drugs, and cars; smuggling; financial crimes; and terrorism.

Organized Crime Laws   Congress has passed a number of laws that have made it easier for agencies to bring transnational gangs to justice. One of the first measures aimed directly at organized crime was the Interstate and Foreign Travel or Transportation in Aid of Racketeering Enterprises Act (Travel Act).[69] The Travel Act prohibits travel in interstate commerce or use of interstate facilities with the intent to promote, manage, establish, carry on, or facilitate an unlawful activity; it also prohibits the actual or attempted engagement in these activities. In 1970, Congress passed the Organized Crime Control Act. Title IX of the act, probably its most effective measure, is the **Racketeer Influenced and Corrupt Organization Act (RICO)**.[70] RICO did not create new categories of crimes but rather new categories of offenses in racketeering activity, which it defined as involvement in two or more acts prohibited by 24 existing federal and 8 state statutes. The offenses listed in RICO include state-defined crimes, such as murder, kidnapping, gambling, arson, robbery, bribery, extortion, and narcotic violations; and federally defined crimes, such as bribery, counterfeiting, transmission of gambling information, prostitution, and mail fraud. RICO is designed to limit patterns of organized criminal activity by prohibiting involvement in acts intended to do the following:

- Derive income from racketeering or the unlawful collection of debts and use or investment of such income
- Acquire through racketeering an interest in or control over any enterprise engaged in interstate or foreign commerce
- Conduct business through a pattern of racketeering
- Conspire to use racketeering as a means of making income, collecting loans, or conducting business

An individual convicted under RICO is subject to 20 years in prison and a $25,000 fine. Additionally, the accused must forfeit to the U.S. government any interest in a business in violation of RICO. These penalties are much more potent than simple conviction and imprisonment.[71]

Why Is It So Difficult to Eradicate Global Crime?

While international cooperation is now common and law enforcement agencies are willing to work together to fight transnational gangs, these criminal organizations are extremely hard to eradicate. The gangs are ready to use violence and well equipped to carry out threats. Take for example the so-called war on drugs. One reason it has proven so difficult for law enforcement to combat the drug cartels is that they use their firepower to intimidate police, judges, and potential witnesses. The shifting alliances and changes of location can confound law enforcement efforts. For example, the Zetas gang, whose core members are former members of the Mexican military's elite Special Air Mobile Force Group (Grupo Aeromovil de Fuerzas Especiales, GAFES), is able to carry out complex operations using their military training and sophisticated weaponry.[72] The Zetas, who began as enforcers for the Gulf cartel, are now their rivals. From their base in Nuevo Laredo, their sphere of influence extends across Mexico and deep into Central America, trafficking in arms, kidnapping, and competing for control of trafficking routes along the eastern half of the U.S.-Mexico border.[73] When they feel threatened, they are quite willing to fight the law.

Racketeer Influenced and Corrupt Organization Act (RICO)
Federal legislation that enables prosecutors to bring additional criminal or civil charges against people engaged in two or more acts prohibited by 24 existing federal and 8 state laws. RICO features monetary penalties that allow the government to confiscate all profits derived from criminal activities. Originally intended to be used against organized criminals, RICO has also been used against white-collar criminals.

LO10 Tell how law enforcement is taking on transnational criminal syndicates

■ Police lead suspected gunmen Domingo Choj, right, and Hector Rolando Toj, back, at an air force base in Guatemala City. Nine gunmen were arrested after hours of fighting in western Guatemala. One of the men is a Mexican national and suspected of being a recruiter for the Zetas. Mexican crime syndicates are spreading their tentacles as never before, using their trademark brutality to take over in places like Guatemala and even Colombia, long the heart of Latin America's drug world. In all, they now operate in 47 countries. The Zetas, former enforcers for the Gulf cartel, are now their rivals.

AP Photo/Moises Castillo

Adding to control problems is the fact that the drug trade is an important source of foreign revenue, and destroying the drug trade undermines the economies of third-world nations. Even if the government of one nation were willing to cooperate in vigorous drug suppression efforts, suppliers in other nations, eager to cash in on the sellers' market, would be encouraged to turn more acreage over to coca or poppy production. Today, almost every Caribbean country is involved with narcotrafficking; illicit drug shipments in the region are worth more money than the top five legitimate exports combined. Drug gangs are able to corrupt the political structure and destabilize countries. Drug addiction and violent crime are now common in Jamaica, Puerto Rico, and even small islands like St. Kitts. The corruption of the police and other security forces has reached a crisis point, where an officer can earn the equivalent of half a year's salary by simply looking the other way on a drug deal.[74] There are also indications that the drug syndicates may be planting a higher yield variety of coca and improving refining techniques to replace crops lost to government crackdowns.

The United States has little influence in some key drug-producing areas such as Helmand Province in Afghanistan—an area still controlled by the Taliban—and in rebel-held areas of Myanmar (formerly Burma).[75] War and terrorism also may make gang-control strategies problematic. After the United States toppled Afghanistan's Taliban government, the remnants began to grow and sell poppy to support their insurgency; Afghanistan now supplies a significant percentage of the world's opium.[76] And while the Colombian guerillas may not be interested in joining or colluding with crime cartels, they finance their war against the government by aiding drug traffickers and "taxing" crops and sales.[77] Considering these problems it is not surprising that transnational gangs continue to flourish.

Ethical Challenge

A tracking device has been developed that can be implanted in every new computer to constantly monitor every web page visited on the Net. This device can record every transaction and activity and automatically send the data to government computers programmed to look for suspicious web activity. The surveillance device would enable the government to keep tabs on what people are doing, what they buy, download, and so on. Once a person becomes suspect in a crime, they can be easily monitored from a distance without danger to any government agent. They cannot hide or escape detection.

Write an essay discussing the pros and cons of employing such a device. You might want to refer to the sections on cyber crime, including etailing fraud and copyright infringement. Even if you approve of the device, what questions might you want answered before it becomes standard equipment on home computers?

L01 Discuss the impact of criminal enterprise crime The crimes of the rich and powerful have the most significant impact on society. Experts place the total monetary value in the hundreds of billions of dollars, far outstripping the expense of any other type of crime. Large-scale investment growth has led to significant growth in the amount of fraud and misconduct seen on Wall Street. Investment firms have engaged in deceptive securities sales that have cost investors billions.

L02 Describe a Ponzi scheme A Ponzi scheme is an investment fraud that involves the payment of purported returns to existing investors from funds contributed by new investors. Fraudsters focus on attracting new money to make promised payments to earlier-stage investors and to use for personal expenses, instead of engaging in any legitimate investment activity.

L03 Be familiar with the mortgage fraud scandal Borrowers provided false information to the mortgage broker and/or lender, enabling them to get loans for which they were not qualified. Those involved in mortgage lending got involved in criminal fraud schemes, including false accounting entries and fraudulently inflated assets and revenues.

L04 Be familiar with the various forms of green crime Green crimes involve the environment. They include such activities as illegal fishing, pollution, dumping, forestry, and the like. In some instances, environmental criminals conduct activities overseas to avoid legal controls and enforcement.

L05 Discuss the various forms of cyber crime Cyber crime typically involves the theft and/or destruction of information, resources, or funds via computers, computer networks, and the Internet. Cyber theft is the use of computer networks for criminal profits. Illegal copyright infringement, identity theft, and Internet securities fraud are examples of cyber theft. Cyber vandalism, or technological destruction, involves malicious attacks aimed at disrupting, defacing, and destroying technology. Cyber war consists of politically motivated attacks designed to compromise the electronic infrastructure of the enemy and to disrupt its economy.

L06 Know what is being done to thwart cyber criminals Numerous organizations have been set up to provide training and support for law enforcement agents. In addition, new federal and state laws have been enacted to help discourage particular types of high-tech crimes. In the future, technological prowess may make it possible to identify cyber criminals and bring them to justice before they can carry out their attacks.

L07 Be familiar with the influence of globalization on crime Globalization has shifted the focus of crime from a local to a world perspective. With money and power to spare, criminal enterprise groups can recruit new members, bribe government officials, and even fund private armies.

L08 Understand the concept of transnational crime Transnational organized crime involves ongoing international criminal enterprise groups whose purpose is personal economic gain through illegitimate means. Transnational gangs are involved in money laundering; human smuggling; cyber crime; and trafficking of humans, drugs, weapons, body parts, or nuclear material. There is also a troubling overseas trade in prostitution. Transnational gangs export women from third-world nations for the purposes of prostitution. Some may be kidnapped or forced into prostitution against their will through violence and threats.

L09 Be familiar with some of the most important transnational crime groups Eastern gangs trace their origin to countries spanning the Baltics, the Balkans, Central/Eastern Europe, Russia, the Caucacus, and Central Asia. Russian organized crime is active in Europe, Africa, Asia, and North and South America. Asian gangs include the Yakuza Japanese criminal group, often involved in multinational criminal activities, including human trafficking, gambling, prostitution, and undermining licit businesses. Chinese groups are also involved in human trafficking—bringing large numbers of Chinese migrants to North America and essentially enslaving them for profit. There are a number of powerful Mexican drug cartels that now dominate the cross-border drug trade into the United States.

L010 Tell how law enforcement is taking on transnational criminal syndicates Efforts to combat transnational organized crime are typically in the hands of federal agencies. One approach is for them to form international working groups to collect intelligence, share information, and plot unified strategies among member nations. U.S. law enforcement agencies have cooperated in cross-border operations to eradicate gang activity.

1. Should people who illegally download movies or music be prosecuted for theft?

2. How can Internet pornography be controlled considering that a great deal of adult content is available on foreign websites?

3. Considering the threat of transnational drug trafficking, should drugs be legalized and controlled by the government?

4. Should the Internet be more closely monitored and controlled to prevent the threat of cyber war?

5. Is there any point to placing economic sanctions on billion-dollar corporations? Should corporate executives be put in prison? Put another way, what is the purpose of incarcerating someone like 72-year-old Bernard Madoff? Is he really a threat to society?

actus reus An illegal act. The *actus reus* can be an affirmative act, such as taking money or shooting someone, or a failure to act, such as failing to take proper precautions while driving a car.

adjudication The determination of guilt or innocence; a judgment concerning criminal charges. The majority of offenders charged plead guilty; of the remainder, some cases are adjudicated by a judge and a jury, some are adjudicated by a judge without a jury, and others are dismissed.

adversarial procedure The process of publicly pitting the prosecution and the defense against one another in pursuit of the truth.

antisocial (sociopathic, psychopathic) personality Individuals who are always in trouble and do not learn from either experience or punishment. They are loners who engage in frequent callous and hedonistic behaviors, are emotionally immature, and lack responsibility, judgment, and empathy.

appeal A request for an appellate court to examine a lower court's decision in order to determine whether proper procedures were followed.

appellate court A court that reconsiders a case that has already been tried in order to determine whether the measures used complied with accepted rules of criminal procedure and were in accordance with constitutional doctrines.

assigned counsel A lawyer appointed by the court to represent a defendant in a criminal case because the person is too poor to hire counsel.

bail The monetary amount for or condition of pretrial release, normally set by a judge at the initial appearance. The purpose of bail is to ensure the return of the accused at subsequent proceedings.

Bail Reform Act of 1984 Federal legislation that provides for both greater emphasis on release on recognizance for nondangerous offenders and preventive detention for those who present a menace to the community.

bench trial The trial of a criminal matter by a judge only. The accused waives any constitutional right to trial by jury.

Bill of Rights The first ten amendments to the U.S. Constitution.

biosocial theory Human behavior is a function of the interaction of biochemical, neurological, and genetic factors with environmental stimuli.

bipolar disorder A psychological condition marked by mood swings between periods of wild elation and deep depression.

blameworthy Culpable or guilty of participating in a particular criminal offense.

blue curtain The secretive, insulated police culture that isolates officers from the rest of society.

boot camp A short-term militaristic correctional facility in which inmates undergo intensive physical conditioning and discipline.

broken windows hypothesis The view that deteriorated communities attract criminal activity.

broken windows model A term used to describe the role of the police as maintainers of community order and safety.

brutalization effect An outcome of capital punishment that enhances, rather than deters, the level of violence in society. The death penalty reinforces the view that violence is an appropriate response to provocation.

Bureau of Alcohol, Tobacco, Firearms, and Explosives (ATF) Federal agency with jurisdiction over the illegal sale, importation, and criminal misuse of firearms and explosives and the distribution of untaxed liquor and cigarettes.

challenge for cause A request that a prospective juror be removed because he or she is biased or has prior knowledge about a case, or for other reasons that demonstrate the individual's inability to render a fair and impartial judgment in a particular case.

Children's Aid Society A child-saving organization begun by Charles Loring Brace; it took children from the streets in large cities and placed them with farm families on the prairie.

child savers Late nineteenth-century reformers in America who developed programs for troubled youths and influenced legislation creating the juvenile justice system.

chivalry hypothesis The view that the low rates of female crime and

delinquency are a reflection of the leniency with which police and judges treat female offenders.

chronic offender A delinquent offender who is arrested five or more times before he or she is 18 and who stands a good chance of becoming an adult criminal; these offenders are responsible for more than half of all serious crimes.

civil law All law that is not criminal, including the law of torts (personal wrongs) and contract, property, maritime, and commercial law.

commitment Decision of judge ordering an adjudicated and sentenced juvenile offender to be placed in a correctional facility.

common law Early English law, developed by judges, that incorporated Anglo-Saxon tribal custom, feudal rules and practices, and the everyday rules of behavior of local villages. Common law became the standardized law of the land in England and eventually formed the basis of the criminal law in the United States.

community-oriented policing Programs and strategies designed to bring police and the public closer together and create a more cooperative working environment between them.

community service restitution An alternative sanction that requires an offender to work in the community at such tasks as cleaning public parks or working with disabled children in lieu of an incarceration sentence.

CompStat A program originated by the New York City police that used carefully collected and analyzed crime data to shape policy and evaluate police effectiveness.

compulsory process Compelling the production of witnesses via a subpoena.

concurrent sentences Prison sentences for two or more criminal acts, served simultaneously and run together.

conflict view of crime The law is controlled by the rich and powerful who shape its content to ensure their continued economic domination of society. The criminal justice system is an instrument of social and economic repression.

confrontation clause A part of the Sixth Amendment that establishes the right of a criminal defendant to see and cross-examine all the witnesses against him or her.

congregate system Prison system first used in New York that allowed inmates to engage in group activities such as work, meals, and recreation.

consecutive sentences Prison sentences for two or more criminal acts, served one after the other.

consensus view of crime The majority of citizens in a society share common ideals and work toward a common good. Crimes are acts that are outlawed because they conflict with the rules of the majority and are harmful to society.

constable In medieval England, an appointed official who administered and supervised the legal affairs of a small community.

contract system The practice of correctional officials selling the labor of inmates to private businesses.

contract system (attorney) Providing counsel to indigent offenders by having attorneys under contract to the county handle all (or some) such cases.

convict-lease system The practice of leasing inmates to a business for a fixed annual fee.

corporate enterprise crime Conspiracies that involve bending the rules of legitimate business and commerce to make illegal profits in the marketplace. Enterprise crimes involve the violation of law in the course of an otherwise legitimate occupation.

corruption Exercising legitimate discretion for improper reasons or using illegal means to achieve approved goals.

court of last resort A court that handles the final appeal on a matter. The U.S. Supreme Court is the official court of last resort for criminal matters.

courtroom work group The phrase used to indicate that all parties in the adversary process work together cooperatively to settle cases with the least amount of effort and conflict.

courts of general jurisdiction State or federal courts that have jurisdiction over felony offenses and more serious civil cases (that is, cases involving more than a dollar amount set by the legislature).

crime A violation of societal rules of behavior as interpreted and expressed by a criminal legal code created by people holding social and political power. Individuals who violate these rules are subject to sanctions by state authority, social stigma, and loss of status.

crime control perspective A model of criminal justice that emphasizes the control of dangerous offenders and the protection of society. Its advocates call for harsh punishments as a deterrent to crime and support availability of the death penalty.

criminal justice process The decision-making points, from the initial investigation or arrest by police to the eventual release of the offender and his or her reentry into society; the various sequential criminal justice stages through which the offender passes.

criminal justice system The law enforcement, court, and correctional agencies that work together to effect the apprehension, prosecution, and control of criminal offenders. They are charged with maintaining order, enforcing the law, identifying transgressors, bringing the guilty to justice, and treating criminal behavior.

criminal procedure The rules and laws that define the operation of criminal proceedings. Procedural law describes the methods that must be followed in obtaining warrants, investigating offenses, effecting lawful arrests, conducting trials, introducing evidence, sentencing convicted offenders, and reviewing cases by appellate courts.

cross-examination The process in which the defense and the prosecution interrogate witnesses for the other side during a trial.

cruel and unusual punishment Physical punishment or punishment that is far in excess of that given to people under similar circumstances and is therefore banned by the Eighth Amendment. The death penalty has so far not been considered cruel and unusual if it is administered in a fair and nondiscriminatory fashion.

cultural transmission The passing of cultural values from one generation to the next.

culture of poverty The crushing lifestyle of slum areas produces a culture of poverty, passed from one generation to the next, marked by apathy, cynicism, feelings of helplessness, and mistrust of social institutions, such as schools, government agencies, and the police.

Customs and Border Protection (CBP) Federal agency responsible for the control and protection of America's borders and ports of entry. Its first priority is keeping terrorists and their weapons out of the United States.

cyber crime The theft and/or destruction of information, resources, or funds via computers, computer networks, or the Internet.

cyber stalking Using the Internet, email, or other electronic communications devices to stalk or harass another person.

cyber theft The use of computer networks for criminal profits. Illegal copyright infringement, identity theft, and Internet securities fraud are examples of cyber theft.

cyber vandalism Malicious attacks aimed at disrupting, defacing, and destroying technology.

cyber war Politically motivated attacks designed to compromise the electronic infrastructure of the enemy and to disrupt its economy.

cynicism The belief that most people's actions are motivated solely by personal needs and selfishness.

day fees A program requiring probationers to pay some of the costs of their treatment.

day fine A fine geared to the average daily income of the convicted offender in an effort to bring equity to the sentencing process.

day reporting center (DRC) A nonresidential community-based treatment program.

deadly force Force that is likely to cause death or serious bodily harm.

decriminalization Reducing the penalty for a criminal act but not actually legalizing it.

deinstitutionalization The policy of removing as many offenders as possible from secure confinement and treating them in the community.

demeanor The way in which a person outwardly manifests his or her personality.

denial-of-service attack Extorting money from an Internet service user by threatening to prevent the user having access to the service.

Department of Homeland Security (DHS) Federal agency responsible for preventing terrorist attacks within the United States, reducing America's vulnerability to terrorism, and minimizing the damage and assisting in recovery from attacks that do occur.

deposit bail The monetary amount set by a judge at a hearing as a condition of pretrial release; the percentage of the total bond required to be paid by the defendant.

detention The temporary care of a child alleged to be a delinquent or status offender who requires secure custody, pending court disposition.

determinate sentence A fixed term of incarceration, such as three years' imprisonment. Many people consider determinate sentences too restrictive for rehabilitative purposes; the advantage is that offenders know how much time they have to serve—that is, when they will be released.

deterrent effect Stopping or reducing crime by convincing would-be criminals that they stand a significant risk of being apprehended and punished for their crimes.

developmental theory Social interactions that are developed over the life course shape behavior. Some interactions (such as involvement with deviant peers) encourage law violations, whereas others (such as marriage and military service) may help people desist from crime.

direct examination The questioning of one's own (prosecution or defense) witness during a trial.

directed patrol A patrol strategy that involves concentrating police resources in areas where certain crimes are a significant problem.

directed verdict The right of a judge to direct a jury to acquit a defendant because the state has not proved the elements of the crime or otherwise has not established guilt according to law.

discretion The use of personal decision making and choice in carrying out operations in the criminal justice system. For example, police discretion can involve deciding whether to make an arrest; prosecutorial discretion can involve deciding whether to accept a plea bargain.

disposition For juvenile offenders, the equivalent of sentencing for adult offenders. The theory is that disposition is more rehabilitative than retributive. Possible dispositions include dismissing the case, releasing the youth to the custody of his or her parents, placing the offender on probation, or sending him or her to a state correctional institution.

diversion A noncriminal alternative to trial, usually featuring counseling, job training, and educational opportunities.

DNA profiling The identification of criminal suspects by matching DNA samples taken from their person with specimens found at the crime scene.

double marginality The social burden African American police officers carry by virtue of being both minority group members and law enforcement officers.

Drug Enforcement Administration (DEA) The federal agency that enforces federal drug control laws.

due process perspective Due process is a basic constitutional principle based on the concept of the privacy of the individual and the complementary concept of limitation on governmental power; it is a safeguard against arbitrary and unfair state procedures in judicial or administrative proceedings. Embodied in the due process concept are the basic rights of a defendant in criminal proceedings and the requirements for a fair trial.

electronic monitoring (EM) Requiring convicted offenders to wear a monitoring device as part of their community sentence. Typically part of a house arrest order, this enables the probation department to ensure that offenders are complying with court-ordered limitations on their freedom.

emotional intelligence "The ability to monitor one's own and others' feelings and emotions, to discriminate among them and to use this information to guide one's thinking and actions."

entrapment A criminal defense that maintains the police originated the criminal idea or initiated the criminal action.

equal justice perspective The view that all people should be treated equally before the law. Equality may best be achieved through individual discretion in the justice process.

equity The action or practice of awarding each person what is due him or her; sanctions based on equity seek to compensate individual victims and society in general for their losses due to crime.

etailing fraud Using the Internet to illegally buy or sell merchandise.

exclusionary rule The principle that prohibits the use, in a trial, of evidence illegally obtained. Based on the Fourth Amendment "right of the people to be secure in their persons, houses, papers, and effects, against unreasonable searches and seizures." The rule is not a bar to prosecution, because legally obtained evidence may be available that may be used in a trial.

Federal Bureau of Investigation (FBI) The arm of the U.S. Justice Department that investigates violations of federal law, seeks to protect America from terrorist attacks, gathers crime statistics, runs a comprehensive crime laboratory, and helps train local law enforcement officers.

felony A more serious offense that carries a penalty of incarceration in a state prison, usually for one year or more. Persons convicted of felony offenses lose such rights as the right to vote, hold elective office, or maintain certain licenses.

fine A money payment levied on offenders to compensate society for their misdeeds.

foot patrol Police patrols that take officers out of cars and put them on a walking beat in order to strengthen ties with the community.

forensic science The use of scientific techniques to investigate questions of interest to the justice system and solve crimes.

forfeiture The seizure of personal property by the state as a civil or criminal penalty.

furlough A correctional policy that allows inmates to leave the institution for vocational or educational training, for employment, or to maintain family ties.

general deterrence A crime control policy that depends on the fear of criminal penalties. General deterrence measures, such as long prison sentences for violent crimes, are aimed at convincing the *potential law violator* that the pains associated with paying for the crime outweigh the benefits.

Gideon v. Wainwright The 1963 U.S. Supreme Court case that granted counsel to indigent defendants in felony prosecutions.

globalization The process of creating a global economy through transnational markets and political and legal systems.

good faith exception The principle that evidence may be used in a criminal trial, even though the search warrant used to obtain it is technically faulty, if the police acted in good faith and to the best of their ability when they sought to obtain it from a judge.

grand jury A type of jury responsible for investigating alleged crimes, examining evidence, and issuing indictments.

grass eaters A term for police officers who accept payoffs when everyday duties place them in a position to "look the other way."

green crime Criminal activity that involves violation of rules and laws designed to protect the environment, including illegal dumping, polluting, fishing, logging and so on.

halfway house A community-based correctional facility that houses inmates before their outright release so they can become gradually acclimated to conventional society.

hands-off doctrine The legal practice of allowing prison administrators a free hand to run the institution, even if correctional practices violate inmates' constitutional rights; ended with the onset of the prisoners' rights movement in the 1960s.

hearsay evidence Testimony that is not firsthand but, rather, relates information told by a second party.

hot spots of crime Places from which a significant portion of all police calls originate. These hot spots include taverns and housing projects.

house arrest A form of intermediate sanction that requires the convicted offender to spend a designated amount of time per week in his or her own home—such as from 5:00 PM Friday until 8:00 AM Monday.

hue and cry In medieval England, a call for assistance. The policy of self-help that prevailed in villages demanded that everyone respond if a citizen raised a hue and cry to get their aid.

hulks Abandoned ships anchored in harbors and used in eighteenth-century England to house prisoners.

hundred In medieval England, a group of 100 families responsible for maintaining order and trying minor offenses.

identity theft Using the Internet to steal someone's identity and/or impersonate the victim in order to conduct illicit transactions, such as committing fraud using the victim's name and identity.

incapacitation The policy of keeping dangerous criminals in confinement to eliminate the risk of their repeating their offense in society.

indeterminate sentence A term of incarceration with a stated minimum and maximum length, such as a sentence to prison for a period of from 3 to 10 years. The prisoner would be eligible for parole after the minimum sentence has been served. Based on the belief that sentences should fit the criminal, indeterminate sentences allow individualized sentences and provide for sentencing flexibility. Judges can set a high minimum to override the purpose of the indeterminate sentence.

indictment The action by a grand jury when it finds that probable cause exists for prosecution of an accused suspect.

indigent Without the means to hire an attorney.

information Charging document filed by the prosecution that forms the basis of the preliminary hearing.

initial appearance A juvenile's first appearance before the juvenile court judge, in which the charges are reviewed and an effort is made to settle the case without a trial. If the child does not have legal counsel, an attorney is appointed.

inmate social code An unwritten code of behavior, passed from older inmates to younger ones, that serves as a guideline to appropriate inmate behavior within the correctional institution.

inmate subculture The loosely defined culture that pervades prisons and has its own norms, rules, and language.

in-presence requirement The condition that in order to make an arrest in a misdemeanor, the arresting officer must have personally witnessed the crime being committed.

insanity A legal defense that maintains a defendant was incapable of forming criminal intent because he or she suffers from a defect of reason or mental illness.

intake The process in which a probation officer settles cases at the initial appearance before the onset of formal criminal proceedings; also, the process in which a juvenile referral is received and a decision is made to file a petition in the juvenile court, release the juvenile, or refer the juvenile elsewhere.

intensive probation supervision (IPS) A type of intermediate sanction involving small probation caseloads and strict monitoring on a daily or weekly basis.

interactionist view of crime Criminal law reflects the values of people who use their social and political power to shape the legal system.

intermediate sanctions Punishments that fall between probation and prison ("probation plus"). Community-based sanctions, including house arrest and intensive supervision, serve as alternatives to incarceration.

internal affairs The branch of the police department that investigates charges of corruption or misconduct on the part of police officers.

jail A place to detain people awaiting trial, to serve as a lockup for drunks and disorderly individuals, and to confine convicted misdemeanants serving sentences of less than one year.

jailhouse lawyer An inmate trained in law or otherwise educated who helps other inmates prepare legal briefs and appeals.

judicial reprieve The common-law practice that allowed judges to suspend punishment so that convicted offenders could seek a pardon, gather new evidence, or demonstrate that they had reformed their behavior.

jury nullification A defense tactic that consists of suggesting that the jury acquit a defendant, despite evidence that he actually violated the law, by maintaining that the law was unjust or not applicable to the case.

jury trial The process of deciding a case by a group of persons selected and sworn in to serve as jurors at a criminal trial, often as a 6- or 12-person jury.

just desert The philosophy of justice asserting that those who violate the rights of others deserve to be punished. The severity of punishment should be commensurate with the seriousness of the crime.

justice of the peace Established in 1326 England, the office was created to help the shire reeve in controlling the county; it later took on judicial functions.

juvenile court A court that has original jurisdiction over persons defined by statute as juveniles and alleged to be delinquents or status offenders.

juvenile delinquency Participation in illegal behavior by a minor who falls under a statutory age limit.

Knapp Commission A public body that led an investigation into police corruption in New York and uncovered a widespread network of payoffs and bribes.

landmark decision A decision handed down by the U.S. Supreme Court that becomes the law of the land and serves as a precedent for resolving similar legal issues.

Law Enforcement Assistance Administration (LEAA) Funded by the federal government's Safe Streets Act, this agency provided technical assistance and hundreds of millions of dollars in aid to local and state justice agencies between 1969 and 1982.

legalization The removal of all criminal penalties from a previously outlawed act.

less-lethal weapons Weapons designed to disable or immobilize rather than kill criminal suspects.

lex talionis Latin for "law as retaliation." From Hammurabi's ancient legal code, the belief that the purpose of the law is to provide retaliation for an offended party and that the punishment should fit the crime.

make-believe family In female institutions, the substitute family group—including faux father, mother, and siblings—created by some inmates.

mala in se A term that refers to acts that society considers inherently evil, such as murder and rape, and that violate the basic principles of Judeo-Christian morality.

mala prohibitum Crimes created by legislative bodies that reflect prevailing moral beliefs and practices.

mandatory sentence A statutory requirement that a certain penalty shall be set and carried out in all cases upon conviction for a specified offense or series of offenses.

Manhattan Bail Project The innovative experiment in bail reform that introduced and successfully tested the concept of release on recognizance.

maximum-security prison A correctional institution that houses dangerous felons and maintains strict security measures, high walls, and limited contact with the outside world.

meat eaters A term for police officers who actively solicit bribes and vigorously engage in corrupt practices.

medical model A correctional philosophy grounded on the belief that inmates are sick people who need treatment rather than punishment in order to help them reform.

medium-security prison A less secure institution that houses nonviolent offenders and provides more opportunities for contact with the outside world.

mens rea Guilty mind. The mental element of a crime or the intent to commit a criminal act.

minimum-security prison The least secure institution, which houses white-collar and nonviolent offenders, maintains few security measures, and has liberal furlough and visitation policies.

Miranda warning The requirement that police officers inform suspects subjected to custodial interrogation that they have a constitutional right to remain silent, that their statements can later be used against them in court, that they can have an attorney present to help them, and that the state will pay for an attorney if they cannot afford to hire one.

misdemeanor A minor crime usually punished by less than one year's imprisonment in a local institution, such as a county jail.

Missouri Plan A way of picking judges through nonpartisan elections as a way to ensure that judges adhere to high standards of judicial performance.

monetary restitution A sanction requiring that convicted offenders compensate crime victims by reimbursing them for out-of-pocket losses caused by the crime. Losses can include property damage, lost wages, and medical costs.

moral entrepreneurs People who wage moral crusades to control criminal law so that it reflects their own personal values.

motivational interviewing A technique that increases the probationer's awareness of his potential problems by asking him to visualize a better future and learn strategies to reach his goals.

National Crime Victimization Survey (NCVS) The ongoing victimization study conducted jointly by the Justice Department and the U.S. Census Bureau that surveys victims about their experiences with law violation.

neighborhood-oriented policing (NOP) Community-oriented policing efforts aimed at individual neighborhoods.

no bill The action by a grand jury when it votes not to indict an accused suspect.

nolle prosequi The term used when a prosecutor decides to drop a case after a complaint has been formally made. Reasons for a *nolle prosequi* include evidence insufficiency, reluctance of witnesses to testify, police error, and office policy.

nondeadly force Force that is unlikely to cause death or significant bodily harm.

nonintervention perspective A view of criminal justice that emphasizes the least intrusive treatment possible. Among its central policies are decarceration, diversion, and decriminalization. In other words, less is better.

obiatry Helping people take their own lives.

official crime statistics Compiled by the FBI in its Uniform Crime Reports, these are a tally of serious crimes reported to police agencies each year.

order maintenance (peacekeeping) The order-maintenance aspect of the police role involves peacekeeping, maintaining order and authority without the need for formal arrest, "handling the situation," and keeping things under control by using threats, persuasion, and understanding.

parens patriae Latin term meaning "father of his country." According to this legal philosophy, the government is the guardian of everyone who has a disability, especially children, and has a legal duty to act in their best interests until they reach the age of majority.

parole The early release of a prisoner from imprisonment, subject to conditions set by a parole board.

Part I crimes The eight crimes for which, because of their seriousness and frequency, the FBI reports their incidence in its annual Uniform Crime Reports. The Part I crimes are murder, rape, assault, robbery, burglary, arson, larceny, and motor vehicle theft.

Part II crimes All other crimes except the eight Part I crimes. The FBI records all arrests made for Part II crimes, including race, gender, and age information.

penitentiary A state or federal correctional institution for the incarceration of felony offenders for terms of one year or more.

penitentiary house Term used for early prisons, so named because inmates were supposed to have penitence for their sins.

Pennsylvania system The correctional model used in Pennsylvania that isolated inmates from one another so they would be prevented from planning escapes, make them easy to manage and give them time to experience penitence.

peremptory challenge The dismissal of a potential juror by either the prosecution or the defense for unexplained, discretionary reasons.

phishing Also known as carding and spoofing, phishing consists of illegally acquiring personal information, such as bank passwords and credit card numbers, by masquerading as a trustworthy person or business in what appears to be an official electronic communication, such as an email or an instant message. The term *phishing* comes from the lures used to "fish" for financial information and passwords.

plea bargaining Nonjudicial settlement of a case in which the defendant exchanges a guilty plea for some consideration, such as a reduced sentence.

police brutality Usually involves such actions as the use of abusive language, the unnecessary use of force or coercion, threats, prodding with nightsticks, stopping and searching people to harass them, and so on.

police chief The top administrator of the police department, who sets policy and has general control over departmental policies and practices. The chief is typically a political rather than a civil service appointee and serves at the pleasure of the mayor.

Ponzi scheme An investment fraud that involves the payment of purported returns to existing investors from funds contributed by new investors.

poor laws Seventeenth-century laws in England that bound out vagrants and abandoned children as indentured servants to masters.

preliminary hearing A hearing that occurs in lieu of a grand jury hearing, when the prosecutor charges via information. Three issues are decided: whether a crime was committed, whether the court has jurisdiction over the case, and whether there is sufficient probable cause to believe the defendant committed the alleged crime.

preponderance of the evidence The level of proof in civil cases; more than half the evidence supports the allegations of one side.

pre-sentence investigation An investigation performed by a probation officer attached to a trial court after the conviction of a defendant.

presentment The report of a grand jury investigation, which usually includes a recommendation of indictment.

pretrial detention Holding an offender in secure confinement before trial.

pretrial diversion A program that provides nonpunitive, community-based alternatives to more intrusive forms of punishment such as jail or prison.

pretrial procedures Critical pretrial processes and decisions, including bail, arraignment, and plea negotiation.

preventive detention The practice of holding dangerous suspects before trial without bail.

prison A state or federal correctional institution for incarceration of felony offenders for terms of one year or more.

prisonization Assimilation into the separate culture in the prison that has its own set of rewards and behaviors, as well as its own norms, rules, and language. The traditional prison culture is now being replaced by a violent gang culture.

proactive policing A police department policy that emphasizes stopping crimes before they occur, rather than reacting to crimes that have already occurred.

probable cause The evidentiary criterion necessary to sustain an arrest or the issuance of an arrest or search warrant; less than absolute certainty or "beyond a reasonable doubt," but greater than mere suspicion or "hunch."

probable cause hearing Term used in some jurisdictions for a preliminary hearing to show cause to bring a case to trial.

probation A sentence entailing the conditional release of a convicted offender into the community under the supervision of the court (in the person of a probation officer), subject to certain conditions for a specified time.

probation rules Conditions or restrictions mandated by the court that must be obeyed by a probationer.

problem-oriented policing A style of police operations that stresses proactive problem solving, rather than reactive crime fighting.

proof beyond a reasonable doubt The standard of proof needed to convict in a criminal case. The evidence offered in court does not have to amount to absolute certainty, but it should leave no reasonable doubt that the defendant committed the alleged crime.

pro se "For oneself"; presenting one's own defense in a criminal trial; self-representation.

prosecutor Representative of the state (executive branch) in criminal proceedings; advocate for the state's case—the charge—in the adversary trial. Examples include the attorney general of the United States, U.S. attorneys, the attorneys general of the states, district attorneys, and police prosecutors. The prosecutor participates in investigations both before and after arrest, prepares legal documents, participates in obtaining arrest or search warrants, and decides whether to charge a suspect and, if so, with which offense. The prosecutor argues the state's case at trial, advises the police, participates in plea negotiations, and makes sentencing recommendations.

psychodynamic view Criminals are driven by unconscious thought patterns, developed in early childhood, that control behaviors over the life course.

public defender An attorney usually employed (at no cost to the accused) by the government to represent poor persons accused of a crime.

public law The branch of law that deals with the state or government and its relationships with individuals or other governments.

racial profiling The practice of police targeting minority groups because of a belief that they are more likely to be engaged in criminal activity.

racial threat hypothesis The view that the percentage of minorities in the population shapes the level of police activity.

Racketeer Influenced and Corrupt Organization Act (RICO) Federal legislation that enables prosecutors to bring additional criminal or civil charges against people engaged in two or more acts prohibited by 24 existing federal and 8 state laws. RICO features monetary penalties that allow the government to confiscate all profits derived from criminal activities. Originally intended to be used against organized criminals, RICO has also been used against white-collar criminals.

rational choice theory People will engage in delinquent and criminal behavior after weighing the consequences and benefits of their actions. Delinquent behavior is a rational choice made by a motivated offender who perceives the chances of gain as outweighing any perceived punishment or loss.

recognizance The medieval practice of allowing convicted offenders to go unpunished if they agreed to refrain from any further criminal behavior.

rehabilitation The strategy of applying proper treatment so an offender will present no further threat to society.

rehabilitation perspective The view that the primary purpose of criminal justice is helping to care for people who cannot manage themselves. Crime is an expression of frustration and anger created by social inequality and can be controlled by giving people the means to improve their lifestyle through conventional endeavors.

relative deprivation The view that extreme social and economic differences among people living in the same community exacerbate criminal activity.

release on recognizance (ROR) A nonmonetary condition for the pretrial release of an accused individual; an alternative to monetary bail that is granted after the court determines that the accused has ties in the community, has no prior record of default, and is likely to appear at subsequent proceedings.

residential community corrections (RCC) A nonsecure facility, located in the community, that houses probationers who need a more secure environment. Typically, residents are free during the day to go to work, school, or treatment, and they return in the evening for counseling sessions and meals.

restitution A condition of probation in which the offender repays society or the victim of crime for the trouble and expense the offender caused.

restorative justice A view of criminal justice that focuses on crime as an act against the community rather than the state. Justice should involve all parties affected by crime—victims, criminals, law enforcement, and the community.

restorative justice perspective A view of criminal justice that advocates peaceful solutions and mediation rather than coercive punishments.

revocation An administrative act performed by a parole authority that removes a person from parole, or a judicial order by a court removing a person from parole or probation, in response to a violation on the part of the parolee or probationer.

risk classification Classifying probationers so that they may receive an appropriate level of treatment and control.

search warrant An order issued by a judge, directing officers to conduct a search of specified premises for specified objects or persons and bring them before the court.

Secret Service Federal agency responsible for executive protection and for investigation of counterfeiting and various forms of financial fraud.

securitization The process in which vendors take individual subprime loans and bundle them into large pools and sell them as securities.

self-defense A legal defense in which defendants claim that their behavior was legally justified by the necessity to protect their own life and property, or that of another victim, from potential harm.

self-report survey A research approach that requires subjects to reveal their own participation in delinquent or criminal acts.

sentencing circle A type of sentencing in which victims, family members, community members, and the offender participate in an effort to devise fair and reasonable sanctions that are ultimately aimed at reintegrating the offender into the community.

sentencing guidelines A set of standards that define parameters for trial judges to follow in their sentencing decisions.

sheriff The chief law enforcement officer in a county.

shire reeve In medieval England, the senior law enforcement figure in a county; the forerunner of today's sheriff.

shock incarceration A short prison sentence served in boot camp–type facilities.

shock probation A sentence in which offenders serve a short prison term before they begin probation, to impress them with the pains of imprisonment.

Sixth Amendment The U.S. constitutional amendment containing various criminal trial rights, such as the right to public trial, the right to trial by jury, and the right to confrontation of witnesses.

social conflict theory Human behavior is shaped by interpersonal conflict, and those who maintain social power use it to further their own interests.

social control The control of an individual's behavior by social and institutional forces in society.

social learning theory Behavior patterns are modeled and learned in interactions with others.

social process theory An individual's behavior is shaped by interactions with key social institutions—family, school, peer group, and the like.

social structure theory A person's position in the social structure controls his or her behavior. Those in the lowest socioeconomic tier are more likely to succumb to crime-promoting elements in their environment, whereas those in the highest tier enjoy social and economic advantages that insulate them from crime-producing forces.

specific deterrence A crime control policy suggesting that punishment should be severe enough to convince *convicted offenders* never to repeat their criminal activity.

split sentence A practice that requires convicted criminals to spend a portion of their sentence behind bars and the remainder in the community.

stalking The willful, malicious, and repeated following and harassing of another person.

stare decisis Latin for "to stand by decided cases." The legal principle by which the decision or holding in an earlier case becomes the standard by which subsequent similar cases are judged.

state courts of limited jurisdiction Courts that have jurisdiction over misdemeanors and conduct preliminary investigations of felony charges.

status offender A juvenile who engages in behavior legally forbidden to minors, such as running away, truancy, or incorrigibility.

sting operation An undercover police operation in which police pose as criminals to trap law violators.

stop and frisk The situation when police officers who are suspicious of an individual run their hands lightly over the suspect's outer garments to determine whether the person is carrying a concealed weapon. Also called a patdown or threshold inquiry, a stop and frisk is intended to stop short of any activity that could be considered a violation of Fourth Amendment rights.

strict liability crime Illegal act whose elements do not contain the need for intent, or *mens rea*; usually, an act that endangers the public welfare, such as illegal dumping of toxic wastes.

subculture A substratum of society that maintains a unique set of values and beliefs.

substantive criminal law A body of specific rules that declare what conduct is criminal and prescribe the punishment to be imposed for such conduct.

substantive rights A number of civil rights that the courts, through a slow process of legal review, have established for inmates, including the rights to receive mail and medical benefits and to practice their religion.

suicide by cop A form of suicide in which a person acts in an aggressive manner with police officers in order to induce them to shoot to kill.

super-maximum-security prison The newest form of a maximum-security prison that uses high-level security measures to incapacitate the nation's most dangerous criminals. Most inmates are in lockdown 23 hours a day.

sureties During the Middle Ages, people responsible for the behavior of an offender released before trial.

suspended sentence A prison term that is delayed while the defendant undergoes a period of community treatment. If the treatment is successful, the prison sentence is terminated.

therapeutic communities Institutions that rely on positive peer pressure within a highly structured social environment in order to create positive inmate change.

time-in-rank system For police officers to advance in rank, they must spend an appropriate amount of time, usually years, in the preceding rank—for example, to become a captain, an officer must first spend time as a lieutenant.

tithing In medieval England, a group of 10 families who collectively dealt with minor disturbances and breaches of the peace.

tort A personal injury or wrong for which an action for damages may be brought.

total institution A regimented, dehumanizing institution such as a prison, in which inmates are kept in social isolation, cut off from the world at large.

transfer hearing The hearing in which a decision is made to waive a juvenile to the criminal court. Waiver decisions are based on such criteria as the child's age, her or his prior offense history, and the nature of the offense.

transnational crime Use of illegal tactics to gain profit in the global marketplace, typically involving the cross-border sale and distribution of illegal commodities.

treatment The rehabilitative method used to effect a change of behavior in the juvenile offender, in the form of therapy, or educational or vocational programs.

true bill of indictment A written statement charging a defendant with the commission of a crime, drawn up by a prosecuting attorney and considered by a grand jury. If the grand jury finds sufficient evidence to support the indictment, it will issue a true bill of indictment.

truth-in-sentencing laws A sentencing scheme requiring that offenders serve at least 85 percent of their original sentence before being eligible for parole or other forms of early release.

Uniform Crime Reports (UCR) The FBI's yearly publication of where, when, and how much serious crime occurred in the prior year.

USA Patriot Act (USAPA) A law designed to grant new powers to domestic law enforcement and international intelligence agencies in an effort to fight terrorism.

U.S. magistrate judge A federal trial judge who is appointed by a district court judge and who presides over various civil cases with the consent of the parties and over certain misdemeanor cases.

U.S. Marshals Service Federal agency whose jurisdiction includes protecting federal officials, transporting criminal defendants, and tracking down fugitives.

venire The group called for jury duty from which jury panels are selected.

vice squad Police officers assigned to enforce morality-based laws, such as those on prostitution, gambling, and pornography.

victim impact statement A post-conviction statement by the victim of crime that may be used to guide sentencing decisions.

vigilantes Groups of citizens who tracked down wanted criminals in the Old West.

voir dire The process in which a potential jury panel is questioned by the prosecution and the defense in order to select jurors who are unbiased and objective.

waiver (juvenile) A practice in which the juvenile court waives its jurisdiction over a juvenile and transfers the case to adult criminal court for trial. In some states, a waiver hearing is held to determine jurisdiction, whereas in others, juveniles may be automatically waived if they are accused of committing a serious crime such as murder.

Walnut Street Jail An eighteenth-century institution that housed convicted criminals in Philadelphia.

warez Copyrighted software illegally downloaded and sold by organized groups without license to do so.

watch system During the Middle Ages in England, men were organized in church parishes to guard at night against disturbances and breaches of the peace under the direction of the local constable.

widening the net of justice The view that programs designed to divert offenders from the justice system actually enmesh them further in the process by substituting more intrusive treatment programs for less intrusive punishment-oriented outcomes.

work release A prison treatment program that allows inmates to be released during the day to work in the community and returned to prison at night.

writ of certiorari An order of a superior court requesting that the record of an inferior court (or administrative body) be brought forward for review or inspection.

writ of *habeas corpus* A judicial order requesting that a person who detains another person produce the body of the prisoner and give reasons for his or her capture and detention. *Habeas corpus* is a legal device used to request that a judicial body review the reasons for a person's confinement and the conditions of confinement. *Habeas corpus* is known as "the great writ."

zero tolerance The practice of seizing all instrumentalities of a crime, including homes, boats, and cars. It is an extreme example of the law of forfeiture.

NOTES

Chapter 1, Crime and Criminal Justice

1. Ian Urbina and Manny Fernandez, "Memorial Services Held in U.S. and Around World," *New York Times*, April 21, 2007.
2. Samuel Walker, *Popular Justice* (New York: Oxford University Press, 1980).
3. Ibid.
4. For an insightful analysis of this effort, see Samuel Walker, "Origins of the Contemporary Criminal Justice Paradigm: The American Bar Foundation Survey, 1953–1969," *Justice Quarterly* 9 (1992): 47–76.
5. President's Commission on Law Enforcement and the Administration of Justice, *The Challenge of Crime in a Free Society* (Washington, DC: Government Printing Office, 1967).
6. See Public Law No. 90-351, *Title I–Omnibus Crime Control Safe Streets Act of 1968*, 90th Congress, June 19, 1968.
7. For a review, see Kevin Wright, "Twenty-Two Years of Federal Investment in Criminal Justice Research: The National Institute of Justice, 1968–1989," *Journal of Criminal Justice* 22 (1994): 27–40.
8. Brian A. Reaves, *Census of State and Local Law Enforcement Agencies 2004* (Washington, DC: Bureau of Justice Statistics, 2007).
9. Federal Bureau of Investigation, *Crime in the United States, 2005* (Washington, DC: Government Printing Office, 2006), Table 29.
10. Matthew R. Durose and Patrick A. Langan, *Felony Sentences in State Courts, 2002* (Washington, DC: Bureau of Justice Statistics, 2004).
11. Matthew Durose, Donald Farole, and Sean Rosenmerkel, *Felony Sentences in State Courts, 2006* (Washington, DC: Bureau of Justice Statistics, 2009), available online at http://bjs.ojp.usdoj.gov/index.cfm?ty=pbdetail&iid=2152 (accessed May 21, 2011).
12. For an analysis of this issue, see William Wilbanks, *The Myth of a Racist Criminal Justice System* (Monterey, CA: Brooks/Cole, 1987); Stephen Klein, Joan Petersilia, and Susan Turner, "Race and Imprisonment Decisions in California," *Science* 247 (1990): 812–816; Alfred Blumstein, "On the Racial Disproportionality of the United States Prison Population," *Journal of Criminal Law and Criminology* 73 (1982): 1259–1281; Darnell Hawkins, "Race, Crime Type, and Imprisonment," *Justice Quarterly* 3 (1986): 251–269.
13. Marilyn Bardsley, Rachael Bell, and David Lohr, *BTK—Birth of a Serial Killer*, truTV Crime Library, www.trutv.com/library/crime/serial_killers/unsolved/btk/index_1.html (accessed May 21, 2011).
14. Herbert L. Packer, *The Limits of the Criminal Sanction* (Stanford, CA: Stanford University Press, 1975), p. 21.
15. Durose and Langan, *Felony Sentences in State Courts, 2002*.
16. James Eisenstein and Herbert Jacob, *Felony Justice* (Boston: Little, Brown, 1977); Peter Nardulli, *The Courtroom Elite* (Cambridge, MA: Ballinger, 1978); Paul Wice, *Chaos in the Courthouse* (New York: Praeger, 1985); Marcia Lipetz, *Routine Justice: Processing Cases in Women's Court* (New Brunswick, NJ: Transaction Books, 1983).
17. Samuel Walker, *Sense and Nonsense About Crime* (Belmont, CA: Wadsworth, 1985).
18. Charles Montaldo, "The Elizabeth Smart Case, Background and Latest Developments," About.com, http://crime.about.com/od/current/a/elizabeth_smart.htm (accessed May 21, 2011).
19. Malcolm Feeley, *The Process Is the Punishment* (New York: Russell Sage, 1979).
20. John DiLulio, *No Escape: The Future of American Corrections* (New York: Basic Books, 1991).
21. Karen Parker and Patricia McCall, "Structural Conditions and Racial Homicide Patterns: A Look at the Multiple Disadvantages in Urban Areas," *Criminology* 37 (1999): 447–448.
22. Francis Cullen, John Paul Wright, and Mitchell Chamlin, "Social Support and Social Reform: A Progressive Crime Control Agenda," *Crime and Delinquency* 45 (1999): 188–207.
23. Jane Sprott, "Are Members of the Public Tough on Crime? The Dimensions of Public 'Punitiveness'," *Journal of Criminal Justice* 27 (1999): 467–474.
24. Packer, *The Limits of the Criminal Sanction*, p. 175
25. "DNA Testing Has Exonerated 28 Prison Inmates, Study Finds," *Criminal Justice Newsletter*, June 17, 1996, 2.
26. Caitlin Lovinger, "Death Row's Living Alumni," *New York Times*, August 22, 1999, 1.
27. Eric Stewart, Ronald Simons, Rand Conger, and Laura Scaramella, "Beyond the Interactional Relationship Between Delinquency and Parenting Practices: The Contribution of Legal Sanctions," *Journal of Research in Crime and Delinquency* 39 (2002): 36–60.
28. Cassia Spohn and David Holleran, "The Effect of Imprisonment on Recidivism Rates of Felony Offenders: A Focus on Drug Offenders," *Criminology* 40 (2002): 329–359.
29. *Doe v. Pryor M.D. Ala*, Civ. No. 99-T-730-N, Thompson, J. 8/16/99.
30. This section is based on Paula M. Ditton and Doris James Wilson, *Truth in Sentencing in State Prisons* (Washington, DC: Bureau of Justice Statistics, 1999).
31. Herbert Bianchi, *Justice as Sanctuary* (Bloomington: Indiana University Press, 1994); Nils Christie, "Conflicts as Property," *British Journal of Criminology* 17 (1977): 1–15; L. Hulsman, "Critical Criminology and the Concept of Crime," *Contemporary Crises* 10 (1986): 63–80.
32. Larry Tifft, foreword to *The Mask of Love*, Dennis Sullivan (Port Washington, NY: Kennikat Press, 1980), p. 6.
33. Christopher Cooper, "Patrol Police Officer Conflict Resolution Processes," *Journal of Criminal Justice* 25 (1997): 87–101.
34. Robert Coates, Mark Umbreit, and Betty Vos, "Responding to Hate Crimes through Restorative Justice Dialogue," *Contemporary Justice Review* 9 (2006): 7–21; Kathleen Daly and Julie Stubbs, "Feminist Engagement with Restorative Justice," *Theoretical Criminology* 10 (2006): 9–28.

35. This section relies heavily on Joycelyn M. Pollock, *Ethics in Crime and Justice: Dilemmas and Decisions*, 4th ed. (Belmont, CA: Wadsworth, 2004).

36. International Association of Chiefs of Police, 2005.

37. Alex Roth, "Story of Plea Attempt Raises Ire of Many," *San Diego Union Tribune*, September 18, 2002, p. 1.

38. Allen Beck and Timothy Hughes, *Prison Rape Elimination Act of 2003, Sexual Violence Reported by Correctional Authorities, 2004* (Washington, DC: Bureau of Justice Statistics, 2005).

Box Source Notes
Contemporary Issues in Criminal Justice: Evidence-Based Justice
Does Monitoring Sex Offenders Really Work?

Kristen Zgoba and Karen Bachar, "Sex Offender Registration and Notification: Research Finds Limited Effects in New Jersey," National Institute of Justice, April 2009, www.ncjrs.gov/pdffiles1/nij/225402.pdf (accessed May 19, 2011).

Criminal Justice and Technology
Using Biometrics to Fight Terrorism: US-VISIT

Sources: "United States Visitor and Immigrant Status Indicator Technology" (Electronic Privacy Information Center), www.epic.org/privacy/us-visit (accessed May 10, 2011); "US-Visit" (Travel and Transportation, U.S. Department of Homeland Security), www.dhs.gov/dhspublic/interapp/content_multi_image/content_multi_image_0006.xml (accessed May 10, 2011).

Chapter 2, The Nature of Crime and Victimization

1. Lizette Alvarez, "Casey Anthony Not Guilty in Slaying of Daughter," *New York Times*, July 5, 2011, www.nytimes.com/2011/07/06/us/06casey.html (accessed July 12, 2011).

2. Mirka Smolej and Janne Kivivuori, "The Relation Between Crime News and Fear of Violence," *Journal of Scandinavian Studies in Criminology and Crime Prevention* 7 (2006): 211–227.

3. Gallup Organization, *The Gallup Poll*, www.gallup.com/poll/1603/Crime.aspx (accessed May 23, 2011).

4. Data provided by the *Sourcebook of Criminal Justice Statistics*, Hindelang Criminal Justice Research Center University at Albany, 2008, www.albany.edu/sourcebook/pdf/t2402007.pdf (accessed May 23, 2011).

5. For a general discussion of Marxist thought on criminal law, see Michael Lynch, Raymond Michalowski, and W. Byron Groves, *The New Primer in Radical Criminology: Critical Perspectives on Crime, Power, and Identity*, 3rd ed. (Monsey, NY: Criminal Justice Press, 2000).

6. Howard Becker, *Outsiders, Studies in the Sociology of Deviance* (New York: Macmillan, 1963).

7. The National Council on Alcoholism and Drug Dependence, www.ncadd.org (accessed May 23, 2011).

8. FBI, *Crime in the United States, 2009* (Washington, DC: U.S. Government Printing Office, 2010), www2.fbi.gov/ucr/cius2009/ (accessed May 23, 2011).

9. FBI, *Crime in the United States*, "Murder," www2.fbi.gov/ucr/cius2009/offenses/violent_crime/murder_homicide.html (accessed May 23, 2011).

10. Data from the NCVS used in this chapter come from Michael Rand and Jennifer Truman, *Criminal Victimization, 2009* (Washington, DC: Bureau of Justice Statistics, 2010), http://bjs.ojp.usdoj.gov/content/pub/pdf/cv09.pdf (accessed May 23, 2011).

11. Michael Rand, *Criminal Victimization, 2007* (Washington, DC: Bureau of Justice Statistics, 2008), http://bjs.ojp.usdoj.gov/content/pub/pdf/cv07.pdf (accessed May 23, 2011).

12. To read about the Monitoring the Future study, go to www.monitoringthefuture.org.

13. Leonore Simon, "Validity and Reliability of Violent Juveniles: A Comparison of Juvenile Self-Reports with Adult Self-Reports," paper presented at the annual meeting of the American Society of Criminology, Boston, November 1995, p. 26.

14. Stephen Cernkovich, Peggy Giordano, and Meredith Pugh, "Chronic Offenders: The Missing Cases in Self-Report Delinquency," *Criminology* 76 (1985): 705–732.

15. See, for example, Spencer Rathus and Larry Siegel, "Crime and Personality Revisited: Effects of MMPI Sets on Self-Report Studies," *Criminology* 18 (1980): 245–251; John Clark and Larry Tifft, "Polygraph and Interview Validation of Self-Reported Deviant Behavior," *American Sociological Review* 31 (1966): 516–523.

16. Alfred Blumstein, Jacqueline Cohen, and Richard Rosenfeld, "Trend and Deviation in Crime Rates: A Comparison of UCR and NCVS Data for Burglary and Robbery," *Criminology* 29 (1991): 237–248.

17. Clarence Schrag, *Crime and Justice: American Style* (Washington, DC: U.S. Government Printing Office, 1971), p. 17.

18. Rand and Truman, *Criminal Victimization, 2009*.

19. Kathleen Maguire and Ann Pastore, *Sourcebook of Criminal Justice Statistics, 1995* (Albany, NY: Hindelang Research Center, 1996), www.druglibrary.org/schaffer/govpubs/sourcebook/1995/ (accessed May 23, 2011).

20. Lloyd Johnston, Patrick O'Malley, Jerald Bachman, and John Schulenberg, *Monitoring the Future: National Results on Adolescent Drug Use, Overview of Key Findings, 2010* (Ann Arbor, MI: University of Michigan, Institute for Social Research, 2011), http://monitoringthefuture.org/pubs/monographs/mtf-overview2010.pdf (accessed May 23, 2011).

21. Steven Levitt, "The Limited Role of Changing Age Structure in Explaining Aggregate Crime Rates," *Criminology* 37 (1999): 581–599.

22. Daniel Mears, Matthew Ploeger, and Mark Warr, "Explaining the Gender Gap in Delinquency: Peer Influence and Moral Evaluations of Behavior," *Journal of Research in Crime and Delinquency* 35 (1998): 251–266.

23. Freda Adler, *Sisters in Crime* (New York: McGraw-Hill, 1975); Rita James Simon, *The Contemporary Woman and Crime* (Washington, DC: Government Printing Office, 1975).

24. Finn-Aage Esbensen and Elizabeth Piper Deschenes, "A Multisite Examination of Youth Gang Membership: Does Gender Matter?" *Criminology* 36 (1998): 799–828.

25. Hubert Blalock, Jr., *Toward a Theory of Minority-Group Relations* (New York: Capricorn Books, 1967).

26. Robin Shepard Engel and Jennifer M Calnon, "Examining the Influence of Drivers' Characteristics during Traffic Stops with Police," *Justice Quarterly* 21 (2004).

27. Malcolm D. Holmes, Brad Smith, Adrienne Freng, and Ed Muñoz, "Minority Threat, Crime Control, and Police Resource Allocation in the Southwestern United States," *Crime and Delinquency* 54 (2008): 128–152; Bradley Keen and David Jacobs, "Racial Threat, Partisan Politics, and Racial Disparities in Prison Admissions," *Criminology* 47 (2009): 209–238.

28. David Jacobs and Katherine Woods, "Interracial Conflict and Interracial Homicide: Do Political and Economic Rivalries Explain White Killings of Blacks and Black Killings of Whites?" *American Journal of Sociology* 105 (1999): 157–190.

29. Robert Agnew, "A General Strain Theory of Community Differences in Crime Rates," *Journal of Research in Crime and Delinquency* 36 (1999): 123–155.

30. Bonita Veysey and Steven Messner, "Further Testing of Social Disorganization Theory: An Elaboration of Sampson and Groves's Community Structure and Crime," *Journal of Research in Crime and Delinquency* 36 (1999): 156–174.

31. Judith Blau and Peter Blau, "The Cost of Inequality: Metropolitan Structure and Violent Crime," *American Sociological Review* 47 (1982): 114–129.

32. Herman Schwendinger and Julia Schwendinger, "The Paradigmatic Crisis in Delinquency Theory," *Crime and Social Justice* 18 (1982): 70–78.

33. Michael Gottfredson and Travis Hirschi, "The True Value of Lambda Would Appear to Be Zero: An Essay on Career Criminals, Criminal Careers, Selective Incapacitation, Cohort Studies and Related Topics," *Criminology* 24 (1986): 213–234. Further support for their position can be found in Lawrence Cohen and Kenneth Land, "Age Structure and Crime," *American Sociological Review* 52 (1987): 170–183.

34. Marvin Wolfgang, Robert Figlio, and Thorsten Sellin, *Delinquency in a Birth Cohort* (Chicago: University of Chicago Press, 1972).

35. Marvin Wolfgang, Terence Thornberry, and Robert Figlio, *From Boy to Man, from Delinquency to Crime* (Chicago: University of Chicago Press, 1996).

36. Kimberly Kempf-Leonard, Paul Tracy, and James Howell, "Serious, Violent, and Chronic Juvenile Offenders: The Relationship of Delinquency Career Types to Adult Criminality," *Justice Quarterly* 18 (2001): 449–478.

37. Victim data used in these sections are from Michael Rand, *Criminal Victimization, 2008* (Washington, DC: Bureau of Justice Statistics, 2009).

38. Centers for Disease Control, "Homicide Among Young Black Males—United States, 1978–1987," *Morbidity and Mortality Weekly Report* 39 (1990): 869–873.

39. Janet Lauritsen and Kenna Davis Quinet, "Repeat Victimizations Among Adolescents and Young Adults," *Journal of Quantitative Criminology* 11 (1995): 143–163.

40. Denise Osborn, Dan Ellingworth, Tim Hope, and Alan Trickett, "Are Repeatedly Victimized Households Different?" *Journal of Quantitative Criminology* 12 (1996): 223–245.

41. Terry Buss and Rashid Abdu, "Repeat Victims of Violence in an Urban Trauma Center," *Violence and Victims* 10 (1995): 183–187.

42. Graham Farrell, "Predicting and Preventing Revictimization," in *Crime and Justice: An Annual Review of Research*, vol. 20, ed. Michael Tonry and David Farrington (Chicago: University of Chicago Press, 1995), pp. 61–126.

43. David A. Ward, Mark C. Stafford, and Louis N. Gray, "Rational Choice, Deterrence, and Theoretical Integration," *Journal of Applied Social Psychology* 36 (2006): 571–585.

44. Brandon C. Welsh and David P. Farrington, *Making Public Places Safer: Surveillance and Crime Prevention* (New York: Oxford University Press, 2008).

45. Stephanie Carmichael and Alex Piquero, "Deterrence and Arrest Ratios," *International Journal of Offender Therapy and Comparative Criminology* 50 (2006): 71–87.

46. Ross Matsueda, Derek Kreager, and David Huizinga, "Deterring Delinquents: A Rational Choice Model of Theft and Violence," *American Sociological Review* 71 (2006): 95–122.

47. Alicia Sitren and Brandon Applegate, "Testing the Deterrent Effects of Personal and Vicarious Experience with Punishment and Punishment Avoidance," *Deviant Behavior* 28 (2007): 29–55.

48. Andrew Klein and Terri Tobin, "A Longitudinal Study of Arrested Batterers, 1995–2005: Career Criminals," *Violence Against Women* 14 (2008): 136–157.

49. Rudy Haapanen, Lee Britton, and Tim Croisdale, "Persistent Criminality and Career Length," *Crime and Delinquency* 53 (2007): 133–155.

50. Todd A. Jusko, Charles R. Henderson Jr., Bruce P. Lanphear, Deborah A. Cory-Slechta, Patrick J. Parsons, and Richard L. Canfield, "Blood Lead Concentrations < 10 µg/dL and Child Intelligence at 6 Years of Age," *Environmental Health Perspectives* 116 (2008): 243–248.; Joel Nigg, G. Mark Knottnerus, Michelle Martel, Molly Nikolas, Kevin Cavanagh, Wilfried Karmaus, and Marsha D. Rappley, "Low Blood Lead Levels Associated with Clinically Diagnosed Attention-Deficit/Hyperactivity Disorder and Mediated by Weak Cognitive Control," *Biological Psychiatry* 63 (2008), 325–331.

51. Lauren Wakschlag, Kate Pickett, Kristen Kasza, and Rolf Loeber, "Is Prenatal Smoking Associated with a Developmental Pattern of Conduct Problems in Young Boys?" *Journal of the American Academy of Child and Adolescent Psychiatry* 45 (2006): 461–467; "Diet and the Unborn Child: The Omega Point," *The Economist*, January 19, 2006.

52. Rick Nevin, "Understanding International Crime Trends: The Legacy of Preschool Lead Exposure," *Environmental Research* 104 (2007): 315–336.

53. Kevin Beaver, John Paul Wright, and Matthew Delisi, "Self-Control as an Executive Function: Reformulating Gottfredson and Hirschi's Parental Socialization Thesis," *Criminal Justice and Behavior* 34 (2007): 1345–1361.

54. Thomas Brown, *Attention Deficit Disorder: The Unfocused Mind in Children and Adults* (New Haven, CT: Yale University Press, 2005).

55. Leonore Simon, "Does Criminal Offender Treatment Work?" *Applied and Preventive Psychology* (Summer, 1998); Stephen Faraone et al., "Intellectual Performance and School Failure in Children with Attention Deficit Hyperactivity Disorder and in Their Siblings," *Journal of Abnormal Psychology* 102 (1993): 616–623.

56. B. Hutchings and S. A. Mednick, "Criminality in Adoptees and Their Adoptive and Biological Parents: A Pilot Study," in *Biosocial Bases of Criminal Behavior*, ed. S. A. Mednick and Karl O. Christiansen (New York: Gardner Press, 1977).

57. August Aichorn, *Wayward Youth* (New York: Viking Press, 1965).

58. Paige Crosby Ouimette, "Psychopathology and Sexual Aggression in Nonincarcerated Men," *Violence and Victimization* 12 (1997): 389–397.

59. Robert Krueger, Avshalom Caspi, Phil Silva, and Rob McGee, "Personality Traits Are Differentially Linked to Mental Disorders: A Multitrait-Multidiagnosis Study of an Adolescent Birth Cohort," *Journal of Abnormal Psychology* 105 (1996): 299–312.

60. Seymour Halleck, *Psychiatry and the Dilemmas of Crime* (Berkeley: University of California Press, 1971).

61. Eric Elbogen, and Sally Johnson, "The Intricate Link Between Violence and Mental Disorder," *Archives of General Psychiatry* 66 (2009): 52–161.

62. David Eitle and R. Jay Turner, "Exposure to Community Violence and Young Adult Crime: The Effects of Witnessing Violence, Traumatic Victimization, and Other Stressful Life Events," *Journal of Research in Crime and Delinquency* 39 (2002): 214–238. See also Albert Bandura, *Aggression: A Social Learning Analysis* (Englewood Cliffs, NJ: Prentice Hall, 1973); Albert Bandura, *Social Learning Theory* (Englewood Cliffs, NJ: Prentice Hall, 1977).

63. U.S. Department of Health and Human Services, *Television and Behavior* (Washington, DC: Government Printing Office, 1982).

64. Elizabeth Cauffman, Laurence Steinberg, and Alex Piquero, "Psychological, Neuropsychological, and Physiological Correlates of Serious Antisocial Behavior in Adolescence: The Role of Self-Control," *Criminology* 43 (2005): 133–176.

65. Shadd Maruna, "Desistance from Crime and Explanatory Style: A New Direction in the Psychology of Reform," *Journal of Contemporary Criminal Justice* 20 (2004): 184–200.

66. Donald Lynam and Joshua Miller, "Personality Pathways to Impulsive Behavior and Their Relations to Deviance: Results from Three Samples," *Journal of Quantitative Criminology* 20 (2004): 319–341.

67. Tony Ward and Claire Stewart, "The Relationship Between Human Needs and Criminogenic Needs," *Psychology, Crime and Law* 9 (2003): 219–225.

68. David Lykken, "Psychopathy, Sociopathy, and Crime," *Society* 34 (1996): 30–38.

69. Gisli Gudjonsson, Emil Einarsson, Ólafur Örn Bragason, and Jon Fridrik Sigurdsson, Personality Predictors of Self-Reported Offending in Icelandic Students," *Psychology, Crime and Law* 12 (2006) 383–393.

70. Rolf Holmqvist, "Psychopathy and Affect Consciousness in Young Criminal Offenders," *Journal of Interpersonal Violence* 23 (2008): 209–224.

71. Lykken, "Psychopathy, Sociopathy, and Crime," 30–38.

72. U.S. Department of Health and Human Service, "The 2011 HHS Poverty Guidelines, One Version of the [U.S.] Federal Poverty Measure," http://aspe.hhs.gov/poverty/11poverty.shtml (accessed June 15, 2011).

73. Ralph Taylor, *Breaking Away from Broken Windows: Baltimore Neighborhoods and the Nationwide Fight Against Crime, Grime, Fear, and Decline* (Boulder, CO: Westview Press, 2001).

74. Lincoln Quillian and Devah Pager, "Black Neighbors, Higher Crime? The Role of Racial Stereotypes in Evaluations of Neighborhood Crime," *American Journal of Sociology* 107 (2001): 717–769.

75. Oscar Lewis, "The Culture of Poverty," *Scientific American* 215 (1966): 19–25.

76. William Julius Wilson, *The Truly Disadvantaged* (Chicago: University of Chicago Press, 1987).

77. Xu Yili, Mora Fiedler, and Karl Flaming, "Discovering the Impact of Community Policing: The Broken Windows Thesis, Collective Efficacy, and Citizens' Judgment," *Journal of Research in Crime and Delinquency* 42 (2005): 147–186.

78. C. L. Storr, C.-Y. Chen, and J. C. Anthony, "'Unequal Opportunity': Neighbourhood Disadvantage and the Chance to Buy Illegal Drugs," *Journal of Epidemiology and Community Health* 58 (2004): 231–238.

79. Rebekah Levine Coley, Jodi Eileen Morris, and Daphne Hernandez, "Out-of-School Care and Problem Behavior Trajectories Among Low-Income Adolescents: Individual, Family, and Neighborhood Characteristics as Added Risks," *Child Development* 75 (2004): 948–965.

80. Stacy De Coster, Karen Heimer, and Stacy Wittrock, "Neighborhood Disadvantage, Social Capital, Street Context, and Youth Violence," *Sociological Quarterly* (2006): 723–753.

81. Lisa Mufti, "Advancing Institutional Anomie Theory," *International Journal of Offender Therapy and Comparative Criminology* 50 (2006): 630–653.

82. Ibid.

83. W. Byron Groves and Robert Sampson, "Critical Theory and Criminology," *Social Problems* 33 (1986): 58–80.

84. Marvin Krohn, Alan Lizotte, and Cynthia Perez, "The Interrelationship Between Substance Use and Precocious Transitions to Adult Sexuality," *Journal of Health and Social Behavior* 38 (1997): 88.

85. Norman White and Rolf Loeber. Bullying and Special Education as Predictors of Serious Delinquency," *Journal of Research in Crime and Delinquency* 45 (2008): 380–397.

Box Source Notes

Contemporary Issues in Criminal Justice
Is the United States Crime Prone?

Jan van Dijk, John van Kesteren, and Paul Smit, "Criminal Victimisation in International Perspective: Key Findings from the 2004–2005 ICVS and EU ICS, 2008, http://rechten.uvt.nl/icvs/pdffiles/ICVS2004_05.pdf (accessed May 22, 2011).

Chapter 3, Criminal Law: Substance and Procedure

1. United States Criminal Code, Chapter 63, "Mail Fraud and Other Fraud Offenses," www.law.cornell.edu/uscode/18/usc_sup_01_18_10_I_20_63.html (accessed May 23, 2011)

2. The CAN-SPAM Act of 2003, 15 U.S.C. 7701, et seq., Public Law No. 108-187, was S.877, www.ftc.gov/os/caselist/0723041/canspam.pdf (accessed May 23, 2011).

3. Code of Hammurabi, available online at http://avalon.law.yale.edu/ancient/hamframe.asp (accessed May 23, 2011).

4. See John Weaver, *Warren—The Man, the Court, the Era* (Boston: Little, Brown, 1967); see also "We the People," *Time,* July 6, 1987, p. 6.

5. *Kansas v. Hendricks,* 117 S.Ct. 2072 (1997); *Chicago v. Morales,* 119 S.Ct. 246 (1999).

6. *City of Chicago v. Morales et al.,* 527 US 41 (1999).

7. Daniel Suleiman, "The Capital Punishment Exception: A Case for Constitutionalizing the Substantive Criminal Law," *Columbia Law Review* 104 (2004): 426–458.

8. *Calder v. Bull*, 3 U.S. 386 (1798).

9. See, for example, *General Laws of Massachusetts, Part II: Real and Personal Property and Domestic Relations. Title III. Domestic Relations*, Section 209 (June 30, 2002).

10. Sheldon Krantz, *Law of Corrections and Prisoners' Rights, Cases and Materials*, 3rd ed. (St. Paul, Minn.: West, 1986), 702; Barbara Knight and Stephen Early Jr., *Prisoners' Rights in America* (Chicago: Nelson-Hall, 1986), chapter 1; see also Fred Cohen, "The Law of Prisoners' Rights—An Overview," *Criminal Law Bulletin* 24 (188): 321–349.

11. See *United States v. Balint*, 258 U.S. 250, 42 S.Ct. 301, 66 L.Ed. 604 (1922); see also *Morissette v. United States*, 342 U.S. 246, 72 S.Ct. 240, 96 L.Ed. 288 (1952).

12. *Regina v. Dudley and Stephens*, 14 Q.B.D. 273 (1884).

13. For a history and analysis of these types of defenses, see Eugene Milhizer, "Justification and Excuse: What They Were, What They Are, and What They Ought to Be," *St. John's Law Review* 78 (2004): 725–895.

14. William Blackstone, *Commentaries on the Law of England*, vol. 1, ed. Thomas Cooley (Chicago: Callaghan, 1899), pp. 4, 26. Blackstone was an English barrister who lectured on the English common law at Oxford University in 1753.

15. Henry Fradella, *From Insanity to Diminished Capacity: Mental Illness and Criminal Defenses of Excuse in Contemporary American Law* (Bethesda, MD: Academic Press, 2007).

16. Samuel M. Davis, *Rights of Juveniles: The Juvenile Justice System* (New York: Boardman, 1974; updated 1993), chapter 2; Larry Siegel and Joseph Senna, *Juvenile Delinquency: Theory, Practice, and Law* (St. Paul, MN: West, 1996).

17. "Criminal Law—Mutual Combat Mitigation—Appellate Court of Illinois Holds that Disproportionate Reaction to Provocation Negates Mutual Combat Mitigation—*People v. Thompson*, 821 N.E. 2d 664 (Ii. App. Ct. 2004)," *Harvard Law Review* 118 (2005): 2437–2444.

18. Florida Statutes, Home Protection; Use of Deadly Force; Presumption of Fear of Death or Great Bodily Harm, www.leg.state.fl.us/statutes/ (accessed May 23, 2011).

19. Patrik Jonsson, "Is Self-Defense Law Vigilante Justice? Some Say Proposed Laws Can Help Deter Gun Violence. Others Worry About Deadly Confrontations," *Christian Science Monitor*, February 24, 2006.

20. 356 U.S. 369, 78 S.Ct. 819, 2 L.Ed.2d 848 (1958); see also *Jacobson v. United States*, 503 U.S. 540, 112 S.Ct. 1535, 118 L.Ed.2d 174 (1992).

21. Matthew R. Lyon, "No Means No?: Withdrawal of Consent During Intercourse and the Continuing Evolution of the Definition of Rape," *Journal of Criminal Law and Criminology* 95 (2004): 277–314.

22. *Lawrence et al. v. Texas*, No. 02-102, June 26, 2003.

23. Marvin Zalman, John Strate, Denis Hunter, and James Sellars, "Michigan Assisted Suicide Three Ring Circus: The Intersection of Law and Politics," *Ohio Northern Law Review* 23 (1997): 230–276.

24. 1992 P.A. 270 as amended by 1993 P.A.3, M.C. L. ss. 752.1021 to 752.1027.

25. Michigan Code of Criminal Procedure, *Assisting a Suicide*, Section 750.329a.

26. National Institute of Justice, *Project to Develop a Model Anti-stalking Statute* (Washington, DC: National Institute of Justice, 1994).

27. National Conference of State Legislators, Identity Theft Statutes, August 31, 2010, www.ncsl.org/?tabid=12538 (accessed May 23, 2011).

28. Environmental Protection Agency, Criminal Enforcement Division, www.epa.gov/compliance/criminal/ (accessed May 23, 2011).

29. Drug Policy Alliance Network, *Medical Marijuana*, www.drugpolicy.org/marijuana/medical/ (accessed May 23, 2011).

30. State of New Jersey 213th Legislature, Senate Bill 119, http://medicalmarijuana.procon.org/sourcefiles/NJS119.pdf (accessed May 23, 2011).

31. *Gonzales v. Raich*, 545 U.S. 1 (2005).

32. 384 U.S. 436, 86 S.Ct. 1602, 16 L.Ed.2d 694 (1966).

33. Daniel Suleiman, "The Capital Punishment Exception: A Case for Constitutionalizing the Substantive Criminal Law," *Columbia Law Review* 104 (2004): 426–458.

34. *Baze and Bowling v. Rees*, 553 U.S. (2008).

35. See "Essay," *Time*, February 26, 1973, p. 95; also, for a tribute to the Bill of Rights and due process, see James MacGregor Burns and Steward Burns, *The Pursuit of Rights in America* (New York: Knopf, 1991).

36. *Boumediene v. Bush*, 553 U.S. (2008).

37. 342 U.S. 165, 72 S.Ct. 205, 95 L.Ed. 183 (1952).

38. *Herring vs. U.S.*, 129 S. Ct. 695, 555 US 135, 172 L. Ed. 2d 496, 555 US ___ (2009).

Chapter 4, Police in Society: History and Organization

1. Jeff Horseman, "Temecula to Plug Budget Gap with Overtime Limits," *Press-Enterprise*, Riverside, CA, February 23, 2010, p. A4.

2. Carrie Johnson, "Double Blow for Police: Less Cash, More Crime," *Washington Post*, February 28, 2009. Available at www.washingtonpost.com/wp-dyn/content/article/2009/02/07/AR2009020701157.html (accessed May 27, 2011).

3. Caitlin Devitt, "Toledo Passes FY 2010 Budget that Unilaterally Amends Police Contract," *The Regions* 371 (2010): 24.

4. David Seifman, "NYPD Cop Count Sinking to 34,000," *New York Post*, March 19, 2011, http://tinyurl.com/4ldyssd (accessed May 27, 2011).

5. This section relies heavily on such sources as Malcolm Sparrow, Mark Moore, and David Kennedy, *Beyond 911: A New Era for Policing* (New York: Basic Books, 1990); Daniel Devlin, *Police Procedure, Administration, and Organization* (London: Butterworth, 1966); Robert Fogelson, *Big City Police* (Cambridge, MA: Harvard University Press, 1977); Roger Lane, *Policing the City, Boston 1822–1885* (Cambridge, MA: Harvard University Press, 1967); J. J. Tobias, *Crime and Industrial Society in the Nineteenth Century* (New York: Schocken Books, 1967); Samuel Walker, *A Critical History of Police Reform: The Emergence of Professionalism* (Lexington, MA: Lexington Books, 1977); Samuel Walker, *Popular Justice* (New York: Oxford University Press, 1980); John McMullan, "The New Improved Monied Police: Reform Crime Control and

Commodification of Policing in London," *British Journal of Criminology* 36 (1996): 85–108.

6. Devlin, *Police Procedure, Administration, and Organization*.

7. McMullan, "The New Improved Monied Police," p. 92.

8. Phillip Reichel, "Southern Slave Patrols as a Transitional Type," *American Journal of Police* 7 (1988): 51–78.

9. Walker, *Popular Justice*, 61.

10. Christopher Thale, "Assigned to Patrol: Neighborhoods, Police, and Changing Deployment Practices in New York City Before 1930," *Journal of Social History* 37 (2004): 1037–1064.

11. Walker, *Popular Justice*, 8.

12. Dennis Rousey, "Cops and Guns: Police Use of Deadly Force in Nineteenth-Century New Orleans," *American Journal of Legal History* 28 (1984): 41–66.

13. Law Enforcement Assistance Administration, *Two Hundred Years of American Criminal Justice* (Washington, DC: Government Printing Office, 1976).

14. National Commission on Law Observance and Enforcement, *Report on the Police* (Washington, DC: Government Printing Office, 1931), pp. 5–7.

15. Pamela Irving Jackson, *Minority Group Threat, Crime, and Policing* (New York: Praeger, 1989).

16. James Q. Wilson and George Kelling, "Broken Windows," *Atlantic Monthly* 249 (1982): 29–38.

17. Frank Tippett, "It Looks Just Like a War Zone," *Time*, May 27, 1985, pp. 16–22; "San Francisco, New York Police Troubled by Series of Scandals," *Criminal Justice Newsletter* 16 (1985): 2–4; Karen Polk, "New York Police: Caught in the Middle and Losing Faith," *Boston Globe*, December 28, 1988, p. 3.

18. Staff of the *Los Angeles Times*, *Understanding the Riots: Los Angeles Before and After the Rodney King Case* (Los Angeles: *Los Angeles Times*, 1992).

19. David H. Bayley, "Policing in America," *Society* 36 (December 1998).

20. Ronald Burns, Keith Whitworth, and Carol Thompson, "Assessing Law Enforcement Preparedness to Address Internet Fraud," *Journal of Criminal Justice* 32 (2004): 477–493.

21. Edward R. Maguire, "Counting Cops: Estimating the Number of Police Departments and Police Officers in the USA," *Policing: An International Journal of Police Strategies and Management* 21 (1998): 97–120.

22. Bruce Smith, *Police Systems in the United States* (New York: Harper & Row, 1960).

23. Brian J. Reaves, *Local Police Departments, 2007* (Washington, DC: Bureau of Justice Statistics, 2010).

24. California Anti-Terrorism Information Center (CATIC), www.ag.ca.gov/antiterrorism/ (accessed May 27, 2011).

25. Reaves, *Local Police Departments, 2007*.

26. Harris County Homeland Security and Emergency Management, www.hcoem.org (accessed May 27, 2011).

27. Montgomery County, Maryland, Homeland Security, www.montgomerycountymd.gov/mcgtmpl.asp?url=/content/homelandsecurity/index.asp (accessed May 27, 2011).

28. Data in this section come from Reaves, *Local Police Departments, 2007*.

29. See, for example, Robert Keppel and Joseph Weis, *Improving the Investigation of Violent Crime: The Homicide Investigation and Tracking System* (Washington, DC: National Institute of Justice, 1993).

30. For an overview of the department's many counterterrorism initiatives, see www.nyc.gov/html/nypd/html/administration/counterterrorism_units.shtml (accessed May 27, 2011).

31. NYPD SHIELD, www.nypdshield.org/public/ (accessed May 27, 2011).

32. Elizabeth E. Joh, "The Paradox of Private Policing," *Journal of Criminal Law and Criminology* 95 (2004): 49–131.

33. Larry Coutorie, "The Future of High-Technology Crime: A Parallel Delphi Study," *Journal of Criminal Justice* 23 (1995): 13–27.

34. This section is based on Derek Paulsen, "To Map or Not to Map: Assessing the Impact of Crime Maps on Police Officer Perceptions of Crime," *International Journal of Police Science and Management* 6 (2004): 234–246; William W. Bratton and Peter Knobler, *Turnaround: How America's Top Cop Reversed the Crime Epidemic* (New York: Random House, 1998), p. 289; Jeremy Travis, "Computerized Crime Mapping," *NIJ News* (National Institute of Justice), January 1999.

35. Arthur Gordon and Ross Wolf, "License Plate Recognition Technology Innovation in Law Enforcement Use," *FBI Law Enforcement Bulletin* 76 (2007), www.fbi.gov/stats-services/publications/law-enforcement-bulletin/2007-pdfs/march07leb.pdf (accessed May 27, 2011).

36. "Spotlight on Computer Imaging," *Police Chief* 66 (1999): 6–8.

37. See, generally, Ryan McDonald, "Juries and Crime Labs: Correcting the Weak Links in the DNA Chain," *American Journal of Law and Medicine* 24 (1998): 345–363; "DNA Profiling Advancement," *FBI Law Enforcement Bulletin* 67 (1998): 24.

Box Source Notes
Careers in Criminal Justice: Border Patrol Agent

U.S. Customs and Border Protection, www.cbp.gov (accessed May 31, 2011).

Criminal Justice and Technology
Fusion Centers

Fusion Center Guidelines: Developing and Sharing Information and Intelligence in a New Era, www.it.ojp.gov/documents/fusion_center_guidelines.pdf (accessed May 31, 2011); Charles R. Swanson, Leonard Territo, and Robert W. Taylor, *Police Administration: Structures, Processes, and Behavior*, 7th ed. (Upper Saddle River, NJ: Prentice Hall, 2008), pp. 77–78.

Chapter 5, The Police: Role and Function

1. State News Service, "Texas Senators Hutchison, Cornyn Request Action from President Obama on Escalating Violence in Mexico," March 17, 2010.

2. "Napolitano: Mexico Violence Hasn't Spread to U.S.," www.msnbc.msn.com/id/42264713/ns/us_news-security (accessed May 28, 2011).

3. Gary Martin, "Customs Chief: Violence Not Crossing Border," *San Antonio Express-News*, April 8, 2010, p. 10A.

4. James Willis, Stephen Mastrofski, and David Weisburd, "Making Sense of COMPSTAT: A Theory-Based Analysis of Organizational Change in Three Police Departments," *Law and Society Review* 41 (2007): 147–188.

5. Matthew Durose and Patrick Langan, *Contacts Between Police and the Public, Findings from the 2005 National Survey* (Washington, DC: Bureau of Justice Statistics, 2007).

6. Brian A. Reaves and Pheny Smith, *Law Enforcement Management and Administrative Statistics, 1993: Data for Individual State and Local Agencies with 100 or More Officers* (Washington, DC: Bureau of Justice Statistics, 1995).

7. American Bar Association, *Standards Relating to Urban Police Function* (New York: Institute of Judicial Administration, 1974), standard 2.2.

8. Albert J. Reiss, *The Police and the Public* (New Haven, CT: Yale University Press, 1971), p. 19.

9. James Q. Wilson, *Varieties of Police Behavior: The Management of Law and Order in Eight Communities* (Cambridge, MA: Harvard University Press, 1968).

10. James Q. Wilson and Barbara Boland, "The Effect of Police on Crime," *Law and Society Review* 12 (1978): 367–384.

11. Robert Sampson, "Deterrent Effects of the Police on Crime: A Replication and Theoretical Extension," *Law and Society Review* 22 (1988): 163–191.

12. Richard Timothy Coupe and Laurence Blake, "The Effects of Patrol Workloads and Response Strength on Arrests at Burglary Emergencies," *Journal of Criminal Justice* 33 (2005): 239–255.

13. Lawrence Sherman, James Shaw, and Dennis Rogan, *The Kansas City Gun Experiment* (Washington, DC: National Institute of Justice, 1994).

14. For a thorough review of this issue, see Andrew Karmen, *Why Is New York City's Murder Rate Dropping So Sharply?* (New York: John Jay College, 1996).

15. Robert Davis, Pedro Mateu-Gelabert, and Joel Miller, "Can Effective Policing Also Be Respectful? Two Examples in the South Bronx," *Police Quarterly* 8 (2005): 229–247.

16. Mitchell Chamlin, "Crime and Arrests: An Autoregressive Integrated Moving Average (ARIMA) Approach," *Journal of Quantitative Criminology* 4 (1988): 247–255.

17. Stewart D'Alessio and Lisa Stolzenberg, "Crime, Arrests, and Pretrial Jail Incarceration: An Examination of the Deterrence Thesis," *Criminology* 36 (1998): 735–761.

18. Perry Shapiro and Harold Votey, "Deterrence and Subjective Probabilities of Arrest: Modeling Individual Decisions to Drink and Drive in Sweden," *Law and Society Review* 18 (1984): 111–149.

19. William Spelman and Dale K. William, *Calling the Police: A Replication of the Citizen Reporting Component of the Kansas City Response Time Analysis* (Washington, DC: Police Foundation, 1976).

20. George Kelling and James Q. Wilson, "Broken Windows: The Police and Neighborhood Safety," *Atlantic Monthly* 249 (1982): 29–38.

21. Catherine Coles and George Kelling, *Fixing Broken Windows: Restoring Order and Reducing Crime in Our Communities* (New York: Free Press, 1998).

22. Anthony A. Braga and Brenda J. Bond, "Policing Crime and Disorder Hot Spots: A Randomized Controlled Trial," *Criminology* 46 (2008): 577–606.

23. Vincent Henry, *The Compstat Paradigm: Management Accountability in Policing, Business and the Public Sector* (New York: Looseleaf Law Publications, 2002).

24. For a view of the modern detective, see William Sanders, *Detective Work: A Study of Criminal Investigations* (New York: Free Press, 1977).

25. Mark Pogrebin and Eric Poole, "Vice Isn't Nice: A Look at the Effects of Working Undercover," *Journal of Criminal Justice* 21 (1993): 385–396; Gary Marx, *Undercover: Police Surveillance in America* (Berkeley: University of California Press, 1988).

26. Martin Innes, *Investigating Murder: Detective Work and the Police Response to Criminal Homicide* (Clarendon Studies in Criminology) (London: Oxford University Press, 2003).

27. John B. Edwards, "Homicide Investigative Strategies," *FBI Law Enforcement Bulletin* 74 (2005): 11–21.

28. Robert Langworthy, "Do Stings Control Crime? An Evaluation of a Police Fencing Operation," *Justice Quarterly* 6 (1989): 27–45.

29. Mary Dodge, Donna Starr-Gimeno, and Thomas Williams, "Puttin' on the Sting: Women Police Officers' Perspectives on Reverse Prostitution Assignment," *International Journal of Police Science and Management* 7 (2005): 71–85.

30. Peter Greenwood and Joan Petersilia, *Summary and Policy Implications*, vol. 1, *The Criminal Investigation Process* (Santa Monica, CA: Rand, 1975).

31. Mark Willman and John Snortum, "Detective Work: The Criminal Investigation Process in a Medium-Size Police Department," *Criminal Justice Review* 9 (1984): 33–39.

32. Janice Puckett and Richard Lundman, "Factors Affecting Homicide Clearances: Multivariate Analysis of a More Complete Conceptual Framework," *Journal of Research in Crime and Delinquency* 40 (2003): 171–194.

33. Police Executive Research Forum, *Calling the Police: Citizen Reporting of Serious Crime* (Washington, DC: Police Executive Research Forum, 1981).

34. John Eck, *Solving Crimes: The Investigation of Burglary and Robbery* (Washington, DC: Police Executive Research Forum, 1984).

35. A. Fischer, "CopLink Nabs Criminals Faster," *Arizona Daily Star*, January 7, 2001; A. Robbins, *PC Magazine* 22 (2003); M. Sink, "An Electronic Cop That Plays Hunches," *New York Times*, November 2, 2002.

36. Paul Johnson and Robin Williams, "Internationalizing New Technologies of Crime Control: Forensic DNA Databasing and Datasharing in the European Union," *Policing and Society* 17 (2007): 103–118.

37. For a general review, see Robert Trojanowicz and Bonnie Bucqueroux, *Community Policing: A Contemporary Perspective* (Cincinnati: Anderson, 1990).

38. Police Foundation, *The Newark Foot Patrol Experiment* (Washington, DC: Police Foundation, 1981).

39. John Worrall and Jihong Zhao. "The Role of the COPS Office in Community Policing," *Policing: An International Journal of Police Strategies and Management* 26 (2003), 64–87.

40. Jihong Zhao, Nicholas Lovrich, and Quint Thurman, "The Status of Community Policing in American Cities," *Policing* 22 (1999): 74–92.

41. Albert Cardarelli, Jack McDevitt, and Katrina Baum, "The Rhetoric and Reality of Community Policing in Small and Medium-Sized Cities and Towns," *Policing* 21 (1998): 397–415.

42. Brian Renauer, "Reducing Fear of Crime," *Police Quarterly* 10 (2007): 41–62.

43. Susan Sadd and Randolph Grinc, *Implementation Challenges in Community Policing* (Washington, DC: National Institute of Justice, 1996).

44. Donald Green, Dara Strolovitch, and Janelle Wong, "Defended Neighborhoods: Integration and Racially Motivated Crime," *American Journal of Sociology* 104 (1998): 372–403.

45. Robin Shepard Engel, *How Police Supervisory Styles Influence Patrol Officer Behavior* (Washington, DC: National Institute of Justice, 2003).

46. Amy Halsted, Max Bromley, and John Cochran, "The Effects of Work Orientations on Job Satisfaction Among Sheriffs' Deputies Practicing Community-Oriented Policing," *Policing: An International Journal of Police Strategies and Management* 23 (2000): 82–104.

47. Venessa Garcia, "Constructing the 'Other' Within Police Culture: An Analysis of a Deviant Unit Within the Police Organization," *Police Practice and Research* 6 (2005): 65–80.

48. Kevin Ford, Daniel Weissbein, and Kevin Plamondon, "Distinguishing Organizational from Strategy Commitment: Linking Officers' Commitment to Community Policing to Job Behaviors and Satisfaction," *Justice Quarterly* 20 (2003): 159–186.

49. Michael Palmiotto, Michael Birzer, and N. Prabha Unnithan, "Training in Community Policing: A Suggested Curriculum," *Policing: An International Journal of Police Strategies and Management* 23 (2000): 8–21.

50. Lisa Riechers and Roy Roberg, "Community Policing: A Critical Review of Underlying Assumptions," *Journal of Police Science and Administration* 17 (1990): 112–113.

51. Yili Xu, Mora Fiedler, and Karl Flaming, "Discovering the Impact of Community Policing: The Broken Windows Thesis, Collective Efficacy, and Citizens' Judgment," *Journal of Research in Crime and Delinquency* 42 (2005): 147–186.

52. Ling Ren, Liqun Cao, Nicholas Lovrich, and Michael Gaffney, "Linking Confidence in the Police with the Performance of the Police: Community Policing Can Make a Difference," *Journal of Criminal Justice* 33 (2005): 55–66.

53. Jihong Zhao, Ni He, and Nicholas Lovrich, "Value Change Among Police Officers at a Time of Organizational Reform: A Follow-up Study of Rokeach Values," *Policing* 22 (1999): 152–170.

54. Herman Goldstein, "Improving Policing: A Problem-Oriented Approach," *Crime and Delinquency* 25 (1979): 236–258.

55. Jerome Skolnick and David Bayley, *Community Policing: Issues and Practices Around the World* (Washington, DC: National Institute of Justice, 1988), p. 12.

56. Lawrence Sherman, Patrick Gartin, and Michael Buerger, "Hot Spots of Predatory Crime: Routine Activities and the Criminology of Place," *Criminology* 27 (1989): 27–55.

57. Ibid., 45.

58. Dennis Roncek and Pamela Maier, "Bars, Blocks, and Crimes Revisited: Linking the Theory of Routine Activities to the Empiricism of 'Hot Spots,'" *Criminology* 29 (1991): 725–753.

59. Sherry Plaster Carter, Stanley Carter, and Andrew Dannenberg, "Zoning Out Crime and Improving Community Health in Sarasota, Florida: 'Crime Prevention Through Environmental Design,'" *American Journal of Public Health* 93 (2003): 1442–1445.

60. Anthony Braga, David Kennedy, Elin Waring, and Anne Morrison Piehl, "Problem-Oriented Policing, Deterrence, and Youth Violence: An Evaluation of Boston's Operation Ceasefire," *Journal of Research in Crime and Delinquency* 38 (2001): 195–225.

61. Bureau of Justice Assistance, *Problem-Oriented Drug Enforcement: A Community-Based Approach for Effective Policing* (Washington, DC: National Institute of Justice, 1993).

62. Ibid., pp. 64–65.

63. William Doerner and Terry Nowell, "The Reliability of the Behavioral-Personnel Assessment Device (BPAD) in Selecting Police Recruits," *Policing* 22 (1999): 343–352.

64. See, for example, Richard Larson, *Urban Police Patrol Analysis* (Cambridge, MA: MIT Press, 1972).

65. Brian A. Reaves, *State and Local Police Departments, 1990* (Washington, DC: Bureau of Justice Statistics, 1992), p. 6.

66. Philip Ash, Karen Slora, and Cynthia Britton, "Police Agency Officer Selection Practices," *Journal of Police Science and Administration* 17 (1990): 258–269.

67. Dennis Rosenbaum, Robert Flewelling, Susan Bailey, Chris Ringwalt, and Deanna Wilkinson, "Cops in the Classroom: A Longitudinal Evaluation of Drug Abuse Resistance Education (DARE)," *Journal of Research in Crime and Delinquency* 31 (1994): 3–31.

Box Source Notes
Contemporary Issues in Criminal Justice
Does Patrol Deter Crime? A Look at the Evidence

George Kelling, Tony Pate, Duane Dieckman, and Charles Brown, *The Kansas City Preventive Patrol Experiment: A Summary Report* (Washington, DC: Police Foundation, 1974); Thomas Marvell and Carlisle Moody, "Specification Problems, Police Levels, and Crime Rates," *Criminology* 34 (1996): 609–646; Colin Loftin and David McDowall, "The Police, Crime, and Economic Theory: An Assessment," *American Sociological Review* 47 (1982): 393–401; John L. Worrall, "The Effects of Policing on Crime: What Have We Learned?" in *Critical Issues in Policing*, 6th ed., R. Dunham and G. Alpert, eds. (Long Grove, IL: Waveland, 2009).

Criminal Justice and Technology
Crime Scene Investigation

K. Daniel Glover, "Facebook Patrol: The Social Police Beat," www.thecrimereport.org/archive/2011-05-facebook-patrol-the-social-police-beat (accessed June 7, 2011); Don Butler, "Facebook Helps Store Owner Track Thief," *Yahoo News*, October 31, 2010; Julie Massis, "Is This Lawman Your Facebook Friend?" *Boston Globe*, www.boston.com/news/local/articles/2009/01/11/is_this_lawman_your_facebook_friend/ (accessed June 7, 2011); www.wired.co.uk/news/archive/2011-02/28/police-facebook (accessed June 7, 2011).

Contemporary Issues in Criminal Justice
"Forensics under the Microscope"

Chicago Tribune, "Forensics under the Microscope," www
.chicagotribune.com/news/specials/chi-forensics-specialpackage,
0,4244313.special (accessed June 2, 2011); National
Academy of Sciences, National Research Council, *Strengthening Forensic Science in the United States: A Path Forward*
(Washington, DC: The National Academies Press), www.nap
.edu/catalog.php?record_id=12589 (accessed June 2, 2011).

Careers in Criminal Justice
Forensic Scientist

Hall Dillon, "Forensics: A Career In," *Occupational Outlook
Quarterly* 1 (Fall 1999), www.bls.gov/opub/ooq/1999/fall/
art01.pdf (accessed June 2, 2011); U.S. Department of Labor,
Bureau of Labor Statistics, "Forensic Science Technicians,"
Occupational Employment and Wages, 2008, www.bls.gov/
oes/2009/may/oes194092.htm (accessed June 2, 2011).

Chapter 6, Issues in Policing: Professional, Social, and Legal

1. *Arizona v. Gant*, No. 07-542 (2009).
2. *New York v. Belton*, 453 U.S. 454 (1981).
3. Jihong Zhao and Nicholas Lovrich, "Determinants
   of Minority Employment in American Municipal Police
   Agencies: The Representation of African American
   Officers," *Journal of Criminal Justice* 26 (1998): 267–278.
4. Brian A. Reaves, *Local Police Departments, 2007*
   (Washington, DC: Bureau of Justice Statistics, 2010).
5. T. David Murphy and John Worrall, "Residency Requirements and Public Perceptions of the Police in Large
   Municipalities," *Policing* 22 (1999): 327–342.
6. Jack Kuykendall and David Burns, "The African
   American Police Officer: An Historical Perspective,"
   Journal of Contemporary Criminal Justice 1 (1980): 4–13.
7. Ibid.
8. Nicholas Alex, *Black in Blue: A Study of the Negro Policeman* (New York: Appleton-Century-Crofts, 1969).
9. Nicholas Alex, *New York Cops Talk Back* (New York:
   Wiley, 1976).
10. David Eitle, Lisa Stolzenberg, and Stewart J. D'Alessio,
    "Police Organizational Factors, the Racial Composition
    of the Police, and the Probability of Arrest," *Justice
    Quarterly* 22 (2005): 30–57.
11. Stephen Leinen, *African American Police, White Society*
    (New York: New York University Press, 1984).
12. Ni He, Jihong Zhao, and Ling Ren, "Do Race and Gender
    Matter in Police Stress? A Preliminary Assessment of the
    Interactive Effects," *Journal of Criminal Justice* 33 (2005):
    535–547.
13. Joseph L. Gustafson, "Tokenism in Policing: An Empiri-
    cal Test of Kanter's Hypothesis," *Journal of Criminal
    Justice* 36 (2008): 1–10.
14. For a review of the history of women in policing, see
    Dorothy Moses Schulz, "From Policewoman to Police Of-
    ficer: An Unfinished Revolution," *Police Studies* 16 (1993):
    90–99; Cathryn House, "The Changing Role of Women in
    Law Enforcement," *Police Chief* 60 (1993): 139–144.
15. Susan Martin, "Female Officers on the Move? A Status
    Report on Women in Policing," in *Critical Issues in*

    Policing, ed. Roger Dunham and Geoffery Alpert (Grove
    Park, IL: Waveland Press, 1988), pp. 312–331.
16. *Le Boeuf v. Ramsey*, 26 FEP Cases 884 (9/16/80).
17. Michael Birzer and Delores Craig, "Gender Differences
    in Police Physical Ability Test Performance," *American
    Journal of Police* 15 (1996): 93–106.
18. Reaves, *Local Police Departments, 2007*.
19. James Daum and Cindy Johns, "Police Work from a
    Woman's Perspective," *Police Chief* 61 (1994): 46–49.
20. Mary Brown, "The Plight of Female Police: A Survey of
    NW Patrolmen," *Police Chief* 61 (1994): 50–53.
21. Matthew Hickman, Alex Piquero, and Jack Greene,
    "Discretion and Gender Disproportionality in Police
    Disciplinary Systems," *Policing: An International Journal of
    Police Strategies and Management* 23 (2000): 105–116.
22. Robin Haarr and Merry Morash, "Gender, Race, and
    Strategies of Coping with Occupational Stress in Polic-
    ing," *Justice Quarterly* 16 (1999): 303–336.
23. Ibid.
24. Eric Poole and Mark Pogrebin, "Factors Affecting the
    Decision to Remain in Policing: A Study of Women
    Officers," *Journal of Police Science and Administration* 16
    (1988): 49–55.
25. See, for example, Gary Cordner and AnnMarie Cordner,
    "Stuck on a Plateau? Obstacles to Recruitment, Selection,
    and Retention of Women Police," *Police Quarterly* (2011),
    forthcoming.
26. Reaves, *Local Police Departments, 2007*.
27. Bruce Berg, "Who Should Teach Police? A Typology and
    Assessment of Police Academy Instructors," *American
    Journal of Police* 9 (1990): 79–100.
28. David Carter and Allen Sapp, *The State of Police Educa-
    tion: Critical Findings* (Washington, DC: Police Executive
    Research Forum, 1988), p. 6.
29. John Krimmel, "The Performance of College-Educated
    Police: A Study of Self-Rated Police Performance Mea-
    sures," *American Journal of Police* 15 (1996): 85–95.
30. See, for example, Richard Harris, *The Police Academy:
    An Inside View* (New York: Wiley, 1973); John Van
    Maanen, "Observations on the Making of a Policeman,"
    in *Order Under Law*, ed. R. Culbertson and M. Tezak
    (Prospect Heights, IL: Waveland Press, 1981),
    pp. 111–126; Jonathan Rubenstein, *City Police* (New
    York: Ballantine Books, 1973); John Broderick, *Police
    in a Time of Change* (Morristown, NJ: General Learning
    Press, 1977).
31. Gary R. Rothwell, "Whistle-Blowing and the Code of
    Silence in Police Agencies: Policy and Structural Predic-
    tors," *Crime and Delinquency* 53 (2007): 605–632; Louise
    Westmarland, "Police Ethics and Integrity: Breaking the
    Blue Code of Silence," *Policing and Society* 15 (2005):
    145–165.
32. Malcolm Sparrow, Mark Moore, and David Kennedy,
    Beyond 911: A New Era for Policing (New York: Basic
    Books, 1992), p. 51.
33. M. Steven Meagher and Nancy Yentes, "Choosing a
    Career in Policing: A Comparison of Male and Female
    Perceptions," *Journal of Police Science and Administration*
    16 (1986): 320–327.
34. Venessa Garcia, "Constructing the 'Other' Within Police
    Culture: An Analysis of a Deviant Unit Within the Police
    Organization," *Police Practice and Research* 6 (2005):
    65–80.

35. Michael K. Brown, *Working the Street* (New York: Russell Sage, 1981), p. 82.

36. Stan Shernock, "An Empirical Examination of the Relationship Between Police Solidarity and Community Orientation," *Journal of Police Science and Administration* 18 (1988): 182–198.

37. John Crank, *Understanding Police Culture*, 2nd ed. (Cincinnati: Anderson, 2003).

38. Eugene Paoline, "Taking Stock: Toward a Richer Understanding of Police Culture," *Journal of Criminal Justice* 31 (2003): 199–214.

39. Crank, *Understanding Police Culture*, pp. 359–363.

40. Egon Bittner, *The Functions of Police in Modern Society* (Cambridge, MA: Oelgeschlager, Gunn & Hain, 1980), p. 63.

41. Richard Lundman, *Police and Policing* (New York: Holt, Rinehart & Winston, 1980); see also Jerome Skolnick, *Justice Without Trial* (New York: Wiley, 1966).

42. Robert Regoli, Robert Culbertson, John Crank, and James Powell, "Career Stage and Cynicism Among Police Chiefs," *Justice Quarterly* 7 (1990): 592–614.

43. William Westly, *Violence and the Police: A Sociological Study of Law, Custom, and Morality* (Cambridge, MA: MIT Press, 1970).

44. Skolnick, *Justice Without Trial*, pp. 42–68.

45. Milton Rokeach, Martin Miller, and John Snyder, "The Value Gap Between Police and Policed," *Journal of Social Issues* 27 (1971): 155–171.

46. Wallace Graves, "Police Cynicism: Causes and Cures," *FBI Law Enforcement Bulletin* 65 (1996): 16–21.

47. Larry Tifft, "The 'Cop Personality' Reconsidered," *Journal of Police Science and Administration* 2 (1974): 268; David Bayley and Harold Mendelsohn, *Minorities and the Police* (New York: Free Press, 1969); Robert Balch, "The Police Personality: Fact or Fiction?" *Journal of Criminal Law, Criminology, and Police Science* 63 (1972): 117.

48. Lowell Storms, Nolan Penn, and James Tenzell, "Policemen's Perception of Real and Ideal Policemen," *Journal of Police Science and Administration* 17 (1990): 40–43.

49. Skolnick, *Justice Without Trial*.

50. Carroll Seron, Joseph Pereira, and Jean Kovath, "Judging Police Misconduct: 'Street-Level' versus Professional Policing," *Law and Society Review* 38 (2004): 665–710.

51. Peter Salovey and John D. Mayer, "Emotional Intelligence," *Imagination, Cognition, and Personality* 9 (1990): 185–211.

52. Michael E. Burnette, *Emotional Intelligence and the Police* (Germany: VDM Verlag, 2008)

53. Ivan Y. Sun, Brian K. Payne, and Yuning Wu, "The Impact of Situational Factors, Officer Characteristics, and Neighborhood Context on Police Behavior: A Multilevel Analysis," *Journal of Criminal Justice* 36 (2008): 22–32.

54. Kenneth Litwin, "A Multilevel Multivariate Analysis of Factors Affecting Homicide Clearances," *Journal of Research in Crime and Delinquency* 41 (2004): 327–351.

55. Robert Kane, "Patterns of Arrest in Domestic Violence Encounters: Identifying a Police Decision-Making Model," *Journal of Criminal Justice* 27 (1999): 65–79.

56. Gregory Howard Williams, *The Law and Politics of Police Discretion* (Westport, CT: Greenwood Press, 1984).

57. Dana Jones and Joanne Belknap, "Police Responses to Battering in a Progressive Pro-Arrest Jurisdiction," *Justice Quarterly* 16 (1999): 249–273.

58. Allison Chappell, John Macdonald, and Patrick Manz, "The Organizational Determinants of Police Arrest Decisions," *Crime and Delinquency* 52 (2006): 287–306.

59. Westly, *Violence and the Police*.

60. Peter Liu and Thomas Cook, "Speeding Violation Dispositions in Relation to Police Officers' Perception of the Offenders," *Policing and Society* (March 15, 2005): 83–88.

61. Joseph Schafer and Stephen Mastrofski, "Police Leniency in Traffic Enforcement Encounters: Exploratory Findings from Observations and Interviews," *Journal of Criminal Justice* 33 (2005): 225–238; Richard Lundman, "Demeanor or Crime? The Midwest City Police–Citizen Encounters Study," *Criminology* 32 (1994): 631–653; Nathan Goldman, *The Differential Selection of Juvenile Offenders for Court Appearance* (New York: National Council on Crime and Delinquency, 1963).

62. David Klinger, "Bringing Crime Back In: Toward a Better Understanding of Police Arrest Decisions," *Journal of Research in Crime and Delinquency* 33 (1996): 333–336; "More on Demeanor and Arrest in Dade County," *Criminology* 34 (1996): 61–79; "Demeanor or Crime? Why 'Hostile' Citizens Are More Likely to Be Arrested," *Criminology* 32 (1994): 475–493.

63. Ambrose Leung, Frances Woolley, Richard Tremblay, and Frank Vitaro, "Who Gets Caught? Statistical Discrimination in Law Enforcement," *Journal of Socio-Economics* 34 (2005): 289–309.

64. Jennifer Schwartz and Bryan D. Rookey, "The Narrowing Gender Gap in Arrests: Assessing Competing Explanations Using Self-Report, Traffic Fatality, and Official Data on Drunk Driving, 1980–2004," *Criminology* 46 (2008): 637–671.

65. R. Steven Daniels, Lorin Baumhover, William Formby, and Carolyn Clark-Daniels, "Police Discretion and Elder Mistreatment: A Nested Model of Observation, Reporting, and Satisfaction," *Journal of Criminal Justice* 27 (1999): 209–225.

66. For a review, see Frank Schmalleger and John L. Worrall, *Policing Today* (Upper Saddle River, NJ: Pearson, 2010), p. 319.

67. Brian Withrow, "Race-Based Policing: A Descriptive Analysis of the Wichita Stop Study," *Police Practice and Research* 5 (2004): 223–240; Brian Withrow, "A Comparative Analysis of Commonly Used Benchmarks in Racial Profiling: A Research Note," *Justice Research and Policy* 6 (2004): 71–92; Amy Farrell, Jack McDevitt, Lisa Bailey, Carsten Andresen, and Erica Pierce, "Massachusetts Racial and Gender Profiling Final Report" (Boston: Northeastern University, 2004), www.racialprofiling analysis.neu.edu/IRJsite_docs/finalreport.pdf (accessed June 3, 2011); Richard Lundman, "Driver Race, Ethnicity, and Gender and Citizen Reports of Vehicle Searches by Police and Vehicle Search Hits," *Journal of Criminal Law and Criminology* 94 (2004): 309–350; Michael Smith and Geoffrey Alpert, "Explaining Police Bias: A Theory of Social Conditioning and Illusory Correlation," *Criminal Justice and Behavior* 34 (2007): 1262–1283; *Interim Report of the State Police Review Team Regarding Allegations of Racial Profiling* (Trenton, NJ: Office of the Attorney General, 1999).

68. David Eitle, Lisa Stolzenberg, and Stewart J. D'Alessio, "Police Organizational Factors, the Racial Composition

of the Police, and the Probability of Arrest," *Justice Quarterly* 22 (2005): 30–57; Matt DeLisi and Robert Regoli, "Race, Conventional Crime, and Criminal Justice: The Declining Importance of Skin Color," *Journal of Criminal Justice* 27 (1999): 549–557; Jon Gould and Stephen Mastrofski, "Suspect Searches: Assessing Police Behavior Under the U.S. Constitution," *Criminology and Public Policy* 3 (2004): 315–362; Joseph Schafer, David Carter, and Andra Katz-Bannister, "Studying Traffic Stop Encounters," *Journal of Criminal Justice* 32 (2004): 159–170; James Lange, Mark Johnson, and Robert Voas, "Testing the Racial Profiling Hypothesis for Seemingly Disparate Traffic Stops on the New Jersey Turnpike," *Justice Quarterly* 22 (2005): 193–223; Geoffrey P. Alpert, Roger G. Dunham, and Michael R. Smith, "Investigating Racial Profiling by the Miami-Dade Police Department: A Multimethod Approach," *Criminology and Public Policy* 6 (2007): 25–56.

69. Mathias Risse and Richard Zeckhauser, "Racial Profiling," *Philosophy and Public Affairs* 32 (2004): 131–170.

70. Karen Kruger and Nicholas Valltos, "Dealing with Domestic Violence in Law Enforcement Relationships," *FBI Law Enforcement Bulletin* 71 (2002): 1–7.

71. Lumb and Breazeale, "Police Officer Attitudes and Community Policing Implementation."

72. Donald Yates and Vijayan Pillai, "Frustration and Strain Among Fort Worth Police Officers," *Sociology and Social Research: An International Journal* 76 (1992): 145–149.

73. For an impressive review, see Richard Farmer, "Clinical and Managerial Implications of Stress Research on the Police," *Journal of Police Science and Administration* 17 (1990): 205–217.

74. Lawrence Travis III and Craig Winston, "Dissension in the Ranks: Officer Resistance to Community Policing and Support for the Organization," *Journal of Crime and Justice* 21 (1998): 139–155.

75. Francis Cullen, Terrence Lemming, Bruce Link, and John Wozniak, "The Impact of Social Supports on Police Stress," *Criminology* 23 (1985): 503–522.

76. Merry Morash, Robin Haarr, and Dae-Hoon Kwak, "Multilevel Influences on Police Stress," *Journal of Contemporary Criminal Justice* 22 (2006): 26–43.

77. Farmer, "Clinical and Managerial Implications"; Nancy Norvell, Dale Belles, and Holly Hills, "Perceived Stress Levels and Physical Symptoms in Supervisory Law Enforcement Personnel," *Journal of Police Science and Administration* 16 (1988): 75–79.

78. Donald Yates and Vijayan Pillai, "Attitudes Toward Community Policing: A Causal Analysis," *Social Science Journal* 33 (1996): 193–209.

79. Harvey McMurray, "Attitudes of Assaulted Police Officers and Their Policy Implications," *Journal of Police Science and Administration* 17 (1990): 44–48.

80. Lawrence Blum, *Force Under Pressure: How Cops Live and Why They Die* (New York: Lantern Books, 2000).

81. Rose Lee Josephson and Martin Reiser, "Officer Suicide in the Los Angeles Police Department: A Twelve-Year Follow-Up," *Journal of Police Science and Administration* 17 (1990): 227–230.

82. Yates and Pillai, "Attitudes Toward Community Policing," pp. 205–206.

83. Ibid.

84. Rosanna Church and Naomi Robertson, "How State Police Agencies Are Addressing the Issue of Wellness," *Policing* 22 (1999): 304–312.

85. Farmer, "Clinical and Managerial Implications," p. 215.

86. Peter Hart, Alexander Wearing, and Bruce Headey, "Assessing Police Work Experiences: Development of the Police Daily Hassles and Uplifts Scales," *Journal of Criminal Justice* 21 (1993): 553–573.

87. Scott R. Senjo and Karla Dhungana, "A Field Data Examination of Policy Constructs Related to Fatigue Conditions in Law Enforcement Personnel," *Police Quarterly* 12 (2009): 123–136.

88. Bryan Vila and Dennis J. Kenney, "Tired Cops: The Prevalence and Potential Consequences of Police Fatigue," *NIJ Journal* 248 (2002): 16–21.

89. Luenda E. Charles, Cecil M. Burchfiel, Desta Fekedulegn, Bryan Vila, Tara A. Hartley, James Slaven, Anna Mnatsakanova, and John M. Violanti, "Shift Work and Sleep: The Buffalo Police Health Study," *Policing* 30 (2007): 215–227.

90. Sean Griffin and Thomas Bernard, "Angry Aggression Among Police Officers," *Police Quarterly* 6 (2003): 3–21.

91. Kim Michelle Lersch and Tom Mieczkowski, "Who Are the Problem-Prone Officers? An Analysis of Citizen Complaints," *American Journal of Police* 15 (1996): 23–42.

92. Samuel Walker, Geoffrey P. Alpert, and Dennis J. Kenney, *Early Warning Systems: Responding to the Problem Police Officer, Research in Brief* (Washington, DC: National Institute of Justice, 2001).

93. Michael D. White, "Controlling Police Decisions to Use Deadly Force: Reexamining the Importance of Administrative Policy," *Crime and Delinquency* 47 (2001): 131.

94. Kevin Flynn, "New York Police Sting Tries to Weed Out Brutal Officers," *New York Times*, September 24, 1999, p. 2.

95. Samuel Walker, *Popular Justice*, 2nd ed. (New York: Oxford University Press, 1997), pp. 48–64.

96. Herman Goldstein, *Police Corruption* (Washington, DC: Police Foundation, 1975), p. 3.

97. Lawrence Sherman, *Scandal and Reform: Controlling Police Corruption* (Berkeley: University of California Press, 1978), p. 194.

98. Barbara Gelb, *Tarnished Brass: The Decade After Serpico* (New York: Putnam, 1983); Candace McCoy, "Lawsuits Against Police: What Impact Do They Have?" *Criminal Law Bulletin* 20 (1984): 49–56.

99. Samuel Walker, *Police Accountability: The Role of Citizen Oversight* (Belmont, CA: Wadsworth, 2001); Liqun Cao and Bu Huang, "Determinants of Citizen Complaints Against Police Abuse of Power," *Journal of Criminal Justice* 28 (2000): 203–213; Peter Finn, "Getting Along with Citizen Oversight," *FBI Law Enforcement Bulletin* 69 (2000): 22–27.

100. For a general review, see Tom McEwen, *National Data Collection on Police Use of Force* (Washington, DC: National Institute of Justice, 1996).

101. Matthew Durose and Patrick Langan, *Contacts Between Police and the Public: Findings from the 2005 National Survey* (Washington, DC: Bureau of Justice Statistics, 2007).

102. Lawrence Sherman and Robert Langworthy, "Measuring Homicide by Police Officers," *Journal of Criminal Law and Criminology* 4 (1979): 546–560.

103. Ibid.

104. James Fyfe, "Police Use of Deadly Force: Research and Reform," *Justice Quarterly* 5 (1988): 165–205.

105. Richard Parent and Simon Verdun-Jones, "Victim-Precipitated Homicide: Police Use of Deadly Force in British Columbia," *Policing* 21 (1998): 432–449.

106. "10 Percent of Police Shootings Found to Be 'Suicide by Cop,'" *Criminal Justice Newsletter* 29 (1998): 1.

107. Colin Loftin, David McDowall, Brian Wiersema, and Adam Dobrin, "Underreporting of Justifiable Homicides Committed by Police Officers in the United States, 1976–1998," *American Journal of Public Health* 93 (2003): 1117–1121.

108. *Tennessee v. Garner*, 471 U.S. 1, 105 S. Ct. 1694, 85 L.Ed.2d 889 (1985).

109. Franklin Graves and Gregory Connor, "The FLETC Use-of-Force Model," *Police Chief* 59 (1992): 56–58.

110. Frank Zarb, "Police Liability for Creating the Need to Use Deadly Force in Self-Defense," *Michigan Law Review* 86 (1988): 1982–2009.

111. Brian A. Lawton, "Levels of Nonlethal Force: An Examination of Individual, Situational, and Contextual Factors," *Journal of Research in Crime and Delinquency* 44 (2007): 163–184.

112. Matthew J. Hickman, Alex R. Piquero, and Joel H. Garner, "Toward a National Estimate of Police Use of Nonlethal Force," *Criminology and Public Policy* 7 (2008): 563–604.

113. *Graham v. Connor*, 490 U.S. 386, 109 S. Ct. 1865, 104 L.Ed.2d 443 (1989).

114. Warren Cohen, "When Lethal Force Won't Do," *U.S. News and World Report* 122 (June 23, 1997): 12.

115. Richard Lumb and Paul Friday, "Impact of Pepper Spray Availability on Police Officer Use-of-Force Decisions," *Policing* 20 (1997): 136–149.

116. Tom McEwen, "Policies on Less-than-Lethal Force in Law Enforcement Agencies," *Policing* 20 (1997): 39–60.

117. *Miranda v. Arizona*, 384 U.S. 436 (1966).

118. *Colorado v. Connelly*, 107 S. Ct. 515 (1986).

119. *Fare v. Michael C.*, 439 U.S. 1310 (1978).

120. *New York v. Quarles*, 467 U.S. 649 (1984).

121. *Oregon v. Elstad*, 470 U.S. 298 (1985).

122. *Colorado v. Connelly*, 479 U.S. 157 (1986).

123. *Moran v. Burbine*, 475 U.S. 412 (1986).

124. *Colorado v. Spring*, 479 U.S. 564 (1987).

125. *Minnick v. Mississippi*, 498 U.S. 146 (1990).

126. *Arizona v. Fulminante*, 499 U.S. 279 (1991).

127. *Davis v. United States*, 512 U.S. 452 (1994).

128. *Chavez v. Martinez*, 538 U.S. 760 (2003).

129. *United States v. Patane*, 542 U.S. 630 (2004).

130. *Missouri v. Seibert*, 542 U.S. 600 (2004).

131. *Maryland v. Shatzer*, 559 U.S. ___ (2010).

132. *Florida v. Powell*, 559 U.S. ___ (2010).

133. *Berghuis v. Thompkins* 560 U.S. ___ (2010).

134. Marvin Zalman and Brad W. Smith, "Attitudes of Police Executives Toward *Miranda* and Interrogation Policies," *Journal of Criminal Law and Criminology* 97 (2007): 873–942; Victoria Time and Brian Payne, "Police Chiefs' Perceptions About *Miranda*: An Analysis of Survey Data," *Journal of Criminal Justice* 30 (2002): 77–86.

135. Ronald Allen, "*Miranda's* Hollow Core," *Northwestern University Law Review* 100 (2006): 71–85.

136. G. Daniel Lassiter, Jennifer Ratcliff, Lezlee Ware, and Clinton Irvin, "Videotaped Confessions: Panacea or Pandora's Box?" *Law and Policy* 28 (2006): 192–210.

137. *Chimel v. California*, 395 U.S. 752 (1969).

138. *Terry v. Ohio*, 392 U.S. 1 (1968).

139. *Illinois v. Wardlow*, 528 U.S. 119 (2000).

140. *Carroll v. United States*, 267 U.S. 132 (1925).

141. *United States v. Ross*, 102 S. Ct. 2147 (1982).

142. Drivers, *Pennsylvania v. Mimms*, 434 U.S. 106 (1977); passengers, *Maryland v. Wilson*, 117 U.S. 882 (1997) and *Arizona v. Johnson*, No. 07-1122 (2009).

143. Mark Hansen, "Rousting Miss Daisy?" *American Bar Association Journal* 83 (1997): 22; *Knowles v. Iowa*, 119 S. Ct. 507 (1998); *Wyoming v. Houghton*, 119 S. Ct. 1297 (1999).

144. *Bumper v. North Carolina*, 391 U.S. 543 (1960).

145. *Ohio v. Robinette*, 117 S. Ct. 417 (1996).

146. Limitations on the plain-view doctrine have been defined in *Arizona v. Hicks*, 107 S. Ct. 1149 (1987); the recording of serial numbers from stereo components in a suspect's apartment could not be justified as being in plain view.

147. *Warden v. Hayden*, 387 U.S. 294 (1967); *Minnesota v. Olson*, 495 U.S. 91 (1990); *Breithaupt v. Abram*, 352 U.S. 432 (1957).

148. *Kentucky v. King*, No. 09-1272 (2011).

149. *Weeks v. United States*, 232 U.S. 383, 34 S. Ct. 341, 58 L.Ed. 652 (1914).

150. *Mapp v. Ohio*, 367 U.S. 643, 81 S. Ct. 1684, 6 L.Ed.2d 1081 (1961).

151. William Greenhalgh, *The Fourth Amendment Handbook: A Chronological Survey of Supreme Court Decisions* (Chicago: American Bar Association Section on Criminal Justice, 1995).

152. *United States v. Leon*, 468 U.S. 897, 104 S. Ct. 3405, 82 L.Ed.2d 677 (1984).

Box Source Notes
Careers in Criminal Justice
Police Officer

"Police and Detectives," *Occupational Outlook Handbook*, 2010–2011 (Bureau of Labor Statistics, U.S. Department of Labor); Princeton Review, "Police Officer/Manager," www.princetonreview.com/Careers.aspx?cid=120 (accessed July 19, 2011).

Chapter 7, Courts, Prosecution, and the Defense

1. Greg Berman and John Feinblatt, Problem-Solving Courts: A Brief Primer (New York: Center for Court Innovation, 2001).

2. Office of National Drug Control Policy, www.whitehousedrugpolicy.gov/enforce/drugcourt.html (accessed June 7, 2011).

3. Center for Court Innovation, www.courtinnovation.org/topic/mental-health (accessed June 7, 2011).

4. Robert LaFountain, Richard Schauffler, Shauna Strickland, William Rafferty, and Chantal Bromage, *Examining the Work of State Courts, 2006* (Arlington, VA: National Center for State Courts, 2007), pp. 69–71.

5. U.S. Constitution, Art. 3, Secs. 1 and 2.

6. David Klein and Robert Hume, "Fear of Reversal as an Explanation of Lower Court Compliance," *Law and Society Review* 37 (2003): 579–607.

7. Roy Schotland, "2002 Judicial Elections," *Spectrum: The Journal of State Government* 76 (2003): 18–20.

8. Sari Escovitz with Fred Kurland and Nan Gold, *Judicial Selection and Tenure* (Chicago: American Judicature Society, 1974), pp. 3–16.

9. Judith McFarlane, Ann Malecha, Julia Gist, Kathy Watson, Elizabeth Batten, Iva Hall, and Sheila Smith, "Protection Orders and Intimate Partner Violence: An 18-Month Study of 150 Black, Hispanic, and White Women," *American Journal of Public Health* 94 (2004): 613–618.

10. Steven Perry, *Prosecutors in State Courts, 2005* (Washington, DC: Bureau of Justice Statistics, 2006).

11. Jessie Larson, "Unequal Justice: The Supreme Court's Failure to Curtail Selective Prosecution for the Death Penalty," *Journal of Criminal Law and Criminology* 93 (2003): 1009–1031.

12. Kenneth C. Davis, *Discretionary Justice* (Baton Rouge: Louisiana State University Press, 1969), p. 180; see also James B. Stewart, *The Prosecutor* (New York: Simon & Schuster, 1987).

13. Barbara Boland, *The Prosecution of Felony Arrests* (Washington, DC: Government Printing Office, 1983).

14. Jeffrey Spears and Cassia Spohn, "The Effect of Evidence Factors and Victim Characteristics on Prosecutors' Charging Decisions in Sexual Assault Cases," *Justice Quarterly* 14 (1997): 501–524.

15. Janell Schmidt and Ellen Hochstedler Steury, "Prosecutorial Discretion in Filing Charges in Domestic Violence Cases," *Criminology* 27 (1989): 487–510.

16. John Worrall, Jay Ross, and Eric McCord, "Modeling Prosecutors' Charging Decisions in Domestic Violence Cases," *Crime and Delinquency* 52 (2006): 472–503.

17. Myrna Dawson and Ronit Dinovitzer, "Victim Cooperation and the Prosecution of Domestic Violence in a Specialized Court," *Justice Quarterly* 18 (2001): 593–622.

18. Rodney Kingsworth, John Lopez, Jennifer Wentworth, and Debra Cummings, "Adult Sexual Assault: The Role of Racial/Ethnic Composition in Prosecution and Sentencing," *Journal of Criminal Justice* 26 (1998): 359–372; *United States v. Armstrong*, 517 U.S. 456 (1996).

19. Michael Edmund O'Neill, "Understanding Federal Prosecutorial Declinations: An Empirical Analysis of Predictive Factors," *American Criminal Law Review* 41 (2004): 1439–1533.

20. Shaila Dewan, "Prosecutors Say Cuts Force Plea Bargains," *New York Times*, March 10, 2003, p. B3.

21. Charles D. Breitel, "Controls in Criminal Law Enforcement," *University of Chicago Law Review* 27 (1960): 427.

22. Cassia Spohn, Dawn Beichner, and Erika Davis-Frenzel, "Prosecutorial Justifications for Sexual Assault Case Rejection: Guarding the 'Gateway to Justice,'" *Social Problems* 48 (2001): 206–235.

23. "Prosecutor Conduct," editorial, *USA Today*, April 1, 1999, p. 14A.

24. *North Carolina v. Pearce*, 395 U.S. 711, 89 S. Ct. 2072, 23 L.Ed.2d 656 (1969).

25. *Blackledge v. Perry*, 417 U.S. 21, 94 S. Ct. 2098, 40 L.Ed.2d 628 (1974).

26. *Bordenkircher v. Hayes*, 434 U.S. 357, 98 S. Ct. 663, 54 L.Ed.2d 604 (1978).

27. *Gideon v. Wainwright*, 372 U.S. 335, 83 S. Ct. 792, 9 L.Ed.2d 799 (1963).

28. *Argersinger v. Hamlin*, 407 U.S. 25, 92 S. Ct. 2006, 32 L.Ed.2d 530 (1972).

29. Carol J. DeFrances, *State-Funded Indigent Defense Services, 1999* (Washington, DC: Bureau of Justice Statistics, 2001).

30. Data compiled by the Bureau of Justice Statistics, www.ojp.usdoj.gov/bjs/ (accessed February 26, 2009); see also Arye Rattner, Hagit Turjeman, and Gideon Fishman, "Public versus Private Defense: Can Money Buy Justice?" *Journal of Criminal Justice* 36 (2008): 43–49.

31. *Strickland v. Washington*, 466 U.S. 668, 104 S. Ct. 2052, 80 L.Ed.2d 674 (1984).

32. *Florida v. Nixon*, No. 03-931 (Decided: 12/13/04).

33. The following sections are based on Ron Bowmaster and John Cariotto, "Information Sharing in Nebraska," National Center for State Courts, 2003, www.ncsconline.org/d_tech/ctc/showarticle.asp?id=69 (accessed June 7, 2011); Fredric I. Lederer, "The Road to the Virtual Courtroom? Consideration of Today's—and Tomorrow's—High-Technology Courtrooms," *South Carolina Law Review* 50 (1999): 799; "Criminal Court Records Go Online," *The Quill* 90 (2002): 39; Donald C. Dilworth, "New Court Technology Will Affect How Attorneys Present Trials," *Trial* 33 (1997): 100–114.

Box Source Notes
Careers in Criminal Justice
Prosecutor

Bureau of Labor Statistics, U.S. Department of Labor, "Lawyers," *Occupational Outlook Handbook, 2010–11 Edition*, www.bls.gov/oco/ocos053.htm (accessed June 8, 2011); Average Prosecutor Salaries, www.simplyhired.com/a/salary/search/q-prosecutor (accessed June 8, 2011).

Contemporary Issues in Criminal Justice
No-Drop Prosecution: Does It Work?

Robert C. Davis, Chris S. O'Sullivan, Donald J. Farole, Jr., and Michael Rempel, "A Comparison of Two Prosecution Policies in Cases of Intimate Partner Violence: Mandatory Case Filing versus Following the Victim's Lead," *Criminology and Public Policy* 7 (2008): 633–662, quote from p. 658; see also John L. Worrall, *Crime Control in America: What Works?* 2nd ed. (Boston, MA: Allyn and Bacon, 2008), pp. 110–111.

Chapter 8, Pretrial and Trial Procedures

1. *District Attorney's Office v. Osborne*, No. 08-6 (2009).

2. *Stack v. Boyle*, 342 U.S. 1 (1951).

3. Data in this section come from Thomas Cohen and Brian Reaves, *Felony Defendants in Large Urban Counties, 2002* (Washington, DC: Bureau of Justice Statistics, 2006).

4. Christopher Stephens, "Bail" section of the Criminal Procedure project, *Georgetown Law Journal* 90 (2002): 1395–1416.

5. Traci Schlesinger, "Racial and Ethnic Disparity in Pretrial Criminal Processing," *Justice Quarterly* 22 (2005): 170–192.

6. Bob Burton, Director of Training and Surety Corporation Liaison, National Institute of Bail Enforcement, personal contact, September 17, 2004.

7. Cohen and Reaves, *Felony Defendants in Large Urban Counties.*

8. Vera Institute of Justice, *1961–1971: Programs in Criminal Justice* (New York: Vera Institute of Justice, 1972).

9. Public Law No. 89-465, 18 U.S.C., sec. 3146 (1966).

10. 18 U.S.C., sec. 3142 (1984).

11. See, generally, Fred Cohen, "The New Federal Crime Control Act," *Criminal Law Bulletin* 21 (1985): 330–337.

12. This section leans on John Clark and D. Alan Henry, *Pretrial Services Programming at the Start of the 21st Century: A Survey of Pretrial Services Programs* (Washington, DC: Bureau of Justice Assistance, 2003).

13. Ric Simmons, "Reexamining the Grand Jury: Is There Room for Democracy in the Criminal Justice System?" *Boston University Law Review* 82 (2002): 1–76.

14. John Gibeaut, "Indictment of a System," *ABA Journal* 87 (2001): 34.

15. Kirke D. Weaver, "A Change of Heart or a Change of Law? Withdrawing a Guilty Plea Under Federal Rule of Criminal Procedure 32(e)," *Journal of Criminal Law and Criminology* 92 (2001): 273–306.

16. Anne Piehl and Shawn Bushway, "Measuring and Explaining Charge Bargaining," *Journal of Quantitative Criminology* 23 (2007): 105–125.

17. George Fisher, "Plea Bargaining's Triumph," *Yale Law Journal* 109 (2000): 857–1058.

18. Fred Zacharis, "Justice in Plea Bargaining," *William and Mary Law Review* 39 (1998): 1121–1189.

19. Nathaniel J. Pallone, "Without Plea-Bargaining, Megan Kanka Would Be Alive Today," *Criminology and Public Policy* 3 (2003): 83–96.

20. William Stuntz, "Plea Bargaining and Criminal Law's Disappearing Shadow," *Harvard Law Review* 117 (2004): 2548–2569.

21. Mike McConville, "Plea Bargaining: Ethics and Politics," *Journal of Law and Society* 25 (1998): 526–555.

22. *Hill v. Lockhart*, 474 U.S. 52 (1985).

23. *Boykin v. Alabama*, 395 U.S. 238 (1969); *Brady v. United States*, 397 U.S. 742 (1970).

24. *Santobello v. New York*, 404 U.S. 257 (1971).

25. *Ricketts v. Adamson*, 483 U.S. 1 (1987).

26. *Bordenkircher v. Hayes*, 434 U.S. 357 (1978).

27. *North Carolina v. Alford*, 400 U.S. 25 (1970).

28. *United States v. Mezzanatto*, 513 U.S. 196 (1995).

29. Jeremy Ball, "Is It a Prosecutor's World? Determinants of Court Bargaining Decisions," *Journal of Contemporary Criminal Justice* 22 (2006): 241–260.

30. Deirdre M. Bowen, "Calling Your Bluff: How Prosecutors and Defense Attorneys Adapt to Plea Bargaining Strategies to Increase Formalization," *Justice Quarterly* 26 (2009): 2–29.

31. Stephen P. Lagoy, Joseph J. Senna, and Larry J. Siegel, "An Empirical Study on Information Usage for Prosecutorial Decision Making in Plea Negotiations," *American Criminal Law Review* 13 (1976): 435–471.

32. Keith Bystrom, "Communicating Plea Offers to the Client," in *Ethical Problems Facing the Criminal Defense Lawyer*, ed. Rodney Uphoff (Chicago: American Bar Association Section on Criminal Justice, 1995), p. 84.

33. American Bar Association, Standards Relating to Pleas of Guilty, standard 3.3; *National Advisory Commission on Criminal Justice Standards and Goals, Task Force Report on Courts* (Washington, DC: Government Printing Office, 1973), p. 42.

34. American Bar Association, *Standards Relating to Pleas of Guilty*, p. 73; see also Alan Alschuler, "The Trial Judge's Role in Plea Bargaining," *Columbia Law Review* 76 (1976): 1059.

35. Barbara Boland and Brian Forst, *The Prevalence of Guilty Pleas* (Washington, DC: Bureau of Justice Statistics, 1984), p. 3; see also Gary Hengstler, "The Troubled Justice System," *American Bar Association Journal* 80 (1994): 44.

36. National Institute of Law Enforcement and Criminal Justice, *Plea Bargaining in the United States*, p. 37–40.

37. For a discussion of this issue, see Michael Tonry, "Plea Bargaining Bans and Rules," in *Sentencing Reform Impacts* (Washington, DC: Government Printing Office, 1987).

38. Franklyn Dunford, D. Wayne Osgood, and Hart Weichselbaum, *National Evaluation of Diversion Programs* (Washington, DC: Government Printing Office, 1982).

39. Sharla Rausch and Charles Logan, "Diversion from Juvenile Court: Panacea or Pandora's Box?" in *Evaluating Juvenile Justice*, ed. James Kleugel (Beverly Hills, CA: Sage, 1983), pp. 19–30.

40. John Hepburn, "Recidivism among Drug Offenders Following Exposure to Treatment," *Criminal Justice Policy Review* 16 (2005): 237–259.

41. *Tumey v. Ohio*, 273 U.S. 510 (1927), at 523.

42. See, for example, Minn. R. Crim. P. 26.03, subd. 13(4).

43. *Riggins v. Nevada*, 504 U.S. 127 (1992).

44. *Diaz v. United States*, 223 U.S. 442 (1912); *Taylor v. Illinois*, 484 U.S. 400 (1988).

45. *Illinois v. Allen*, 397 U.S. 337 (1970).

46. *Maryland v. Craig*, 497 U.S. 836 (1990).

47. *Washington v. Texas*, 388 U.S. 14 (1967).

48. *Baldwin v. New York*, 399 U.S. 66 (1970).

49. *Scott v. Illinois*, 440 U.S. 367 (1979).

50. *Shelton v. Alabama*, 122 U.S. 1764 (2002).

51. *Faretta v. California*, 422 U.S. 806 (1975).

52. See American Bar Association, *Standards Relating to Speedy Trial* (Chicago: ABA, 1995).

53. *Klopfer v. North Carolina*, 386 U.S. 213 (1967).

54. *Wilson v. Layne*, 526 U.S. 603 (1999).

55. See *Brinegar v. United States*, 338 U.S. 160 (1949); *In re Winship*, 397 U.S. 358, 90 (1970).

56. Ibid., at 174.

57. See *In re Winship*, at 397.

58. Ibid., at 371, 90 S. Ct. at 1076.

59. Brian Kalt, "The Exclusion of Felons from Jury Service," *American University Law Review* 53 (2003): 65–189.

60. George Hayden, Joseph Senna, and Larry Siegel, "Prosecutorial Discretion in Peremptory Challenges: An Empirical Investigation of Information Use in the Massachusetts Jury Selection Process," *New England Law Review* 13 (1978): 768.

61. *Batson v. Kentucky*, 476 U.S. 79 (1986); see also Alan Alschuler and Randall Kennedy, "Equal Justice—Would Color-Conscious Jury Selection Help?" *American Bar Association Journal* 81 (1995): 36–37.

62. John Schwartz, "As Jurors Turn to Web, Mistrials Are Popping Up," *New York Times*, March 17, 2009, http://www.nytimes.com/2009/03/18/us/18juries.html (accessed June 13, 2011).

63. Arie Rubenstein, "Verdicts of Conscience: Nullification and the Modern Jury Trial," *Columbia Law Review* 106 (2006): 959–993.

64. David Pepper, "Nullifying History: Modern-Day Misuse of the Right to Decide the Law," *Case Western Reserve Law Review* 50 (2000): 599–643.

65. *Chapman v. California*, 386 U.S. 18 (1967).

66. *Douglas v. California*, 372 U.S. 353 (1963).

Box Source Notes
Contemporary Issues in Criminal Justice
The *CSI* Effect

Donald E. Shelton, "The '*CSI* Effect': Does It Really Exist?" *National Institute of Justice Journal* 259 (2008): 1–7; Donald E. Shelton, Young S. Kim, and Gregg Barak, "A Study of Juror Expectation and Demands Concerning Scientific Evidence: Does the '*CSI* Effect' Exist?" *Vanderbilt Journal of Entertainment and Technology Law* 9 (2007): 331–368; Young S. Kim, Gregg Barak, and Donald E. Shelton, "Examining the '*CSI* Effect' in the Cases of Circumstantial Evidence and Eyewitness Testimony: Multivariate and Path Analyses," *Journal of Criminal Justice* 37(2009): 452–460; Zap2It, TV by the Numbers, "'CSI: Crime Scene Investigation' Is the Most-Watched Drama Series in the World!" http://tvbythenumbers.zap2it .com/2011/06/13/csi-crime-scene-investigation-is-the-most-watched-drama-series-in-the-world/95460/ (accessed July 20, 2011).

Careers in Criminal Justice
Court Reporter

S. E. Lambert and D. Regan, "Court Reporter," *Great Jobs for Criminal Justice Majors* (New York: McGraw-Hill, 2001), pp. 159–161; Bureau of Labor Statistics, U.S. Department of Labor, "Court Reporters," *Occupational Outlook Handbook, 2008–09 Edition*, www.bls.gov/oco/ocos152.htm (accessed June 13, 2011).

Chapter 9, Punishment and Sentencing

1. *Thompson v. McNeil*, No. 08-7369 (2009), cert. denied.

2. Death Penalty Information Center, *The Death Penalty in 2008: Year End Report*, available at www.deathpenaltyinfo .org/2008YearEnd.pdf (accessed June 27, 2011); see also www.deathpenaltyinfo.org/time-death-row (accessed June 27, 2011).

3. Among the most helpful sources for this section were Benedict Alper, *Prisons Inside-Out* (Cambridge, MA: Ballinger, 1974); Gustave de Beaumont and Alexis de Tocqueville, *On the Penitentiary System in the United States and Its Applications in France* (Carbondale, IL: Southern Illinois University Press, 1964); Orlando Lewis, *The Development of American Prisons and Prison Customs, 1776–1845* (Montclair, NJ: Patterson-Smith, 1967); Leonard Orland, ed., *Justice, Punishment, and Treatment* (New York: Free Press, 1973); J. Goebel, *Felony and Misdemeanor* (Philadelphia: University of Pennsylvania Press, 1976); Georg Rusche and Otto Kircheimer, *Punishment and Social Structure* (New York: Russell & Russell, 1939); Samuel Walker, *Popular Justice* (New York: Oxford University Press, 1980); Graeme R. Newman, *The Punishment Response* (Piscataway, NJ: Transaction Publishers, 2008); David Rothman, *Conscience and Convenience* (Boston: Little, Brown, 1980); George Ives, *A History of Penal Methods* (Montclair, NJ: Patterson-Smith, 1970); Robert Hughes, *The Fatal Shore* (New York: Knopf, 1986); Leon Radzinowicz, *A History of English Criminal Law*, vol. 1 (London: Stevens, 1943), p. 5.

4. *Crime and Punishment in America, 1999*, Report 229 (Washington, DC: National Center for Policy Analysis, 1999).

5. Matthew Durose and Patrick Langan, *Felony Sentences in State Courts, 2004* (Washington, DC: Bureau of Justice Statistics, 2007).

6. Patrick Langan and David Levin, *Recidivism of Prisoners Released in 1994* (Washington, DC: Bureau of Justice Statistics, 2002).

7. Faith Lutze, "The Influence of Shock Incarceration Program on Inmate Adjustment and Attitudinal Change," *Journal of Criminal Justice* 29 (2001): 255–266.

8. Tomislav Kovandzic and Lynne Vieraitis, "The Effect of County-Level Prison Population Growth on Crime Rates," *Criminology and Public Policy* 5 (2006): 213–244.

9. Raymond Liedka, Anne Morrison Piehl, and Bert Useem, "The Crime-Control Effect of Incarceration: Does Scale Matter?" *Criminology and Public Policy* 5 (2006): 245–276.

10. Ibid.

11. Charles Logan, *Criminal Justice Performance Measures for Prisons* (Washington, DC: Bureau of Justice Statistics, 1993), p. 3.

12. Alexis Durham, "The Justice Model in Historical Context: Early Law, the Emergence of Science, and the Rise of Incarceration," *Journal of Criminal Justice* 16 (1988): 331–346.

13. Andrew von Hirsh, *Doing Justice: The Choice of Punishments* (New York: Hill and Wang, 1976).

14. Shawn Bushway, "The Impact of an Arrest on the Job Stability of Young White American Men," *Journal of Research in Crime and Delinquency* 35 (1998): 454–479.

15. Lawrence W. Sherman, David P. Farrington, Doris Layton MacKenzie, Brandon Walsh, Denise Gottfredson, John Eck, Shawn Bushway, and Peter Reuter, *Evidence-Based Crime Prevention* (London: Routledge and Kegan Paul, 2002); see also Arnulf Kolstad, "Imprisonment as Rehabilitation: Offenders' Assessment of Why It Does Not Work," *Journal of Criminal Justice* 24 (1996): 323–335.

16. Francis Cullen, John Paul Wright, Shayna Brown, Melissa Moon, and Brandon Applegate, "Public Support for Early Intervention Programs: Implications for a Progressive Policy Agenda," *Crime and Delinquency* 44 (1998): 187–204; Richard McCorkle, "Research Note: Punish and Rehabilitate? Public Attitudes Toward Six Common Crimes," *Crime and Delinquency* 39 (1993): 240–252; D. A. Andrews, Ivan Zinger, Robert Hoge, James Bonta, Paul Gendreau, and Francis Cullen, "Does Correctional Treatment Work? A Clinically Relevant and Psychologically Informed Meta-Analysis," *Criminology* 28 (1990): 369–404.

17. Paula Ditton and Doris James Wilson, *Truth in Sentencing in State Prisons* (Washington, DC: Bureau of Justice Statistics, 1999).

18. Jo Dixon, "The Organizational Context of Criminal Sentencing," *American Journal of Sociology* 100 (1995): 1157–1198.

19. Michael Tonry, *Reconsidering Indeterminate and Structured Sentencing Series: Sentencing and Corrections: Issues for the 21st Century* (Washington, DC: National Institute of Justice, 1999).

20. *Blakely v. Washington*, 124 S. Ct. 2531 (2004).

21. *United States v. Booker*, No. 04–104, decided January 12, 2005.

22. Michael Tonry, "The Failure of the U.S. Sentencing Commission's Guidelines," *Crime and Delinquency* 39 (1993): 131–149.

23. Sean Nicholson-Crotty, "The Impact of Sentencing Guidelines on State-Level Sanctions: An Analysis Over Time," *Crime and Delinquency* 50 (2004): 395–410.

24. United States Sentencing Commission, "Final Report on the Impact of *United States v. Booker* on Federal Sentencing," March 2006, www.ussc.gov/Legislative_and_Public_Affairs/Congressional_Testimony_and_Reports/Submissions/200603_Booker/Booker_Report.pdf (accessed June 27, 2011).

25. Jeffrey T. Ulmer, Megan C. Kurlychek, and John H. Kramer, "Prosecutorial Discretion and the Imposition of Mandatory Minimum Sentences," *Journal of Research in Crime and Delinquency* 44 (2007): 427–458.

26. See, for example, John L. Worrall, *Crime Control in America: What Works?* (Boston: Allyn and Bacon, 2008), pp. 193–199.

27. Marc Mauer, *Americans Behind Bars: The International Use of Incarceration, 1992–93: Part II* (Washington, DC: The Sentencing Project, 1994).

28. For a review of the literature, see John L. Worrall, *Crime Control in America: What Works?* 2nd ed. (Boston: Allyn and Bacon, 2008), pp. 198–199.

29. Thomas B. Marvell and Carlisle E. Moody, "The Lethal Effects of Three-Strikes Laws," *Journal of Legal Studies* 30 (2001): 89–106; Thomas Kovandzic, John J. Sloan, III, and Lynne M. Vieraitis, "Unintended Consequences of Politically Popular Sentencing Policy: The Homicide-Promoting Effects of 'Three Strikes' in U.S. Cities (1980–1999)," *Criminology and Public Policy* 1 (2002): 159–201.

30. *Lockyer v. Andrade*, 538 U.S. 63 (2003).

31. *Ewing v. California*, 538 U.S. 11 (2003).

32. Ditton and Wilson, *Truth in Sentencing in State Prisons*.

33. See, for example, Matthew Durose and Patrick Langan, *Felony Sentences in State Courts, 2006* (Washington, DC: Bureau of Justice Statistics, 2009), http://bjs.ojp.usdoj.gov/content/pub/pdf/fssc06st.pdf (accessed June 27, 2011).

34. Ibid.

35. Brent Smith and Kelly Damphouse, "Terrorism, Politics, and Punishment: A Test of Structural-Contextual Theory and the Liberation Hypothesis," *Criminology* 36 (1998): 67–92.

36. Stewart D'Alessio and Lisa Stolzenberg, "Socioeconomic Status and the Sentencing of the Traditional Offender," *Journal of Criminal Justice* 21 (1993): 61–77.

37. Cecilia Saulters-Tubbs, "Prosecutorial and Judicial Treatment of Female Offenders," *Federal Probation* 57 (1993): 37–41.

38. See, generally, Janet Johnston, Thomas Kennedy, and I. Gayle Shuman, "Gender Differences in the Sentencing of Felony Offenders," *Federal Probation* 87 (1987): 49–56; Cassia Spohn and Susan Welch, "The Effect of Prior Record in Sentencing Research: An Examination of the Assumption that Any Measure Is Adequate," *Justice Quarterly* 4 (1987): 286–302; David Willison, "The Effects of Counsel on the Severity of Criminal Sentences: A Statistical Assessment," *Justice System Journal* 9 (1984): 87–101.

39. Cassia Spohn, Miriam DeLone, and Jeffrey Spears, "Race/Ethnicity, Gender, and Sentence Severity in Dade County, Florida: An Examination of the Decision to Withhold Adjudication," *Journal of Crime and Justice* 21 (1998): 111–132.

40. Ellen Hochstedler Steury and Nancy Frank, "Gender Bias and Pretrial Release: More Pieces of the Puzzle," *Journal of Criminal Justice* 18 (1990): 417–432.

41. Shimica Gaskins, "Women of Circumstance—The Effects of Mandatory Minimum Sentencing on Women Minimally Involved in Drug Crimes," *American Criminal Law Review* 41 (2004): 1533–1563.

42. Shawn Bushway and Anne Morrison Piehl, "The Inextricable Link between Age and Criminal History in Sentencing," *Crime and Delinquency* 53 (2007): 156–183.

43. Dean Champion, "Elderly Felons and Sentencing Severity: Interregional Variations in Leniency and Sentencing Trends," *Criminal Justice Review* 12 (1987): 7–15.

44. Darrell Steffensmeier, John Kramer, and Jeffery Ulmer, "Age Differences in Sentencing," *Justice Quarterly* 12 (1995): 583–601.

45. Darrell Steffensmeier, Jeffery Ulmer, and John Kramer, "The Interaction of Race, Gender, and Age in Criminal Sentencing: The Punishment Cost of Being Young, Black, and Male," *Criminology* 36 (1998): 763–798.

46. Tracy Nobiling, Cassia Spohn, and Miriam DeLone, "A Tale of Two Counties: Unemployment and Sentence Severity," *Justice Quarterly* 15 (1998): 459–486.

47. Shawn Bushway and Anne Morrison Piehl, "Judging Judicial Discretion: Legal Factors and Racial Discrimination in Sentencing," *Law and Society Review* 35 (2001): 733–765.

48. Michael Tonry, *Malign Neglect: Race, Crime, and Punishment in America* (New York: Oxford University Press, 1995), pp. 105–109.

49. John Wooldredge, "Neighborhood Effects on Felony Sentencing," *Journal of Research in Crime and Delinquency* 44 (2007): 238–263.

50. Cassia Spohn, "Thirty Years of Sentencing Reform: A Quest for a Racially Neutral Sentencing Process, in *Policies, Processes, and Decisions of the Criminal Justice System*, vol. 3, *Criminal Justice 2000* (Washington, DC: U.S. Department of Justice, 2000), pp. 455–456.

51. Ibid.

52. Bruce Western, *Punishment and Inequality in America* (New York: Russell Sage Foundation, 2006).

53. *Payne v. Tennessee*, 111 S. Ct. 2597, 115 L.Ed.2d 720 (1991).

54. Robert Davis and Barbara Smith, "The Effects of Victim Impact Statements on Sentencing Decisions: A Test in an Urban Setting," *Justice Quarterly* 11 (1994): 453–469; Edna Erez and Pamela Tontodonato, "The Effect of Victim Participation in Sentencing on Sentence Outcome," *Criminology* 28 (1990): 451–474.

55. Rodney Kingsworth, Randall MacIntosh, and Jennifer Wentworth, "Sexual Assault: The Role of Prior Relationship and Victim Characteristics in Case Processing," *Justice Quarterly* 16 (1999): 276–302.

56. *Coker v. Georgia*, 433 U.S. 584 (1977); see also *Lockett v. Ohio*, 438 U.S. 586 (1978).

57. For more on this issue, read Hugo Adam and Paul Cassell, *Debating the Death Penalty: Should America Have Capital Punishment? The Experts on Both Sides Make Their Best Case* (London: Oxford University Press, 2003).

58. Stephen Layson, "United States Time-Series Homicide Regressions with Adaptive Expectations," *Bulletin of the New York Academy of Medicine* 62 (1986): 589–619.

59. James Galliher and John Galliher, "A 'Commonsense' Theory of Deterrence and the 'Ideology' of Science: The New York State Death Penalty Debate," *Journal of Criminal Law and Criminology* 92 (2002): 307.

60. Steven Stack, "The Effect of Well-Publicized Executions on Homicide in California," *Journal of Crime and Justice* 21 (1998): 1–12.

61. David Friedrichs, "Comment—Humanism and the Death Penalty: An Alternative Perspective," *Justice Quarterly* 6 (1989): 197–209.

62. Kathleen Maguire and Ann L. Pastore, eds., *Sourcebook of Criminal Justice Statistics, 2002*, www.albany.edu/sourcebook/pdf/t2512010.pdf (accessed June 27, 2011).

63. For an analysis of the formation of public opinion on the death penalty, see Kimberly Cook, "Public Support for the Death Penalty: A Cultural Analysis," paper presented at the annual meeting of the American Society of Criminology, San Francisco, November 1991.

64. Alexis Durham, H. Preston Elrod, and Patrick Kinkade, "Public Support to the Death Penalty: Beyond Gallup," *Justice Quarterly* 13 (1996): 705–736.

65. Samuel R. Gross, Kristen Jacoby, Daniel J. Matheson, Nicholas Montgomery, and Sujata Patil, "Exonerations in the United States: 1989 through 2003," *Journal of Criminal Law and Criminology* 95 (2005): 523–560.

66. David Stewart, "Dealing with Death," *American Bar Association Journal* 80 (1994): 53.

67. "The Innocence Protection Act," editorial, *America* 187 (September 23, 2002): 2–3.

68. Erik Lillquist, "Absolute Certainty and the Death Penalty," *American Criminal Law Review* 42 (2005): 45–92.

69. Elizabeth Purdom and J. Anthony Paredes, "Capital Punishment and Human Sacrifice," in *Facing the Death Penalty: Essays on Cruel and Unusual Punishment*, ed. Michael Radelet (Philadelphia: Temple University Press, 1989), pp. 152–153.

70. Kimberly Cook, "A Passion to Punish: Abortion Opponents Who Favor the Death Penalty," *Justice Quarterly* 15 (1998): 329–346.

71. Julian Roberts, "Capital Punishment, Innocence, and Public Opinion," *Criminology and Public Policy* 4 (2005): 1–3.

72. Kathleen Maguire and Ann Pastore, *Sourcebook of Criminal Justice Statistics, 1995* (Washington, DC: Government Printing Office, 1996), p. 183.

73. James Unnever and Francis Cullen, "Executing the Innocent and Support for Capital Punishment: Implications for Public Policy," *Criminology and Public Policy* 4 (2005): 3–37.

74. Scott Vollum, Dennis Longmire, and Jacqueline Buffington-Vollum, "Confidence in the Death Penalty and Support for Its Use: Exploring the Value-Expressive Dimension of Death Penalty Attitudes," *Justice Quarterly* 21 (2004): 521–546.

75. Gennaro Vito and Thomas Keil, "Elements of Support for Capital Punishment: An Examination of Changing Attitudes," *Journal of Crime and Justice* 21 (1998): 17–25.

76. Denise Paquette Boots, Kathleen Heide, and John Cochran, "Death Penalty Support for Special Offender Populations of Legally Convicted Murderers: Juveniles, the Mentally Retarded, and the Mentally Incompetent," *Behavioral Sciences and the Law* 22 (2004): 223–238.

77. James Unnever and Francis Cullen, "The Racial Divide in Support for the Death Penalty: Does White Racism Matter?" *Social Forces* 85 (2007): 1281–1301.

78. Walter C. Reckless, "Use of the Death Penalty," *Crime and Delinquency* 15 (1969): 43; Thorsten Sellin, "Effect of Repeal and Reintroduction of the Death Penalty on Homicide Rates," in *The Death Penalty*, ed. Thorsten Sellin (Philadelphia: American Law Institute, 1959); Robert H. Dann, "The Deterrent Effect of Capital Punishment," *Friends Social Service Series* 29 (1935): 1; William Bailey and Ruth Peterson, "Murder and Capital Punishment: A Monthly Time-Series Analysis of Execution Publicity," *American Sociological Review* 54 (1989): 722–743; David Phillips, "The Deterrent Effect of Capital Punishment," *American Journal of Sociology* 86 (1980): 139–148; Sam McFarland, "Is Capital Punishment a Short-Term Deterrent to Homicide? A Study of the Effects of Four Recent American Executions," *Journal of Criminal Law and Criminology* 74 (1984): 1014–1032; Richard Lempert, "The Effect of Executions on Homicides: A New Look in an Old Light," *Crime and Delinquency* 29 (1983): 88–115.

79. Jon Sorenson, Robert Wrinkle, Victoria Brewer, and James Marquart, "Capital Punishment and Deterrence: Examining the Effect of Executions on Murder in Texas," *Crime and Delinquency* 45 (1999): 481–493.

80. Isaac Ehrlich, "The Deterrent Effect of Capital Punishment: A Question of Life or Death," *American Economic Review* 65 (1975): 397.

81. For a review, see William Bailey, "The General Prevention Effect of Capital Punishment for Non-Capital Felonies," in *The Death Penalty in America: Current Research*, ed. Robert Bohm (Cincinnati: Anderson, 1991), pp. 21–38.

82. Bijou Yang and David Lester, "The Deterrent Effect of Executions: A Meta-Analysis of Thirty Years after Ehrlich," *Journal of Criminal Justice* 36 (2008): 453–460.

83. Jonathan R. Sorensen and Rocky L. Pilgrim, "An Actuarial Risk of Assessment of Violence Posed by Murder Defendants," *Journal of Criminal Law and Criminology* 90 (2000): 1251–1271.

84. Rick Ruddell and Martin Urbina, "Minority Threat and Punishment: A Cross-National Analysis," *Justice Quarterly* 21 (2004): 903–931.

85. Marian Williams and Jefferson Holcomb, "Racial Disparity and Death Sentences in Ohio," *Journal of Criminal Justice* 29 (2001): 207–218.

86. Jon Sorenson and Donald Wallace, "Prosecutorial Discretion in Seeking Death: An Analysis of Racial Disparity in the Pretrial Stages of Case Processing in a Midwestern County," *Justice Quarterly* 16 (1999): 559–578.

87. Marian R. Williams, "Understanding the Influence of Victim Gender in Death Penalty Cases: The Importance of Victim Race, Sex-Related Victimization, and Jury Decision Making," *Criminology* 45 (2007): 865–891;

Catherine Lee, "Hispanics and the Death Penalty: Discriminatory Charging Practices in San Joaquin County, California," *Journal of Criminal Justice* 35 (2007): 17–27.

88. Jefferson Holcomb, Marian Williams, and Stephen Demuth, "White Female Victims and Death Penalty Disparity Research," *Justice Quarterly* 21 (2004): 877–902.

89. Lawrence Greenfield and David Hinners, *Capital Punishment, 1984* (Washington, DC: Bureau of Justice Statistics, 1985).

90. Gennaro Vito and Thomas Keil, "Capital Sentencing in Kentucky: An Analysis of the Factors Influencing Decision Making in the Post-*Gregg* Period," *Journal of Criminal Law and Criminology* 79 (1988): 483–508.

91. Geoffrey Rapp, "The Economics of Shootouts: Does the Passage of Capital Punishment Laws Protect or Endanger Police Officers?" *Albany Law Review* 65 (2002): 1051–1084.

92. William Bailey, "Disaggregation in Deterrence and Death Penalty Research: The Case of Murder in Chicago," *Journal of Criminal Law and Criminology* 74 (1986): 827–859.

93. Gennaro Vito, Pat Koester, and Deborah Wilson, "Return of the Dead: An Update on the Status of Furman-Commuted Death Row Inmates," in *The Death Penalty in America*, ed. Bohm, pp. 89–100; Gennaro Vito, Deborah Wilson, and Edward Latessa, "Comparison of the Dead: Attributes and Outcomes of Furman-Commuted Death Row Inmates in Kentucky and Ohio," in *The Death Penalty in America*, ed. Bohm, pp. 101–112.

94. John Cochran, Mitchell Chamlin, and Mark Seth, "Deterrence or Brutalization? An Impact Assessment of Oklahoma's Return to Capital Punishment," *Criminology* 32 (1994): 107–134.

95. William Bailey, "Deterrence, Brutalization, and the Death Penalty: Another Examination of Oklahoma's Return to Capital Punishment," *Justice Quarterly* 36 (1998): 711–734.

96. *Hill v. McDonough*, 547 U.S. 573 (2006).

97. Robert Johnson, *Death Work: A Study of the Modern Execution Process* (Pacific Grove, CA: Brooks/Cole, 1990).

98. LiYing Li, "The Tainted Milk Scandal: Punishing Economic Criminals in China," unpublished paper (Denver: Metropolitan College of Denver, 2011).

99. Tracy L. Snell, *Capital Punishment, 2009* (Washington, DC: Bureau of Justice Statistics, 2010), p. 12.

100. See, for example, Ernest Van Den Haag, *Punishing Criminals: Concerning a Very Old and Painful Question* (New York: Basic Books, 1975), pp. 209–211; Walter Berns, "Defending the Death Penalty," *Crime and Delinquency* 26 (1980): 503–511.

101. Thoroddur Bjarnason and Michael Welch, "Father Knows Best: Parishes, Priests, and American Catholic Parishioners' Attitudes toward Capital Punishment," *Journal for the Scientific Study of Religion* 43 (2004): 103–118.

102. Franklin Zimring, *The Contradictions of American Capital Punishment* (London: Oxford University Press, 2003).

103. Vance McLaughlin and Paul Blackman, "Mass Legal Executions in Georgia," *Georgia Historical Quarterly* 88 (2004): 66–84.

104. Austin Sarat, "Innocence, Error, and the 'New Abolitionism': A Commentary," *Criminology and Public Policy* 4 (2005): 45–53.

105. *Furman v. Georgia*, 408 U.S. 238 (1972).

106. *Gregg v. Georgia*, 428 U.S. 153 (1976).

107. Ibid., at pp. 205–207.

108. *Ring v. Arizona*, 536 U.S. 584 (2002).

109. *Coker v. Georgia*, 430 U.S. 349 (1977); *Kennedy v. Louisiana*, 554 U.S. 407 (2008).

110. *Ford v. Wainwright*, 477 U.S. 399 (1986).

111. *Atkins v. Virginia*, 536 U.S. 304 (2002).

112. *Roper v. Simmons*, 543 U.S. 551 (2005).

Chapter 10, Community Sentences: Probation, Intermediate Sanctions, and Restorative Justice

1. UPI.Com, "Lawrence Taylor Gets Probation in Sex Case," March 22, 2011, www.upi.com/Sports_News/2011/03/22/Lawrence-Taylor-gets-probation-in-sex-case/UPI-92091300814565/ (accessed June 16, 2011).

2. Starpulse.com, "Mel Gibson Gets Probation, Must Undergo Counseling," March 11th, 2011, www.starpulse.com/news/index.php/2011/03/11/mel_gibson_gets_probation_must_undergo (accessed June 16, 2011).

3. Ken Lee, "Chris Brown Avoids Jail Time in Rihanna Assault," People.com, June 22, 2009, www.people.com/people/article/0,,20286732,00.html (accessed June 16, 2011).

4. Brandon Applegate, Hayden Smith, Alicia Sitren, and Nicolette Fariello Springer, "From the Inside: The Meaning of Probation to Probationers," *Criminal Justice Review* 34 (2009): 80–95.

5. For a history of probation, see Edward Sieh, "From Augustus to the Progressives: A Study of Probation's Formative Years," *Federal Probation* 57 (1993): 67–72.

6. Ibid.

7. David Rothman, *Conscience and Convenience* (Boston: Little, Brown, 1980), pp. 82–117.

8. *Gall v. United States*, 552 U.S. 38 (2007).

9. Lauren Glaze, Thomas Bonczar, and Fan Zhang, *Probation and Parole in the United States, 2009* (Washington, DC: Bureau of Justice Statistics, 2010), http://bjs.ojp.usdoj.gov/content/pub/pdf/ppus09.pdf.

10. Sean Rosenmerkel, Matthew Durose and Donald Farole, Jr., *Felony Sentences in State Courts, 2006* (Washington, DC: Bureau of Justice Statistics, 2009), http://bjs.ojp.usdoj.gov/content/pub/ascii/fssc06st.txt (accessed June 16, 2011).

11. Tracey Kyckelhahn and Thomas Cohen, *Felony Defendants in Large Urban Counties, 2004* (Washington, DC: Bureau of Justice Statistics, 2008).

12. Heather Barklage, Dane Miller, and Gene Bonham, Jr., "Probation Conditions vs. Probation Officer Directives," *Federal Probation* 70 (2006), www.uscourts.gov/uscourts/FederalCourts/PPS/Fedprob/2006-12/probationconditions.html (accessed July 27, 2011).

13. Karl Hanson and Suzanne Wallace-Carpretta, "Predictors of Criminal Recidivism among Male Batterers," *Psychology, Crime and Law* 10 (2004): 413–427.

14. *Higdon v. United States*, 627 F.2d 893 (9th Cir., 1980).

15. *United States v. Lee*, No. 01-4485 01/07/03, *United States v. Lee*, PICS N. 03-0023.

16. *United States v. Gallo*, 20 F.3d 7 (1st Cir., 1994).

17. Todd Clear and Edward Latessa, "Probation Officers' Roles in Intensive Supervision: Surveillance versus Treatment," *Justice Quarterly* 10 (1993): 441–462.

18. Paul von Zielbauer, "Probation Dept. Is Now Arming Officers Supervising Criminals," *New York Times*, August 7, 2003, p. 5.

19. Jeffrey Lin, Joel Miller, and Mayumi Fukushima, "Juvenile Probation Officers Dispositional Recommendations: Predictive Factors and Their Alignment with Predictors of Recidivism," *Journal of Crime and Justice* 31 (2008): 1–34.

20. Melinda Schlager, "Validity of the Level of Service Inventory—Revised (LSI-R) among African American and Hispanic Male Offenders," *Criminal Justice and Behavior* 34 (2007): 545–554; Carolin Kröner, Cornelis Stadtland, Matthias Eidt, and Norbert Nedopil, The Validity of the Violence Risk Appraisal Guide (VRAG) in Predicting Criminal Recidivism," *Criminal Behaviour and Mental Health* 17 (2007): 89–100.

21. Lawrence Sherman, "Use Probation to Prevent Murder," *Criminology and Public Policy* 6 (2007): 843–849.

22. Diana Wendy Fitzgibbon, "Deconstructing Probation: Risk and Developments in Practice," *Journal of Social Work Practice* 22 (2008): 85–101.

23. Fox News Chicago, "Rape Victim's Mom Sues Attacker and Probation Chief," January 26, 2011, www.myfoxchicago.com/dpp/news/metro/acurie-collier-rape-victim-mom-sues-attacker-probation-officer-20110126 (accessed June 16, 2011).

24. National Law Enforcement Corrections Technology Center, "Community Corrections Directions," *Tech Beat* (Spring 2007), http://198.77.71.164/TechBeat%20Files/CommunityCorrections.pdf (accessed July 27, 2011).

25. Mary McMurran, "Motivational Interviewing with Offenders: A Systematic Review," *Legal and Criminological Psychology* 14 (2009): 83–100; Scott Walters, Amanda Vader, Norma Nguyen, Robert Harris, and Jennifer Eells, "Motivational Interviewing as a Supervision Strategy in Probation: A Randomized Effectiveness Trial," *Journal of Offender Rehabilitation* 49 (2010): 309–323.

26. *Minnesota v. Murphy*, 465 U.S. 420, 104 S.Ct. 1136, 79 L.Ed.2d 409 (1984).

27. *Griffin v. Wisconsin*, 483 U.S. 868, 107 S.Ct. 3164, 97 L.Ed.2d 709 (1987).

28. *United States v. Knights*, 122 S.Ct. 587 (2001).

29. *Mempa v. Rhay*, 389 U.S. 128, 88 S.Ct. 254, 19 L.Ed.2d 336 (1967).

30. *Morrissey v. Brewer*, 408 U.S. 471, 92 S.Ct. 2593, 33 L.Ed.2d 484 (1972).

31. *Gagnon v. Scarpelli*, 411 U.S. 778, 93 S.Ct. 1756, 36 L.Ed.2d 656 (1973).

32. *Beardon v. Georgia* 33 CrL 3101 (1983).

33. *United States v. Granderson*, 114 Ct. 1259, 127 L.Ed.2d 611 (1994).

34. *Probation and Parole, 2009.*

35. M. Kevin Gray, Monique Fields, and Sheila Royo Maxwell, "Examining Probation Violations: Who, What, and When," *Crime and Delinquency* 47 (2001): 537–557.

36. Nancy Rodriguez and Vincent Webb, "Probation Violations, Revocations, and Imprisonment: The Decisions of Probation Officers, Prosecutors, and Judges Pre- and Post-Mandatory Drug Treatment," *Criminal Justice Policy Review,* 2007 (18): 3–30.

37. Kevin Minor, James Wells, and Crissy Sims, "Recidivism among Federal Probationers—Predicting Sentence Violations," *Federal Probation* 67 (2003): 31–37.

38. Cassia Spohn and David Holleran, "The Effect of Imprisonment on Recidivism Rates of Felony Offenders: A Focus on Drug Offenders," *Criminology* 40 (2002): 329–359.

39. Christopher Krebs, Kevin Strom, Willem Koetse, and Pamela Lattimore, "The Impact of Residential and Non-residential Drug Treatment on Recidivism among Drug-Involved Probationers: A Survival Analysis," *Crime and Delinquency* 55 (2009): 442–471.

40. Eladio Castillo and Leanne Alarid Fiftal, "Factors Associated with Recidivism among Offenders with Mental Illness," *International Journal of Offender Therapy and Comparative Criminology* 55 (2011): 98–117.

41. Joan Petersilia, Susan Turner, James Kahan, and Joyce Peterson, *Granting Felons Probation: Public Risks and Alternatives* (Santa Monica, CA: Rand, 1985).

42. Spohn and Holleran, "The Effect of Imprisonment on Recidivism Rates of Felony Offenders."

43. Paula M. Ditton, *Mental Health and Treatment of Inmates and Probationers* (Washington, DC: Bureau of Justice Statistics, 1999).

44. Kathryn Morgan, "Factors Associated with Probation Outcome," *Journal of Criminal Justice* 22 (1994): 341–353.

45. Naomi Freeman, "Predictors of Rearrest for Rapists and Child Molesters on Probation," *Criminal Justice and Behavior* 34 (2007): 752–768.

46. Kathryn Morgan, "Factors Influencing Probation Outcome: A Review of the Literature," *Federal Probation* 57 (1993): 23–29.

47. Diana Wendy Fitzgibbon, "Deconstructing Probation."

48. Joan Petersilia, "Probation in the United States," in *Crime and Justice: A Review of Research* 21 (Chicago: University of Chicago Press, 1997), p. 185.

49. "Law in Massachusetts Requires Probationers to Pay 'Day Fees,'" *Criminal Justice Newsletter*, September 15, 1988, p. 1.

50. Peter Finn and Dale Parent, *Making the Offender Foot the Bill: A Texas Program* (Washington, DC: National Institute of Justice, 1992).

51. State of Arizona, Senate Bill 1476 (2008), www.votesmart.org/billtext/18014.pdf (accessed June 16, 2011).

52. Nicole Leeper Piquero, "A Recidivism Analysis of Maryland's Community Probation Program," *Journal of Criminal Justice* 31 (2003): 295–308.

53. Todd R. Clear, "Places Not Cases: Rethinking the Probation Focus," *Howard Journal of Criminal Justice* 44 (2005): 172–184.

54. Andrew Klein and Ann Crowe, "Findings from an Outcome Examination of Rhode Island's Specialized Domestic Violence Probation Supervision Program," *Violence against Women* 14 (2008): 226–246.

55. Roberto Hugh Potter and Timothy Akers, "Improving the Health of Minority Communities through Probation-Public Health Collaborations: An Application of the Epidemiological Criminology Framework," *Journal of Offender Rehabilitation* 49 (2010): 595–609.

56. Private Probation Services, www.privateprobationservices.com (accessed June 16, 2011).

57. Christine Schloss and Leanne Alarid, "Standards in the Privatization of Probation Services: A Statutory Analysis," *Criminal Justice Review* 32 (2007): 233–245.

58. "HOPE in Hawaii: Swift and Sure Changes in Probation," National Institute of Justice, 2008, www.ncjrs.gov/pdffiles1/nij/222758.pdf (accessed June 16, 2011).

59. "Evaluating Delaware's Decide Your Time Program for Drug-Using Offenders Under Community Supervision," National Institute of Justice, 2011, www.nij.gov/nij/topics/corrections/community/drug-offenders/decide-your-time.htm (accessed June 16, 2011).

60. Todd Clear and Patricia Hardyman, "The New Intensive Supervision Movement," *Crime and Delinquency* 36 (1990): 42–60.

61. Norval Morris and Michael Tonry, *Between Prison and Probation: Intermediate Punishments in a Rational Sentencing System* (New York: Oxford University Press, 1990).

62. Ibid., p. 8.

63. For a thorough review of these programs, see James Byrne, Arthur Lurigio, and Joan Petersilia, eds., *Smart Sentencing: The Emergence of Intermediate Sanctions* (Newbury Park, CA: Sage, 1993). Hereinafter cited as *Smart Sentencing*.

64. Michael Tonry and Richard Will, *Intermediate Sanctions* (Washington, DC: National Institute of Justice, 1990).

65. Sally Hillsman and Judith Greene, "Tailoring Fines to the Financial Means of Offenders," *Judicature* 72 (1988): 38–45.

66. George Cole, "Monetary Sanctions: The Problem of Compliance," in *Smart Sentencing*, pp. 51–64.

67. *Tate v. Short*, 401 U.S. 395, 91 S.Ct. 668, 28 L.Ed.2d 130 (1971).

68. Doris Layton MacKenzie, "Evidence-Based Corrections: Identifying What Works," *Crime and Delinquency* 46 (2000): 457–472.

69. John L. Worrall, "Addicted to the Drug War: The Role of Civil Asset Forfeiture as a Budgetary Necessity in Contemporary Law Enforcement," *Journal of Criminal Justice* 29 (2001): 171–187.

70. C. Yorke, *Some Consideration on the Law of Forfeiture for High Treason*, 2d ed. (1746), pp. 26, cited in David Fried, "Rationalizing Criminal Forfeiture," *Journal of Criminal Law and Criminology* 79 (1988): 328–436.

71. Fried, "Rationalizing Criminal Forfeiture," p. 436.

72. James B. Jacobs, Coleen Friel, and Edward O'Callaghan, "Pension Forfeiture: A Problematic Sanction for Public Corruption," *American Criminal Law Review* 35 (1997): 57–92.

73. Worrall, "Addicted to the Drug War."

74. For a general review, see Burt Galaway and Joe Hudson, *Criminal Justice, Restitution, and Reconciliation* (New York: Criminal Justice Press, 1990); Robert Carter, Jay Cocks, and Daniel Glazer, "Community Service: A Review of the Basic Issues," *Federal Probation* 51 (1987): 4–11.

75. Frederick Allen and Harvey Treger, "Community Service Orders in Federal Probation: Perceptions of Probationers and Host Agencies," *Federal Probation* 54 (1990): 8–14.

76. Gail Caputo, "Community Service in Texas: Results of a Probation Survey," *Corrections Compendium* 30 (2005): 8–12.

77. Sudipto Roy, "Two Types of Juvenile Restitution Programs in Two Midwestern Counties: A Comparative Study," *Federal Probation* 57 (1993): 48–53.

78. Joan Petersilia, *The Influence of Criminal Justice Research* (Santa Monica, CA: Rand, 1987).

79. Ibid.

80. Jodi Lane, Susan Turner, Terry Fain, and Amber Sehgal, "Evaluating an Experimental Intensive Juvenile Probation Program: Supervision and Official Outcomes," *Crime and Delinquency* 51 (2005): 26–52.

81. Greg Warchol, "Intensive Supervision Probation: An Impact Evaluation," *Justice Professional* 13 (2000): 219–232.

82. James Byrne and Linda Kelly, "Restructuring Probation as an Intermediate Sanction: An Evaluation of the Massachusetts Intensive Probation Supervision Program," final report to the National Institute of Justice, Research Program on the Punishment and Control of Offenders, Washington, DC, 1989.

83. James Ryan, "Who Gets Revoked? A Comparison of Intensive Supervision Successes and Failures in Vermont," *Crime and Delinquency* 43 (1997): 104–118.

84. Angela Robertson, Paul Grimes, and Kevin Rogers, "A Short-Run Cost-Benefit Analysis of Community-Based Interventions for Juvenile Offenders," *Crime and Delinquency* 47 (2001): 265–284.

85. Linda Smith and Ronald Akers, "A Comparison of Recidivism of Florida's Community Control and Prison: A Five-Year Survival Analysis," *Journal of Research in Crime and Delinquency* 30 (1993): 267–292.

86. Robert N. Altman, Robert E. Murray, and Evey B. Wooten, "Home Confinement: A 90s Approach to Community Supervision," *Federal Probation* 61 (1997): 30–32.

87. Omnilink Systems, www.omnilink.com (accessed June 16, 2011).

88. William Burrell and Robert Gable, "From B. F. Skinner to Spiderman to Martha Stewart: The Past, Present and Future of Electronic Monitoring of Offenders," *Journal of Offender Rehabilitation* 46 (2008): 101–118; Hugh Downing, "Emergence of Global Positioning Satellite (GPS) Systems in Correctional Applications," *Corrections Today* 68 (2006): 42–45.

89. Edna Erez and Peter Ibarra, "Making Your Home a Shelter: Electronic Monitoring and Victim Re-Entry in Domestic Violence Cases," *British Journal of Criminology* 47 (2007): 100–120.

90. Matthew DeMichele, Brian Payne, and Deeanna Button, "Electronic Monitoring of Sex Offenders: Identifying Unanticipated Consequences and Implications," *Journal of Offender Rehabilitation* 46 (2008): 119–135.

91. Kathy Padgett, William Bales, and Thomas Blomberg, "Under Surveillance: An Empirical Test of the Effectiveness and Consequences of Electronic Monitoring," *Criminology and Public Policy* 5 (2006): 61–91.

92. Burrell and Gable, "From B. F. Skinner to Spiderman to Martha Stewart."

93. William Bales, Karen Mann, Thomas Blomberg, Gerry Gaes, Kelle Barrick, Karla Dhungana, and Brian McManus, "A Quantitative and Qualitative Assessment of Electronic Monitoring," Florida State University, College of Criminology and Criminal Justice, Center for Criminology and Public Policy Research, January 2010, www.ncjrs.gov/pdffiles1/nij/grants/230530.pdf (accessed June 16, 2011).

94. See, generally, Edward Latessa and Lawrence Travis III, "Residential Community Correctional Programs," in *Smart Sentencing*, pp. 65–79.

95. Dale Parent, *Day Reporting Centers for Criminal Offenders: A Descriptive Analysis of Existing Programs* (Washington, DC: National Institute of Justice, 1990); Jack McDevitt and Robyn Miliano, "Day Reporting Centers: An Innovative Concept in Intermediate Sanctions," in *Smart Sentencing*, pp. 80–105.

96. David Diggs and Stephen Pieper, "Using Day Reporting Centers as an Alternative to Jail," *Federal Probation* 58 (1994): 9–12.

97. Michael Ostermann, "An Analysis of New Jersey's Day Reporting Center and Halfway Back Programs: Embracing the Rehabilitative Ideal Through Evidence Based Practices," *Journal of Offender Rehabilitation* 48 (2009): 139–153.

98. Dae-Young Kim, Hee-Jong Joo, and William McCarty, "Risk Assessment and Classification of Day Reporting Center Clients: An Actuarial Approach, *Criminal Justice and Behavior* 35 (2008): 792–812.

99. Amy Craddock, "Day Reporting Center Completion: Comparison of Individual and Multilevel Models," *Crime and Delinquency* 55 (2009): 105–133; Sudipto Roy and Shannon Barton, "Convicted Drunk Drivers in Electronic Monitoring Home Detention and Day Reporting Centers," *Federal Probation* 70 (2006), www.uscourts.gov/uscourts/FederalCourts/PPS/Fedprob/2006-06/drunkdrivers.html (accessed July 27, 2011).

100. Kathleen Daly and Russ Immarigeon, "The Past, Present, and Future of Restorative Justice: Some Critical Reflections," *Contemporary Justice Review* 1 (1998): 21–45.

101. John Braithwaite, *Crime, Shame, and Reintegration* (Melbourne, Australia: Cambridge University Press, 1989).

102. Gene Stephens, "The Future of Policing: From a War Model to a Peace Model," in *The Past, Present and Future of American Criminal Justice*, ed. Brendan Maguire and Polly Radosh (Dix Hills, NY: General Hall, 1996), pp. 77–93.

103. Kay Pranis, "Peacemaking Circles: Restorative Justice in Practice Allows Victims and Offenders to Begin Repairing the Harm," *Corrections Today* 59 (1997): 74.

104. Carol LaPrairie, "The 'New' Justice: Some Implications for Aboriginal Communities," *Canadian Journal of Criminology* 40 (1998): 61–79.

105. David R. Karp and Beau Breslin, "Restorative Justice in School Communities," *Youth and Society* 33 (2001): 249–272.

106. Paul Jesilow and Deborah Parsons, "Community Policing as Peacemaking," *Policing and Society* 10 (2000): 163–183.

107. Aidan Wilcox, Richard Young, and Carolyn Hoyle, "Two-Year Resanctioning Study: A Comparison of Restorative and Traditional Cautions," British Home Office, 2004, http://webarchive.nationalarchives.gov.uk/20110220105210/rds.homeoffice.gov.uk/rds/pdfs04/rdsolr5704.pdf (accessed June 16, 2011); Lynette Parker, "Evaluating Restorative Programmes: Reports from Two Countries," Restorative Justice.org, June 2005, www.restorativejustice.org/editions/2005/june05/evaluations (accessed June 16, 2011); Aidan Wilcox and Richard Young, "How Green Was Thames Valley? Policing the Image of Restorative Justice Cautions," *Policing and Society* 17 (2007): 141–163.

108. Australian Institute of Criminology, *Restorative Justice: An Australian Perspective*, www.aic.gov.au/meta-data/categories/classification/crime%20and%20the%20community/restorative%20justice.aspx (accessed July 27, 2011).

109. Gordon Bazemore and Curt Taylor Griffiths, "Conferences, Circles, Boards, and Mediations: The 'New Wave' of Community Justice Decision Making," *Federal Probation* 61 (1997): 25–37.

110. Mark Umbreit and Rina Ritter, "Arab Offenders Meet Jewish Victim: Restorative Family Dialogue in Israel," *Conflict Resolution Quarterly* 24 (2006): 99–109.

111. John Braithwaite, "Setting Standards for Restorative Justice," *British Journal of Criminology* 42 (2002): 563–577.

112. Nancy Rodriguez, "Restorative Justice, Communities, and Delinquency: Whom Do We Reintegrate?" *Criminology and Public Policy* 4 (2005): 103–130.

113. John Braithwaite, "Setting Standards for Restorative Justice."

114. David Altschuler, "Community Justice Initiatives: Issues and Challenges in the U.S. Context," *Federal Probation* 65 (2001): 28–33.

115. Lois Presser and Patricia Van Voorhis, "Values and Evaluation: Assessing Processes and Outcomes of Restorative Justice Programs," *Crime and Delinquency* 48 (2002): 162–189.

116. Sharon Levrant, Francis Cullen, Betsy Fulton, and John Wozniak, "Reconsidering Restorative Justice: The Corruption of Benevolence Revisited? *Crime and Delinquency* 45 (1999): 3–28.

117. Dean Gromet and John Darley, "Restoration and Retribution: How Including Retributive Components Affects the Acceptability of Restorative Justice Procedures," *Social Justice Research* 19 (2006): 395–432.

118. Michael E. Smith, *What Future for "Public Safety" and "Restorative Justice" in Community Corrections?* (Washington, DC: National Institute of Justice, 2001).

Box Source Notes
Careers in Criminal Justice
Probation Officer

Andrew Alpert, "Probation Officers and Correctional Treatment Specialists," *Occupational Outlook Quarterly* 45 (2001), www.bls.gov/opub/ooq/2001/Fall/art05.pdf (accessed June 16, 2011); Bureau of Labor Statistics, "Probation Officers and Correctional Treatment Specialists—Working to Rehabilitate Offenders," www.bls.gov/opub/ted/2001/sept/wk4/art05.htm (accessed June 16, 2011).

Contemporary Issues in Criminal Justice:
Evidence-Based Justice
Treating Probationers with Cognitive Behavioral Therapy

Sesha Kethineni and Jeremy Braithwaite, "The Effects of a Cognitive-Behavioral Program for At-Risk Youth: Changes in Attitudes, Social Skills, Family, and Community and Peer Relationships," *Victims and Offenders* 6 (2011): 93–116; Patrick Clark, "Preventing Future Crime with Cognitive Behavioral Therapy," *National Institute of Justice Journal* 265 (2010), www.ojp.usdoj.gov/nij/journals/265/therapy.htm (accessed June 17, 2011); Martin Lipsey, "The Primary Factors that Characterize Effective Interventions with Juvenile Offenders: A Meta-analytic Overview," *Victims and Offenders* 4 (2009): 124–147; Nana Landenberger and Martin Lipsey, "The Positive Effects of Cognitive-behavioral Programs for Offenders: A Meta-analysis of Factors Associated with Effective Treatment," *Journal of Experimental Criminology* 1 (2005): 451–476.

Chapter 11, Corrections: History, Institutions, and Populations

1. *Graham v. Florida*, No. 08-7412, www.law.cornell.edu/supct/html/08-7412.ZS.html (accessed June 21, 2011).
2. William Sabol, Heather West, and Sarah Greenman, *Prisoners in 2009* (Washington, DC: Bureau of Justice Statistics, 2010), http://bjs.ojp.usdoj.gov/content/pub/pdf/p09.pdf (accessed June 21, 2011).
3. See David Fogel, *We Are the Living Proof*, 2d ed. (Cincinnati: Anderson, 1978); Andrew von Hirsch, *Doing Justice: The Choice of Punishments* (New York: Hill and Wang, 1976).
4. Francis Cullen, "The Twelve People Who Saved Rehabilitation: How the Science of Criminology Made a Difference," *Criminology* 43 (2005): 1–42.
5. Malcolm Feeley and Jonathan Simon, "The New Penology: Notes on the Emerging Strategy of Corrections and Its Implications," *Criminology* 30 (2006): 449–474.
6. Thomas Stucky, Karen Heimer, and Joseph Lang, "Partisan Politics, Electoral Competition, and Imprisonment: An Analysis of States over Time," *Criminology* 43 (2005): 211–247.
7. Among the most helpful sources in developing this section were Mark Colvin, *Penitentiaries, Reformatories, and Chain Gangs* (New York: St. Martin's Press, 1997); Benedict Alper, *Prisons Inside-Out* (Cambridge, MA: Ballinger, 1974); Harry Elmer Barnes, *The Story of Punishment*, 2d ed. (Montclair, NJ: Patterson-Smith, 1972); Gustave de Beaumont and Alexis de Tocqueville, *On the Penitentiary System in the United States and Its Applications in France* (Carbondale: Southern Illinois University Press, 1964); Orlando Lewis, *The Development of American Prisons and Prison Customs, 1776–1845* (Montclair, NJ: Patterson-Smith, 1967); Georg Rusche and Otto Kircheimer, *Punishment and Social Structure* (New York: Russell and Russell, 1939); Samuel Walker, *Popular Justice* (New York: Oxford University Press, 1980); Graeme Newman, *The Punishment Response* (Philadelphia: J. B. Lippincott, 1978); David Rothman, *Conscience and Convenience* (Boston: Little, Brown, 1980).
8. Frederick Pollock and Frederick Maitland, *History of English Law* (London: Cambridge University Press, 1952).
9. Marvin Wolfgang, "Crime and Punishment in Renaissance Florence," *Journal of Criminal Law and Criminology* 81 (1990): 567–584.
10. John Howard, *The State of Prisons*, 4th ed. (1792; reprint, Montclair, NJ: Patterson-Smith, 1973).
11. Alexis Durham III, "Newgate of Connecticut: Origins and Early Days of an Early American Prison," *Justice Quarterly* 6 (1989): 89–116.
12. Dario Melossi and Massimo Pavarini, *The Prison and the Factory: Origins of the Penitentiary System* (Totowa, NJ: Barnes and Noble, 1981).
13. Lewis, *Development of American Prisons and Prison Customs*, p. 17.
14. See, generally, David Rothman, *The Discovery of the Asylum* (Boston: Little, Brown, 1970).
15. Ibid., p. 144.
16. Walker, *Popular Justice*, p. 70.
17. Ibid., p. 71.
18. Beverly Smith, "Military Training at New York's Elmira Reformatory, 1880–1920," *Federal Probation* 52 (1988): 33–41.
19. William Parker, *Parole: Origins, Development, Current Practices, and Statutes* (College Park, MD: American Correctional Association, 1972); Samuel Walker, *Popular Justice*.
20. This section leans heavily on David Rothman, *Conscience and Convenience*.
21. Ibid., p. 23.
22. Ibid., p. 133.
23. 18 U.S.C. 1761.
24. Barbara Auerbach, George Sexton, Franlin Farrow, and Robert Lawson, *Work in American Prisons: The Private Sector Gets Involved* (Washington, DC: National Institute of Justice, 1988), p. 72.
25. See, generally, Jameson Doig, *Criminal Corrections: Ideals and Realities* (Lexington, MA: Lexington Books, 1983).
26. Todd Minton, *Jail Inmates at Midyear 2010: Statistical Tables* (Washington, DC: Bureau of Justice Statistics, 2011), http://bjs.ojp.usdoj.gov/content/pub/pdf/jim10st.pdf (accessed June 21, 2011).
27. National Institute of Corrections and the National Center on Institutions and Alternatives (NCIA), *National Study of Jail Suicide: 20 Years Later (2010)*, /www.ncianet.org/suicideprevention/documents/SuicideStudy-20YearsLater.pdf (accessed July 28, 2011).
28. Brandon Applegate, Ray Surette, and Bernard McCarthy, "Detention and Desistance from Crime: Evaluating the Influence of a New Generation of Jail on Recidivism," *Journal of Criminal Justice* 27 (1999): 539–548.
29. *Justice Expenditure and Employment in the United States, 2006* (Washington, DC: Bureau of Justice Statistics, 2007), http://bjs.ojp.usdoj.gov/index.cfm?ty=tp&tid=5 (accessed June 21, 2011).
30. Human Rights Watch, *Prison Conditions in the United States*, www.hrw.org/wr2k2/prisons.html (accessed June 21, 2011).
31. "Suit Alleges Violations in California's 'Super-Max' Prison," *Criminal Justice Newsletter*, September 1, 1993, p. 2.
32. Jody Sundt, Thomas Castellano, and Chad Briggs, "The Sociopolitical Context of Prison Violence and Its Control: A Case Study of Supermax and Its Effect in Illinois," *Prison Journal* 88 (2008): 94–122.
33. Daniel Mears, "An Assessment of Supermax Prisons Using an Evaluation Research Framework," *Prison Journal* 88 (2008): 43–68 ; Daniel Mears and Jennifer Castro, "Wardens' Views on the Wisdom of Supermax Prisons," *Crime and Delinquency* 52 (2006): 398–431; Daniel Mears and Jamie Watson, "Towards a Fair and Balanced Assessment of Supermax Prisons," *Justice Quarterly* 23 (2006): 232–270.
34. James Anderson, Laronistine Dyson, and Jerald Burns, *Boot Camps: An Intermediate Sanction* (Lanham, MD: University Press of America, 1999), pp. 1–17.
35. Ibid., 328–329.
36. Doris Layton Mackenzie, "Boot Camp Prisons: Components, Evaluations, and Empirical Issues," *Federal Probation* 54 (1990): 44–52; see also "Boot Camp Programs Grow in Number and Scope," *NIJ Reports* (November/December 1990): 6–8.
37. Doris Layton Mackenzie and James Shaw, "The Impact of Shock Incarceration on Technical Violations and New Criminal Activities," *Justice Quarterly* 10 (1993): 463–487.

38. Vanessa St. Gerard, "Federal Prisons to Eliminate Boot Camps," *Corrections Today* 67 (2005): 13–16.

39. Correctional Research Associates, *Treating Youthful Offenders in the Community: An Evaluation Conducted by A. J. Reiss* (Washington, DC: Correctional Research Associates, 1966).

40. Kevin Krajick, "Not on My Block: Local Opposition Impedes the Search for Alternatives," *Corrections Magazine* 6 (1980): 15–27.

41. Corrections Corporation of America, www.cca.com (accessed June 28, 2011).

42. GEO Corporation, www.thegeogroupinc.com/facilityoperations.asp (accessed June 28, 2011).

43. Richard Harding, "Private Prisons," in *Crime and Justice: An Annual Edition*, ed. Michael Tonry (Chicago: University of Chicago Press, 2001), pp. 265–347.

44. William Bales, Laura Bedard, Susan Quinn, David Ensley, and Glen Holley, "Recidivism of Public and Private State Prison Inmates in Florida," *Criminology and Public Policy* 4 (2005): 57–82; Lonn Lanza-Kaduce, Karen Parker, and Charles Thomas, "A Comparative Recidivism Analysis of Releases from Private and Public Prisons," *Crime and Delinquency* 45 (1999): 28–47.

45. Charles Thomas, "Recidivism of Public and Private State Prison Inmates in Florida: Issues and Unanswered Questions," *Criminology and Public Policy* 4 (2005): 89–99; Travis Pratt and Jeff Maahs, "Are Private Prisons More Cost-Effective than Public Prisons? A Meta-Analysis of Evaluation Research Studies," *Crime and Delinquency* 45 (1999): 358–371.

46. Ira Robbins, *The Legal Dimensions of Private Incarceration* (Chicago: American Bar Association, 1988).

47. Danica Coto, "Medical Care Company Named in Numerous Jail Lawsuits," *Charlotte Observer*, August 30, 2004.

48. Sabol, West, and Greenman, *Prisoners in 2009*.

49. Pew Foundation, *1 in 31: The Long Reach of American Corrections*, www.pewcenteronthestates.org/uploadedFiles/PSPP_1in31_report_FINAL_WEB_3-26-09.pdf (accessed June 21, 2011).

50. Pew Charitable Trusts, *Collateral Costs: Incarceration's Effect on Economic Mobility* (Washington, DC: Pew Charitable Trusts, 2010), www.pewtrusts.org/uploadedFiles/wwwpewtrustsorg/Reports/Economic_Mobility/Collateral%20Costs%20FINAL.pdf (accessed June 21, 2011).

51. Caroline Wolf Harlow, *Education and Correctional Populations* (Washington, DC: Bureau of Justice Statistics, 2003).

52. Greg Greenberg and Robert Rosenheck, "Homelessness in the State and Federal Prison Population," *Criminal Behaviour and Mental Health* 18 (2008): 88–103.

53. Seena Fazel and John Danesh, "Serious Mental Disorder in 23,000 Prisoners: A Systematic Review of Sixty-Two Surveys," *Lancet* 359 (2002): 545–561.

54. West, Sabol, and Greenman, *Prisoners in 2009*.

55. Sean Nicholson-Crotty, The Impact of Sentencing Guidelines on State-level Sanctions: An Analysis over Time," *Crime and Delinquency* 50 (2004): 395–411.

56. Todd Clear, *Harm in American Penology: Offenders, Victims, and Their Communities* (Albany: State University of New York Press, 1994).

57. Benjamin Steiner and John Wooldredge, "Comparing State- versus Facility-level Effects on Crowding in U.S. Correctional Facilities," *Crime and Delinquency* 54 (2008): 259–290.

58. Thomas P. Bonczar and Allen J. Beck, *Lifetime Likelihood of Going to State or Federal Prison* (Washington, DC: Bureau of Justice Statistics, 1997).

Box Source Notes
Careers in Criminal Justice
Corrections Counselor

Bureau of Labor Statistics, U.S. Department of Labor, "Correctional Counselor," *Occupational Outlook Handbook, 2010–11 Edition*, www.bls.gov/oco/ocos265.htm.

Criminal Justice and Technology
Technocorrections: Contemporary Correctional Technology

Philip Bulman, "Using Technology to Make Prisons and Jails Safer," *NIJ Journal* 262 (March 2009), www.ojp.usdoj.gov/nij/journals/262/corrections-technology.htm (accessed June 22, 2011); John Ward, "Jump-Starting Projects to Automate Correctional Processes," *Corrections Today* 68 (2006): 82–83; Debbie Mahaffey, "Security and Technology: The Human Side," *Corrections Today* 66 (2004): 8; Frank Lu and Laurence Wolfe, "Automated Record Tracking (SMART) Application," *Corrections Today* 66 (2004): 78–81

Chapter 12, Prison Life: Living in and Leaving Prison

1. Mark S. Hamm, "Prisoner Radicalization: Assessing the Threat in U.S. Correctional Institutions," *NIJ Journal* 261 (2008), www.nij.gov/nij/journals/261/prisoner-radicalization.htm (accessed July 1, 2011).

2. Sarah Lawrence and Jeremy Travis, *The New Landscape of Imprisonment: Mapping America's Prison Expansion* (Washington, DC: Urban Institute, 2004), www.urban.org/UploadedPDF/410994_mapping_prisons.pdf.

3. James Stephan and Jennifer Karberg, *Census of State and Federal Correctional Facilities, 2000* (Washington, DC: Bureau of Justice Statistics, 2003, updated 2008).

4. Timothy Hughes and Doris James Wilson, "Reentry Trends in the United States: Inmates Returning to the Community After Serving Time in Prison," Bureau of Justice Statistics, http://bjs.ojp.usdoj.gov/content/pub/pdf/reentry.pdf (accessed July 1, 2011).

5. Ros Burnett and Shadd Maruna, "So 'Prison Works,' Does It? The Criminal Careers of 130 Men Released from Prison under Home Secretary Michael Howard," *Howard Journal of Criminal Justice* 43 (2004): 390–404.

6. Richard Berk, Heather Ladd, Heidi Graziano, and Jong-Ho Baek, "A Randomized Experiment Testing Inmate Classification Systems," *Criminology and Public Policy* 2 (2003): 215–242.

7. James A. Paluch, Jr., *A Life for a Life: Life Imprisonment (America's Other Death Penalty)* (Los Angeles: Roxbury Press, 2004), p. 4.

8. Manop Kanato, "Drug Use and Health among Prison Inmates," *Current Opinion in Psychiatry* 21 (2008): 252–254.

9. Gresham Sykes, *The Society of Captives* (Princeton, NJ: Princeton University Press, 1958).

10. Karen Lahm, "Inmate-on-Inmate Assault: A Multilevel Examination of Prison Violence," *Criminal Justice and Behavior* 35 (2008): 120–137.

11. Hamm, "Prisoner Radicalization."

12. Robert Johnson, *Hard Time: Understanding and Reforming the Prison* (Monterey, CA: Brooks/Cole, 1987), p. 115.

13. John D. Wooldredge, "Inmate Lifestyles and Opportunities for Victimization," *Journal of Research in Crime and Delinquency* 35 (1998): 480–502.

14. Attapol Kuanliang, Jon Sorensen, and Mark Cunningham, "Juvenile Inmates in an Adult Prison System: Rates of Disciplinary Misconduct and Violence," *Criminal Justice and Behavior,* 35 (2008): 1186–1201.

15. Mark Kellar and Hsiao-Ming Wang, "Inmate Assaults in Texas County Jails," *Prison Journal* 85 (2005): 515–534.

16. Benjamin Steiner and John Wooldredge, "Inmate versus Environmental Effects on Prison Rule Violations," *Criminal Justice and Behavior* 35 (2008): 438–456.

17. T. J. Parsell, *Fish: A Memoir of a Boy in a Man's Prison* (Cambridge, MA: Da Capo Press, 2007).

18. Christopher Hensley, Mary Koscheski, and Richard Tewksbury, "Examining the Characteristics of Male Sexual Assault Targets in a Southern Maximum-Security Prison," *Journal of Interpersonal Violence* 20 (2005): 667–679.

19. Wilbert Rideau and Ron Wikberg, *Life Sentences: Rage and Survival Behind Bars* (New York: Times Books, 1992), pp. 78–80.

20. Hensley, Koscheski, and Tewksbury, "Examining the Characteristics of Male Sexual Assault Targets in a Southern Maximum-Security Prison."

21. Mark Fleisher and Jessie Krienert, *The Myth of Prison Rape: Sexual Culture in American Prisons* (Lanham, MD: Rowman & Littlefield, 2009).

22. Kristine Levan Miller, "The Darkest Figure of Crime: Perceptions of Reasons for Male Inmates to Not Report Sexual Assault," *Justice Quarterly* 27 (2010): 692–712.

23. Tonisha Jones and Travis Pratt, "The Prevalence of Sexual Violence in Prison," *International Journal of Offender Therapy and Comparative Criminology* 52 (2008): 280–295.

24. Allen Beck, Paige Harrison, Marcus Berzofsky, Rachel Caspar, and Christopher Krebs, *Sexual Victimization in Prisons and Jails Reported by Inmates, 2008–09* (Washington, DC: Bureau of Justice Statistics, 2010), available at http://bjs.ojp.usdoj.gov/content/pub/pdf/svpjri0809.pdf (accessed August 1, 2011).

25. Nancy Wolff and Jing Shi, "Patterns of Victimization and Feelings of Safety Inside Prison: The Experience of Male and Female Inmates," *Crime and Delinquency* 57 (2011): 29–55.

26. Mark Fleisher and Jessie Krienert, *The Culture of Prison Sexual Violence* (Washington, DC: U.S. Department of Justice, National Institute of Justice, 2006).

27. S. 1435[108]: Prison Rape Elimination Act of 2003; Public Law No: 108-79.

28. John Irwin, "Adaptation to Being Corrected: Corrections from the Convict's Perspective," in *Handbook of Criminology,* ed. Daniel Glazer (Chicago: Rand McNally, 1974), 971–993.

29. Donald Clemmer, *The Prison Community* (New York: Holt, Rinehart & Winston, 1958).

30. Gresham Sykes and Sheldon Messinger, "The Inmate Social Code," in *The Sociology of Punishment and Corrections,* ed. Norman Johnston, Leonard Savitz, and Marvin Wolfgang (New York: Wiley, 1970), pp. 401–408.

31. Ibid., p. 439.

32. James B. Jacobs, ed., *New Perspectives on Prisons and Imprisonment* (Ithaca, NY: Cornell University Press, 1983); James B, Jacobs, "Street Gangs Behind Bars," *Social Problems* 21 (1974): 395–409; James B. Jacobs, "Race Relations and the Prison Subculture," in *Crime and Justice,* vol. 1, ed. Norval Morris and Michael Tonry (Chicago: University of Chicago Press, 1979), pp. 1–28.

33. Nicole Hahn Rafter, *Partial Justice* (New Brunswick, NJ: Transaction Books, 1990), pp. 181–182.

34. Kathryn Watterson and Meda Chesney-Lind, *Women in Prison: Inside the Concrete Womb* (Boston: Northeastern University Press, 1996).

35. Merry Morash, Robin Harr, and Lila Rucker, "A Comparison of Programming for Women and Men in U.S. Prisons in the 1980s," *Crime and Delinquency* 40 (1994): 197–221.

36. Pamela Schram, "Stereotypes about Vocational Programming for Female Inmates," *Prison Journal* 78 (1998): 244–271.

37. Morash, Harr, and Rucker, "A Comparison of Programming for Women and Men in U.S. Prisons in the 1980s."

38. Vernetta Young and Rebecca Reviere, *Women Behind Bars: Gender and Race in U.S. Prisons* (Boulder, CO: Lynne Rienner Publishers, 2006).

39. Lauren Sharkey, "Does Overcrowding in Prisons Exacerbate the Risk of Suicide among Women Prisoners?" *Howard Journal of Criminal Justice* 49 (2010): 111–124.

40. Seena Fazel and John Danesh, "Serious Mental Disorder in 23,000 Prisoners: A Systematic Review of 62 Surveys," *Lancet* 359 (2002): 545–561.

41. Gary Michael McClelland, Linda Teplin, Karen Abram, and Naomi Jacobs, "HIV and AIDS Risk Behaviors among Female Jail Detainees: Implications for Public Health Policy," *American Journal of Public Health* 92 (2002): 818–826.

42. Christine Grella and Lisa Greenwell, "Correlates of Parental Status and Attitudes toward Parenting among Substance-Abusing Women Offenders," *Prison Journal* 86 (2006): 89–113.

43. Lee Ann Slocum, Sally Simpson, and Douglas Smith, "Strained Lives and Crime: Examining Intra-Individual Variation in Strain and Offending in a Sample of Incarcerated Women," *Criminology* 43 (2005): 1067–1110.

44. Beck, Harrison, Berzofsky, Caspar, and Krebs, *Sexual Victimization in Prisons and Jails Reported by Inmates, 2008–09.*

45. Meda Chesney-Lind, "Vengeful Equity: Sentencing Women to Prison," in *The Female Offender: Girls, Women, and Crime,* ed. Medea Chesney-Lind and Lisa J. Pasko (Thousand Oaks, CA: Sage, 1997).

46. General Accounting Office, *Women in Prison: Sexual Misconduct by Correctional Staff* (Washington, DC: Government Printing Office, 1999).

47. Rebecca Trammell, "Relational Violence in Women's Prison: How Women Describe Interpersonal Violence and Gender," *Women and Criminal Justice* 19 (2009): 267–285.

48. Candace Kruttschnitt and Sharon Krmpotich, "Aggressive Behavior among Female Inmates: An Exploratory Study," *Justice Quarterly* 7 (1990): 370–389.

49. Candace Kruttschnitt, Rosemary Gartner, and Amy Miller, "Doing Her Own Time? Women's Responses to Prison in the Context of the Old and New Penology," *Criminology* 38 (2000): 681–718.

50. Mark Pogrebin and Mary Dodge, "Women's Accounts of Their Prison Experiences: A Retrospective View of Their Subjective Realities," *Journal of Criminal Justice* 29 (2001): 531–541.

51. Shanhe Jiang and L. Thomas Winfree, Jr., "Social Support, Gender, and Inmate Adjustment to Prison Life," *Prison* Journal 86 (2006): 32–55.

52. Edna Erez, "The Myth of the New Female Offender: Some Evidence from Attitudes toward Law and Justice," *Journal of Criminal Justice* 16 (1988): 499–509.

53. Robert Ross and Hugh McKay, *Self-Mutilation* (Lexington, MA: Lexington Books, 1979).

54. Dianna Newbern, Donald Dansereau, and Urvashi Pitre, "Positive Effects on Life Skills Motivation and Self-Efficacy: Node-Link Maps in a Modified Therapeutic Community," *American Journal of Drug and Alcohol Abuse* 25 (1999): 407–410.

55. Rose Parkes and Charlotte Bilby, "The Courage to Create: The Role of Artistic and Spiritual Activities in Prisons," *Howard Journal of Criminal Justice* 49 (2010): 97–110.

56. Steven D. Vannoy and William T. Hoyt, "Evaluation of an Anger Therapy Intervention for Incarcerated Adult Males," *Journal of Offender Rehabilitation* 39 (2004): 40.

57. Retrieved from University of South Australia, School of Psychology, Social Work and Social Policy, www.unisa.edu.au (accessed July 1, 2011).

58. Byron R. Johnson, "Religious Programming, Institutional Adjustment and Recidivism among Former Inmates in Prison Fellowship Programs," *Justice Quarterly* 21 (2004): 329–354.

59. Charles McDaniel, Derek Davis, and Sabrina Neff, "Charitable Choice and Prison Ministries: Constitutional and Institutional Challenges to Rehabilitating the American Penal System," *Criminal Justice Policy Review* 16 (2005): 164–189.

60. Lawrence T. Jablecki, "A Critique of Faith-Based Prison Programs," *The Humanist* 65 (2005): 11–16.

61. Ibid.

62. Janeen Buck Willison, Diana Brazzell, and KiDeuk Kim, *Faith-Based Corrections and Reentry Programs: Advancing a Conceptual Framework for Research and Evaluation* (Washington, DC: Urban Institute, 2010), www.ncjrs.gov/pdffiles1/nij/grants/234058.pdf (accessed July 1, 2011).

63. Dawn Daggett, Scott Camp, and Okyun Kwon, "Faith-Based Correctional Programming in Federal Prisons: Factors Affecting Program Completion," *Criminal Justice and Behavior* 35 (2008): 848–862.

64. Philip R. Magaletta, Pamela M. Diamond, Beth M. Weinman, Ashley Burnell, and Carl G. Leukefeld, "Preentry Substance Abuse Services: The Heterogeneity of Offender Experiences," *Crime and Delinquency* first published online on April 28, 2010.

65. Kate Dolan, James Shearer, Bethany White, Zhou Jialun, John Kaldor, and Alex Wodak, "Four-Year Follow-up of Imprisoned Male Heroin Users and Methadone Treatment: Mortality, Re-Incarceration and Hepatitis C Infection," *Addiction* 100 (2005): 820–828.

66. Clayton Mosher and Dretha Phillips, "The Dynamics of a Prison-Based Therapeutic Community for Women Offenders: Retention, Completion, and Outcomes," *Prison Journal* 86 (2006): 6–31.

67. Sheldon X. Zhang, Robert E. L. Roberts, and Kathryn E. McCollister, "Therapeutic Community in a California Prison: Treatment Outcomes After 5 Years," *Crime and Delinquency* 57 (2011): 82–101; J. Mitchell Miller and Holly Ventura Miller, "Considering the Effectiveness of Drug Treatment Behind Bars: Findings from the South Carolina RSAT Evaluation," *Justice Quarterly* 28 (2011): 70–86.

68. Wayne Welsh, "A Multisite Evaluation of Prison-Based Therapeutic Community Drug Treatment," *Criminal Justice and Behavior* 34 (2007): 1481–1498.

69. Daniel Werb, Thomas Kerr, Will Small, Kathy Li, Julio Montaner, and Evan Wood, "HIV Risks Associated with Incarceration among Injection Drug Users: Implications for Prison-Based Public Health Strategies," *Journal of Public Health* 30 (2008): 126–132.

70. Karen Lahm, "Educational Participation and Inmate Misconduct," *Journal of Offender Rehabilitation* 48 (2009): 37–52.

71. Rosa Minhyo Cho and John H. Tyler, "Does Prison-Based Adult Basic Education Improve Postrelease Outcomes for Male Prisoners in Florida?" *Crime and Delinquency*, published online on November 30, 2010.

72. Bill Conlon, Scott Harris, Jeffrey Nagel, Mike Hillman, and Rick Hanson, "Education: Don't Leave Prison without It," *Corrections Today* 70 (2008): 48–52; David Wilson, Catherine Gallagher, and Doris MacKenzie, "A Meta-Analysis of Corrections-Based Education, Vocation, and Work Programs for Adult Offenders," *Journal of Research in Crime and Delinquency* 37 (2000): 347–368.

73. Howard Skolnik and John Slansky, "A First Step in Helping Inmates Get Good Jobs after Release," *Corrections Today* 53 (1991): 92.

74. Federal Bureau of Prisons web page concerning UNICOR Federal Prison Industries, www.unicor.gov/fpi_contracting/ (accessed July 1, 2011).

75. Courtesy of the Prison Industry Authority, 560 East Natoma St., Folsom, CA, 95630-2200.

76. Douglas Lipton, Robert Martinson, and Judith Wilks, *The Effectiveness of Correctional Treatment: A Survey of Treatment Evaluation Studies* (New York: Praeger, 1975).

77. James Wilson and Robert Davis, "Good Intentions Meet Hard Realities: An Evaluation of the Project Greenlight Reentry Program," *Criminology and Public Policy* 5 (2006): 303–338.

78. Paula Smith, Paul Gendreau, and Kristin Swartz, "Validating the Principles of Effective Intervention: A Systematic Review of the Contributions of Meta-Analysis in the Field of Corrections," *Victims and Offenders* 4 (2009): 148–169.

79. Paul Gendreau and Robert Ross, "Effective Correctional Treatment: Bibliotherapy for Cynics," *Crime and Delinquency* 27 (1979): 463–489.

80. Mark W. Lipsey and Francis T. Cullen, "The Effectiveness of Correctional Rehabilitation: A Review of Systematic Reviews," *Annual Review of Law and Social Science* 3 (2007): 297–320.

81. Lucien X. Lombardo, *Guards Imprisoned* (New York: Elsevier, 1981); James Jacobs and Norma Crotty, "The Guard's World," in *New Perspectives on Prisons and Imprisonment*, ed. James Jacobs (Ithaca, NY: Cornell University Press, 1983), pp. 133–141.

82. Richard Tewksbury and Elizabeth Mustaine, "Correctional Orientations of Prison Staff," *Prison Journal* 88 (2008): 207–233.

83. Mike Vuolo and Candace Kruttschnitt, "Prisoners" Adjustment, Correctional Officers, and Context: The Foreground and Background of Punishment in Late Modernity," *Law and Society Review* 42 (2008): 307–335.

84. Eric Lambert, Nancy Hogan, and Irshad Altheimer, "An Exploratory Examination of the Consequences of Burnout in Terms of Life Satisfaction, Turnover Intent, and Absenteeism among Private Correctional Staff," *Prison Journal* 90 (2010): 94–114.

85. Stephen Owen, "Occupational Stress among Correctional Supervisors," *Prison Journal* 86 (2006): 164–181; Eugene Paoline, Eric Lambert, and Nancy Hogan, "A Calm and Happy Keeper of the Keys: The Impact of ACA Views, Relations with Coworkers, and Policy Views on the Job Stress and Job Satisfaction of Jail Staff," *Prison Journal* 86 (2006): 182–205.

86. Dana Britton, *At Work in the Iron Cage: The Prison as Gendered Organization* (New York: New York University Press, 2003), Ch. 6.

87. *San Antonio Express News,* March 28, 2008.

88. David Duffee, *Corrections, Practice and Policy* (New York: Random House, 1989), p. 305.

89. Randy Martin and Sherwood Zimmerman, "A Typology of the Causes of Prison Riots and an Analytical Extension to the 1986 West Virginia Riot," *Justice Quarterly* 7 (1990): 711–737.

90. Benjamin Steiner, "Assessing Static and Dynamic Influences on Inmate Violence Levels," *Crime and Delinquency* 55 (2009): 134–161.

91. David Allender and Frank Marcell, "Career Criminals, Security Threat Groups, and Prison Gangs," *FBI Law Enforcement Bulletin* 72 (2003): 8–12.

92. Terri Compton and Mike Meacham, "Prison Gangs: Descriptions and Selected Intervention," *Forensic Examiner* 14 (2005): 26–31.

93. Jon Sorensen and Mark Cunningham, "Conviction Offense and Prison Violence: A Comparative Study of Murderers and Other Offenders," *Crime and Delinquency* 56 (2010): 103–125.

94. Benjamin Steiner and John Wooldredge, "Inmate versus Environmental Effects on Prison Rule Violations," *Criminal Justice and Behavior* 35 (2008): 438–456.

95. Attapol Kuanliang, Jon R. Sorensen, and Mark Cunningham, "Juvenile Inmates in an Adult Prison System: Rates of Disciplinary Misconduct and Violence," *Criminal Justice and Behavior,* 35 (2008): 1186–1201.

96. Jon Sorensen and Mark Cunningham, "Conviction Offense and Prison Violence: A Comparative Study of Murderers and Other Offenders, *Crime and Delinquency* 56 (2010): 103–125.

97. Grant Harris, Tracey Skilling, and Marnie Rice, "The Construct of Psychopathy," in *Crime and Justice: An Annual Edition,* ed. Michael Tonry (Chicago: University of Chicago Press, 2001), pp. 197–265.

98. For a series of papers on the position, see A. Cohen, G. Cole, and R. Baily, eds., *Prison Violence* (Lexington, MA: Lexington Books, 1976).

99. Lahm, "Inmate-on-Inmate Assault."

100. Scott Camp and Gerald Gaes, "Criminogenic Effects of the Prison Environment on Inmate Behavior: Some Experimental Evidence," *Crime and Delinquency* 51 (2005): 425–442.

101. Hans Toch, "Cumulative Default: The Cost of Disruptive Prison Careers," *Criminal Justice and Behavior* 35 (2008): 943–955.

102. Bert Useem and Michael Resig, "Collective Action in Prisons: Protests, Disturbances, and Riots," *Criminology* 37 (1999): 735–760.

103. Prison Litigation Reform Act P.L. 104-134, 110 Stat. 1321 (2006); 42 U.S.C. § 1997e (1994 ed. and Supp. II).

104. *Booth v. Churner*, U.S. 731 (2001); *Porter v. Nussle*, 534 U.S. 516 (2002).

105. ACLU, "Know Your Rights: The Prison Litigation Reform Act (PLRA)," www.aclu.org/images/asset_upload_file79_25805.pdf (accessed July 1, 2011).

106. *Shaw v. Murphy* (99-1613), 2001.

107. *Newman v. Alabama*, 92 S.Ct. 1079, 405 U.S. 319 (1972).

108. *Estelle v. Gamble*, 429 U.S. 97 (1976).

109. Ibid.

110. Lester Wright, "Health Care in Prison Thirty Years after *Estelle v. Gamble*," *Journal of Correctional Health Care* 14 (2008): 31–35.

111. *Trop v. Dulles*, 356 U.S. 86, 78 S.Ct. 590 (1958); see also *Furman v. Georgia*, 408 U.S. 238, 92 S.Ct. 2726, 33 L.Ed.2d 346 (1972).

112. *Weems v. United States*, 217 U.S. 349, 30 S.Ct. 544, 54 L.Ed. 793 (1910).

113. *Lee v. Tahash*, 352 F.2d 970 (8th Cir., 1965).

114. *Estelle v. Gamble*, 429 U.S. 97 (1976).

115. *Robinson v. California*, 370 U.S. 660 (1962).

116. *Gregg v. Georgia*, 428 U.S. 153 (1976).

117. *Jackson v. Bishop*, 404 F.2d 571 (8th Cir. 1968).

118. *Johnson v. California*, 543 U.S. 499 (2005)

119. *Bell v. Wolfish*, 99 S.Ct. 1873–1974 (1979); see "Bell v. Wolfish: The Rights of Pretrial Detainees," *New England Journal of Prison Law* 6 (1979): 134.

120. *Farmer v. Brennan*, 144 S.Ct. 1970 (1994).

121. *Rhodes v. Chapman*, 452 U.S. 337 (1981); for further analysis of *Rhodes*, see Randall Pooler, "Prison Overcrowding and the Eighth Amendment: The Rhodes Not Taken," *New England Journal on Criminal and Civil Confinement* 8 (1983): 1–28.

122. Kristin Preston "Right Place, Right Time: GPS Monitoring in Pinellas County," *Geography and Public Safety* 2 (2009): 3–5, www.ojp.usdoj.gov/nij/maps/gps-bulletin-v2i1.pdf (accessed July 1, 2011).

123. Joel Caplan and Susan Kinnevy, "National Surveys of State Paroling Authorities: Models of Service," *Federal Probation* 74 (2010): 34–42.

124. Lauren Glaze and Thomas Bonczar, *Probation and Parole in the United States, 2009* (Washington, DC: Bureau of Justice Statistics, 2010), http://bjs.ojp.usdoj.gov/content/pub/pdf/ppus09.pdf (accessed July 1, 2011).

125. Patrick A. Langan and David J. Levin, *Recidivism of Prisoners Released in 1994* (Washington, DC: Bureau of Justice Statistics, 2002).

126. Pew Center on the States, *State of Recidivism: The Revolving Door of America's Prisons* (Washington, DC: Pew Charitable Trusts, April 2011), www.pewtrusts.org/uploadedFiles/wwwpewtrustsorg/Reports/sentencing_and_corrections/State_Recidivism_Revolving_Door_America_Prisons%20.pdf (accessed July 1, 2011).

127. Stephen Duguid, *Can Prisons Work? The Prisoner as Object and Subject in Modern Corrections* (Toronto: University of Toronto Press, 2000).

128. Beth Huebner and Mark Berg, "Examining the Sources of Variation in Risk for Recidivism," *Justice Quarterly* 28 (2011): 146–173; Beth Huebner, Christina DeJong, Jennifer Cobbina, "Women Coming Home: Long-Term Patterns of Recidivism," *Justice Quarterly* 27 (2010): 225–254.

129. Catherine Hamilton, Louise Falshaw, and Kevin D. Browne, "The Link between Recurrent Maltreatment and Offending Behavior," *International Journal of Offender Therapy and Comparative Criminology* 46 (2002): 75–95.

130. Brent Benda, "Gender Differences in Life-Course Theory of Recidivism: A Survival Analysis," *International Journal of Offender Therapy and Comparative Criminology* 49 (2005): 325–342.

131. J. E. Ryan, "Who Gets Revoked? A Comparison of Intensive Supervision Successes and Failures in Vermont," *Crime and Delinquency* 43 (1997): 104–118.

132. Thomas E. Hanlon, David N. Nurco, Richard W. Bateman, and Kevin E. O'Grady, "The Response of Drug Abuser Parolees to a Combination of Treatment and Intensive Supervision," *Prison Journal* 78 (1998): 108.

133. Joan Petersilia, *When Prisoners Come Home: Parole and Prisoner Reentry* (New York: Oxford University Press, 2003); Joan Petersilia, "Hard Time Ex-Offenders Returning Home after Prison," *Corrections Today* 67 (2005): 66–72; Joan Petersilia, "When Prisoners Return to Communities: Political, Economic, and Social Consequences," *Federal Probation* 65 (2001): 3–9.

134. Michael Ostermann, "How do Former Inmates Perform in the Community? A Survival Analysis of Rearrests, Reconvictions, and Technical Parole Violations," *Crime and Delinquency,* published online on February 18, 2011.

135. Micheal Ostermann, "Parole? Nope, Not for Me: Voluntarily Maxing Out of Prison," *Crime and Delinquency,* published online on September 8, 2010.

136. Megan Kurlychek, Andrew Wheeler, Leigh Tinik, and Cynthia Kempinen, "How Long After? A Natural Experiment Assessing the Impact of the Length of Aftercare Service Delivery on Recidivism," *Crime and Delinquency,* published online on November 4, 2010.

137. Stephen Metraux and Dennis Culhane, "Recent Incarceration History among a Sheltered Homeless Population," *Crime and Delinquency* 52 (2006): 504–517.

138. Petersilia, "Hard Time Ex-Offenders Returning Home after Prison."

139. Hanlon, Nurco, Bateman, and O'Grady, "The Response of Drug Abuser Parolees to a Combination of Treatment and Intensive Supervision."

140. Paul Hirschfield and Alex Piquero, "Normalization and Legitimation: Modeling Stigmatizing Attitudes Toward Ex-Offenders," *Criminology* 48 (2010): 27–55.

141. Mark Berg and Beth Huebner, "Reentry and the Ties that Bind: An Examination of Social Ties, Employment, and Recidivism," *Justice Quarterly* 28 (2011): 382–410; Andy Hochstetler, Matt DeLisi, and Travis C. Pratt, "Social Support and Feelings of Hostility Among Released Inmates," *Crime and Delinquency* 56 (2010): 588–607.

142. National Drug Strategy Network, "HUD Announces '"One Strike' Rules for Public Housing Tenants," May 1996, www.ndsn.org/may96/onestrik.html (accessed July 1, 2011).

143. Pew Charitable Trusts, *Collateral Costs: Incarceration's Effect on Economic Mobility* (Washington, DC: Pew Charitable Trusts, 2010), www.pewtrusts.org/uploadedFiles/wwwpewtrustsorg/Reports/Economic_Mobility/Collateral%20Costs%20FINAL.pdf (accessed July 1, 2011).

144. Richard Seiter, "Prisoner Reentry and the Role of Parole Officers," *Federal Probation* 66 (2002): 50–54.

145. Charis Kubrin and Eric Stewart, "Predicting Who Reoffends: The Neglected Role of Neighborhood Context in Recidivism Studies," *Criminology* 44 (2006): 165–197.

146. Ryken Grattet, Joan Petersilia, and Jeffery Lin, *Parole Violations and Revocations in California* (Washington, DC: National Institute of Justice, 2008).

147. John Hipp, Joan Petersilia and Susan Turner, "Parolee Recidivism in California: The Effect of Neighborhood Context and Social Service Agency Characteristics," *Criminology* 48 (2010): 947–979.

148. Jeremy Travis, Anna Crayton, and Debbie Mukamal, "A New Era in Inmate Reentry," *Corrections Today* 71 (2009): 38–41.

149. Hanlon, Nurco, Bateman, and O'Grady, "The Response of Drug Abuser Parolees to a Combination of Treatment and Intensive Supervision."

150. Kathleen Olivares, Velmer Burton, and Francis Cullen, "The Collateral Consequences of a Felony Conviction: A National Study of State Legal Codes Ten Years Later," *Federal Probation* 60 (1996): 10–17.

151. Maryland State Department of Education, www.marylandpublicschools.org/msde (accessed June 29, 2011).

152. Stacy Adams, "Richmond Program Helps Former Female Inmates," *Crisis* 113 (2006): 8.

153. Anthony Braga, Anne Piehl, and David Hureau, "Controlling Violent Offenders Released to the Community: An Evaluation of the Boston Reentry Initiative," *Journal of Research in Crime and Delinquency* 46 (2009): 411–436.

Box Source Notes
Careers in Criminal Justice: Correctional Officer

Bureau of Labor Statistics, U.S. Department of Labor, "Correctional Officers," Occupational Outlook Handbook, 2008–09 Edition, www.bls.gov/oco/ocos156.htm (accessed July 1, 2011); Stephen Lambert and Debra Regan, "Corrections Officer," in *Great Jobs for Criminal Justice Majors* (New York: McGraw-Hill, 2001): 193–196.

Contemporary Issues in Criminal Justice: Evidence-Based Justice
Getting Ready Program

Dora Schriro, "Getting Ready: How Arizona Has Created a 'Parallel Universe' for Inmates," *National Institute of Justice Journal* 263 (2009), www.nij.gov/journals/263/getting-ready.htm (accessed July 1, 2011).

Chapter 13, Juvenile Justice in the Twenty-First Century

1. Patricia Wen, "Odgren Sentenced to Life in Prison," *Boston Globe,* May 1, 2010, http://articles.boston.com/

2010-05-01/news/29302884_1_first-degree-murder-parole-option-lincoln-sudbury-regional-high-school (accessed April 12, 2011).

2. Federal Bureau of Investigation, *Crime in the United States, 2005* (Washington, DC: U.S. Government Printing Office, 2006).

3. David S. Tanenhaus, *Juvenile Justice in the Making* (New York: Oxford University Press, 2004); Lawrence Stone, *The Family, Sex, and Marriage in England: 1500–1800* (New York: Harper & Row, 1977); Philippe Aries, *Century of Childhood: A Social History of Family Life* (New York: Vintage Press, 1962); Douglas R. Rendleman, *"Parens Patriae: From Chancery to the Juvenile Court," South Carolina Law Review* 23 (1971): 205–229; Anthony M. Platt, "The Rise of the Child-Saving Movement: A Study in Social Policy and Correctional Reform," *Annals of the American Academy of Political and Social Science* 381 (1979): 21–38; Robert S. Pickett, *House of Refuge: Origins of Juvenile Reform in New York State, 1815–1857* (Syracuse, NY: Syracuse University Press, 1969).

4. Anthony Platt, *The Child Savers: The Invention of Delinquency* (Chicago: University of Chicago Press, 1969), pp. 11–38.

5. See, generally, Anne Meis Knupfer, *Reform and Resistance: Gender, Delinquency, and America's First Juvenile Court* (London: Routledge, 2001).

6. This section is based on material from the New York State Archives, *The Greatest Reform School in the World: A Guide to the Records of the New York House of Refuge: A Brief History 1824–1857* (Albany: New York State Archives, 2001); Sanford J. Fox, "Juvenile Justice Reform: A Historical Perspective," *Stanford Law Review* 22 (1970): 1187.

7. Pickett, *House of Refuge*.

8. LaMar T. Empey, *American Delinquency: Its Meaning and Construction* (Homewood, IL: Dorsey Press, 1978), p. 515.

9. Public Law 93–415 (1974).

10. For a comprehensive view of juvenile law, see, generally, Joseph J. Senna and Larry J. Siegel, *Juvenile Law: Cases and Comments*, 2nd ed. (St. Paul, MN: West, 1992).

11. Erika Gebo, "Do Family Courts Administer Individualized Justice in Delinquency Cases?" *Criminal Justice Policy Review* 16 (2005): 190–210.

12. Federal Bureau of Investigation, *Crime in the United States, 2009*, www2.fbi.gov/ucr/cius2009/data/table_32.html (accessed July 3, 2011).

13. Richard J. Lundman, "Routine Police Arrest Practices," *Social Problems* 22 (1974): 127–141; Robert E. Worden and Stephanie M. Myers, *Police Encounters with Juvenile Suspects* (Albany: Hindelang Criminal Justice Research Center and School of Criminal Justice, State University of New York, 2001).

14. *Fare v. Michael C.*, 442 U.S. 707 (1979).

15. Ana Abrantes, Norman Hoffmann, and Ronald Anton, "Prevalence of Co-occurring Disorders among Juveniles Committed to Detention Centers," *International Journal of Offender Therapy and Comparative Criminology* 49 (2005): 179–194.

16. Nancy Rodriquez, "Juvenile Court Context and Detention Decisions: Reconsidering the Role of Race, Ethnicity, and Community Characteristics in Juvenile Court Processes," *Justice Quarterly* 24 (2007): 629–656.

17. Barry Holman and Jason Ziedenberg, *The Dangers of Detention: The Impact of Incarcerating Youth in Detention and Other Secure Facilities* (Washington, DC: Justice Policy Institute, 2006), http://www.cfjj.org/Pdf/116-JPI008-DOD_Report.pdf (accessed July 3, 2011).

18. *Schall v. Martin*, 467 U.S. 253 (1984).

19. See Juvenile Justice and Delinquency Prevention Act of 1974, 42 U.S.C., sec. 5633.

20. Catherine Van Dijk, An Nuytiens, and Christian Eliaerts, "The Referral of Juvenile Offenders to the Adult Court in Belgium: Theory and Practice," *Howard Journal of Criminal Justice* 44 (2005): 151–166.

21. *Kent v. United States*, 383 U.S. 541 (1966).

22. *Breed v. Jones*, 421 U.S. 519 (1975).

23. John Burrow, "Reverse Waiver and the Effects of Legal, Statutory, and Secondary Legal Factors on Sentencing Outcomes for Juvenile Offenders," *Crime and Delinquency* 54 (2008): 34–64.

24. Alan Karpelowitz, *State Legislative Priorities—1995* (Denver, CO: National Conference of State Legislatures, 1995), p. 10.

25. Howard N. Snyder, Melissa Sickmund, and Eileen Poe-Yamagata, *Juvenile Transfers to Criminal Court in the 1990s: Lessons Learned from Four Studies* (Washington, DC: Office of Juvenile Justice and Delinquency Prevention, 2000).

26. James Austin, Kelly Dedel Johnson, and Maria Gregoriou, *Juveniles in Adult Prisons and Jails* (Washington, DC: Bureau of Justice Assistance, 2000).

27. Aaron Kupchik, "The Correctional Experiences of Youth in Adult and Juvenile Prisons," *Justice Quarterly* 24 (2007): 247–270.

28. Benjamin Steiner and Emily Wright, "Assessing the Relative Effects of State Direct File Waiver Laws on Violent Juvenile Crime: Deterrence or Irrelevance?" *Journal of Criminal Law and Criminology* 96 (2006): 1451–1477.

29. Benjamin Steiner, "The Effects of Juvenile Transfer to Criminal Court on Incarceration Decisions," *Justice Quarterly* 26 (2009): 77–106; Megan Kurlychek and Brian Johnson, "The Juvenile Penalty: A Comparison of Juvenile and Young Adult Sentencing Outcomes in Criminal Court," *Criminology* 42 (2004): 485–517.

30. Barry Feld, "The Juvenile Court Meets the Principle of the Offense: Legislative Changes in Juvenile Waiver Statutes," *Journal of Criminal Law and Criminology* 78 (1987): 471–533; see also John Kramer, Henry Sontheimer, and John Lemmon, "Pennsylvania Waiver to Adult Court," paper presented at the annual meeting of the American Society of Criminology, San Francisco, November 1991; authors confirm that juveniles tried in adult courts are generally male, age 17 or older, and disproportionately minorities.

31. Jeffrey Fagan, Martin Forst, and T. Scott Vivona, "Racial Determinants of the Judicial Transfer Decision: Prosecuting Violent Youth in Criminal Court," *Crime and Delinquency* 33 (1987): 359–386; J. Fagan, E. Slaughter, and E. Hartstone, "Blind Justice: The Impact of Race on the Juvenile Justice Process," *Crime and Delinquency* 53 (1987): 224–258; J. Fagan and E. P. Deschenes, "Determinants of Judicial Waiver Decisions for Violent Juvenile Offenders," *Journal of Criminal Law and Criminology* 81 (1990): 314–347; see also James Howell, "Juvenile Transfers to Criminal Court," *Juvenile and Family Justice Journal* 6 (1997): 12–14.

32. Anne L. Stahl, *Delinquency Cases in Juvenile Courts, 1997* (Washington, DC: Office of Juvenile Justice and Delinquency Prevention, 2000).

33. Dale Parent, *Key Issues in Criminal Justice: Transferring Serious Juvenile Offenders to Adult Courts* (Washington, DC: National Institute of Justice, 1997).

34. *In re Gault*, 387 U.S. 1 (1967).

35. See Joseph Goldstein, Anna Freud, and Albert Solnit, *Beyond the Best Interest of the Child* (New York: Free Press, 1973).

36. See Michael Serrill, "Police Write a New Law on Juvenile Crime," *Police Magazine* (September 1979): 47; see also A. Schneider and D. Schram, *Assessment of Juvenile Justice Reform in Washington State*, vols. 1–4 (Washington, DC: Department of Justice, Institute of Policy Analysis, 1983); T. Castellano, "Justice Model in the Juvenile Justice System—Washington State's Experience," *Law and Policy* 8 (1986): 479.

37. Emily Gaarder, Nancy Rodriguez, and Marjorie Zatz, "Criers, Liars, and Manipulators: Probation Officers' Views of Girls," *Justice Quarterly* 21 (2004): 547–578.

38. Office of Juvenile Justice and Delinquency Prevention, *Juveniles in Corrections*, http://ojjdp.ncjrs.gov/ojstatbb/corrections/qa08201.asp (accessed July 3, 2011).

39. Ibid.

40. J. David Hawkins, Richard F. Catalano, and associates, *Communities that Care: Action for Drug Abuse Prevention* (San Francisco: Jossey-Bass, 1992).

41. Richard F. Catalano, Michael W. Arthur, J. David Hawkins, Lisa Berglund, and Jeffrey J. Olson, "Comprehensive Community- and School-Based Interventions to Prevent Antisocial Behavior," in *Serious and Violent Juvenile Offenders: Risk Factors and Successful Interventions*, ed. Rolf Loeber and David P. Farrington (Thousand Oaks, CA: Sage, 1998).

42. David Smith, "The Effectiveness of the Juvenile Justice System," *Criminal Justice: International Journal of Policy and Practice* 5 (2005): 181–195.

43. Barry C. Feld, *Bad Kids: Race and the Transformation of the Juvenile Court* (New York: Oxford University Press, 1999).

44. Alexes Harris, "Diverting and Abdicating Judicial Discretion: Cultural, Political, and Procedural Dynamics in California Juvenile Justice," *Law and Society Review* 41 (2007): 387–428.

45. John Johnson Kerbs, "(Un)equal Justice: Juvenile Court Abolition and African Americans," *Annals, AAPSS*, 564 (1999): 109–125.

46. Howard N. Snyder and Melissa Sickmund, *Juvenile Offenders and Victims: 2006 National Report* (Washington, DC: Office of Juvenile Justice and Delinquency Prevention, 2006), http://ojjdp.ncjrs.gov/ojstatbb/nr2006/downloads/NR2006.pdf (accessed July 3, 2011).

47. Ibid.

48. National Council on Crime and Delinquency, *And Justice for Some: Differential Treatment of Minority Youth in the Justice System*, January 2007, www.nccd-crc.org/nccd/pubs/2007jan_justice_for_some.pdf (accessed July 3, 2011).

Box Source Notes
Contemporary Issues in Criminal Justice
Are Teen Courts Effective?

National Association of Youth Courts, *Youth Court List by State*, www.youthcourt.net/?page_id=40 (accessed July 6, 2011); Jeffrey Butts, Janeen Buck, and Mark Coggeshall, *The Impact of Teen Courts on Young Offenders* (Washington, DC: Urban Institute, 2002); Jeffrey A. Butts and Janeen Buck, "Teen Courts: A Focus on Research," *Juvenile Justice Bulletin October 2000* (Washington, DC: Office of Juvenile Justice and Delinquency Prevention, 2000); Kevin Minor, James Wells, Irinia Soderstrom, Rachel Bingham, and Deborah Williamson, "Sentence Completion and Recidivism among Juveniles Referred to Teen Courts," *Crime and Delinquency* 45 (1999): 467–480; Paige Harrison, James R. Maupin, and G. Larry Mays, "Teen Court: An Examination of Processes and Outcomes," *Crime and Delinquency* 47 (2001): 243–264.

Chapter 14, Crime and Justice in the New Millenium

1. John F. Burns and Ravi Somaiya, "WikiLeaks Founder on the Run, Trailed by Notoriety," *New York Times*, October 23, 2010, www.nytimes.com/2010/10/24/world/24assange.html (accessed July 3, 2011).

2. Nikos Passas and David Nelken, "The Thin Line between Legitimate and Criminal Enterprises: Subsidy Frauds in the European Community," *Crime, Law, and Social Change* 19 (1993): 223–243.

3. For a thorough review, see David Friedrichs, *Trusted Criminals* (Belmont, CA: Wadsworth, 1996).

4. FBI, "Ponzi Scheme Indictments: Five Charged in $7 Billion Ploy," June 19, 2009, www.fbi.gov/page2/june09/stanford_061909.html (accessed July 3, 2011).

5. FBI, "2009 Financial Crimes Report," www.fbi.gov/stats-services/publications/financial-crimes-report-2009 (accessed July 3, 2011).

6. Ibid.

7. Securities and Exchange Commission, "SEC Charges Bernard L. Madoff for Multi-Billion Dollar Ponzi Scheme," December 11, 2008, www.sec.gov/news/press/2008/2008-293.htm (accessed July 3, 2011); Joe Lauria, "Life Inside the Weird World of Bernard Madoff," *The Times*, March 22, 2009, http://business.timesonline.co.uk/tol/business/industry_sectors/banking_and_finance/article5949961.ece (accessed July 3, 2011).

8. FBI, *Mortgage Fraud Report*, 2009, "Year in Review," www.fbi.gov/stats-services/publications/mortgage-fraud-2009 (accessed August 1, 2011).

9. FBI, "2009 Financial Crimes Report," www.fbi.gov/stats-services/publications/financial-crimes-report-2009 (accessed August 1, 2011).

10. Kurt Eichenwald, "Ex-Andersen Partner Pleads Guilty in Record-Shredding," *New York Times*, April 12, 2002, p. C1; John A. Byrne, "At Enron, the Environment Was Ripe for Abuse," *Business Week* (February 25, 2002): 12; Peter Behr and Carrie Johnson, "Govt. Expands Charges against Enron Execs," *Washington Post*, May 1, 2003, p. 1.

11. Sean Rosenmerkel, "Wrongfulness and Harmfulness as Components of Seriousness of White-Collar Offenses," *Journal of Contemporary Criminal Justice* 17 (2001): 308–328.

12. Jonathan Lechter, Daniel Posner, and George Morris, "Antitrust Violations," *American Criminal Law Review* 39 (2002): 225–273.

13. Mark Cohen, "Environmental Crime and Punishment: Legal/Economic Theory and Empirical Evidence on Enforcement of Federal Environmental Statutes," *Journal of Criminal Law and Criminology* 82 (1992): 1054–1109.

14. Attorney General Bill McCollum press release, "Miami-Dade Mortgage Fraud Task Force Announces Series of Arrests in $4.5 Million Mortgage Fraud Operation," April 16, 2009, www.myfloridalegal.com/newsrel.nsf/mortgage/878FC08EA1B2C41B8525759A0045BD71 (accessed July 3, 2011).

15. Thomas Catan and Guy Chazan, "Spill Draws Criminal Probe," *Wall Street Journal*, June 2, 2010, http://online.wsj.com/article/SB10001424052748704875604575280983140254458.html (accessed July 3, 2011); Environmental Protection Agency press release, "Exxon to Pay Record One Billion Dollars in Criminal Fines and Civil Damages in Connection with Alaskan Oil Spill," March 13, 1991, www.epa.gov/history/topics/valdez/02.html (accessed August 1, 2011); Tyson Slocum, "BP: The Worst Safety and Environmental Record of All Oil Companies Operating in the United States," *Monthly Review*, http://mrzine.monthlyreview.org/2010/slocum060510.html (accessed July 3, 2011).

16. Helene Cooper and Peter Baker, "U.S. Opens Criminal Inquiry Into Oil Spill," *New York Times*, June 1, 2010, www.nytimes.com/2010/06/02/us/02spill.html (accessed July 3, 2011).

17. Alternative Fines Act, 18 U.S.C. § 3571(d).

18. 15 U.S.C. §§ 78dd-2(g)(3), 78dd-3(e)(3), 78ff(c)(3).

19. Michael J. Lynch and Paul Stretesky, "Green Criminology in the United States," in *Issues in Green Criminology*, ed. Piers Beirne and Nigel South (Portland, OR: Willan, 2008), pp. 248–269, at 249.

20. Michael M. O'Hear, "Sentencing the Green-Collar Offender: Punishment, Culpability, and Environmental Crime," *Journal of Criminal Law and Criminology* 95 (2004): 133–276.

21. This section relies on Duncan Brack, *Illegal Logging* (London: Chatham House, 2007), www.illegal-logging.info/uploads/1_Illegal_logging_bp_07_01.pdf (accessed July 3, 2011).

22. Ibid.

23. World Wide Fund for Nature, "Fishing Problems: Pirate Fishing," http://wwf.panda.org/about_our_earth/blue_planet/problems/problems_fishing/illegal_fishing/ (accessed July 3, 2011).

24. Carole Gibbs, Edmund F. McGarrell, and Mark Axelrod, "Transnational White-Collar Crime and Risk: Lessons from the Global Trade in Electronic Waste," *Criminology and Public Policy* 9 (2010): 543–560.

25. Andrew Oliveira, Christopher Schenck, Christopher Cole, and Nicole Janes, "Environmental Crimes (Annual Survey of White-Collar Crime)," *American Criminal Law Review* 42 (2005): 347–380.

26. Environmental Protection Agency, Criminal Investigation Division, www.epa.gov/compliance/criminal/ (accessed June 26, 2011).

27. Statement of Michael A. Vatis, director, National Infrastructure Protection Center, Federal Bureau of Investigation, on cyber crime before the Senate Judiciary Committee, Criminal Justice Oversight Subcommittee, and House Judiciary Committee, Crime Subcommittee, February 29, 2000, www.cybercrime.gov/vatis.htm (accessed July 3, 2011).

28. VoGon Interntational, www.vogon-international.com/ (accessed July 3, 2011).

29. Michael Arrington, "Internet Porn Stats," TechCrunch, www.techcrunch.com/2007/05/12/internet-pornography-stats/ (accessed August 1, 2011).

30. Ben Fritz, "Tough Times in the Porn Industry," *Los Angeles Times*, August 10, 2009, www.latimes.com/news/local/la-fi-ct-porn10-2009aug10,0,3356050.story (accessed July 3, 2011).

31. Katrin Bennhold, "In Child Sex Case, More Facets than Meet the Eye," *New York Times*, April 25, 2011, www.nytimes.com/2011/04/26/world/europe/26iht-abuse26.html (accessed July 3, 2011).

32. This section relies heavily on CERT® Coordination Center Denial of Service Attacks, www.cert.org/tech_tips/denial_of_service.html (accessed July 3, 2011).

33. Jim Wolf, "Internet Scams Targeted in Sweep: A 10-Day Crackdown Leads to 62 Arrests and 88 Indictments," *Boston Globe*, May 22, 2001, p. A2.

34. These sections rely on "Phishing Activity Trends Report," June 2005, Anti-Phishing Working Group, www.ncjrs.org/spotlight/identity_theft/publications.html#phishing (accessed July 3, 2011).

35. Identity Theft Resource Center (ITRC), "Scams and Consumer Alerts," www.idtheftcenter.org (accessed July 3, 2011).

36. National Center on Addiction and Substance Abuse at Columbia University, "'You've Got Drugs!' V: Prescription Drug Pushers on the Internet," May 2008, www.casacolumbia.org/download.aspx?path=/UploadedFiles/2zlhtwsh.pdf (accessed July 3, 2011).

37. Anne Branscomb, "Rogue Computer Programs and Computer Rogues: Tailoring Punishment to Fit the Crime," *Rutgers Computer and Technology Law Journal* 16 (1990): 24–26.

38. Heather Jacobson and Rebecca Green, "Computer Crimes," *American Criminal Law Review* 39 (2002): 272–326.

39. United States Department of Justice, "Cyberstalking: A New Challenge for Law Enforcement and Industry, a Report from the Attorney General to the Vice President," August 1999, www.usdoj.gov/criminal/cybercrime/cyberstalking.htm (accessed July 3, 2011).

40. Janis Wolak, David Finkelhor, Kimberly Mitchell, and Michele Ybarra, "Online 'Predators' and Their Victims: Myths, Realities, and Implications for Prevention and Treatment," *American Psychologist* 63 (2008): 111–128.

41. This section leans heavily on *Justin Patchin and Sameer Hinduja*, "Bullies Move Beyond the Schoolyard: A Preliminary Look at Cyberbullying," *Youth Violence and Juvenile Justice* 4 (2006): 148–169.

42. Ibid.

43. Mark Pollitt, "Cyberterrorism—Fact or Fancy?" FBI Laboratory, www.cs.georgetown.edu/~denning/infosec/pollitt.html (accessed July 3, 2011).

44. Barry C. Collin (2004), "The Future of CyberTerrorism: Where the Physical and Virtual Worlds Converge," http://afgen.com/terrorism1.html (accessed July 3, 2011).

45. James Lewis, "Assessing the Risks of Cyberterrorism, Cyber War, and Other Cyber Threats," report submitted to the Center for Strategic and International Studies (CSIS), Washington, DC, 2002, p. 1.

46. William J. Broad, John Markoff, and David E. Sanger, "Israeli Test on Worm Called Crucial in Iran Nuclear

Delay," *New York Times*, January 15, 2011, www.nytimes.com/2011/01/16/world/middleeast/16stuxnet.html (accessed July 3, 2011).

47. Heather Jacobson and Rebecca Green, "Computer Crime," *American Criminal Law Review* 39 (2002): 273–326; Identity Theft and Assumption Act of 1998 (18 U.S.C. S 1028(a)(7)); Bruce Swartz, Deputy Assistant General, Criminal Division, "Justice Department Internet Fraud Testimony Before the House Energy and Commerce Committee, May 23, 2001"; Comprehensive Crime Control Act of 1984, PL 98-473, 2101-03, 98 Stat. 1837, 2190 (1984), adding 18 USC 1030 (1984); Counterfeit Active Device and Computer Fraud and Abuse Act Amended by PL 99-474, 100 Stat. 1213 (1986) codified at 18 U.S.C. 1030 (Supp. V 1987); Computer Abuse Amendments Act 18 U.S.C. section 1030 (1994); Copyright Infringement Act 17 U.S.C. section 506(a) 1994; Electronic Communications Privacy Act of 1986, 18 U.S.C. 2510–2520 (1988 and Supp. II 1990).

48. Computer Fraud and Abuse Act (CFAA), 18 U.S.C. section 1030 (1998).

49. Digital Millennium Copyright Act, Public Law 105-304 (1998).

50. Title 18, United States Code, section 2319.

51. Title 17, United States Code, section 506.

52. Identity Theft and Assumption Deterrence Act, as amended by Public Law 105-318, 112 Stat. 3007 (October 30, 1998).

53. *Ashcroft v. Free Speech Coalition*, 535 U.S. 234 (2002).

54. Prosecutorial Remedies and Other Tools to End the Exploitation of Children Today, 18 USC 1466A (2003).

55. *United States v. Williams*, 553 U.S. 285 (2008).

56. PL 98-473, Title H, Chapter XXI, [sections] 2102(a), 98 Stat. 1837, 2190 (1984).

57. "Statement of Mr. Bob Weaver, Deputy Special Agent in Charge, New York Field Office, United States Secret Service, Before the House Financial Services Committee, the Subcommittee on Financial Institutions and Consumer Credit and the Subcommittee on Oversight and Investigations, U.S. House of Representatives, April 3, 2003."

58. Andrew Nikiforuk, *Pandemonium: How Globalization and Trade Are Putting the World at Risk*, (Queensland, NZ: University of Queensland Press, 2007).

59. David Friedrichs and Jessica Friedrichs, "The World Bank and Crimes of Globalization: A Case Study," *Social Justice* 29 (2002): 13–36.

60. Louise Shelley, "The Globalization of Crime and Terrorism," State Department's Bureau of International Information Programs (IIP,) 2006, www.america.gov/st/business-english/2008/June/20080608103639xjyrreP4.218692e-02.html (accessed July 3, 2011).

61. United Nations, *The Globalization of Crime, 2010* (New York: United Nations Publications, 2010), www.unodc.org/unodc/en/data-and-analysis/tocta-2010.html (accessed August 1, 2011).

62. Ibid.

63. U.S. Department of State, "Trafficking in Persons Report 2010," www.state.gov/g/tip/rls/tiprpt/2010/ (accessed July 3, 2011).

64. Louise Shelley, "The Globalization of Crime and Terrorism."

65. Ibid.

66. Louise I. Shelley, "Crime and Corruption: Enduring Problems of Post-Soviet Development," *Demokratizatsiya* 11 (2003): 110–114; James O. Finckenauer and Yuri A. Voronin, *The Threat of Russian Organized* Crime (Washington, DC: National Institute of Justice, 2001).

67. Omar Bartos, "Growth of Russian Organized Crime Poses Serious Threat," *CJ International* 11 (1995): 8–9.

68. Colleen Cook, "Mexico's Drug Cartels, Congressional Research Service, 2007," http://ftp.fas.org/sgp/crs/row/RL34215.pdf (accessed August 1, 2011).

69. 18 U.S.C. 1952 (1976).

70. Public Law 91-452, Title IX, 84 Stat. 922 (1970) (codified at 18 U.S.C. 1961–68, 1976).

71. Ibid.

72. William Booth, "Mexican Azteca Gang Leader Arrested in Killings of 3 Tied to U.S.," *Washington Post*, March 30, 2010, www.washingtonpost.com/wp-dyn/content/article/2010/03/29/AR2010032903373.html (accessed August 1, 2011).

73. Angela Kocherga, "Zeta Leader Captured in Mexico," KVUE News, July 4, 2011, www.kvue.com/home/Zeta-leader-captured-in-Mexico--124979219.html (accessed August 1, 2011).

74. Orlando Patterson, "The Other Losing War," *New York Times*, January 13, 2007.

75. Declan Walsh, "Afghan Province to Provide One-Third of World's Heroin," *The Guardian*, June 14, 2006, www.guardian.co.uk/world/2006/jun/14/afghanistan.drugstrade (accessed August 1, 2011).

76. Office of National Drug Control Policy, "Source Countries and Drug Transit Zones: Afghanistan," www.whitehousedrugpolicy.gov/international/afghanistan.html (accessed August 1, 2011).

77. Francisco Gutierrez, "Institutionalizing Global Wars: State Transformations in Colombia, 1978–2002: Colombian Policy Directed at Its Wars, Paradoxically, Narrows the Government's Margin of Maneuver Even as It Tries to Expand It," *Journal of International Affairs* 57 (2003): 135–152.

Box Source Notes
Contemporary Issues in Criminal Justice
Global Sex Trafficking

United Nations, "The Globalization of Crime: Trafficking in Persons, 2010," www.unodc.org/unodc/en/data-and-analysis/tocta-2010.html (accessed July 5, 2011); U.S. Department of State, "Trafficking in Persons Report 2010," www.state.gov/g/tip/rls/tiprpt/2010/ (accessed July 5, 2011); Linda Williams and Jennifer Ngo, "Human Trafficking," in *Encyclopedia of Interpersonal Violence*, ed. Claire Renzetti and Jeffrey Edelson (Thousand Oaks, CA: Sage Publications, 2007).

CASE INDEX

NAME INDEX

Hansen, Mark, 365n
Hanson, Karl, 371n
Hanson, Rick, 378n
Harding, Richard, 376n
Hardyman, Patricia, 373n
Harlow, Caroline Wolf, 376n
Harr, Robin, 377n
Harris, Alexes, 382n
Harris, Grant, 379n
Harris, Michael R., 287
Harris, Richard, 362n
Harris, Robert, 318, 372n
Harris, Scott, 378n
Harrison, Paige M., 323, 377n, 382n
Hart, Peter, 364n
Hartley, Tara A., 364n
Hartstone, E., 381n
Hassall, Kayla, 319
Hawkins, Darnell, 354n
Hawkins, J. David, 382n
Hayden, George, 367n
Hayward, George, 145
He, Ni, 361n, 362n
Headey, Bruce, 364n
Heffernan, Tim, 296
Heide, Kathleen, 370n
Heimer, Karen, 357n, 375n
Henderson, Charles R., Jr., 356n
Henry, D. Alan, 367n
Henry, Vincent, 360n
Henry II, 256
Hensley, Christopher, 377n
Hepburn, John, 367n
Hernandez, Daphne, 357n
Hernandez, Peter (Bruno Mars), 241, 242
Herring, Bennie Dean, 70
Hickman, Matthew, 362n, 365n
Hileman, Susan, 5
Hillman, Mike, 378n
Hills, Holly, 364n
Hillsman, Sally, 373n
Hinduja, Sameer, 383n
Hinners, David, 371n
Hipp, John, 380n
Hirschfield, Paul, 299, 380n
Hirschi, Travis, 356n
Hochstetler, Andy, 380n
Hoffmann, Norman, 381n
Hogan, Brooke, 211
Hogan, Hulk, 211
Hogan, Nancy, 379n
Hogan, Nick, 211
Hoge, Robert, 368n
Holcomb, Jefferson, 370n, 371n
Holleran, David, 354n, 372n
Holley, Glen, 376n
Holman, Barry, 381n
Holmes, Malcolm D., 356n
Holmqvist, Rolf, 357n
Hoover, Herbert, 7
Hope, Tim, 356n
Horseman, Jeff, 358n

Horton, Willie, 264
House, Cathryn, 362n
Howard, John, 203, 257, 375n
Howell, James, 356n, 381n
Hoyle, Carolyn, 374n
Hoyt, William T., 378n
Huang, Bu, 364n
Hudson, Joe, 373n
Huebner, Beth, 380n
Hughes, Lorine, 36
Hughes, Robert, 368n
Hughes, Timothy, 355n, 376n
Huizinga, David, 356n
Hulsman, L., 354n
Hume, Robert, 365n
Hunter, Denis, 358n
Hureau, David, 380n
Hutchings, B., 356n
Hutchinson, Kay Bailey, 94

I

Ibarra, Peter, 373n
Immarigeon, Russ, 374n
Innes, Martin, 101, 360n
Irvin, Clinton, 365n
Irwin, John, 377n
Ives, George, 368n

J

Jablecki, Lawrence T., 378n
Jackall, Robert, 103
Jackson, Dexter, 170
Jackson, Pamela Irving, 359n
Jacob, Herbert, 354n
Jacobs, David, 356n
Jacobs, James, 373n, 377n, 378n
Jacobs, Naomi, 377n
Jacobson, Heather, 383n, 384n
Jacoby, Kristen, 370n
James, Jesse, 6
James, Kevin, 277–279
Janes, Nicole, 383n
Jesilow, Paul, 374n
Jialun, Zhou, 378n
Jiang, Shanhe, 378n
Joh, Elizabeth E., 359n
Johns, Cindy, 362n
Johnson, Brian, 381n
Johnson, Byron R., 378n
Johnson, Carrie, 358n, 382n
Johnson, Donnell, 47
Johnson, Kelly Dedel, 381n
Johnson, Lyndon, 7
Johnson, Mark, 364n
Johnson, Paul, 360n
Johnson, Robert, 221, 371n, 377n
Johnson, Sally, 357n
Johnson, William, 199
Johnston, Janet, 369n
Johnston, Lloyd, 355n
Johnston, Michael, 131
Johnston, Norman, 377n
Jones, Dana, 363n

Jones, Tonisha, 377n
Jonsson, Patrik, 358n
Joo, Hee-Jong, 374n
Jordan, Samuel, 326
Joseph, Deon, 125
Josephson, Rose Lee, 364n
Jusko, Todd A., 356n

K

Kahan, James, 372n
Kaldor, John, 378n
Kalt, Brian, 367n
Kanato, Manop, 376n
Kane, Robert, 363n
Kanka, Megan, 19, 65–66, 181, 367n
Karberg, Jennifer, 376n
Karmaus, Wilfried, 356n
Karmen, Andrew, 360n
Karp, David R., 374n
Karpelowitz, Alan, 381n
Kasza, Kristen, 356n
Katz-Bannister, Andra, 364n
Kazmierczak, Steven, 5
Keen, Bradley, 356n
Keil, Thomas, 370n, 371n
Kellar, Mark, 377n
Kellems, Kevin, 304–305
Kelling, George, 99–100, 359n, 360n, 361n
Kelly, Debra, 44
Kelly, Linda, 373n
Kemmler, William, 259
Kempf-Leonard, Kimberly, 356n
Kempinen, Cynthia, 380n
Kendall, George, 215
Kennedy, David, 358n, 361n, 362n
Kennedy, Randall, 367n
Kennedy, Thomas, 369n
Kenney, Dennis J., 364n
Keppel, Robert, 359n
Kerbs, John, 327, 382n
Kerr, Thomas, 378n
Kesteren, John van, 357n
Kethineni, Sesha, 237, 374n
Kevorkian, Jack, 65
Kim, Dae-Young, 374n
Kim, KiDeuk, 378n
Kim, Young S., 368n
King, Rodney, 81, 359n
Kingsworth, Rodney, 369n
Kinkade, Patrick, 370n
Kinnevy, Susan, 379n
Kircheimer, Otto, 368n, 375n
Kivivuori, Janne, 355n
Klein, Andrew, 356n, 372n
Klein, David, 365n
Klein, Stephen, 354n
Kleugel, James, 367n
Klinger, David, 126, 363n
Klostreich, Chelsea, 232
Knight, Barbara, 358n
Knobler, Peter, 359n
Knottnerus, G. Mark, 356n

Smith, Brent, 369n
Smith, Bruce, 359n
Smith, David, 382n
Smith, Douglas, 377n
Smith, Erica, 132
Smith, Hayden, 371n
Smith, Linda, 373n
Smith, Michael, 363n, 374n
Smith, Michael R., 364n
Smith, Paula, 378n
Smith, Pheny, 360n
Smith, Sheila, 366n
Smolej, Mirka, 355n
Snell, Tracy, 371n
Snortum, John, 360n
Snyder, Howard N., 381n, 382n
Snyder, John, 363n
Soderstrom, Irinia, 382n
Solnit, Albert, 382n
Somaiya, Ravi, 382n
Sontheimer, Henry, 381n
Sorensen, Jon, 377n, 379n
Sorensen, Jonathan R., 370n
Sorensen, Jon R., 379n
Sorenson, Jon, 292, 370n
South, Nigel, 383n
Sparks, Hal, 30
Sparrow, Malcolm, 358n, 362n
Spears, Jeffrey, 366n, 369n
Spelman, William, 360n
Spielberg, Steven, 332
Spohn, Cassia, 354n, 366n, 369n, 372n
Springer, Nicolette Fariello, 371n
Sprott, Jane, 354n
St. Gerard, Vanessa, 376n
Stack, Steven, 370n
Stadtland, Cornelis, 372n
Stafford, Mark C., 356n
Stahl, Anne L., 381n
Stanford, Robert Allen, 332
Starr-Gimeno, Donna, 360n
Steffensmeier, Darell, 369n
Steinberg, Laurence, 357n
Steiner, Benjamin, 291, 321, 376n, 377n, 379n, 381n
Stephan, James, 376n
Stephens, Christopher, 366n
Stephens, Gene, 374n
Steury, Ellen Hochstedler, 366n, 369n
Stevens, John Paul, 199
Stewart, Claire, 357n
Stewart, Courtney, 59
Stewart, David, 370n
Stewart, Eric, 354n, 380n
Stewart, James B., 366n
Stewart, Martha, 246
Stolzenberg, Lisa, 360n, 362n, 363n, 369n
Stone, Lawrence, 381n
Storms, Lowell, 363n
Storr, C. L., 357n
Strate, John, 358n
Strauss-Kahn, Dominique, 11, 158

Stretesky, Paul, 383n
Strickland, Shauna, 365n
Strolovitch, Dara, 361n
Strom, Kevin, 372n
Stubbs, Julie, 354n
Stucky, Thomas, 375n
Stuntz, William, 367n
Suleiman, Daniel, 358n
Sullivan, Dennis, 354n
Sullivan, John, 73
Sun, Ivan, 363n
Sundt, Jody, 375n
Surette, Ray, 375n
Swanson, Charles R., 359n
Swartz, Bruce, 384n
Sykes, Gresham, 281, 376n, 377n

T

Tanenhaus, David S., 381n
Taylor, Lawrence, 229, 371n
Taylor, Ralph, 357n
Taylor, Robert W., 359n
Tenzell, James, 363n
Teplin, Linda, 377n
Territo, Leonard, 359n
Tewksbury, Richard, 377n, 379n
Tezak, M., 362n
Thale, Christopher, 359n
Thomas, Charles, 376n
Thomas, Clarence, 199
Thompson, Carol, 359n
Thomson, Scott, 108
Thornberry, Terence, 356n
Thurman, Quint, 360n
Tifft, Larry, 354n, 355n, 363n
Time, Victoria, 365n
Timmendequas, Jesse, 181
Tinik, Leigh, 380n
Tippett, Frank, 359n
Tobias, J. J., 358n
Tobin, Terri, 356n
Toch, Hans, 379n
Tocqueville, Alexis de, 368n, 375n
Toj, Rolando, 351
Tonry, Michael, 214, 356n, 369n, 373n, 376n, 377n, 379n
Tontodonato, Pamela, 369n
Tracy, Paul, 356n
Traina, Chuck, 165
Trammell, Rebecca, 283, 377n
Travis, Jeremy, 359n, 376n, 380n
Travis, Lawrence, III, 364n, 373n
Treger, Harvey, 373n
Tremblay, Richard, 363n
Trickett, Alan, 356n
Trojanowicz, Robert, 360n
Truman, Jennifer, 355n
Turjeman, Hagit, 366n
Turner, Anthony, 209
Turner, R. Jay, 357n
Turner, Susan, 354n, 372n, 373n, 380n
Tyler, John H., 378n

U

Ulmer, Jeffrey T., 369n
Umbreit, Mark, 354n, 374n
Unnever, James, 370n
Unnithan, N. Prabha, 361n
Uphoff, Rodney, 367n
Urbina, Ian, 354n
Urbina, Martin, 370n
Useem, Bert, 368n, 379n

V

Vader, Amanda, 372n
Valltos, Nicholas, 364n
Van Dijk, Catherine, 381n
Van Maanen, John, 362n
Vannoy, Steven D., 378n
Van Voorhis, Patricia, 374n
Vatis, Michael A., 383n
Ven Den Haag, Ernest, 371n
Verdun-Jones, Simon, 365n
Veysey, Bonita, 356n
Victoria (queen), 61
Vieraitis, Lynne, 368n, 369n
Vila, Bryan, 364n
Violanti, John M., 364n
Vitaro, Frank, 363n
Vito, Gennaro, 370n, 371n
Vivona, T. Scott, 381n
Voas, Robert, 364n
Vollmer, August, 79
Vollum, Scott, 370n
von Hirsh, Andrew, 368n, 375n
von Zielbauer, Paul, 372n
Vos, Betty, 354n
Votey, Harold, 360n
Vuolo, Mike, 289, 379n

W

Wadsworth, Tim, 36
Wakschlag, Lauren, 356n
Walker, Samuel, 14–15, 354n, 358n, 359n, 364n, 368n, 375n
Wallace, Donald, 370n
Wallace-Carpretta, Suzanne, 371n
Walsh, Brandon, 368n
Walsh, Declan, 384n
Walters, Scott, 372n
Wang, Hsiao-Ming, 377n
Warchol, Greg, 373n
Ward, David A., 356n
Ward, John, 376n
Ward, Tony, 357n
Ware, Lezlee, 365n
Waring, Elin, 361n
Washington, James, 47
Washington, Levar, 277, 279
Waterman, Megan, 37
Watson, Jamie, 269, 375n
Watson, Kathy, 366n
Watterson, Kathryn, 377n
Wearing, Alexander, 364n
Weaver, Bob, 384n
Weaver, John, 357n

biosocial theory, 45–46
bipolar disorder, 46
BJA, 7
Black in Blue (Alex), 118
Black Muslims, 282
blacks. *See* African Americans
blameworthy, 205
blood, corruption of, 243
blue curtain, 122
bobbies, 76–77
body-scanning screening system, 268
bondsmen, 173
boot camp, 270–271
border patrol agents, 84–85
Boston Social Club, 79
bounty hunters, 173
Bow Street Runners, 76
B-PAD, 113
BP oil spill, 336–337
bribery, 131
Brideswell-type workhouses, 202
broken windows model, 99–100
brutality, 81, 129–130
Bureau of Alcohol, Tobacco, Firearms, and Explosives (ATF), 83
Bureau of Justice Assistance (BJA), 7
Bureau of Justice Statistics, 280
burglaries
    asportation in, 60
    incarceration rate for, 204
    larceny, 31
    motor vehicle theft, 31
    reports, 32
    statistics on, 32, 34

C

cannibalism, 61
CAN-SPAM, 53
capital punishment, 68, 224
    age, 223
    arguments against, 217–221
    arguments for, 215–217
    bias, 220
    causes more crime than deters, 220–221
    cruel and inhuman, 221
    delays, 200
    deterrence, 215–216, 219
    developed countries' abandonment, 221
    expense, 221
    gender, 220
    jury, 223
    legal issues, 222–223
    mental illness, 223
    misplaced vengeance, 218
    moral correctness, 216–217, 221
    possibility of error, 217–218
    proportional to crime, 217
    public opinion, 217, 218–219
    race, 220
    rates, 215–216
    rehabilitation, 220

by state, 216
    unfair use of discretion, 218
    unlikely chance of error, 217
carding, 342
career patterns, 41–42, 51
career profiles
    Beranis, Ann, 226–227
    Bishopp, Stephen, 72–73
    Curcio, Gina, 227
    Kellems, Kevin, 304–305
    Martin, Ralph C., II, 2–3
    Martinez, Carlos, 143–144
    Martino, Ruben Andres, 142–143
    Mongeau, Daisy, 1–2
    O'Hara, Samantha J., 2
    Sullivan, John, 73
careers in criminal justice
    border patrol agent, 84–85
    correctional officer, 290
    corrections counselor, 227–228, 257
    court reporter, 196
    forensic scientist, 109–110
    municipal police officer, 72–73
    police officers, 120–121
    probation officer, 234
    prosecutor, 157
    state trooper, 73
case management, 166–167
castle exception, 64
Castle Island prison, 258
causes of crime
    bisocial theory, 45–46
    choice theory, 45
    developmental theory, 50
    psychological theory, 46–48
    social conflict theory, 50
    social process theory, 49–50
    social structure theory, 48–49
cautioning, restorative, 251
CBP, 83–85
CBT, 237
CCA, 272
Central European Working Group, 349
certifying juvenile cases, 320
certiorari, writ of, 150
CFAA, 344
CFCs, 338
challenge for cause, 190
The Challenge of Crime in a Free Society, 7
chancery courts, 308
charging, 10
charging the defendant, 176–179
Chicago Crime Commission, 6
chief probation officer (CPO), 233
child abuse, 28, 64, 102
    jury overturn on, 70
    kiddie porn, 341, 345
    pedophiles, 145
Child Pornography Prevention Act (1996) (CPPA), 345
children, 46
    of prison inmates, 271, 284, 300
    See also juvenile justice

children in need of supervision (CHINS), 312
Children's Aid Society, 310
child savers, 308–309
China, 221
CHINS, 312
chivalry hypothesis, 213
chlorofluorocarbons (CFCs), 338
choice theory, 45
Christopher Commission, 131
chronic offenders, 41–42
circuit courts, 148–150
circumstantial evidence, 192
citizen review boards, 131–132
civil forfeiture proceedings, 243
civil law, 54
civil rights, 236–237
    inmates, 296
Civil Rights Act, 42 U.S.C. 1983, 293–294
Civil Rights Act of 1964, 119
Civil War, 261
claims court, 149
classifications, of crime, 57–58
class patterns, 40
Clean Water Act (1972), 339
clear and convincing, 188
clerk, 151, 153, 190
Clinton Prison, 263
closed-circuit television, 166
closing arguments, 192–193
Code of Hammurabi, 55
cognitive behavioral therapy (CBT), 237
cognitive theory, 47–48
collective violence, 292–293
colonial America, 77
commitment, 322–323
common law, 55–56
common pleas, court of, 148
communication, 78, 166
    fusion centers, 91
    terrorism, 87
community notification laws, 65–66
community-oriented policing, 106–112, 115
    challenges, 110–111
    effectiveness, 112
    implementation, 108
    police role, 108, 110
    police values, 111
    recruitment, 111–112
    supervisors, 111
    training, 111
Community Oriented Policing Services (COPS), 108
community service restitution, 243–244
community treatment, 184, 231, 314
    probation as, 324
competence
    defense attorney, 164–165
    at trial, 185
CompStat, 99–100
compulsory process, 185

Evaluation of Teen Courts Project, 323
evidence
    circumstantial, 192
    exculpatory, 218
    hearsay, 185
    preponderance of, 188
    presentation, 166
    questionable, 107
    search, 117
    sufficient, 188
    types, 192
evidence-based prosecution policies, 159
evidentiary standards of proof, 188
e-waste, 338
exception circumstances doctrine,
    294–295
excessive bail, 68, 171
excluded offense waiver, 320
exclusionary rule, 67–68, 138–140
exculpatory evidence, 218
excuse defenses, 61–63
exigent circumstances, 138
exile, 201
expected punishment, 203–204
ex post facto laws, 57
extortion, 131
extralegal factors, 126–127
extraordinary trial court errors, 195

F

Facebook, 105
facial recognition, biometric, 91, 268
failure to act, 59
faith-based programs, 285
family court, 148, 153, 312–313
farm inmates, 270
fatigue, 128–129
faulty question format, 32
FBI, 82–83
Federal Alternative Fines Act, 336–337
Federal Bureau of Investigation (FBI),
    82–83
federal courts
    courts of appeals, 149, 150
    district courts, 149–150
    Supreme Court, 70–71, 148–149,
        150–151
federal involvement in criminal
    justice, 7
federal judges, 154
federal law enforcement agencies,
    82–85
Federal Law Enforcement Training
    Center, 133–134
Federal Prison Industries (UNICOR), 287
federal prosecutor, 156
Federal Sentencing Guidelines, 231
Federal Trade Commission, 335
felony conviction rate, 12
felony crimes, 12, 58
    discretion, 158
    incarceration, 212
    prior convictions, 213

probation, 12, 239
    serious, 15
felony probation rate, 12
female corrections systems
    adapting to, 283–284
    inmates, 282–283
    sexual violence in, 283
female police officers, 119, 121, 140
Fifth Amendment, 68, 176
financial restitution, 244
fines, 242
fingerprint identification systems
    (AFIS), 91, 107
finger scans, 23
First Amendment, 345
FISA, 67
Fish (Parsell), 279–280
fishing, illegal, 337–338
Fishkill Correctional Facility, 47
Folsom Prison, 263
foot patrol, 108
force
    deadly, 132–134
    nondeadly, 134
    use of force, 114, 132–134
Force-Related Integrity Testing program,
    129–130
forcible rape, 31
Foreign Intelligence Surveillance Act
    (FISA), 67
forensic science, 105–106, 107
    career, 108–109
forestry camp inmates, 270
forfeiture, 145, 243
48 Hours Mystery, 193
Fourteenth Amendment, 68
Fourth Amendment, 67–68, 117
fraudulent offerings of securities,
    341–342
freedom of press and expression, 294
freedom of the yard, 263, 279
Free Venture Program, 288
Fuk Ching, 347
full cash bail, 172
furloughs, 287–288
fusion centers, 91

G

galley slavery, 202
gangs, 35
    Asian, 347–348
    nineteenth century, 6
    road gangs, 270
Gangster Disciples, 282
GED, 286–287, 302
gender
    abortion, 35
    capital punishment, 220
    chivalry hypothesis, 213
    correctional officers, 289, 291
    male-female arrest ratio, 39
    police officers, 119, 121, 140
    prostitution, 37, 170

    sentencing, 213
    social class, 212–213
    victim patterns, 42
gender patterns, 39
general deterrence, 203–204
general educational development
    (GED), 286–287, 302
general jurisdiction, state courts of, 147
genetic factors, 46
GEO Corporation, 272
Getting Ready Program, 302
globalization, 346
good faith exception, 140
good-time credits, 209
GPR, 268
grand jury, 10, 176–178
grass eaters, 130–131
Great Meadow Prison, 263
green crime, 352
    definition, 336
    enforcing environmental laws, 339
    forms of, 337–338
    illegal dumping, 338
    illegal fishing, 337–338
    illegal logging, 337, 338
    illegal polluting, 338
ground-penetrating radar (GPR), 268
Group 4 Securicor, 88
Guantánamo prisoners, 69, 195
guardians, 262
guarding the institution, 289–291
guidelines for sentencing, 207–208, 231
guilty by ordeal, 55
guilty mind, 58
guilty plea, 179
guns, 5, 29, 35, 98–99

H

habeas corpus, writ of, 69, 195
hacking, 340
halfway houses, 271
Halliburton, 336
Hammurabi, 55
hands-off doctrine, 293
harmless error, 136, 195
harm requirement, 60
hearsay evidence, 185
heartbeat monitoring, 268
Heijin, 347
Hierarchy Rule, 32
historical overview
    correctional systems, 256–265
    criminal justice, 6–7
    criminal law, 55–56
    juvenile justice, 308–310
    police/policing, 75–79
    punishment, 200–203
history of prior violence, 291–292
HIV/AIDS treatment, 286
homicide
    criminal, 31
    drunk drivers, 59
    See also murders

homicide rate, 34
hormone imbalances, 45–46
HotSpot probation, 240
hot spots of crime, 89–90, 112
house arrest, 246
House of Reformation, 309
House of Refuge, 309
Hudson Dusters, 6
hue and cry, 75, 76
hulks, 257
hundred, 75, 76
hung jury, 194

I

IACP, 23, 79
ICE, 305
identification, 90–91, 104, 107
identity theft, 342, 344–345
Identity Theft and Assumption
    Deterrence Act (1998), 344–345
Identity Theft Penalty Enhancement Act
    (2004), 345
ignorance of the law, 61
ignorance or mistake, 61
illegal touting, 342
Illinois Juvenile Court Act, 310, 312
ILO, 348
immediate-impact studies, 219
immigration, 35
    transnational crime, 347
Immigration and Customs (ICE), 305
impartial jury, 185–186
incapacitation, 204–205
incarceration
    burglaries, 204
    felony crimes, 212
    shock, 270–271
    See also corrections
income, 42
indenture, 308
indeterminate sentence, 206–207
indictment, 176–177
    true bill of, 10
indigent, 161–163
indigent defense, 163, 168
inferior courts, 148–150
information, 10, 114
    process, 177–178
    prosecutor, 177
    sharing, 167
information technology (IT), 105
information theft, 340
infractions, 58
infrastructure protection, 83, 87, 345
initial appearance, 321–322
initial contact, 9
inmate-balance theory, 292
inmate populations, 272–274
inmate social code, 280–281, 303
inmate subculture, 280
innocence movement, 217
in-presence requirement, 10
insanity, 61–63

Insanity Defense Reform Act, 63
institutionalization, 325
instructions to jury, 193–194
intake, 233
intensive probation supervision (IPS),
    245–246
interactionist view of crime, 30
Interagency Council on Women, 348
Interagency Telemarketing and
    Internet Fraud Working Group,
    345–346
intermediate appellate courts, 148
intermediate sanctions, 241, 253
    concept summary, 248
    day fines, 242
    DRCs, 248
    EM, 246–247
    fines, 242
    forfeiture, 243
    house arrest, 246
    IPS, 245–246
    RCC, 247–248
    restitution, 243–244
    shock probation, 244–245
    split sentence, 244–245
internal affairs, 113–114
internal corruption, 131
International Association of Chiefs of
    Police (IACP), 23, 79
International Labor Organization
    (ILO), 348
Internet, 167, 190–191
    etailing fraud, 342
    pornography, 340–341, 345
    surveillance, 351
    See also cyber crime
Internet securities fraud, 341–342
interrogations, 135–137
Interstate and Foreign Travel or
    Transportation in Aid of
    Racketeering Enterprises Act
    (Travel Act), 350
intoxication, 62
    public, 58
investigation, 10
    evaluation, 103
    pre-sentence, 233
    support, 102
investigation function, 115
    detective work, 101–103
    evaluating investigations, 103
    forensic science, 105–109
    sting operation, 103–104
    technology, 105
investigators, 1–2, 305
    See also detectives
Investments Advisers Act of
    1940, 333
IPS, 245–246
IQ tests, race, and crime, 50
Iran, 344
irresistible impulse, 63
IT, 105

J

jails, 172
    conditions, 265–266
    definition, 256
    juveniles in, 265
    new-generation, 266–267
    populations and trends, 265
    race, 265
    suicide, 265–266
    Walnut Street Jail, 258, 286
    See also correctional systems
Jao Pho, 347
JJDP Act, 311–312
J-Net, 167
job stress, 127–128, 289
Joint Terrorist Task Force, 88
judges, 151–152, 165, 167
    appeals and, 195
    example, 142–143
    federal, 154
    impartial, 185
    plea bargaining, 182
    state, 154–155
Judicial Act of 1789, 149
judicial reprieve, 230
judicial support staff, 153
judicial waiver, 320
judiciary, 151–155
jury
    capital punishment, 223
    CSI effect on, 193
    grand, 10, 176–178
    hung, 194
    impartial, 185–186
    instructions to, 193–194
    overturn, 70
    race and, 190
    sequestering, 194
jury nullification, 194–195
jury selection, 190–191
jury staff, 153
jury trial, 151, 186, 189
just desert, 205, 224
justice
    perspectives on, 16–21
    "wedding cake" model of, 14–16, 26
    See also criminal justice; juvenile
        justice
Justice Department, U.S., 82–83
justice of the peace, 76, 148
justice policy, 36
Justice Policy Institute, 317
justification defenses, 63–65
juvenile correctional process, 324–327
juvenile court, 310–312
juvenile delinquency, 312
juvenile justice, 265
    adjudication, 321–322
    adult court, 320
    adult justice system comparison,
        314–315
    aftercare, 325–326
    bail, 318

sufficient evidence, 188
suicide
    jails, 265–266
    juvenile, 320
    physician-assisted, 65
    prison, 282
suicide by cop, 132
Sumners-Ashurst Act (1940), 263
superior courts, 148
super-maximum-security prisons,
    267–269
Supreme Court, U.S., 70–71, 148–149,
    150–151
sureties, 230
surety bail, 173
suspended sentence, 231

T

Taliban, 351
technology
    backscatter imaging system for
        concealed weapons, 268
    biometrics, 23, 91, 268
    body-scanning screening
        system, 268
    closed-circuit television, 166
    CompStat, 99–100
    computerized crime mapping,
        89–90, 92
    control of, 66
    DNA testing and profiling, 18,
        90–91, 105, 170, 218
    early, 78
    facial recognition, 91, 268
    fingerprint identification,
        23, 91, 107
    fusion centers, 91
    GPR, 268
    heartbeat monitoring, 268
    law enforcement, 89–91
    less-lethal weapons, 134
    license plate recognition, 89–90
    LPR, 89–90
    medical, 36
    personal alarm location system, 268
    ProLaser III, 113
    WikiLeaks, 331
    See also court technology
teen courts, 323
television
    closed-circuit, 166
    violence, 47
terrorism, 60, 277
    biometrics against, 23, 91
    communication, 87
    criminal investigator, 305
    fight against, 67
    New York City, 83, 88
    state law enforcement, 85–86
    suspect detention, 195
    Taliban, 351
    USAPA, 67, 69
testimonial evidence, 192

Texas Rangers, 85
therapeutic communities, 285
thief takers, 76
three-strikes laws, 208–209
ticket-of-leave, 262
time-in-rank system, 96–97
time-series analysis, 219
tithings, 75, 76
torts, 54–55
torture, 261
    as punishment, 201–202
total institution, 278, 303
traffic patrol, 113
traffic violations, 58
training
    police, 111, 114, 133–134
    vocational, 287
transfer hearing, 319–320
transnational crime, 352
    Asian gangs, 347–348
    drug trade, 347
    drug trafficking, 347–349, 351
    eradication difficulties, 350–351
    groups, 347–349
    human organs, 347
    immigration, 347
    Mexican drug cartels, 94, 349–350
    organized crime, 346
    organized crime laws, 350
    pornography, 347
    profits, 347
    Russian groups, 348–349
    sex trafficking, 348
    types, 346–347
Transocean Drilling Corporation, 336
transportation, 78, 202, 262, 350
Travel Act, 350
treatment, 12
    community, 184, 231, 314, 324
    correctional systems, 284–289
    drugs, 285–286
    HIV/AIDS, 286
    individual and group, 284–286
    juvenile justice, 322–324
    probation, 235–236
"Treatment of Youth of Color in the
    Justice System," 327–328
triads, 347
trial, 11, 195
    bench, 184
    competence at, 185
    jury, 151, 186, 189
    juvenile compared to adult, 322
    legal rights, 185–188
    public, 186–187
    Sixth Amendment, 68
trial process, 197
    appeals in, 195
    closing arguments, 192–193
    criminal defense, 191–192
    deliberation and verdict, 194–195
    instructions to jury, 193–194
    jury selection, 188–191

opening statements, 191
prosecution's case, 191
sentence, 195
Trojan horses, 343
true bill of indictment, 10
truth in sentencing, 20, 209
truth-in-sentencing laws, 20
Tucson massacre, 5
tunnel vision, 218
Twitter, 105
2011 Defense Authorization Bill, 69

U

UCR, 31–32, 51
underreporting, 32
unemployment, 35
UNICOR, 287
Uniform Crime Reports (UCR), 31–32, 51
unsecured bail, 173
Urban Institute, 323
USAPA, 67, 69
USA Patriot Act (USAPA), 67, 69
use of force, 133–134
    African Americans, 132
    ethical challenge, 114
US-VISIT, 23

V

vehicle searches, 117, 138
vengeance, 218
venire, 190
Vera Institute of Justice, 174–175
verdicts, 191, 194–195
Vice Lords, 282
vice squad, 103
victims
    NCVS, 32–34
    plea bargaining, 182
    prosecutorial discretion, 159
    sentencing, 214–215
victim impact statement, 214–215
victimless crime, 19, 139, 181, 205
victim patterns
    African Americans, 43
    age, 40–41
    ecological factors, 43
    ethnic/racial diversity, 43
    gender, 42
    income, 42
    marital status, 43
    repeat victimization, 44
    victim-offender relationships,
        43–44
vigilantes, 77, 78
vindictive prosecutors, 161
violations, 58
    curfew, 313
violence, 129–130
    collective, 292–293
    correctional systems, 291–293, 303
violent crime
    decline, 34
    interest, 28–29